Administrative Procedures
for the **Canadian Office**

Ninth Edition

Administrative Procedures
for the Canadian Office

Lauralee Kilgour
Northern Alberta Institute
of Technology

Edward Kilgour
Management Support
& Services (MSS)

Marie Rutherford
Georgian College

Blanche Rogers
College of the North Atlantic

Sharon Burton
Brookhaven College

Nelda Shelton
Tarrant County College

Ninth Edition

PEARSON

Toronto

Vice-President, Editorial Director: Gary Bennett
Editor-in-Chief: Nicole Lukach
Marketing Manager: Leigh-Anne Graham
Team Leader, Development: Madhu Ranadive
Developmental Editor: Rachel Stuckey
Project Manager: Richard di Santo
Production Editor: Vijaykumar Sekar, Jouve
Copy Editor: Anne Sussman
Proofreader: Trish O'Reilly-Brennan
Photo and Permissions Researcher: David Strand
Compositor: Jouve
Art Director: Julia Hall
Interior and Cover Designer: Anthony Leung
Cover Image: Masterfile

Credits and acknowledgments for materials borrowed from other sources and reproduced, with permission, in this textbook appear on the appropriate page within the text, and on page 461.

Original edition *Office Procedures for the 21st Century,* published by Pearson Education, Inc., Upper Saddle River, New Jersey, USA. Copyright © 2008 Pearson Education, Inc. This edition is authorized for sale only in Canada. If you purchased this book outside the United States or Canada, you should be aware that it has been imported without the approval of the publisher or the author.

10 9 8 7 6 EBM

Library and Archives Canada Cataloguing in Publication

Administrative procedures for the Canadian office/Lauralee Kilgour ... [et al.]. — 9th ed.

Includes index.
Revised ed. of: Secretarial procedures for the automated office/Lucy Mae Jennings, Lauralee Kilgour.
ISBN 978-0-13-216437-5

1. Office practice—Textbooks. 2. Office procedures—Textbooks. I. Kilgour, Lauralee G. (Lauralee Gail), 1953–

HF5547.5.J465 2013   651.3'74   C2013-900085-2

ISBN 978-0-13-216437-5

*To all my students; past and present for providing the
inspiration to undertake this endeavour.
A special thanks to my husband Ray, my mother Maureen,
and my son Christopher for your encouragement
and patience.
Finally, thanks to all who made this project an adventure.*

— Marie Rutherford

Brief Contents

Detailed Contents

Part II Office Services 86

6 Office Technology

7 Web-Based Tools and Security

8 Incoming and Outgoing Mail

Preface

Welcome to the ninth edition of *Administrative Procedures for the Canadian Office*!

Administrative assistants are relied on for their diverse technological, interpersonal, and office procedure skills. An essential component of working in today's Canadian office is the ability to make critical business decisions, as the administrative assistant is often the eyes and ears of an organization.

Excellent soft skills and a positive attitude are in demand now more than ever. It is essential that administrative assistants have highly developed personal skills and a positive work ethic to ensure a successful career in a diverse and global environment.

Revisions that appear in this ninth edition are reflective of developments in technology and the constantly evolving role of the administrative assistant. The text expands its focus on emerging technologies and explores varied employability requirements. A greater emphasis has been placed on the development of cultural diversity understanding, and the international business operational content has been fine-tuned. Working in a global economy makes it essential for administrative assistants to develop knowledge of broad business practice. These additions facilitate greater competency and equip graduates to meet forthcoming challenges.

NEW FOR THIS EDITION

To keep up with new trends in business, new developments in technology, and new ways of looking at the world, the contemporary office is constantly changing. These changes are reflected in the text through the addition and/or expansion of numerous topics, of which only the *major* changes are listed below.

- Recognition of specialized role for medical and legal assistants (Intro)
- Recognition of multiculturalism (Chapter 2)
- Recognition of cultural diversity in the workplace (Chapter 2)
- International business relations (Chapter 2)
- Using digital devices (Chapter 6)
- Troubleshooting computers (Chapter 6)
- Online connectivity options (Chapter 7)
- Functionality of intranets and extranets (Chapter 7)
- Exploring Web 2.0 tools (Chapter 7)
- Search engines (Chapter 7)
- Security on the internet (Chapter 7)
- End of chapter problem solving and special reports using Web 2.0 in action (Chapter 7)
- Electronic mail options (Chapter 8)
- Exploring Project management concepts (Chapter 9)
- Identify challenges related to project management (Chapter 9)
- End of chapter exercises exploring project management resources and challenges (Chapter 9)
- Four classification for records retention (Chapter 10)
- Maintaining records in medical and legal offices (Chapter 10)
- Clients booking appointments online (Chapter 11)
- Passport application process and e-passport options (Chapter 12)
- E-tickets, electronic boarding passes and mobile device boarding passes (Chapter 12)
- Using m-banking in business (Chapter 15)
- Guidelines for payroll processing (Chapter 15)
- Overview of the budget process (Chapter 15)
- Additional tips on dressing for success (Chapter 16)
- Additional insight into addressing salary issues during an interview (Chapter 16)
- Updated MS certifications available (Chapter 17)
- Chapter-specific, content-relevant material on the issue of ethics throughout the text
- Chapter-specific, content-relevant material on international business issues throughout the text
- Additional and revised learning objectives and end-of-chapter questions in heavily revised chapters
- Updated and new Weblinks at the end of each chapter

FEATURES

Administrative Procedures for the Canadian Office has many features to inspire students and help them learn, as well as support the instructor.

- Each chapter opens with a **Graduate Profile** that focuses on a successful office administration graduate.
- The boxed **pro-Link** features highlight professional tips on specific topics.
- **Self-Check** questions appear after short segments of text throughout the chapters, allowing students to evaluate their knowledge at appropriate intervals.
- **Questions for Study and Review** help students review the chapter's content.
- **Everyday Ethics** cases found in each chapter are excellent for class discussion and give students an opportunity to evaluate their personal and professional moral codes of conduct. The cases explore ethical and moral judgments, and pose light problem-solving questions to help students improve their decision-making skills.
- **Problem Solving** cases encourage students to think critically and develop their problem-solving and decision-making skills.
- **Special Reports** provide the opportunity for more in-depth research into particular topics.
- The practical exercises provided in the **Production Challenges** encourage students to apply the knowledge they have gained. Many Challenges refer to **Working Papers**: these are provided in hard copy at the back of the book.
- A list of updated and expanded **Weblinks** at the end of each chapter leads students to further explore the ideas presented within the text and to learn independently.
- Throughout the text, **key terms** are highlighted in boldface. These boldfaced terms are included in the **Glossary** at the back of the book.
- The appendix introduces students to a list of **Common Proofreaders' Marks**.

SUPPLEMENTS

Administrative Procedures for the Canadian Office, Ninth Edition, is accompanied by the following supplements:

Companion Website (978-0-13-309939-3) To supplement the book, we have prepared a Companion Website (www.pearsoned.ca/kilgour) for instructors and students. The site provides a great source of valuable information, including Windows-based Exercises, Internet Exercises, Working Papers, Quizzes, Spelling and Grammar reinforcement, a Glossary, and Weblinks.

Instructor's Manual (978-0-13-309940-9) The Instructor's Manual includes teaching suggestions, ideas for related activities, and suggested solutions to the Everyday Ethics Cases, Questions for Study and Review, Problem Solving Cases, and Production Challenges. The Instructor's Manual can be downloaded from Pearson's online catalogue (www.pearsoncanada.ca/highered).

Test Item File (978-0-13-324834-0) This test bank offers a test for each chapter with multiple-choice, fill-in-the-blank, matching, and short-answer questions, along with an answer key for instructors. The Test Item File can be downloaded from Pearson's online catalogue (www.pearsoncanada.ca/highered).

PowerPoint Presentations (978-0-13-309941-6) A collection of slides specifically designed to complement chapter content is available in PowerPoint software from Pearson's online catalogue (www.pearsoncanada.ca/highered).

CourseSmart for Instructors (978-0-13-338458-1) CourseSmart goes beyond traditional expectations, providing instant online access to the textbooks and course materials you need at a lower cost for students. And even as students save money, you can save time and hassle with a digital eTextbook that allows you to search for the most relevant content at the very moment you need it. Whether you're evaluating textbooks or creating lecture notes to help students with difficult concepts, CourseSmart can make life a little easier. See how when you visit www.coursesmart.com/instructors.

CourseSmart for Students (978-0-13-338458-1) CourseSmart goes beyond traditional expectations, providing instant online access to the textbooks and course materials you need at an average savings of 60 percent. With instant access from any computer and the ability to search your text, you'll find the content you need quickly, no matter where you are. And with online tools such as highlighting and note-taking, you can save time and study efficiently. See all of the benefits at www.coursesmart.com/students.

Technology Specialists Pearson's Technology Specialists work with faculty and campus course designers to ensure that Pearson technology products, assessment tools, and online course materials are tailored to meet your specific needs. This highly qualified team is dedicated to helping schools take full advantage of a wide range of educational resources, by assisting in the integration of a variety of instructional materials and media formats. Your local Pearson sales representative can provide you with more details on this service program.

Acknowledgements

The publisher and authors would like to thank Tammy Burns and Rachel Stuckey for contributing the new Graduate Profile features in this edition.

Thanks are also due to the following reviewers who provided valuable feedback that helped to shape the ninth edition:

Nancy Breen
Nova Scotia Community College

Carolyn Clark
Lethbridge College

Kellie Hayward
Sheridan Institute of Technology and Advanced Learning

Doug McLean
Vancouver Island University

Janine Violini
SAIT Polytechnic

Charlene Wyatt
Okanagan College

Introduction

A Career as an Office Professional

Learning Outcomes

After completion of this chapter, the student will be able to:

1 Describe current office trends.

2 Explain the background of the title *secretary*.

3 Differentiate between the role of an executive assistant and that of a personal assistant.

4 Define the role of the administrative assistant.

5 Describe the role of the legal and the medical administrative assistant.

6 Explain how the Information Age has affected the role of the office professional.

7 Describe ways the administrative assistant uses electronic equipment to accomplish the job.

8 Describe the expected future for employment of the office professional.

9 Review this textbook to locate pertinent information.

WHAT'S HAPPENING?

The office of today is constantly evolving, and the role of the administrative professional continues to evolve with it. A survey conducted by OfficeTeam found that "nearly three-quarters (73 percent) of managers polled said responsibilities for support professionals have increased in the last five years" ("The Ever-Expanding Administrative Role," *OfficePro* 68, no. 4 [May 2008]: 8). The changing nature of the office environment means that administrative support staff need to be ready and able to adapt to their changing roles and responsibilities. If you don't adapt and simply rely on what you've learned in the past, your technical skills will become obsolete and your attitude will likely be considered inconsistent with the corporate vision.

Employers are looking for well-rounded administrative assistants. They need support professionals who have initiative and can be proactive in their approach to the ever-shifting demands and increasing workflow of the contemporary office.

Current Office Trends

Here is a description of current office trends to which office professionals must adapt:

1. Administrative assistants are considered full team members whose skills are absolutely essential to the operation of the business. The role of an administrative assistant is highly specialized, and both advanced technical training and human relations skills are paramount. The administrative assistant is a contributing team member who must make valuable decisions within the realm of her/his authority.

2. The level of skill and responsibility has changed. Administrative assistants use sophisticated hardware and software as well as coordinate a myriad of details. They are expected to handle people as deftly as they handle computers. In fact, many administrative assistants perform what a decade ago were considered strictly managerial responsibilities. The gap between management and administrative assistant is closing.

Graduate Profile

Hilda J. Broomfield Letemplier
President, Pressure Pipe Steel Fabrication Ltd.

College Graduation:
Secretarial Science Program
Labrador Community College
Happy Valley–Goose Bay, Labrador
1992

Hilda Letemplier is president and chief financial officer of Pressure Pipe Steel Fabrication Ltd. (PPSF), an Inuit-owned company that provides steel fabrication and welding services to a growing number of industrial clients in the fast-expanding economy of Labrador. She and her husband, Lionel, a high-pressure welder, started the company in 1991. Hilda and Lionel's youngest son, Travis, has joined the company as their sales manager. The company now has ten employees and works with clients and suppliers across Canada and beyond.

Although Hilda left high school at the age of 14, and started her family at the age of 17, she still understood the importance of education. She worked hard to obtain her high school equivalency and started her administrative studies with a vocational school clerk-typist course. After living for a time in Sherbrooke, Quebec, the Letemplier family moved back to their community in Labrador, where Hilda completed the Secretarial Science Program at Labrador Community College.

The skills Hilda learned at school were important, particularly those related to financial management and reporting, but she also needed to learn about the actual products and services that the company was selling. Most of this knowledge was learned on the job, working with her husband.

The first five years of the business were the hardest. Hilda was taking courses and working part-time, and later worked for the college as an administrative assistant, all while working evenings and weekends at the business and looking after her young family. Starting a business is a big risk—both Hilda and her husband made sacrifices in work-life balance and even remortgaged their home. As Hilda says, there were times when "Kraft Dinner was a regular menu item."

Today PPSF is very successful and supplies some of the largest resource development projects in Labrador; with the signing of the Nunatsiavut Land Claims Agreement, resource companies are obliged under Inuit Impact Benefit Agreements to work with Inuit suppliers of products and services.

Hilda believes strongly in giving back to the community to help others become successful in business. She is a longtime member of the Newfoundland and Labrador Organization of Women Entrepreneurs (NLOWE), an organization that helps women entrepreneurs start, grow, and advance successful businesses; she is currently serving as NLOWES's regional director for Labrador. Hilda is also a member of WEConnect, a nonprofit organization that helps women-owned businesses expand their opportunities. PPSF was the first company from Labrador to become certified and registered with WEConnect. As well, PPSF was the first company to become certified and registered in all of Newfoundland and Labrador with the Canadian Aboriginal Minority Suppliers Council (CAMSC).

Hilda's secret for success consists of not taking no for an answer and putting in a 100 percent effort—along with being a lifelong learner who takes calculated risks. Her determination has paid off: today Hilda is an award-wining businesswoman, recently selected by Pauktuutit Inuit Women of Canada for a case study project profiling five Inuit women in business across the country. PPSF has also won a National Award from WEConnect. And in 2012, PPSF won CAMSC's Small Business of the Year Award, granted to an aboriginal or minority-owned business based on business growth and development, export sales and growth, and major accomplishments during the previous year.

3. Working hours have become very flexible. The concept of working 9 a.m. to 5 p.m. Monday to Friday is disappearing. With computer networking, many office professionals perform some of their responsibilities from their home computer on a Saturday or Sunday, or even at 4 a.m. on a weekday. Flexible time works well for parents who want to shift their working day to meet family needs. The mode of working from home and having flexible hours means that employees have become managers of their own time. Self-discipline for these office professionals is an essential skill.

4. Companies have become more employee friendly, with wellness programs and quality-management programs that require input and recommendations from the staff. So office specialists cannot simply bring problems to the attention of management. Instead, they are

required to bring recommendations and solutions to the table.

5. Office specialists have the opportunity and need to become entrepreneurial. Where once we settled into long-term employment with benefits and eventual retirement, we now see more short-term contracts available and fewer jobs with company benefits. Therefore, the administrative assistant must be constantly ready for change, in search of new assignments, and ready to upgrade technical expertise. Fortunately, the skills of an administrative assistant lend themselves to an entrepreneurial approach, giving assistants the ability to open their own businesses offering office support to individuals or corporations.

6. Technology will continue to remove routine tasks from the office. Instead, administrative assistants will take a higher level of responsibility.

7. The practice of payment for actual work performed as opposed to payment for a job title is popular. Many human resource departments rate each task listed on each separate job description. Each task is given a score based on importance and difficulty. Therefore, two administrative assistants from the same office but performing different responsibilities will receive different rates of pay.

8. Employees are expected to demonstrate cultural awareness and sensitivity; these qualities are no longer considered to be exceptional traits found exclusively in people with good public relations skills. Electronic communication has made the business world a much smaller place, so that office professionals are routinely in contact with clients or colleagues located in other countries. In addition, international travel is a requirement for many executives, and arranging face-to-face meetings and hosting international guests is now simply a routine responsibility for administrative professionals.

9. It is essential today for a company to have a strong digital presence. Social media is part of this digital presence, and administrative professionals now have responsibility for managing these sites. This involves maintaining and updating information as well as promoting business-related activities. It also often involves handling customer/client feedback—a critical task, since responding effectively can help to preserve a company's positive reputation.

10. Corporate responsibility regarding social and environmental issues is gaining greater focus. Companies are examining their business practices and looking for ways to give back to their communities and to protect the environment. Involvement in community projects, fundraisers, and green-based initiatives is now critical for promoting a strong corporate image.

11. Businesses are encouraging employees to achieve a better balance between work and life. Some companies provide employees with portable wireless tools, giving them greater control over their work schedules. This, in turn, enables employees to balance and prioritize work and personal commitments. The lines between work and life are more integrated because professionals can perform many tasks at home during what can be considered personal time.

The future is bright, and the opportunities are infinite. Office professionals should always be looking for new opportunities, responsibilities, and possibilities.

WHAT DOES YOUR TITLE MEAN?

Over time, the roles and titles of office professionals have changed. The title of **secretary** was originally intended to refer to people requiring complex organizational and supervisory skills. One of the earliest uses of the word *secretary* came from the Roman Empire, where the secretary was a close confidant to the emperor. The term seems to have different meaning depending on the culture and country using it. For example, in Japan, most office professionals are called assistants, but they would like to be called secretaries since the position of secretary is a top management position that is often influential. In North America, however, the term *secretary* has in the past been inappropriately used to refer to office workers handling repetitive and simple tasks.

Many office professionals have become dissatisfied with the misuse of the title *secretary* and, as a result, have insisted on alternative titles that better reflect their responsibilities and distinguish them from workers who perform routine tasks. A wide range of titles are used, such as *personal assistant, executive assistant, office coordinator, office specialist, administrative assistant*, and *office professional*.

Specialized roles, rather than general expertise, are reflected in the many new titles now assigned to administrative assistants. Specialized titles can include *executive*, *legal*, and *medical* administrative assistant. Additionally, according to *Office of the Future 2020*, a research study released by OfficeTeam, new titles have emerged to describe jobs previously considered part of an administrative assistant's duties, such as resource coordinator, workflow controller, and knowledge manager. These roles require advanced administrative skills and training.

To eliminate confusion, the term **administrative assistant** has been used throughout this text to designate all classifications of office professionals.

Executive and Personal Assistants

The titles of *executive assistant* and *personal assistant* hold a high status in the realm of office employment. Along with every title comes responsibility, salary, status, and opportunity that relate to that title. So if the titles of personal assistant and executive assistant hold a high status, what responsibilities and challenges do these professionals handle?

An executive assistant usually works for one or more senior staff of an organization. Responsibilities can include almost any type of office work from keying reports, to organizing meetings, to handling budgets. The position is well respected and generally pays at the top end of the office professional pay scale.

The position of personal assistant is somewhat different. It too is well respected, and remuneration for it is at the top end of the office professional pay scale. However, the responsibilities often extend to personal work as well. A busy executive may need an efficient and capable office professional who, in addition to handling office-related work, also assists with the executive's personal life. This could mean making travel arrangements for a family vacation, handling the executive's personal banking, or even organizing social functions that don't relate to the office.

Legal and Medical Assistants

Legal and medical administrative assistants perform highly specialized work requiring knowledge of technical terminology and procedures. For instance, legal assistants prepare correspondence and legal documents such as summonses, complaints, motions, responses, and subpoenas. They may also assist with legal research.

Medical assistants transcribe dictation, prepare correspondence, and assist physicians or medical scientists with reports, speeches, articles, and conference proceedings. Most medical assistants need to be familiar with billing practices as well as hospital and laboratory procedures.

WHAT IS THE ROLE OF AN ADMINISTRATIVE ASSISTANT?

Today's office is a dynamic place to work. Electronic equipment has automated procedures at all levels of the office (see Figure In-1). Advanced information technology enables office professionals to perform their jobs better and faster than ever before. However, having strong technical skills is not enough; without effective management and people skills, the administrative assistant will be unsuccessful.

Modern technology has led the way for the revolution known as the **Information Age**, in which there is an abundant and rapid flow of information available for decision making. The administrative assistant must provide the human element in the rapid and unceasing flow of information in today's business world. Clearly, communication is an important part of every administrative assistant's role.

The Information Age has made the administrative assistant's profession one that is exciting and challenging, and also one that requires fine-tuned technical, administrative, and human relations skills. Administrative assistants

Figure In-1 Technology has automated procedures at all levels of the office.

are the lifeblood of an organization. They are information and people managers, and no company could be successful without them.

Dynamic Communications

The communications functions in an office demand that an administrative assistant have excellent technical as well as personal skills. Because there is a constant demand for information to flow faster, the administrative assistant must use high-tech skills and automated tools to be productive and efficient.

Following are examples of how administrative assistants use electronic tools to stay efficient. They:

1. handle photocopying, printing, faxing, and filing
2. manage electronic calendars by setting/cancelling appointments and by sending meeting reminders to participants
3. compose and send email correspondence
4. process, revise, and proofread documents using word processing software
5. maintain and compile spreadsheets
6. use presentation software to create colourful and dynamic presentations that illustrate company statistics on bar graphs and pie charts
7. access, update, and maintain data using database software
8. design reports, flyers, letterhead, business cards, and other promotional material using desktop publishing software
9. create company or department newsletters, and write articles for them

Figure In-2 The administrative assistant provides the communication link between people and technology.

10. use the internet to collect and post data
11. create, maintain, and update company web/social media sites
12. prepare and coordinate mailings

Will There Be a Job for You?

There has always been employment for skilled office professionals. Today is no exception. The skills of an office professional are portable, flexible, transferable, and in demand.

Every office needs personnel who can handle computers, administration, and people. If you live in a community where employment is scarce, don't be discouraged. Remember that your skills are portable enough to keep you employed just about anywhere in the world. This gives you choices and opportunities. Businesses require professional office skills at every level, and your skills are flexible and transferable enough to have you performing document processing in one job, selling office software in the next, training new office staff in another, or running your own business.

Statistics indicate that in the future there may be fewer long-term jobs with benefits and retirement packages. On the other hand, there will be more contract assignments and work on an **ad hoc** basis. This means it will be necessary to keep your skills upgraded, be the best at your profession, and have an entrepreneurial spirit. This will be the winning formula for continuous employment.

WHAT'S THE NEXT STEP?

By now, you have an understanding of the responsibilities of an administrative assistant and the possibilities for future employment. Are you still interested in pursuing this exciting career? If you are, then take the next step—work through the chapters in this textbook.

What Will You Learn?

The information, exercises, and challenges in this book will help you to learn:

1. how to be an efficient and effective administrative assistant—organizing work, managing time, maintaining desirable attitudes, and setting priorities
2. electronic office concepts—sending and receiving email, using the internet, arranging meetings with an electronic calendar, organizing electronic conferences, using voice mail, making effective use of a personal digital assistant, and maintaining online databases
3. where to access information on Canada's privacy laws and how to deal with confidential issues

4. what the Conference Board of Canada considers to be employability skills

5. procedures for preparing and processing written communications—transcribing, composing letters, processing incoming and outgoing mail, and preparing reports

6. procedures and guidelines for dealing with people—locally and internationally—face-to-face in the office or in meetings or over the telephone, and for making appointments and travel arrangements

7. how to rely on office equipment—computers, copiers, fax machines, telephones—for effective job performance

8. how to use published sources and databases for finding facts

9. information management—filing procedures, rules, systems, supplies, equipment, retention, storage, and retrieval

10. ways that office commerce is used by administrative assistants

11. the importance of a job campaign and how to launch a successful one

12. how to supervise others

QUESTIONS FOR STUDY AND REVIEW

1. Discuss six trends that exist in the modern office.
2. Explain the background of the title *secretary*.
3. Differentiate between the role of an executive assistant and a personal assistant.
4. Discuss how the Information Age has affected the administrative assistant's role.
5. Describe how legal and medical administrative assistants have specialized roles.

EVERYDAY ETHICS

What Did You Call Me?

You are employed by Image, a fast-paced and well-known publishing company, in Winnipeg. When you started working for Image two years ago, you were given the title of administrative assistant. At that time, the title was suitable for the responsibilities you were expected to perform. However, over time you took on much greater challenges. Six months ago, you began working exclusively for the chief executive officer (CEO). In addition to the traditional administrative responsibilities, you have been organizing the CEO's family vacations and arranging social events that take place at her home, as well as handling all the professional responsibilities associated with her position. You love your new job.

Last month you met with the CEO and expressed how much you were enjoying your new role. You then recommended that you receive a job title change from administrative assistant to personal assistant (PA) and that you

be paid a salary increase consistent with the new title. She rejected the suggestion of salary change, saying that the budget could not handle a salary for a personal assistant. She agreed to change your title to personal assistant as long as you continued to perform the PA responsibilities but that you would have to do so on your original salary. You accepted this offer but said that you would like to revisit the salary issue in the future, when you would make a stronger case for an increase. She agreed.

Soon after your meeting, you notice that one of the other administrative assistants is being called upon to perform the PA responsibilities for the CEO. You, on the other hand, are being asked to do less and less executive work. Today, the CEO brought a client out of her office and introduced you as her administrative assistant.

■ What should you do?

Problem Solving

1. The organization for which you recently started to work has invited a consultant to hold a seminar for administrative assistants on "The Dos and Don'ts of Electronic Messages." You read the first announcement and wanted to attend, but you did not apply because you were new to your job. Today another announcement was distributed, saying there is room for three more administrative assistants to attend. You have decided to tell your manager you want to go to the seminar. Write the statements you will use when you make the request.

2. You work in a law office. More than 35 percent of the material you are asked to key is presented to you in longhand. You have difficulty reading the longhand of one writer. This writer often sends you lengthy material. Because you have so much difficulty reading the writer's longhand, your production is very slow. What should you do?

3. You worked as an administrative assistant on your first job for four years before the organization merged with another organization. At that time, you were offered a job as a document specialist. You accepted it and have now been on the job one year, but you strongly dislike the work. On a daily basis, you spend between six and seven hours keying; you are not getting the experience you want. You have gone to Human Resources several times requesting a job similar to the one you had before the two organizations merged, but this type of position is not available. What are your alternatives?

Special Reports

1. Read and prepare a one-page summary of a magazine article discussing the role of the office professional. Use a current issue of *OfficePro* magazine.
2. Volunteer to be a class representative to visit the main office at your school. Find answers to questions such as these: How many administrative assistants work in the main office? What are the principal types of work performed at the main office? What equipment and software are used? What records are kept of the work performed? Report your findings to the class.

PRODUCTION CHALLENGES

Production Challenges will appear at the end of each chapter. In each Production Challenge, consider that you are an administrative assistant with

Millennium Appliances, Inc.
3431 Bloor Street
Toronto, ON M8X 1G4

Millennium Appliances, Inc. manufactures and sells its own line of innovative refrigerators, microwave ovens, conventional and convection ovens, garbage compactors, freezers, dishwashers, clothes washers and dryers, and pure water dispensers.

You work for Mr. William Wilson, Vice-President of Marketing (email wwilson@millennium.ca), and his four assistant vice-presidents:

Mr. Jack R. Rush
Assistant Vice-President of Marketing
Eastern Region
Extension 534
jrush@millennium.ca

Mrs. Linda Yee
Assistant Vice-President of Marketing
Midwestern Region
Extension 535
lyee@millennium.ca

Mr. Sid Levine
Assistant Vice-President of Marketing
Northwestern Region
Extension 536
slevine@millenium.ca

Ms. Charlene Azam
Assistant Vice-President of Marketing
Western Region
Extension 537
cazam@millennium.ca

Most of your communications are with the following managers of the four regional sales offices:

Ms. Joanna Hansen
Manager, Sales Office
Eastern Region
197 Queen Street
Fredericton, NB E3B 1A6
jhansen@millennium.ca

Mr. John Reddin
Manager, Sales Office
Midwestern Region
3436 College Avenue
Regina, SK S4T 1W4
jreddin@millennium.ca

Mrs. Mary Karlovsky
Manager, Sales Office
Northwestern Region
9129 Jasper Avenue
Edmonton, AB T5H 3T2
mkarlovsky@millennium.ca

Ms. Karuna Singe
Manager, Sales Office
Western Region
3152 West 45th Avenue
Vancouver, BC V6N 3M1
ksinge@millennium.ca

Please refer to Figure In-3 to view the regional organization chart for the Marketing Division of Millennium Appliances, Inc.

In-A Searching for Information
Supplies needed:
- *Plain paper*
- *This textbook*

Figure In-3 Organization chart for the Marketing Division of Millennium Appliances.

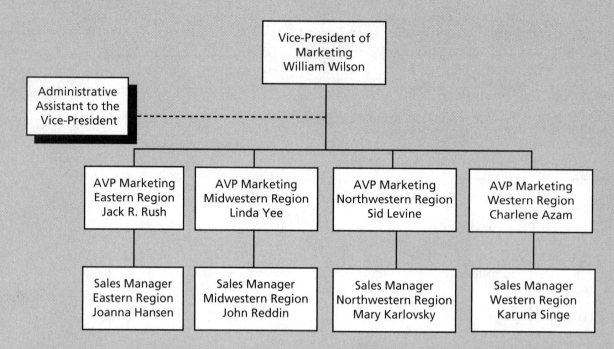

Millennium Appliances employs 24 administrative assistants. Mr. Wilson would like to propose that the company provide some resource materials for each assistant's workstation. He hands you this textbook and asks you to search the book to see if it contains information on the following topics. He suggests that you create a table showing the topic and the exact page number where that topic is discussed in the book.

- dealing with difficult customers
- working as an office team
- screening telephone calls
- placing international telephone calls
- dealing with customer abuse
- working with difficult team members
- coping with stress
- setting up a wellness program for employees
- acting ethically in the office
- dealing with office politics
- planning for the day's work
- controlling a large project
- organizing office supplies
- reading an organizational chart
- filing business correspondence
- setting up a video conference
- hosting international guests
- arranging flight tickets through the internet
- choosing the most efficient mail services
- preparing minutes of meetings
- giving effective presentations
- banking through the internet
- getting professional certification for administrative assistants
- accessing information on Canada's privacy laws

Weblinks

IAAP OfficePro
www.iaap-hq.org
This is the home page of the International Association of Administrative Professionals®. Articles from *OfficePro* magazine containing techniques, tips, and advice can be accessed from this page.

Deskdemon
http://us.deskdemon.com/pages/us/indexus
Resources, articles, and information for administrative professionals of all types are available. Also offered is a free monthly e-magazine.

Gaebler Ventures
www.gaebler.com/Office-Managers.htm
Tips and advice on how to run a small business office are abundant on this site. Topics include how to set up a conference call, how to run a meeting, common administrative assistant complaints, and hiring an office administrator.

Chapter 1
Human Relations

Learning Outcomes

After completion of this chapter, the student will be able to:

1 Define desirable interpersonal skills.

2 Identify 11 interpersonal skills that professionals display in the workplace.

3 Describe how to cope with nonproductive behaviours within a team.

4 Discuss guidelines for giving and receiving constructive criticism.

5 Give examples of information that is private and should be kept confidential.

6 Describe what is meant by *personal qualities* and explain why they are important in the workplace.

7 Recognize positive and negative behaviours associated with office politics.

8 Identify unethical office practice and determine how to deal with it.

9 Explain why change is inevitable in the office and how office professionals should handle it.

10 Identify strategies for dealing with stress.

11 Recognize the appropriate types of humour to use in the office environment.

12 Decide how to deal with romantic relationships in the professional environment.

13 Practise guidelines for dining etiquette during a business luncheon.

14 Recommend ideas for an employee wellness program.

Business offices are connected to virtually the entire world by the telephone, written communications, and telecommunication systems. Administrative assistants never know what situations they will encounter until they answer the telephone, access their email, read incoming faxes, listen to their voice mail, open the postal mail, or greet visitors at their desks. Whatever the situation, they are expected to respond in a manner that will keep, or make, friends for their organization.

Administrative assistants spend much of their time either directly in contact with people or producing and channelling information that will affect people. They collect, analyze, transmit, and store information, either through their computer system or manually. However they manage their work, administrative assistants are always connecting with colleagues or clients.

To be an effective administrative assistant, it will be necessary for you to possess the hard skills required in today's office. **Hard skills**, or technical skills, include working with a variety of technological equipment, using technology to produce and manage information, and maintaining and troubleshooting problems as they arise.

Graduate Profile

Jenny Bascur
Executive Assistant to the
Honourable Senator Percy E. Downe

Senate of Canada
Ottawa, Ontario

College Graduation:
Office Administration—Executive and Legal
  (Honours)
Algonquin College
Ottawa, Ontario

2005

"Networking is absolutely key."

Jenny Bascur worked as a legal assistant for six years in both medium-size and national law firms before accepting a position as an executive assistant to the Honourable Percy E. Downe at the Senate of Canada. Her responsibilities include composing, editing, and proofreading correspondence; assisting the senator with speeches and news releases; coordinating the senator's calendar and travel arrangements; managing the senator's office and travel budgets; and conducting research on a variety of issues according to the senator's needs.

To accomplish these tasks efficiently, Jenny relies on email—including messages received via her BlackBerry—and the telephone as her main communication tools. In fact, she handles between 50 and 75 email messages per day and could not work efficiently without the use of her computer and BlackBerry. She also uses various search engines every day to access media available online through the Parliament of Canada.

A key professional skill in the smooth operation of this busy office is organization—Jenny must manage the huge amount of information that arrives at her desk by way of email, faxes, news releases, and postal mail. She must sort through every item and ensure that those of importance are handled appropriately.

When Jenny took on her current position, she had to perform functions for which she had no previous experience, adding new challenges to her role. Managing personnel in the office is an example of a skill that Jenny has added to her repertoire since joining Senator Downe's staff. She has learned to effectively supervise the work of others by using tact and open-mindedness and by respecting the ideas of her co-workers.

Jenny feels professionally fulfilled in her current position supporting Senator Downe to the best of her ability, and she looks forward to taking on more research-oriented duties in the future. She advises future graduates to look for ways to continue their education, even in small ways, through classes, associations, and personal effort: "Read, read, read—keep yourself informed on your industry and the growth that takes place, as this makes you invaluable to an employer."

Jenny adds that the constant need for impeccable attention to detail can be challenging. This first-rate quality, however, is required at the executive level of administration, and is a good reminder for all administrative professionals to maintain an optimal degree of accuracy in their work.

More importantly, though, employers are placing greater emphasis on the **soft skills** that are necessary for success on the job. Success in gaining employment may be relatively easy, but the likelihood of your continued employment with the company might well depend on your highly developed soft skills.

Human relations soft skills include **personal qualities** such as having a positive attitude, being dependable, being responsible, having a positive self-image, being a self-starter, displaying integrity and honesty, and projecting a professional image. In addition to valued personal qualities, soft skills that employers seek include well-developed **interpersonal skills**, or the ability to

interact effectively with others. Examples of interpersonal skills include working as part of a team, teaching others, interacting with customers, negotiating agreements, and respecting diversity.

Employees can learn hard, or technical, skills with time and practice, but development of soft skills requires a genuine desire on the part of the employee to develop a positive attitude and to leave a positive impression with every person with whom he or she communicates. Possessing excellent human relations skills, both personal and interpersonal, will ensure you are recognized as a professional and as a valuable asset to your company.

DEVELOPING INTERPERSONAL SKILLS

To be an effective administrative assistant, you must be aware at all times that each person you meet, whether customer or co-worker, is forming an image of the organization, your manager, and you. You must rely on your business personality to communicate effectively with everyone you come in contact with in your business activities.

You cannot depend on knowledge, skills, and abilities alone for success in your job. Your performance as an effective office professional and your happiness on the job will be closely linked to your ability to communicate and to get along with people. This, in turn, will depend on your understanding the importance of interpersonal skills. Consider what happened to an administrative assistant named Violeta.

Violeta was one of several administrative assistants at a large travel agency. The manager and assistant manager were discussing which of the administrative assistants should be promoted to office manager to replace the present office manager, who had been promoted to travel agent after she received her certification. The manager mentioned that Violeta should be selected for the office manager position. He stated that she had less experience than the other four administrative assistants and had adequate technical skills, but that she would make a great office manager. The assistant manager said he thought that Anita would make a better office manager. Anita knew more about the computer system being used and had several years of experience with the travel agency. The first manager said, "I agree that Anita has better technical skills and more experience, but I have personally seen Violeta resolve several difficult problems. Violeta has terrific people skills and works really well with customers as well as the rest of the office staff." The assistant manager said, "Yes, you are right. Let's promote Violeta. We can keep Anita in mind as our second choice."

Situations like this happen all the time in the workplace. Often a person is promoted simply because he or she has good interpersonal skills combined with adequate technical skills. You should strive to display good interpersonal skills at all times. Do not depend solely on your technical skills and knowledge, even if they are superior skills.

Interpersonal skills are not just about getting along with people. When you promote an atmosphere that encourages idea sharing and that recognizes experiences and individual differences, your interpersonal skills are further enhanced. Your reward is personal satisfaction, the respect of others, and your co-workers' recognition of you as a true professional.

Figure 1-1 shows how you can improve your interpersonal skills by working on one skill at a time. Here are some of the interpersonal skills to help you succeed in the workplace.

Figure 1-1 Improving your interpersonal skills one step at a time can help you to achieve a professional image.

Be a Team Player

Teamwork has replaced individual work as the basic building block of organizations. Teamwork is viewed as an effective and efficient way to accomplish work, to build harmony in the office, to increase individual and group knowledge, and to strengthen the organization. In fact, employers value team skills so highly that they search for new employees who can contribute to the corporate team just as much as they can contribute independently.

As you contribute effectively to team efforts, your membership on other teams will become a desirable commodity. The more teams to which you contribute, the more opportunities you will have to expand your knowledge, responsibilities, and career opportunities.

Setting ground rules is an essential part of ensuring a productive and effective work team. (Refer to the section "Team Meetings" in Chapter 13 for examples of ground rules.)

Some of the many team behaviours that lead to productivity and can serve as a basis for ground rules are:

- treating every member with respect
- basing decisions on fact rather than opinion
- communicating clearly and honestly
- balancing participation among all team members at meetings
- staying on topic and not allowing digressions during meetings

- seeking creative ways to solve problems through brainstorming

- summarizing decisions at the end of team meetings

- committing to do equal work

- believing that every member has talents that will contribute to the team's work

- not personalizing criticism of the project; remember, it's a team effort

Become a role model by displaying these positive team behaviours. In return, you will earn the respect of your team members.

As an administrative assistant, take every opportunity to work in a team. This will increase your knowledge, job satisfaction, and value to the company. Take full responsibility for your part of the workload and for any problems that arise within the team. If you think in terms of what you can contribute rather than of what you can get, you will earn greater acceptance by the office team and a greater sense of self-satisfaction. Strive for excellence, and be enthusiastic about your team responsibilities. When the team is successful, every individual will be successful.

The benefits of teamwork are numerous. Consider:

- An effective group can accomplish more work than an effective individual.

- Teams provide social interaction.

- During stressful periods of work, the team will provide emotional support for its members.

---

pro-Link
Swearing Supervisors

Like any relationship, the manager-assistant relationship will have its ups and downs. Here are some positive points to help you deal with a manager who shouts and uses profanities:

- This is unacceptable behaviour, but the yelling may have nothing to do with your performance. Most people shout to vent built-up frustration from a variety of sources.
- Keep calm and use a warm tone in your voice.
- Think of a parent-child relationship and, without being condescending, deal with the situation like a clever parent.
- Don't get engaged in the shouting or the expletives.
- Let the manager know that this behaviour is not appreciated, but don't show that you are rattled or distressed. Stay on top!

- As team members share information, the knowledge and experience of the team members grow.

- The company values employees who contribute to the organization's goals and decision making through teamwork.

Good teamwork consists of clear and full communication as well as trust. A successful team will be one that informs all its members as well as management. A high level of disclosure leads to trust between team members and between management and the team. Trust is essential if the team members and the team as a whole are to be **empowered** and capable.

Nonproductive Behaviours

No matter how well-intentioned your team is, nonproductive behaviours may still exist. The following are descriptions of some of the nonproductive behaviours encountered in many teams. Also provided are some suggested remedies.

1. **Dominant or Reluctant Team Members.** When one or more members of a team monopolize discussions, or when you have a member who is reluctant to discuss the team's issues for whatever reason, you need to work at balancing the participation. While treating all members with courtesy and respect, you should point out the ground rule where you agreed to balance and share the team discussions. As a team leader, you could encourage a balanced discussion by interjecting with comments such as "Carole, thanks for sharing that information. Rima, we haven't heard from you. What are your feelings on the . . . ?"

2. **Lack of Direction.** When team members lack direction, members do not know how to get started or what the next step should be. If the team establishes an action plan in the early stages of the process, the members will find it easier to stay on track.

3. **Digressing.** Not staying on topic is a common team problem. When the conversation starts to drift, tactfully make the team aware of it, and ask the members to focus on the topic at hand. For example, you might say, "Getting back to the agenda item we were discussing . . ." or "Mark, getting back to the point you were making on . . ." or simply "Getting back to Item #3. . . ." This should be enough to bring the team back to the topic being discussed.

4. **Quarrelling.** When two or more team members begin to argue, the other team members are left feeling uncomfortable and frustrated by the team's lack of productivity. If this should occur, act as the mediator. Mediation may take the form of speaking privately to

the members involved. However, you might simply compare their behaviour to the ground rule discouraging such behaviour and remind them that their actions are unproductive.

5. **Discounting.** People sometimes discount the work and opinions of others through their unkind criticism, lack of attention, poor body language, and so on. Every person deserves respect and attention. If you sense that someone on your team is being discounted, support that person. Comments that show consideration and attention are not difficult to make.

Recognize Individual Differences

To deal effectively with others in the workplace, it is necessary to recognize that people have individual differences—different capabilities, needs, and interests. The purpose of learning and understanding about individual differences in personality types is to help you build better working relationships and establish rapport with others.

Learn to Work with Difficult People

Even if you are congenial, cooperative, and a strong team player, you will encounter people with whom it is difficult to interact effectively. Many types of difficult people have been identified. Here are a few common types and some suggestions on how to cope with them.

The Bully The bully uses intimidation to gain control by making others angry or afraid. The bully tries to push all your buttons by yelling, name-calling, sarcasm, mocking, putting down, belittling, embarrassing, or negativity to cause these reactions in others.

Coping:

- Think only about the positive attributes of the bully—what you like about her when she is not bullying.

- Look her straight in the eye. Using a calm, normal voice and "I" and not "you" words, say exactly what you don't like about her behaviour. For instance, you might say, "I do not like it when people raise their voices at me. I feel as if I am being treated like a child. I am not a child. I am an adult and want to be treated as such."

The Gossip The gossip goes from person to person spreading negative rumours about others, whether true or not, and trying to set one person against the other. He looks for people who will listen and agree with him. He feels open to use anyone's name who listens to him; he says such things as, "I just talked to Jo and she told me. . . ." It makes him feel powerful.

Coping:

- When the gossip begins telling his rumour, break into the conversation and say something positive about the person or situation.

- Each time the gossip resumes by saying, "Yes, but . . . ," break in again and give a positive statement about the person or situation. Gossips dislike talking to people who always find the good in others or in situations.

- If you refuse to listen, sooner or later the gossip will get the message.

The Know-It-All The know-it-all believes she is the expert. She has opinions about everything, but when she is found to be wrong, she passes the buck or becomes defensive.

Coping:

- Deal with her on a one-on-one basis, not in a group setting.

- Check the facts, be sure they are correct, and then state your facts.

- Do not put down the know-it-all.

- Give the person a way out so she can save face.

The Backstabber The backstabber will try to get you to discuss a problem or situation in which you are involved. He appears to befriend you and encourages you to talk freely. Later, he goes to the person or supervisor with whom he knows he can cause the most damage to you, and he repeats what you told him, often embellishing the information. He wants to discredit you to others.

Coping:

- Do not retaliate by talking about the backstabber. It may appear as if you are the backstabber.

- Always think before you speak. Don't say anything to anyone in the office you wouldn't want repeated.

- Keep an accurate record of what happens. If the backstabber is your boss, you need verification of what was said—date, time, conversation, and anyone else who heard it.

The Blamer The blamer never solves her own problems. When faced with a problem, she thinks someone else caused it—the supervisor, a group member, or you.

Coping:

- Attempt to get the blamer to answer the question, "Whose responsibility was it for (whatever the problem is)?" Answering that question gets to the heart of the problem.

Difficult people tend to bring out the worst in us. Many know how to "push our buttons" to cause us to react emotionally, to cause us distress, or simply to create tension. Here is a plan to follow to help you deal with these difficult situations:

1. Do not react emotionally; stand back and take a look at the situation. If you do not have to respond immediately, take time to write down everything in as much detail as possible.

2. Analyze the behaviour of the difficult person. Identify exactly what was said that caused you to feel threatened or upset. What do you believe motivated the person to make the statement or to create the situation?

3. Analyze your behaviour and emotional response (e.g., anger, frustration, disappointment).

4. Decide exactly what behaviour—all or part—you believe you must acknowledge and respond to and why.

5. Define all the ways you might respond.

6. Decide on a plan: What will you say (making sure you form the statements using "I" and not "you"), where will you say it, and when will you say it?

7. Imagine how the person might respond.

The more experience you gain in dealing with difficult people, the easier it will be to maintain a positive attitude throughout adverse experiences.

Teach Others

Often the opportunity will arise on the job for you to help others learn new techniques, processes, software, equipment, or other new skills. Seize every opportunity to volunteer when the need arises to help others learn. In addition to creating an environment of cooperation, your actions will highlight you as a highly skilled and valuable employee with potential for leading others. Helpful hints to successfully teach others include:

■ Do not give the impression that you think you "know it all," which could lead to resentment from the co-worker whom you are helping.

■ Be patient; not everyone learns at the same rate.

■ Recognize that some learn by doing rather than by just being told.

■ Don't view others' learning as a threat to your job.

■ Recognize that in the process of teaching others, you often learn from them as well. Let your co-workers know that you have learned through teaching them.

Offer Exceptional Customer Service

Exceptional customer service is helping customers, clients, or co-workers with a willingness to put their needs first in order to resolve their problems. Some of these skills are:

■ Smile and be friendly.

■ Offer to help before being asked.

■ If you can't help, locate someone who can.

■ If the person is upset, let him or her vent frustration; then show empathy and understanding.

■ Go the extra mile above and beyond what would normally be expected of you.

These highly desirable skills will promote your professional image and the customers-first image of the company. Customer service does not mean just offering excellent service to those customers outside your business; it also means you see each person within your organization as a customer as well and treat him or her as such.

Exercise Leadership

Exercising leadership means communicating your position on certain matters clearly and effectively, persuading or convincing others, and responsibly challenging existing procedures and policies when necessary. A good leader shows self-confidence and intelligence, follows the rules, stands behind his or her word, is trustworthy, and has a sense of humour.

It has been said that good leaders are made, not born. If you have the desire and the willingness to become a leader, your chances of attaining that goal will improve by developing effective leadership skills. Good leaders develop through a never-ending process of self-study, education, training, and experience. Remember, power does not make you a good leader; power just means you are the boss. A good leader influences employees to want to do a good job by leading rather than just bossing people around.

Negotiate Effectively

Negotiating means the process of exchanging ideas, information, and opinions with others to work toward agreements; consequently, policies and programs are formulated, and decisions, conclusions, or solutions are the result of a joint effort. A good negotiator:

■ Thinks before he or she begins. Do your homework so you will know the other's side, and then develop a plan and write it down. Know the minimum and maximum for which you are willing to settle.

- Is ready to compromise. Identify the benefits of your offer. Even getting a little of what you want makes you a winner.
- Displays excellent people skills. You must observe the other person and be ready to adjust to his or her personality.
- Is a good listener. Develop the habit of summarizing what the other person says to make sure you understand his or her intent.

Embrace Constructive Criticism

Constructive criticism is the process of offering one's opinion about the work of another. The criticism should involve both positive and constructive comments, and the comments should be offered in a friendly manner rather than a confrontational one. Some people tend to take criticism negatively; we should embrace constructive criticism, even welcome it, because it can help us improve.

When giving constructive criticism:

1. Be genuine. Criticism is only constructive if the person giving it truly means to help the person receiving it and feels it is important.

2. Always give criticism in private.

3. Don't sound threatening. Avoid statements that start with "I think you should" or "You have to" or "You had better." It would be better to say, "Let's take a look at what has been happening and see if, between the two of us, we can work out a solution. What do you think?"

4. Focus on the problem, not the person.

When receiving constructive criticism:

1. Welcome the criticism. See it as a way for you to improve.

2. Listen carefully to the criticism; restate the criticism when necessary.

3. Focus on the problem, not the person giving it.

4. Understand that this dialogue can help improve the interpersonal relationship between you and the person giving the criticism.

Keep Confidential Information Confidential

Whatever management system you work in, you will always have to practise discretion when it comes to confidential information.

Refrain from repeating the opinions of your management. In fact, most activities that take place in your office should be kept confidential. To gain the trust of your organization, manager, and co-workers, never discuss company business outside the office.

If there is an upcoming company announcement and you are aware of it, keep it confidential. Managers should make company announcements.

Be careful not to give away confidential information to your colleagues or to your company's competitors. Sometimes just one isolated fact obtained from you is all the information that a competitor needs. Confidential information is often given away without intent. For example, you are proud of where you work and the decisions that management is making. As a result, you discuss this information with new acquaintances at a social event. When this happens, however, you never know where the information will end up and how it will be used. Always use good judgment and discretion when sharing company information.

Be Considerate

"Good morning" is viewed by some people as only a necessary, routine greeting. But a pleasant and cheerful greeting is appreciated when it is sincere and optimistic. Take the high road! Speak first and call other people by name. Be pleasant and respectful of everyone, from the cleaning staff to the owner of the company. Make an effort to get acquainted with as many co-workers as possible. People prefer to work with upbeat people. Be one of them.

Other people will see you as approachable if you are pleasant, courteous, and responsive. Listen attentively when someone is talking with you. Be responsive to what is going on around you. Avoid being condescending when giving instructions. Suggest rather than command. Request rather than demand.

Be considerate of others by doing the following:

1. Stop at the administrative assistant's desk when you go in to see his or her manager.

2. Wait your turn to use the office copier.

3. When you must interrupt someone, time your interruption so it will have the least impact on the people being interrupted.

4. Remember that everyone has personal interests and pursuits. These might include family, education, and leisure activities. Inquiring about these nonbusiness topics shows diplomacy.

Knowing what *not* to say is as important as knowing what to say. Be very careful when discussing sensitive subjects such as religion, money, morals, or politics; you don't want to offend a co-worker. You can gain trust of others by:

- keeping general criticism to yourself
- treating others as you wish to be treated
- talking positively about colleagues
- not making negative remarks about co-workers
- not prying into others' personal affairs
- not criticizing your employer, colleagues, or management at any time
- thinking and then speaking; otherwise, your statements may come out wrong and place you in an embarrassing position
- being cooperative and doing more than is expected of you

Create a pleasant, businesslike atmosphere by establishing good rapport with employees and customers at all levels. Besides creating a pleasant atmosphere in which to work, your thoughtfulness will help you enjoy your relationships with others.

Be Sociable

Sociable people demonstrate understanding, friendliness, adaptability, empathy, and politeness in group settings. Some employees develop social bonds with certain co-workers. You may find others with whom you work who have interests similar to your own, and, because of these similar interests, you will become closer to them. You should, however, strive to be friendly toward each person in your work group. A pleasant smile and an acknowledgment of each individual will continually show others that you are a friendly, pleasant co-worker.

Always take part in office get-togethers such as birthday celebrations, lunches, or holiday celebrations. Your attendance and participation will demonstrate that you belong to the office group and will show your desire to support your co-workers.

Self-Check

1. List five important interpersonal skills.
2. What are three benefits of teamwork?
3. What are five nonproductive team behaviours?
4. What is meant by individual differences?
5. How would you deal with a backstabber?
6. List any interpersonal skills you plan to improve.

DEVELOPING PERSONAL QUALITIES

When you accept a position with a company, management expects you to do the best job you can and to get along with everyone to the best of your ability. Remember that your contribution is essential to a smooth-running, productive, and efficient office. By upholding a high standard of personal qualities, you will demonstrate excellent human relations skills to those around you, and your role will become a central one on the office team (see Figure 1-2).

Be Responsible

Responsibility means accepting the assignment of duties. When you accept a position, you are being entrusted with and assigned many duties. You are expected to perform these duties to the best of your ability. To be responsible, you must answer to someone for your actions, and on the job this means your supervisor. Displaying responsibility is one of the key human relations skills.

Be Dependable

Dependability means being consistent and reliable in your behaviour. For instance, you would display dependability by having an excellent attendance record and by being prompt in arriving at work each morning and in returning on time to your workstation after each break and lunch. Dependability helps create a desirable office atmosphere.

Figure 1-2 Personal qualities needed to project a professional image.

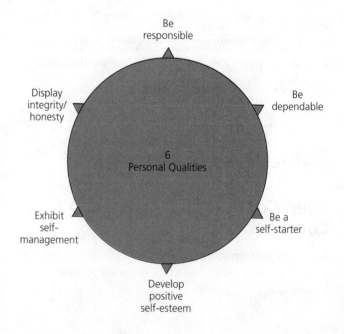

Each employee in your office depends on every person being there. When someone is absent, no matter the reason, or is late returning from lunch or a break, someone in the office must cover for that person. When someone is covering for another individual, that person is not getting his or her own work completed. Hostile feelings can grow quickly toward any people who do not carry their workloads and are not dependable.

Be a Self-Starter

Self-starters take the initiative to begin tasks for which they are responsible. Don't wait for your manager to ask you to do something—be observant and anticipate what you are expected to do without having to be told.

When you finish your work, ask if you can help someone else. Everyone feels overworked and underpaid; and when someone sits idly by while others are swamped, a negative attitude builds toward the person who is not busy. You can't just say, "It isn't my job," because it is your job to help anyone at any time you are not busy. You are paid to work a full day's work, and you should project the image of always wanting to help when help is needed.

Develop Positive Self-Esteem

Self-esteem is the opinion you have of yourself. As you perform a task or handle a situation well, you gain confidence that you can do it well again. With practice and success, your confidence will grow. Once you have gained self-confidence, you will rely on your competence and the strength of your own judgment.

The following list identifies some of the concepts that affect your self-esteem:

- the value you place on yourself as a person
- the opinion you believe others hold of you
- your strengths and weaknesses
- your social status and how you relate to others
- your ability to be independent

Low self-esteem is when you view one or more of these items negatively, which results in a poor self-image. High self-esteem is just the opposite and causes you to be confident and believe in your ability to succeed. Having positive self-esteem is critical to your living a happy life both at home and in the workplace. People who are self-confident rely on the correctness of their own judgment and competence in spite of the discouragement and influence of others.

Confident people can maintain **composure** even under pressure. Composure is a sense of calmness or tranquillity. Confident people also exhibit **poise**, which denotes ease and dignity of manner. Keep the following tips in mind:

1. Believe in your abilities and remain in control of your reactions. Be consistent in maintaining your composure. There is no place in the professional world for a temperamental person. If your colleagues cannot rely on you to be cooperative and pleasant, they will avoid working with you. A temperamental attitude is a serious barrier to effectiveness and cooperation in the office.

2. You cannot control all the circumstances that surround your work. Most of the daily happenings in the office—new problems, minor changes, major changes, new situations, emergencies—are beyond your control. However, how you react to them is within your control. Don't overreact. Turn challenges into opportunities for growth.

3. When you feel impatient, don't show it! Be patient, take time to distinguish fact from fiction, and withhold judgment until you have all the facts.

4. Develop a sense of humour and use it at the right time. Laugh *at* yourself, but laugh *with* others. Do not take yourself or your problems too seriously. Suggestions for practising humour in the workplace are discussed later in this chapter in the section "Manage Stress."

Exhibit Self-Management

Self-management means that you set personal goals, monitor your progress, assess yourself accurately, and exhibit self-control. Your goals may be for self-improvement in certain areas, attempting something new, or working on a personal problem.

When you are faced with difficult situations in the workplace, you should always exhibit self-control. You know yourself better than anyone else; therefore, if this is an area you need to work on, set self-management goals to develop the ability to react as you should in stressful situations. When you are in a tense situation, stop and think before you speak. Give yourself time to analyze the reactions of others to what you might say. This time can allow you to organize your thoughts and response, help you develop the desired attitude, and avoid reacting inappropriately.

You should seek to cultivate attitudes and traits that will contribute to your success. When you succeed in displaying an appropriate attitude or trait in a difficult situation, you will be able to apply that experience in coping with the next difficult situation.

Display Integrity/Honesty

Integrity and honesty both involve being sincere and trustworthy. No one wants to work with someone who does not possess these characteristics. The lack of these characteristics can lead to termination of employment. Just as you set these standards for yourself, you should expect the same standards from everyone with whom you work. Integrity encompasses sound moral or ethical principles, fairness, honesty, sincerity, and the courage to stand up for these moral precepts. Strength of character, the behaviour that demonstrates you live by your values, and integrity are among the most important traits a person can possess.

You will be respected if your dealings with others are fair, honest, and sincere. Not all aspects of business are as ethical as they should be. When you face a serious ethical situation, rely on your strength of character to make your decision. Your only alternative may be to change employment. Whatever your decision, never cover for another person's transgression. You must be accountable for your actions.

Remember to Always Project a Professional Image

What is professionalism? **Professionalism** is aspiring to meet the highest possible standards of your profession rather than a set of minimum requirements. Embrace these opportunities rather than shying away from them.

First impressions are everything, and the first impression you want to make is by projecting a positive professional image. A professional image reflects:

- an educated and skilled employee
- a team player who contributes valuable ideas
- a polished individual with a neat, groomed appearance and a clear, concise communication style
- a person who can solve problems and integrate ideas
- a person who takes pride in each piece of work he or she produces
- an employee who works for the betterment of the organization and is not self-serving
- a person who takes pride in his or her career and who has aspirations for the future
- an employee who manages assignments by applying quality standards
- an employee who is willing to work hard and accept new and more challenging responsibilities
- an employee who is willing to learn and grow professionally

- one who seeks to learn about professional organizations such as the International Association of Administrative Professionals (IAAP; see Chapter 17)

Sir Walter Scott said, "Success or failure is caused more by mental attitude than by mental capacity." You should approach life and your job with a positive attitude. Periodically take inventory of your needs and your accomplishments. Set new goals and keep reaching. Your rewards will be many, including physical vitality, an alert mind, and an optimistic attitude toward life.

Self-Check

1. Rank the six personal qualities in order with the most important listed first and the least important last.
2. List any personal qualities you plan to improve.

WHAT ABOUT OFFICE POLITICS?

Office politics can be defined simply as actions taken by office employees to influence others for personal reasons. Depending on how you react to office politics, it can work either to your advantage or your disadvantage.

Recognize It

These attempts to influence others are often exhibited in some of the following ways:

- **Withholding or Selectively Sharing Information.** If an employee chooses to pass along damaging information, it can seriously affect the careers of other employees. The same is true when accurate information is withheld.
- **Creating Political Networks.** When a person cultivates a relationship with someone for the purpose of getting advancement in the office, gaining information, getting approval on a project, or reaching other personal objectives, it is referred to as political networking. If you are excluded from the office social network, you may become quite powerless.
- **Accusing Other People.** Sometimes one employee will repeatedly place blame on a particular employee. This action might be to target a person who is in a desirable position. Eventually management may be convinced that the employee being blamed is detrimental to the staff. In this case, the accused person may lose his/her job, leaving the job open for the accuser.

- **Forming Groups.** How often have we heard the expression "strength in numbers"? When two or more people with a common purpose join together to force a change in the office, they are acting politically. This group may attempt to change office procedures or even to change management decisions.

Being able to recognize office politics is important. But for many people, this skill is acquired only with some firsthand experience.

Good or Bad?

We acknowledge that office politics exists, but is it a good thing or is it a bad thing for the office?

If you become politically involved in your company for the good of others, especially your co-workers or subordinates, you will be favourably recognized. An example would be creating a political network that allows you to grow close to management personnel. Your association with management may get your department an increase in budget. Subsequently, that budget increase might create some new work in your department, allowing your co-workers to keep their jobs. On the other hand, the people who lose at the game of office politics or are the victim of another person's political gain will view office politics as unfavourable.

Whether you approve of office politics or not, it does exist. The best policy is to stay away from politics that will adversely affect others. However, some healthy political maneuvers that bring success to your team and are not at the expense of other people are characteristic of good leadership.

Self-Check

1. Give three examples of "good" office politics.
2. Give three examples of "bad" office politics.

WORKPLACE ETHICS

The concept of ethics is difficult to understand. Cultures have wrestled with it for millennia without developing a set of rules describing what is good and what is bad. Whether you act ethically or unethically at work will depend on several factors, including the way you were raised, your individual values, personality, and experience. It will also have a lot to do with the organization's culture and the issue in question.

Ethical Practice

Many common practices are questionable in the workplace. They are often associated with irresponsible work practice and the theft of time and resources.

Examples of questionable behaviour are:

- doing something unethical based on a request by your manager—for example, shredding documents to hide the fact that they ever existed
- altering information on documents to falsify information
- not reporting incidents, such as accidents, in a manufacturing company

Along with these common practices comes the rationalization: the devil made me do it, they don't pay me enough, I put so much time in here anyway, and I write reports at home . . . I think "they" should supply the paper! But employees, regardless of their roles, are ethically obliged to follow the ethical law at work just as they are legally obliged to follow civil law. Obviously, we should not steal, lie, or harass others in the workplace. We should treat others with respect and expect the same consideration in return.

Employees are obliged to fulfill the terms of their contract. If they are hired to work eight hours a day, they should work that amount of time. They should work conscientiously according to the terms of their contract. We are obliged to consider the interests of the organization for which we work. These obligations are sometimes spelled out in employment contracts and job descriptions.

Without rules, good ethical practice becomes **ambiguous**. Codes of ethical practice are an increasingly popular tool for reducing that ambiguity. A **code of ethics** is a formal document developed by your organization that states the organization's primary values and ethical rules of conduct. The best ones are specific and not only guide employees in what they are supposed to do but also allow employees the freedom to exercise judgment in their decisions.

Decisions, especially ambiguous ones, can be tested by asking yourself questions such as:

- What benefit and what harm will my decision produce?
- What rights do the other people have that are involved in my decision, and what can I do to respect those rights?
- Which decision treats everyone the same and does not show favouritism or discrimination?
- Does my decision benefit most people in the organization or just me?
- Does my decision consider my ideas of honesty, compassion, integrity, fairness, and good sense?

Figure 1-3 Good teamwork consists of clear and full communication.

Adopting a code of corporate ethics is popular for many contemporary organizations. If a code of ethics exists at the organization where you work, read it and commit to its principles. If used well, the code will guide you through those ambiguous decisions. Codes of ethics can be effective depending on whether the organization supports them and how employees are treated when they break the code. In the end, as an employee you have the responsibility to do the right thing based upon your own judgment and personal principles.

Work, Time, and Resources

Good judgment and discretion are much more than keeping information confidential. Their foundation lies in sound ethical conduct, which has a far-reaching effect in the contemporary business office. Let's review ethical responsibilities as they relate to the office. If you find yourself considering any of the following activities, recognize that your organization's policies and trust are likely to be compromised.

With Regard to Work

- plagiarizing
- harassing co-workers
- exaggerating on your résumé
- pretending to be ill
- spreading untrue information
- endangering others
- deceiving others

- acting unreasonably
- speaking negatively in public about the organization

With Regard to Time

- taking extended breaks
- arriving late
- leaving early
- wasting time
- talking at length on personal telephone calls
- checking your personal email during company time

With Regard to Resources

- exaggerating on expense claims
- playing games on the company computer
- downloading software for personal use
- conducting personal research on the internet
- taking supplies for personal use at home
- using the photocopier for personal documents

Consider your company's code of ethics as well as your own standards of loyalty, fairness, and truthfulness. Then ask yourself if you would be comfortable if your actions were published on the front page of the office newsletter. After this simple test, you'll know whether or not you have compromised any codes or standards.

Self-Check

1. List two additional examples of unethical situations.

Figure 1-4 A confident person maintains composure even under pressure.

CHANGE IN THE WORKPLACE
Change Is Constant

Change has become the expectation in the office. Change, both organizational and technological, is an important part of doing business and cannot be avoided.

Changes come about rapidly because of the relentless updating of office technology, competition between companies, and the restructuring of organizations to become more efficient. Newer technology is enabling administrative assistants to produce more with greater speed and ease than in the past. Organizations keep replacing old equipment with state-of-the-art equipment, so accept the fact that the equipment and software you learn to operate today will be replaced by new technology tomorrow.

The pressure of competition has increased because of international trade. Telecommunications and the **internet** have made competing in the **global marketplace** common practice.

Another major change has been the restructuring of organizations. Companies are constantly striving to outdo their competition, a process that involves combining or eliminating functions and buying equipment that will improve their operations. All of this results in changes in procedures.

As well, company **mergers** and **buyouts** occur, resulting in a duplication of jobs and positions that must be addressed. In a merger, the two companies agree on the restructuring. In a buyout, one company buys out the other and there may be less agreement on restructuring.

Regardless of where you work, change is inevitable. Anticipate it, and realize that change is the way of the future. Expect yourself to suddenly be using new equipment and new software, to be assigned an entirely new job within your organization, or to be looking for employment with another organization. Instead of wasting energy over changes you cannot avoid, direct your energy toward getting in step with the new arrangements. If an opportunity to use new equipment or software presents itself, or a chance to participate in further training or new responsibilities arises, grasp the opportunity. You should always welcome new possibilities for growth, since professional development prepares you for steady employment and improves your prospects for career advancement.

Adapt to New Management

You can expect to have more than one change in management as well as a variety of roles and possibly a variety of careers in your lifetime. Your challenge is to prove yourself in all situations. Never expect a new management team to be like the last one. No two managers are exactly alike. The best advice to handle changes in management is to be flexible, adaptable, and tolerant (FAT). Show tolerance to different ideas and beliefs expressed by the new management team.

Management can change rapidly, but successful managers do share some of the same qualities. For example, all good managers have a capacity for hard work and are dedicated to the job and the team. They are never satisfied with the status quo; they can't afford to be.

Respect your manager's position. A managerial job involves continual problems that are not always easy to solve. You can contribute by listening and offering solutions instead of problems. Whenever you need to address an issue with the manager, always be prepared to offer viable solutions.

You should be as dependable and accountable to the new management as to the previous management. At all levels of management, loyalty is rated as one of the most desirable traits an employee can possess. Being loyal means supporting the organization's policies and actions. Being loyal can be difficult when you believe management is not working in the best interests of the organization. If you find yourself in this situation, don't jump to conclusions. Not all managers are good managers and many lose their positions because of poor management skills. Working for a manager who does not perform the job well will be difficult. However, by being loyal to the company, diplomatic, and tolerant, you should be able to preserve your own job.

A promotion for you could mean working for new management. Be flexible. Be willing to accept change and to adjust to new situations. View change as the opportunity for new and exciting challenges. The more you demonstrate your ability to accept the challenges of your new assignments, the more professional opportunities will come your way.

MANAGE STRESS

Jobs in contemporary offices can be very stressful. But some people seem to thrive on **stress** while others crumble under it. The difference is that those who cope well with stress have control over their jobs. This control enables them to meet their own deadlines, as well as deadlines set for them by others. Having a positive attitude toward work helps people to deal with stress.

Wellness in the Workplace

Although the workplace may seem to be safe, hazards abound. Ergonomic illnesses such as repetitive stress injuries, neck strain, eye stress, and muscle strain are just the beginning. The most common workplace illness in the professional environment is mental stress.

Companies are well aware of the effect of stress on the employee. They are equally aware of the cost to the company when workers are away from their jobs either through physical illness or mental stress leaves. It is in the company's best interest to take good care of its employees. That's why programs for prevention of workplace illness are in place at many organizations. Some of the common programs include:

- free access to wellness counsellors, social workers, and psychologists
- company-sponsored memberships for health clubs
- health seminars held at lunchtime
- health videos, CDs, and books available in the company library
- company-paid massage therapy
- company-sponsored healthcare and dental plans
- health food in the company cafeteria
- fitness programs offered at the company's own gym or courts

Figure 1-5 Recognize when your co-workers are under stress.

What Causes Stress in the Office?

What makes office work stressful? This question is difficult to answer since what causes negative stress for one person is stimulating and positive to the next worker. The following is a list of reported sources of work-related stress for many office professionals:

- Some office workers are hired to complete temporary assignments. In these cases, there is very little long-term employment security.
- Technology improves rapidly, requiring constant retraining.
- Management styles and organizational structures continue to change. Companies have flattened their management and downsized their staff, causing insecurity for workers. In these cases, employees work under the constant threat of losing their jobs.
- The responsibilities of office professionals have broadened and intensified.
- Workloads have become heavier as companies cut back their budgets and expect to do more with fewer resources.
- In order to keep up with the workload, many office professionals work through the day without taking time for lunch, refreshments, or even washroom breaks.

Handle It

People often blame the company or their jobs for causing their high levels of stress. In fact, stress leave is a common request for people believing they need relief from their work. However, work is not the only source of negative stress. People who carry a lot of responsibility outside their employment often suffer from stress because they are trying to do too much—balancing the responsibilities for family and home, community work, continued education and training, and so on.

To cope with stress, analyze what is happening to you. Often it is not the situation that causes stress but how you react to it and what you do about it.

A certain amount of stress helps us to be alert, efficient, and creative. Here are some suggestions for handling stress that becomes *too* great:

1. Recognize what your body is telling you, and recognize that anger and frustration are energy wasters. Keep notes on what is happening and the cause.
2. Organize your work and your time for the entire day. Assign priorities to your work; don't plan more than is possible to do in a day.
3. When faced with an overload of work, analyze it and discuss it with your supervisor. Offer solutions. By facing a situation, you will relieve stress and ensure that you don't become overwhelmed.

4. Don't be overly critical of your own work and don't expect impossible levels of work from others. Strive for excellence, but at times be pleased with an acceptable performance.

5. Slow down! This is good advice for office professionals who race around doing their work at turbo speeds. You will accomplish more and also eliminate stress by working at a comfortable pace—one that enables you to keep mistakes to a minimum, to relate well with others, and to avoid backtracking and revising.

6. Avoid taking on too much. Learn to say "no" tactfully. Don't hesitate to refuse outside organizations that ask you to do volunteer work. Consider hiring help for home and family responsibilities.

7. Talk out your stressful problems. Find someone in whom you can confide—someone away from the job, someone who is a good listener. Simply talking out your problem can be helpful.

8. Eat nourishing food regularly and in moderate amounts.

9. Program relaxation into your schedule. Use lunch and coffee breaks to relax. Don't use these breaks to rush around on personal errands. During your breaks, be quiet, and practise relaxation techniques until you feel yourself relaxing. Use waiting time to relax. Allow yourself a quiet hour at home. Schedule some time for a hobby.

10. Get regular exercise. Exercise is one of the best ways to shed stress.

11. Escape to a movie, to your favourite TV program, to spend time with others, or to do something for someone in need.

Humour Is Helpful

Work should be fun. If you dislike getting ready for work and going to your office each morning, it's time to take action. You can either terminate your employment or enhance your employment. When there is a healthy dose of humour in the office, productivity and enthusiasm increase; and the workplace becomes an appealing place to be. Humour need not detract from a professional atmosphere. In the correct proportion, inoffensive humour can actually strengthen the professional environment.

Laughter promotes teamwork and reduces stress. Research indicates that laughter is healthy not only mentally, but also physiologically, since laughter actually massages our internal organs. But knowing when to refrain from using humour is paramount. Use your common sense to judge when and where humour is appropriate. Good timing and good taste are essential.

Assess your office and consider how to make the environment more enjoyable without losing the professional climate.

Here are some ideas to consider:

1. Purchase a joke book; occasionally select a joke. With discretion, key it up, and send it to your manager and co-workers through email.

2. Hold contests—for example, "The Month's Most Embarrassing Situation."

3. Hold an annual kickoff meeting where humorous awards are given to all staff members for any activities they participated in.

4. When a staff member has a birthday, prepare a cake with a humorous message. Invite the staff to share cake and coffee together for a few minutes.

5. At the annual Christmas party, exchange inexpensive but humorous gifts.

6. Once a year, select a good sport in your office and hold a roast. The staff will enjoy participating.

7. Watch for humorous articles in magazines and circulate them among the staff.

8. Share anything humorous that you have acquired. Humorous cards, books, and magazine articles work well on a circulation list.

Self-Check

1. What is meant by "Laugh *at* yourself, but laugh *with* others"?

SOCIAL SKILLS

For the office professional, it's not enough to be just technically competent, an excellent office administrator, and a tactful communicator in the office. The responsibilities of many business professionals extend outside the walls of the office. Many administrative assistants find themselves entertaining customers of the company, and most administrative assistants socialize with company personnel or customers outside the office. These social situations require a special set of skills. It may be difficult in some social situations to retain your professionalism and ethical correctness. A common ethical dilemma is office romance.

Keep Personal Relationships Private

The professional office is an obvious place to meet new friends and to establish romantic relationships. Many professionals with fast-paced jobs spend more time at work than they do away from work. Work brings people with common goals and interests into the same environment, an environment where people look their best, perform at their best, work cohesively together, and show respect for each other. This environment makes the office an appealing place to find a partner for a romantic relationship.

However, in general, organizations do not condone romantic relationships in the working environment. Romantic relationships are seen as getting in the way of work goals and productivity.

So before you enter a romantic relationship with a colleague, ask yourself if the positives outweigh the negatives. Whatever you perceive to be the advantages, consider the following questions:

- How will this relationship affect your professionalism and productivity on the job?
- How will the romance affect your working relationships with other colleagues?
- Will you be able to refrain from sharing confidential work-related issues with your partner?
- Do you share interests outside of work, or will your social conversation be restricted to only work topics?
- If your partner is dismissed from work, how will this affect the security of your job or your desire to continue with the same company?
- If your romantic relationship ends, will you be able to continue working together professionally?

The best advice for people involved romantically with a colleague is to keep the personal relationship private. If it becomes common knowledge that you are partners, don't deny it, but beyond that, avoid sharing information about your social activities, your future plans, and personal information about your partner. Once your colleagues learn that you have no intention to share this kind of private information, they will stop asking for it and will respect you for your confidentiality.

Let's Do Lunch!

Knowing how to care for a guest and displaying good manners at a business lunch are desirable social skills for any office professional. Management may expect you to take new employees or customers for lunch, you might attend a business lunch for an association you belong to, or you might be attending a luncheon at a conference or business meeting. Whatever the occasion, you will want to make the right impression.

Entire books have been devoted to the subject of using proper manners. This short section is not meant to be a detailed guide; rather, the intent here is to help you avoid making embarrassing mistakes. The following are some simple but important guidelines for business dining:

1. When escorted by the restaurant host to a table, your guest should walk ahead of you and behind the host.

2. If you take a guest to a restaurant that has open seating, lead the way to an appropriate table.

3. Unless you intend to negotiate with your guest during lunch, offer your guest the best seat at the table; remember, your objective is to make your guest feel comfortable. Often the best seat is the one facing the main eating area. Never seat guests so they are facing the exit doors, or the kitchen or washroom doors.

4. Place your napkin on your lap only *after* everyone has arrived and is seated; once the meal begins, the napkin should not be placed on the table until the meal is finished.

5. Guests will get an idea of acceptable price range from the meal you suggest or order. Having your guest order first is a courteous gesture; but, unless your guest knows what you plan to eat, you may be placing your guest in an awkward position.

6. When the server takes your order, refer to the other party as your guest ("I will let my guest order first," or "My guest would like to order . . ." or similar). This is a clue to the server that you would like the bill brought to you.

7. Let hot food cool naturally; do not blow on your food, stir soup or coffee that is too hot, or fan your food. These activities are distracting and considered rude and unbusinesslike behaviour.

8. Begin eating only after everyone has been served. Often meals will arrive at the table a few minutes apart. It is considered rude to begin eating while someone is left sitting without a meal.

9. If you reach for something, such as a condiment or breadbasket, offer the item to your guest before you serve yourself.

10. Table settings are often confusing, and leave a person wondering which glass or fork to use. The general rule for utensils is *outside in*. If there is a series of forks or spoons, simply begin by using the one on the outer edge of your table setting and work inward toward your plate. Your glass will be at the top of your knife on the right side of your plate; your bread and butter plate will be to your left.

11. Never chew with your mouth open or talk with food in your mouth. It's wise to take only small bites so that you can carry on a conversation.

12. If the need arises to remove something undesirable from your mouth (such as a seed, bone, pit, or partially chewed food), you should use a utensil rather than your fingers to catch the food. Lift your napkin to your mouth at the same time to conceal the unwanted food.

13. The proper way to eat any form of bread is to break it off as needed, into bite-sized pieces.

14. When you are finished eating, never remove or stack dishes for the server. You want to maintain a professional business image.

15. Never primp at the table. If you wish to apply cosmetics, comb your hair, straighten your clothing or—worst of all—blow your nose, do so in the washroom.

Following these general guidelines will increase your confidence and pleasure at any business lunch.

Self-Check

1. What are two rules of etiquette when hosting a business lunch? Can you think of one more?

QUESTIONS FOR STUDY AND REVIEW

1. Describe the administrative assistant's role in forming the image of the organization.

2. Suggest five ground rules that may help make a team more effective.

3. State five nonproductive team behaviours and explain how you, as a team member, might influence a positive change in each of these behaviours.

4. Describe what it means to create political networks.

5. Consider two possible reasons why a person might withhold or selectively share information in an office.

6. List three unethical behaviours that are commonly found in office environments.

7. Explain how the term "strength in numbers" could be interpreted as office politics.

8. Give examples of healthy office politics that could bring success to your office team.

9. What is a code of ethics?

10. State five guidelines for keeping work-related information confidential.

11. State five unethical practices that relate to each of the following: work, time, and resources.

12. Give six examples of actions you can take to develop respectful relationships in the office.

13. What is meant by "maintaining composure"?

14. If an office professional has integrity, what traits might he or she display?

15. Why is change constant in the office?

16. Give examples of how you can be flexible, adaptable, and tolerant with new management.

17. If you believe that management is not working in the best interests of the organization, what should you do?

18. Discuss six measures a company could take to reduce stress in the workplace.

19. State reasons why the work of an office professional may be stressful.

20. Suggest eight strategies you might employ to reduce stress.

21. What are two factors that you should weigh in determining whether humour is appropriate in the office?

22. Why do many companies discourage personal relationships between employees?

23. Suggest ten guidelines you might follow when taking a guest for a business lunch.

Problem Solving

1. You work for Miramar Cosmetics as an executive assistant. The longer you work for this organization, the more often you have to make decisions about whether the behaviour of you and your colleagues is ethical or unethical. What will you do when the following situations occur?

    a. As a part of your professional responsibilities, you make many long-distance calls from the telephone in your office. These calls are not tracked. You would like to use your office telephone to make a personal call long distance to your mother.

    b. Your company policy states that it deducts wages for people who come to work late or leave early. One of your assistants works very hard, accomplishes a great deal, and is essential to your success at work. Her only method of transportation is the public bus service. To make her transportation convenient, she arrives 15 minutes late every day. It's your responsibility to deduct her salary.

   c. You are responsible for hiring a new receptionist. Your friend really needs the job but is not the most qualified person who applied.

   d. During a sales meeting with a client, the sales representative presents false information about a company product. This information leads to the signing of a contract during that meeting.

2. You are an administrative assistant in the purchasing department. Another administrative assistant, Janice McCall, is getting married on November 18. The purchasing department employs 12 office workers, two of whom are administrative assistants. According to a rumour, Janice is not coming back to work after the wedding, and two of the office workers want to apply for her position. They have come to you to find out if the rumour is true. You have not seen an official announcement about Janice's employment plans after she gets married. However, Janice did tell you that she does not plan to come back to work after the wedding. What should you say to your two co-workers?

3. You and Chris met at work three years ago, and you have now been married for one year. Your main social group is made up of your office colleagues. The company is going through a reorganization, and, unfortunately, Chris has been given notice for the end of next month. Chris is bitter about the company's decision; and, as a result, he has been outspoken and critical about company policy and management. How should you react to this?

EVERYDAY ETHICS

Dating the Boss

Alex has been Patti's supervisor for the last three years. They started dating over a year ago and agreed to keep their relationship confidential and quite separate from their professional lives. It's worked well so far because Patti is working as a senior administrative assistant in another department quite separate from Alex.

However, a great, new executive assistant opportunity has occurred—working directly for Alex! The problem is that Isabelle, the only other competitor for the new position, has seen Patti and Alex together socially.

Not surprisingly, Isabelle has spread the rumour that Patti is dating the boss and that she, Patti, will obviously have an unfair advantage when interviews begin.

■ Do you see any *potential* harm in this scenario?

■ What should Patti do in this situation?

Special Reports

1. Think of someone whose personality you admire. Make a list of this person's personality traits that you like and then select the most outstanding traits and describe them in detail. Try to decide why these traits appeal to you. Do you think they would appeal to others? Share your ideas by writing an email with your comments to your instructor.

2. Organize a restaurant lunch for your classmates and your instructor. During the lunch, sit at tables in groups of no more than three or four people. Determine who are the guests and who are the administrative assistants. Role-play having a business lunch. During lunch discuss and practise the business lunch guidelines given in this book.

3. Select two different companies where you would like to work. Research the policies of both companies on hiring people when their spouses are already employed within the company. Do they have a policy covering retention of two single employees who marry? Do these hiring policies affect your desire to work for either of these companies? Why or why not?

PRODUCTION CHALLENGES

1-A Exercising Ethics

Supplies needed:

- *Personal Values, Form 1-A, page 380*

Everyone needs to develop their own personal framework of ethics. To do this, consider what you value the most and what you value the least. Refer to Form 1-A in your Working Papers, where you will rank 15 different values by placing the number 1 next to the item you value the most and the number 15 next to the item you value the least. You must give each item a number. Do not repeat any of the numbers. This is a very difficult exercise. There are no right or wrong answers. This will simply encourage you to think about your own values.

1-B Challenging Personalities

Supplies needed

- *Difficult Personalities, Form 1-B, page 381*

Mr. Wilson has asked you to attend a workshop to learn more about challenging personalities and the conflicts that may arise within teams because of the challenges.

The workshop is held at your local college. When you arrive, your instructor puts you into small groups and asks you to discuss specific personality types and to come up with possible coping strategies. Refer to Form 1-B in your Working Papers, and in small groups (consisting of your classmates) discuss personality behaviours.

When you return to your office, Mr. Wilson tells you that he is looking forward to learning about the insights you have gained from this workshop. He asks you to prepare a report on what you have discovered about challenging personalities, and to include a copy of the form you have completed.

Weblinks

Business Ethics
www.businessethics.ca
This site offers access to a wide variety of Canadian resources for business ethics including articles, case studies, and more.

Publications for Corporate Wellness
www.personalbest.com
The topics on this site are devoted to corporate wellness. It advertises self-help publications for organizations.

Table Manners
www.charlestonschoolofprotocol.com
Here's a site that provides online professional table manners training.

Office Politics
www.managementhelp.org
Here you will find various perspectives on many topics from interpersonal skills to evaluations to personal development.

Stress Management
http://www.helpguide.org/mental/stress_management_relief_coping.htm
Topics dealing with how to reduce, prevent, and cope with stress are featured on this site along with links to many other valuable resources on the topic.

Chapter 2
Cultural Diversity and International Business Relations

Learning Outcomes

After completion of this chapter, the student will be able to:

1 Describe multiculturalism.

2 Comprehend the importance and benefits of diversity.

3 Describe cross-cultural competence.

4 Describe methods for developing cross-cultural awareness.

5 Identify ways for improving international communication across cultures.

6 Discuss the importance of international business relations.

7 State important considerations when travelling to foreign countries and hosting international visitors.

MULTICULTURALISM IN CANADA

Multiculturalism can be defined as the integration and acceptance of multiple cultures in a specific place or demographic location. In Canada, our society is made up of people and groups with various traditions and racial origins. With the arrival of the *Canadian Multiculturalism Act* in 1971, Canada became the first country in the world to declare multiculturalism an official state policy. This bold step charted the path to a vibrant and changing cultural mosaic built on mutual respect for Canadians of all backgrounds and ancestry.

The roots of multiculturalism in Canada can be seen in the country's origins, as three founding cultures—aboriginal, British, and French—were soon joined by many others from around the world. Today, multiculturalism is a key element of Canadian national identity. In fact, individuals who have neither French nor British heritage now make up the largest part of Canadian society. Policies and standards are in place in Canada encouraging cultural integration in the workplace and in society.

Diversity and Equity

Diversity encompasses acceptance and respect for others, as well as an understanding that each individual is unique. It involves recognizing individual differences, including race, ethnicity, gender, sexual orientation, socioeconomic status, age, physical abilities, and religious beliefs. It entails moving beyond simple tolerance to embracing and celebrating the dimensions of diversity found within each individual. As a wise person once said, "Always remember that you're unique. Just like everybody else."

Successful businesses embrace and encourage diversity in the workplace. The concept of workplace diversity incorporates awareness of, and respect for, differences in the way people communicate, approach tasks, and interact. To be effective in business an administrative assistant must take steps necessary to develop an awareness of diversity. Building connections with people is often essential to the success of an organization. In your role you will play a key part in developing and sustaining successful business relations. Oftentimes the administrative assistant is the first point of contact in an office, so it is imperative to ensure all visitors and callers are always treated courteously and made to feel important.

Diversity adds a special richness to the workplace, but it also raises some challenges. These challenges are addressed under specific Canadian statutes. Canada is committed to ensuring equitable and fair treatment of all citizens in and outside of the workplace. This is evidenced by the *Canadian Charter of Rights and Freedoms* as well as the *Canadian Human Rights Act*.

Jade Jocko
Executive Project Support

Shell Canada Limited
Calgary, Alberta

College Graduation:
Administrative Information Management (AIM)
Diploma
SAIT Polytechnic
2010

"Your work will always speak for itself."

Jade started at Shell Canada in Calgary in the events management department after completing her practicum in June 2010. She quickly proved herself by taking charge of one of the largest events in the department's history—a ten-day workshop for 500 employees. "Looking back it was an incredible amount of work, and definitely had its challenges given the size of the event and the logistics involved; however, the event was a smashing success!" says Jade. Her supervisors took notice, and she was soon offered new positions within the company and now works under senior management.

Shell is a global corporation with over 100 000 employees in over 90 countries and territories worldwide. In her current role, Jade is working on two major projects that provide support to the Calgary operations. The first is a project to innovate the workspace and office layouts in an effort to change the way departments and employees work together. The second is a town hall meeting with 350 employees, a project that requires her to liaise with the Shell head office in the Netherlands. "The Project Management course at SAIT gave me a fantastic foundation for utilizing project software," says Jade.

Working in such a large company makes email the main form of communication—it works best across time zones and locations, and it also provides a record of communication. On an average day, Jade reads and responds to emails, attends meetings with stakeholders, and prepares materials and makes plans for upcoming events. Some of her specialized responsibilities include managing project plans and creating process flow charts—and she also works closely with senior leadership.

In fact, Jade is constantly dealing with her co-workers and clients, so she must always be "on"—that can be a real challenge. "And because we have an open office plan, rarely do you have the opportunity to have quiet, alone time that you need sometimes to finish a task such as a presentation" says Jade. But, she adds, the best part of her job is that she gets to work with people: "I know myself, and I would be unhappy doing an analyst/data job where I had little interaction with others."

Jade is an unofficial ambassador for SAIT's AIM program: "I think that people don't understand how diverse the curriculum is. The practical skills you learn are highly valued in the workplace, so it is important to generate information about the program to industry."

Now that she's been working in the industry for a few years, Jade thinks a degree in business might be her best option for advancement and professional development.

Human Rights and Equity Standards

The *Canadian Human Rights Act* is a statute passed by the Parliament of Canada in 1977. The goal of this act is to ensure equal opportunity to individuals who may be victims of discrimination based on set prohibited grounds such as gender, disability, or religion. The *Canadian Human Rights Act* outlined the creation of the Canadian Human Rights Commission, which investigates claims of discrimination. The protections offered by this legislation extend into the workplace: in the Canadian workplace we have the right to be treated fairly, free from discriminatory practices. A discriminatory practice might involve not hiring someone for a job based on age, gender, race, physical abilities, or religious beliefs.

In 2005, the Government of Canada established the Racism-Free Workplace Strategy, which promotes a fair and inclusive workplace, one free of discriminatory barriers to the employment and advancement of members of visible minorities and aboriginal peoples. This strategy is educational in nature, as it helps businesses adapt to Canada's ever-changing demographics. Workshops have been created for employers covering topics such as dealing with diversity, building inclusive workplaces, and understanding the challenges facing visible minorities in the workplace. In 2008, three years after the implementation of the strategy, nine racism prevention officers were hired in different regions across Canada to assist employers in creating racism-free workplaces.

Discrimination in the workplace can also stem from stereotyping. **Stereotypes** are standardized and simplified conceptions of groups based on prior assumptions. We could consider stereotyping as a type of bias we form based either on preconceptions or on personal experience. Stereotyping can turn into discrimination if acted upon in a negative manner. Take, for example, a situation in which two equally qualified individuals are applying for the same job. One candidate is a mother with two children and the other candidate is childless. If the employer treats these two candidates differently, or assumes that the mother will miss a lot of time at work or be preoccupied with her children, this would be a case of negative stereotyping.

In order to ensure equity in the Canadian workplace, a variety of protective standards have been established under the *Employment Equity Act*. A key element of this law is the duty to accommodate; this provision refers to the obligation of an employer to take measures to eliminate disadvantages to employees and prospective employees that result (or may result) from a rule, practice, or physical barrier. The employer must make reasonable accommodations so that individuals with differing needs can work to the best of their ability. Differences that must be accommodated include gender, ethnic or cultural origin, physical ability, or religious affiliation. For example, a violation could involve an employer prohibiting an employee from wearing an item of clothing required by his or her religious practices, or otherwise not respecting this need.

CULTURAL COMPETENCE AND AWARENESS

Advances in modern technology have brought the world much closer. Today's working environment often spans numerous cultures. Businesses can expand their operations globally, and administrative assistants will find themselves communicating remotely or face-to-face with individuals from diverse cultural regions or backgrounds. Understanding one's own culture and the impact of culture on the actions of others is essential for effective business interactions.

Culture refers to a system of shared values, beliefs, morals, and social standards embraced by a group of people. This system is usually passed from one generation to another. Cultural systems encompass features such as languages, religious practices, and social interactions. Something as simple as social distance varies greatly among cultures. For example, in North America we generally like to have a distance of 18 inches in a social situation, while in Japan the ideal distance is 36 inches. Communication can immediately break down if we don't make a considerable effort to be aware of subtle differences.

Developing an understanding of cultural differences will enable you to be a productive and contributing member of your organization. As an administrative assistant, take the opportunity to develop knowledge of cultural practices.

Figure 2-1 Joining hands.

Cross-Cultural Competence

Cross-cultural competence involves the ability to interact effectively with people from a variety of different cultural backgrounds. Good communication skills are the cornerstone of all business interactions, and this is particularly true when dealing with individuals from different cultures. Cross-cultural communication skills are best developed through practice and experience. Moreover, cross-cultural competence involves more than merely obtaining cultural information; we must understand how to apply this knowledge effectively. This level of understanding is not something we are naturally born with. It is developed over time with considerable effort. Adapting to different cultural beliefs and practices requires flexibility and a respect for others' viewpoints.

The need for cross-cultural competence in today's business environment has never been greater. Not only has the workplace become more diverse, but business is increasingly conducted on an international scale. The stronger your cross-cultural competence, the less likely it is that you will fall victim to cross-cultural misunderstandings or make unfortunate blunders.

By putting aside our own cultural mindsets and assumptions we remove barriers to cross-cultural communication in the workplace. It is especially important to avoid cultural stereotyping, or treating others on the basis of a preconceived belief about their culture, which can prevent us from creating solid relationships. By the same token, setting aside these stereotypes will allow us to work more effectively with individuals from a wide range of backgrounds. Although it may not be easy to give up some of our own cultural assumptions, doing so will enable us to have more successful and productive business relationships. In fact, you may eventually be selected for international assignments because of your well-honed skills in cross-cultural communication.

Cultural competence can be developed at both the professional and social levels. One way to develop cultural competence is to participate in activities that expose you to other cultures. Choose to become involved in community activities that may expose you a network of people with diverse cultural backgrounds. You may also want to be involved with meetings that involve international business relations. Cross-cultural competence requires us to investigate new cultures by keeping an open mind and removing some of our personal prejudices. When interacting with a new culture, we need to avoid judging it—and its values—by comparing it to our own. Instead, we need to bridge our own cultural insights with new ones; this skill is at the heart of all cross-cultural competency.

However, there is no one recipe for cultural competency. Developing cultural competence is an ongoing process, as we continually adapt and reevaluate our practices, assumptions, and outlook.

Developing Cultural Awareness

Workplace cross-cultural awareness has become an increasingly important aspect of business. The term *cross-cultural awareness* refers to the development of an understanding of and sensitivity to other cultures. We are raised with a set of beliefs and practices, and as a result, sometimes we don't view beliefs that are different from ours as acceptable. It is important to remember, however, that we usually have more similarities than differences.

The first step in developing cross-cultural awareness or cultural competence is to be aware of and examine your own beliefs through self-discovery. Consider some of these suggestions for developing cross-cultural awareness:

- **Become more self-aware.** Don't think that your way is the only way. Have an open mind when presented with new opportunities to explore diverse ways of doing things.
- **Avoid stereotyping.** Your expectations of another person's behaviour may be based on a stereotype that simply is not true.
- **Don't generalize.** Everybody is unique.
- **Ask questions.** By keeping these questions professional you will minimize misunderstandings and keep lines of communication open.

- **Be positive and enthusiastic.** Your willingness to work together will be apparent, and your co-workers will appreciate your cooperative approach.

Self-Check

1. What are two goals of the *Canadian Human Rights Act*?
2. State why it is important to develop cross-cultural awareness.

Guidelines for Cross-Cultural Encounters

Following some basic principles will greatly limit the potential for misunderstandings. Here are some tips to follow in cross-cultural encounters:

- **Greeting.** It is critical you acknowledge the other person. In some cultures, you may need to make direct eye contact, shake hands, and exchange a few words. In general, no matter what the culture, it is rude not to acknowledge the other person. Ask how to address the other person. In some cultures the use of nicknames is an acceptable practice, while in others it might be considered impolite. Be upfront and ask.
- **Responsiveness.** Show the person you want to get to know him or her. This attitude is critical in cross-cultural communication as it shows a willingness to understand why someone does something perhaps a little differently from what you are used to.
- **Clarity.** Be transparent in your communication with others. You can avoid misunderstandings by giving as much detail as possible.
- **Create a Connection.** Be friendly. Show that you really want to connect with the other person by asking questions that initiate interaction.
- **Flexibility.** You may need to send a message using a variety of methods of communication, including appropriate use of body language.

UNDERSTANDING THE BENEFITS OF DIVERSITY

At no other time has there been a more complex array of cultures within the workplace. In Canada, we have many cultures living and working together. There are significant advantages to diversity in the workplace. By integrating workers from culturally diverse backgrounds into the workforce, organizations become much stronger. Diversity needs to be seen as an integral part of the business plan, essential to successful operation of the organization. This is especially true in today's global marketplace, as companies interact with different cultures and clients.

By embracing diversity initiatives a company can show that it recognizes and celebrates the differences associated with different backgrounds. By recognizing the value of each individual, a company can encourage employees to make worthy contributions to the organization. Indeed, when a company actively works toward achieving diversity in the workplace, it can increase productivity and overall morale.

The benefits of workplace diversity are numerous:

- Fairness and equality can be achieved by having open lines of communication where each contribution is appreciated and respected. No one is favoured over another.

- Hiring and promotional policies are based on qualifications and performance. This ensures that the most qualified individuals are recognized for what they have to offer.

- New ideas and varying perspectives are shared. When we encourage an atmosphere where all team members are involved in the creative process, individuals will be comfortable in sharing ideas.

- Utilization of the strengths and talents of team members can be realized, since people from diverse backgrounds often have assorted skills and abilities.

- Differences can be harnessed and made to work for the organization in positive ways.

DIVERSITY IN THE GLOBAL BUSINESS ENVIRONMENT

Diversity can be a challenge in any business environment. With the massive growth of the global marketplace, understanding how business is done internationally is critical to organizational success. In order to be productive on a global scale, we must explore the business culture of those countries or regions where we wish to conduct business. Business culture is a model or style of business operations. The business culture determines how staff interacts with each other and how employees deal with clients.

The leadership role—and how members of an organization perceive that role—is a critical element of business culture. Depending on our cultural background, we may have certain expectations of the leader that may or may not be shared by all members within an organization. In countries such as Canada, Germany, and Russia, for example, there is a tendency to elevate the role of the leader almost to a glorified

status. By contrast, in the Netherlands the position of the leader is often regarded with skepticism; indeed, if someone is employed as a manager, he or she typically will not brag about it. Given the globalization of the working environment, it is essential to understand cultural leadership differences. What may be acceptable in one culture may not be in another. This creates a substantial challenge for the office of today. Being aware of the perceptions we have in relation to leadership may help to foster a harmonious working environment.

Contract negotiations may also need to be approached differently when performed on a global scale. We can't assume because of our traditions and beliefs that others will judge, behave, perceive, and reason as we do. Managers cannot negotiate successfully if they neglect other countries' cultures, beliefs, and rituals. Therefore, managers need to learn how cultures and traditions differ in the countries where their company operates so that they can efficiently and effectively negotiate and be able to manage across cultures and borders.

Time Management in Culture

The essence of time management—organizing and sequencing tasks—may be perceived by cultures in different ways. For example, imagine you are a local employee in the home office in Dubai, and a Canadian employee from the Burnaby, British Columbia, office comes by for her 2 p.m. appointment. She arrives promptly, and, as you greet and begin to help her, you also handle a telephone call, answer a coworker's question, and send a fax to someone else. From your point of view and in keeping with your perception of time management, you consider that you are very efficient; you are, after all, accomplishing several other tasks in addition to dealing with the visitor. However, from your visitor's point of view, your activity may appear unfocused and inefficient. Your visitor may perceive your multitasking while meeting with her as an indication that you regard her visit as unimportant or as a disruption to your routine; she may even feel that it has not been given the appropriate attention. In Canada business success is often judged on the ability to balance time efficiently while still meeting the needs of clients. For instance, if a project is not completed on time as promised the organization will lose profits and its reputation may suffer.

To understand how the perception of time can differ in various cultures consider the following examples: in India and Japan, people tend to favour coordinating work on related tasks rather than tackling them consecutively. In France, two-hour lunches are considered normal. In Japan, Saturday is considered a standard workday, while in Muslim countries the workweek ends on Thursday evening and Sunday is a workday. Holiday time standards vary among countries throughout the world.

Figure 2-2 Clock.

Interpersonal Communication in the Global Market

When conducting business globally we may encounter language barriers that will require us to make some adjustments in our communication methods. Even if someone speaks your language it does not mean they have the same understanding of the verbal message that you are sending. Sometimes language barriers result because we apply mental filters to the messages others send to us. The term *mental filter* describes our capacity to accept some facts and ideas and to screen out others—perhaps those that are unfamiliar or that are different from our own. The mental filters we use are closely related to the unique way each of us views the world. When faced with some of these barriers we should practice some of the following basic guidelines:

- **Learn common greetings and responses.** For example, "hello" in French is spelled "bonjour" and is pronounced "bone-zhoor"; "thank you" in Spanish is spelled "gracias" and is pronounced "gRAH-see-ahs."

- **Use simple English.** It has been said that English is one of the most difficult languages to learn. Use simple words in short sentences. For example, use *little* rather than *petite*, *like* rather than *resemble*. Avoid using puns, slang, jargon, and sports or military references.

- **Speak slowly and enunciate.** If you are speaking in a rush toned many words may be lost in your message. By taking the time to clearly pronounce words, you will ensure your message is heard and better understood.

- **Watch for blank stares.** A blank stare or a glazed expression tells you the listener may not comprehend your message.

- **Ask the listener to paraphrase.** When the listener can repeat your message, there is a better chance it is being understood. Giving your listener the opportunity to paraphrase what you've said will also allow you to correct any misunderstandings.

- **Accept blame for misunderstanding.** Accepting blame will make the listener feel less embarrassed about not understanding your message. Doing so will also allow him or her to "save face."

- **Listen without interrupting.** Don't help the speaker finish his or her sentences. Finishing sentences only points out what a poor command the speaker has of the language; it also indicates impatience on the part of the listener.

- **Follow up in writing when negotiating.** A follow-up message that summarizes an agreement will confirm the results of your negotiation and minimize misunderstandings. A person with limited English-speaking skills may have very good reading comprehension. In some countries, people are taught how to read and write English but often have limited opportunities to practise speaking it.

- **Observe nonverbal messages.** Examples of nonverbal messages are the use of personal space and eye contact, as discussed earlier in this chapter. Watch your gestures: some gestures may seem harmless in Canada but can have a very different interpretation elsewhere. Take, for instance, the symbol commonly used to mean "okay" in North America, the thumb and index finger forming a circle and the other fingers raised. In France this gesture means "zero," it is a symbol for money in Japan, and it carries a vulgar connotation in Brazil.

Managing International Client Relations

Recent innovations in communication technology have allowed employees to work more closely with international clients and teams than ever before. Being separated by location and often culture, however, can present some unique challenges. Simple things like the time difference can make communication a lot trickier, depending on what areas of the world and nationalities you are dealing with. You will need to pay attention to time zones so you just don't pick up the phone to call your client in Paris, for example, or you might wake him up in the middle of a good night's sleep. Keep track of your customers' time zones by checking an online tool like the World Clock (http://www.timeanddate.com/worldclock/), which tells you the current time in countries around the world. Prearrange a time that works for both of you.

Pay attention to cultural differences. Before working with an international client, do some research on his or her local customs and etiquette. You may find that in some cultures people don't like to talk about pricing upfront, so you might need to customize the way you discuss your estimate for a project. Take extra care when interpreting emails and other communications. Whether or not your client is from an English-speaking country, you're likely to notice differences in language and local slang. If you're not certain exactly what your client is telling you or asking for, be sure to ask for further clarification via email, stating what you think the client is saying, and then asking whether your interpretation is correct.

Working on International Teams

Working with teams across continents can be exciting and rewarding, but it also presents some challenges. Research suggests some of these challenges include differences in culture, language, business practices, and attitudes. Face-to-face communication is highly valued in European countries, while in Canada there is a greater acceptance of virtual communication. It may be wise to plan for an initial face-to-face meeting when first working together. If that is not practical perhaps a videoconference can be arranged to allow people to visit team members virtually so they can associate faces with names. Most companies have access to web tools that help to facilitate this initial meeting. You also may want to consider rotating communication times to be considerate of time differences between countries. Team leaders of international virtual teams must be aware and sensitive to differences and take appropriate action to ensure optimal performance and results.

Working in a Foreign Country

Every year, thousands of Canadians relocate to foreign countries to work and acquire new skills. Many companies are "going global," and this may mean that you will need to relocate to another country for an extended period of time. You will require special permission from the Canadian government to work abroad. Permission must be granted by the country you wish to work in as well. Find out the requirements well in advance of deciding to relocate.

Working abroad can enhance and diversify your administrative skills. A wide variety of international work opportunities exist around the world. Alan Cumyn's *What in the World Is Going On?*, published by the Canadian Bureau of International Education, is a useful source when planning to work abroad.

You will need a passport before working abroad. A work visa or special permission in the form of a work permit will be required. If you are planning to go for a long time you may also require a residency permit. Additionally,

some countries may require a medical certificate as an entry requirement. Another consideration may be obtaining an international driver's license.

Before You Go The department of Foreign Affairs and International Trade Canada is committed to providing services throughout the world to Canadians working and travelling abroad. There are more than 260 offices worldwide, and it would be wise to find a list of where these offices are located prior to your departure. This department can also provide information on documentation needed, as well as travel reports and warnings.

Look to employment agencies, the internet, newspapers, and magazines to find international opportunities. If you are offered a job overseas, it is important to evaluate it carefully before you accept it. Find out as much as you can about the organization by visiting the company website. Talk to others who you know may have worked for the business, or ask to speak to someone who is currently working for the company.

Cross-Cultural Workplace Challenges Relocating to live and work in a foreign country can be an exciting experience. Many times, however, we may not be as prepared for the extent of cultural dissimilarity we encounter. This phenomenon is referred to culture shock. In order to be successful, we need to adapt to the new culture. When relocating we often go through stages prior to reaching the point of adaptation.

Initially we go through a short stage after arriving in our new country where the excitement and newness of our environment is a delight. Normally, these feelings wear off after some time. Then feelings of culture shock begin to set in. Culture shock can best be described as the emotional and sometimes physical reaction experienced while settling into a new culture. Homesickness, irritability, and depression are some of the symptoms people may experience as they adapt to their new environment. These are normal reactions to relocation, and in most cases these feelings pass. As you psychologically adapt to the new culture, which involves participating in the local culture and learning the language, you should begin to enjoy your new life.

Taking the following steps will help you to adapt to your host country:

1. **Work Etiquette.** Learn your host country's workplace etiquette. This involves knowing how to introduce yourself and how to address others. Find out if religion plays a role in daily work. Determine if there are items of clothing considered appropriate or inappropriate.

2. **Work Environment.** Learn about expectations in terms of work commitment. Are you expected to work extra hours? Will you need to take work home? What

are the cultural views about social engagement in and outside of the workplace?

3. **Importance of Time.** Learn about how time is handled in the host country. Is punctuality important? How are lunch and breaks handled? What days of the week are considered workdays?

4. **Laws.** Learn about workplace legislation. What rights do you have as a worker? How are rights enforced?

5. **Pay.** Learn how you will be paid. Determine if you will need to open up a bank account. Find out what deductions are made and what benefits are provided to you.

6. **Language.** Learn the language in which business is normally conducted in your host country. Be aware that certain phrases may be considered offensive.

7. **Women in the Workplace.** Learn the cultural view of women in the workplace. Depending on the host country, views of women in the workplace can differ greatly.

8. **Supervisory.** Learn the host country's cultural view toward authority. In some countries, criticism of your supervisor is unacceptable and grounds for dismissal.

Self-Check

1. Describe culture shock.
2. What documents might be required prior to accepting a work assignment in a foreign country?

Hosting International Visitors

If your manager travels to meet international clients, it's very possible those clients will also visit your office. Being able to build positive relationships with international clients is highly desirable and worth achieving. Your office may also host international employees, and they may want to tour your office while in town.

Here are some tips for your success when hosting international visitors:

1. Take the time to learn a few courteous words in your visitor's language if different from your own. Expressions like "good morning," "welcome," "please," and "thank you" spoken in the visitor's language will be interpreted as a gesture of goodwill and will set a positive tone for the visit.

2. Locate the client's nearest consulate's office. As a courtesy to your international clients, have handy the nearest consulate's location, phone number, and ambassador's name for reference should you need them.

Figure 2-3 Professional Greeting.

3. Research what cultural attitudes exist about time management. As you learned earlier, different cultures treat time differently. Time does not have the same priority in all cultures. Some have a much more relaxed view of time. In fact, in some cultures people do not work in the afternoon and prefer to have only morning and evening meetings. This can create the need to make some adjustments in terms of scheduling meetings, completing projects, and closing deals. Keep this in mind when scheduling meetings, and be as flexible as possible.

4. Learn the preferred eating habits of the country. Although many international visitors are open to experimenting with new foods, many are not. For example, in some cultures people do not eat pork. In this case, it would be a gross error to arrange a meal where pork is on the menu. Be certain coffee and lunch breaks include food and beverages the international clients will enjoy.

5. Consider international differences in customs when greeting visitors. Greetings in North America are done with a firm handshake, whereas in many other cultures bowing and kissing are the norms. In some cultures, men and women do not touch. Although women and men in these cultures do not shake hands, members of the same gender may deliver a very warm and physical greeting.

6. Be aware of body language. A friendly hand gesture in one country can be obscene in the next and even illegal in another. Be sure to pay close attention to how others use certain gestures (movements of the hands, arms, legs, or head) to convey a message.

7. Learn to pronounce names correctly. In some cultures, such as China and Korea, the family's surname is stated first and then the given name. Show your respect by

using names correctly. Learn the titles of respect that go with names and when it is appropriate to use them.

8. Take the time to research national holidays and important events in the visitor's country of origin. Be respectful of those occasions and avoid scheduling meetings or activities at times that would give the impression of disrespect or disregard for the visitor's culture. Acknowledging your understanding of the importance of those occasions in your visitor's culture will in turn gain respect for your organization.

9. Determine if physical space is of importance. When receiving visitors from outside your culture, pay attention to what is considered an appropriate distance between you and the visitor when talking. With some visitors, standing too far away may be interpreted as being unconcerned, too formal, or too distant. On the other hand, if you stand too close to a visitor, it may be interpreted as being too casual or too informal. Learn how to use space or distance to your advantage so as not to offend visitors.

10. Recognize that your international visitor may not be familiar with your city and will likely want to do some sightseeing. Prepare a portfolio that includes maps of the area, recommended restaurants, special-interest sites, and special events. Ask if there are any attractions the visitor would like to explore, and offer to arrange for a tour guide.

The bottom line is that you want your international visitor to have a pleasant, positive visit to Canada, a visit that produces a profitable yet cordial relationship. With more and more international trade between Canadian and foreign companies, developing your skills in this area will be viewed favourably by your manager and increase your value as a knowledgeable employee.

---

pro-Link
Avoiding Cultural Blunders

In your busy working day you are bound to meet and greet many people from diverse cultural backgrounds. Planning in advance how to handle these situations will help you to eliminate cultural blunders. Of course, you can't avoid all blunders, but the way you manage yourself will go far to reduce their occurrence and impact.

- Accept the fact that you will make some blunders, so if you make a mistake don't focus on it; focus on what you can do differently in the future.

- Stay focused on communication. Note what is said, how it is said, and what is not said.

- Watch for gestures that may convey a message and will help you correct your blunder. You can tell by a facial reaction that demonstrates surprise that you may have asked or answered a question incorrectly.

- Avoid questions on age, marital status, and income.

- Don't ignore hierarchy in the workplace. Buy gifts according to rank and seniority.

Remember that you want your guests to feel comfortable and welcome in your place of business. By avoiding cultural blunders, you will help to ensure the success of their visit.

QUESTIONS FOR STUDY AND REVIEW

1. When did Canada officially adopt the *Multicultural Act*?
2. Define the term *culture*.
3. Explain why an administrative assistant should have an understanding of cultural diversity.
4. Distinguish between cultural and workplace diversity.
5. Suggest three benefits of workplace diversity.
6. Suggest four ways you could develop more cross-cultural awareness.
7. Explain how people may have different expectations of a leader depending on their cultural background.
8. List four suggestions for improving international communication.
9. Suggest how gestures can impact the communication process when involving international relations.
10. State three important considerations when thinking about working in another country.
11. Discuss how the perception of time management varies depending on cultural standards.
12. List four suggestions for hosting international visitors.
13. Suggest additional steps you could take to ensure your international visitor has a pleasant experience.
14. State three factors to consider if you or your manager is travelling for business.
15. State the importance of becoming familiar with the social norms and acceptable practices of your international visitor's home country.
16. What is culture shock? What can someone do to adapt to a new work culture?

EVERYDAY ETHICS

Gender Matters

You have been working as an executive assistant to Ms. Simmons, the CEO of a prominent marketing company in Canada. Recently, Ms. Simmons has decided to do business with a Saudi Arabian firm. You have been in contact with administrative counterparts at the Saudi firm, exchanging information on the services your marketing firm can provide. Things have been progressing well until a meeting is set up between Ms. Simmons and Mr. al-Ghamdi, the owner of the Saudi business. This meeting will involve Ms. Simmons travelling to Saudi Arabia to meet directly with Mr. al-Ghamdi and his management team. When Mr. al-Ghamdi discovers the CEO of your firm is female, he refuses to meet with her for the negotiation process and insists on meeting with a man from your organization. Women are not often found in leadership roles in Saudi Arabia, and this situation creates a conflict with Mr. al-Ghamdi's cultural values.

Your company does not want to lose this contract, and a solution must be found.

■ What can be done to resolve this situation?

■ Is there something that could have been done in advance to prevent this situation from arising?

Gift Giving

Your company has strict rules on gift giving. The company practice reflects the belief that gift giving can be perceived as a form of bribery, and your company wants to ensure this perception is never invited. Your supervisor is travelling to Italy on business where gift giving is expected and is often considered necessary for establishing and building a trusting relationship. Your supervisor has asked you to order a nice pen with the recipient's name and your company logo engraved on it. You will need to submit this purchase to accounting, and questions will be raised about it.

■ What should you do?

■ How can this matter be handled in a mutually satisfying manner?

Problem Solving

1. Your telecommunications company has spent a significant amount of time trying to attract new international clients Finally, Mr. Chang has agreed to make the trip from China to tour your office and meet extensively with your supervisor, Alan Jacobs. As the administrative assistant, you have responsibility for coordinating the schedule of events for Mr. Chang's visit. You have also arranged an interpreter for Mr. Chang, as he speaks a limited amount of English. The day before Mr. Chang is due to arrive in Canada the interpreter has a family emergency and will need to travel out of the country, which means that he can no longer help you with Mr. Chang's visit. What can you do on such limited notice to ensure Mr. Chang has a good visit?

2. Your company is hosting three business associates from India for one week. Your manager has purchased a bottle of wine for each of the visitors. As you are preparing for their arrival you realize that one of your visitors is Hindu. Because you have researched beliefs and cultural values surrounding the Hindu culture, you realize that alcohol is not an appropriate gift. What should you do?

Special Reports

1. Interview an office professional to determine how workplace diversity is handled and promoted in his or her organization. Report your findings to the class or to the instructor.

2. Research three countries to determine how business gift giving and receiving is handled in these cultures. Prepare a memo for your instructor detailing your findings.

3. Search online for two international employment opportunities that may be suitable for you to apply to. Provide a brief report detailing the job location, qualifications, and method for applying for this position. Present your findings to your instructor.

4. Using the information you obtained by completing Question 3, research four business culture practices of one of the international employment opportunities you have discovered and prepare a memo for your instructor detailing your findings.

PRODUCTION CHALLENGES

2-A Cultural Self-Awareness

Supplies needed:

- *Exploring Your Own Cultural Background, Form 2-A, page 382*

One of the first steps in developing cultural awareness is to learn about your own cultural beliefs and values. This exercise will help you understand how your own personal cultural exposures have an impact on how you react to and view other cultures. Share your findings with your classmates.

2-B Cultural Understanding

Supplies needed:

- *Plain paper*

Develop an interactive activity that can be used with a group of people in your class that will explore and celebrate the rich diversity of backgrounds of the people in your classroom.

1. Plan this activity to last for approximately 10 to 15 minutes.

2. Carefully consider all aspects of the activity to ensure it is fun and engaging, but be sure not to include anything that may make a person feel embarrassed.

2-C Celebrations (Cultural Awareness)

Supplies needed:

- *Plain paper*

Respond to the following questions, drawing on your personal background. Answering these questions will help you to appreciate the importance of being aware of your own cultural practices and will thus help you to understand the importance of traditions in all cultures.

1. Describe your favourite family tradition.
2. How did this tradition begin?
3. Why is this tradition important to you?
4. Write down a traditional celebration you are aware of that another culture in your community practices.
5. Do you know why this practice is important to this culture?

Weblinks

Business without Borders
www.bwob.ca
This Canadian site provides useful information on conducting business in a global marketplace. Topics such as gift giving and arranging interpreters are explored.

Citizenship and Immigration Canada
www.cic.gc.ca/english/multiculturalism
This Canadian site provides multicultural information. It addresses a variety of subjects, including multicultural programs, and it provides links to select publications.

Diversity in the Workplace
http://www.diversityintheworkplace.ca/
This is an online publication dealing with diversity in the workplace. The site publishes monthly newsletters and also sponsors webinars that explore issues surrounding workplace diversity.

Canada's International Gateway
www.canadainternational.gc.ca
This site offers information about culture, travel, and doing business in Canada.

Newspapers and Magazines
www.ipl.org/div/news
This site provides links to newspapers and magazines around the world. This is beneficial for an international job search.

Passport Canada
www.passportcanada.gc.ca
This is a Government of Canada website providing information about acquiring a passport as well as locations of local passport offices.

Centre for Intercultural Learning
www.intercultures.gc.ca
This is a Government of Canada website that provides information about countries around the world. The site provides geographical statistics about the country, language spoken, religion, and ethnicity.

Chapter 3

Management of Work, Time, and Resources

Learning Outcomes

After completion of this chapter, the student will be able to:

1 Define the concept of the Quality approach.

2 Explain the difference between working efficiently and working effectively.

3 Outline methods for working efficiently.

4 Explain the importance of taking time to think through problems and make valuable contributions.

5 Assign priorities to the tasks of an administrative assistant.

6 Identify ways of overcoming the habit of procrastination.

7 List the procedures that ensure accuracy when proofreading keyed work.

8 Describe ways to avoid interruptions and to handle interruptions without wasting time.

9 Understand the importance of preparing for the next day's work.

10 Determine the normal working areas at a desk and the appropriate placement of equipment and supplies.

11 State suggestions for organizing both the office supplies and the workstation.

12 Discuss the options and advantages of nontraditional work arrangements.

13 Suggest methods for practising environmental consciousness in an office.

14 Prepare a daily plan chart.

15 Prepare and summarize a time distribution chart.

16 Efficiently prepare requisitions to order office supplies.

Administrative assistants work with a constant and rapid flow of information. Good organizational skills are required to process the flow. Administrative assistants must be able not only to organize work and to manage their time, but also to evaluate their own effectiveness and efficiency and to look for ways to continuously improve their contributions to the organization.

Systematic methods of organizing work, managing time, and managing resources provide indicators with which to measure your accomplishments each day, regardless of your long-term goals. This chapter identifies tools and techniques that may help you to become a more effective administrative assistant.

Graduate Profile

Warren Murphy
Executive Director

Fort McMurray Youth Soccer Association
Fort McMurray, Alberta

College Graduation:
Office Administration Diploma
Keyano College
Fort McMurray, Alberta

Prior to completing the Office Administration Diploma at Keyano College, Warren Murphy had worked extensively in the retail industry gaining valuable customer service skills. This experience, coupled with Warren's training in office administration, caught the attention of a college faculty member who held a board position with the Fort McMurray Youth Soccer Association. Warren was offered the Executive Director position and says, "The job turned out to be a good fit for me."

The day-to-day operations of this nonprofit association are handled by Warren and a co-worker who are directed by a ten-member Board of Directors. To meet the wants and needs of the different groups with whom he interacts, Warren draws on the professionalism he gained from his former customer service positions. He understands that effective communication is vital to the success of the soccer association and the satisfaction of its stakeholders. In the office, communication is mostly handled face to face, but also by telephone and email. The telephone is an essential tool during soccer registration, when Warren fields up to 50 calls per day.

Another indispensable communication tool is the internet, which Warren uses to answer and send email messages continuously throughout the day. He relies on his concern for quality and attention to detail as he completes various government forms online and as he uses web banking to handle payroll, bills, and government remittances. Updating the association website with current information is another task that Warren performs on a regular basis.

He explains that his most difficult responsibility is registering 1200 children for soccer in a two-week timeframe. He adds, "Making schedules for the leagues can be difficult since it is hard to please everybody." A common challenge for nonprofit organizations is the ability to attract volunteers to hold key positions, and the soccer association is no exception. If volunteers are not found to take on certain functions, staff members "pick up the ball and run with it" to help fill in the gaps.

Warren takes a realistic view of his abilities and realizes that not everything can be perfect with a job like his. At the end of the day, he knows he has done his best. If something has not been completed, it will always be there for him to complete the next day. Generally, Warren does not let work interfere with his free time but does not mind working some overtime during the busy periods to handle important tasks.

His current career goals are to keep improving at his job and his skills. Warren plans to achieve these goals by learning as much as he can and becoming the best administrator he can be. He advises future graduates to pursue the jobs they feel are most comfortable for them and believes there are jobs suitable for all working styles.

QUALITY APPROACH

Through globalization, new markets have opened both in Canada and abroad. To stay competitive in this global marketplace, many businesses have adopted a sound and effective approach for achieving success. This fundamental business methodology, known as the Quality approach, is practised through four basic principles:

1. customer focus
2. continuous improvement and learning
3. strategic planning and leadership
4. teamwork

The Quality approach recognizes the customer as the real judge of the quality of a company's products or services. Companies that adopt Quality not only plan for strategic business improvement but also encourage learning and new leadership ideas from their employees. As an administrative assistant in a company that embraces this approach to business, you are likely to become a member of a problem-solving team, or a team working to improve a business process somewhere in the organization. Most certainly you will be empowered to make broader decisions within your sphere of work.

In the office, Quality means that each employee is involved with office teamwork and focused on customer satisfaction. Employees at every level are encouraged to find new and innovative ways of doing their jobs more effectively, and to be flexible enough to assist others. You may be empowered—that is, given more autonomy and broader responsibilities—with the goal of simplifying office operations. You will be given responsibility for making decisions that will have an impact on your own effectiveness and performance.

You will be judged on your team contribution and on your innovation: If the filing system does not correspond to the operation—change it! If your colleague is having difficulty completing a project—help out! If a customer has a complaint—resolve it!

As an example, the administrative assistant may be invited to become part of a team that reviews the problem of products that aren't being delivered to the customer on time. The team would consist of employees who are directly involved in the delivery process under review. In this case, all members of the team would have equal responsibility and an equal voice in identifying all the steps and problems involved in the delivery cycle.

Refer to the section "Team Meetings" in Chapter 13 for details of how to participate in a team meeting. The problem must be clearly understood and stated in written form. All the issues that team members consider important are recorded. Team members then prioritize (by vote) the stated problems. The problem that is deemed the most significant is the first one the team deals with.

This first-priority problem is then thoroughly examined. Each step of the current procedure is analyzed for its effectiveness and necessity. The process of examining the entire procedure will inspire improvements. Additionally, each member will feel that he or she has contributed to a solution for improving customer satisfaction.

This team problem-solving approach is typical of process-improvement activities that organizations conduct as part of their Quality approach. Let's review a sequence of events that might occur as a cross-functional team is formed to address a late delivery problem:

1. A team of employees who are directly involved in the order and delivery process is formed. This team may include the administrative assistant.
2. A team leader is selected to chair the meeting.
3. All input is documented by a designated recorder.
4. A facilitator may be involved to organize the team members' input.
5. The general problem is clearly defined during the first team meeting.
6. Each team member has an equal opportunity to state what he or she believes to be the contributing factors to the general problem. This step, which allows the employees the freedom of open suggestion without criticism, is known as **brainstorming**. In this case, examples of contributing factors to the general problem may be:
   a. The person who places the orders is often away from work.
   b. When the orders are placed, the suppliers do not have ready stock; they must get stock from foreign markets.
   c. When suppliers deliver stock, it is sometimes in damaged condition and therefore must be reordered.
7. The team members now vote on what they believe to be the most important specific problems (contributing factors). In this case, the most significant factor may be that the stock is often received in poor condition and must be reordered.
8. Next, each team member helps outline the exact steps that take place in the process. In the case of goods arriving in damaged condition, it may be discovered that the foreign suppliers are not packing the goods carefully enough.
9. As the process is completely identified, team members provide input about possible changes until an improved process is developed. In this case, employees might suggest that proper packaging and careful handling of goods would expedite the delivery of the product to the customer.
10. The team will now make a recommendation to management for improving the delivery process.

EFFECTIVENESS AND EFFICIENCY

For the administrative assistant, being effective and being efficient are equally important. However, these two qualities are often confused with each other. These terms, while interrelated, are separate and distinct. Effectiveness is often defined as *doing the right things*, efficiency as *doing things right*.

What's the Difference?

Effectiveness means producing a definite or desired result. **Efficiency** means producing the desired result with a minimum of effort, expense, and waste. While it is possible to be effective without being efficient, the cost of inefficiency is usually too great for profit-making organizations; they must couple efficiency with effectiveness.

Whether administrative assistants work for one manager or for more than one, they must always do the following three things to organize their work so that they can perform efficiently:

1. Divide large projects into manageable segments of work.
2. Group related isolated tasks to reduce the time consumed in changing from one unrelated task to another.
3. Match the work to the time frames in which it must be performed, by classifying it as work that must be done today, work that must be done this week, or work that has no specific deadline.

Time management involves developing work habits that result in maximum efficiency; acquiring knowledge, skills, and equipment to extend performance beyond present capabilities; controlling attitudes and emotions that have a tendency to steal time; and developing an effective reminder method for following through on each task at the appropriate time. There will always be something critical demanding time. The key is to know how to prioritize work and complete work within an appropriate time frame.

Establish Efficient Work Habits

You can boost your own morale by increasing your organizational skills and by managing your time and working efficiently.

Be a self-starter; that is, take the initiative to begin a task for which you are responsible. Don't wait for your supervisor to prompt you. You also need to be a finisher. If you have many tasks started and none finished, your workload will seem heavier than it actually is. As you face a load of unfinished tasks, you may become less efficient. If you fall behind in your work and you can't catch up during regular

hours, work overtime. As you lighten your load by completing unfinished tasks, you will feel more relaxed and find it easier to cope and be effective.

It's much easier to complete your work if you have an exemplary attendance record, arrive on time each day, keep focused while at work, and put in the full expected hours.

An administrative assistant often works under the pressure of juggling priorities. One of the most difficult parts of your job will be learning how to judge these priorities. You will have to learn what degree of importance to place on each task and when to shift quickly to another task and apply extra effort.

Timing is an important factor in efficiency; a job must be performed not only well but also at the right time. To make time for urgent priorities and to feel that you are in control of your job, work willingly and with enthusiasm.

Self-Check

1. What does "effectiveness" mean?
2. What does "efficiency" mean?

TAKE CHARGE OF YOUR TIME

There is no single "right way" for managing time on the job. The rules are often job-specific and change from organization to organization. Exactly what constitutes successful time management is difficult to define without reference to specific examples from the workplace. There is no doubt that effective employees establish recognizable work *patterns*, but no two employees necessarily follow the *same* pattern. Nevertheless, the ideas presented in this chapter can be used as a guide to establish your own work habits and time-management techniques. It is important to remember, though, that this is only a guide. You will have to work hard and think about how best to adapt these rules and suggestions to your own situation.

For example, balancing family responsibilities and work responsibilities is a significant challenge for many administrative assistants. Some organizations have developed employee-friendly policies and support systems that provide flexible work schedules and permit more work-at-home and telecommuting options.

In a type of schedule design known as **flextime**, employees work a set number of hours each day but vary the starting and ending times. Flextime allows management to relax some of the traditional "time clock" control of employees' time. Similarly, working from home and telecommuting present an extraordinary opportunity to take charge of your own time.

Learn the Job

The organization expresses its objectives—the tasks to be accomplished—in terms of short-range, intermediate, and long-range goals. Management focuses its attention on achieving organizational objectives by accomplishing those goals. In any given week, your manager will devote time to both dealing with the work at hand and also addressing longer-range goals. As you join this dynamic environment, be as flexible, adaptable, and tolerant as you can in order to provide real value-added assistance.

In a new job, you will have to understand how your manager works. Organize your day's work so that it dovetails with that of your manager; do not expect your manager to adjust to your work schedule. At first:

1. Concentrate on learning.
2. Be cautious about taking initiative until you understand what is expected of you.

Someone will explain your new job to you. This might be the outgoing administrative assistant or your supervisor. Take full advantage of this **orientation**. You should listen, take notes, and ask questions that will increase your understanding of your new job. Try to remember the names of people you meet and what their roles are in the organization.

In addition to learning new procedures to follow, it may be prudent to inquire about:

1. supporting information
2. location of supplies
3. priority items
4. your manager's preferences

Every day, make an effort to learn more about your job and exactly how your manager prefers the work done. Learn the job not just for the current week and the next but for three months to a year in advance. Become familiar with the information in your office. For example:

1. Carefully study all the instructions left for you by the previous administrative assistant.
2. Check on the different kinds of stationery and forms in your desk and determine when each is to be used.
3. Read instruction sheets that have been prepared for certain assignments you are to perform.
4. Study the office manual, if given one.
5. Find out what is in the active files.
6. Refer to the directory of the organization to learn the names of the **executives** and other employees and their titles.

When you report to work, the former administrative assistant may not be there to train you. Perhaps there will not be an office manual describing your responsibilities. In this situation your manager will direct you. You will have to rely heavily on your own resourcefulness and use good judgment in seeking and finding answers. Keep in mind that you may not be fully effective until you understand the scope and responsibilities of your new job.

Take Time to Think

After working overtime the evening before, you arrive at work early the next morning to try to get a head start on some of your priorities. Instead, you find an urgent request left on the seat of your chair and messages on adhesive notes stuck to the screen of your computer. Your telephone message light is blinking, and before you can remove your coat, your telephone is ringing. The day is young and already you feel stressed!

With this level of pressure, responsibility, and expectations, how can administrative assistants find the time and the right environment to think clearly? We often underestimate the importance of taking time to think; but, without clear thinking, office professionals cannot improve office procedures, streamline office policies, or provide creative solutions to problems. Improving procedures, streamlining policies, and being creative about solving problems are as much the responsibility of the administrative assistant as they are of the executive.

Many office professionals find it challenging and exhausting just keeping up with the daily demands of the office and so leave strategic thinking to their managers. Get involved! You need to contribute by putting improvements and solutions forward. Your recommendations for improving office procedures will add to the big picture of the organization. As well, they let your organization know that you are valuable. Your contribution counts.

Finding the Time So just how do you find the time for creative thinking and planning? You could ask yourself the same question about where you will find the time to answer the telephone or reply to emails. Solving problems and making improvements should be as much a part of your job as answering the telephone. So schedule thinking time into your working day.

Creating the Environment Solving problems and developing better procedures are often done best as a team. When you have a definite problem or procedure that needs attention, call an informal brainstorming session with people who are involved in the problem. If you need to think through a problem or procedure on your own, put the telephone on hold, shut the door, and ask a co-worker to cover your desk for the next half hour while you move to a place void of interruption. If this is impossible, do your creative thinking on a scheduled break or early before others arrive. It's your job to think.

Thoughts on Thinking Where do you do your best thinking? When do you do your best thinking? How do you do your best thinking? Doodling on paper? Staring at a wall? Listening to music? Sitting in complete silence? Drinking a cup of coffee? Discussing ideas with others?

Experts say that the most creative thought happens differently for individuals. While one person gets his best inspiration in the shower, the next person does her best thinking while listening to rock and roll, and yet another while sitting in complete silence. Studies indicate that most students study better in a quiet environment with no interruptions. However, this solitude won't work for everyone. The environment most conducive for your thinking could be very distracting to the next person.

Assign Priorities

Setting **priorities** could be the most challenging part of organizing your work and assigning your time.

Although you are guided by general policies about priorities, you will need to make judgments concerning performing the work in the most beneficial way for others and for the organization. Performing the work in the order in which it is submitted to you will not always be feasible; some tasks will have more pressing deadlines than others. An example of a low-priority item is a memorandum written only as a matter of record. It can be keyed and filed at any time.

The demands of managers will be the overriding factor in how you divide your time. When you are working for two executives, one may have a lot of work for you and the other very little. When you work for a group, it may be made up of managers who are out of the office much of the time. Each one may have very little work for you, but each one will expect you to do it on the day he or she returns to the office. Under this arrangement, prepare a schedule a week in advance showing who will be in the office on which days of the week. This information may not be easy to obtain, but it will be helpful when it comes to answering the telephone and anticipating your own workload.

Eventually you will learn how much time you will need to perform each person's work. For your own use, keep a record of how you spend your time. Prepare a **time distribution chart**, as shown in Figure 3-1. The time distribution chart is designed to show the distribution of work and time for several workers performing related office tasks; however, with

Figure 3-1 Time distribution chart.

Dorothy Auvigne											_Week of: 20— 03 23_
					TIME DISTRIBUTION CHART						
MAJOR ACTIVITIES	Napoli	hrs.	Carson	hrs.	Jones	hrs.	Parker	hrs.	Ramos	hrs.	For Group	hrs.	TOTAL
Mail											Open and distribute	1 1/2	1 1/2
Research	Internet	1 1/2			Internet	1/2							2
Keying	Letters	1/2	Report	1/2			Letters	1/4	Memos	1/4			1 1/2
Setting Appointments	By electronic calendar	1/2					Telephone and in person	1/2					1
Payroll											Time sheets distribute cheques	1/2	1/2
Misc.											Handle calls	1/2	1/2
TOTAL		2 1/2		1/2		1/2		3/4		1/4		2 1/2	7

minor changes it can be used to show the distribution of time and duties performed by one worker for several others. At the top of the columns, write the names of those for whom you perform work. Enter the time used and a brief description of the task performed in the columns below the names.

After keeping the charts for several weeks, total the time used on behalf of each person and compute percentages. Your analysis will give you some estimate of how much work to expect from each person, and it will reflect what you are doing that could be channelled elsewhere. When you have so much work to be done that some of it must be reassigned, your charts will be especially helpful to you and your manager in deciding which duties can be handled by someone else.

Most administrative assistants who work for groups comprising employees of different ranks give highest priority to the work of the top manager in their group, second priority to the manager next in rank, and so on. This arrangement may ensure a good relationship with your manager, but it may also create problems, particularly if some of the employees in the lower ranks feel that they can never get their work done on time or at all. Eventually they will complain. Avoid this problem by learning how to assess the urgency of the work of the senior managers in the group. You will discover that some of their work can wait. Make your own judgment without discussing it with anyone and proceed with performing the tasks. However, when your work is backed up to the extent that it must be discussed formally, the most senior manager has the responsibility of assessing the total workload and determining the need for extra help.

Some people, in an effort to gain priority for their requests, will label all requests RUSH. In each case you will have to judge what is a rush item and what is not. When you sense that these employees are under a lot of pressure, you might occasionally prevent a disruption by giving priority to their work; however, this practice must not become the norm. By giving priority to managers who mark all items RUSH, you are encouraging this behaviour at the expense of other managers' work. Those managers who decrease the stress in the office by practising effective time management should not be penalized. Deal with this issue in a diplomatic way. The best advice is to collect facts before you approach the problem. How many rush items are you receiving? Which managers are giving you the rush items? What are the rush items? Exactly what dates are you being given the rush items, and when are the deadlines? The time distribution chart will assist with collection of these data.

You can maintain more control over your work schedule by relying on your own judgment about the order in which work should be done, instead of trying to follow rigid rules. Your judgment must be good, and you should be as concerned about your rapport with the members of the group as you are about the quality of the work you perform.

Some administrative assistants aspire to work for only one manager. There are advantages and disadvantages to such a situation.

Advantages of Working with Only One Manager

1. You are often viewed as having more status within the company.

2. You do not have to adjust to conflicting management styles.

3. Your manager has a clearer idea of your time constraints. Where several managers share the same assistant, the managers often are not aware of pressures being placed on you by their colleagues.

Disadvantages of Working with Only One Manager

1. Your responsibilities may be more routine. Where an assistant works for more than one manager, the assistant often receives a greater variety of projects to complete. Remember—the more experience you receive, the more marketable you become.

2. An assistant who works for only one manager gains business contacts from only that source. If you work for a number of managers, your chances of networking are improved; this, of course, could improve your future employment opportunities.

3. Working for only one manager may not allow you to practise your organizational skills to the same degree that working for multiple managers would.

The preference is a personal one. Both positions may offer equal challenges. If the challenges do not present themselves, find them!

Adopt a Flexible Plan

There's an adage that advises, "Plan your work then work your plan." This is good advice for the overtaxed administrative assistant.

You must plan for the ideal distribution of your time, but your plan must be flexible. Use your plan as an overall guide, but do not become discouraged if you cannot follow it closely. Your reputation of being flexible, adaptable, and tolerant with your plan will serve you well for the rest of your career.

One of your major responsibilities is to save your manager's time. To accomplish this, decrease interruptions or at least schedule them, and assist your manager by collecting and verifying facts and assembling materials that he or she will need to accomplish the task. To enable both you and your manager to perform with maximum efficiency, tackle the most pressing or important job first and keep adjusting your plan so that you can meet the corresponding deadlines.

There are three ways that you may learn the order of priority:

1. Ask questions of those involved in the process.

2. Listen to your manager's requests to determine a "pattern."

3. Keep a record of how work flows in and out of the office.

For example, know when routine reports are due and how much in advance to request work from service departments, learn mail pickup and transportation schedules, and be cognizant of the most convenient times to reach executives by telephone.

You must recognize that your work schedule is not truly your own. Your work schedule is governed not only by your manager's objectives and deadlines but also by the organization's schedule and need for information. For example:

■ You may plan to devote the morning hours to starting a lengthy assignment only to discover that your manager wants you to process a new expense summary in order to meet a scheduled payroll run.

■ A telephone call from corporate head office requesting critical information may take precedence over everything else.

■ The deadline for sending the department's weekly and monthly revenue report is based on a routine and defined schedule.

■ Whenever an associated department with which your work is interrelated changes its schedule, you must adjust your schedule to accommodate the department.

Manage Details

You, like every other administrative assistant, will be faced with the problem of keeping up with a myriad of details. In fact, you will be forced to devise methods for managing them. Not only must you record them immediately, but you must put them in a form that will enable you to locate and use these details later.

To capture details, use notebooks or forms. Use a separate notebook or form to record telephone dialogue or voice mail messages and subsequent action or conversations. Use another notebook or form to record reminders to yourself of actions you must take; this is commonly referred to as a **to do list**. Refer to Figure 3-2.

The computer may also manage details and reminders. Forms and simple templates are readily available in software

Figure 3-2 To do list.

applications enabling administrative assistants to store the recorded detail in electronic format. Refer to the electronic task list in Figure 3-3.

The advantage of an electronic format is that the detail is easily changed or modified, and that its distribution to other staff is simple.

To decrease the time you spend recording certain kinds of information, design a form in which you key and duplicate the constant information and leave space to write in the variable information. Forms bring related information together in one place and prompt the user to record all the essential facts.

Recording facts as soon as they become available to you is an important aspect of capturing details. You will discover that the practice of "do it now" is in conflict with the concept of grouping tasks to save time and energy; nevertheless, you need to capture details at the precise moment they arise in order to keep up with them.

Actually, the means you devise for keeping up with details can vary from task to task according to the work involved and your personal preferences. That being said, recognize in all your work:

■ the importance of having some method for capturing details

■ the need to be consistent in following your method

You can use check marks, initials, codes, and symbols to indicate the status of each detail that you want to capture. For instance:

1. The date stamp you place on a piece of incoming mail will tell you that you have already seen it.

2. The check mark by the enclosure notation on the file copy of a letter will remind you that you did include the enclosure.

Figure 3-3 Electronic task list.

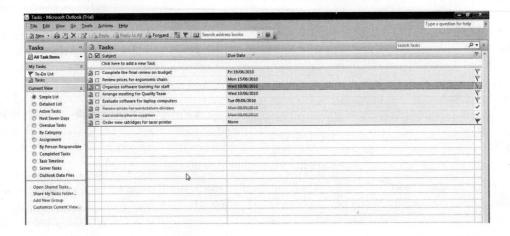

3. The electronic date and time attached to a computer file will indicate when the file was last updated.

In addition, be consistent in using each type of notation to convey its respective meaning. The absence of an appropriate notation will alert you to give attention to that particular item.

When you encounter a new task, spend a little time deciding how you are going to manage the details, and then be consistent in doing so.

Details arranged in the chronological order in which they were originally recorded usually are not in their most usable form. Details must be arranged so that they can be located quickly. The arrangement can range from simple indexing on cards to computer information search tools.

Organizing the details you need to keep—such as the names of new contacts, telephone numbers, changes of address, and schedule changes—can be done with great efficiency with a computer as you only need to record them once. Not everything you jot down needs to be transferred; this is especially true of reminders of things to do or other temporary items. Cross out the reminders as you complete the tasks, but go over your list carefully and transfer the reminders of tasks yet to be done to your to do list for the following day.

Self-Check

1. List four ways to become familiar with the information in your office.

2. Why is setting priorities one of the most challenging parts of organizing your work and assigning your time?

3. What are two advantages of working with only one manager? Two disadvantages?

4. What is a to do list?

Work at One Task at a Time

Schedule your work so that you can stay with one task until you finish it. Jumping from one task to another is confusing. Furthermore, reviewing work to figure out where to begin and recalling what has and has not been done results in wasted time and energy.

As you work, thoughts about other tasks will come to mind. Write down each usable thought on your to do list and continue to concentrate on the work at hand. Learn how to handle interruptions and shift back quickly to the immediate task; coping with interruptions is discussed in the section "Excuse Me!" found later in this chapter.

Form the habit of working at an uncluttered desk. On the immediate work area of your desk, put out only the materials you need for the one task on which you are working. Since you can give attention to only one main task at a time, put the other work aside, carefully organized and labelled.

Start the Day with a Difficult Task

Begin your day in an unhurried way so that you will not need the first 30 minutes at the office to "pull yourself together." If you commute and often find yourself worrying about your transportation being late, try to improve your day by taking earlier transportation. If you drive to work, allow yourself an extra five or ten minutes to get a head start on the morning rush hour. Arrive early, go over your plans for the day (which you prepared the day before), and then tackle a task that requires concentration and effort on your part. Tackle either a task that is difficult or one that you dislike. It will seem easier when you have energy and your mind is clear.

Make the first hour one of accomplishment, not one in which you simply get ready to work. Perhaps your first tasks will be to listen to your voice mail, to take down messages, or to read your email. As soon as you finish these regular responsibilities, start a challenging task. Of course, there will be times when you use the first hour to complete unfinished work from the day before.

Some office workers claim that they perform best early in the day; others, in the afternoon; and still others claim that they concentrate best very late in the day. In fact, psychologists have confirmed that every person has her or his own preferred work cycle. If you consider yourself an afternoon performer, use your afternoon hours for your most creative and challenging work, but force yourself to make the first hour a brisk one. Workers who waste time getting started are only putting themselves under unnecessary pressure to accomplish their work in what remains of the day. At any rate, do not use the beginning of the day to perform those easy tasks that can provide relaxation at intervals during the day.

Group Similar Tasks

You can save time and energy by not shifting from one task to another. For example, replenish your supplies once a week or less often. If supplies are delivered to you, fill out one requisition for all the supplies you will need for several weeks.

Different tasks require different degrees of concentration and, in turn, different speeds. Therefore, in order to control your pace, group together the tasks that require the same degree of concentration. Letters or emails to grant appointments and to make routine requests are favourable in tone, usually short, and easy to write. Group these messages and compose them rapidly.

In addition, group tasks to increase effectiveness. For example, making a telephone call should not be a routine task to be sandwiched between other work in an offhand way. A telephone call conveys an impression of the organization to the receiver. By grouping your telephone calls, you can give them your complete attention and project your personality in a thoughtful, businesslike way.

Avoid Procrastination

Procrastination is an unproductive behaviour pattern that causes you to delay working on your most important assignments and to focus on tasks that aren't priorities. We all procrastinate to some degree at certain times, but to some people it is a habit. To break the habit of procrastination, you must first gain an understanding of your behaviour and then work to overcome it. You can gain a better understanding of this behaviour by:

1. Admitting that you are procrastinating.
2. Asking yourself what types of projects cause you to procrastinate. Some office workers might see a major

project as a horrendous task, while others might find the daily routine tasks too much to face.

3. Asking yourself why you avoid these projects or tasks. Are you bored with the routine or afraid of the challenge? Are you avoiding interaction with certain office workers or authority figures? Do you fear failing at greater responsibility?

After answering these questions, you will be better prepared to overcome this unproductive behaviour. The following tips will help you avoid procrastination and become more productive.

1. Ask yourself what is the worst thing that can happen while you perform this task. Once you think it through, you will find that the risk created by the project is not that great; in fact, the benefits of completing the project will far outweigh the difficulties.

2. If the project is large, divide it into smaller sections. Several small tasks always appear to be easier to accomplish than one large task.

3. Reward yourself often. Allow yourself a break or a more pleasant task once you have completed a portion of the work. Small and frequent rewards work better for procrastinators than one large reward after completion of a very strenuous task.

4. Ask yourself what is the downside of not completing the task on time—or worse, not completing the task at all. Does not doing the project mean the loss of your job, a demotion, or the loss of respect from your peers and managers? This alone may encourage you to get started.

5. If you are a perfectionist, you may be avoiding a simple task because of your working style. Remember that not all work must be flawless. Working *smarter*, instead of *harder*, means recognizing the difference between work that must be perfect and work that can contain minor flaws, and acting on it.

Build Relaxation into Your Schedule

Most organizations provide a lunch hour and short morning and afternoon breaks during a regular workday. With these exceptions, employees are expected to perform efficiently throughout the day.

To maintain your best performance throughout the day and the week, experiment with alternating difficult and easy tasks to establish the best combination for conserving your energy. Observe which tasks consume a great deal of energy and which ones seem to require little energy. Rotate tasks that require a great deal of concentration and effort with tasks that require less thought and energy. Whether a task is difficult or easy for you to perform will depend on your ability, your experience in performing the given task, and your attitude toward it.

Performing an undesirable task requires an extra expenditure of energy. Repetitive tasks are often disliked. Here the dislike arises from the repetition rather than from the work itself. Fortunately, new computer technology and software have introduced interesting and productive methods of accomplishing tasks.

Once you discover which tasks are easy for you, save them to perform between difficult tasks. Use them to provide relaxation as you work. Start your day with a difficult task and work at a vigorous pace. Keep at one task for at least two hours or until you reach a stopping place. Throughout the day, alternate difficult tasks with easy ones. When possible, also alternate sitting with standing tasks. When you cannot change the task, change your pace. After lunch and after your morning and afternoon breaks, tackle difficult tasks.

Save easy tasks for late in the day. When you are estimating the time needed for performing a long, complicated task, allow for a decrease in production as you continue working. You cannot expect to perform at your maximum rate for six or seven hours. Your productivity will be highest when you can keep fatigue to a minimum. Discover and maintain a pace that will make it possible for you to do your best work.

Because of the pressure of work, you may forgo your morning or afternoon break and shorten your lunch hour. You will possibly stick to the difficult task and postpone other work. You may be asked to work overtime, and others in the office may be asked to assist you. You may feel that you have no control over your work schedule. When you face these situations, evaluate your working plan. Establish the duration of the peak load, how often it will occur, and what you can do about it. Determine what preparation you can make in advance to lessen the peak load. If there is no letup in the work, either you are not approaching your job in the right way or you need assistance. Discuss the situation with your manager, but be prepared to offer viable solutions.

Do It Right the First Time

To produce acceptable work on the first try, plan each task before you begin, focus on the exactness of the details as you perform, and then check each finished task for correctness and completeness before you release it.

Remember that waste results when work that could have been completed correctly on the first try must be redone.

Before you start performing a task, make sure you understand the instructions; then review the facts, visualize the work in its finished form, and make a plan. Spend sufficient time determining exactly what you are expected to

do: do not guess. You will discover that the extra minutes needed to perform the task correctly the first time are fewer than you would spend redoing the task. Work at a pace that will result in the most productivity for you.

The speed with which business information flows places a premium on accuracy. An error that has been released is difficult to retrieve. Problems created by errors that are released into the channels of information are not only time-consuming to correct, but can also result in losses to the organization. So check your work carefully. Be sure that every detail is correct and that each item is complete before you transmit it. On the job, you will discover ways to check the various tasks you perform to ensure their correctness. Develop your own checkpoints and guidelines for each task. Here are a few guidelines that should be observed for checking printed work:

1. Edit the copy for meaning. At the same time, watch for typographical, spelling, and punctuation errors. Do this while the copy is still on the screen so that making corrections will be easy.

2. Go over the copy a second time, scanning it for figures such as dates and amounts of money. Then check their accuracy.

3. Use a calculator to check a long list of keyed figures that have been totaled.

4. When a long series appears, count the items and compare the number with the list in the original.

5. When you must proofread a document that you have copied from keyed material, follow the original line by line, using a ruler to keep your place.

6. Always proofread the two-letter provincial abbreviations and the postal codes in addresses. One wrong stroke at the keyboard, if not caught, can mean a delayed letter.

Prepare in Advance

With the exception of routine tasks, office work requires planning. The amount of planning time needed depends on how complicated the job is, the length of it, and whether or not the person doing the work has ever performed similar tasks.

Executives in successful organizations plan three to five years in advance. Managers at all levels plan at least one year in advance. Observe how your manager and others in your organization think ahead, and then apply some of their techniques to your own assignments. The time you spend thinking through what needs to be done will save you minutes and hours of redoing work.

Take time to study a job until you can visualize it to its completion regardless of how complicated or lengthy it is. People who work aimlessly seldom reach the goals toward which they should have been working. Ask yourself what the expected outcome and purpose of the specific assignment is. When an assignment is new and you find it difficult to visualize it through to completion, ask your team manager for guidance.

The most critical parts of an assignment are the ones that require other people—either to supply information or to actually perform certain tasks. Begin your preparation with the segments of the work that involve others.

Figure 3-4 illustrates a Gantt chart. This chart is an excellent tool for comparing your planned work schedule against the actual time that is required to complete a task.

Complete a Task

You will be doubly rewarded when you stay with a task until it is complete:

1. You will feel satisfaction at having finished the task.
2. You will experience the emotion of accomplishment.

Always think more about what you have accomplished than about what you still must get done. Enjoy the satisfaction that one naturally experiences from completing an assignment or reaching a goal. When you are working on a lengthy project that seems endless, break the assignment into segments that you can complete in a morning or an afternoon, or into even smaller parts that you can complete in an hour or two. Plan on stopping occasionally to measure your accomplishment by the number of segments completed. Don't get sidetracked. If you stay focused on one task there is less likelihood of errors occurring. If you must put work aside unfinished, make detailed notes of what still needs to be done. Make your notes carefully so that you can rely on them.

Avoid Interruptions

Every challenging position that demands a variety of responsibilities will be punctuated by interruptions. There are ways of avoiding some interruptions.

1. Practise avoidance by organizing your work area so that it is less accessible to co-workers who wish to socialize during work hours. Try moving extra chairs away from your desk, or moving or angling your desk so that it cannot easily be seen by passers-by.

Figure 3-4 Gantt chart.

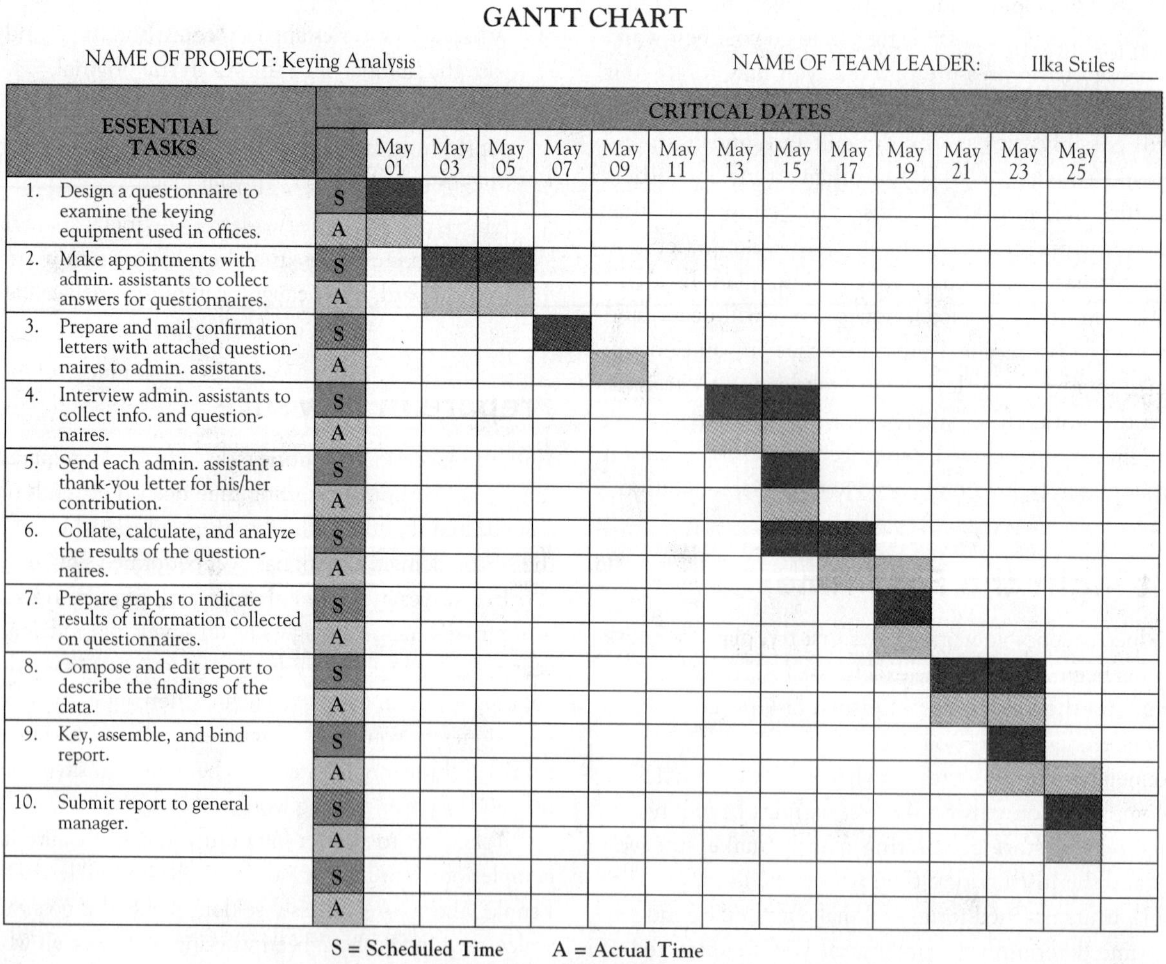

GANTT CHART

NAME OF PROJECT: Keying Analysis   NAME OF TEAM LEADER: Ilka Stiles

S = Scheduled Time   A = Actual Time

2. Interruptions are often caused by noise. You can avoid this type of interruption by having noisy equipment relocated away from your desk.

3. When you are working on a project that requires your full attention, ask another administrative assistant to handle your telephone calls; explain the urgency of your task to co-workers, and then move to a location away from your desk.

Excuse Me!

Your success in coping with interruptions will depend on your attitude toward them and your ability to handle them and then resume work quickly.

You know that interruptions cannot always be prevented—the telephone will ring, a visitor will walk in, a co-worker will ask you a question, your manager will need assistance. What you do not know is the precise moment when the interruption will occur.

Recognize that interruptions are a part of the job, and allow time for them in your planning. Keep a record of the number of telephone calls you receive in a typical day, the number of visitors you receive, and the number of times you assist your manager and co-workers. Estimate the time consumed by these duties, and determine how much time you have left for other tasks. Do not create your own frustrations by planning to accomplish more than you can get done.

Don't resent interruptions. Keep calm; do not allow yourself to become upset. You will feel less frustrated if you know how much time you will need to perform each of your normal tasks. For example, keep a record of how long it takes to key a two-page letter, to compose a one-page memo, to develop a 12-page formal report, and to process the daily mail. This is useful information for future planning and scheduling. If you discover that you are running out of time to meet a deadline, decide for yourself which work can be postponed. Use your time for the priority item.

Give adequate time to handling each interruption. Do not appear to be rushed. Be courteous, but do not waste time because of an interruption. To reduce the time used for each interruption, proceed in the following way:

1. Mark your place as soon as you are interrupted—a light, erasable check mark in the margin with a soft lead pencil will suffice.

2. Once you are interrupted, handle the interruption immediately if it can be dealt with in only a few minutes. If a co-worker asks for information, look it up and supply the information while the co-worker is at your desk. In response to a telephone call you can handle, follow through on the caller's request, even looking up information if you can do so without keeping the

caller waiting a noticeable length of time. However, if the interruption requires prolonged attention, you may have to postpone action on it. Realize, however, that each time you must postpone following through on a request, you are creating a new item for your to do list.

3. Quickly resume work where you left off at the time of the interruption. Do not encourage co-workers to linger in your office. Be courteous, but do not continue a telephone conversation beyond the time actually necessary to handle the call.

4. Avoid interrupting yourself because of lack of planning.

5. Keep a pencil in your hand, or keep your hands on the keyboard. These actions inform the visitor that you are eager to continue your work.

6. Do not get involved in office gossip. Small talk creates big interruptions.

7. When a co-worker drops into your office for a visit, stay standing. Often a person feels invited to sit if you are sitting. If the visitor sits down and you feel the need to sit, do so on the edge of your desk. This does not invite the visitor to become too comfortable.

8. When possible, hold meetings in another person's office. This allows you to leave as soon as the business is complete. Meeting with visitors in reception areas or conference rooms helps to keep the meeting short, since these areas often do not provide the privacy of an office.

When you must interrupt others, be considerate. Wait until the other person is at a break in her or his work. Direct your questions to the correct person, and do not interrupt others unnecessarily. Do not ask others to answer questions if you can find the answers yourself by looking them up. Accumulate the questions you must ask your manager; then ask several at one time to cut down on interrupting her or him. A concise memo or electronic message enumerating your questions is an excellent way to avoid a direct interruption and to obtain a quick response.

Make a Daily Plan

At the end of the day, review the work you must do the following day. Estimate the time each of your tasks will take and fit them one by one into time slots. Go through the same steps daily, and then leave your office with the satisfaction of knowing that your work is well organized for the following day. To prepare a systematic daily plan, you could proceed as follows:

1. Verify that everything you have entered into the computer during the day has been saved.

2. If you use an **electronic calendar** or desk calendar pads, make sure the appointment entries in your manager's calendar and yours are identical.

3. Go over your to do list. If something on the list must be carried out the following day, enter it in your daily calendar. As you are planning your work, you will think of other tasks that must be done some time during the day. Put notes about these on your to do list.

4. Prepare a list of your manager's activities for the following day. Include on it all appointments, showing with whom, the purpose, the time, and where (if it is not in your manager's office). At the bottom of the sheet, add reminders of work your manager must complete during the day.

5. Locate the reports, correspondence, and other items to which you know your manager will need to refer during conferences, or before he or she places a telephone call, writes a report, or carries out other responsibilities. Flag these with coloured stickers so that you can retrieve them quickly the following day. Likewise, locate the information you will need in order to proceed with your own work. Also make computer printouts of information you and your manager will need.

6. Complete your filing, and lock the files. As a part of your filing routine, transfer copies of completed work and the related supporting data from your work-in-progress folder to the file. All papers should be stored in cabinets, for protection from fire or perusal.

7. Clear your desk, putting everything in place.

The next morning, do the following:

1. Review the entries in your daily appointment calendar.

2. Place your manager's list of activities on his or her desk if you did not place it there the day before.

By using this system, you will be well prepared to start your work immediately. You will enjoy the satisfaction of having a plan for your tasks and priorities.

Operate within Easy Reach

Normal and maximum working areas at a desk have been established through time and motion studies. Materials and tools should be positioned within the normal working area if the worker is to attain maximum efficiency.

You can determine the *normal* working area of the desk for either the right or the left hand by swinging the extended hand and forearm across the desk. You can determine the *maximum* working area for either the right or the left hand by swinging the extended hand and the entire arm across the desk.

Before you begin a task at a desk or a table, place the equipment, supplies, and tools you will need in the normal working area.

Use the space in your desk to store supplies, stationery, and work in progress. Materials should pass across the top of your desk but should not be stored on it. Keep a minimum of items on top of your desk.

File all your work in progress together in one drawer, unless your manager is working on a project that generates so much paperwork that the materials must be subdivided into several folders. Allocate separate space in a vertical file drawer for a project of this magnitude. Never put a single folder of pending material in an unusual place—relocation of this material can lead to confusion and wasted time.

In case you might be absent, let your manager know where you keep the correspondence folder and other work in progress. If the work in progress is highly confidential, you may have to store it in file cabinets with special locks at night.

If you have a drawer that is not deep enough to hold file folders in vertical positions, keep it empty. Use it as a temporary storage when you want to clear your desk to store the papers on which you are currently working—for instance, while you sort the mail or go to lunch.

Self-Check

1. What does "procrastinating" mean?

2. What determines whether a task is easy or difficult for you to perform?

3. When might you use a Gantt chart? Why?

OFFICE ORGANIZATION

By organizing office supplies and the workstation, an administrative assistant can save a great deal of time, as well as save the company money. Following are some suggestions for getting the office supplies and workstation organized.

Organize the Office Supplies

1. Label the shelves where supplies are kept. This way staff members know where to look without interrupting you. This procedure also helps you keep track of supplies on hand.

2. Make sure that one person is responsible for controlling inventory and ordering supplies. This is a task that a senior administrative assistant will often delegate.

3. Develop your own requisition form. Keep these forms in the supply room. Staff will be expected to complete the form if they notice a product is running low. Be sure the form has room for a full description. Encourage the staff to fill in as much information as possible (descriptions, quantities, colours, sizes, unit numbers, and so on). This will simplify your work when it comes to completing the requisition for ordering.

4. Compose a list of all items you use on a regular basis. Include the item unit numbers, unit prices, descriptions, colours available, and so on. Post this list in the supply room along with a stack of the requisition forms you have developed. This is necessary if you expect staff members to partially complete the requisition forms.

5. Discourage staff members from placing verbal orders with you. This type of interruption can be very time-consuming: you must stop your work, listen to the request, write down the information, check the supplies, and perhaps get back to the staff members for further clarification. Insist that all orders be completed on requisition forms.

6. When staff members have rush orders, request that they fill in a requisition, mark it RUSH, and bring it to your desk.

7. Take inventory on a regular basis. Taking inventory once or twice a month on a designated day works well for most offices.

8. Before placing an order, compare prices between the office supply catalogues and advertisements sent to you. The office supply market is a competitive one, and you may be able to order your items on sale.

9. Ordering items in standard package sizes may save you money. Ordering items one at a time is short-sighted and expensive.

10. Do not over-order supplies, unless you are ordering supplies in standard-size packages. Too many supplies will cause confusion. Because space is often at a premium, excess supplies tend to create a storage problem. As well, some supplies have a shelf life: if not used before a certain date, they become less useful.

11. When you place an order, be prepared with all the required information. Having requisition forms returned or needing to make a follow-up telephone call to clarify an order will delay delivery.

Organize the Workstation

A cluttered desk gives clients, co-workers, and managers the impression that you are disorganized. A cluttered desk is not necessarily a sign that you are busy; in fact, a cluttered desk simply adds to your workload. It is essential that you purge any extraneous materials and then organize the materials you intend to keep.

Purge Unnecessary Items One of the first steps to take in organizing your desk is to eliminate all that you don't need. Each time you pick up a document from your desk and wonder where to file it, ask yourself whether there's a law that says you must keep it. If not, consider the recycling box or the garbage bin.

If any of the following applies to a document, you have just cause to purge yourself of paper:

1. Another co-worker has filed it where you can access it if needed.

2. You will not really use the information; it is just *nice* to have. Remember that libraries have incredible amounts of reference materials that can be easily accessed.

3. The document is a duplicate. Once you get organized, one copy is all you need of any document.

4. The document is out of date. Newer information is usually better information. You can always get current information from the internet or from the reference section of the library. If the document pertains to your company, historical records may be kept in the central registry.

5. Chances are you will never find the time to read the information. If the information is "nice to know" rather than essential, rid yourself of it until you are organized.

You will find that you work much more efficiently after you have organized your desk.

Organize Necessary Items Ridding your workstation of excess paper is only the first step in getting organized. The importance of a highly organized workstation cannot be emphasized enough.

One of the most frustrating time-wasters is searching for information that has been filed incorrectly or has simply disappeared. Of course, employing the correct ARMA filing rules is imperative; these rules are discussed in Chapter 10. However, there is much more to organizing your workstation. When your workstation is organized, you save valuable time.

The following are some suggestions to help you get started:

1. If your workstation is currently in a cluttered condition, plan several uninterrupted hours you can use to attack the problem.

2. Once you have organized the workstation, take a mental snapshot of it and vow that you will never leave it disorganized at the end of the day. Start the day with a clear mind and a clear desk. Many offices now practise a **clean desk policy**, which stipulates that each evening employees must leave their desks in either a totally clear or very tidy condition.

3. If your office does not have a paper shredder, approach your manager about purchasing one. Employees are often reluctant to discard confidential material, so they let it accumulate in what eventually becomes a very thick folder tucked into a corner of the desk. Compact shredders can be placed on top of wastebaskets.

4. A basket placed in your workstation to hold work that is pending often becomes a storage bin. If you do not intend to work on a document immediately, file it in its appropriate labelled folder. Then place the folder in the file cabinet and make a comment in your calendar on the day this document must be dealt with. This way the phrase "out of sight—out of mind" will not apply.

5. Use one calendar for all your appointments. If you keep your personal appointments separate from your business appointments, you will constantly be referring to two calendars. This is a time-waster and will result in disorganization. Take your calendar with you to every meeting and seminar you attend. Tuck your calendar into your briefcase at the end of each day so that you can continue to record personal appointments.

6. Compose documents at your keyboard. By using a computer screen to compose documents, you avoid excess paper with letters and memos scratched on them. If the documents you compose can be mailed and filed electronically, you will never have to add a piece of paper to your filing cabinet.

7. Wherever you store information—drawers, cabinets, folders, baskets, and so on—affix a label that describes the type of information that should be stored in this location. While you are getting organized you will have stacks of paper. Organize them by placing a temporary label on the top of the pile. Not only will the labels assist you in locating information, but they will also assist others in your absence.

8. Attempt to follow this rule: *Never handle a piece of paper more than once.* At times this rule may be unrealistic, but it will force you to make a decision rather than procrastinate, then rehandle and reread a document.

9. Never use the surface of your desk as storage space. Your desk is a work area; you need all of it available to remain organized while you conduct your work.

10. Keep your computer reference information current. If names, addresses, and telephone numbers are indexed on your computer system, consider it a priority to update the system as often as possible. You cannot enjoy the efficiency of using a computer system unless it provides correct information.

11. Continually organize, purge, and alphabetize your filing system. When you discover a document out of place or out of date, take action immediately. Your filing cabinet is a work area you should take pride in. Refer to Chapter 10 for filing strategies.

12. Create a reference for frequently called telephone or fax numbers. Place this reference list nearby or code the numbers into the memory of the telephone or fax machine.

13. Place reference sources (books, CD-ROMs, portable media storage devices) at an arm's length from your work area. These references should include a dictionary, a thesaurus, an administrative assistant's reference manual, office manual, telephone directories, and the like.

14. Paper clips are not a reliable tool for keeping pages together. In fact, your files should contain no paper clips. When you want to avoid pages being separated, staple them.

15. Do you really know what is in your desk and cabinets? Schedule 15 minutes every month to purge your current bookshelves, desk drawers, and cabinets. You must keep current with the contents of your workstation. Keep the wastebasket and recycling box handy; you should constantly purge your workstation of unwanted materials.

16. If there is a bulletin board in your workstation, be sure the information is current and well organized. If the bulletin board is not easy to use, it is just occupying space and adding to the office clutter.

17. After you take a telephone message, place the message in a designated location, off your desk. In this way you have dismissed the task immediately. You are then free to continue with your other tasks, and your desk is less cluttered.

18. Use coloured paper to coordinate your tasks. This will assist you in locating categories of information. Coloured paper draws attention. For example, you will be able to quickly spot blue telephone messages or green memos in a pile of white documents. Not only will the coloured paper help you get organized, but it will also draw the attention of others to requests for action or information that you place on their desks. Try using fluorescent-coloured paper when you want your interoffice requests to get immediate attention.

19. Keep the equipment you rely upon the most within easy reach; you should be able to slide your chair easily between the telephone, the computer, fax machine, and so on.

20. Your workstation will require drawer space for office supplies. Store only a limited supply at your desk; store larger amounts away from your workstation in a supply cabinet. The small supplies you keep at your desk (stapler, tape, pens, clips, adhesive notes, and the like) can

be stored with drawer organizers, which are sold at stationery stores. Letterhead, envelopes, forms, and other major paper supplies should be placed in drawer trays, not left out in visible stacks.

21. Your personal items need a place too; but do not crowd your desk surface with family photos. Leave the desk surface as clear as possible and place the photos on top of your **credenza** or filing cabinet. Coats and spare shoes should be stored in the coatroom. Lunches and tea bags belong in the lunchroom. Awards belong on the walls. If your office contains plants, place small ones on the window ledge, credenza, and so on, and large ones on the floor. Keep personal items to a minimum. The workstation is professional space, not personal space.

Self-Check

1. What does "purge" mean?
2. List three suggestions that you will adopt to help you organize your workstation.

NONTRADITIONAL ARRANGEMENTS

Why do we believe that working in an office means working 9 a.m. to 5 p.m., with two refreshment breaks and one lunch hour? Many organizations offer flexible working arrangements for administrative assistants. Flexible working hours, job sharing, and working outside the office are popular and yet still considered nontraditional work arrangements.

Good managers know that allowing employees to have working arrangements that better suit their lifestyles means happier and more productive employees.

Flextime

For administrative assistants with front-line reception responsibilities, working face-to-face with other employees and with clients is a priority. In this case, it is essential to have standardized working hours that match those of the organization's business hours.

However, where there is more than one administrative assistant with similar responsibilities there is an opportunity for flexible hours. A cooperative working arrangement between administrative assistants will mean that there is always at least one person available to handle clients and employees and generally cover administrative work

while another assistant is enjoying the benefits of flextime. Managers often approve an arrangement in which employees have extended working hours for nine days and then are given the tenth day as a holiday. Flexible hour arrangements thus offer an excellent opportunity for frequent long weekends. Another advantage of flextime is that one can avoid rush-hour traffic by starting work early or finishing late.

Job Sharing

An office with a cooperative team environment lends itself to job sharing. Where employees have a good understanding of what must be accomplished and the procedures for handling the work, it is possible for two or more people to share one job. Many office professionals have a lifestyle that suits a part-time working arrangement. In this case, job sharing is an excellent option.

Workplaces

What about office professionals whose roles do not include front-line reception and who work more with document production, travel arrangements, or project and event management? Is it necessary for these employees to perform all their work at the office? The answer is probably no.

It is so convenient and effective to communicate using email, voice mail, and other forms of instant messaging. Without question, cell phones allow people to stay in touch much better than stationary desk telephones. Laptop and tablet computers offer ease of internet access, which allows work to be done almost anywhere and anytime. So with the cooperation of management, office professionals with the correct electronic tools may be able to maximize their performance by working away from the office.

Self-Check

1. List three nontraditional work arrangements.
2. Give an example of each nontraditional arrangement.

ENVIRONMENTAL MANAGEMENT

Administrative assistants can take the lead in making the office an environmentally conscious workplace. Consider the opportunities for recycling, reusing, and reducing that present themselves each workday.

Many organizations take their environmental responsibilities so seriously that it is often written into their vision, mission, and values statements. Individual offices are similarly taking a more responsible approach to managing resources. Most companies make a serious effort to recycle and reuse materials, reduce waste, and purchase products that have been recycled.

Become Part of an Environmentally Conscious Office

If your office has not yet committed itself to becoming environmentally conscious, you should initiate this change. Here are some suggestions:

1. First look at the coffee/lunchroom. Is the office still using paper or polystyrene plates and cups? If so, don't replace them when the supply is depleted. A set of reusable dishes is not expensive. Request that staff clean their own dishes after using them. Washing dishes is not the responsibility of an administrative assistant; recycling is everyone's responsibility!

2. Consider your duplication procedures. Are you still copying single-sided documents? Duplex whenever possible.

3. When a number of office personnel need the same document, don't duplicate it. Place a routing slip on it, or scan and email it.

4. Before you copy or print anything, check and double-check the document. This way, you won't have to discard a multiple set of documents if you find an error after the copying is complete.

5. When you must discard paper, ask yourself if the paper can be recycled. Special paper trays and bins for the collection of recyclable paper should be set around the office in convenient locations. See Figure 3-5, which

shows the difference between a product that is recyclable and one that is recycled.

6. It is easier to simply discard the used toner cartridges from copiers and printers than to return them to the manufacturer for recycling; however, discarding cartridges is a wasteful practice. Most manufacturers welcome the return of cartridges for recycling. In some cases, manufacturers and suppliers will refill your used cartridge and return it to your office, thereby reducing costs and waste.

7. If a vending machine selling canned or bottled drinks is used in the office, place a box next to the machine. Post a sign asking the staff to drop empty cans or bottles in the box. The cans will add up quickly. You can offer the cans or the proceeds from them to a local charity, or use the proceeds to buy the reusable dinnerware for your lunchroom.

8. When ordering office supplies, make a conscious effort to purchase recycled products; but keep in mind that the term *recycled* can be vague. Canadian manufacturers are expected to publish the percentage of recycled material in the product along with the recycled logo (see Figure 3-6).

If you cannot buy recycled products, buy those that are recyclable.

Your office personnel will have more ideas about responsible resource management that might pertain to your office. Continue to explore these options. Welcome their ideas and publish them in a monthly newsletter. Of course, the newsletter can be printed on recycled paper and rotated on a circulation slip. Remember, not everyone needs a separate copy.

Figure 3-6 Sample of product displaying percentage of recycled material.

Figure 3-5 Signs depicting recycled or recyclable materials.

Recycled

Recyclable

This envelope is made of
100% recycled paper
and is recyclable

*Cette enveloppe est
fabriquée de papier
100% recyclé et est
recyclable*

QUESTIONS FOR STUDY AND REVIEW

1. Distinguish between effectiveness and efficiency.

2. What effect will a manager's work preferences have on the way the administrative assistant's daily work is organized?

3. Who should establish an understanding of priorities with all the members of the office team?

4. List categories of information that an administrative assistant should concentrate on as the new job is being explained.

5. Suggest ways that an administrative assistant can take initiative in learning a new job.

6. Explain how you can justify taking time at your desk for creative thinking.

7. Suggest four ways you can create an environment that is conducive to creative thinking while you are located at your workstation.

8. Should all segments of the working day be structured? Explain.

9. Why should details be recorded immediately?

10. What are the advantages of keeping the work you have in progress carefully organized?

11. Describe how to get a head start on the day's work.

12. Give examples of similar tasks that can be grouped.

13. What does the phrase "work smarter, not harder" mean?

14. Describe how to organize your work throughout the day so that you can maintain your best performance.

15. In order to get work right the first time, what should you do before actually performing the task?

16. Make a list of routine tasks that can be performed between major tasks.

17. What is the primary advantage of focusing on a task until it is finished?

18. Suggest three ways to avoid interruptions before they occur.

19. Suggest three ways to deal successfully with interruptions once they have occurred.

20. Why should you discourage staff members from verbally placing supply requests?

21. Suggest five ways to determine whether a piece of paper should be discarded rather than filed.

22. State two things you could do to make a quiet environment if you wanted time to think and be creative.

23. Suggest five ways to demonstrate environmental consciousness in your office.

EVERYDAY ETHICS

Smoking Supervisor

You are the office supervisor for a respected consulting firm in Saskatoon. You supervise four administrative assistants. The office hours are from 8:00 a.m. until 4:30 p.m. five days a week. All your employees respect the established office hours and the allotted time for lunch. In addition to lunch, everyone is allowed two 30-minute refreshment breaks.

One of the people you supervise, Kylie, is a good friend, and you see each other socially outside the office. You and Kylie are the only smokers on staff. Because your office is a nonsmoking environment, you take an average of four additional breaks per day, each break taking about ten minutes.

Do the math! You and Kylie are taking 40 extra minutes on breaks every day. By the end of every working week you and Kylie have each spent more than three and a half hours away from work. By the end of the month, you each have spent almost two extra days on breaks.

Your three nonsmoking employees come to you with this issue of Kylie's time. They say that Kylie is working fewer hours than they are working. They report that the other administrative assistants handle the clients and managers that come to Kylie's desk while she is on smoking breaks. They have spoken to Kylie several times about the issue, and Kylie's response has always been, "See my supervisor." The nonsmoking administrative assistants recommend that they too be given equivalent time away from their desks.

■ What are you going to do?

Problem Solving

1. You have a new job. You have been working for three weeks. Each afternoon before leaving work, you carefully plan your work for the next day. You are having difficulty sticking to your plan because the telephone rings continually. You seem to be spending a lot of time on the telephone. In fact, you are becoming frustrated because you must answer so many telephone calls. What are the solutions to your problem?

2. When you started working for Mr. Chow, he suggested that filing was a low-priority item. He said you should let filing go until you do not have other work to do. You have followed his suggestion for four weeks, and the papers

in your filing baskets are about to reach the ceiling. You never seem to find the time to file. The problem is compounded when Mr. Chow calls for a paper and you must go through the unfiled stacks to find what he wants. What can you do to solve your filing problem?

3. Your manager, Ms. Polowski, writes many reports. She usually works on the reports on Monday, Tuesday, and Wednesday. On Thursday morning she hands you enough material written in longhand to keep you keying all day. The final reports are prepared by the junior office assistants, who request that all material coming to them be keyed in rough-draft form.

On Friday as soon as the completed reports come back, you spend about two hours checking them to make sure they are accurate and that everything has been included.

You enjoy keying the drafts and proofreading the reports. However, you are becoming frustrated because you are letting your other work go. What are the solutions to this problem? What can you do to relieve your frustration?

4. Five weeks ago you were promoted to administrative assistant for the Sales Department. There are 25 salespeople in the department, and you are having difficulty prioritizing your work. This morning one of the salespeople shouted, "You never get my work done by the time I need it. You are always doing work for Kristien and Adam." Kristien and Adam do give you more work than the other salespeople, and you are aware that you've spent much of your time doing their work. What can you do to ensure that you allocate a fair portion of your time to doing the work of the other salespeople?

Special Reports

1. Interview an office professional who works for more than one person—several executives, everyone within a department, or everyone within a division. Request an interview in order to ask questions about how the office professional organizes and handles the work. Phrase your questions in advance. Develop your questions carefully. As you formulate your questions, be sure to inquire about priorities for completing work, standards of acceptability, telephone and data management responsibilities, problems encountered, and suggestions that might be helpful to you on the job. Do not limit your questions to the ideas given here. Report your findings to the class or to the instructor.

2. How many unfinished projects do you have? Are you burdened with the thought that "everything is started and nothing is finished"? Make a list of your unfinished projects and tasks. Select the one you can finish in the least amount of time and complete it. Select another task that you can complete in a few minutes and then complete it. Notice how you lighten your load by finishing tasks. Use what you have discovered to remind yourself to finish

tasks as soon as possible, thus leaving your mind free to tackle new assignments. Write a memorandum to your instructor about what you learned.

3. Are you using your time effectively? To find out, keep a record. Begin by keeping a list of minor tasks that you perform between major tasks. Leave space to the right of each item on your list. As you complete each minor task, jot down the date, the time, and the number of minutes used. For example, did you pay unplanned attention to the postage? Did you package up literature for transfer to another branch office? Did you search for stationery that was not found in the appropriate location? At the end of one week, analyze your list for similar tasks, for redundant tasks, and for those tasks that were the result of interruptions. Add the time spent for each category and then multiply the time by 52 for an estimate of the time spent in a year. Write a brief report for your instructor that summarizes your findings and suggests methods to manage your minor-task time more effectively.

PRODUCTION CHALLENGES

3-A Setting Priorities

Supplies needed:

- Daily Plan Chart, Form 3-A, page 383

The time is 9 a.m., Monday, June 2, and you have enough work to keep you busy for one week. Mr. Wilson is leaving on a business trip at noon today. At 8 a.m., Mr. Wilson used speech recognition software to dictate three letters and discussed with you work to be done in his absence.

Here are the notes you took during your conference with Mr. Wilson:

1. Send copies of the combined sales report for the week of May 19 to the four regional managers. (You will use a copier to make copies of the sales summary from a computer printout.)

2. Call J. R. Rush, Assistant Vice-President of Marketing, Eastern Region, extension 534, and ask him to see

David Walters, an out-of-town supplier, who had an appointment with Mr. Wilson on Wednesday, June 4, at 10 a.m.

3. Review, edit, and mail the letter to Allen Fitzgerald that Mr. Wilson dictated earlier. Mr. Wilson stressed that it must be mailed today. The letters to Nancy Evans and Robert Berger may be mailed tomorrow.

4. Make a daily digest of the incoming mail. Hold all mail for Mr. Wilson to answer. Call Mr. Wilson if something is urgent.

5. Key a letter to Nancy Cromwell, Regina, advising her that Mr. Wilson will accept her invitation to speak at the National Sales Conference in Regina on November 28 at 2:30 p.m.

6. Rekey the last two pages of the talk that Mr. Wilson gave at the local chamber of commerce and send a copy of the talk to Art Winfield so that he will receive it by Friday afternoon. (Art Winfield has a local address.)

7. Call Sid Levine, Assistant Vice-President of Marketing, Northwestern Region, extension 536, to remind him that Mr. Wilson will be out of town for the week. Mr. Wilson counts on Sid Levine to represent him when Mr. Wilson cannot attend weekly Executive Committee meetings, held every Wednesday at 10 a.m.

8. Make copies of an article on time management and distribute them to the four assistant vice-presidents of marketing.

9. Call Creighton's Restaurant at 555-0611 to set up a luncheon meeting on Monday, June 9, at 12:30 p.m. for 12 members of the planning committee for the November Sales Seminar.

10. Call Air Canada at 555-1414 to cancel Mr. Wilson's reservation to Vancouver on Wednesday, June 4.

The assistant vice-presidents have left the following work in your in-basket:

A. A six-page report written by Linda Yee to be keyed in final form by Wednesday afternoon.

B. A note from J. R. Rush asking you to obtain online the sales figures for the four regions for the week of May 26. He wrote, "Please key the figures on cards so that I may refer to them in a staff meeting at 10 a.m. on Tuesday."

C. A note from Sid Levine asking you to copy the figures he has circled in red on the computer printout. He wrote, "I need this information by 2 p.m. today (Monday). Just key them on a couple of cards."

D. A revised 12-page report written by Charlene Azam. She needs to receive the completed report on Friday to review it before she presents it to Mr. Wilson on Monday, June 9. (You stored the first draft of this report on a flash drive. You will need to key the revisions.)

Before you begin working on these tasks, take a Daily Plan Chart, Form 3-A, from your desk, write down the work to be done, and assign priorities to the items.

3-B Correcting Letters

Supplies needed:
- *Plain paper*

Correct the spelling and capitalization errors in the following two letters. List the incorrect words, correctly spelled, on a separate sheet of paper. Key the two letters in an acceptable letter style.

(Current date) Mrs. M. M. Freedman, Financial Manager, Super Stove Store, 4909–50 Avenue, Red Deer, AB, T4N 4A7. Each year Millennium Appliances, Inc., provides you with a complete anual statement of the debits and credits made with our company. However, the statement we are curenntly enclosing includes all tranactions that occured during this past year, with the exception of those for the month of September and October. (P) You will recall that during those months, we ofered our retail customers a 30 percent discount on all colored appliances. Unfortunately, however, we neglected to include this discount on our new computerized accounting system. Therefore, your statement does not reflect this discount; when this oversite is corrected, we will forward an updated statement to you. We expect to have your corected statement in the mail within the next too weeks. Please except our apologies for any inconvenience this may cause. (P) If you have any additional conserns about the statement, please call our office. We look forward to your continued business in the year a head. Sincerely, William Wilson, Vice President of Marketing.

(Current date) Lori Anderson, 630 Beach Blvd., Hamilton, ON, L8H 6Y4. Thank you for submiting your oficial transcript and resume as applicant for the position of administrative assistent. (P) This year their have been many well qualified canidates expressing intrest in employment at Millennium Appliances, Inc. We have not fill all the positions for administrative assistents. Because of the definate promise you education and experience reflect, we know you have much to offer and employer. (P) In the mean time we shall keep your credantials on active file for six months in case another opening ocurrs for which you qualify. You interest in applying for employment with our organization and your cooperation in submiting the neccesary information requested of you is appreciated. Cordially Yours, William Wilson, Vice-President of Marketing.

3-C Distribution of Time

Supplies needed:

- *Time Distribution Chart, Form 3-C-1, page 384*
- *Notes on time spent during week of May 19–23, Form 3-C-2, pages 385 and 386*
- *Plain paper*

You know you can plan your work more efficiently if you keep a record of the demands on your time. You want to know how much time you spend working for some of your managers.

Your notes on the time spent are in Form 3-C-2. You have already prepared the Time Distribution Chart, Form 3-C-1. Under the heading Major Activities, use broad categories such as processing mail and word processing.

Processing the postal mail, handling telephone calls, and filing is done for the entire group. The email and voice mail you handle is your own.

Summarize the information given in Form 3-C-2. Enter the categories of tasks performed in the Major Activities column of the distribution chart. Enter the total time spent working for each person.

Optional—Create your own distribution chart that will summarize the amount of time spent on each activity.

3-D Requisitioning Supplies

Supplies needed:

- *Millennium Requisition for Supplies, Forms 3-D-1 and 3-D-2, page 387*

You had a note from Jack Rush saying, "Please get me six ruled office pads, 21.5 cm x 28 cm, white."

You decided to check the supplies you had on hand and to requisition what you needed. The following supplies were low: ruled office pads, letterhead, self-stick notepads, index cards, and ballpoint pens.

All the employees at Millennium Appliances, Inc. requisition office supplies from the Stationery and Supplies Department. You have the authority to sign your own requisitions for office supplies. Your location is office 216, on the second floor. The requisition number is 21.

Here is what you requested: six ruled office pads, 21.5 cm x 28 cm, white; one ream of letterhead; five packages of removable self-stick notepads, yellow, 76 mm x 127 mm; four packages of index cards, 7.5 cm x 12.5 cm, white; six ballpoint pens, black, fine point.

Prepare the requisition.

Weblinks

Tools of the Trade

www.mindtools.com

Mind Tools' extensive information base includes articles on time management, stress management, creativity tools, tips on effective management, techniques for effective decision making, and more.

Time Management

http://sbinfocanada.about.com/od/timemanagement

This Canadian site gives useful links for information on time management skills, software, tools, and tips.

http://www.getmoredone.com/tips.html

This site provides useful tips for managing your time personally and professionally. Use the Tabulator link to compare how you are spending your time to how you would like to spend your time and to how others in your category spend theirs.

www.daytimer.com

This site includes Day-Timer's product information as well as articles with time management tips.

World Environmental Organization

www.world.org/weo/recycling

The World Environmental Organization's website provides links to other environmentally conscious sites including Earth's 911 and Canadian Centre for Pollution Prevention.

Where to Recycle Computers

www.sbinfocanada.about.com/od/environmentbiz/a/comprecycling1.htm

In addition to helpful information on recycling computers in Canada, this site also includes links to other informative sites on recycling in general.

Chapter 4
Reference Sources

Learning Outcomes

After completion of this chapter, the student will be able to:

1   Identify the services provided by libraries.

2   Classify reference titles used in business.

3   Recommend sources to consult to find articles in print.

4   Identify the purpose of different directories.

5   Explain the benefit of an online computer search.

6   Identify and avoid plagiarism.

7   Reference a book source with one author using the APA, MLA, and Harvard referencing styles.

8   Develop an office procedure manual.

In their day-to-day responsibilities, office professionals use information that comes from many sources. Most information comes from sources within the organization; some comes from external sources, but all must be current and accurate. In order to locate such information, an administrative assistant must have an understanding of the variety of sources and methods of locating such information. One popular method of capturing sources located on the internet is to record the address of the source as a "bookmark" or as a "favourite" in your web browser. Once located, a record of favourite sources and those that suit your special needs should be made. Update your record frequently as the volume of information and the selection of reliable sources change constantly. Knowing where to locate information rapidly is often as important as actually knowing the facts.

At a correspondingly rapid rate, technology is providing us with faster and broader opportunities to search for information than previously possible. Networked computers, virtual reference libraries, CDs, and other textual databases have enabled the administrative assistant to become a virtual researcher from the desktop.

Tracking down information is time-consuming. Effective research depends upon your knowledge of reliable resources and how to use them efficiently. Traditional sources of information such as books and periodicals are still available at libraries throughout Canada. However, the same material is often committed to more technologically based media and supplements traditional sources. CD and the internet provide the easiest and, perhaps, first access to find your information. To be sure of the most current reference resource, you should consult with a skilled reference librarian.

LIBRARIES AND LIBRARIANS
Support and Assistance

Thousands of Canadian business organizations maintain their own libraries, which are staffed with professionally trained librarians. If you work for one of these organizations, direct your search for facts to your organization's librarians. If they do not have the information in their library, they will contact other libraries to obtain it.

The internet provides an important in-house alternative to the organization's librarian. With a good internet search engine, a broader, less time-consuming search for information can be achieved. To start a broad search, visit www.worldcat.org first. WorldCat is a large, comprehensive catalogue database maintained by over 9000 libraries

Cheryl Giff
Campus Administrative Officer

Algonquin College Heritage Institute
Perth, Ontario

College Graduation:
Office Administration—Executive
Algonquin College Heritage Institute
Perth, Ontario
2003

Cheryl takes pride in being a lifelong learner, setting and carrying out goals—and adjusting them along the way to accommodate changes in her life.

Following high school graduation, Cheryl Giff obtained her hairstylist license and worked in a shop for a few years. She then transferred her skills to a bank, where she was employed for the next six years. After the birth of her second child, Cheryl stayed at home until her children were both in school. She returned to hairstyling for a couple of years but felt that she needed a change. As a 30-something mother of two, Cheryl seized the opportunity to enroll in the Office Administration—Executive Diploma program.

While studying, Cheryl learned the skills to enable her to obtain, and function effectively in, her current position with Algonquin College—her initial career goal. However, she notes that employers may have in-house software programs that can only be learned on the job and that there are always things to be learned with a new job.

This multi-tasking administrative professional finds budget preparation and year-end responsibilities such as purchasing and receiving to be her most difficult tasks. Completing quarterly budget reviews and resolving unexpected problems are also challenging but enjoyable responsibilities. Cheryl's days can be unpredictable, and she must prioritize in order to keep organized and meet deadlines. She must also keep a close eye on the budget, which can be affected by facility maintenance issues such as repairs. Her job description also includes routine tasks that Cheryl handles quickly and efficiently such as payroll, leave reports, maintaining spreadsheets, and accounts payable.

Communication is key in this fast-paced office and usually takes place face to face with co-workers. While staff communicate by email and telephone, email is particularly useful, as Cheryl receives up to 25 messages per day compared with an average of about seven phone calls daily.

Cheryl relies on the computer to help carry out her responsibilities; she uses the internet and intranet, BUS, PeopleSoft, HRIS, and Genesis. Microsoft Outlook is used daily to keep track of deadlines, expiry dates, meetings and other items. She uses MS Word to create flyers and brochures for events such as open houses and golf tournaments.

The college intranet has proved to be an important tool for Cheryl, and she uses it extensively. "I am linked to our main campus by an intranet connection. I can go on our college site and get forms, staff extensions and email addresses, human resources data, college event information, purchasing records, and much more—almost anything I need to know regarding the college."

In order to achieve a balanced lifestyle, Cheryl tries not to take work home with her. She explains, "When I leave the campus at the end of the day, I leave my work at the office and focus on being a mom." She is currently employed as a maternity leave replacement, and her goal is to stay employed by the college at the end of her contract. To enhance her chances of reaching that goal, Cheryl plans to "do my job to the best of my ability and acquire as many skills as I can, so when something comes up, hopefully, I will have the skills needed to fill the position."

Cheryl offers the following advice to future graduates. "Hang in there; the hard work is well worth it. The skills you acquire will prepare you for many administrative positions. [An Office Administration program] opens doors for you that you may not expect and is the solid foundation you need to reach your career goals. It was the best decision I made regarding my career; I am right where I want to be."

and institutions, and contains millions of online records for books, e-books, journals, magazines, newspapers, sheet music, CDs, DVDs, films, and more. Given some information about the item you are searching for together with your postal code, WorldCat will find a public library in your vicinity where the item may be located. WorldCat also has an app for accessing information on mobile devices, which may be obtained by visiting www.worldcat.org/mobile.

You may also use the public library. Every library maintains a catalogue of what is housed in the library; this is a ready reference for users. Most catalogues are available at the library on the library computer or online through the internet.

All libraries have reference books and many other valuable reference sources that you can use by request. The internet will provide access to virtual libraries, which will allow you to identify titles that are in the library system and, occasionally, will allow you to download selected information to your desktop computer.

Whether you visit the reference library in person or via the internet, library staff are always helpful. They welcome the opportunity to assist those who have bona fide requests. When you are unsure of your request, tell the librarian what your need is; you can depend on the librarian to suggest an appropriate approach.

Many private and special libraries are located in cities and towns throughout Canada. The Government of Canada publishes the *Canadian Library Gateway*, a comprehensive directory of Canadian libraries that may be searched by province. This directory lists federal, university, and special libraries. Private and special libraries are not open to the public. However, it is possible to make special arrangements to borrow materials from them and to get help from their librarians.

Great cooperation exists among public and private libraries. Public libraries, college and university libraries, libraries of business organizations, and private libraries in a given community participate actively in interlibrary loans. They also borrow from libraries in other communities. Through interlibrary loans, you can obtain books and photocopies of articles that your organization's library or the public library does not have. This service is provided for a small charge; some libraries charge only for the photocopying involved. If the organization for which you work does not have a library, make your request through the public library.

Among the private libraries in your community might be:

- a law library in a federal court building or at a college of law
- an industrial library at the local chamber of commerce
- a Canadian commerce library, if your city has a regional office of Industry Canada
- a specialized library at an art or historical museum
- a medical library at a hospital or a college of medicine
- a technical library maintained by a professional society
- an international business library at a local or regional International Trade Organization centre

---

Self-Check

1. What listings would you find in the *Canadian Library Gateway*?
2. List examples of private libraries that might be found in your area.

QUICK SOURCES OF REFERENCE

Office professionals often consult references such as almanacs, yearbooks, dictionaries, encyclopedias, atlases, biographical publications, and financial directories. You will find the titles referred to in this chapter in most large public libraries.

Some reference sources discussed are available from three different sources: online, CD, and hard copy. However, there is a publishing industry trend to move away from the hard-copy form of material to the more cost-effective and environmentally friendlier media of online and CD. This technology adds a completely new dimension to reference resources; it precludes many of the traditional, laborious methods of research. With a CD, the researcher

- no longer carries large reference books
- has access to more current information
- has faster access to information
- can access information enhanced by sound and graphics

Reference Databases

Most larger libraries have available several reference databases. Using these, you can quickly and easily locate a broad range of information from periodicals and other sources.

Several years' worth of information may be contained on a database. Databases can easily be searched by subject, title, source, date, or even text abstracts. Once found, search results often can be printed at a nominal cost or downloaded onto a local storage device.

Guides to References

There are many good reference sources available on the internet these days. Librarians use a variety of these sources depending on their region and approved reference source. One such reference source is the Special Libraries Association's Library Resource Centre. This site provides a selective and searchable collection of resources; it links to other search engines, topical guides, ready references, and other databases. Subject-specific categories also present resources focused on specific topics.

Similarly, Concordia University Libraries provides *Canadian Sources of Information*, including a directory of French websites (Bibliothèque Nationale du Québec). If a trip to the library is still in order, then search out a copy of *Canadian Business and Economics: A Guide to Sources of Information*. Both English and French titles are included. As with all reference sources, it is important to look for the current version of each guide to references.

Books in Print

All libraries and many bookstores have up-to-date sources about books that are available from publishers. These sources give all the information needed for ordering publications, including the date and the price. Since these sources are used for ordering, they are kept in the catalogue section of the library. Sources to look for are:

- *Canadian Books in Print* (University of Toronto Press). This is a standard library reference that can also be found online and on CD.

- *Whitaker's Books in Print* (J. Whitaker & Sons). An authoritative source of information about books available in print from the United Kingdom.
- *Quill & Quire* (Key Publishers). Reviews new Canadian books.

Almanacs and Yearbooks

Almanacs and yearbooks contain the latest statistics and facts on all types of human activity. They are updated annually. Most of them are available in both hardcover and paperback, and may be purchased at many local bookstores. Consider these sources:

- *The Corpus Almanac and Canadian Source Book*. The standard Canadian book of facts.
- *Canadian Global Almanac 20xx*. This title is published annually and is an excellent source of recent Canadian facts.
- *Canadian Almanac and Directory* (Micromedia).
- *Whitaker's Almanack* (J. Whitaker & Sons).
- *Canada Year Book* (Statistics Canada). Published as a result of each Canadian census. *Canada Year Book* statistics are also available online in downloadable PDF format.

As with all annualized reference sources, ensure that you have the most current issue.

Dictionaries, Encyclopedias, and Atlases

Dictionaries For your own desk, choose the latest edition of an **abridged** or **unabridged** dictionary such as:

- *Canadian Oxford Dictionary*
- *Webster's New Collegiate Dictionary*
- *Random House Dictionary of the English Language* (College Edition)

Abridged dictionaries will fit easily on your desk and are easy to use. Some of these resources are also available online through a business or institutional subscription. You will require a login to use these resources.

Encyclopedias Encyclopedias are useful for researching a variety of general and unrelated facts. Available in practically every library is the *Encyclopaedia Britannica* (Encyclopaedia Britannica, Inc.), an internationally acclaimed source of dependable facts. The last print edition of the *Encyclopaedia Britannica* was published in 2010; it is now available in digital format. Also popular are:

- *The Canadian Encyclopedia*, from Historica, is an online encyclopedia promoting Canadian history education.

Also available in most public libraries in CD format, it serves as an excellent classroom resource.

- *The Columbia Encyclopedia* is offered as one of the online references from Bartleby (www.bartleby.com), which provides a compendium of encyclopedic data.

Atlases As with most published reference material, atlases are becoming readily available online and in CD format. If your geographic search includes dynamic facts such as migration, climate, or territorial borders, reference to a good online or CD atlas database may provide more current information. The most comprehensive atlas for Canadians is the *Atlas of Canada*, published by Natural Resources Canada, which features maps of climate, population, income, forestry, industries, transportation, and trade. A **gazetteer** (an index of geographical names) may also be helpful.

Biographical Information

Many sources have been compiled to provide biographical information about notable people and other individuals who have made contributions in their respective fields.

A valuable classroom resource of over 28 000 profiles of prominent people may be found in the *Biographical Dictionary*.

For information about men and women living today, consult the following:

- *The Canadian Who's Who* (University of Toronto Press). This contains comprehensive biographies on leading and influential Canadians.
- *The Blue Book of Canadian Business* (Morris and Mackenzie, Inc.), which contains biographies of the chief executive officers of 2500 prominent Canadian firms. This book ranks major Canadian companies by their net worth. This book is also available as an online resource.

Financial Information

There are many sources of financial data. The four best-known publishers of financial information are:

- Dun & Bradstreet
- The Financial Post Data Group
- Moody's Investors Service
- Standard & Poor's

Dun & Bradstreet is widely known for its credit ratings, which are published bimonthly and made available to subscribers only in the *Dun & Bradstreet Reference Book*. In addition to credit and capital ratings, this book gives type of business, address, and a brief history for each listing.

The Financial Post Data Group deals with Canadian companies whose securities are actively traded on the stock market.

Moody's services to investors are numerous. Among them are *Moody's Manual of Investment, American and Foreign*. Bound annually, it is divided into separate manuals covering the following fields:

- industrial
- transportation
- utilities
- banks, insurance, real estate, and investment trusts
- government and municipal bonds

These manuals include financial statements, descriptions of plants and products, officers, history, and other pertinent information. These publications cover foreign companies, including Canadian companies, listed on American stock exchanges.

Among the publications offered by Standard & Poor's is *Standard and Poor's Register of Corporations, Directors, and Executives*, listing approximately 34 000 leading American and Canadian corporations.

Due to the nature of corporate and financial information, there is a vast range of literature available.

Etiquette Books and Quotation Sources

Other sources of information that an administrative assistant will find useful are books on **etiquette**. If your responsibilities include helping to prepare speeches, oral presentations, or articles, books of quotations will also be useful.

The etiquette books are helpful in all areas of gracious living, but they are especially helpful to the administrative assistant in search of suggestions for writing: formal invitations, acceptances, and regrets; thank-you letters; and letters of congratulations and condolence. Among the available books are:

- *Business Etiquette: 101 Ways to Conduct Business with Charm & Savvy*, by Ann Marie Sabath (Career Press, 2010).
- *Subtle Differences, Big Faux Pas*, by Elizabeth Vennekens-Kelly (Summertime, 2012).

When your manager wants to support his or her ideas with well-known quotations or to add a clever statement, look to a book of quotations. Many such books are available, and every library has some of them.

The contents of these books, alphabetized by subject, vary widely, so you may have to consult several to locate the quotation you are seeking. Try these:

- *The Oxford Dictionary of Quotations*, by Elizabeth Knowles (Oxford University Press, 2009).

- *The Forbes Book of Business Quotations*, by Forbes Inc. (Blackdog & Leventhal, 2007).

No list of references would be complete without mention of *Robert's*.

In a business environment, the application of the guidelines found in *Robert's Rules of Order* is to assist a meeting to accomplish, in the most orderly way, the purpose of the meeting. To do this, it is often necessary to curb individuals or groups from "hijacking" the meeting and, in the end, defeating its purpose. On the other hand, contributions even from the most boisterous participant should not be totally eliminated; they too may be valuable. Proceedings may be controlled in an orderly fashion based on respected methods of organization, meetings, and rules. *Robert's Rules of Order* is one of the most popular procedural guides for business, club, and organizational meetings. Familiarization with these procedures could be very helpful to the administrative assistant who is called upon to take minutes of formal or informal meetings.

Perseus Books publishes a revised version of *Robert's Rules of Order* in hard-copy and CD-ROM formats. For a comprehensive review of the Rules of Order (Part I) and Organization, Meetings, and Legal Rights of Assemblies (Part II), go to www.constitution.org/rror/rror--00.htm.

Self-Check

1. List three advantages of online and CD media over hard-copy references.

2. What information can be found in *Robert's Rules of Order*?

3. What information would you find in *The Blue Book of Canadian Business*? *The Canadian Encyclopedia*? *The Canadian Who's Who*?

4. Suggest two reasons why an administrative assistant might consult a book of etiquette.

PERIODICAL AND NEWSPAPER INDEXES

Your office will probably subscribe to several professional journals. An effective approach to keeping up with the array of publications will be either to develop and maintain an office library or to develop a systematic disposal system for the journals after a prescribed period of time. The latter should include an effective recycling process.

Check if the professional journals are available at the local reference library and if the office staff refers to back issues infrequently. If either is the case, it may not be necessary to subscribe to these journals.

You may want to save and file the annual indexes to the magazines you dispose of. With many periodicals, once a year one issue contains an index to all the articles it published during the previous year. In addition, before you dispose of technical or specialized magazines, find out if your organization's library or another local library needs extra copies of the magazines you have on hand.

The most efficient way to search for magazine and newspaper articles is to consult an index in the reference section of a library. The *Canadian Periodical Index* (Thomson Gale) is a widely used periodical, newspaper, and business index available both online and in CD format. There are many other indexes besides that one. As the occasion arises, become familiar with the indexes in the libraries that you use.

Periodical Indexes

Administrative assistants who prepare speeches and articles for publication need to know how to locate articles that have been published on a given subject. The fastest way to locate a magazine or journal article is to consult the general or specialized index. When doing research, consult both types, for articles on popular technical topics appear in general periodicals as well as in specialized journals and periodicals.

Many libraries now have online periodical indexes. For example:

- *Canadian Business and Current Affairs* (CBCA) (Thomson Gale) carries listings for periodical and newspaper articles.
- *Ulrich's International Periodicals Directory* (Ovid) can be used to locate business and general periodicals published in other parts of the world.

Consult specialized indexes to locate articles of a technical or specialized nature. For example, the H.W. Wilson Company publishes the *Readers' Guide*, which provides a guide to more than 300 periodicals and abstracts.

Periodical librarians maintain master lists of the periodical holdings of their libraries and the dates of the available periodicals. They will also be able to tell you whether each periodical is in bound form or is stored on **microfilm**. You may obtain this information over the telephone.

The usual procedure is to read the periodicals at the library and take notes. If an entire article or a considerable portion of it will be of value to your manager, you can often make a copy for research purposes. Copying machines are available in libraries. Use a microfilm reader to read an article on microfilm, but rather than taking copious notes, request a hard copy of the article. The charge for copies is by the page, but it is nominal when you think of the time you save.

When making copies, as when taking notes, be sure to obtain the exact title of the article, the source, the date of the source, and the page number. In your notes, place quotation marks around direct quotations to distinguish them from paraphrased material. Take notes in such a way that you will be able to interpret them at a later date. Plan your note taking carefully. Write on only one side of a card or page. Do not make notes about two topics on the same page.

Newspaper Indexes Generally, newspaper indexes can be found on the Library Database Network as part of the comprehensive CBCA index. CBCA is an excellent broad information source; other sources provide direct and local information.

One means of quickly locating information through news events is through www.onlinenewspapers.com. This site indexes more than 300 major Canadian newspapers.

Libraries in major Canadian cities may have an index solely for the city's own newspaper, or they may have a publicly available facility for searching newspaper articles online. Most major newspapers provide online information free of charge. Others produce an annually revised CD that includes the full text.

Similarly, the full texts of Southam newspapers are available through CanWest Interactive (the electronic publishing arm of Southam newspapers), the internet, CDs, telephone, and other digitized distribution formats. The following short list identifies some of those available:

- *Edmonton Journal*
- *Calgary Herald*
- *The Province* (Vancouver)
- *Vancouver Sun*
- *National Post*
- *Ottawa Citizen*
- *The Gazette* (Montreal)
- *Windsor Star*

Searching for a Specific Newspaper Article For a comprehensive list of newspapers available in full text, reference the internet at www.onlinenewspapers.com. If you need to search a selection of Canadian newspapers for a specific article, go to http://www.onlinenewspapers.com/canada-province-newspapers.htm.

CANADIAN GOVERNMENT PUBLICATIONS

The Canadian government is one of the largest publishers in the country. Many of its publications, which cover nearly all subject areas, are available for a nominal price. All libraries except specialized libraries keep some government publications on file. Some libraries are depository libraries for government publications; that is, they are designated by law to receive all material published by the government in certain broad categories.

Canadian government publications are not usually included in *Canadian Books in Print* or in periodical indexes. The official publisher of the Government of Canada is Canadian Government Publishing (CGP), a division of Communications Canada, which provides a wide range of topics in various formats. It not only maintains a central ordering and distribution source, but, through its associated network of bookstores and retailers across Canada and abroad, it ensures that publications are easily and readily available. CGP can be contacted through http://publications.gc.ca; or 1-800-635-7943.

DIRECTORIES

Hundreds of business directories are published in Canada each year. Directories that administrative assistants should not overlook are:

- local and out-of-town telephone directories, including Canadian Yellow Pages Directory
- *Canadian Almanac and Directory* (Micromedia) available in print and online
- Canada's Postal Code Directory (Canada Post)
- directories of chambers of commerce

Also useful to you might be *Scott's Directories* (Southam). These directories list manufacturers in four Canadian geographic areas. As well, see the "Weblinks" section at the end of this chapter for an index of trade and occupational magazines and product information ranging from the automotive market to the occupational health and safety market.

Telephone Directories

Telephone directories list the names, addresses, and telephone numbers of subscribers. Because telephone directories are usually published annually, they are useful for verifying addresses. You will find them to be an excellent source for locating a street address when the address you have is incomplete. Because of their tabular form, telephone directories can easily be produced in CD format. *CanadaPhone* is one such directory; it includes information from both White and Yellow Pages and is updated quarterly. Similar international phone directories are also available.

The business office of the local telephone company and the local public library both keep on file telephone directories from a number of other cities in your own and other

provinces. For a moderate charge, you may call your local telephone company for a specific listing.

Alternatively, there are many free internet services that provide international directories for both White and Yellow Pages. Canada 411 is an example of an internet directory service. See "Weblinks" for the address.

City Directories

City directories may include links to the following:

- a buyer's guide and classified directory
- an alphabetical street directory of householders and businesses (street numbers are listed in consecutive order with the occupant's name and telephone number)
- a numerical telephone directory, which gives the name of the person at each telephone number listed

Canadian Parliamentary Guide

The Canadian Parliamentary Guide, published and maintained by Desmarais Library, Laurentian University, lists the members of the Senate and the House of Commons, of the provincial governments, and of the Supreme Court, as well as other high-ranking public officials. It also contains some biographical material. It is available in hardcover and e-book versions.

Chamber of Commerce Directories

Most towns of any size in Canada have an active chamber of commerce. Each local chamber of commerce publishes a list of its members. If your manager is chairing a convention or coordinating a regional sales meeting in another city, the chamber of commerce directory for that city is helpful for locating business personnel who take a special interest in the community. If you wish to obtain information from a chamber of commerce in another city, contact your local chamber of commerce, which will supply the telephone number and address for the chamber of commerce you are requesting.

ONLINE LIBRARY SEARCH

Most large libraries provide online computer-search services. These services give you remote access to hundreds of commercially supplied databases containing references and documents on many subjects. This method of searching for information is a highly efficient way of obtaining:

- citations from magazines, newspapers, or research reports
- abstracts

- full-text documents

Canadian libraries use two main database sources:

- *Infomart,* which contains the full text of major Canadian newspapers; company product and trademark information; legal and fax information; and business directories. No subscription is necessary.

- *Dialog,* which consists of almost 600 databases containing worldwide literature references in categories such as:

  - agriculture
  - business
  - computers
  - education
  - environment
  - energy
  - medicine

Reference librarians will conduct an academic- or business-focused search for subscribers who call with their search criteria. Online searching is usually performed by trained library staff using your search criteria. There will be a charge for this service. Some libraries allow their members access to their databases through subscription or by debit to the member's library account. Charges are based on the length of time of the search.

To access the databases, the user needs access to the internet, a subscription to the database, and a printer or screen to receive information.

An online database is a database that is accessible from a computer or device with internet access. Many online databases are accessible from the internet. However, access to specialized databases such as Dialog may require permission and a subscription through your library.

Usually, answers to online database queries can be received in a few minutes. Users can save time and money by identifying the precise words that will give the desired information. Keep this in mind when you are obtaining information from an online database.

Self-Check

1. List three directories that are very useful to an administrative assistant.

2. What information is contained in a city directory?

3. How might you find contact information for a chamber of commerce in another city?

PLAGIARISM
Recognition and Avoidance

Both in business and at college, we continually absorb information and ideas from other people: we discuss them at meetings, research them on the internet, or read about them in books and magazines. Often, we use the information or idea as our own and incorporate it in our writing. However, using information and ideas from others without giving them credit for their work is a serious offence and is known as **plagiarism**. Plagiarism occurs when you fail to credit the original source for:

1. information that is not common knowledge

2. drawings, statistics, or graphs that you did not develop

3. direct quotations of spoken or written words

4. texts that you paraphrase rather than quote

5. viewpoints or theories of other people, or ideas that gave you inspiration

When consciously writing to avoid plagiarism, one of the more difficult tasks is to determine which information is common knowledge. Common knowledge is generally found in many places and is known by many people but is mostly limited to historical facts and geographical data. So, for example, while most Canadians know Wayne Gretzky is a hockey player, we must cite the source from where we learn the number of career goals he scored.

There are a few general rules to keep us safe from plagiarism:

1. Use your own words and credit all sources. Try to:
   a. Cite information and ideas that are new to you.
   b. Paraphrase instead of copying word for word.
   c. Take notes as you are reading material, including title, author, and date of publication.

2. Give credit for adopted, paraphrased, and copied work. Do *not*:
   a. make minor cosmetic changes without citing
   b. assume everything is common knowledge

3. Learn to cite properly.
   a. Be clear when you are using a direct quotation.
   b. Write a full list of references and a bibliography when you are developing lengthy documents.

One method of successfully paraphrasing is to read the information you want to include in your work, taking notes in the margin or on notepaper as you progress. When your reading is complete, cover up the original text and summarize the margin notes in good grammatical form. Now check this paraphrased version against the original text to make sure you have not used the same words or phrases. Don't forget to reference the original author's work.

Providing a reference to others' information and ideas will allow readers to refer back to the original source for further study. It also provides credibility to your work by suggesting that your information is based on integrity and thorough research. Schools and colleges are particularly sensitive to the issue of plagiarism because rampant plagiarism not only damages the reputation of the school but also devalues the diploma that students work so hard to achieve.

Your college may publish guidelines and responsibilities for students in its Plagiarism Policy; take note, as the penalty for plagiarism is often severe and can lead to expulsion. **Copyright** violation is the business equivalent of plagiarism. Companies or individuals may not use original material or products of others without permission. The law deals with copyright violations.

Referencing Styles

There are many referencing styles used at colleges—your instructor will tell you the style that your college prefers to use. Referencing styles attempt to standardize the format of a reference. Three of the most widely used styles are:

- APA—The American Psychological Association www.apastyle.org/
- MLA—Modern Language Association www.mla.org/
- The Harvard System www.bournemouth.ac.uk/library/citing_references/docs/Citing_Refs.pdf

Following are examples of a single book with a single author as a reference and will illustrate the differences of each style:

APA Style Format Author(s). (Year of Publication). *Title of book*. Place of Publication: Publisher.

Example:

Colt, R. C. (1991). *ABC guide to preparing publications*. Washington, DC: American Writers Guild.

MLA Style Format Author(s). *Title of Book*. Place of Publication: Publisher, Year of Publication.

Example:

Harris, Mary. *The Swinbourn Tale*. Denver: Thompson, 1999.

Harvard Style Format Author(s). Year of publication, *Book Title*, Publisher, Place of publication.

Example:

Horner, P. T. 1997, *Marketing Principles and Practices*, Pearson, Sydney.

All styles of reference require:

1. name of author(s)
2. full title of the publication

---

pro-Link
When "Cut 'n' Paste" Gets Sticky

So, you've been charged with the responsibility of writing a report to justify next year's sales conference in your town. Finally! You have an opportunity to apply all of those great skills you learned in the OA program: keying, desktop publishing, research, and internet surfing! With a few *key word* searches, a little cut here, a little paste there . . . you'll have a great report ready in no time.

STOP! Ever heard of *plagiarism*? Plagiarism is not illegal if the work you're copying is not copyrighted . . . but it is unethical. To plagiarize is to present someone else's ideas and words as if they were your own. Even if you change phrases and words of the original work without referencing the source . . . it's plagiarism!

Here are a few tips to help you avoid plagiarism:

1. Brainstorm your ideas on paper before you begin.
2. Have confidence in your report and let your own words tell the story.
3. Only use someone else's work when it adds value to your report.
4. Do not use existing material to repeat what you've already said.
5. When quoting, use the original author's exact words.
6. If the material you wish to copy is copyrighted, seek permission.
7. Provide references for all copied, quoted, and paraphrased material.

Most colleges and universities have strict penalties for plagiarists: expulsion! In the office, at worst you'll be sued for copyright violation. But, if your report is received as a well-written, well-researched document, both your credibility and your confidence will be well served.

---

3. date of publication
4. publisher
5. place of publication

When referencing business reports, you should also include as many of the following details as possible:

1. title of report
2. report number (if it has one)
3. name of organization issuing the report
4. province or city headquarters of the issuing organization
5. report date

Figure 4-1 An office manual helps office professionals to follow preferred formats and procedures.

Figure 4-2 Sample of electronic procedure manual.

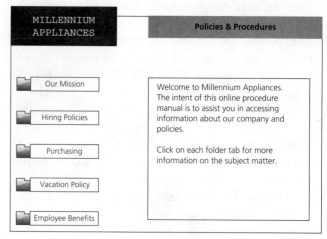

Remember, if you are unsure, it is better to reference a source than to risk any suggestion of plagiarism.

OFFICE MANUALS

A critical resource for any office is an office manual. If the manual is current, well-organized, and easy to follow, it will assist office staff in performing work correctly and efficiently. Refer to Figures 4-2 and 4-3.

Often it is the responsibility of an administrative assistant to prepare this reference resource. The purpose of an office manual is not only to smooth the transition for your

Most of these details will be available with any credible publication. At a minimum, you should include these details in your references and be consistent in your style.

Figure 4-3 Sample of procedure manual.

Procedure Manual Outline

Chapter #		Description	Page
Chapter 1 Company Overview			
1.A	Mission Statement	Our goals and objectives	1
1.B	Letter from the President	Letter of welcome	2
1.C	Organizational Chart	Description of roles	3 & 4
Chapter 2 HR Policies			
2.A	Employment Process	Hiring process for candidates	5
2.B	Interview Process	Description of the interview process	6
2.C	Vacation Policy	Request for vacation process	7
Chapter 3 Mail Handling			
3.A	Outgoing Mail	How to handle outgoing mail	8
3.B	Incoming Mail	How to handle incoming mail	9
3.C	Sorting Mail	How to sort and present mail	10
Chapter 4 Purchasing Policy			
4.A	Supplies ordering	Process for ordering supplies	11
4.B	Suppliers	Approved list of suppliers	12
4.C	Purchase Order Form	Form to be completed for orders	13

successor and to help co-workers who cover your temporary absences, but also to provide consistent procedures for everyone in the office. The office manual provides guidance for everyone who might need to know those procedures.

The office manual should be available in hard copy, as a desk manual, and also in a soft-copy version for ease of maintenance. Many companies have their own intranet and will upload an electronic version of the procedure manual. This helps to ensure access to and currency of information. The list of administrative procedures that may be included in an office manual is endless. It may be useful to include some of the following:

- handling the switchboard
- receiving and sending fax messages
- preparing correspondence
- processing incoming and outgoing mail

- making appointments
- booking the conference centre
- preparing travel expenses
- ordering office supplies

This is a very brief list; the choice of tasks to be included in an office manual will depend on the range of responsibilities held by the administrative assistant.

Self-Check

1. What are three of the most common referencing styles used in colleges and businesses?

2. List three administrative procedures other than those listed that would be appropriate to include in an office manual.

QUESTIONS FOR STUDY AND REVIEW

1. What type of service would it be reasonable to expect from a librarian by telephone?

2. What services are available through interlibrary loans?

3. State four ways that multimedia (online and CD) has changed the traditional methods of research.

4. What source do librarians use to learn about reference books with which they are not familiar?

5. Briefly compare the content of *Canadian Who's Who* and the *Blue Book of Canadian Business*.

6. What useful information, other than financial, can administrative assistants obtain from financial manuals and directories?

7. What should you do with back issues of periodicals that are of no further interest to the office staff?

8. What department should you call to find out if a library has a specific issue of a magazine you are seeking?

9. Where might you look to find a particular article published in England about a business you are researching?

10. What is the source of information for locating or ordering publications of the Canadian government?

11. Name the two main database sources used by Canadian libraries.

12. From what local source can an administrative assistant obtain the telephone number or street address of a person or organization in another town in the same province?

13. What is an online database?

14. State five causes of plagiarism.

15. State three general rules for avoiding plagiarism.

EVERYDAY ETHICS

The "Cover Letter"

Jeanie knew it would happen one day. Her manager, Cynthia Bell, asked her to write a 40-second speech for delivery the following day. Cynthia planned to read the speech to a selection committee as part of a proposal. "It should be something like reading a cover letter," Cynthia explained.

Fortunately, Jeanie didn't despair—she had learned to research in her Office Administration course—she was sure she could come up with something! Next day, just before

the selection committee meeting, Jeanie gave the speech to Cynthia for presentation. It read as follows:

Ladies and Gentlemen of the Proposal Committee,

I'm just preparing my impromptu remarks and fear that the length of this document defends it well against the risk of its being read. However, the proposal that I put before you today is not only revolutionary in design but also marks another improvement in the way we do things; an improvement to the processes that are not serving us well today.

To improve is to change; to be perfect is to change often. So, I suggest to you that this is not the end. It is not even the beginning of the end. But it is, perhaps, the end of the beginning.

While Cynthia was pleased with the writing style and the composition, the committee failed to be impressed. Even though the concept and timing were perfect, something else bothered them. What do you think that was?

- Do some research on the words and phrases found in Jeanie's composition. (Just enter phrases and quotes into a search engine to get results.)
- Why was the committee uncomfortable with Cynthia's presentation?
- What do you think the consequences of the committee's discomfort could be?
- How might Jeanie have avoided the problem?

Problem Solving

1. Today your manager asked you to provide information on three of the most common business services provided by the local public library. She has told you that she needs this information by tomorrow. How will you check on this?

2. Your manager, William Wilson, has been asked to give a 15-minute presentation on ethical behaviour in the workplace to a group of management trainees. He has asked you to research this topic and find three sources he could reference in his presentation. Where would you start?

3. Your manager has asked you to locate and provide two business directories used in the United States. He would like you to evaluate these directories and provide some reasons as to why he might find each of them useful. How will you begin?

4. The speech that Jeanie wrote in this chapter's Everyday Ethics feature was given to you to correctly reference. Rewrite the speech giving proper credit, where appropriate, to Sir Winston Churchill.

PRODUCTION CHALLENGES

4-A Selecting Quotations

Supplies needed:

- *Cards*
- *Access to the internet or a library*

William Wilson is giving the keynote address at Career Day for graduating high school students. He asked you to find two quotations that will impress on students the importance of continuing their education. Use quotation sources from the library or internet to select your quotations. Key each quotation verbatim and its source on a 7.6 cm × 12.7 cm card.

4-B Finding Information

Supplies needed:

- *Plain paper*
- *Access to the internet*

For each of the following internet activities, reference the source of your information using the appropriate APA format.

1. Visit dMarie Time Capsule and determine the significant events that were occurring on the date of your birth. Key a brief report of the significant events and present it to your instructor.

2. Reference the Government of Canada's report on *Planning for a Sustainable Future: A Federal Sustainable Development Strategy for Canada* and rekey the government's section on Why Sustainable Development Matters. Be sure to reference the source correctly.

3. What was Otto Eduard Leopold von Bismarck otherwise known as? For what was he most famous?

4. Conduct an internet search for Donovan Platt's article "Viewpoint: Elevator Etiquette." Paraphrase Platt's 11 rules and add one more rule of your own. Key a memo of recommendation to adopt the 12 rules and present the memo to your instructor. Be sure to share your new rule with the rest of your class.

5. Conduct biographical research on a Canadian whose name is often in the national news. Write three interesting facts about this person.

4-C Developing an Office Manual

Supplies needed:

- *Procedure template (course site)*

Using the information presented in this chapter, develop a component that will go into an office manual for your company, Millennium Appliances, that covers procedures for conducting effective research both in print and online. You will prepare a one-page document that lists a minimum of five steps necessary for effective research and that specifies an acceptable citation style your company will use when referencing material.

4-D Team Research (Collaborative Exercise)

Supplies needed:

- *Email template (course site)*
- *Access to the internet or a library*

For this exercise, form a team with three of your classmates. Each team member should find an online reference that will help you to identify and avoid plagiarism. Each of you will then prepare an email to your other team members recommending the resource you have found and describing why it would be beneficial to use. Use the email template provided.

Weblinks

Yahoo! Canada—Reference

http://dir.yahoo.com/Regional/Countries/Canada/Reference/

This site provides links to many reference sites relating to almanacs, dictionaries, encyclopedias, libraries, maps, phone numbers, postal information, quotations, thesauri, and so on, and includes the Canadian Geographical Name Server.

My Virtual Reference Desk

www.refdesk.com

This is a comprehensive source for facts on the internet.

Canada 411

www.Canada411.ca

Here you may locate a person or business in Canada from over 12 million listings.

Canadian Yellow Pages

www.yellowpages.ca

Canadian Yellow Pages maintains a database of over one million Canadian businesses with over 97 000 live links in 6300 business classifications. You can search by broad parameters such as business classification, or by very defined parameters such as a phone number or postal code. There is also a searchable database of 14 million residential listings.

Newspapers and Magazines of the World

http://www.world-newspapers.com

This site lists all online English-language media—newspapers, magazines, television stations, colleges, visitor bureaus, governmental agencies, and more.

Canadian Federal Government Site

www.canada.gc.ca

The Government of Canada's primary site, available in both English and French, contains links to a government overview, federal organizations, programs and services, a search engine, and other services.

H.W. Wilson

www.hwwilson.com

This site provides several search tools that allow subscribers to retrieve records of interest in Wilson databases. They include full text, catalogues, abstracts, and indexes.

Virtual Library

http://www.virtualreferencelibrary.ca/vrl/

Toronto Public Library's website has excellent links to many other Canadian reference sites. Offerings include access to librarian-selected websites; online magazine, journal, and newspaper articles; and self-guided research support. Special focus is placed on Canadian and Ontario information.

Chapter 5
Organization Structure and Office Layout

Learning Outcomes

After completion of this chapter, the student will be able to:

1 Compare the structure of a simple line organization with the structure of a line-and-staff organization.

2 Compare participatory management with the line-and-staff management style.

3 Interpret an organization chart.

4 Describe the physical features of the landscaped office.

5 Assess the advantages and disadvantages of working in an open office.

6 Describe how office ergonomics involve furniture, lighting, acoustics, and position of equipment.

All organizations have three things in common: goals, people, and structure. Organizational goals are those goals developed by senior management to provide direction for people working in the organization. Organizational structure is a systematic way of subdividing tasks and allocating resources to best accomplish the organizational goals. Traditional organizations are **bureaucratic** in nature, and **hierarchy** and job specialization are seen as the most effective approach to accomplishing those goals. In contrast, contemporary organizations are designed to accommodate change and expect their people to be both effective and flexible in their activities.

The people who handle the flow of paperwork that accompanies the activities of the organization have individual **workspaces** or offices. The workspace should be arranged to suit individual needs and comfort in order to contribute to the effectiveness of the flow of information; consequently, modern offices are carefully designed to accommodate these demands.

ORGANIZATION STRUCTURE

Traditional organizational structures are designed for managers and supervisors to organize workers within a chain of command, where each lower level of the organization is controlled by a higher one. The person with most formal authority occupies the topmost position in the organization with lower layers of management responsible to that person. Many organizations are structured in this way, where each worker is assigned tasks from a supervisor and is expected to perform the task and report to the supervisor. In such organizations, the subdivision of work is based on job specialization and departments where people use their specialized skills and knowledge to contribute toward the organizational goals. Responsibilities and duties of people within the organization are clearly defined and respected.

Some of the most common ways to organize a company by department are shown in Figure 5-1, where the structure reflects order around a specialization. For example, an organization that is structured around the functions within that company may have engineering, manufacturing, or marketing departments. Similarly, an organization that is structured around customer specialization may choose to organize around retailers, wholesalers, or institutional customers.

Contemporary organizational structures, on the other hand, are more logically formed and come together as a result of naturally interrelated functions. They are more adaptable and work well in less bureaucratic environments.

Graduate Profile

Carolyne Rickett
Property Assistant
Forestry and land management industry

College Graduation:
Applied Business Technology
Vancouver Island University
Nanaimo, British Columbia

2011

"In this industry and this department, constant change is the norm, not the exception. I am constantly challenged to think outside the box, to be resourceful, and to adapt."

With over 20 years of experience in sales and administration, Carolyne knew she had the skills—but without the credentials she found it difficult to land a job. "Employers today want certificates, diplomas, and typing speeds" says Carolyne. Going back to school was the only way to take advantage of new career opportunities. Graduates of the Applied Business Technology program at Vancouver Island were in demand, and the college has an email list with potential job opportunities.

Shortly after graduating, Carolyne started working with the real estate division of a timber and land management company and the largest private landowner in western Canada. Her main responsibility is to process the contracts, agreements, and permit requests for access to the company's land, or for the company's access to Crown or other private lands.

The company is large with multiple offices and divisions. There are many stakeholders, and Carolyne's real estate office has to consult with multiple departments regarding various aspects of the agreements and permits she must process. It can also be difficult to coordinate with co-workers who are in the field; the company owns over 300 000 hectares of land! It's not a surprise that on a typical day, most of Carolyne's communication is via email and over the phone, with only a limited amount of face-to-face communication.

In addition to the typical administrative tasks such as distributing mail and organizing files, the average day for Carolyne includes using specialized software for invoicing, digital file management, and GIS mapping. Carolyne also creates databases, updates internal manuals, and liaises with ministry offices to administer land claims. She works in an open concept office, so distraction can be an issue—it can be daunting to stay focused in the midst of many ongoing conversations.

But perhaps the most challenging part of Carolyne's work is understanding and working with the wording of the contracts she processes—precision and accuracy are key requirements: "Working with legal documents and sending them out with your name attached to them is a bit overwhelming at first." Although she wishes she'd taken a legal administration course, she never saw herself in a legal environment. But Carolyne is up to the challenge—and she hopes to obtain a certificate in legal administration soon and eventually go back to school for either business or paralegal studies.

Carolyne says it's important to think outside the box and be resourceful. She advises recent graduates to look for their own answers, not to be afraid to ask questions, and to be life-long learner in order to stay up to date on business technology.

Figure 5-1 Typical departmental structures by organization.

ORGANIZED BY	DEPARTMENTAL STRUCTURE
Function	Marketing, Engineering, Manufacturing
Customer Group	Commercial, Retail, Manufacturers, Institutions
Process	Cutting, Tailoring, Dyeing
Product	College Texts, Technical Texts, Novels
Geographic Region	European Division, Canadian Division, Far East Division

In these organizations, workers are expected to be flexible and adaptable in order to enable the organization's success. Individual workers may find themselves reporting to more than one supervisor at the same time when called for by the organization: for example, a worker might normally work in one department but report to someone else while serving on a cross-functional team to complete a special project (see discussion of the Matrix Organization, on the following page).

Regardless of the structural approach used, authority and responsibility within the organization must be established.

Classifications of Authority

Three main types of authority can be found within a typical organization. These types of authority exist to enable managers to perform their duties effectively and are traditionally classified as:

1. line authority
2. staff authority
3. functional authority

Line managers are those who contribute directly to the organization's goals. They are said to have *line authority*, which is an authority that follows an organization's direct chain of command. In a **line organization**, staff managers provide advice and expertise in support of the line managers. They are considered to be contributing indirectly to achieving the organization's goals. Staff managers have *staff authority*.

Staff managers usually advise and assist line managers and make recommendations based on their areas of expertise: marketing research, human resources, and legal counselling, for example. However, line managers usually have the final say in accepting or rejecting the recommendations of staff managers, as their authority flows in a straight *line* from the president of the organization to the supervisor.

The most frequently established formal structure in larger organizations provides a combination of these management roles in a **line-and-staff organization**. The line-and-staff organization is effective because the staff managers are specialists in their areas and are available to support the line managers throughout the organization.

Functional authority allows staff managers to broaden their authority to limited line authority relating directly to staff expertise. The authority of functional managers reaches throughout the organization to wherever their specialized knowledge or skills are being applied.

Figure 5-2 identifies where typical line-and-staff functions interact and provides typical examples of functional authority. Also refer to Figure 5-3, in which the vice-president of human resources is shown as having functional authority over human resources personnel as well as other functional divisions of the organization.

The ability to wisely use the authority and empowerment that is granted you will be a measure of your maturity and professionalism. Prepare yourself by first studying your company's organization chart to determine where the formal authority lies (see example in Figure 5-3). Be observant, adaptable, and tolerant of your ever-changing environment.

Participatory Management

The concept of **participatory management** has existed for a long time, but in the past was used only on a small scale and was often experimental. In isolated situations, project teams were formed, bringing together employees who had special skills to participate in specific projects.

Organizations today, in an effort to increase productivity and meet competition, are focusing more on the customer. To be more responsive to customer needs, the participatory management style is in contrast to the traditional line-and-staff management style. Employees working

Figure 5-2 Functional authority: Examples of line-and-staff functions.

LINE FUNCTION	STAFF FUNCTION	FUNCTIONAL AUTHORITY
Production	Human Resources	Vice-President of Human Resources has functional authority over Human Resource personnel in departments.
Customer Service	Corporate Accounting	Corporate accounting reviews departmental budgets.
Marketing	Legal	Legal counsel endorses contracts between suppliers of services and departments.

Figure 5-3 Organization chart.

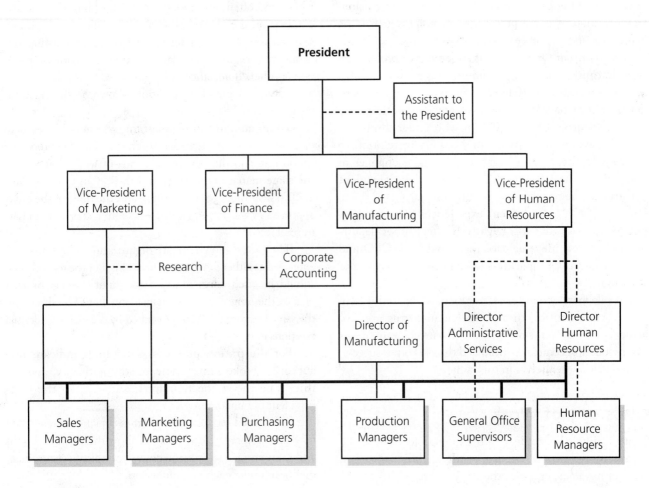

in smaller units or teams within the larger organization are encouraged to communicate freely with different levels of management. Employees are asked for input about their areas of responsibility and often are brought together in management conferences to discuss and offer solutions to organizational issues. In this environment, managers share the decision making with the teams; however, the managers still maintain final authority.

Under participatory management, each employee reports to someone in the structure, but at the same time may report to the manager of a team focusing on a specific project for the organization.

You should be aware that opportunities to launch initiatives, serve on teams, participate in group discussions, and offer constructive suggestions may also exist where you work. You should not only embrace the opportunity, but also accept your responsibility for making valuable contributions.

CONTEMPORARY ORGANIZATIONS

In today's changing environment, many organizations are reducing their bureaucracy to better serve the customer

and to reduce costs. They reorganize themselves to become neither fully bureaucratic nor organic and emerge as a new kind of organization. Current trends are toward smaller, more flexible structures that allow quicker responses yet that remain focused on the customer's needs and on the organization's goals. Descriptions of three popular modifications to the traditional organization follow.

The *Matrix Organization* is a structure that retains both line and staff authority, but specialists from different departments are temporarily brought together to work on special projects. In fact, they share time between their **functional department**, where they perform their normal tasks, and the special project. They continue to report to their functional departmental managers but also report to the project manager for issues relating to the project. When the project is complete, the specialists return to their functional department and to their normal tasks. This type of organization is frequently found in creative environments such as software development firms or architectural design companies.

The *Process (Horizontal) Organization* is designed to focus on filling an order from the customer in the most efficient way; this structure supports teams of people who focus on accomplishing the task from beginning to end. Examples of this form of organization can be found in the car manufacturing industry or any process-driven business such as the vehicle registration office.

The *Circular Organization* is structured to protect the organization's cash flow by monitoring all interrelated activities at the same time through functional managers. Functional managers, in this case, report directly to the Chief Executive Officer (CEO), who understands the implications of one department's activity in relation to another. In this form of organization, major changes in one department will not occur without other dependent departments being aware of its cash flow impact on them. For example, if a department experiences an unforeseen project expense that will negatively affect other departments in the achievement of their goals, the CEO and other managers can quickly and strategically control the situation.

While many industrial organizations aspire to this form of "cash flow control" through the circular structure, few achieve it. However, smaller, more dynamic organizations like production companies (film and theatre) often successfully structure themselves in this fashion.

Divisions of Work

Work is divided according to the main objectives of the organization, and then further subdivided into *divisions*, *departments, units*, or some other appropriate title.

The main activities being carried out govern the divisions of work. For example, a manufacturer of clothes would be concerned with procurement of raw materials, the actual manufacture of the clothes, and distribution and sales. Natural divisions of work would be purchasing, manufacturing, and sales. The manufacturing division could be further subdivided according to the kinds of clothes manufactured: children's wear, ladies' fashion, and rainwear, for example. The divisions of work in a hospital could similarly be made according to the services rendered—for instance, a cardiac unit, a dialysis unit, and a plastic surgery unit.

Other work divisions are needed to support the main functions of the organization. Many organizations have a human resources department and a finance department. Administration departments are needed to carry out support activities such as office operations, mail processing, data processing, security, and building maintenance.

Organization Chart

Most organizations draw charts that describe the relationship of people and their tasks in the organization. An organization chart graphically describes who reports to whom and often describes their responsibility through the position on the chart (see Figure 5-3). To understand an organization chart, look for lines of authority, existing divisions of work, and the relationship of the work groups to one another. If an office manual exists, descriptions of the work divisions and of the positions shown on the organization chart will be provided.

As an administrative assistant, you may be asked to update or draw an organization chart. Begin by preparing an outline showing those functions of work that are on the same management level and those that are subordinate. To save time, get the outline and the draft of the chart approved by the proper executive before you print the chart in final form.

The titles shown in an organization chart may be expressed as either functions or positions, but the form chosen should be used consistently throughout. Functions that occupy the same level of management should be shown on the same horizontal line, as illustrated by the vice-presidential positions in Figure 5-3.

For illustration purposes, solid lines indicate line authority, broken lines indicate staff authority, and the thick line shows the functional authority of the vice-president of human resources.

A crowded organization chart is difficult to read. You may have to prepare one chart to show the main functions and then provide supporting charts to indicate subordinate functions under each main function.

Informal Organization

Informal organization is a natural grouping of individuals according to personality preferences and interests. Informal organization, or grouping, is not created; it exists in every situation in which individuals are relating to one another. Members of workgroups or departments that get together occasionally would constitute an informal organization.

Informal organization satisfies certain social needs; it also can become a channel of communication, referred to as the **grapevine**. The grapevine is used extensively where the official channels are not meeting the informal organization's communication needs, such as with rumours or the premature release of information.

An informal leader usually exists within every informal organization. This leader is not designated—she or he becomes the leader as a natural outgrowth of the needs of the group. The group looks to the leader for guidance, and the leader is its spokesperson.

Managers in the formal structure need the support of the informal organization and often use it as a supplementary means for carrying out the objectives of the organization or for propagating information.

Managers have the ability to change the formal organization because they created it. However, they cannot change the informal organization or make it go away. Wise managers will be aware of the natural groupings of individuals. They should also be aware of the influence these groupings have on one another, and of the influence they have in furthering or impeding the objectives of the organization. Recognize that managers need the support of the informal organization, but beware of your own involvement. Many office professionals are privy to confidential information that should not find its way to the grapevine. Unauthorized distribution of such information will be seen as a serious violation of trust and professional responsibilities, and may result in dismissal.

Figure 5-4 Open office layout.

Self-Check

1. What are the three main types of authority that can be found within a typical organization?
2. Define participatory management.

OFFICE LAYOUT

In recent years the popular office layout has been the **open office**, designed without conventional walls, corridors, or floor-to-ceiling partitions (see Figure 5-4). The open office is often referred to as a **landscaped office** when it has a layout that has been well designed.

The open office concept grew out of the need for:

1. better work and communication flow
2. better and more flexible use of space
3. improved ventilation and lighting
4. a cooperative environment

A well-planned design results in an attractive environment and improved employee morale. Also, open offices cost less to construct and reconfigure than enclosed offices.

For those whose work is of a confidential nature, or for personnel who need privacy in order to concentrate and be creative, the traditional private office is still more practical. Employees with special needs must also be provided with user-friendly access and workspace.

Arrangement of the Open Office

The workspace of employees whose work is related because of the kind of information being processed is often located in the same area. This is especially true when employees are primarily dealing with hard-copy material such as drawings, preprinted forms, or models.

Freestanding partitions are used to form individual workspace. The partitions usually do not go to the ceiling, but are high enough to eliminate distractions and provide some privacy. Workers have the feeling of being with others. In some open offices, file cabinets and large plants are also used as space dividers.

Workspaces are arranged at angles in various configurations, in contrast to the monotonous effect of rows of separate enclosed offices. The arrangement of the workspace follows the natural flow of the work being processed. Workers who need to talk to each other about their tasks are placed in close proximity.

The **supervisor** may occupy a semiprivate office close to the workspace area under his or her supervision. It is usually private enough for conferences, yet open for those seeking advice or direction.

Many offices have adopted a mixed layout. This allows for a combination of open spaces, with private meeting areas for discussions and closed offices for the higher-ranking employees where privacy is essential in order to meet the organization's objectives.

In a well-planned office, ample space is provided for easy movement from one workstation to another. Aisles follow the natural traffic pattern, which is usually not a straight line. Lighting, heating, air conditioning, and humidity are easier to control when the partitions do not go to the ceiling. Short partitions also facilitate the diffusion of ambient overhead lighting for the benefit and comfort of all workers. Task lighting may be used in addition to the ambient overhead lighting, to provide additional lighting where required. Better airflow and reduced energy costs should result from the open plan.

Decor

Colours that blend tastefully are used throughout each land-scaped area. The colour scheme is harmonious, yet many contrasting colours are used to break up the monotony of look-alike workstations.

The partitions may be curved, adding grace to the design. The wall-to-wall carpeting and the fabric surfaces of the partitions add elegance. Growing plants are placed throughout the area to provide privacy, individuality, and beauty.

Living decorations, such as plants and aquariums stocked with tropical fish, add to personal enjoyment and interpersonal comfort during working hours.

Decorative appointments such as attractive light fixtures are also used. Because the decor of the landscaped area is artistically planned, it is **esthetically** pleasing—an important factor in maintaining employee morale and productivity.

Consider the High-Tech Office

When electronic equipment is brought into the office, many challenges accompany it.

Electronic equipment such as monitors, printers, and computers often do not fit on traditional office desks. Fortunately, purpose-built office furniture can be purchased to provide a more efficient use of available space. Regardless of your office furnishings, always make sure that you

- position your monitor, keyboard, mouse, and telephone in positions that work best for you
- organize your desk according to the natural flow of the tasks you handle
- ensure that equipment you use most often, such as telephone and mouse, is within easy reach

Most organizations recognize the importance of an environmentally friendly office; many work actively to improve conditions to make the office a better place to work. Management will often seek your advice in the design and optimal positioning of operational equipment such as computers, printers, and copiers. The proactive office professional will be prepared to make positive contributions to issues pertaining to office design and layout.

Research indicates that workers who spend long periods of time at a computer workstation may suffer from a number of health problems. For this reason you must ensure that you will take periodic breaks to reduce the possibility of discomfort and fatigue. Complaints arise about eyestrain, backaches, muscle tension in the shoulders and neck, and headaches. The most common complaints of high-tech office workers are those symptoms associated with carpal tunnel syndrome

(CTS). CTS is caused by inflammation of the tendons in the tunnel at the base of the hand, which can normally be attributed to repetitive use of the hand and wrist.

CTS is, in fact, a repetitive strain injury (RSI) and can affect anyone whose work calls for long periods of steady hand movement. RSIs tend to come with work that involves prolonged and repetitive movement, such as keying. Typically, swelling occurs in the wrist sufficient to cause the median nerve to be pressed up against a ligament in the wrist, which may then result in numbness, tingling in the hand, clumsiness, or pain.

ERGONOMICS

The science of adapting the workplace to suit the worker is called **ergonomics**; it was previously known as *human factors engineering*. The office environment should be as safe, healthy, comfortable, and productive as possible. Everything that affects the worker must be taken into consideration—furniture, lighting, amount of space, quality of air, heating and cooling, acoustics, and placement of the equipment in relation to the worker.

Furniture

Office furniture manufacturers have designed **modular furniture** to carry out the landscaped office concept. Modular furniture consists of separate components that can be fitted together in various arrangements to meet the needs of users.

Modern desks are narrower than conventional ones, and have fewer drawers. Some of them resemble tables with modesty panels. However, the modern workstation usually provides more working space than that available in a conventional office. Modular furniture can be arranged in many different configurations, giving the worker additional space on one side of the desk, behind the worker, or both. Some desks are adjustable.

If the work flow changes, creating a need for a change in working surface, the modular furniture can easily be rearranged.

The chair is one of the most important pieces of furniture in the office. A poorly designed or incorrectly adjusted chair can be a major contributor to physical discomfort. The height of the chair seat should be easily adjustable to accommodate the individual's height and size; the chair should provide adequate back support.

When the worker is seated, the angle at the knee should be 90 degrees, thighs should be parallel to the floor; the buttocks, not the thighs, should support most of the worker's weight.

Storage space may be integrated; easy-to-reach shelves can be added above the desk. Sometimes shelves are hung

Figure 5-5 A sample workstation arrangement.

on a partition at the back of the desk. Credenzas can be included in the arrangement. However, storage space for files, or for manuals and books not currently in use, is not provided at a workstation. In open office environments, separate workspace is often provided for processing mail, assembling materials, and performing other highly repetitive jobs. See Figure 5-5 for a sample workspace arrangement.

Lighting

In addition to the diffused lighting over the entire area, referred to as **ambient lighting**, light fixtures are provided over individual workstations so that the intensity and direction of light for each worker's needs can be controlled. This is referred to as **task lighting**.

Natural light from windows is the greatest source of computer screen reflection and associated reading problems. A screen that faces directly into or away from a window can cause eyestrain. For this reason, adjustable blinds should cover windows. Most modern monitors are built with antiglare screens; however, antiglare shields may be purchased to reduce or even eliminate glare from older technology screens.

Proper placement of lighting is also crucial; a light source directly behind the computer screen causes stress on the eyes of the worker, who must face the light source while at the workstation. The opposite case is also a problem: a light source directly behind the worker will result in direct glare on the screen. If you suffer from eyestrain or headaches while working, you can check for undue glare by switching off your monitor to determine what is reflected on your screen. The best way to deal with glare is to eliminate the source by closing the blinds or by tilting or moving your monitor. For optimum comfort, lower the ambient lighting and provide task lighting for deskwork.

Generally, the best orientation for a light source is for it to shine over the left shoulder of a right-handed worker (or over the right shoulder of a left-handed worker). The reason for this has to do with the shoulder action of the employee. A right-handed worker tends to lean forward in such a way that the right shoulder blocks light coming from the right side; this creates a shadow on the documents in front of the body.

Acoustics

The Canadian Centre for Occupational Health and Safety (CCOHS) suggests that noise is one of the most common occupational health hazards. Annoyance, stress, and interference with speech communication are the main concerns in noisy offices. To prevent adverse outcomes of noise exposure, noise levels should be reduced to acceptable levels.

CCOHS suggests that if you can answer "yes" to any of the following questions, your workplace may have a noise problem:

- Do people have to raise their voices?
- Do people who work in noisy environments have ringing in their ears at the end of their shift?
- Do they find when they return home from work that they have to increase the volume on their car radio higher than they did when they went to work?
- Does a person who has worked in a noisy workplace for years have problems understanding conversations at parties or restaurants, or in crowds where there are many voices and "competing" noises?

If there is a noise problem in a workplace, then a noise assessment or survey should be undertaken to determine the sources of noise, the amount of noise, and who is exposed and for how long. Temporary equipment such as earmuffs and earplugs may be used, but engineers and office designers must plan proper acoustical control so that unwanted sound does not disturb office work and conversations cannot be easily overheard.

Wall-to-wall carpeting, because of its sound-absorbing qualities, is used throughout the typical open office. The freestanding partitions are covered with carpeting or fabric. Ceilings are equipped with baffles. Sound-reflecting surfaces are limited or avoided.

Although manufacturers today are making electronic office equipment that runs more quietly than earlier models, much more has to be done to control noise in the office environment. For example, **white noise**, a continuous background noise evenly distributed, can be generated by electronic equipment. Installing floor-to-ceiling partitions can help to combat the problem of office noise.

Position and Posture

In addition to the office environment, good work habits, correct keying techniques, and proper posture are important for prevention of musculoskeletal injuries. Musculoskeletal disorders (MSDs) include injuries that affect muscles, nerves, tendons, ligaments, joints, cartilage, blood vessels, and disks. They are the result of RSIs and are one type of injury attributed to ergonomic problems. For example, CTS, discussed above in "Consider the High-Tech Office," belongs to this category. Figure 5-6 illustrates proper posture at the computer, which can only be achieved with the correct positioning of equipment. Note that the chair and keyboard are set so that the thighs and forearms are parallel to the floor and that the wrists are straight and level. If the table is too high to permit this, you should find an adjustable chair; or you may need to put the keyboard in your lap.

While you are keying, your wrists should not rest on anything and should not be bent up, down, or to the side. You should use your arms to move your hands around instead of resting your wrists and stretching to hit keys with the fingers. When you stop keying for a while, rest your hands in your lap and/or on their sides instead of leaving them on the keyboard. Wrist rests are available and give you a place to rest your hands when pausing from keying. They are not designed to rest your wrists while you are keying.

In the illustration, you will note that the worker is sitting straight, not slouching, and does not have to stretch forward to reach the keys or read the screen. Good posture is not just about your hands and arms, but also about the use or misuse of your shoulders, back, and neck. These areas are equally as important as what is happening down at your wrists.

Anything that creates awkward reaches or angles in the body may create discomfort. However, even a perfect posture may result in problems if it is held rigidly for long periods of time.

Figure 5-6 Proper posture at the computer.

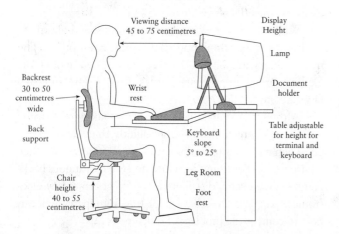

Here are basic tips to avoid discomfort while keying:

- Relax.
- Use a light touch. Do not "pound" on the keys.
- Move and shift positions frequently.
- Wrists should not be bent to the side, but instead your fingers should be in a straight line with your forearm as viewed from above.
- Use an adjustable keyboard tray that permits optimal positioning, or tilt the back edge of your keyboard down and slightly away.
- Use two hands to perform double-key operations like Ctrl-C or Alt-F, instead of twisting one hand to do it.
- Move your whole hand to hit function keys with your fingers instead of stretching to reach them.
- Stretch and relax frequently. Momentary breaks every few minutes and longer breaks every hour or so work well.
- Hold the mouse lightly; do not grip it hard or squeeze it when **mousing**. Place it where you don't have to reach

---

pro-Link
Work Away from Work

The popularity of virtual offices—offices located wherever employees happen to be—has increased the number of office professionals who work outside the confines of the traditional office building. These telecommuters—travellers by way of telecommunications technology—must choose their workspaces carefully. It is quite possible that you will become a telecommuter, perhaps working from home, so here are a few planning tips for *your* new home office:

- Locate the office as far away from temptation as possible: the cookie jar, the fridge, et cetera.
- Give yourself some business atmosphere: put a clock on the wall; provide a coffee station or a water cooler.
- Buy comfortable, purpose-built office furniture—you'll be spending a lot of time at the desk.
- Treat yourself to a decent sound system, but don't install a television.
- Make full use of available technology: a fast and capable computer, fax machine, telephone company services, or a wireless headset, for example.
- Use your telephone company's voice mail and conference services—they appear more professional.
- Ensure you have adequate and timely support for the technology on which you will depend.

up or over. Place it close to the keyboard or learn and use keyboard equivalent commands.

■ Keep your arms and hands warm. Cold muscles and tendons are at much greater risk for overuse injuries, and many offices are overly air conditioned.

■ Do not tuck the telephone between your shoulder and your ear so that you can type and talk on the phone at the same time. This common practice aggravates your neck, shoulders, and arms.

■ Pay attention to your body. Aches and pains are your body's signal that it is in discomfort. Learning what is comfortable or awkward for your body before you are in pain may prevent injury.

QUESTIONS FOR STUDY AND REVIEW

1. Why is a formal organization structure established within businesses and institutions?
2. Compare line authority and staff authority management functions.
3. Why might it be difficult for an observer to determine the authority of a staff manager?
4. Who in the *Circular Organization* would know about changes as they happen?
5. What is an organization chart?
6. Describe how functional authority might help a staff manager who is located in the organization's head office.
7. What is meant by informal organization?
8. What is the grapevine? How can managers use the grapevine effectively?
9. Why should an administrative assistant be aware of informal organization?
10. What is the open office designed to accomplish?
11. What is meant by "living decorations"?
12. Suggest three problems that accompany the introduction of electronic equipment into the office.
13. What is the meaning of the term *ergonomic*?
14. Differentiate between task lighting and ambient lighting.
15. Describe the proper physical position for a person seated at a keyboard.
16. State three ways to reduce the risk of CTS.
17. Give four suggestions to avoid discomfort while keying.

EVERYDAY ETHICS

Sitting Pretty

Sally Chow, the office supervisor at Apogee Designs, has been with the organization for 12 years. Sally is respected for her knowledge of the processes and procedures in the office and, as a matter of fact, she authored the office's procedures manual. Unfortunately, it has not been updated for a few years because Sally is far too busy. She has a lot of control in the office, mainly because she has been working there for longer than most. Office personnel these days are mainly bright young graduates who fear upsetting the status quo, and Sally.

Over time, Sally has been given the authority to make direct purchases and orders from suppliers, including office supplies and furnishings. While it was no surprise to find Sally's workspace is a "cut above" that of other personnel, it was a huge disappointment to discover that one supplier and, indeed, one salesperson had serviced the office needs for quite a while. It was Bruce Bell, Sally's husband! Sally and Bruce have had a confidential and exclusive supply "arrangement" with Apogee Designs for the past eight years.

Bruce's supplies and furniture are okay, but you have noticed that service is mediocre and the quality of his furniture is not the best—except for that in Sally's workspace.

Clearly, both Bruce and Sally are benefiting from this long-standing arrangement, but is that true for Apogee?

■ What, if anything, should you do about this situation?

Problem Solving

1. Your manager, Robert Wrigley, has 35 employees reporting to him. When he receives a memorandum from top management, he edits portions of it by condensing much of the material, and asks you to rekey and make copies of what he has edited for distribution to the 35 employees. The employees often do not understand the summaries distributed to them and come to you for clarification. One co-worker, James Ellis, has demanded that he see the original memorandum. Should you show him the original memorandum or discuss the situation with Robert first? Why do you think your manager always rewrites the communications from top management before distributing them?

2. You work in an open office area. The area works well for you most of the time. A concern you do have is that most of your colleagues are located several aisles away from you. The walk is not convenient when you are in a developmental thinking mode. You ask to meet your manager, Amber Rose, to discuss moving you closer to your colleagues. What reasons will you give for your request?

3. One of your temporary administrative assistants, Martie Evans, is upset because she saw a memorandum written by a staff member in the Human Resources Department recommending that all temporary workers throughout the organization be laid off at the end of September. You suggested that she talk with your manager, Anthony Roberts, before reacting to the memorandum. You tried to reassure her by saying you could not produce all the work that was stacking up on your desk. Were you justified in suggesting to Martie that she talk with Anthony? Explain. Who will make the final decision about Martie's employment?

Special Reports

1. Research two prominent Canadian businesses, locating their organization charts. Review each chart and then prepare a short report for your instructor addressing how many levels of management exist within each company. In your report, discuss the similarities and differences of the two companies' organizational structures.

2. Consider the participatory management style and explain in a short essay why it may, or may not, suit your own work style.

3. Ask the testing questions provided by The Canadian Centre for Occupational Health and Safety, with respect to acoustics, on its website (see the "Weblinks" section at the end of the chapter). From the results, support your answer to the question, "Do you have a noisy classroom?"

PRODUCTION CHALLENGES

5-A A Personnel Problem

Supplies needed:

- *Plain paper*

Recently your office was redesigned and redecorated. The partitions that formed the private offices were removed, and a landscaped office design with smaller partitions and modular furniture was used. The office is beautiful. You work in a modular arrangement with Marge Stevens, administrative assistant in purchasing, and Ann Compton, administrative assistant in financial planning.

Marge and Ann spend much of their time talking. They remain at their workstations and shout over the "masking noise" in order to be heard. Their talking has decreased your productivity. The first week you tried to overlook the interruptions and worked overtime to keep up with your work. Later Mr. Wilson asked you to plan your work so that you would not have to work overtime. You did not tell Mr. Wilson why you were working overtime. The next day you asked Marge and Ann to refrain from talking so much, but they have ignored your request.

You are getting so far behind with your work that you are taking it home with you.

Today you again asked Marge and Ann to stop talking so loudly and so much. Ann retorted, "Don't be such a nag." You became so upset that you felt ill. You took the afternoon off. All afternoon you worried about your work piling up and your inability to concentrate while Marge and Ann are talking loudly.

What are the solutions to your problem? You decide that you need help with it. Jot down what you are going to do and what you will say.

5-B An Organization Chart Change

Supplies needed:

- *Organization chart template for the Marketing Department of Millennium Appliances, Inc., Form 5-B, page 388*

- *Original organization chart for the Marketing Division of Millennium Appliances, Inc., Figure In-3, page 8*

Millennium Appliances, Inc. is in the process of reorganizing itself to become leaner and more efficient. The Vice-President of Manufacturing has resigned and there are no plans to replace him or the position. As a temporary step, the President of Millennium has asked William Wilson, the Vice-President of Marketing, to oversee the activities of the two manufacturing plants. The President has also asked Jim Schultz, Director of Manufacturing, to report directly to William Wilson. Jim Schultz directs the operations of the western and midwestern manufacturing plants through Raymond Jones and Eugene Liam.

Their names, titles, and addresses are as follows:

Jim Schultz
Director of Manufacturing
Corporate Office
Millennium Appliances, Inc.
320 Apogee Way
Winnipeg, MB R2R 4H6

Raymond Jones
Plant Manager
Midwestern Manufacturing
2202 Logan Avenue
Winnipeg, MB R2R 0J2

Eugene Liam
Plant Manager
Western Manufacturing Plant
836 Carnarvon Street
New Westminster, BC V3M 1G1

William Wilson has asked you to revise the marketing organization chart to reflect the temporary changes. Be sure to update the revision number on the organization chart.

Weblinks

Canadian Centre for Occupational Health and Safety
http://www.ccohs.ca/oshanswers/ergonomics/
Canada's national occupational health and safety resource provides information on a wide variety of occupational health and safety issues, including ergonomics.

Ergonomic Issues at the Workstation
http://www.healthycomputing.com/
This site has information specific to office administrators as well as a page on mobile device ergonomics.

Ergonomic Tips for Laptop Users
www.uhs.berkeley.edu/Facstaff/pdf/ergonomics/laptop.pdf
This site offers practical ergonomic suggestions to help reduce the health risks when using your laptop computer for short or long periods of time.

HR World
www.hrworld.com/features/workstation-ergonomics-guide-100107
This site contains ten easy tips regarding workstation ergonomics and numerous links to useful sites on the topic.

UCLA Ergonomics
www.ergonomics.ucla.edu
UCLA's website contains "How To . . ." tips on setting up your workstation, exercises, a computer workstation online self-evaluation, and much more ergonomic advice.

Exercises
www.mydailyyoga.com
Simple exercises you can do in your office or at your desk.

Chapter 6
Office Technology

Learning Outcomes

After completion of this chapter, the student will be able to:

1 Explain the administrative assistant's role in using a computer in the office.

2 Identify digital communication devices used in business.

3 Identify possible methods of computer input and computer output that may be functional in the office.

4 Understand the importance of computer troubleshooting.

5 Describe the importance of accurate data input.

6 Discuss application software as it relates to word processing, spreadsheets, desktop publishing, and presentations.

7 Describe the administrative assistant's role in desktop publishing.

8 Define telecommunications.

9 Identify three call management services offered by the local telephone company.

10 Identify office telephone equipment.

11 Research information for the most cost-effective, high-volume copier.

Technology has an incredible impact on the way business performs. A fundamental skill identified by the Conference Board of Canada and, indeed, an expectation of every employer, is a broad understanding of office technology, its scope, and its application. Office professionals also need to keep up to date with new developments. Changing technologies encompass new and innovative computer **hardware** and **peripherals** as well as new and improved versions of application **software** that serve to improve productivity in the office. More importantly, office professionals need to understand how technology can enhance their productivity when used appropriately.

Office technology is acquired for different purposes and often may not be fully utilized in the contemporary office. Lack of utilization is often due to insufficient training, budget (to acquire the latest technology), or even time to learn the full extent of the technology's capability. It is the investment of time to learn the benefits of office technology that will eventually save you time with your tasks. This chapter explores a broad range of technologies, their application, and the potential productivity improvements they offer.

COMPUTERS AND DIGITAL DEVICES

Types of Computers

Desktop Computers (PCs) Desktop computers were designed for use by one person at a time and can be found at individual workstations in most offices. They are provided so that each member of that organization may share and distribute information and contribute to corporate goals.

Laptop Computers (Notebooks) Many office workers and business travellers will use a **laptop computer (notebook)** to retrieve and process information from the

Laura Keast
EMR Specialist and Healthcare Educator

Choice Learning Inc.
Wasaga Beach, Ontario

College Graduation:
Office Administration—Medical
Georgian College
Barrie, Ontario
1995

"There is nothing you can't accomplish."

With technology changing at such a rapid pace, keeping up with new programs and systems isn't just a nice skill to have—it's a requirement in the workplace. For administrative professionals, this can mean learning new software programs, adapting to new systems, and frequently updating office procedures to comply with these new programs. And, depending on the industry, technological advances present unique challenges specific to that field.

Laura Keast's career has taken her from medical office administration to a role as a hospital and outpatient clinical instructor and into a position as a trainer specializing in electronic medical records (EMR). It's a path that has required her to constantly update her technological skills to keep pace with the healthcare industry. "There are many advances in healthcare every year," she says. "Keeping yourself apprised of all that is changing in technology is key, to keep you relevant and competent in your field."

To keep her skills in top shape, Laura regularly attends workplace training and continuing education courses—something she says has helped her achieve success in her career. Laura also points to her college education as an important primer for the workplace. "My education taught me confidentiality, professionalism, accountability, and multitasking, and prepared me for my chosen career," she says.

In her role as an EMR specialist, Laura provides software training and technical support to instructors and students. As such, she has had to learn how to use various software programs—not just to a level at which she can use them, but to a level that enables her to teach them to others. She says that this has been one of the most difficult tasks she has undertaken in her job, but it is also essential to her work, especially given the pace at which technology is changing in the healthcare field.

"Electronic medical records have changed the role of a health office professional," she says. "The role has evolved into much more responsibility. We now manage the health information so that it can be data-mined and the information used for advanced OHIP billing and preventive healthcare."

In addition to the technical side of her work, Laura carries out customer support, curriculum development, marketing, and bookkeeping and other financial tasks, and makes onsite visits to Ontario colleges to meet instructors and students. She says she plans to one day run her own business with a focus on bringing up-to-date medical office administration training to Ontario colleges.

Her advice to those looking to enter the healthcare field is to keep building your skills. "There is nothing you can't accomplish," she says. "Reach for the stars!"

office, as it can offer 24/7 mobile computing (see Figure 6-1). More and more business professionals are using the laptop computer at the office instead of a desktop PC. A businessperson can easily transport the laptop back and forth between office and home rather than having to move a work file from the PC to a laptop or external storage for access at home.

The laptop computer has many advantages over the desktop computer. Not only is it portable, but it offers the user the flexibility to **sign on** from locations remote to the workplace. Almost every laptop has wireless capability and requires only a location that provides wireless service. Many hotels provide wireless internet access in their guest rooms. Airports commonly offer wireless internet access, allowing business travellers to stay in touch with their offices. Access may be provided throughout the airport or may be restricted to specified areas such as a designated room or waiting area.

Tablet Computers A **tablet computer** is a portable personal computer equipped with a touch screen that has a virtual keyboard for data input in place of a traditional keyboard. Tablet computers are lightweight and smaller than typical laptops (see Figure 6-1). A tablet, because of its wireless capability, can be used to access emails, download files, and browse websites.

Figure 6-1 Common digital devices (laptop, tablet, and PDA).

Smartphones A **smartphone** is a mobile phone that works on a mobile computing platform (see Figure 6-2). These portable devices are much more than phones. They have built-in features such as cameras, music players, and global positioning systems (GPSs). Many smartphones have high-resolution touch screens and can access high-speed data using Wi-Fi (wireless fidelity) and mobile broadband technology. Application programming interfaces (APIs) allow smartphone users, depending on the operating system, to subscribe to third-party applications. For example, some of these applications allow users to track items they have shipped or to view and edit documents without a standard computer. Some additional features include the following:

■ international data roam capabilities (allowing the travelling businessperson to stay connected with the office

Figure 6-2 Smartphones like this are handheld PCs designed to provide business people with remote access to their workplace computers.

while out of the country without changing phones or phone numbers)

■ videoconferencing capability

■ instant messenger

■ desktop synchronization (synchronizes email and calendar information between smartphone and office computer)

■ capacity to send and receive email attachments

■ voice recognition capability

■ Bluetooth wireless technology for compatible accessories such as headsets (for further discussion of Bluetooth technology, see the section "Wireless Networks," below)

Personal Digital Assistants Personal digital assistances (PDAs) made their appearance in the business world in 1986. They are referred to as palmtop computers because they can manage personal information such as scheduling but are also compact and portable. The traditional PDA has many of the same features as a smartphone, but it lacks the phone capability. In fact, smartphones are the present-day PDAs.

Computer Basic Functions

The amount of special terminology surrounding computer technology is immense, but basic functions and vocabulary are useful to learn for simple communication purposes. Refer to Figure 6-3 for the visual concept of the following descriptions:

Processing The **central processing unit (CPU)**, commonly thought of as the brain of the computer, is a **microprocessor chip**. The commercial computer was made possible in 1971 by the introduction of a silicon chip that was smaller than a dime and contained 2250 transistors. Chips today contain the equivalent of millions of transistors and can be found in many forms throughout the computer and its peripherals.

It is the CPU that seeks and interprets instructions from programs temporarily stored in **memory**. Based on its interpretation of the program instructions, the CPU directs all other functions of the computer, including the timing of **input** and **output** data. The CPU interprets millions of instructions and directions each second.

Input External information must be provided to the computer's central processing unit in a form that it can understand. Specially designed input devices change a keystroke or a **mouse** "click" into a computer-understandable form. Commonly used input devices are the **keyboard**, mouse, and **scanner** (see Figure 6-4). Other "input" may come from an externally connected PC, smartphone, or digital camera.

Output Various means of retrieving information from a computer are used, but you will be most familiar with the

Figure 6-3 Input, processing, and output concept.

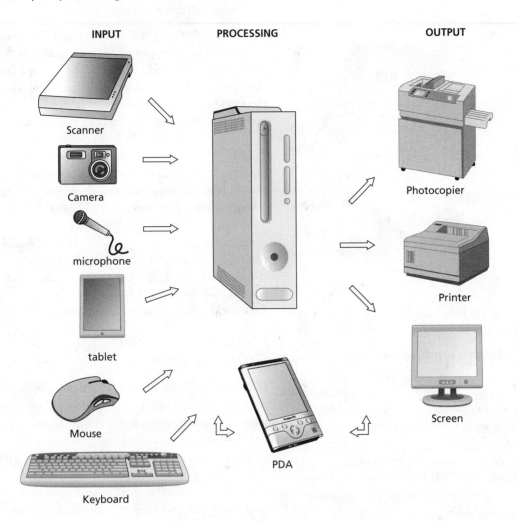

video **display** terminal (VDT) and **printer**. VDTs are more commonly known as "**monitors**" or "screens" and essentially display the information processed by the computer. Similarly, the printer displays a permanent, or printed, version of the information from the computer. There is no

Figure 6-4 Document scanner.

output until the computer is instructed to display, print, or send it to another peripheral. Smartphones (see the section "Smartphones," above) may serve as another input and output device when the user is synchronizing. (A common form of printer used is the **laser printer**; see Figure 6-5.)

Operating System The **operating system** gives fundamental operating instructions to the computer. It contains a number of internal **commands** needed to operate the computer. The operating system must be loaded into the computer's memory *before* **application programs** such as Word or Excel because the operating system is what enables the application program to make full use of the computer.

The application program must be **compatible** with the operating system of the computer being used. For example, Microsoft Windows is an operating system in which most common application programs that are **Windows** compatible can run; it is used widely in Canada. Mac OS X is an operating system developed by Apple Inc. and is now installed on all Macintosh computers being sold. It accommodates application programs that are compatible with

Figure 6-5 An administrative assistant using a laser printer.

Apple computers and is more widely used in the United States than in Canada.

Internal Memory This is the place where information and the instructions that tell the CPU what to do with the information are stored. There are two types of internal memory. One type is **random-access memory (RAM)**, also known as main memory. It is the primary memory in which information is held when being processed. Any data stored in RAM is lost when the computer is shut down.

Read-only memory (ROM) is the other form of internal memory that is used when **processing** information. It is used to store items that the computer needs in order to run when it is first turned on or when a program such as Word is used. ROM is permanent and is not lost when the computer is turned off.

External Memory In order to retain data that is created when using the computer and that must be kept permanently or for a period of time (e.g., a Word document), the data must be saved to an external memory device. Examples of external memory devices include the following:

■ **Hard disk drive** (usually housed within the computer unit but sometimes outside). Some businesses choose to back up their critical files using external removable drives. The typical external drive usually connects via a USB port with plug-and-play capability. Data storage capacity for an external drive usually ranges from 160 gigabytes to 2 terabytes.

■ **CD-ROMs**, in either CD-R format (compact disc-recordable; you can save data only once regardless of whether or not the CD is full) or CD-RW format (compact disc-rewritable; data can be saved and erased more than once, similar to a flash drive).

■ USB (universal serial bus) **flash drives** (sometimes called pen drives or memory keys).

Flash drives plug into, or out of, any USB port on your computer. The miniaturized technology used in flash drives enables this wafer-sized (approximately 7 cm × 2 cm × 1 cm) device to provide up to 256 **gigabytes** (and are moving toward 2 **terabytes**) of permanent **removable storage** space. Once information has been stored on the flash drive, it can be removed and transported easily. Administrative assistants will find the flash drive most convenient for transporting selective information from workstation to workstation, or simply for backing up critical data. In contrast to the flash drive, CD-ROMs have a storage capacity of approximately 700 **megabytes**.

A recent popular alternative for document data storage is cloud computing. Users access cloud-based applications through a web browser, allowing them to store and share documents. Individual users' data is stored on servers at remote locations. Users can synchronize their mobile devices to gain access to and update their documents.

Going Online

Users of computers gain access to online functionality through a coaxial cable connected to workstations; this is referred to as **broadband** connectivity. Signals are transmitted digitally to permit high-speed connection. Dial-up or analogue connections may be found in some offices. This technology is considered very slow, but it is a cheaper alternative to broadband. Dial-up connectivity requires a telephone line and modem connected to a workstation. This arrangement of communicating is called **remote access** (see Figure 6-6).

Online Capability PCs, when appropriately connected, allow users to communicate with each other and with a mainframe server **online**. Administrative assistants are among those who communicate with mainframe servers to obtain more information than is available on the local PC alone.

Several users may request information from the mainframe server at the same time. In theory, each user makes a request to the mainframe server quite independently, but due to the high speed of the mainframe server, it appears that all users obtain their requested information back simultaneously. This is called **time-sharing**.

The online capability that provides instantaneous updating of data is known as real-time transaction processing. Updating takes place as the transaction happens. Commercial airlines' use of computer terminals for making airline reservations is one well-known example of time-sharing and real-time transactions.

With an online database or inventory control system, the inventory balance is immediately available. A sales

Figure 6-6 A remote PC online with a mainframe computer.

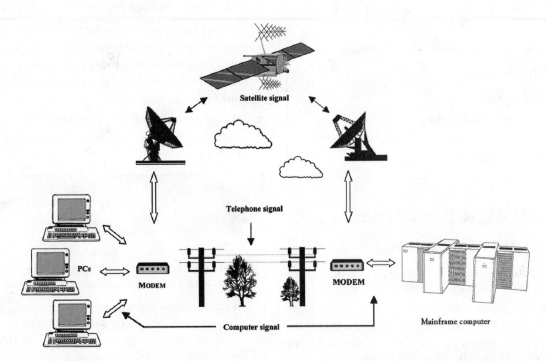

representative in a remote branch office can enter an order directly into the home office computer. An executive or administrative assistant can request desired data from remote computer files and receive an instantaneous response. The administrative assistant who has access to an online terminal will rely on it as an effective means of communication. For instance, if a customer calls about the status of his or her account, the administrative assistant can consult the computer and obtain virtually instantaneous information for the customer. The process is so seamless that the user is not conscious that the information is being retrieved from a remote source.

Networking Computers

Many organizations use **local area networks (LANs)** for connecting their internal computers. LANs are designed not only to provide a means of communication between users of computers but also to facilitate the sharing of common documents, hardware, and software.

LANs typically connect computers that are in the same area. The computers may be connected by fibre optic or coaxial cable (to permit higher transmission speeds) or by simple telephone cable. For enhanced capabilities, LANs are commonly connected to a mainframe computer. LANs can also be connected to other **networks**, such as a metropolitan area network (MAN), which, as the name implies, provides networking facilities within a town or city. In much the same way, a **wide area network (WAN)** provides networking facilities over a yet wider area (perhaps an entire country, or even the entire world).

Wireless Networks Developed by a consortium of companies including IBM, Intel, Nokia, Toshiba, and Microsoft, Bluetooth™ is one of the latest technologies in wireless communications. It is a short-range communications technology that can replace the cables connecting office computer hardware and peripherals while maintaining high levels of security. Offices can become virtually wireless by purchasing Bluetooth-enabling products and turning on, or enabling, the Bluetooth technology that is integrated into the products. Bluetooth is not a wireless service that you purchase but rather is integrated into products by the manufacturer. In order for two devices to communicate wirelessly using Bluetooth, both must have the Bluetooth technology integrated and enabled. Laptops can communicate with printers, desktop PCs with laptops, and smartphones with office hardware over short distances without unsightly cables. This is especially advantageous in open offices, where wires can be an eyesore and a safety issue, and in small working areas such as work cubicles.

Through the use of networks, an administrative assistant can now:

1. communicate with other employees through electronic mail or by memo

2. send draft copies of documents to individuals for validation or correction before committing them to final form

3. route a document for approval both sequentially and electronically

4. co-author or co-edit large documents

5. conduct **virtual** meetings
6. use the server as a common space where data can be saved and shared with authorized users

---

Self-Check

1. List two input devices.
2. What does an operating system do?
3. Explain internal memory versus external memory.
4. What is Bluetooth technology?

COMPUTERS IN THE OFFICE

The Versatile Computer

When computers became an integral part of the office, they were used for word processing more than for any other application. But as the speed and versatility of computers increased, so did the number of uses we found for them.

Over time, a variety of new software versions have been developed for word processing. Each new release is an improvement on what was previously available. Also, computer hardware is continually being improved. These improvements in the computer and in word processing software have established the computer as essential office equipment.

The computer's versatility is apparent in the range of software now available for business use: there is software on the market to handle **spreadsheets**, graphics, electronic presentations, file and information management, telecommunications, accounting, and **desktop publishing (DTP)**. As well, your reliance on the speedy output of computers for decision making will increase as you begin to need it for tasks such as budgeting, scheduling, and general planning.

The computer is a powerful tool for increasing productivity. Managers rely on computers for planning production, monitoring and controlling manufacturing processes, and analyzing sales reports. The administrative assistant who has learned how to analyze and interpret data will also be an invaluable asset to any organization that employs these more advanced processes.

Computer Troubleshooting

When working in a computer-based environment, it is inevitable that some challenges will arise. It is beneficial to understand some basic troubleshooting techniques to alleviate frustration and maintain productivity. Troubleshooting a computer problem involves knowing how to isolate the problem and then possibly fixing it. In an organization, it might not always be practical or cost-efficient to contact a technician when you have a computer problem. In this

case, knowing the basics of troubleshooting can be helpful. Consider these recommendations:

- Always check your computer cables if you are having connectivity issues. Many issues originate when a cable or cord is unplugged or simply loose. A problem like the computer monitor not turning on might easily be due to a loose cable.
- When programs are running slowly, try closing and restarting the program. Check for any updates for the program.

---

pro-Link
Learning Lingo

Confused by computer terminology? Here are some descriptions of commonly used terms that may, at least, put computer information terminology in perspective for you:

- A **directory** is a way to organize information. In your computer system, a directory contains a group of related files that are separated from other directories by a unique name. A familiar everyday example is the Yellow Pages telephone directory. Directories are also known as *catalogues* or *folders*.
- A **file** is a related collection of *records*. For example, you might keep a record on each of your customers in a file.
- A **record** consists of *fields* of individual data items, such as customer name, customer number, and customer address. A customer record contains all details of the customer.
- A **field** is an area within a record that has a fixed size. By providing the same *information* in the same fields in each record (so that all records are consistent), the customer file may be easily used by a computer program.
- **Information** is synonymous with *data*. Data is information translated into a form that is more convenient to manipulate by computers. It is often referred to in terms of *bits* and *bytes*.
- A **bit** is the smallest unit of data in a computer. A bit has a single binary value, either 0 or 1. In most computer systems, there are eight bits in a byte.
- A **byte** is a unit of information that is eight *bits* long. A byte is the unit most computers use to represent one character, such as a letter, number, or symbol.
- A **kilobyte** means approximately 1000 (1 K) bytes or characters.
- A **megabyte** refers to 1 000 000 (1 M) bytes.
- A **gigabyte** refers to 1 000 000 000 (1 G) bytes.
- A **terabyte** refers to 1 000 000 000 000 (1 T) bytes.

- When a program is unresponsive, try using the task manager to end it. (In Windows systems, you can open the task manager by pressing the ctrl, alt, and delete keys and then selecting the task manager.)

- Check computer or software manuals, as they may offer a solution to a problem.

- Finally, if you can't resolve the problem, make a note of any error messages and follow up with a technician. Know who to call in this situation.

Accuracy of Input Information

Most Canadians are familiar with the expression, "Garbage in, garbage out" (or **GIGO**). This expression is particularly significant when applied to the use of computers.

The usefulness of output information from the computer is only as good as the accuracy of the input information. Accuracy and completeness of the input information, or data, is the key to obtaining accurate results. If the user provides inaccurate or incomplete input data to the computer, inaccurate or incomplete output data will result.

Consider for a moment the speed at which a computer processes information (typically millions of instructions each second). Inaccurate input data is processed and distributed so rapidly that the results may create long-term and difficult-to-correct problems. If an address is entered incorrectly it will impact reports generated and documents created. In company terms, such problems have the potential to negatively affect the customer or financial records on which the company's survival depends.

Data input is often taken from source documents. Source documents include orders, invoices, incoming cheques, time cards, and sales tickets. Source documents are often assembled in originating departments and then submitted for processing. Regardless of where the data entry specialist is located, the originating department is responsible for ensuring the accuracy and completeness of the source documents before turning them over to the data entry specialist.

Similarly, the data entry specialist is responsible for accurately entering source documents into the computer.

Do everything you can to decrease errors in source document information. If errors are detected, keep a record of the:

- frequency of errors
- types of errors that occur
- originator(s) of the errors

Analyze the problem to determine how to:

- decrease the frequency of errors
- eliminate errors altogether
- improve the process

Your responsibility as an employee and your role as an administrative professional include both preventing problems and attempting to resolve those that do occur. If the internal or external customer who has been a victim of a "computer error" calls you, be attentive to that customer's position. Demonstrate your commitment to customer support and your willingness to help correct the problem. Customer follow-up should be exercised any time there is an inconvenienced or dissatisfied customer. For the sake of retaining the customer's patronage, a written response or telephone call should be made by an appropriate company representative.

Using Computer Storage

Office workers are ever hopeful that paper files will gradually be replaced by computer-based and computer-assisted filing systems. These systems use media that require much less space than traditional paper files and storage systems. Unfortunately, for the foreseeable future, paper is here to stay; but a variety of information technology-based storage media is now available to hold the use of paper in check. Typically, the choice of medium will depend upon availability and your specific requirements. Figure 6-7 provides a practical guide to computer-based storage media;

Figure 6-7 Relative capacities of computer-based storage.

COMPUTER-BASED	CAPACITY*	APPROXIMATE EQUIVALENT IN FULL PAGES OF TEXT
CD-ROM (writable)	700 Megabytes	189 000 000
Pen drive (flash memory)	2 Gigabytes	540 000 000
Hard (disk) drive	1 Terabyte	270 000 000 000

*In operation, 10 percent to 15 percent of the capacity of each medium would be used for directory and page-formatting information.

it illustrates capacities of both computer-based storage and the approximate equivalence in full pages of text.

Both information access and retrieval speed are dramatically improved by computer-based and computer-assisted filing systems. However, the fact that those systems are susceptible to loss or damage is a definite disadvantage; the loss of information on one flash drive or CD could result in hours or even weeks of work. Consequently, making a **backup** copy of your information and storing information in two places are essential. Figure 6-8 provides examples of online data storage options, which often prove more reliable than traditional storage methods.

Self-Check

1. Have computer-based filing systems replaced paper files? Defend your answer.

2. List two steps to take when troubleshooting a computer problem.

APPLICATION PROGRAMS

Application programs, often referred to collectively as "application *software*," are written to perform specific tasks such as word processing, spreadsheet production, graph and/or desktop publishing, and information management. Electronic mail usually requires its own special application program such as Outlook, a comprehensive time manager, calendar, and email application from Microsoft.

Word Processing

In most organizations, text editing is one of the main administrative responsibilities. In preparation for your career, you need to acquire word processing skills and to learn about

Figure 6-8 Online data storage options.

Service	Initial Capacity
A Drive	50 GB
Alfresco®	10 GB
Box	5 GB
Dropbox	2 GB
Flip Drive	1 GB
Google drive	5 GB
Open Drive	5 GB
Skydrive	7 GB

the capabilities of word processing equipment and software. Word processing may include creating, editing, storing, printing, and even transmitting documents to other word processing equipment. Remember, the goals of organizations that install text-editing equipment are to increase productivity and to improve communication.

Input for Word Processing Information in its original form is called **raw data**. Raw data for word processing can be obtained from any of the following sources:

- keyed data
- form letters or documents—the author of text material dictates the variables (addresses, dates, amounts of money, etc.)
- flash drives
- CD-ROMs on which information has been stored before processing
- document scanner (optical character reader)
- voice input

The flash drive or CD-ROM containing stored material must not only be compatible with the equipment being used, but the data itself must be in—or converted to—the correct format for the word processing application in use.

A document scanner reads printed material that has been keyed with a font style the scanner can recognize. As the keyed material is scanned, it is transferred to the memory of the computer.

Computer **voice-recognition software** converts recognizable voice input into computer data and presents it to the word processor as text.

Impact of Word Processing The use of word processing has resulted in improved document accuracy and a decrease in the time needed to produce documents. Document originators are no longer reluctant to make revisions when they know that the entire document does not have to be rekeyed.

Administrative professionals enjoy working with word processing applications because most mundane tasks are eliminated. Word processing software can, for example, establish margins and tabs, paginate, assemble a table of contents, and tabulate endnotes and footnotes. Word 2010 software converts typed lists of items seamlessly into attractive graphic representations of the data using the SmartArt feature. One result might be a professional-looking organization chart showing the hierarchy of employees in an organization. Merging variable information such as names and addresses with form letters is known as **mail merge**, and is one of the most valuable word processing features that support the administrative assistant. The administrative professional can key and store the variables to be merged; the system can then produce hundreds of letters while the administrative professional is focused on another task.

Advanced word processing features allow administrative assistants to produce brochures, sales bulletins, and other documents with a variety of headings, columns, graphics, and designs to standards that come close to matching those of professional printing companies.

You will need to plan your work carefully in order to increase your productivity. Be sure to save what you have keyed. When you work with revisions, make sure that what is to be moved, deleted, added, or changed is clearly marked on the hard-copy draft. Make sure that if you saved the original data in two locations, you update both locations to avoid accidentally retrieving and using the unrevised data at a later date. You need to understand and use proofreaders' marks. The appendix illustrates the most commonly used proofreaders' marks.

Spreadsheets

Spreadsheet applications—simply called spreadsheets—are computer programs that enable you to create and manipulate the numbers in a spreadsheet electronically. In a spreadsheet application, each number occupies a "cell." You can define what type of number is in each cell and how different cells depend on one another. This defined relationship between cells is called a "formula" and the names of cells are called "labels."

Once you have defined the cells and the formulas for linking them together, you can enter your numbers. You can then modify your numbers to see how all the other related numbers change accordingly. This enables you to study various "what-if" scenarios. (See Figure 6-9.)

A simple example of a useful spreadsheet application is one that calculates loan payments for a car. You would define five cells:

1. total cost of the car
2. deposit
3. interest rate
4. term of the loan
5. monthly payment

Once you define how these five cells depend on one another, you could enter numbers and play with various possibilities. There are a number of spreadsheet applications available, Excel and Quattro Pro being the most popular. The more powerful spreadsheet applications provide graphic features that enable you to produce sophisticated charts and graphs from the data.

Desktop Publishing

Desktop publishing is the process of using your PC to develop and print professional-looking literature, a task that was once the exclusive domain of professional printers. Some desktop publishing can be achieved by using word processing applications, but the special visual and printing features of this application software allow you to develop a more professional look for your design.

Desktop publishing is best done with a PC, special desktop publishing software (Microsoft Publisher or Adobe Illustrator, for example), and a high-quality printer. With this combination, you can combine text and graphics to produce documents such as newsletters, brochures, books, and graphic advertisements (see Figure 6-10).

Desktop publishing software is an excellent tool for the professional administrative assistant to create visual communications for the office. However, training on this software is invariably required for optimal use.

Importance of Learning Desktop Publishing

Mastering the skill of desktop publishing benefits the administrative assistant in a number of significant ways.

Figure 6-9 An active spreadsheet.

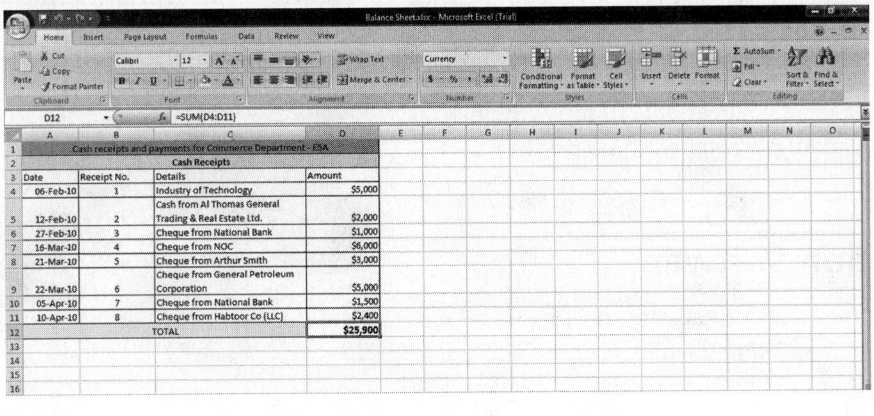

Figure 6-10 An administrative assistant uses technology and graphics software to produce a publication.

The following list states some of these benefits:

1. DTP allows the user to exercise creative skills. A great deal of personal satisfaction is derived in this way. DTP brings enjoyment to what might have been a mundane task.

2. DTP increases the effectiveness of the document. The professional appearance will attract attention and increase credibility.

3. Illustrations and charts can be added to documents without difficulty. These deliver the message more clearly than words alone.

4. The turnaround time is shorter when documents are produced in-house. Before desktop publishing, professional-looking documents could only be produced by sending the project out to a typesetter.

5. Professional documents can be prepared at lower cost when the administrative assistant can produce them in-house.

6. Students who master the art of desktop publishing will have a competitive edge when applying for administrative assistant positions. Desktop publishing is a highly respected skill, and one that will impress prospective employers.

7. Administrative assistants who are adept at desktop publishing have greater career opportunities. Employers seek administrative assistants who have diverse software training.

Presentation Software

Oral or written presentations accompanied by visual representation of information in the form of charts and graphs are more quickly and easily absorbed and understood than when presented in written or verbal form only. Augmenting a speech or an oral presentation with graphics and charts created using **electronic presentation software** is now considered routine practice in the workplace. You, as the administrative assistant, will likely be required to convert an outline of your manager's speech into an electronic format using presentation software such as Microsoft PowerPoint. The software is used to prepare an electronic slideshow of the main points of a speech and incorporate graphics, illustrations, and graphs to enhance the audience's understanding of the material (see Figure 6-11). Animation, music, and sound effects, as well as video clips, can be added to the presentation for additional emphasis.

Integrating Application Software

As an administrative assistant, you will be expected to create spreadsheets using spreadsheet software, to create business documents using word processing software, and to create electronic presentations using electronic presentation software. But, more than that, you will also be expected to have expertise in **integrating application software**, that is, connecting data created in one software program (e.g., Excel) with another (e.g., PowerPoint) in its original form. For example, you might be asked to create a spreadsheet in Microsoft Excel that shows estimated quarterly sales profits for the year. You might then be required to create an electronic presentation that would include a slide containing that spreadsheet in its Excel form. This can be done by either embedding or linking (hyperlinking) the original spreadsheet to the presentation. When there is a hyperlink created between the spreadsheet and the electronic presentation, if the values in the original spreadsheet cells are changed, they will be updated automatically in the electronic presentation when it is next activated. This

Figure 6-11 Electronic presentation software enhances oral presentation.

automated feature can save valuable time, and being skilled in using those advanced software features will increase your value to the organization.

Increasing Your Productivity

When you enter the job market, you will possess skills in keying and word processing; and you will be familiar with application programs for spreadsheets, electronic presentations, and desktop publishing. You may also have skills in information management, project management, and accounting applications. Whatever your set of job entry skills, many opportunities to learn more on the job will be available to you. Be receptive to the opportunities and challenges that come your way. Accept change readily.

Learn new computer applications. Develop a plan for improving and maintaining your technical skills. Take advantage of in-house training sessions. Study manuals, read technical magazines, and attend night classes. Continually search for ways that the computer can help you perform your job.

The speed with which the computer handles information will enable you to be more productive. Master the flow of information in and out of your office. Plan your work carefully; set priorities. Use spare time to think, to listen to customers' needs, to communicate, to solve problems, and to be creative.

Self-Check

1. What is one of the most important impacts of word processing software on the business office?
2. List two desktop publishing software programs.
3. How is electronic presentation software used? What is the benefit to the audience over strictly written or oral presentations?
4. Give an example of how integrating two different application software programs might benefit a business.

TELEPHONE TECHNOLOGY

Most contemporary businesses are dependent on their ability to communicate with the outside world. The same businesses face a myriad of choices from competing telephone companies since the Canadian Radio-television and Telecommunications Commission (CRTC) permitted competition, but the decision is an important one to ensure the culture and nature of the business are properly complemented.

Telecommunications is a term used to describe sending information over a distance. This can include not only telephone communications, but also fax transmissions, radio, and television.

Advances in technology have brought about significant changes in telecommunications. For instance, until recently all telephone systems worked by sending an analogue signal. Today, almost all telephone systems are digital. The advantage of digital service is that it doesn't require wires dedicated for use on your phone system. It usually utilizes the internet to send voice signals. Voice over Internet Protocol, or VoIP, enables people to make voice and video calls over an internet connection. VoIP is sometimes referred to as IP Telephony, or internet protocol telephone system. This type of service can greatly reduce the cost of calls, especially international calls, since VoIP not only provides inexpensive call rates but also allows users on the same network to make free calls. To set up and use VoIP communications one must have an internet connection and VoIP-provider software.

Interconnect Equipment

Interconnect equipment is the term used to refer to telephone equipment that organizations purchase or lease from suppliers other than the telephone companies. The manufacturers of telephone interconnect equipment have placed new switchboards and other equipment with hundreds of features on the market.

Most of the new features of modern telephone systems are controlled at the central office (previously known as the *telephone exchange*), usually owned by the local telephone company. These modern (electronic) digital exchanges replaced old mechanical equipment at the central office and are program-controlled, offering users a variety of services. These are collectively known as **call management services** and include features such as:

- displaying the caller's number on your telephone
- forwarding your call to another number when you are busy or away from your desk
- having the telephone system monitor a busy number and inform you when that number becomes free

Other call management features can enhance your telephone effectiveness:

- A special button feature will allow the administrative assistant to speed-dial a predefined number.
- A previously dialled number may be redialled by pressing a single designated key.
- A list of names and/or numbers may be stored in the electronic memory of most contemporary telephones for convenient recall and dialling.

Figure 6-12 A lightweight headset containing a miniaturized mouthpiece allows the administrative assistant to communicate with hands free.

Figure 6-13 Telephone with advanced features including digital display.

With the electronic memory feature, frequently used numbers may be recorded and reused for dialling automatically and accurately.

Many more telephone features are gaining popularity as enhancements to productivity: bilingual displays, built-in cameras, and supplemental features such as lightweight headsets that enable the user to work hands-free (see Figure 6-12). Some additional features available include bilingual alphanumeric displays (see Figure 6-13), game play, and the provision to check email through the telephone set.

When the personal touch is not necessary, companies often use Interactive Voice Response (IVR). When the electronic voice answers a call, it may instruct you to press a dial pad button (such as # or *) or a certain digit sequence to reach the specific person with whom you wish to speak. After a code or digit has been pressed, a recorded voice message of the party you are calling may be heard. It might request that you leave a message. A person wishing to hear the messages received by the electronic system can telephone from a remote location, receive the messages electronically, and dictate a response, which the electronic system can deliver anywhere, anytime.

We make no attempt here to discuss all the new features that have been introduced by the interconnect industry; instead, we discuss the basic concepts of office telephone systems and telephone equipment. If you are using interconnect equipment, study the operator's manual to learn how to operate the special features.

Common Telephone Equipment

Touch-Tone Telephones Most regular telephones are touch-tone activated. The touch-tone telephone provides both regular telephone service and tone transmission of data through a 12-button keypad. Ten buttons represent the numbers 0 through 9 and the alphabet. The other two buttons, showing the # and the * symbols, generate unique tones that may be connected to special telephone company services. An example of such a service is *repeat dial*, which will redial the last number used.

The touch-tone telephone provides tone transmissions of data, which can be received and converted by the central office. In this way, you communicate with the central office and access the call management services mentioned earlier in the section "Interconnect Equipment."

Key Telephones Key telephones, or key-sets, provide flexibility in making and receiving multiple calls simultaneously. Key-sets are often used in smaller office environments as small office telephone exchanges. Key-sets have multiple buttons, and the buttons on one phone set are the same as those on all the other sets in an office. A number of calls from both inside and outside the office may be made and/or received simultaneously.

The basic key telephone is a regular telephone with push-button keys corresponding to the number of telephone lines terminating in the telephone. The push buttons flash on and off to indicate incoming calls on the lines. To answer a call, push the key that is flashing and lift the receiver. If a second call comes in while the first is in progress, suspend the conversation properly, push the hold button, then push the flashing key of the incoming call and answer the call. To suspend this call and get back to the first call, push the hold button again, and then push the key of the first incoming call. When a push-button key glows steadily, it indicates that the line is in use.

Wireless Telephones
Wireless telephone service (commonly called mobile phone service) provides mobile communication. This telephone network uses radio waves rather than telephone wires to transmit messages. However, mobile telephone users may communicate with conventional telephone users, since wireless systems interconnect with local and long-distance telephone networks.

Mobile phone users can take advantage of most of the features offered to regular telephone users, including voice mail. Technology has enabled owners to use cell phones as remote internet terminals, digital cameras, and global positioning system (GPS) receivers. (See earlier section on "Smartphones" for more detail.)

For those office professionals and management who travel beyond North America, a global wireless telephone may provide the reach and direct access required for calling back to the office. Currently, the Iridium wireless telephone will allow its users to call from anywhere in the world provided the telephone signal has a direct line of sight to a satellite. From the satellite, the signal is relayed from satellite to satellite to reach its destination.

Telephone Messages

Organizations often make arrangements for the telephone to be answered after regular business hours or when it is inconvenient for employees to answer the telephone. Commonly used systems are automatic recording machines, answering services, and voice mail.

Automatic Recording Machines
With a telephone answering machine, a user can turn on a recorded message at the end of the business day. The message may tell callers when the office will be open and invite the callers to leave their number or a message. Sometimes, customers are encouraged to place orders at night by leaving their requests on the automatic recording machine.

Answering Services
A telephone answering service is a switchboard attended by an operator who answers subscribers' telephones at designated hours. The operator takes messages, records numbers to be called, and judges whether or not to reach the subscriber during after-business hours. For example, the telephones of many doctors are answered after regular hours by telephone answering services.

If you work for a manager whose telephone is answered when nobody is in the office, one of your early-morning tasks may be to listen to the automatic recording machine and transcribe the messages or to call a telephone answering service for messages.

Voice Mail
Voice mail (VM) is by far the most popular form of telephone messaging system in use today. In fact, it's essential. From the technological point of view, VM is a computer-based system that processes incoming and outgoing telephone calls by converting speech patterns into digital data, which are then stored and manipulated in the computer.

Hardware for VM systems may be independently purchased and programmed for the organization that intends to use it. Alternatively, the local telephone service provider may provide the service, keeping all hardware-related equipment on their premises.

Self-Check
1. What is interconnect equipment?
2. Give three examples of call management services.
3. How/when are the two symbol buttons on a touch-tone telephone used?
4. How does a key telephone differ from a regular telephone?
5. Can you use a wireless telephone to call your office via long distance?
6. How is an automatic recording machine different from an answering service?

THE INTERNET

The most popular means of communicating and researching information is the internet. The internet is a public global communications network that enables people to exchange information through a computer.

Internet Networking

In its simplest form, the internet is a global network of computer-based information available to anyone with a computer, a modem, and a subscription to an Internet Service Provider (ISP). More accurately, the internet is a network of networks with international telecommunications facilities connecting them.

The telecommunications data network that links the internet together employs **routers**, devices that route information from one network to another. Routers allow independent networks to function as a large **virtual network** so that users of any network can reach users of any other.

While there are many private commercial computer networks, the internet is the largest collection of networks in the world.

Unlike traditional voice or data networks, there is no charge for the long-distance component of the internet.

There is also no charge for exchanging information on the internet. However, internet providers will charge users a fee for the local connection to the internet.

Uses for the Internet

What can you do with the internet? Some of the main basic activities that people participate in on the internet are as follows:

1. Sending and receiving email, or electronic text, that can be addressed to another internet user anywhere on the global network.

2. Transferring data files. Data file transfers allow internet users to access remote computers and retrieve programs or text.

3. Joining newsgroups. A newsgroup is a collection of users who exchange news and debate issues of interest.

4. Joining social networking services. Wikipedia defines a social network service as one that "focuses on building online communities of people who share interests and activities, or who are interested in exploring the interests and activities of others." Users of online social networks such as Facebook interact through various media including email and instant messaging. Sharing of photographs and videos, as well as posting messages on other users' pages, are popular activities. Social networks can be used as a marketing tool for business. Personal use of social networks is often frowned upon in the workplace.

5. Performing remote computing. Those programmers and scientists who need the power of remote computers, or those who need to tap into large information databases, do remote computing.

6. Researching topics of interest. Students and business professionals alike research topics of interest. Clearly, the internet supplements more familiar resources, such as books and periodicals.

7. E-commerce. These activities focus on buying and selling products on the internet.

Collectively, these seven basic activities provide a vast and rich resource for the administrative assistant. Office productivity is directly influenced by such activities as email, research, information feeds, the delivery of large document files, and office commerce. The resulting influence of the internet has enabled greater office productivity.

In addition to the seven basic internet activities already discussed, the following activities are also popular in the business world:

Webcasting (or Netcasting) Webcasting (or netcasting) is broadcasting live or recorded audio and/or video transmissions via computer. For example, a business might record a videotape of a news release to be aired as a webcast at a designated time simultaneously on several media websites. Similarly, your local TV channel will likely record, and make accessible via the internet, webcasts of its news broadcasts. This will enable the public to "watch the news" at their convenience.

Web Conferencing Using web conferencing software, employees can take part in real-time conferencing via the internet from their own computers, much as they would take part in teleconferencing via their own office telephones. In some instances, access to the conference is gained using downloaded application software, either free or purchased through a vendor. See Chapter 7 for more information.

WHAT ARE REPROGRAPHICS?

The term **reprographics** refers to reproduction processes from the highest-quality **offset printing** to the simplest photocopying. The reprographics industry produces a vast array of high-tech products; however, the reprographics equipment most often used by administrative assistants is a copier. For this reason, the following discussion will focus on copiers only.

Copiers

In its simplest form, a copier is used to reproduce exact copies of original documents. At the other end of the spectrum, a copier will:

■ act as a fully active unit in the office network so it can receive documents and instructions directly from all office computers

■ act as a multifunctional device permitting scanning and faxing of documents through the office network

■ format a document from a computer file so the end product is in book format with adjusted headers, footers, margins, and page numbers

■ print in colour so well that the copy looks just like the original

■ print and bind the document so it has the professional appearance of a brochure or booklet

■ **duplex** the document

■ staple and hole-punch the papers

■ enlarge or decrease the size of the document

■ use a variety of sizes, weights, and qualities of paper

And the list goes on. Copiers are classified as low-, mid-, and high-volume machines. The differences between categories are evident in the following discussion.

Personal Low-Volume Copiers Low-volume copying machines, called **convenience copiers** or personal copiers, are mostly used in home offices, small businesses, or in decentralized areas to save the user travel time. These compact copiers have numerous features. Low-volume copiers can:

- be networked into the office system for two to four users
- receive documents and instructions directly from computers
- print in good-quality colour
- reduce and enlarge documents
- accommodate a variety of paper sizes
- automatically feed documents
- print 15–25 pages per minute

Low-volume copiers used in small businesses are often multifunctional units that include any of the following features: fax, copier, printer, and/or scanner (see Figure 6-14).

Mid-Volume Copiers Mid-volume copiers have all the features of the low-volume copiers, along with some additional features. Most mid-volume copiers are appropriate for 5 to 20 users and can:

- operate through touch control screens
- accommodate more paper sizes and weights
- store multiple instructions
- print in high-quality colour
- sort and stack multiple copies

Figure 6-14 A combination fax, copier, and scanner.

Figure 6-15 High-volume copier.

- staple and hole-punch documents
- bind documents into book-style covers
- centre an image on the paper
- print 36–55 pages per minute

High-Volume Copiers With all that low- and mid-volume copiers can do, is there more that high-volume copiers can handle? High-volume copiers (see Figure 6-15) are appropriate for 20 or more users and can:

- produce documents in book format with adjusted headers, footers, margins, and page numbers
- hold large supplies of paper
- sort at faster speeds
- insert tabs and coversheets where programmed to do so
- print in colour with even better quality
- produce 95–105 pages per minute

How to Select a Copier Given all the available features, how do you select the right office copier for your office needs? To begin, determine your current and future needs.

Collecting input from the people who use the office copier would be a good way to find out the needs of the office.

To find the office copier needs:

1. Form a group of people who use the office copier.

2. Together, create a survey that will solicit information about current and future copier needs.

3. Give the survey to all people who use the copier.

4. Collect the surveys and collate the data.

Refer to Figure 6-16 for a sample survey. Your group should create your own survey to suit your office and co-workers.

Find the Right Vendor Once you know your requirements, it's time to talk to the right vendor in order to find the right product.

1. Ask other people who have recently purchased or leased copiers what vendor they recommend.

2. Research products and vendors through the internet, newspapers, et cetera, to determine what products and vendors appeal to you.

3. Contact vendors and set up appointments to view their products.

4. During appointments, share the results of your survey with the sales representatives.

Figure 6-16 Sample survey to determine copier needs.

Copier Needs
Interoffice Survey

Instructions: In order to determine our office needs for a new copier, we are soliciting your input. Would you please answer the following questions by checking the appropriate lines. Then return the completed survey to Narges Abdalla's office mailbox no later than August 10. Your cooperation and input are greatly appreciated. If you have any questions, please contact Narges at extension 444.

1. **How many copies do you make on an average week? Check only one response.**

    _____ 100 to 500   _____ 1000 to 2000
    _____ 500 to 1000   _____ Over 2000

2. **What special paper requirements do you have? Check all that apply.**

    _____ Transparencies
    _____ Card stock
    _____ Photo stock
    _____ Other (Please specify paper. _____)

3. **What paper sizes do you use? Check all that apply.**

    _____ Letter size
    _____ Legal size
    _____ Other (Please identify size. _____)

4. **Where do your copied documents go? Check only one response.**

    _____ Internal use   _____ External use
    _____ Both internal and external use

5. **Which of the following features do you require? Check all that apply.**

    _____ Control from the office network
    _____ Printing colour   _____ Scanning documents
    _____ Binding   _____ Printing book format
    _____ Storing instructions   _____ Duplexing
    _____ Enlarging/reducing sizes   _____ Stapling
    _____ Other (Please specify feature. _____)

5. Keep in mind that it is the sales representative's job to help you solve your problem—the problem of finding the right copier for your office.

6. Get more than just a sales demonstration. Try the equipment yourself.

Find the Right Service When you think you have found the right equipment, you're not finished. The company must be prepared to provide the best service too. What should you look for in service?

■ The machine should have a warranty that covers all parts and labour for at least one full year.

■ There must be a service agreement that includes routine maintenance calls as well as on-call emergency service with a quick turnaround time. It's acceptable to wait four hours for the repairperson to arrive, but it's not acceptable to wait four days. All parts should be available within 24 hours.

Find the Right Price Prices will vary depending on the company, the product, and whether you are planning to purchase or lease the equipment. Shop around for the best product, service agreement, and price.

Self-Check

1. What is a multifunctional device?
2. Differentiate between low-volume, medium-volume, and high-volume copiers.

QUESTIONS FOR STUDY AND REVIEW

1. What are the four basic functions of a computer?
2. Which input devices are widely used in offices?
3. Name two types of removable storage.
4. Which type of computer-based storage has the greatest capacity?
5. Define bit, byte, character, and terabyte.
6. Give three examples of application software.
7. Why has the computer placed such a premium on accuracy?
8. What are source documents? Why should they be checked for accuracy and completeness?
9. What advantage does word processing provide document originators?
10. State two reasons why VoIP or IP Telephony could be a good choice for business.
11. How would you describe the internet in terms of networking computers?
12. Consider yourself an administrative assistant who is seeking employment. How will the acquired skill of desktop publishing benefit you?
13. What basic hardware is required to do desktop publishing?
14. What is the administrative assistant's role in desktop publishing?
15. State two things you would check if you were troubleshooting a computer that would not turn on.
16. What is meant by the term *reprographics*?
17. List steps to take in determining the copier needs of an office.
18. List four questions that might appear on a survey designed to determine the copying needs of an office.
19. What are four important steps in selecting the correct vendor when purchasing or leasing a copier?
20. Discuss why the service agreement is so important when selecting the right equipment vendor.
21. State two factors you should look for in a service agreement.

EVERYDAY ETHICS

Long-Distance Code

Tessa has been employed as an administrative assistant for the last three years with a small but growing manufacturing company. About six months ago business was expanded beyond Canada. As overseas business has increased so has the need to make a significant amount of long-distance phone calls to coordinate orders and deliveries. Tessa was given a special authorization code to key into the phone system whenever she makes a long-distance call. When employees use the long-distance codes the company receives a reduction in the actual cost for the call. In the last few weeks Tessa has started using her code for some personal long-distance calls before or after her shift. Tessa has mentioned that she is using the company code to make some personal calls, and she doesn't believe she is doing anything wrong because she is not making the calls on company time.

- Do you see anything fundamentally wrong with her reasoning?
- What might be unprofessional about Tessa's attitude?

Problem Solving

1. You are administrative assistant to the general sales manager in an organization that has four sales regions. You are responsible for seeing that the appliances requested by the regions are shipped promptly from the manufacturing plants. You operate a PC that is connected online to the offices of the sales regions and the manufacturing plants. Recently the regions have been receiving the correct number of the appliances ordered, but the colours have not been the ones that were requested. You analyze the input data that you have used for the past month. What should you look for in your analysis? What recommendations could you make to improve your accuracy?

2. You are teaching an assistant to input data. This week she has entered the input for all the orders. Every Friday the main computer prints a summary of all the orders for the week. This Friday the computer did not print the summary of your orders for the week. What do you do now to obtain a summary? What else should you do?

3. The day started well. Everyone in the office was able to start their computers, find their work, and continue from yesterday. Then it happened. At about 11 a.m., all PCs in the accounting department stopped communicating with other departments. Interestingly, the order entry group and the administrative assistants could still communicate both with the internet and with each other. Luckily, each group was able to continue using their application software. Mr. Wilson heard about the situation and asked you to phone the appropriate technical support to resolve the issue. Would you call the local communications provider or the computer support people? Why?

Special Reports

1. Research online which operating systems are currently being used with three tablet computers. Report what you have learned to the class

2. Compare the features of two smartphones and identify which one you would recommend using. Prepare a table for your instructor showing your comparisons. .

3. As a result of your local office expansion from 15 to 28 permanent employees, you are tasked with the research and evaluation of an appropriate telephone exchange system to support the expanded staff. Develop a brief report comparing features and benefits of the various systems described in this chapter. Conclude your report with a recommendation.

4. Interview an administrative assistant and ask the following questions about the office copier(s) he or she uses:
   a. Is your office copier connected into the office network?
   b. Would you consider the copier(s) to be small-, mid-, or high-volume?
   c. Does your copier print in colour? If so, what printing restrictions, if any, has management placed on people using the colour cartridge?
   d. What features are used most often?
   e. What are the most sophisticated features the copier(s) performs?
   f. Report your findings to your instructor.

PRODUCTION CHALLENGES

6-A Preparing Final Draft of Material on Copier/Printer Project

Supplies needed:

- *Draft on Online Copier/Printer project, Form 6-A, pages 389 to 390*
- *Common Proofreaders' Marks, Appendix, page 453*

George Andrews is a procurement officer for Millennium Appliances and is frustrated by the indecision over a new online copier/printer purchase plan that seems to have stalled. George has drafted a memorandum to the CEO in an attempt to get the stalled project moving again. Form 6-A is a draft of what he has written, including notations that he made in the margins of the draft copy. Proofread the draft memorandum and rekey the corrected copy. Perform this job in three steps:

1. Using (the draft copy) Form 6-A on page 389, the Common Proofreaders' Marks appendix on page 453, and your pen, carefully mark all the edits that George has indicated in the margins of Form 6-A before you begin to key.

2. Using your edited copy, key the complete document in its edited form.

3. Print one copy of your final document. Give your instructor the printed copy of your final document as well as Form 6-A with the penned edits.

6-B Inserting Proofreaders' Marks

Supplies needed:

- *Memorandum about the copier/printer project, Form 6-B, page 393*
- *Common Proofreaders' Marks, Appendix, page 453*

Using the proofreaders' marks in the appendix, mark the memorandum on Form 6-B so that it is ready for processing. Check your copy to be sure that you have marked all the corrections needed. Next, key the memo in final form.

Weblinks

Microsoft Office Tools
www.office.microsoft.com
This site provides the latest downloads, how-to articles, and more.

Desktop Publishing Reviews
www.consumersearch.com/desktop-publishing-software
This site reviews various desktop publishing software, including programs such as Microsoft Publisher and Adobe InDesign CS2.

PC Webopedia
http://webopedia.internet.com
This online dictionary and search engine for computer and internet technology includes, among other things, a text messaging abbreviations listing.

PC Magazine
www.pcmag.com
This site allows users to access technological product guides, tips, news, product reviews, and test drives.

Hello Direct
http://telecom.hellodirect.com
This site presents product reviews, including evaluations and comparisons, of a selection of current office telecommunications equipment. Information on Bluetooth wireless technology is also available here.

Computer Hope
http://www.computerhope.com/basic.htm
This site provides information on how to troubleshoot common computer issues.

The Phone Lady
www.thephonelady.ca
This site provides articles and tips on telephone management as well as techniques for marketing business effectively using telecommunications.

Chapter 7
Web-Based Tools and Security

Learning Outcomes

After completion of this chapter, the student will be able to:

1 Identify common methods and equipment required for internet connectivity.

2 Contrast uses of intranets and extranets.

3 Describe search engines and their intended use.

4 Discuss the difference between Web 1.0 and Web 2.0.

5 Identify Web 2.0 tools.

6 Explain webcasting, podcasting, and web conferencing.

7 Suggest methods for conducting an effective webinar.

8 Recognize organizational concerns regarding the use of Web 2.0 tools.

9 Understand and identify potential internet security threats.

10 Discuss the importance of internet security and the consequences of having no security.

11 Recognize strategies to combat internet security issues and to keep data secure.

The phenomenal success of the internet continues to stir a great deal of discussion. Business users want the internet to be financially viable, academics want to take advantage of the intellectual tools it offers, and each level of government has an interest in regulating it. Most parties agree, however, that the internet offers a wealth of opportunity. The federal governments of Canada and the United States have recognized the value of the internet in the delivery of education and social programs and in regional communication. Both governments have committed themselves, financially and otherwise, to making the technological advancements necessary to keep pace with the mass transfer of data.

In this changing environment, the office professional must also keep pace with the benefits and opportunities that the internet offers. This chapter provides an overview of basic internet functions as well as some of the more advanced tools that are available on the web today. The chapter also discusses steps you can take to safeguard your company's internet security.

GETTING CONNECTED
Joining the Internet

The internet is an enormous collection of computer networks that allows millions of computers to connect on a global scale. The **World Wide Web** (www) provides the medium necessary to access information on the internet. To retrieve and present information, individuals and organizations often use a specialized application software called a web browser. Firefox, Safari, and Internet Explorer are examples of just some of the browsers available.

As internet technology evolves, so does our need for efficient and fast internet connections. The need for speed has driven changes for consumers and businesses alike in terms of how—and how fast—we can connect to the internet.

To join the internet, you need to first start with a computer, tablet, personal digital assistant (PDA) or

smartphone, and an internet service provider (ISP). Your ISP will offer a variety of ways to connect, each with varying speed and cost.

Dial-up or Analogue

In a dial-up connection, data is sent over an analogue, public telephone network. This type of connection is economical but slow. A **modem** is connected to a computer and the modem is connected to a normal telephone line. Then the modem converts the analogue signal to a digital one, which is the typical form for computer data communication. With this type of service, the user must dial in to a telephone number provided by the ISP in order to connect. The downside of dial-up is that it can tie up the user's telephone line when he or she is online. However, it remains a viable option in locations where high-speed internet connectivity is unavailable.

Digital Subscriber Line

The connection provided by a **digital subscriber line (DSL)** is always on, meaning there is no need to dial in to a telephone number as with analogue access. This service uses a two-wire copper telephone line that transmits a digital signal. The user can still access the telephone line to make phone calls because DSL uses specialized hardware that does not interfere with voice audio frequency.

DSL is up to 50 times faster than dial-up. It is known as a broadband or high-speed connection, because it has high bandwidth (the ability to carry data). In addition to offering a high-speed connection, one of the advantages of DSL is that several users can access the internet at the same time without impacting the bandwidth.

Cable

By using a cable modem a user can access broadband internet service over TV lines. A coaxial cable is connected to the computer's modem, which enables data transmission. This is another type of connection that is always on. Separate TV channels are reserved by the service provider for uploading and downloading data.

A disadvantage to this type of access is that bandwidth may be limited, depending on the number of users accessing the service at the same time. That is, the more people accessing the service at the same time the slower will be the data transmission speed.

Fibre Optic Cable Fibre optic cable is a technology that uses glass (or plastic) threads (fibres) to transmit data. A fibre optic cable consists of a bundle of glass threads, each of which is capable of transmitting messages modulated onto light waves. Fibre optic cables have a much greater bandwidth than metal cables or DSL; this means that they can carry more data than a standard metal cable. In addition, telephone companies are steadily replacing traditional telephone lines with fibre optic cables, clearly because of the advantages fibre offers over metal cables.

Satellite A satellite is an object that orbits the earth transmitting a two-way digital signal to satellite dishes located on earth. A satellite connection is another form of broadband (high-speed) connection. It is usually 10 times faster than a typical modem but not as fast as DSL or cable. Satellite offers an option for high-speed internet access in locations where DSL and cable may not be available.

Wireless Wireless is another form of broadband connectivity. Instead of using a cable or a telephone line to connect to the internet a wireless connection uses radio frequency. Users will remain consistently connected providing they stay within the prescribed network coverage range. Of course, the greatest benefit of wireless is the mobility it provides. Users can move about from location to location within the organization and access many resources connected to the network without needing to plug in.

Wireless fidelity (Wi-Fi) is a wireless network set up for public access. In places like a library, airport, or even a coffee shop you may find a connection for your mobile device. A **hotspot** is a site that provides a wireless local area network through the use of a router connected to a link to an ISP. Recently, some concerns have been raised about possible health risks associated with this type of technology, prompting some to discontinue its use.

Intranets

Organizations sometimes set up a private computer network to share proprietary websites, information, and resources. Such a network is known as an intranet. By using an intranet, a company can ensure that internal communication

and collaboration access are restricted to only those within the organization. In many cases, intranets are protected from unauthorized external access by means of a network firewall (see "Internet Security" section). An intranet's websites look and act just like other websites, but the firewall surrounding an intranet fends off unauthorized access.

Extranets

An extranet provides various levels of accessibility to outsiders. Commonly, a user can access an extranet only if he or she has a valid username and password. Sometimes an organization will determine which components of the extranet a user can view, based on his or her identity. An organization may also set up an extranet to communicate with suppliers and customers alike.

Search Engines

A search engine is a program that enables the user to search online for information. By entering key words or phrases, users can generate real-time results, including online databases, documents, and web pages. There are many search engines available, and it is important to note that results generated by one search engine may not be the same as another one. Here is a list of some available search engines:

- Google
- Bing
- Yahoo!
- AOL
- Dogpile

Self-Check

1. List two ways you can get connected to the internet.
2. State one benefit of an intranet.
3. What is a hotspot?

WEB TOOLS

Given the popularity and globalization of the internet, it is essential that the administrative assistant understand web tools. According to *Office of the Future: 2020*, a study conducted by OfficeTeam, an administrative assistant should demonstrate a "willingness to be an early adopter of new devices, researching the best technology solutions for an organization and training teams how to use them" (http://www.officeofthefuture2020.com/portal/site/oof-us/menuitem.c836330f3f1143b4adbd6f5ca48fbfa0/).

Web 2.0

When the web was first introduced it was very linear. That is, a webmaster would create a web page and the viewer would visit the site and read the information, and very little interaction was possible. Those early days of the internet are often referred to as Web 1.0.

Today, we just don't use the web; we connect with it: it is engaging, interactive, and social. All this integration is referred to as Web 2.0. Web tools (see Figure 7-1) that have enabled this dynamic assimilation include the following:

Blog A **blog** is a term that is short for weblog. A blog can best be described as a journal available on the web. It is updated on a regular basis by the person or organization responsible for it. A business blog is the perfect resource to give a company an official and authoritative voice on the web. Moreover, it can give customers or clients a way to discover more about what a business offers.

Wiki A **wiki** is a collaborative website that allows its users to add, modify, or delete its content via a web browser. Designed as a simple-to-use cooperative tool, wikis have risen through the ranks of content management systems. Businesses have found that wikis are a perfect tool for groups to share information (for example, human resource policies) with larger groups within the organization. Companies may also use a wiki to share or answer frequently asked questions (FAQs) raised by their internal and external customers.

Social Media **Social media** is a general term used to describe web-based tools that encourage exchange of information by users. Some examples of social media sites include YouTube, Twitter, Flickr, and Facebook. What distinguishes social media sites from ordinary websites is that they are based on user-generated content (UGC). Businesses have discovered social media can provide significant opportunities to showcase services, events, and community initiatives. It is also worth noting that in recent years there has been a tremendous shift in how employers view employee use of social media. Although previously it was discouraged, it is now strongly encouraged.

Figure 7-1 Web 2.0 tools.

Live Meeting Depending on the system the office has in place, this tool can be used to conduct meetings with a facilitator who has the ability either to share his own desktop image or to have attendees share theirs. This tool is great for hosting a meeting across multiple sites and locations, and it is often used as a virtual training tool.

SharePoint Developed by Microsoft, SharePoint is an online database where documents can be stored and then shared throughout an organization. For instance, administrative assistants from multiple locations may need to work together on an annual budget for the management teams they support. Instead of each individual administrative assistant having his or her own copy, and tasking someone with rounding them all up and combining them each month, SharePoint allows for one report to be updated by many individuals while maintaining the report in one location. This also simplifies the process and allows each user to see progress as it is made.

Slide Share SlideShare is an online presentation management system. Users can upload a slideshow presentation to be viewed publicly or privately depending on preference. Users can search topics of interest and download or remix slide presentations. SlideShare and similar tools promote collaboration and idea sharing with a wider audience.

Quick Response (QR) Code QR Code is software that allows camera-equipped mobile devices to read and scan special barcodes. A user can quickly scan the barcode, and the information on the barcode is then automatically entered into his/her device (see Figure 7.2). Some companies have placed a QR code on promotional t-shirts using the technology as a marketing tool to promote their corporate image.

Web Conferencing

Web conferencing is, as its name suggests, a way of conducting a conference online. Participants gain access to the conference from their own computers, from the comfort of their own offices. Web conferencing is ideal for small collaborative groups or meetings where the participants must not only hear or view a presentation but be able to communicate with each other.

To use this online meeting tool, participants enter a given URL (website address) at a specified time. They can then view the presentation online and also take part in the conference. Audio is captured and transmitted through users' phone lines or Voice over Internet Protocol (VoIP). Depending on the technical resources available, participants may be able to take part in a question-and-answer session using either an ordinary telephone or computer audio software. In some circumstances, webcams are used for two-way video hook-up during a web conference.

Figure 7-2 Quick Response Code.

In some cases, a web conference platform also requires users to download proprietary software before accessing the presentation and/or sharing content.

Webcasting

A webcast is a media file distributed over the internet using streaming media technology to distribute a single content source simultaneously to many listeners/viewers. Often a webcast has accompanying PowerPoint slides. A webcast may either be distributed live or on demand.

Essentially, webcasting is "broadcasting" over the internet. Ideal for engaging larger online audiences, webcasting is a "one-to-many" form of communication, in which one speaker or panel of speakers presents to many attendees. Since it is broadcast over the internet, it can accommodate thousands of viewers simultaneously.

Webcasts are browser-based and require no additional software download. Because audio is integrated into the platform, no phone line is needed. A user can listen to the presentation through speakers or headphones.

Typically, a webcast is a professionally produced program in itself, or it might involve coverage of a live event, streamed with almost any combination of interactive features, from question-and-answer tools to surveys, polls, and social media sharing.

Podcasting

A podcast involves transmission of media files via the internet; the files are then synced or downloaded to an MP3 player, handheld computer, laptop, or desktop computer for listening at the user's convenience. The files are usually received by subscribing to what is called a podcast feed. The key benefit of podcasts is that the files are portable.

Webinar

A webinar is a seminar delivered over the web, and it is a strategic application often used for marketing and training. To transmit the webinar, either a webcast or web conference platform is used. Webinars typically include interactive features to allow viewers to submit questions to speakers and participate in polls. Other tools relied on in conducting webinars include registration pages to capture audience information, reminder emails to encourage good attendance, source-tracking URLs to monitor how users are finding the program, and departure surveys to collect immediate feedback from attendees. If your organization is planning a webinar, all of these features should be integrated into any webcast or web conference platform you use. In addition, consider the following tips for hosting a successful webinar:

- Send out reminders to your participants reminding them of the time and date of the presentation; this gives participants an opportunity to ask questions, such as how many other individuals will be taking part in the webinar.

- Set up and check in early. You may want to have your presenters online 10 to 15 minutes before the session begins to avoid any last-minute technical issues.

- Do a roll call to make sure all participants are able to connect.

- Once ready to begin review the agenda.

- During the webinar, ensure the conversation is kept on track; discussion can easily be hijacked if not controlled.

- Collect feedback.

- After the session, follow up. You may want to send thank-you emails or notes to speakers.

- Use feedback for planning future seminars.

Appropriate Use of Web 2.0

As wonderful as Web 2.0 tools are, consideration must be given to appropriate use of this technology within the context of a business environment. Employers have been prompted to develop new policies and procedures addressing concerns related to user security, privacy, and representation of corporate image. A useful model in this regard is the policy standard published in 2011 by the Government of Canada, *Guideline for External Use of Web 2.0* (available at http://www.tbs-sct.gc.ca/pol/doc-eng.aspx?id=24835&section=text). Companies need to have

employee-friendly policies governing the use of this technology, but they also need to maintain their security. Some questions companies have to consider include the following:

- How do we protect confidentiality and intellectual property?

- How do we protect our brand while promoting it?

- How do we avoid public relations disasters while still engaging our staff and customers?

Web Authoring Tools

A **web authoring tool** is a category of software enabling the user to develop or edit a website. In many organizations reliance on the administrative assistant to maintain a dynamic web presence is becoming routine. Consider some of the commonly used tools for developing and editing web pages:

- Adobe Dreamweaver®, a web design and editing program utilizing WYSIWYG (what you see is what you get)

- Web Studio®, web design software

- Adobe Photoshop®, a graphics editing program

Additional training may be required to effectively use these programs, but rest assured, most are user friendly.

---

pro-Link
Web 2.0 Lingo

With the explosion of Web 2.0, and especially social media, understanding some basic terminology will help you to get the most of this powerful tool. Here are some key terms:

- **Algorithm**—a set a formulas that allow programs like Facebook to develop content-sharing platforms
- **B2B**—Business to business
- **B2C**—Business to consumer
- **Hashtag**—a word or string of characters that starts with a number sign; usually used with Twitter
- **HootSuite**—a social media management system that helps businesses streamline campaigns across several social media sites
- **Mashup**—the use of two or more sources to create a new graphic, presentation, or audio or other media file
- **RSS (Real Simple Syndication) Feed**—also called web feed; a personal delivery system for news content from several places
- **Traffic**—the number of visitors to a website
- **Trend**—an indication of how many users are viewing the same article or link
- **Viral**—a term to describe a video made popular through internet sharing.

Self-Check

1. Provide two suggestions for conducting a success-ful webinar.
2. List two Web 2.0 tools.
3. What is a web authoring tool used for?

SECURITY ON THE INTERNET

Every day, new threats appear on the internet. An intruder who breaches your computer's security can discover every-thing you have done online, including websites you have visited and emails you have sent. If your company's com-puter security is compromised, unauthorized individuals might learn confidential information about your organ-ization. The consequences of a security breach include the cost of correcting the breach, client notification, network repairs, and lost revenue. It is essential, therefore, that you familiarize yourself with the various types of internet secur-ity risks, as well as measures you can take to protect yourself and your organization.

Security Risks

A risk all businesses and individuals take when using the internet is that unauthorized parties might access private or sensitive information. Following are some of the ways your computer's security might be jeopardized:

Computer Viruses Viruses are destructive programs written and designed to load and run undetected by users. Viruses can delete or corrupt files and programs, duplicate themselves, travel across networks and via email, and even destroy operating systems and shut down computers.

Worms and Trojan Horses Worms and Trojan horses are often inaccurately described as computer viruses, but they are in fact different in some important ways. A worm, unlike a virus, needs no human action; it can travel unassisted. For instance, a worm can send out messages to all the contacts in your computer email system. Likewise, a Trojan will first present itself on the computer as useful and helpful software. Once activated, however, it will do significant damage to your computer.

Hacking A hacker is a slang term referring to someone with an advanced understanding of computers and com-puter networks. Hacking allows the hacker to benefit by exposing weaknesses in a computer or computer network. Whether motivated by protest or profit, hacking can unleash significant havoc for a computer network, often corrupting or permanently destroying data.

Malware Short for malicious software, malware is soft-ware used or created by hackers to disrupt computer oper-ation, gather sensitive information, or gain access to private computer systems. Malware includes computer viruses, worms, Trojans, spyware, adware, and other malicious programs.

Phishing Phishing is the practice of fraudulently attempting to obtain secure information, such as a password, by masquerading as a trusted source. This is considered a method of potential identity theft. The scam often works by sending out an email that looks like an authentic request for information from a bank or credit card company, asking you to use a link or pop-up and enter confidential information.

Spam Spam is the use of electronic messaging systems to send unwelcome bulk messages. The most widely recog-nized form of spam is email spam. Many organizations are aware of the extensive influx of spam and have responded by investing in **spam filtering software**. This software is designed to detect or block unwanted messages from reach-ing a user's in-box.

Bluejacking The Bluejacker program was originally designed to share information, such as cell phone contacts, from device to device through Bluetooth technology. However, it has become a method of sending anonymous, unwanted messages to other users with Bluetooth-enabled mobile phones or devices. Bluejacking is relatively harm-less and can be more bothersome then malicious. For instance, a bluejacker might send out offensive or obscene material.

Figure 7-3 Web security.

Cookies Cookies are files stored on your computer that allow websites to remember your information. They can compromise your confidentiality, as others may be able to review your computer search history, but cannot steal your data.

Mousetrapping This security threat prevents the user from leaving a website. The user will sometimes be directed to a fake website. After the user attempts repeatedly to quit, another browser will open showing the same site from which the user is trying to escape. The best way to avoid this is by using a favourite bookmark for your frequently visited sites.

Page-jacking Page-jacking involves web page links that direct the user to navigate to another web page for more information. The new page is often a duplication of a real page. Many times scammers use this to advertise a service and generate more revenue, as some sites are paid per visitor.

Pharming Pharming redirects the user from a legitimate website to a fraudulent copy, allowing scammers to steal any information you enter at the bogus website.

Maintaining Internet Security

Internet security is a central concern for businesses in every industry. The following tools can help users to protect the security of company as well as personal data:

Antiviral Programs This software can prevent, detect, and immobilize potential threats such as viruses or spyware. Internet service providers frequently recommend or offer

Figure 7-4 Login security.

software at significantly discounted pricing. To maximize the benefits of antiviral software, take the following steps:

- Activate real-time continuous scanning.
- Schedule regular system scans.
- Check frequently for updates.
- Ensure renewal when necessary.

Passwords The purpose of a password is to ensure privacy and security on computer networks (see Figure 7-4). Many hackers, however, can be successful in their attempts to steal your information because they can figure out your password. Here are some tips to consider for password security:

- Avoid simple and short passwords; choose a password at least seven characters in length.
- Choose a password that is easy to remember but hard for others to figure out.
- Use a combination of uppercase, lowercase, and numerical characters
- Change your password frequently, since this reduces the opportunity for detection.
- Do not write your passwords down, as they can be found and used by unauthorized individuals.
- Never give your password out in an email.

Figure 7-5 Common security issues and possible solutions.

Common Security Issues & Possible Solutions

Threat	Issue	Solution
Intrusion/Hacking	Unauthorized access to network	Firewall
Virus	Destruction of files and programs	Antivirus software
Malware	Disrupt computer activity, steal information	Antimalware software
Denial of Service Attack	Attempts to make a network resource unavailable	Intrusion prevention systems
Spam	May trick user into buying nonexistent service	Antispam software
Stolen Laptop/ Mobile Device	Access to confidential files stored on device	Encrypt files
Click Jacking (Social media)	Tricked into clicking on a fake web page	Avoid visiting non work related sites

- Consider using a password manager program to store multiple passwords; this way you only have to remember the password for the program.

- Use a password strength analyzer. This free software will classify your password as weak, fair, or strong.

Data Encryption Software When information is transmitted, **encryption software** can scramble the data to make it unreadable if intercepted. A password supplied by the sender will convert the data to plain text to be viewed by the intended recipient.

Firewall A **firewall** is hardware or software used to control network traffic. A firewall will have preset determinates directing what can pass in or out of the network it is protecting. Intranets utilize firewalls to prevent external networks from breaking through.

Clearing the Cache This is a tool that requires no special program. Your browser's memory is called the cache; every time you visit a website a copy of it is saved in your computer's cache. After each internet session, close your browser to ensure the cache is cleared.

Website Site Advisor This is a browser plug-in that will check the safety of a website before you actually select it to use. A rating icon is displayed indicating the website's level of risk.

QUESTIONS FOR STUDY AND REVIEW

1. List five methods of internet connectivity.
2. Why do most businesses that have access to other connectivity methods not use dial-up?
3. Name two benefits of wireless technology.
4. State how intranets are used in business to enhance collaboration.
5. Why might a company set up an extranet?
6. In what form are results generated from a search engine?
7. How does Web 1.0 differ from Web 2.0?
8. Describe four web tools.
9. Provide two reasons a business would host a webinar.
10. Explain why a company would adopt a Web 2.0 usage policy.
11. Identify three potential threats that might place the security of your computer or computer network at risk.
12. Suggest three strategies to employ when working with passwords.
13. How does a firewall protect computers and computer networks?
14. Describe three ways to maximize your antiviral program.
15. What purpose does data encryption software serve?
16. What does clearing the cache mean?

EVERYDAY ETHICS

Sick Day

You work as an administrative assistant for McMillan & Partners, a medium-size law firm located in Calgary. You get along well with most of your co-workers and for the most part enjoy your work. You work closely with another administrative assistant, Suzanne. Often you cover each other's phone lines when you take lunch or have a break. Last Thursday, Suzanne called in sick. She took the day off, and you did your best to pitch in and help out where you could.

You and Suzanne have embraced using social media, and you both have access to each other's Facebook page.

On Saturday, you were updating your Facebook page and noticed an update from Suzanne that caught your attention. It was a picture of Suzanne sitting on the beach sipping her favourite drink. The caption read, "Having a great 'sick day.'" Naturally you were shocked and surprised.

- Will you ask Suzanne about what you saw on Facebook?

- Should you say anything to your supervisor? Why or why not?

- Do you think it is a good idea to "friend" a co-worker? Why or why not?

Problem Solving

1. It is your first month on the job. Your supervisor, Samuel Barnes, Vice-President of Marketing, met with you today to discuss your performance this past month. Overall, he is very pleased with your administrative skills and your take-charge attitude. He especially likes how computer and internet savvy you are. Based on this, Mr. Barnes would like you to find and recommend two online programs for creating slideshow presentations. Because Mr. Barnes spends so much of time away from the office meeting customers and making presentations, he wants a dynamic tool that he can access online anytime on any of his mobile devices. He also wants to be able to import presentations he has already created into the new program. What steps would take to find a program that would work for Mr. Barnes?

2. You are training a new receptionist for the group medical practice you manage. So far, the training has gone well, and you believe the new person will fit well with the team. Today, you happen to notice a slip of paper sitting by the new receptionist's workstation when she is out for lunch. You pick up the piece of paper and quickly realize the patient database login is written on the piece of paper, along with the password. It has been a very busy day, with three of the five physicians and 60 to 70 visitors in the office. Since you have no idea if anyone else has seen this information, what should you do?

3. It is almost the end of a busy workweek. You feel you have been confronted by every challenge imaginable. You just received a panicked call from your immediate supervisor, Julianne Kwong, who is leaving on a business trip to Germany in a few hours. She is taking her tablet computer and plans to remotely access all the documents she will need by using the company intranet. Ms. Kwong has just realized, however, that she does not know how to do this, or even if it is possible to do this, and she has asked you to find out if and how she can access her documents remotely. You are now going to contact the IT Department. What information do you believe they will want to know before giving you an answer? What questions will you ask?

Special Reports

1. Research two live meeting programs. List the advantages and disadvantages of both and present your findings to the class.

2. Interview an administrative assistant and ask the following questions:
   a. How is your office connected to the internet?
   b. Does your organization have a social media presence? If yes, what programs are used?
   c. How often are you required to change your password?
   d. Do you know what measures are in place to protect internet security when you go online?

3. Conduct online research using three of the search engines listed in this chapter. Use the following key phrases:
   a. Latest in cloud computing
   b. Computer viruses
   c. Internet security

   Write a summary of your findings, identifying the similarities and the differences.

4. Inquire about the media services available at your school. Determine if your school is equipped to conduct a webinar. Find out what technical support is available if you have any trouble. Report your findings to the class.

PRODUCTION CHALLENGES

7-A Identifying Appropriate/Inappropriate Use of Technology

Supplies needed:

- *Identifying Appropriate/Inappropriate Use of Technology, Form 7-A, page 394*

Review Form 7-A. Decide whether the examples provided are appropriate or inappropriate uses of technology in the workplace. Hand in your completed form to your instructor.

7-B Web 2.0 in Action

Supplies needed:

- *Plain bond paper*
- *Access to the internet*

Visit two of the following three blogs written by administrative assistants (or ones of your choosing):

1. http://secretaryhelpline.blogspot.ca/
2. http://www.theeffectiveadminblog.com/
3. http://www.theprofessionalassistant.net/

Your supervisor, Mr. Barnes, has decided a blog would be a great tool for announcing events and generating interest in the company. He would like you to review the listed blogs and write a one-page report outlining your findings.

Weblinks

Audio, Video, and Networking Products
www.polycom.com
Polycom is a leading producer of networking systems that enhance office voice and video communication. Specification and application information may be found at this site.

Norton Antivirus Software
www.symantec.com
Information on Norton software products, including antivirus and anti-spyware software, can be found at this site.

McAfee Antivirus Protection
www.mcafee.com/us
Visit this site to find information on McAfee software products including antivirus and anti-spyware software.

BlackBerry
ca.blackberry.com
BlackBerry's website provides background on the company and links to their wireless products.

SlideShare
http://www.slideshare.net/
This website offers slideshow presentations on a number of topics.

Center for Internet Security
http://www.cisecurity.org/
The Center for Internet Security (CIS) is a site providing useful information regarding issues related to internet security.

Bitdefender Resource Centre
http://www.bitdefender.com/resourcecenter/virus-encyclopedia/
This site displays a searchable encyclopedia of computer viruses. It indicates the level of threat as low, medium, or high. The site also lists the date the virus was discovered.

Public Security Canada (Canada's Cyber Security Strategy)
http://www.publicsafety.gc.ca/prg/ns/cybr-scrty/ccss-scc-eng.aspx
This site provides insight into Canada's commitment to fostering cybersecurity.

Chapter 8
Incoming and Outgoing Mail

Learning Outcomes

After completion of this chapter, the student will be able to:

1 Identify the benefits of electronic mail.

2 Compare different methods of technology-based mail.

3 Explain the procedures for processing incoming mail.

4 Describe the duties involved in answering mail when your employer is absent.

5 Discuss the privacy expectations that accompany your role as an administrative assistant.

6 Describe the special mailing services available from Canada Post (CP).

7 State what items are prohibited from being mailed.

8 List postal services for international mail.

9 Demonstrate proper envelope addressing.

10 Describe methods of delivery that are alternatives to those offered by CP.

Whether you are an administrative assistant in a large organization or a small one, mail will arrive daily—probably more than once during each business day. Electronic mail, courier services, and other distribution alternatives have seen a significant increase in recent years. At the same time, traditional mail services still provide an effective means of moving information from one location to another.

Each mail transaction represents a contact with someone outside or within your organization, and the promptness with which you and your manager answer the mail is an important factor in building goodwill and increasing the effectiveness of your organization.

As administrative assistant, you may or may not have direct contact with the post office—this may depend on whether or not the organization for which you work has a central mailing department. Nevertheless, you should become knowledgeable about all distribution and shipping services, because as you prepare outgoing mail you will have to indicate how it is to be sent. Become familiar with the Canada Post (CP) website (www.canadapost.ca). As postal rates and services are subject to frequent change, you will find this site an invaluable tool and a source of current information.

While far from comprehensive, this chapter introduces alternatives and advice for dealing with selective technology-based mail services, as well as the traditional incoming and outgoing mail. See Figure 8-1 for an overview of general distribution services.

Jennifer Allen
Senior Legal Assistant

Oatley, Vigmond Personal Injury Lawyers
Barrie, Ontario

College Graduation:
Legal Administration
Georgian College
Barrie, Ontario
2006

"I highly recommend volunteering in an office to gain hands-on experience you don't get in the classroom."

Approximately 40 emails and 10 to 20 phone calls. That's what Jennifer Allen has to manage and respond to every day. As a senior legal assistant for a personal injury law firm, Jennifer has numerous responsibilities, from drafting court documents to arranging meetings to resolving clients' concerns. Her duties also include ensuring that all correspondence coming into the office is received and responded to promptly. She must determine what needs to be forwarded to the lawyers and what she can handle herself. It's a task that requires a thorough understanding of what her office does and of the legal profession in general. It also requires solid time management skills—and persistence.

"When a piece of mail comes in that I can answer myself, I deal with it right away and try not to let my in-box get piled up," she says. "If it is something that I have to forward on to a lawyer for their response, I will email it to them and set a reminder in my calendar to follow up with them. I will continue to follow up by email, phone calls, or by speaking with them directly until the matter has been dealt with."

Jennifer warns that not managing the mail properly can have serious consequences, especially in the legal profession, where there are time limitations imposed by the *Rules of Civil Procedure,* the provincial law governing the court system. "Without responding to the mail efficiently, a file can be at a standstill or even slip through the cracks, and a limitation may be missed," she says. "Having a good bring-forward system in place is very important."

To keep the system moving, Jennifer responds to mail and telephone calls herself when she can. But doing so requires that she clearly understand her own responsibilities and what the firm expects of her. It also means that she needs to be familiar with each case as a whole—not an easy task, she says, since each file is unique and what falls within her authority can change depending on the case. However, Jennifer says these challenges can also be rewarding. She says speaking with clients about their cases and explaining the status of their files in a way they can understand is one of the most enjoyable parts of her job.

While Jennifer admits her career can be stressful at times, she says that focusing on work, minimizing distractions, and taking breaks as needed help her to maintain a proper work-life balance. She also tries not to let the stress get to her, and she tells her colleagues the same thing. "I think it's important to accept at the outset that there are times when the circumstances are out of your hands," she says. "Either a task cannot get done that day or overtime is needed—and it isn't your fault. I have two mottos I share with the staff I mentor: 'Don't sweat the small stuff' and 'It will always be there tomorrow.'"

HANDLING OFFICE TECHNOLOGY

Electronic Mail

Because of its speed and accessibility, **electronic mail (email)** is the most popular and cost-effective mail system found in business. Many companies use a private email system known as an **intranet**, which connects employees' computers together. Companies usually also subscribe to the larger, external internet (see Chapter 6), but in either case, employees are given a unique email address to which both internal and external users may send email.

Email systems vary widely both in configuration and screen appearance, but all have certain controls in common.

Most commercial email systems run within a Windows™ operating system in which controls and options are presented to the user in an **icon** format.

If the user is *sending* an email, the system will present the send screen, or template (see Figure 8-2A). Certain fields on the send template will already have information added, such as the date, time, and the sender's network address. These are already recorded by the computer's operating system.

However, to prepare the message for sending, you must provide certain information. Specifically, you must enter:

1. the name or unique email address of the intended recipient

2. the names and unique email addresses of any users who are to receive a copy of your email

3. the subject title of your message

4. the message text

Options such as *mark as urgent*, *acknowledge*, or *cancel* may also be selected from this screen.

When options (if any) are selected and the message is complete, the user may instruct the computer to "send" the message across the network to the addressee.

Figure 8-1 Overview of general distribution services.

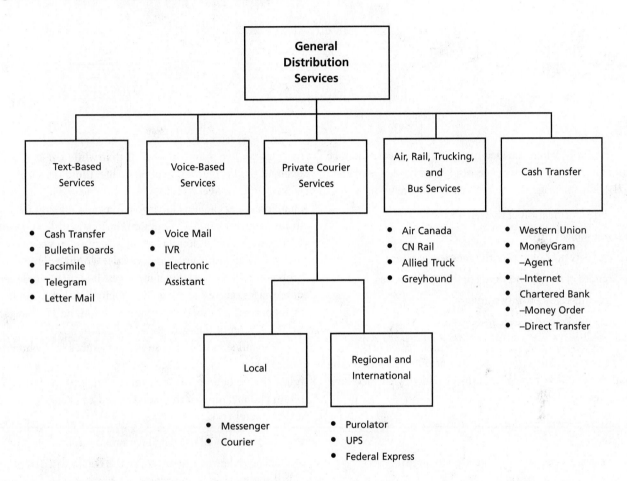

Figure 8-2A An email message being composed for sending.

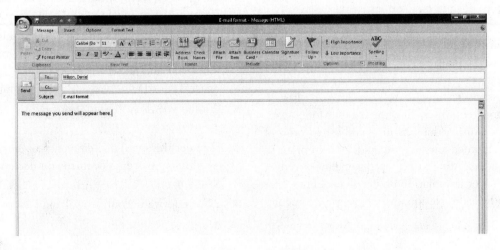

Figure 8-2B An incoming email message.

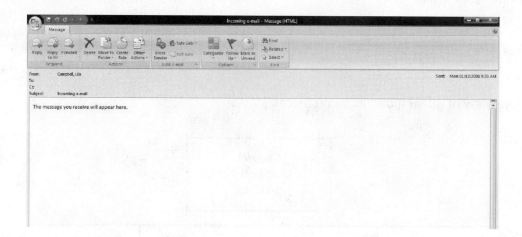

Similarly, when you read incoming email, your message will be displayed in a message display template (see Figure 8-2B). The message will be received complete with:

1. the identification of the sender
2. the subject title
3. the date and time that the message was sent
4. names of those who were copied on the message
5. the message's priority status
6. the incoming message itself

The recipient is not given the option to edit incoming mail directly, but typical options provided with incoming messages may be:

1. Reply—Reply to the originator using the same subject title.
2. Forward—Forward this message to another user.
3. Delete—Erase the message.
4. Print—Print the message on a printer.
5. File—Copy the message to a separate file (storage location).

The administrative assistant must quickly become familiar with the email system used in order to communicate effectively. However, the explosive growth of electronic messaging through communication tools such as email presents its own challenging issues. More organizations are recognizing that emailing and other forms of electronic communications require guidelines in order to be effective, and many have developed guidelines to cover those practices. For information on email guidelines refer to "The Core Rules of Netiquette" at www.albion.com/netiquette.

Researchers have discovered that while the exchange of email has become a way of office life, there is a surprising lack of concern over its risks. Unacceptable and inconsistent email practices can develop into potential problems ranging from system overload to public relations and legal issues. Unless the organization has a policy in place, users may not know they are using email incorrectly. Unintentional email problems include overuse of messages, inappropriate length of messages, failure to credit the original author, impulsive or inappropriate use, poor communication, and a disregard for the impact of one-way communication.

The office professional should remember that while the printed word has long been governed by widely accepted rules, the guidelines for using email are still evolving. To retain the meaning of the message and to ensure it will be read, remember to:

- Learn to use all the email features appropriately.
- Clearly identify the subject so the reader can determine if the message is important. Be similarly clear and precise in your message.
- Avoid using bold, italics, or fancy lettering as they may be misinterpreted by the reader as expressive or denoting urgency, even when this is not your intent.
- Avoid using special formatting. Special formatting commands in email word processing programs are not universal and may be garbled during transmission to readers who do not have identical programs.
- Ensure you do not send emails with spelling or grammatical errors.
- Temper the speed and efficiency of email by carefully proofreading every document for accuracy, tone, and content.
- Never forward confidential mail to others without obtaining permission.

- Avoid sending highly emotional, sensitive, or controversial information.

- Make sure you do not burden the receivers with unnecessary information.

Implementing suggestions like these will be easier if you remind yourself that a person, not just a computer, is on the receiving end of your electronic message.

Electronic Bulletin Board

Much like their corkboard predecessors, **electronic bulletin boards** are public message centres that appear on computer networks. While email is intended for addressed recipients, electronic bulletin board messages are intended for anyone and everyone with access to the network. Electronic bulletin boards are also an integral part of such commercial networks as America Online (AOL) and Delphi Forums.

Facsimile

The **facsimile**, commonly known as the *fax machine*, remains an essential piece of office equipment (see Figure 8-3). Fax machines can electronically send copies of original documents from one location to another. The fax machine will send almost any kind of hard-copy document—keyed text, charts, photographs, drawings, longhand messages, and so on. The document will be reproduced on paper at the destination fax or computer.

Figure 8-3 Fax system.

Faxing is a quick way to get a document across the city, country, or even the world. It is generally more expensive than CP Lettermail service but less expensive than most courier services, depending on the size of the document.

Although the fax machine continues to be a fixture in many offices, many online tools also now exist for sending faxes. In this case, hard copies of documents must first be scanned in before they can be faxed.

Fax transmission uses telephone lines or internet services to send documents—in fact, sending a fax is as easy as making a telephone call. Fax machines operate automatically, allowing you to send documents without first notifying the recipient. The general procedure is very simple:

1. Place the document to be transmitted in the sending fax unit.

2. Dial the fax number of the receiver.

3. Press the send button.

Each fax being transmitted should be accompanied by a cover page, called a **transmittal sheet** (see Figure 8-4). The transmittal sheet gives full details of who the sender is and who the receiver should be.

If you work for a small company that does not own a fax machine, one can be leased. Many pharmacies, copy shops, and CP outlets are equipped with fax machines for public use. Hotels will allow their guests to use their fax machines and often locate a fax machine in the lobby for public use. Most courier services are equipped with fax equipment that can be used for a fee.

Feature-rich fax machines are quite affordable for small businesses and home offices. The newest and most advanced fax machines provide both cost and time savings to the office. The following is a discussion of some of their features.

1. *Dialling.* For fax numbers that are dialled frequently, the administrative assistant may enter the telephone numbers into the machine's memory so that for future calls only one or two digits need be keyed to retrieve the original number.

   This is a real time-saver because it means that the sender of the fax does not need to look up and dial long number sequences.

   When the administrative assistant attempts to send a fax, and the receiving line is busy, the document may be left in the machine for transmittal. The assistant may use the *automatic redial* feature to have the fax machine continually redial the number, and transmit when the line becomes available.

   Fax messages, like telephone calls, cost less to send outside business hours. For this reason, another

Figure 8-4 Fax transmittal sheet.

MILLENNIUM APPLIANCES

3431 BLOOR STREET, TORONTO, ON M8X 1G4
www.millennium.ca

Fax

To: _____   From: _____

Fax: _____   Pages: _____

Phone: _____   Date: _____

Re: _____   CC: _____

o **Urgent**   o **For Review**   o **Please Comment**   o **Please Reply**   o **Please Recycle**

• **Message:**

The information contained in this message is confidential. It is intended for the stated addressee(s) only. Please treat this communication as confidential and deliver to the addressee. If the addressee is not known to you, please inform us immediately at Millennium Appliances, Inc., a Canadian registered company.

popular feature is delayed auto dialling, whereby the administrative assistant can program the fax machine to send the message long after the staff have left for the evening. Leaving the hard copy in the machine is not always necessary, since some feature-rich machines can scan the document and electronically store the image until the designated transmittal time.

2. *Security*. One of the problems with a basic fax machine is that documents transmitted via a fax may receive little or no confidentiality. Companies often avoid sending confidential information by fax, since the document may be read by whoever collects the printouts. However, more advanced and feature-rich machines have solved this problem. An advanced feature now allows the message to print only after the correct security code has been keyed. When sending a fax containing confidential information, the sender should telephone the receiving company immediately prior to the transmission and ask that the appropriate person wait at the fax machine for the transmitted document to arrive. The sender must remain at the fax machine until the transmission is completed successfully.

Another precaution to take may be the inclusion of a *confidentiality request statement* at the foot of the cover sheet (see Figure 8-4). The administrative assistant may wish to modify the confidentiality request statement or have a separate set of fax cover sheets for critical or confidential faxes.

3. *Broadcasting*. An administrative assistant who often needs to send the same message to many different offices would require a fax machine with the *broadcast* feature. The assistant would preprogram the fax numbers of the recipients and send the message only once. The same fax message would be sent to all the preprogrammed destinations at the time the assistant designated. The assistant need not be present when the fax is transmitted, since the fax machine can store the message in memory until the required transmittal time.

Faxes may be received at any time during the day or night. Those received at night should be processed at the beginning of the next business day. Others should be delivered to the recipients as soon as the faxes arrive or according to a designated schedule.

Sending Money Electronically

If you wish to send or receive money over a distance, it may be done through most chartered banks using their internet and mobile device services. You can also use a service such as Western Union or MoneyGram. These services require the sender to provide funds through a major credit or debit card. The initial transfer of funds may be limited to a maximum amount of $1000. Transfers of sums larger than $1000 are permitted, but are sometimes subject to additional restrictions. In more populated centres, transfers are almost immediate; in the worst case of a remote location, the complete transfer and notification process might take as long as a few days.

Electronic Services

Canada Post (CP) has invested heavily in technology to meet the evolving needs of contemporary business and consumers. CP has combined its long experience of moving mail with advanced technology to develop a unique Mail Production and Delivery™ service that simply requires you to provide CP with mailing information, and CP can look after the rest.

These comprehensive electronic services may assist with your mailing lists, mail processing, custom programming and artwork, formatting and printing of your mail, and delivery, either electronically or in hard-copy format.

Original information in electronic data format may be sent to CP via:

- bulletin board
- PosteCS™
- file transfer protocol (FTP)
- CD-ROM
- tapes

Once CP has received your information, it offers consultation and production options that include:

- mail printing
- custom programming
- design and layout
- information management
- address management
- return mail management

Finally, more options provide your organization with a choice of delivering its information electronically or in hard copy.

The two electronic services provided by CP are known as:

- epost™—for bill payment and receipt
- SmartFlow™—a document management service

These services automate high-volume document production for secure internet delivery. Examples of their use include secure invoices, monthly bank statements, and bill presentation and payment, all of which can be managed with confidence as a result of CP's focus on providing internet security for its clients.

The three hard-copy delivery services are known as:

- Lettermail™
- Addressed Admail™
- Incentive Lettermail™

These options provide a hassle-free alternative to the volume "printing, production, and delivery" projects that are common tasks of the administrative assistant.

Electronic Post Office

CP provides the ability to send and receive mail electronically. Mail, in this case, refers to invoices, forms, and other correspondence that would normally be delivered as physical mail. The Electronic Post Office uses the internet to deliver your mail to a secure virtual electronic post office box known as an epost™ box. Individuals and participating companies send mail to your epost™ box just as they would send physical mail to a letter mailbox. You can store documents up to seven years in your mailbox.

You will choose the invoices you want to receive electronically from the list of participating companies. You may pay the bills in a number of ways: directly from your organization's bank account, a credit card, or by forwarding your invoices to your financial institution's banking facility.

All personal and confidential information remains secure because of encrypted codes and passwords. Only the sender and the recipient are able to see the contents of your mail. The electronic mail is stored on CP's own secured servers and not on public internet servers.

From the participating company's point of view, the Electronic Post Office eliminates the cost of paper and postage. The company may also maintain accurate records of mail and invoices as they are already presented in electronic format.

Electronic mail sent via the Electronic Post Office increases the flow of information in and out of the office. Since speed of communication is the main advantage of using electronic mail, the administrative assistant must be alert to email that arrives on his or her system but is intended for someone else in the office. Deliver or transfer the email without delay; however, if this type of email is received frequently, delivery schedules should be worked out.

Electronic Lettermail may arrive in the regular mail and should be processed along with the other items. However, the fact that it is electronic mail indicates that there is some urgency for its receipt.

Voice Mail

Because of its name, **voice mail** must be mentioned in this chapter.

In its simplest form, voice mail allows callers to access or record voice information from a list of prerecorded options. To better understand this technology, refer to Chapter 11, "Front-Line Reception."

Self-Check

1. Define the term *intranet*.
2. What information must you provide when sending an email?
3. Define the term *electronic bulletin board*.
4. How might you ensure the confidentiality of a fax you are sending when it arrives at the recipient's company?

HANDLING INCOMING MAIL

Although most organizations now use email, every office continues to receive paper mail, and handling the mail is a high priority for an administrative assistant. When the mail is handled accurately and expeditiously, other office employees are able to respond more efficiently to the needs addressed in the items of mail.

The information provided here on incoming mail is extensive. For an administrative assistant to perform all these steps would be too time-consuming. While it is not expected that every office will handle mail with this degree of care, the administrative assistant is certain to perform at least some of the steps listed below:

1. sorting mail
2. opening mail
3. inspecting the contents
4. date-time stamping mail
5. reading and annotating mail
6. presenting mail to the manager
7. distributing and routing mail

Some large organizations have central mailing departments, although with the decreased volume of paper mail, one encounters fewer of these. Such departments are responsible for receiving *all* of the organization's mail and for routing it to the correct departments or individuals. Usually, the mailing department provides at least one pickup and delivery to each department every day. At one time, central mailing departments opened, date-time stamped, and distributed the mail. They rarely do so now; instead, recipients open their own mail, or the administrative assistant performs this task for the executives or for the whole department.

When the mail is delivered to one location, someone must sort the mail and deliver it to the appropriate workstations. If this task should be assigned to you, sort and make the deliveries at once so that other administrative assistants may start processing their own mail.

Sorting Mail

Mail may come to your desk unopened. When it does, read the information on the envelopes, and sort it into the following groups:

1. mail sent with urgency (electronic or courier)
2. Lettermail, including bills and statements
3. interoffice mail
4. personal mail
5. newspapers and periodicals
6. booklets, catalogues, and other advertising materials
7. parcels

The administrative assistant may have to sign for couriered mail and other insured, registered, or expedited pieces of mail before they can be received. Keep the priority mail separate from the rest of the mail, open it as soon as it arrives, and then put it on the addressee's desk in a way that calls attention to it. Priority mail refers to electronic mail, couriered mail, and all CP mail that is delivered via an expedited service.

In the stack of mail to be opened immediately, assemble Lettermail and interoffice memoranda. All interoffice mail is important. Each item either requires a reply or provides your manager with information she or he needs.

Do not open your manager's personal mail. Definitely do not open letters marked *Confidential, Personal,* or *Private.* Unless you receive explicit instructions to open them, place the personal letters on your manager's desk unopened.

Do not open, but quickly distribute, any mail specifically addressed to another employee in your work area. Any mail that has been delivered to you by mistake should be promptly forwarded to its intended recipient or returned to the post office.

You will have to decide whether mail addressed to an employee who is no longer with the organization is personal or business correspondence. If the letter appears to be personal, write the forwarding address clearly on the item and put it in the outgoing mail. If the letter is addressed by

title to someone no longer with the organization, you can assume that it is a business letter. When you distribute the mail, deliver it unopened to the new employee who has this title or is responsible for the work implied by the title.

As you sort, put all circulars, booklets, advertisements, newspapers, and periodicals aside until you have opened and processed the more urgent mail.

Opening Mail

Before you begin opening the mail, assemble the supplies you will need: opener, date-time stamp, pencils, stapler, transparent tape, paper clips, your Mail-Expected Record, and your to do list.

Slit the envelopes of all the important mail before you remove the contents from any of them. To reduce the possibility of cutting the contents, tap the lower edges of the letters on the desk so that the contents fall to the bottom.

Should you open a letter by mistake, seal the envelope with transparent tape, write "Opened by mistake" and your initials on the envelope, and distribute or forward the letter to the addressee.

Inspecting the Contents

Be certain to remove *all* the contents from envelopes. A thorough inspection is necessary to avoid throwing enclosures out with the envelopes. Keep the envelopes until you are certain that all the enclosures and addresses are accounted for. Save the interoffice envelopes (sometimes called interdepartmental envelopes) for further use (see Figure 8-5).

Inspect each letter for the address and signature of the sender, the date, and enclosures. If the sender's address *or* signature is missing from a letter, look for the address on the envelope. If it is there, staple the envelope to the back of the letter. When a letter is not signed, the envelope may help identify who wrote the letter.

When a letter is not dated, write the postmark date on the letter and staple the envelope to the back of the letter. Also, if you notice a major discrepancy between the date on the letter and the date of arrival, staple the envelope to the letter.

Check the enclosures received against the enclosure notations. If an enclosure is missing, inspect the envelope again; if you do not find the enclosure, make a note on the face of the letter beside the enclosure notation that the enclosure is missing. Underline the reference to it and add a note in the margin. You will have to fax or telephone the sender to request the missing enclosure; enter a reminder on your to do list at once.

Figure 8-5 Interdepartmental envelope.

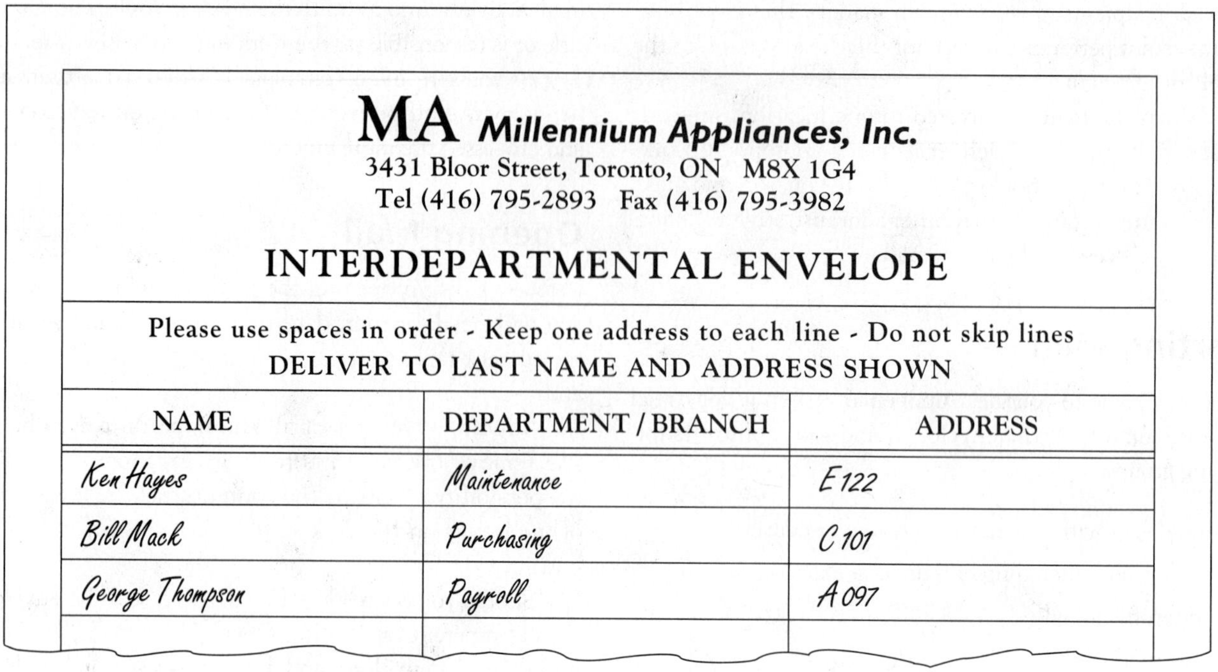

MA Millennium Appliances, Inc.
3431 Bloor Street, Toronto, ON   M8X 1G4
Tel (416) 795-2893   Fax (416) 795-3982

INTERDEPARTMENTAL ENVELOPE

Please use spaces in order - Keep one address to each line - Do not skip lines
DELIVER TO LAST NAME AND ADDRESS SHOWN

NAME	DEPARTMENT / BRANCH	ADDRESS
Ken Hayes	Maintenance	E 122
Bill Mack	Purchasing	C 101
George Thompson	Payroll	A 097

When appropriate, if enclosures are letter-size or larger, staple them to the back of the letter. Fasten small enclosures to the front of a letter. Use paper clips to fasten an item temporarily that a staple would mutilate—for example, a cheque or a photograph. Fold a small piece of paper over a photograph to protect it from the paper clip.

Date-Time Stamping Mail

The time of arrival of certain correspondence has legal significance. For example, the date a payment is received is a factor in allowing a cash discount, and a specific time of day is set for opening bids. When correspondence is received too late for the recipient to comply with a request, the date received is protection for the addressee.

Organizations do not prejudge which correspondence should be date-time stamped. With the exception of a few documents that should not be marred in any way, organizations stamp all incoming mail either with the date or with both the date and the hour of arrival. The entry is made in one of three ways:

1. By writing the date in abbreviated form, such as 21/9/2013, in pencil.

2. By stamping the word *Received* and the date with a mechanical date stamp, on which the date must be changed daily.

3. By stamping the minute, hour, and date of arrival with a date-time recorder. Mailing departments use a date-time recorder, which has a clock built in with the printing device.

Stamp or write the date received on each piece of correspondence in an area of white space at the edge. If you date-stamp all the mail as you read it, you will know as soon as you see the stamp that you have already seen and read a particular piece of correspondence. Consistently stamp booklets, catalogues, and periodicals on either the front or the back.

Reading and Annotating Mail

You can save a lot of time for your manager and yourself by marking and grouping correspondence according to the next step to be taken for each piece. You do this by reading the correspondence in search of the important facts, underlining key words and dates, and writing notes in the margins. In some cases, you will not know what the next step should be; in other cases, your manager will not agree with your notations. Even so, by using good judgment you can organize the correspondence so that your manager can spend time on the letters and memoranda that truly need attention.

Some managers prefer that nothing be underlined or written in the margins of incoming letters. For this reason, Post-It Notes or Info Notes have become a popular alternative to writing notes in the margin of a letter.

Read the correspondence rapidly, concentrating on the content and using a systematic method of making notes on which you can rely for following through. Develop a questioning attitude—one that will ensure that you pick out significant facts and help you decide what the next step should be. For instance, keep your eyes open for letters that:

1. contain the date of an appointment that must be entered in the appointment calendars
2. mention that a report is being mailed separately
3. confirm a telephone conversation
4. request a decision that cannot be made until additional information is obtained

Use a pencil to underline and make notes. Underline sparingly; otherwise your attempt to emphasize will lose its effectiveness. Underline key words and figures that reveal who, what, when, and where.

Provide your manager with additional information in the form of notes. This is called **annotating**. Use small handwriting and make your notations brief. See Figure 8-6 for an example of an annotated letter.

Jot down what you would remind your manager of if you were talking to him or her about it. For example, if the letter is a reminder to send a booklet that was requested earlier and it has been mailed, write "Mailed" and the date of mailing. If an item referred to in a letter arrived separately, write "Received."

Annotating is preferable to verbally reminding your manager. The use of marginal notes eliminates interruption; as well, your manager is able to refer to those notes as she or he answers the correspondence. On the other hand, she or he might prefer that no marks be made on a letter—for example, in cases when that letter might be presented to a manager for consultation and action, or if the letter might be circulated. Marginal notes can confuse readers, and underlining can irritate the readers to whom a letter is circulated. Although your usual practice may be to underline and annotate, refrain from marking certain letters. When in doubt, do not mark them.

As you read correspondence, pay close attention to the items that require following up. Make the entries in the proper places in your reminder system. Your follow-up plan needs to be foolproof; do not rely on your memory. Use a to do list.

If you discover that your manager will need previous correspondence, make a note in your to do list to obtain it. As soon as you have finished reading the mail, obtain the earlier correspondence and attach it to the back of the respective incoming letters. However, do not delay getting the mail to your manager. You can obtain earlier correspondence, locate facts, and verify figures while your manager is reading the mail.

Be sure to enter reminders on your to do list to request missing enclosures. Occasionally the sender will discover that an enclosure was omitted and will send it separately. Unless an enclosure is urgently needed, wait a day to request it. At other times the enclosure will be needed immediately, and you will need to fax a message or make a telephone call to check on it.

If an enclosure is money, make sure the amount received matches the amount mentioned in the letter. When it does not, indicate the amount received and the difference in the margin of the letter.

Presenting Mail

When placing mail on your manager's desk, follow these simple rules:

1. Remember that the mail is a priority; act on it as quickly as possible.
2. Place the most urgent items on top and the least urgent items on the bottom. When items are couriered or faxed they may be urgent; however, you will need to determine this by reading the content. The longer you have worked for a particular organization or manager, the better your judgment will be in separating urgent mail from routine mail.
3. Mail should be placed in such a way that it is not visible to people visiting your manager's office in his or her absence. Often, you can protect the confidentiality of the mail by placing it in a large envelope or a folder.

Self-Check

1. Which mail should you never open without receiving explicit instructions?
2. Why is it important to inspect the contents of all envelopes?
3. How should you handle a letter that has no address or signature when you open it?

Handling Packages, Publications Mail, and Advertising by Mail

Packages should receive priority over newspapers, periodicals, and advertising materials. Expedited parcels should receive the same priority as Lettermail. In some cases, you will be watching for the arrival of packages. Packages that have letters attached or that are marked "Letter Enclosed" should be processed with the important mail. However, do not open a package or separate a letter from it until you

Figure 8-6 Sample annotated letter.

MILLENNIUM APPLIANCES

3431 BLOOR STREET, TORONTO, ON M8X 1G4
www.millennium.ca

28 August 2004

Mr. Kyle Rhodes
Manager, Sales Office
Millennium Appliances, Inc.
3152 - 45th Avenue
Vancouver, BC V6N 3M1

Dear Mr. Rhodes

NOVEMBER SALES SEMINAR

One of the speakers for the November Sales Seminar is in the hospital. Therefore, he will be unable to present a program for the Sales Seminar.

The members of the Executive Committee of the November Sales Seminar have suggested that you would make an excellent substitute speaker. If you accept our offer to speak, you will receive VIP hospitality and an honorarium to cover all out-of-pocket expenses that you may incur.

The dates for the Seminar are Tuesday, November 11 and Wednesday, November 12. We would ask that you present your topic twice, once on each day.

Your presentation should last approximately one hour and would be delivered to an audience of 50 sales professionals. May we suggest that your topic relate to your successful methods of team building? I am enclosing a list of topics that will be used by other speakers at the Seminar.

Your acceptance of this invitation would be greatly appreciated.

Sincerely

W. Wilson

W. Wilson
Chairperson, Sales Seminar

lr
Enclosure

No enclosure was sent.

You have a conference planned for Nov. 11, with H. Thomas and B. Ross.

have time to check the contents carefully against the packing slip or invoice. Always avoid opening a package with the intention of checking the contents later.

Unwrap newspapers and try to flatten them. On the front cover of newspapers and periodicals, affix circulation lists. Circulation lists are a type of routing slip (for more information on routing slips, see the following section, "Distributing Mail").

If the manager wishes to see the newspapers and periodicals before they are circulated to the rest of the staff, key his or her name at the top of each list. Otherwise, names are commonly arranged in alphabetical order or according to the staff hierarchy.

As people pass the newspaper or periodical to the next person on the list, they should draw a line through their name on the circulation list.

Do not throw advertising materials away until your manager has had a chance to glance at them. Managers want to know about new products in their fields; perusing advertising materials is one way to become aware of what is new. If your manager asks you to screen advertising materials, be sure you clearly understand which items she or he has no interest in.

After your manager has seen the advertising materials, booklets, catalogues, and so on, you will have to decide what to do with them. Which ones should you keep? Which ones should you route to someone who has an interest in a particular subject? Which ones should you throw away? Ask your manager to initial anything that might be looked at again.

Figure 8-7 shows a sample Mail-Expected Record. Many offices use these to track packages and expected mail to ensure proper follow-up procedures are used to locate mail, especially those that are time sensitive in nature.

Distributing Mail

A manager distributes mail to others to:

1. obtain information so that she or he can reply
2. ask someone else to reply directly
3. keep others informed

Important mail can be delayed and can even get "lost" on someone else's desk. Nevertheless, top management expects mail to be answered. Your manager is still responsible for the reply to a letter, even when the actual writing of it has been delegated to someone else.

As a general rule, your manager will make notations on letters or send memoranda asking others to comment, provide information, or to reply directly. Some managers attach "Action Requested" or routing slips as they read the mail so that they don't have to handle the same pieces of correspondence again. However, much of this responsibility can be handled by an administrative assistant. When given the responsibility for making requests, realize that a considerate tone will play a significant part in getting someone to comply. In contrast, a demanding tone will detract from your efforts and sometimes result in the letter getting "lost."

For informal requests for action, use an Action Requested slip similar to the one shown in Figure 8-8. For example, attach an Action Requested slip to a letter that has been misdirected to your manager and obviously should

Figure 8-7 Mail-Expected Record.

MAIL-EXPECTED RECORD			
EXPECTED FROM	DESCRIPTION OF DOCUMENT	DATE RECEIVED	FOLLOW-UP SENT
L. Crawford	map	Nov. 1	—
D. Duggin	photos	Nov. 16	yes — thank you
I.B.M.	brochures		
Unitel	annual report		

Figure 8-8 Action Requested slip.

ACTION REQUESTED!

TO: *Janice Miller*

FROM: *Edward Kaye*

DATE: *May 2*

✓	**PLEASE RUSH** – immediate action necessary!
	For your information; no need to return.
	Let's discuss.
	Note and return to me.
	Note and file.
	Please handle as you see appropriate.
	Please respond to this document.
	Your comments, please.
	Other –

COMMENTS:

The Kentworth Project can't go ahead without the third communiqué. We need to push this through.

Please complete action by *May 2*

pro-Link
Snail Mail

How would you handle a bad rep? More specifically, what would you do if you had a bad reputation with 33 million people?

Well, Canada Post (CP) dealt with it by facing the issues and dragging their aged and ailing corporation into the 21st century. Change was the name of the game: a change of management, philosophy, attitude, strategy, and partners.

"We recognized that the delivery business had become more competitive . . . we saw a need to be more efficient and invited other companies to help us streamline our operations," a CP spokesperson said. The legendary mail monolith became a hotbed of innovation and technology by partnering with other industry experts.

These days, CP is clearly well into the e-commerce biz with millions of Canadians signed up to deal with their mail and bills electronically. Continuous quality improvement has enabled CP to deliver mail with fast and predictable service times too—guaranteed! They're also experimenting with a web-based vehicle tracking system and environmentally friendly electric vehicles.

CP is also collaborating with the National Quality Institute to roll out their "healthy workplace" initiative. They want to be a workplace of choice.

So, next time you believe you have a bad rep, remember Canada Post's approach. Identify the problem, collaborate with friends, and move on, leaving skeptics in the dust. Think "Dynamic Dispatch," not "Snail Mail."

be handled in another department. Write the recipient's name, and check "Please handle."

Sometimes a letter requires two types of action, one of which your manager can handle and another that someone in another department must handle. When this situation arises, let the other person know precisely which part of the letter she or he is to answer. In the margin of the letter, indicate the part on which your manager will follow through.

Decide whether the person who is to reply will require earlier correspondence. If you think she or he will need it, attach it to the letter being distributed.

To obtain information, you will be dealing with co-workers in numerous departments throughout the organization. Make an effort to get acquainted with them, at least by telephone. When you must obtain information from a service department, you should be aware of the work schedule followed by that department. Find out how much time must elapse between the time you place a request and the time the material will be ready. Often you will be pressed by a deadline, and you must communicate this. You may have to request special service in order to meet your deadline.

When you ask someone who is not following a predetermined schedule to assemble facts for you, request that the information be ready by a designated time. Suggest a realistic deadline. Often, work that can be done when it is convenient to do it gets relegated to the bottom of the stack.

Attach a routing, or circulation, slip to mail that is to be distributed to more than one person. A routing slip is a small sheet of paper on which are listed the names of the people to whom an item is to be distributed. Each recipient should initial and date the slip after she or he has seen the material, and then forward it to the next person on the list.

When mail is often circulated to the same people, the names can be preprinted. On a pre-printed slip, you can change the order in which material is to be circulated by writing numbers in front of the names on the list. For an

Figure 8-9 Routing or circulation slip.

ROUTING SLIP			
SEQUENCE	TEAM MEMBER	DATE	INITIAL
4	J. Adams		
	A. Arnolds		
	K. Best		
	L. Davenport		
	M. Franzen		
3	L. Gatez		
	H. Hatherly		
1	E. Kaye		
	A. Kohut		
	L. Mann		
	J. Newman		
	L. Minchuk		
5	W. Roberts		
	K. Stansbury		
	B. Taylor		
2	C. Winters		
This routing slip was initiated on	*Feb. 2*		
Please return to J. Waye by	*Feb. 20*		

illustration, see Figure 8-9. Be sure to include "Return to" near the bottom of a routing slip.

When you distribute a letter, memorandum, or report to inform others, you will have to decide whether to attach to the original a routing slip listing the names of the recipients, make a copy and attach a routing slip, or make a copy for each person on the list. When deciding, consider the important factors, such as the number of pages, whether each person on the list must be informed at the same time, your immediate need for the original, and the risk that the original will be lost while it is being circulated. Also consider paper wastage when you ask yourself how many copies are actually necessary.

Your records should show what information has been disseminated. When a circulated item is returned to you, staple the routing slip to the document. This makes a permanent record of who saw the item and the date she or he saw it. When you do not use a circulation or routing slip, and must make separate copies for each individual, write on your file copy the names of the people to whom you sent the item.

Answering Mail in the Manager's Absence

What happens to the mail when your manager is away from the office depends on his or her preferences and length of absence, and on the time and attention she or he can give—or chooses to give—to what is going on at the office while she or he is away.

Email may be dealt with in a number of ways: auto response, remote access, or with the direct support of the administrative assistant. Contemporary email systems provide an auto notice function that will automatically inform every email correspondent that the intended recipient, your manager in this case, is away from the office and that a full response will not be forthcoming until his or her return date. Alternatively, your manager may want to deal with his or her email while away from the office by accessing the office email system remotely. With the use of appropriate connections and passwords, your manager may access and deal with email as if he or she were in the office.

Active businesses of all types maintain their pace based on the free flow and exchange of critical information through email. If you are charged with the responsibility of monitoring and responding to email in the manager's absence, it will first be prudent to understand the nature and deemed priority of your manager's email. Determine which, if any, email should be forwarded to the manager or a higher authority during the manager's absence from the office. What remains in your manager's email is that which requires a response or that which can be saved until your manager returns.

You should process the postal mail as promptly when your manager is out of the office as when she or he is there. The first steps are always the same: classifying and sorting; opening, removing, and inspecting contents; date-time stamping; reading and annotating; and rerouting mail that does not belong in your department.

You will have the additional responsibilities of making a summary of all incoming mail, answering and acknowledging letters yourself, and seeing that correspondence requiring immediate action receives it.

If your manager is away from the office for only a day or two, his or her preference probably will be for you to put aside all the mail you cannot answer. However, never put aside correspondence that must be handled immediately. If there is no one at the office who is authorized to reply to an urgent message, call your manager.

Send letters that require immediate action to the person designated to answer them; make copies of these letters and write the name of the person receiving each one on the letter itself. Put the copies in a folder for your manager marked *Correspondence to Be Read*.

Answer the letters that you can answer. Acknowledge nearly all the Lettermail not being answered immediately, indicating that your manager will be back in the office on a specific date and that the sender can expect a reply soon after she or he returns. Note and reply to the email address (if any) on the incoming mail. This form of response is expedient and can provide a concise record of your actions. If no email address is evident, write a brief letter to explain the situation. The recipient of your acknowledgment will either wait for your manager's reply or contact someone else within your organization. You may say that your manager is on vacation, but do not say where. When your manager is on a business trip, remember that you would be giving out confidential information if you told where she or he is. (See Chapter 14 for examples of acknowledgment letters.)

Organize in folders all the business mail that accumulates during your manager's absence. Place the folders, along with your summary of the mail, on your manager's desk in the order listed below. Keep personal mail in a separate folder and put it on your manager's desk in a separate place. The folders might be labelled:

- *Correspondence for Signature*—for letters you prepared for his or her signature.
- *Correspondence Requiring Attention*—for all correspondence your manager must answer.
- *Correspondence to Be Read*—for copies of letters you and others have answered, and copies of your replies. Often, as a courtesy, the people answering will send your manager a copy of their replies. When they do, staple these replies to the letters they answered.
- *Reports and Informational Memos*—for all informational items.
- *Advertisements*—for advertising brochures and other literature for your manager's perusal.

When dealing with your manager's email and postal mail, always remain cognizant of the expectations and individual rights surrounding privacy. Chapter 1, "Human Relations," under "Keep Confidential Information Confidential," discusses confidentiality and the responsibilities that accompany your critical role as an administrative assistant. If you wish to find out more about this topic, the Office of the Privacy Commission of Canada has prepared a guide for individuals to learn about their rights and the rights of others under the *Personal Information Protection and Electronic Documents Act* (*PIPEDA*), Canada's private sector privacy law. This guide for individuals may be found at www.privcom.gc.ca. For more discussion on *PIPEDA*, see Chapter 10, "Information Management."

Self-Check

1. List three reasons why your manager would distribute mail to others.
2. When would you use a routing slip? An Action Requested slip?
3. How should you process mail when your manager is away from the office?

HANDLING OUTGOING MAIL[1]

Outgoing mail handled by Canada Post (CP) may have a domestic destination, a US destination, or an international destination. **Domestic mail** is mailable matter that is transmitted within Canada; this includes the ten provinces,

---

[1] Information for the "Handling Outgoing Mail" section has been extracted from the *Canadian Postal Guide and Reference Tools* and the *Addressing Guidelines*, both published by Canada Post.

Yukon Territory, Northwest Territories, and Nunavut. Mail addressed to a point in any state of the United States, or to any US territory or possession, is considered **USA mail**. Mail addressed to any destination outside Canadian or US territory is considered **international mail**. These three destination groupings determine the cost of the mailing service. Of course, the size, weight, and delivery service required will also all have a bearing on the cost of the delivery. See Figure 8-10 for an overview of business services provided by CP.

CP publishes brochures that provide product and price information for these three destinations. However, because rates change rapidly, as do definitions of services, CP now provides a toll-free number and a comprehensive website for Canadians to visit. If you require the most current information on services provided by CP to any destination, call 1-888-550-6333. If your office requires a printed document with detailed information and rates for all services available from CP, the *Canadian Postal Guide* is available for reference at all Canadian postal outlets. Or, you may review and print it by contacting CP's online information website at www.canadapost.ca/common/tools/pg/default-e.asp.

Types of Domestic Mail

The basic types of domestic mail are Lettermail, Publications Mail, Admail, and Parcels. Your knowledge of available services should enable you to choose expeditious and economical means of sending mail.

Figure 8-10 Business services from Canada Post.

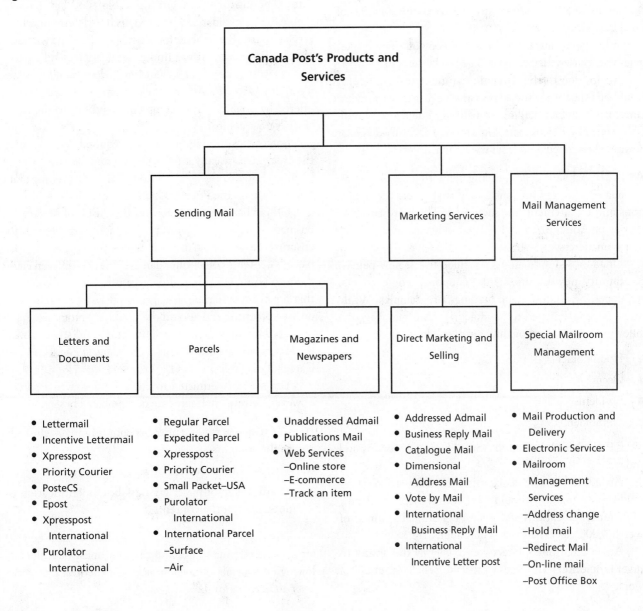

Lettermail Among the items classified as Lettermail are:

■ letters, postcards, or similar communications completely or partly keyed or handwritten

■ receipts, invoices, or similar financial statements relating to a specified sum of money

■ any other mail that the sender chooses to post at Lettermail rates of postage

Lettermail items mailed without sufficient postage are returned to the sender. If the item has no return address, it is forwarded to the addressee for collection of the deficient postage and an administrative charge.

Publications Mail To be eligible for mailing at the publications rate, a newspaper, magazine, or newsletter must be produced at least twice a year and mailed in Canada for delivery in Canada. Further qualifications require the publication to be either individually addressed or in bundles of unaddressed copies.

When you want to mail a single copy of a newspaper, magazine, or newsletter, you should use Lettermail.

Again, due to the dynamic nature of this service, it would be prudent for the administrative assistant to review current criteria for a mailing to qualify for Publications Mail. For a copy of CP's *Customer Guide*, call 1-800-267-1177, or download the document from www.canadapost.ca.

Admail Admail is advertising mail that is posted in Canada for delivery in Canada and that meets the conditions and requirements for such mail. There are two categories of Admail: Admail that is addressed and Admail that is unaddressed.

Unaddressed Admail may include flyers, newspapers, community newspapers, cards, coupons, single sheets, envelopes, brochures, co-op mailings, and samples. While this service is designed to be unaddressed, it may bear the following wording without any further address:

■ Householder

■ Occupant

■ Resident

■ Boxholder

CP delivers Unaddressed Admail between Monday and Friday.

An administrative assistant who wishes to send an unaddressed mailing should first contact the local post office for specifications and prices. For annual volumes of over 100 000 pieces, discounts may apply.

Addressed Admail offers your company the ability to target promotional messages to specific people or groups of people.

Parcels Parcel service is used to send goods, merchandise, and so on. CP will accept parcels within a broad range of sizes and weights. To be accepted, parcels must conform to the packaging requirements of CP and must not contain dangerous or prohibited articles.

Parcel service includes:

1. *Commercial Parcels.* Commercial parcels are those the mailer has weighed and applied sufficient postage to, before bringing them to CP for mailing.

2. *Counter Parcels.* Counter parcels are those parcels that the CP counter staff must weigh and calculate postage for.

The minimum acceptable size for a parcel is a small packet; the maximum size depends on the length, width, and depth of the package. Within certain limits, oversize items may be acceptable, but these may be charged higher rates. The maximum weight allowable is 30 kg. Refer to Figure 8-11 for guidance when you need to determine which service to use. Remember, for exact specifications you must check CP's website. If you find it necessary to send a package exceeding the size or weight limits, you should consider alternatives to CP. Among these alternatives are services offered by private courier companies, and by airline, train, truck, or bus companies.

Sometimes special services are required. When this is the case, items usually sent as parcels may be sent Priority Courier. Refer to the next section of this chapter for more information on the Priority Courier service.

CP publishes information on the *ABCs of Mailing* for business, which recommends proper packaging methods for ensuring the safe arrival of goods. Unless properly packaged, a parcel's contents could suffer damage; they could even cause harm to postal workers and damage other mail. Remember that a parcel containing damaged goods is a poor reflection on your company and also on the product it promotes.

To determine precise weights, sizes, and standards for the service you are using, refer to the *Canada Postal Guide* or Canada Post's website.

You are not permitted to enclose a letter in a parcel; however, certain enclosures are acceptable. These include:

■ an invoice or statement of account relating exclusively to the contents

■ a return card, envelope, or wrapper

■ a card or slip of paper giving a brief identification or directions for the contents

When a letter is enclosed or attached, it must be paid for at the Lettermail rate, and the item must bear the following endorsement: *Amount includes Lettermail postage for letter attached/enclosed.*

Figure 8-11 Maximum and approximate sizes for Canada Post mail services.

	Example of Content	Maximum Weight	Maximum Size
Standard Letter	Letter	50 grams	245 mm × 156 mm × 5 mm
Oversized Letter	Book	500 grams	380 mm × 270 mm × 20 mm
Parcel	Notebook Computer	30 kilograms	Length 1 metre Length + girth = 3 metres
Oversized Item	Small Furniture	30 kilograms	Length 2 metres Length + girth = 3 metres

To determine precise weights, sizes, and standards for the service you are using, refer to the *Canada Postal Guide* or Canada Post's website.

Priority Courier Priority Courier is CP's top-priority service. It is a guaranteed delivery service for urgent, time-sensitive items. Priority Courier items, deposited at a post office in any major Canadian location and addressed to another major Canadian location, will be delivered on the next business day. However, this one-day Priority Courier guarantee applies only to shipments within Canada. For international courier delivery service, Canada Post offers service through Purolator™ International. This service guarantees on-time delivery of time-sensitive documents and packages to the United States and to over 220 countries worldwide.

The fee for Priority Courier covers $100 worth of insurance; additional insurance can be purchased up to a maximum of $5500. If you require further details, contact your local service and sales representative at CP.

Xpresspost Xpresspost™ service combines speed with verification of delivery. CP guarantees that Xpresspost™ will be delivered in one business day for local destinations and in two business days between major Canadian urban centres. Xpresspost™ can also be used for time-sensitive delivery to the United States and other parts of the world. Service delivery is guaranteed within three to five days for the United States and four to six days internationally. It is intended to be faster than regular delivery and less expensive than Priority Courier.

It is available for both documents and packages up to 30 kg. Because an identification number and access code are printed on the sender's receipt, the customer may access information on the delivery status by using CP's tracking system. Refer to the "Registered Mail" section, below, for the toll-free numbers and internet address.

Because Xpresspost envelopes are prepaid, they may be dropped in any street letterbox. However, the money-back guarantee for expeditious delivery applies only when the Xpresspost is given to a CP official at a postal outlet—not when it is dropped into a mailbox. You can purchase and print your Xpresspost labels from your workstation.

Self-Check

1. Define *domestic mail, USA mail,* and *international mail.*
2. List the types of domestic mail.
3. Define *commercial parcels* and *counter parcels.*
4. What is the name of Canada Post's top-priority service?

Supplemental Services

As an administrative assistant who prepares outgoing mail, you should know what special services are available from CP and when to use them. The following is a discussion of some of the services that enable office workers to handle correspondence effectively and efficiently. CP has an increasing number of services. If you require a service that is not discussed below, contact your local CP sales and service representative or review CP's website.

Registered Mail Registered mail is an option with most of CP's services. For an additional fee, registered mail provides mailing and delivery confirmation for valuable mail items such as:

- important letters: for example, confirmation of appointment or a message from a dignitary
- critical documents: for example, contracts or land titles
- jewellery and other negotiable items: for example, stocks, bonds, precious stones and metals

It also includes built-in insurance for loss or damage to the mail piece.

Registered mail is coded with a red identification sticker and is available for Lettermail services both domestically and internationally. You can also print registered mail barcodes directly on your mail items, using your own computer and printer. Check with your IT department to ensure your systems are capable of printing the required barcodes.

The sender's receipt bears an identification number that enables the sender to track the delivery status of domestic items through either:

- the CP **automated inquiry system** at 1-888-550-6333, or
- www.canadapost.ca

Partial tracking of US and international items is also available.

Registered items must be turned in at an authorized postal outlet or given to a rural mail courier; they may not be dropped into a mailbox. On the delivery end, CP must obtain a signature from the addressee or the addressee's representative before delivery is considered complete. The receiver may inquire as to the name and address of the sender but may not inspect the contents before accepting receipt of the item.

For registered items going to the United States or international destinations, an optional Advice of Receipt is available at the time of mailing. This card accompanies the registered item and will be returned to the sender with the date and signature of the addressee.

Advice of Receipt An Advice of Receipt provides proof of delivery (including the date and signature of the addressee) in hard copy. For selective services, Advice of Receipt can be purchased at the time of mailing. The actual advice receipt card is attached to the mailed item and returned to the sender by the destination postal administration.

The Advice of Receipt service is only available for registered mail to the United States and other international destinations.

Insurance CP offers insurance coverage on its distribution services. Coverage for loss or damage of $100 is built into the fee charged for many distribution services including:

- Priority Courier
- Xpresspost™
- Purolator International

Additional coverage is available up to a maximum of $5000 for domestic services and $1000 for US and international services, depending on the destination country. Again, it is important to reference CP's website for current and complete insurance details.

Articles to be insured must be handed in at the post office or given to a rural mail courier. They may not be dropped into a street letter box.

For insured items, a receipt for proof of mailing is always given to the sender. As with registered mail, the codes given on the sender's receipt permit the sender to access the tracking system in order to check the status of delivery. Refer to the section on "Registered Mail," above, for the correct telephone number and internet address.

In all cases, the signature copy of the receipt is available to the sender for an additional fee and will be forwarded by Lettermail or faxed within three days.

COD By means of *collect on delivery* service (COD), the seller who wishes to mail an article for which she or he has not been paid may have the price of the article and the postage fee collected from the addressee when the article is delivered. COD articles must be sent by parcel only or at parcel rates. However, customers wishing to use the COD service for letter-size packages may pay Xpresspost service plus the COD fee.

CP will collect payment up to $1000 for a cash payment on a COD item. A cheque or money order is also accepted up to a maximum of $25 000. When the addressee makes payment by cash or by cheque, CP will forward a Postal Money Order payable to the sender. This service cannot be used to collect on items that were not ordered or requested by the addressee or to collect money owing on previous accounts. The CP official acts only as a type of liaison in the transaction—delivering the goods, collecting the payment, and forwarding the money to the sender.

This service is available only for domestic mail. The item may be mailed at any postal outlet in Canada, and may be delivered to any postal outlet or mail delivery route in Canada.

Return To Sender Domestic business Lettermail is returned to sender:

- if it does not bear a sufficient address
- if the addressee has moved without providing a forwarding address

- if it is refused by the addressee, or
- if the addressee does not pay the postage on demand (no return address shown on cover)

Depending on the type of mail, the cost to the sender can vary from no charge, a fixed or negotiated amount, or an amount equal to the original postage.

Dangerous Goods

Articles or substances that could be dangerous to postal workers and postal equipment, or that could damage other mail, are prohibited from being mailed both domestically and to points outside Canada. It is an offence to use the domestic service to deliver:

- explosives
- flammable solids and flammable liquids
- radioactive material
- gases, oxidizers, and organic peroxides
- corrosives
- toxic and infectious substances
- miscellaneous dangerous goods, such as asbestos, airbags, and dry ice

A list of restricted items is available for international mail as well. If you are in doubt about any item you wish to mail, contact CP at 1-800-267-1177 for a complete list of prohibited mail.

US and International Mail

CP offers a number of services for Lettermail, Admail, parcels, and other items subject to customs clearance and duty.

Purolator International courier service provides guaranteed delivery to 19 000 US cities and over 220 countries worldwide. It also includes:

- online tracking
- convenience packaging
- Saturday delivery to selected US zip codes

Xpresspost–US offers:

- guaranteed service of three to five days between major centres in Canada and the United States
- availability for both documents and packages

Specific item barcodes and documentation for customs clearance in the United States are required. Like their domestic counterparts, delivery confirmation is available by using CP's tracking system.

As CP's US and international mail services are designed in conjunction with other international postal services and are therefore subject to frequent change, it is advisable to obtain current and complete details of specific services from:

- Distribution Service Customer Guide
- Customer Service at 1-888-550-6333, or
- www.canadapost.ca

Other Delivery Options

Courier Services Courier service is available for sending documents or packages across town or across the world. It guarantees expeditious delivery; however, the cost of this service is high relative to that of CP's Priority Courier. Courier services are privately owned and represent strong competition for CP.

Many courier services offer one-hour pickup and delivery in the same city, overnight delivery to all major cities in Canada and the United States, and door-to-door delivery of sensitive packages and business documents (see Figure 8-12). When an administrative assistant is responsible for having an item delivered within a very short time, a courier service is often the best option.

Airline Services Canada's airlines offer competitive delivery service to all destinations they serve. If urgency of delivery is not the major factor, you may ship documents and goods via air cargo services. This service will transport almost any size of cargo, and pickup and delivery are available. Shipments are guaranteed to move on the first

Figure 8-12 Courier service provides expeditious delivery to international and domestic locations.

available flight. This service is much more economical than express services.

However, if you wish to ensure that your shipments arrive the next business day, you should use the airline express or priority services. Of course, these services cost more.

Bus Express The most rapid means of delivering a package to a small town in your geographic area (or to more distant points not served by an airport) may be *bus express*. Most bus companies offer a shipping service on a round-the-clock basis, including Sundays and holidays. Packages often get same-day or next-day delivery. Call the local offices of bus companies for information on rates, restrictions, and schedules. Also inquire about pickup and delivery services.

Freight Shipments Freight service is used for sending heavy, bulky goods in large quantities. Carriers include railway companies, trucking companies, and shipping lines. Airline transport is not as economical but is more expeditious. If the decision to ship goods by freight is based on economics alone, the sender will likely choose the railway, trucking, or shipping lines.

Self-Check

1. When would you send correspondence via registered mail?

2. What is Canada Post's COD service? How does it work?

3. Give three examples of dangerous goods that are prohibited from being mailed both domestically and to points outside Canada.

4. What are three mail delivery options besides Canada Post for sending non-electronic mail?

Proper Addressing

CP uses computerized systems that can scan a wide range of addressing styles; this includes both handwritten and keyed addresses. To increase the speed and efficiency of mail handling, CP has designed a consistent format for users. CP requests that we use this *optimum* format whenever possible, but recognizes some other formats as acceptable for computerized scanning. This is especially important for mail addressed in some languages other than English. Especially important in Canada is the fact that the *acceptable* formats encompass the accents, upper- and lowercase characters, full spellings, and punctuation used in the French language. For the sake of brevity, this textbook will deal only with the optimum format as defined by CP.

Canada Post's *Addressing Guidelines* can be found and downloaded from CP's website at www.canadapost.ca/tools/pg/manual/PGaddress-e.asp. This comprehensive guide provides illustrated examples of different types of addresses including:

- civic
- post office box
- rural route
- general delivery
- bilingual
- military
- US
- international

The *Addressing Guidelines* also provide acceptable bilingual names and abbreviations for:

- street types
- street directions
- unit designators (flat, apartment, etc.)
- province and territory symbols
- US and possessions symbols
- English and French country names

Properly addressed mail saves time and avoids errors in delivery. While the following information is designed to help the administrative assistant properly prepare addressed mail, the *Addressing Guidelines* will remain an essential professional reference.

Address Format The sequence of components (see Figure 8-13) for mail originating in and addressed to a destination within Canada is as follows:

Addressee Information

Delivery Address Information

Municipality Province Postal Code

1. The bottom lines of the address are the most critical, since the automated equipment scans from the bottom lines upwards.

2. Attention or information data must always appear at the top of the address block.

3. Addressee information, delivery address information, municipality, province, and postal code must always be the bottom three or four lines of the address block.

4. Address components and elements on the same line will be separated from each other by one blank space. The postal code, however, must be separated from the province by two blank spaces and must contain one space between the first three and last three characters.

Figure 8-13 Guidelines for addressing envelopes.

Adapted from the Canadian Postal Guide.

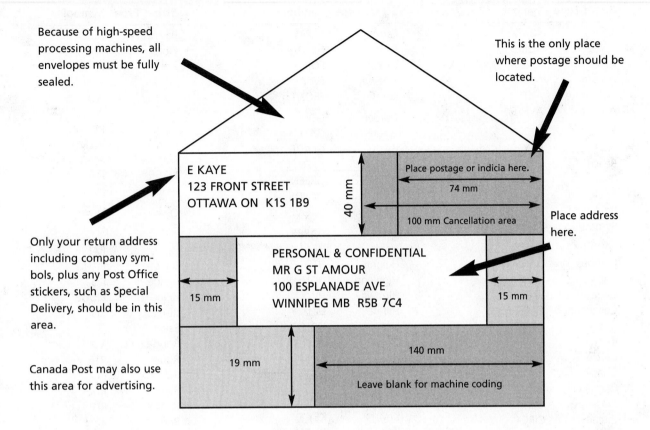

Because of high-speed processing machines, all envelopes must be fully sealed.

This is the only place where postage should be located.

E KAYE
123 FRONT STREET
OTTAWA ON K1S 1B9

40 mm

Place postage or indicia here.

74 mm

100 mm Cancellation area

Place address here.

Only your return address including company symbols, plus any Post Office stickers, such as Special Delivery, should be in this area.

PERSONAL & CONFIDENTIAL
MR G ST AMOUR
100 ESPLANADE AVE
WINNIPEG MB R5B 7C4

15 mm

15 mm

Canada Post may also use this area for advertising.

19 mm

140 mm

Leave blank for machine coding

5. Where symbols exist for address elements, these should be used rather than full names.

6. Province and state names should always be written in the two-letter abbreviation format. Refer to Figure 8-18 on page 144 for a complete list of these abbreviations.

7. All lines of the address should be formatted with a flush-left margin.

8. Uppercase letters are preferred on all lines of the address block.

9. Punctuation such as the number sign (#) should not be used as a delimiter between address elements. Use punctuation marks only where they are a part of the place name (for example, ST. ALBERT).

10. The name of the addressee is the last line scanned; this means that the automated equipment has already determined the destination before it reads the addressee's name. Therefore, punctuation is acceptable on this line. However, for consistency this text will adhere to the rule of all capital letters, and no punctuation, except where these are part of the place name. Both of these are quite acceptable:

MR. W. ROSS

or

MR W ROSS

11. The return address should follow the same format as the main address. This is of little value in the original scanning for sorting and delivery of the item; remember, however, that if the address cannot be deciphered, the item may need to be returned to the sender. Use the same format, since the CP staff are accustomed to it. For items leaving the country, be sure to include the country of origin as part of the return address.

Non-Address Data Non-address data refers to any additional information that you put on the envelope. This data should be located above all other lines in the address. Refer to the following sample.

ATTN: MR B CLARKE

MARKETING DEPARTMENT

Figure 8-14 List of street types and corresponding symbols.

Street Type	Symbol	Street Type	Symbol	Street Type	Symbol
Abbey	ABBEY	Farm	FARM	Pathway	PTWAY
Acres	ACRES	Field	FIELD	Pines	PINES
Allee	ALLEE	Forest	FOREST	Place	PL (E)
Alley	ALLEY	Freeway	FWY	Place	PLACE (F)
Autoroute	AUT	Front	FRONT	Plateau	PLAT
Avenue	AVE (E)			Plaza	PLAZA
Avenue	AV (F)	Gardens	GDNS	Point	PT
		Gate	GATE	Pointe	POINTE
Bay	BAY	Glade	GLADE	Port	PORT
Beach	BEACH	Glen	GLEN	Private	PVT
Bend	BEND	Green	GREEN	Promenade	PR
Boulevard	BLVD (E)	Grounds	GRNDS		
Boulevard	BOUL (F)	Grove	GROVE	Quay	QUAY
By-pass	BYPASS			Quai	QUAI
Byway	BYWAY	Harbour	HARBR		
		Heath	HEATH	Ramp	RAMP
Campus	CAMPUS	Heights	HTS	Rang	RANG
Cape	CAPE	Highlands	HGHLDS	Range	RG
Carre	CAR	Highway	HWY	Ridge	RIDGE
Carrefour	CARREF	Hill	HILL	Rise	RISE
Centre	CTR (E)	Hollow	HOLLOW	Road	RD
Centre	C (F)			Rond-point	RDPT
Cercle	CERCLE	Ile	ILE	Route	RTE
Chase	CHASE	Impasse	IMP	Row	ROW
Chemin	CH	Inlet	INLET	Rue	RUE
Circle	CIR	Island	ISLAND	Ruelle	RLE
Circuit	CIRCT			Run	RUN
Close	CLOSE	Key	KEY		
Common	COMMON	Knoll	KNOLL	Sentier	SENT
Concession	CONC			Square	SQ
Corners	CRNRS	Landing	LANDING	Street	ST
Cote	COTE	Lane	LANE	Subdivision	SUBDIV
Cour	COUR	Limits	LMTS		
Court	CRT	Line	LINE	Terrace	TERR
Cove	COVE	Link	LINK	Terrasse	TSSE
Crescent	CRES	Lookout	LKOUT	Thicket	THICK
Croissant	CROIS	Loop	LOOP	Towers	TOWERS
Crossing	CROSS			Townline	TLINE
Cul-de-sac	CDS	Mall	MALL	Trail	TRAIL
		Manor	MANOR	Turnabout	TRNABT
Dale	DALE	Maze	MAZE		
Dell	DELL	Meadow	MEADOW	Vale	VALE
Diversion	DIVERS	Mews	MEWS	Via	VIA
Downs	DOWNS	Montee	MONTEE	View	VIEW
Drive	DR	Moor	MOOR	Village	VILLGE
		Mount	MT	Villas	VILLAS
Echanger	ECH	Mountain	MTN	Vista	VISTA
End	END			Voie	VOIE
Esplanade	ESPL	Orchard	ORCH		
Estates	ESTATE			Walk	WALK
Expressway	EXPY	Parade	PARADE	Way	WAY
Extension	EXTEN	Parc	PARC	Wharf	WHARF
		Park	PARK	Wood	WOOD
		Parkway	PKY	Wynd	WYND
		Passage	PASS		
		Path	PATH		

IMPERIAL OIL LTD
PO BOX 9070 STN B
ST. JOHN'S NL A1A 2X6

Civic Addresses

Civic Addresses In an English address, the street type always follows the street name. See the complete list of symbols in Figure 8-14. In a French address, the street type appears before the street name unless the street type is numeric, in which case the street type follows the street name. The street type should always be identified by the official CP symbols. Two samples follow; in the first the French address has a street name, and in the second the street type is numeric.

B GUTHRIE
225 **RUE** FLEURY O
MONTREAL QC H3L 1T8

R MANN
2061 36E **RUE**
SHAWINIGAN QC G9N 5J9

Street Direction Street direction, where required, should be identified by a one- or two-character symbol, as shown below.

W WEEKS
548 GEORGIA ST **E**
VANCOUVER BC V6A 1Z9

For a complete list of CP's street direction symbols, refer to Figure 8-15.

Unit Designator This designator indicates the type of unit, such as an apartment or suite, and should be identified by the official CP symbol.

MRS A DALE
415 HERITAGE CRES **SUITE** 102
SASKATOON SK S7H 5M5

Where the number of characters is too long on a line, the unit information may be placed on a line by itself above the street information. Refer to the following example.

MME R HUGHES
UNITE 509
169 RUE NOTRE-DAME-DES-VICTOIRES
STE. FOY QC G2G 1J3

Unit Identifier The unit identifier is the specific number of an apartment, suite, house, or building. It must appear in numeric format; therefore, you would never see an identifier written as SUITE TWO.

MRS A DALE
415 HERITAGE CRES **SUITE 102A**
SASKATOON SK S7H 5M5

Where the unit designator is not stated in the address, the unit identifier may be placed before the street information. The proper separation between the identifier and the street information is a single hyphen. Refer to the example below.

Figure 8-15 List of street directions and corresponding symbols.

STREET DIRECTIONS AND SYMBOLS

English Street Type	Symbol	French Street Type	Symbol
East	E	Est	E
North	N	Nord	N
North East	NE	Nord-est	NE
North West	NW	Nord-ouest	NO
South	S	Sud	S
South East	SE	Sud-est	SE
South West	SW	Sud-ouest	SO
West	W	Ouest	O

MR W RIDDELL
104-2701 23RD AVE
REGINA SK S4S 1E5

Mode of Delivery The mode of delivery refers to postal boxes, rural routes, general deliveries, and so on. The official CP symbols should be used (see Figure 8-16). The numeric identifier is separated from the mode of delivery designator by one space. Do not use a number sign (#) before the mode of delivery identifier. Refer to the following examples.

Sometimes the identifier is alphanumeric, as in the next example.

MS B COLLINS

SS 4

SPRUCE GROVE AB T7X 2V1

MR BRIAN HUNTER

PO BOX 6001 LCD 1

VICTORIA BC V8P 5L1

Postal Code A unique alphanumeric code is used to identify the delivery address for a mail item. It is the first set of alphanumeric characters that CP's high-speed sorting equipment reads. The purpose of the **postal code** is to enable the automatic sorting equipment to read and sort millions of items each day. As the sorting process is an integral part of delivery, a speedier delivery of the mail item can take place. Addresses are considered incomplete if the postal code is missing. The sequence for the characters in Canadian postal codes is letter, number, letter, space, number, letter, number.

Since the postal code is read by a scanner, it is important that the characters not overlap each other or other parts of the address.

Canada has 19 postal code zones. The letter for each zone begins all six-character postal codes within that zone. The next two characters represent a region within that zone. The last three characters of the postal code identify a smaller section of the area. A correct postal code will lead the mail carrier to the correct side of a specific street, or even to an exact building. Canada's postal code zones are shown in Figure 8-17.

Postal codes are now available from a number of sources:

- Some telephone books publish the postal codes for all areas under the jurisdiction of the telephone book.

- Postal code software that has been recognized by CP is available for purchase.

- The *Canada Postal Code Directory* is available by contacting the local divisional office of CP. If you require

Figure 8-16 List of delivery address symbols.

DELIVERY ADDRESS SYMBOLS

ENGLISH DELIVERY INSTALLATION TYPE	SYMBOL	FRENCH DELIVERY INSTALLATION TYPE	SYMBOL
Letter carrier depot	LCD	Poste des facteurs	PDF
Post office	PO	Bureau de poste	BDP
Retail Postal Outlet	RPO	Bureau auxiliaire	BA
Station	STN	Comptoir postal	COP
		Succursale	SUCC

ENGLISH DELIVERY MODE TYPE	SYMBOL	FRENCH DELIVERY MODE TYPE	SYMBOL
General Delivery	GD	Poste Restante	PR
Mobile Route	MR	Itinéraire motorisé	IM
Post Office Box (for lock box/bag service)	PO BOX	Case postale (pour service de cases postales/sacs)	CP
Rural Route	RR	Route rurale	RR
Suburban Service	SS	Service suburbain	SS

Figure 8-17 Map of Canada showing postal code areas.

the address or telephone number, simply call the toll-free customer service number, 1-888-550-6333.

■ A very effective postal code lookup search engine can be found on CP's website at www.canadapost.ca/cpotools/apps/fpc/personal/findByCity?execution=e1s1.

The postal code should be placed on the same line as the municipality and the province unless the line is too long; in this case the code may be placed on the line below. Refer to the following examples.

MS DULAC
GD
COLD LAKE AB **T0A 0V0**

MARIELLE HOBBS
913 RUE DES MARRONNIERS
ST-JEAN-CHRYSOSTOME-DE-LÉVIS QC
G6Z 3B1

The lists in Figure 8-18 on page 144 show the preferred two-letter abbreviations for the provinces, territories, states, and districts.

Country The country name is used only on mail items to be delivered outside Canada. Use the official English- or French-language spelling for the country name. It should appear alone on the last line of the address block.

An administrative assistant may be called upon to prepare envelopes for delivery to foreign countries. For this reason, it is important to know the regulations that pertain to international addresses. CP defines *international mail* as mail items addressed to countries other than Canada and the United States. During processing of international mail, CP equipment reads only the country name.

Canada carries on a great deal of trade with the United States; an administrative assistant in Canada may often have to prepare envelopes for delivery in that country. The CP processing equipment reads the country name, municipality, state, and zip code. Therefore, the lines that include these pieces of information should follow the CP regulations for envelopes being delivered in Canada. Other information in the address block is used by the US Postal Service and should be prepared according to US standards. The American standards are very similar to those used in Canada:

1. The full municipality name should be separated from the two-letter state abbreviation by two blank spaces.

Figure 8-18 Two-letter abbreviations for destinations in Canada and the USA.

CANADA
(Provinces and Territories)

Alberta	AB	Nunavut	NU
British Columbia	BC	Ontario	ON
Manitoba	MB	Prince Edward Island	PE
New Brunswick	NB	Quebec	QC*
Newfoundland and Labrador	NL	Saskatchewan	SK
Northwest Territories	NT	Yukon Territory	YT
Nova Scotia	NS		

Note that the province of Quebec uses QC as its official abbreviation. In the past, both PQ and QC were acceptable; however, PQ is no longer considered correct.

UNITED STATES
(States and Possessions)

Alabama	AL	Kansas	KS	Northern Mariana	
Alaska	AK	Kentucky	KY	Islands	MP
American Samoa	AS	Louisiana	LA	Ohio	OH
Arizona	AZ	Maine	ME	Oklahoma	OK
Arkansas	AR	Marshall Islands	MH	Oregon	OR
Armed Forces Africa	AE	Maryland	MD	Palau	PW
Armed Forces Americas	AA	Massachusetts	MA	Pennsylvania	PA
Armed Forces Canada	AE	Michigan	MI	Puerto Rico	PR
Armed Forces Europe	AE	Micronesia	FM	Rhode Island	RI
Armed Forces Pacific	AP	Minnesota	MN	South Carolina	SC
California	CA	Minor Outlying Islands	UM	South Dakota	SD
Colorado	CO	Mississippi	MS	Tennessee	TN
Connecticut	CT	Missouri	MO	Texas	TX
Delaware	DE	Montana	MT	Utah	UT
District of Columbia	DC	Nebraska	NE	Vermont	VT
Florida	FL	Nevada	NV	Virgin Islands	VI
Georgia	GA	New Hampshire	NH	Virginia	VA
Guam	GU	New Jersey	NJ	Washington	WA
Hawaii	HI	New Mexico	NM	West Virginia	WV
Idaho	ID	New York	NY	Wisconsin	WI
Illinois	IL	North Carolina	NC	Wyoming	WY
Indiana	IN	North Dakota	ND		
Iowa	IA				

2. The zip code will appear on the same line as the municipality name and state abbreviation. Separate the state abbreviation from the zip code with two blank spaces.

3. The zip code will be either five or nine digits in length. When the zip code is nine digits, a single hyphen is used to separate the fifth and sixth digits.

4. The guidelines for names and street addresses in the United States are the same as those in Canada.

MR B ROSS
4417 BROOKS ST NE
WASHINGTON DC 20019-4649
UNITED STATES OF AMERICA

MR THOMAS CLARK
17 RUSSELL DR
LONDON W1P 6HQ
GREAT BRITAIN

KARL HAUSER
LANDSTRASSE 15
4100 DRUSBURG 25
GERMANY

Bilingual Addressing Bilingual addressing is the use of address information in both English and French. The standard bilingual format is two side-by-side address blocks: the left block in French, the right block in English. The address blocks should be separated by a solid black line at least 0.7 mm thick. The following sample illustrates bilingual addressing.

MASTER CARD	MASTER CARD
BANQUE DE MONTREAL	BANK OF MONTREAL
CP 6044 SUCC A	PO BOX 6044 STN A
MONTREAL QC H3C 3X2	MONTREAL QC H3C 3X2

Return Address A mail item should display a return address that includes a postal code. The return address should appear in the upper left-hand corner of the face of the mail item. The same rules regarding components and format of the mailing address apply to the return address. Sender's name, address information, municipality, province, and postal code lines are mandatory.

Metered Mail

Many organizations use in-house postage meters. Metered mail need not be cancelled when it reaches the post office; however, it must be turned in at a postal outlet counter and not simply dropped into a mailbox.

Metered mail is sent directly for sorting, since it does not need cancelling by CP. **Cancelling mail** refers to the process of printing bars over the stamps, as well as printing the date, time, and municipality where mail processing has occurred. This process prevents a person from reusing the postage; more importantly, it also allows the receiver to track the actual time, date, and place where processing occurred.

Since properly prepared metered mail can go directly to the sorting machine in the postal centre, it may be dispatched slightly sooner than mail that must be cancelled. However, the real advantage to the user is the convenience of not using stamps but being able to apply whatever amount of postage is needed. Additionally, not waiting in line at the postal outlet is a great time-saver. Postage meter machines vary in size from lightweight desk models to fully automatic models that feed, seal, and stack envelopes in addition to printing the postage, the postmark, and the date of mailing.

Manufacturers of postage meter machines must have the approval of CP before distributing the machines. The meter impression die is the property of CP. Only an authorized representative of CP may set, lock, and seal a postage meter.

The user of a basic postage meter must take the meter to the post office and pay for a specified amount of postage. The meter dials are then set for this amount by a CP agent. Each time an envelope is imprinted with an amount of postage, the unused balance on the meter is decreased by that amount. When the unused balance runs low, the meter must be taken to the post office to be reset.

Most offices use a computerized postage machine that provides real efficiency (see Figure 8-19). These machines have a number of features, including electronic weighing, metering, and sealing. Computerized postage machines are leased from an authorized dealer. They are designed so that you can buy postage electronically without having to go to CP. Because the service is computerized, you can purchase postage at any time, even when the leasing agents are closed. The Electronic Postage Setting System (EPSS) allows the user of designated postage meters to reset meters at his or her place of business. The customer can remotely reset these meters over the telephone. The meter supplier provides the customer with a code via telephone, which allows the customer to reset the meter.

The following examples apply to mail prepared in Canada to be delivered to countries other than Canada.

If you use a postage meter, check the manual dials or electronic readout to make sure the correct postage will be printed on the mail. Also check the date to be certain it is the correct date of mailing, not the previous day's date.

In order to work efficiently, group your mail, and stamp all mail requiring the same denomination in one batch. Put pieces of mail requiring irregular amounts of postage aside until the rest of the mail is stamped.

Figure 8-19 Computerized mailing system.

After you have processed all the mail, reset the machine so that the next user will not waste postage because the meter was set for the wrong amount.

Try to avoid making mistakes when stamping mail, but if you do make a mistake, you can request credit from the leasing agent. When complete and legible meter stamps cannot be used because of misprints, spoiled envelopes or cards, and the like, the agent will credit the postage. You should note that in order to receive a credit, you must supply the complete envelope as proof, not just the meter impression.

Self-Check

1. When addressing envelopes for domestic mail, what information should appear in the last line of the address block?
2. What does the first letter in a Canadian postal code represent?
3. What does *cancelling mail* mean?

EXCEPTIONS

The mail does not always go through without problems. What happens to undelivered mail? Is it possible to recall a piece of mail or to refuse mail? As an administrative assistant, you will encounter these situations, and you will have to make decisions regarding what to do when there is an exception or a change in procedure.

Changing an Address

When the organization for which you work changes its address, someone within the organization must notify the local postal outlet of the change. If doing this is your responsibility, ask CP for a *SmartMoves* booklet. This booklet will include a Change of Address Notification form (see Figure 8-20) and great moving tips. You can order announcement cards through CP in quantities of 250. It is advisable to submit the completed form to CP at least two weeks before the move takes place. To safeguard the company's mail, two pieces of acceptable identification must be presented when submitting the request. You must also have written authorization from your company that allows you to redirect the mail to the new address. CP will redirect your company's mail to the new address for a fee that covers six months of service.

In the event that you are sharing your address with more than two other businesses, CP will not be able to accept your change of address, and different arrangements will have to be made. Such arrangements are usually made in cooperation with company mailroom personnel or the person that accepts the mail on your company's behalf.

Returning Undelivered Mail

Keep mailing lists up to date, and address envelopes and labels with absolute accuracy to avoid the cost and delay involved when mail is returned. A returned letter must be placed in a fresh envelope, correctly addressed with new postage.

If the addressee has moved or simply refuses to accept mail, if there is insufficient postage or an incorrect or incomplete address, or if for other reasons the mail cannot be delivered, CP will return the item to the sender. Where the item is sent as Lettermail and contains a return address, the item is returned to sender at no charge.

However, charges may apply to other types of mail that must be returned to the sender. For example, if for any reason unaddressed Admail items cannot be delivered, they may be returned to the sender by specific request. The cost for this additional service is the applicable regular parcel counter price. Conversely, all Admail pieces that do not have the proper endorsement are disposed of locally.

Figure 8-20 Change of address guide and announcement.

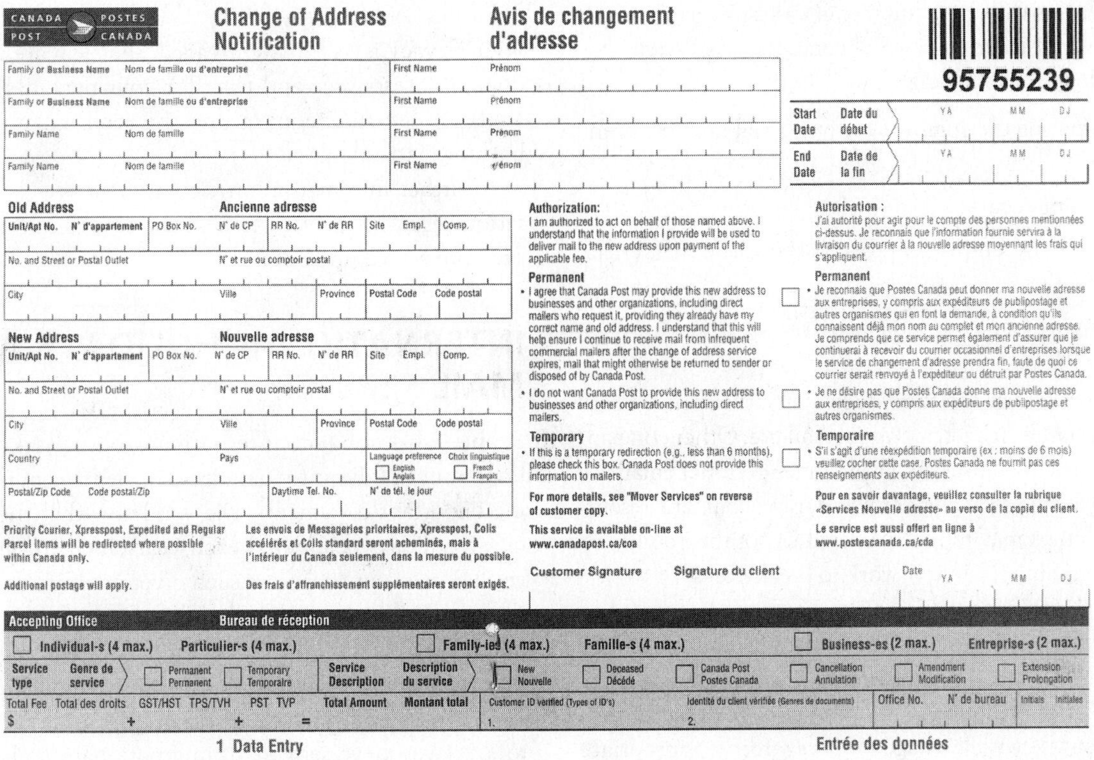

CANADA POST / POSTES CANADA

Change of Address Notification / **Avis de changement d'adresse**

95755239

Family or Business Name / Nom de famille ou d'entreprise — First Name / Prénom

Family or Business Name / Nom de famille ou d'entreprise — First Name / Prénom

Family Name / Nom de famille — First Name / Prénom

Family Name / Nom de famille — First Name / Prénom

Start Date / Date du début — YA MM DJ

End Date / Date de la fin — YA MM DJ

Old Address / **Ancienne adresse**

Unit/Apt No. / N° d'appartement — PO Box No. / N° de CP — RR No. / N° de RR — Site — Empl. — Comp.

No. and Street or Postal Outlet / N° et rue ou comptoir postal

City / Ville — Province — Postal Code / Code postal

New Address / **Nouvelle adresse**

Unit/Apt No. / N° d'appartement — PO Box No. / N° de CP — RR No. / N° de RR — Site — Empl. — Comp.

No. and Street or Postal Outlet / N° et rue ou comptoir postal

City / Ville — Province — Postal Code / Code postal

Country / Pays — Language preference / Choix linguistique — English / Anglais — French / Français

Postal/Zip Code / Code postal/Zip — Daytime Tel. No. / N° de tél. le jour

Priority Courier, Xpresspost, Expedited and Regular Parcel items will be redirected where possible within Canada only.

Les envois de Messageries prioritaires, Xpresspost, Colis accélérés et Colis standard seront acheminés, mais à l'intérieur du Canada seulement, dans la mesure du possible.

Additional postage will apply.

Des frais d'affranchissement supplémentaires seront exigés.

Authorization:
I am authorized to act on behalf of those named above. I understand that the information I provide will be used to deliver mail to the new address upon payment of the applicable fee.

Permanent
- I agree that Canada Post may provide this new address to businesses and other organizations, including direct mailers who request it, providing they already have my correct name and old address. I understand that this will help ensure I continue to receive mail from infrequent commercial mailers after the change of address service expires, mail that might otherwise be returned to sender or disposed of by Canada Post.
- I do not want Canada Post to provide this new address to businesses and other organizations, including direct mailers.

Temporary
- If this is a temporary redirection (e.g., less than 6 months), please check this box. Canada Post does not provide this information to mailers.

For more details, see "Mover Services" on reverse of customer copy.

This service is available on-line at www.canadapost.ca/coa

Autorisation :
J'ai autorité pour agir pour le compte des personnes mentionnées ci-dessus. Je reconnais que l'information fournie servira à la livraison du courrier à la nouvelle adresse moyennant les frais qui s'appliquent.

Permanent
- Je reconnais que Postes Canada peut donner ma nouvelle adresse aux entreprises, y compris aux expéditeurs de publipostage et autres organismes qui en font la demande, à condition qu'ils connaissent déjà mon nom au complet et mon ancienne adresse. Je comprends que ce service permet également d'assurer que je continuerai à recevoir du courrier occasionnel d'entreprises lorsque le service de changement d'adresse prendra fin, faute de quoi ce courrier serait renvoyé à l'expéditeur ou détruit par Postes Canada.
- Je ne désire pas que Postes Canada donne ma nouvelle adresse aux entreprises, y compris aux expéditeurs de publipostage et autres organismes.

Temporaire
- S'il s'agit d'une réexpédition temporaire (ex : moins de 6 mois) veuillez cocher cette case. Postes Canada ne fournit pas ces renseignements aux expéditeurs.

Pour en savoir davantage, veuillez consulter la rubrique «Services Nouvelle adresse» au verso de la copie du client.

Le service est aussi offert en ligne à www.postescanada.ca/cda

Customer Signature / Signature du client — Date YA MM DJ

Accepting Office / **Bureau de réception**

Individual-s (4 max.) / Particulier-s (4 max.) — Family-ies (4 max.) / Famille-s (4 max.) — Business-es (2 max.) / Entreprise-s (2 max.)

Service type / Genre de service — Permanent / Permanent — Temporary / Temporaire — Service Description / Description du service — New / Nouvelle — Deceased / Décédé — Canada Post / Postes Canada — Cancellation / Annulation — Amendment / Modification — Extension / Prolongation

Total Fee / Total des droits $ — GST/HST TPS/TVH + — PST TVP + — Total Amount / Montant total = — Customer ID verified (Types of ID's) / Identité du client vérifiée (Genres de documents) 1. 2. — Office No. / N° de bureau — Initials / Initiales

1 Data Entry — Entrée des données

Lettermail and Parcel items that are without a return address are sent to CP's National Undeliverable Mail Office. If necessary, CP will open the items to look for an address and, if one is found, will return the item to the sender. There is a fee for returning these items. If no return address is found, mail with no obvious value is destroyed. If the item contains cash, the money is deposited to the credit of CP. Saleable merchandise found in the undeliverable items is sold, and again, the monies are deposited to the credit of CP; merchandise that is not saleable is destroyed. Customers wishing to inquire about undeliverable mail should contact CP's customer service department.

Refusing Mail

The recipient of unsolicited mail, such as books and other items of some value, is not obligated to pay for the item or to return it. However, if unsolicited mail arrives at your desk and you wish to return it, you may do so without paying postage if you have not opened it. Simply write "Return to Sender" in clear words on the exterior of the item and drop it in the local mailbox. However, often mail becomes solicited without intention. Be certain to read the fine print carefully before agreeing to receive information through the mail. Often when people agree to receive information, they are also agreeing to receive merchandise that has a cost.

Self-Check

1. What happens to mail that has insufficient postage?
2. What happens to mail that cannot be delivered and has no return address?

ETHICAL ISSUES REGARDING EMAIL

Every office employee should be aware of just how public their office email system is and take responsibility for learning their company's expectations regarding monitoring of email and other computer activity such as web browsing. While Canadian laws recognize an employer's right to monitor employees' email and internet use at work or while using company resources, controversy continues over what can be considered "reasonable" levels of surveillance. One factor to be considered in determining reasonable monitoring might be the reason for the surveillance.

Employers will cite a number of valid reasons to justify surveillance of their employees' computer use. Their concerns include the following:

1. maintaining the company's professional reputation and image

2. increasing security

3. preventing employee disclosure of confidential information

4. improving employee productivity

Companies vary in their degree of surveillance. Some companies rarely, if ever, monitor email use. Other companies may restrict any internet browsing or personal email use by employees while at work or while using company resources. Still others may restrict personal use of the employer's computer resources while at work to break times.

What is an acceptable balance between security and employee privacy? Companies are struggling to establish a balance between the two. If your company has no formal guidelines or policies regarding personal email/internet use, check with management regarding appropriate behaviour in these areas. Volunteer to work on a team to develop reasonable policies that would be acceptable to both employer and employee. Without a doubt, employees will be more likely to buy into the practice of surveillance if they understand the logical reasoning behind the measure.

Company policy or not, play it wise. Use company email for company use only. Set up your own email account through a provider such as Yahoo! and use it exclusively for personal correspondence. Furthermore, access that account only outside the office. That way, regardless of company policy, you will be confident that your privacy is not being invaded, that you are not using company resources and time for your personal use, and that you are not jeopardizing the security of the company's electronic data.

Further information on Government of Canada legislation regarding privacy laws and access to information is presented in Chapter 10.

INTERNATIONAL HOLIDAYS AND MAIL SERVICE

People who conduct international business know how important holiday information can be when mailing or faxing important documents. Did you know that the dates of many holidays celebrated each year change from year to year? Some countries have such diverse ethnic populations that they observe religious holidays for ten or more major religions. How does this knowledge affect the way you and your manager conduct your business communications?

A surprisingly common reason for getting no response to a fax you have sent to an international number is that you are faxing the document on that country's national or local holiday. Conducting business may be difficult if people take extra days off from work in order to take advantage of the long holiday. Before you try to mail or fax an important document or package to a country outside Canada, check out that country's schedule of holidays. For a current list, access a search tool such as Google, and search under the key words *international holidays*.

QUESTIONS FOR STUDY AND REVIEW

1. List five guidelines that you might employ to make your email more meaningful.

2. What information should a fax transmittal form contain?

3. Explain the meaning of the terms *fax automatic redial* and *fax broadcasting*.

4. What does the abbreviation *PIPEDA* stand for?

5. What is an epost™ box?

6. Explain why nobody but the sender and recipient is able to see the contents of a subscriber's epost™ box.

7. What should you do with a personal letter addressed to a former employee of your department?

8. What are the correct steps to take if you open a letter by mistake?

9. Why is date-time stamping important?

10. What is annotating? Why is it helpful?

11. The recommended methods for placing mail on the executive's desk are to put it in a folder or in an envelope. Why?

12. Give reasons for opening booklets and advertising mail daily.

13. What information should be recorded in a Mail-Expected Record? Why is the follow-up significant?

14. Suggest ways to group mail that has arrived in your manager's absence before presenting it to him or her.

15. State what happens to Lettermail items that are mailed without sufficient postage.

16. What are the eligibility criteria for Publications Mail?

17. Provide two examples of two types of unaddressed Admail.

18. If you wish to include a letter in a parcel, mailed at parcel rates, what must you do?

19. What advantages do private courier services offer over Canada Post?

20. Can registered mail be put in a street letterbox, or must it be handed in at the post office?

21. Provide two reasons why you would send an item registered mail.

22. State five items that would be considered dangerous goods.

23. Where does the attention line go on a properly addressed envelope? Where does the postal code go on a properly addressed envelope?

24. What punctuation is acceptable in the address on an envelope?

25. What is the rule for bilingual addressing on an envelope?

26. Why do many organizations use electronic postage meters?

27. What would be the most economical and fastest method of sending a bulky parcel to Whitehorse, Yukon?

EVERYDAY ETHICS

Trick or Treat?

Could it be that dogs recognize the shape of their biscuits? Canada Post believes they do!

Recently, Canada Post successfully lobbied Pet Valu Canada, a chain of pet stores in Manitoba and Ontario, to stop selling their most popular dog biscuits. The Bark Bar, a biscuit made in the United States, comes in several flavours and shapes. Most popular are those manufactured in the shapes of cats and letter carriers—traditional adversaries of the domestic canine.

The president of Pet Valu agreed to discontinue the Bark Bar after he received a persuasive letter from Canada Post's legal department. Pet Valu and its executive were accused of being insensitive to the dangers posed to letter carriers by dogs that ate the Bark Bar. Interestingly, there were no formal complaints from cat lovers.

For Canada Post, the whole affair was very serious and in very bad taste considering the hazards that letter carriers face each day. Pet Valu, on the other hand, reported that the product had not been withdrawn from any other market. In fact, some letter carriers in the United States are reportedly carrying Bark Bars to pacify their would-be archenemy.

- Is this a David and Goliath story?
- Did Canada Post take advantage of its overwhelming profile for other reasons?
- Did Pet Valu have any moral reason to stop selling Bark Bars?
- Was Canada Post morally responsible to protect its letter carriers in this case?
- What do you think? Support your answer with good reasoning.

Problem Solving

1. Desmond Clive is an administrative assistant at a very busy office. He handles correspondence for five managers. When he processed the mail today he opened a letter for one of his managers. He soon realized it was of a very personal nature even though it was not marked *personal*. How should he handle any letters he receives in the future from the same return address?

2. Your manager, who is head of the Accounting Department, forwarded a letter to the sales manager requesting that she reply. The situation is difficult to handle. The customer is dissatisfied with a product and has threatened to send it back rather than pay for it. Your manager is convinced that the sales manager must handle the problem. Here is the chain of events that follow: The sales manager's administrative assistant immediately sends the letter back to you. You attach an Action Requested slip to it and send it right back to the sales manager. The sales manager's administrative assistant calls you on the telephone and says, "We just sent this back to you, and here it is on my desk again." She demands that your manager answer the letter. What should you say to her? What should you do next?

3. As you open the mail, you find the following items:
   a. a letter that mentions two enclosures, but that only contains one enclosure
   b. a confirmation of an appointment your manager requested by letter
   c. a reference to a catalogue being sent separately
   d. a memorandum requesting forms that you supply to others
   e. a memorandum from your manager's superior, reminding your manager that she wants to approve the final draft of a sales bulletin before she leaves town on Thursday afternoon

f. a second letter from a customer whose first letter was sent to another department a week ago requesting a reply

g. a letter being sent to another department requesting a reply to one part of it

h. a letter including a price quotation that you requested by telephone.

What notations would you make and on which document or form?

Special Reports

1. Research online international rates and fees from CP.

Find:

a. the rates for sending a letter to China, Portugal, Russia, and Taiwan

b. the cost of sending a parcel weighing 1 kg to Australia, Israel, Spain, Great Britain, and Peru

2. Using information from CP, find the cost of the following:

a. an Advice of Receipt obtained at the time of mailing

b. an Advice of Receipt requested after the item has been mailed

c. a letter-size Xpresspost travelling to a destination 500 km away

d. insurance for a package valued at $60

e. registration for an item with a declared value of $2700

f. a 4.50 kg parcel mailed within your local postal zone

3. By searching the CP website, determine the service standards for:

- Incentive Lettermail
- Addressed Admail
- Unaddressed Admail
- Newspapers and Periodicals

PRODUCTION CHALLENGES

8-A Processing Incoming Mail

Supplies needed:

- *Notes on Incoming Mail for Monday, July 14, Form 8-A-1, page 395*
- *Mail-Expected Record, Form 8-A-2, page 396*
- *To Do list, Form 8-A-3, page 397*
- *Routing Slips, Forms 8-A-4, 8-A-5, 8-A-6, and 8-A-7, pages 398 and 399*
- *Plain paper*

Mr. Wilson is out of the office during the week of July 14. You are processing the mail on Monday morning, July 14. Mr. Wilson always wants mail from a region routed to the respective assistant vice-president for the region. However, Mr. Wilson expects you to open the letters and to keep a record of the mail forwarded to the assistant vice-presidents. You route magazines and advertising letters from other organizations to the assistant vice-presidents. On your to do list, put reminders to yourself and notes about items that you should follow up on. Put the other letters, memoranda, and important items in a folder for Mr. Wilson. For your instructor, make a list of the items you will put in a folder for Mr. Wilson.

8-B Correcting Addresses and Postal Codes

Supplies needed:

- *Access to CP's website and the Postal Code Look Up web page*

- *List of names and addresses from William Wilson, Form 8-B, page 400*
- *Plain paper*

A. Privately, William Wilson is organizing a high school reunion. He has asked you to help in your spare time. The challenge is that while Mr. Wilson knows the names of his old classmates really well, he has vague recollection of their last known addresses. That's where you can help. Using CP's Postal Code Look Up web page, determine the full, correct address. Key the address in the way that it will appear on an envelope, including the correct format and postal code. You will find the address information from Mr. Wilson on Form 8-B.

B. Martin Beard will be the treasurer of the high school reunion. William Wilson has asked you to determine the closest postal outlet to Martin's location to enable cash transfers. Provide the complete address of the postal outlet to William Wilson in the form of a memo.

8-C Checking Postal Services

Supplies needed:

- *Information from CP*
- *Postal Services question sheet, Form 8-C, page 401*

Collect information from CP. Read and interpret the information in order to answer the questions on the question sheet, Form 8-C.

8-D Determining Which Service Is Best

Supplies needed:

- *Mail Service Options , Form 8-D-1, page 402*
- *Mail Service Selections, Form 8-D-2 page 403*

Determine which class of mail or special service you would use to send the items listed on Form 8-D-1. Arrange each item on Form 8-D-2 indicating the service you would use and why.

Weblinks

Netiquette
www.albion.com/netiquette
This site provides information on the ten core rules of netiquette.

Canada Post
www.canadapost.ca
Here users may locate rates, access product information, track mail items, obtain postal code information, and link to Canadian retailers online.

FedEx
www.fedex.com/ca_english
Federal Express's Canadian site provides details of online services, free software, shipment tracking, delivery options and rates, international shipping documentation, and much more.

PIPEDA
www.privcom.gc.ca/information/02_05_d_08_e.pdf
This site from the Office of the Privacy Commission of Canada contains a guide on individual rights under the *Personal Information Protection and Electronic Documents Act* (*PIPEDA*).

Western Union
www.westernunion.ca

This site lists the company's business solutions services plus its messaging services such as Money Transfer.

Purolator
www.purolator.com
This site lists Purolator's online shipping products and services, including shipping estimates, shipment tracking, and an online shipping demo. Purolator™ International is a courier delivery service offered by Canada Post, as an agent for Purolator. This service provides on-time delivery of time-sensitive documents and packages to the United States, and to over 220 countries worldwide. Details may be found on the Canada Post website.

UPS
www.ups.com
This site lists the UPS products and services and allows you to find out whether and when your package was delivered and who signed for it.

Greyhound Courier Express
www.shipgreyhound.ca
This site provides information on Greyhound's shipping services. The company offers domestic and international shipping services

Chapter 9
Project Management

Learning Outcomes

After completion of this chapter, the student will be able to:

1 Recognize the difference between a project and ongoing work.

2 Understand concepts related to the theory of project management.

3 Define the role of the project manager and the project assistant.

4 Describe the five phases of a project's life cycle.

5 Explore project management certifications.

6 Discuss project management tools.

7 Identify project management software options.

8 Understand common project management terminology.

Today, in addition to their ongoing daily responsibilities, administrative professionals are often called upon to work with their managers on special projects. These projects typically involve individuals from different departments and areas of an organization who work together for a limited time; usually these activities are directed by a project manager.

As an administrative assistant, you will be expected to support your manager's participation on such projects. When your manager is supervising a special project, you may be asked to serve as a project assistant. This will demand a large investment of time, and it will require you to stretch your skills—to coordinate the work of many people, gather resources, and assist your manager in setting goals and identifying project requirements.

This chapter will explore key theoretical concepts related to project management, the roles and responsibilities of project managers and assistants, essential tools for project management, and some of the challenges associated with managing special projects.

WHAT IS PROJECT MANAGEMENT?

To understand **project management**, we first need to understand what a project is. A project typically has a defined goal and a set outcome. The Project Management Institute

(PMI) describes a project as "temporary in that it has a defined beginning and end in time, and therefore defined scope and resources" ("What Is Project Management?," *Project Management Institute*, http://www.pmi.org/About-Us/About-Us-What-is-Project-Management.aspx). For example, planning the Olympics would be considered a project to be managed that has a defined beginning and ending. Projects differ from ongoing work or tasks in that they often bring together, for a limited time period, people who normally wouldn't work together. Projects may also draw on a variety of organizational resources. A project is considered successful when its promised outcome is delivered, within budget, and on schedule.

According to the PMI, project management is "the application of knowledge, skills, tools and techniques to a broad range of activities in order to meet the requirements of a particular project" ("Project Management: A Proven Process for Success," *Project Management Institute Educational Foundation*, www.pmi.org/pmief/learningzone/provenprocess.asp).

A project manager has the responsibility of planning, implementing, and concluding the project. The chief challenge facing the project manager is to achieve the project goal while dealing with constraints of time and resources.

Linda Flory
Executive Assistant

Catalyst Paper
Port Alberni, British Columbia

College Graduation:
Office Administration Diploma, 2000
Administrative Office Management Program—
Applied Business Technology Diploma, 2004
North Island College
Port Alberni, British Columbia

"Your attitude should always be positive."

After six years with a major food retailer, Linda Flory was laid off. One year and another major food retailer later, Linda was laid off again. Linda saw a pattern developing and decided that she was in a "go nowhere" career, so she enrolled in an Office Administration Diploma program.

Just before her courses started, she went back to work to help out a friend. She attended classes during the week and worked at her friend's store each weekend. With one semester left, Linda began taking Administrative Office Management courses two nights a week, in addition to her weekend job and daytime classes. This busy student was also a single parent to her young son and daughter.

Linda juggled her various roles well, and she completed her diploma with honours in December 1999. She began temporary work at Pacifica Papers (Catalyst Paper's predecessor) and, by the fall of 2000, had applied and been selected for the position of Executive Assistant to the company Vice-President and his six department directors. Her goal had been to reach this position within five years of graduating, so she was pleased to be offered the job well in advance of that timeframe. Linda attributes her swift advancement to the additional knowledge and skills she gained by continuing her education during the evenings. She attained a second honours diploma in Applied Business Technology that earned her an outstanding student award in the Administrative Office Management Program.

As Executive Assistant, Linda relies on her strong organizational skills to carry out administrative tasks. She is effective at handling the routine responsibilities of her position; and

she skilfully manages the more challenging items, such as preparing the weekly production reports for her division and ensuring that accurate information is reported to the corporate office. She has also experienced substantial corporate changes at Catalyst Paper, including employee downsizing and two company name changes. She says adjusting to the name changes is a huge undertaking which affects signage, logo usage, document design, advertising, and much more.

To keep the department running smoothly, Linda and her co-workers communicate via email, the telephone, and in person, as well as at meetings. She receives between 30 and 50 emails daily and handles up to 30 phone calls per day.

Linda knows that communication with her family is also important, and that communication helps her to balance home and work commitments. However, work takes priority at times of heightened demands. The cooperation of her family has enabled her to achieve and maintain her career goal of becoming the Executive Assistant to the Vice-President and Senior Management Team of Catalyst Paper. Linda loves her job and the changes and challenges it presents to her.

To future administrative program graduates, Linda encourages: "Learn as much about your business as you can. Networking with others that do similar work can become invaluable. Be willing and capable of change and always strive for success. Stay current with the world around you and keep your skills sharp—proofread everything."

The administrative assistant serves a vital role in meeting this challenge. As a project assistant (PA), you will work closely with the project manager from conception to completion of the project. Seamless collaboration between the project manager and the PA is essential for a successful outcome of the project.

Phases of Project Management

Each project has a life cycle, and within this life cycle there exist five distinct phases. Here are working descriptions of the project management phases (see also Figure 9-1).

1. *Initiation.* When an idea for a project is considered it needs to be carefully evaluated to determine how it will benefit the organization. This evaluation usually takes the form of a business case that defines the project's objectives, scope, and purpose, as well as the deliverables to be produced. Some questions addressed in this phase include the following:

- Why do we need to do this project?
- Who will partner with us?
- What is the feasibility of this project?

Figure 9-1 Phases of project management.

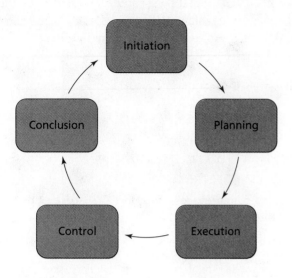

As part of this process, an organization will usually undertake a feasibility study to determine solutions for the business problem or need identified. Within the range of the study, a number of possible pathways will be reviewed and considered. Potential risks for each pathway will also be highlighted. Once the study is completed, a report is compiled and presented in order to gain the support necessary to move forward.

2. *Planning.* Once approval is given to move forward with the project and the team is assembled, the planning phase of project management begins. This phase involves putting the plans in place to guide the team through the project process. In addition to creating an overall schedule for the project, there are several individual plans created during this phase, including the following:

- financial plan
- resource plan
- risk plan
- communication plan
- suppliers' plan

Together, these plans are known as the project plan. Not only does the project plan enable the team to focus on the project's goals, but it also helps in the management of staff and external factors to ensure that the project is delivered on time and within budget.

3. *Execution.* This is the part of the project and product life cycle where the tasks that build the deliverables are executed or launched. Project execution should be in accordance with the approved project plan. In this phase you know what needs to be done and when it needs to be done. The start of one activity is dependent on the completion of another activity. This is why it is essential, during the planning phase, to create an effective schedule. Tracking the progress of completed activities is also a focus of project execution. Once work is completed by a contractor or supplier, it must be approved, or validated, to confirm the work meets the plan specifications.

4. *Control.* The PMBOK® (Project Management Body of Knowledge) defines project control as "a project management function that involves comparing actual performance with planned performance and taking appropriate corrective action (or directing others to take this action) that will yield the desired outcome in the project when significant differences exist." Controlling also involves anticipating possible challenges that could affect project cost, completion target, and outcome. Projects usually fail because challenges are not anticipated and effectively controlled. It is also important to remember that Phases 2, 3, and 4 will be continuous interactive activities throughout the project.

5. *Concluding.* This phase involves the finalization and acceptance of the project. The project manager will ensure the deliverables are handed over to the customer. All contracts related to the project are settled. Sometimes a post-project review is conducted to assess the lessons learned through the process itself and to prepare for future project initiatives.

Self-Check

1. What is a project?
2. What role does the administrative assistant play in project management?
3. List the five phases of project management.

THE PROJECT TEAM
The Project Manager

Successful project management is a collaborative team effort, and a results-oriented team leader is vital in order for the mission to attain its goals. The leader is often referred to as the project manager. Since the administrative assistant will work closely with the manager, an understanding of this role is essential. The primary duties and responsibilities of a project manager are described below.

Staffing and Development To effectively lead a team, a project manager must:

- Build the project team by recruiting, selecting, orienting, and assigning duties to members.
- Establish all procedures.
- Provide training and coaching where needed.
- Lead and motivate the team and provide support for the client.
- Resolve conflicts between team members and relieve client concerns.

Plan Management To ensure that the project stays on track, the manager must:

- Arrange resources by securing equipment, tools, and appropriate contracts.
- Establish project timelines.
- Meet financial objectives.
- Provide updates on project progress while identifying problems and solutions.
- Work directly with project stakeholders.

Interpersonal management In addition to the practical skills listed above, the project manager should have soft skills, or people skills, that will allow team members to interact productively. A project manager should:

- Communicate clearly and concisely.
- Maintain a positive attitude, even when things do not go according to plan.
- Provide leadership in order to manage by example (MBE).
- Be influential. With this skill the manager can often remove roadblocks presented by others in the department or organization.
- Delegate responsibilities to other members of the team. Managers will often fail when they fail to delegate.

Although simplified, this list provides a general overview of the duties and responsibilities of a project manager.

Administrative Assistant's Duties

As support staff, the project assistant (PA) must be able to assume a wide range of responsibilities. The PA may be expected to clarify the objectives of a particular project and to assist in its overall operation. Duties can include handling the logistics of gathering information for progress reports, collecting and tracking time sheets, preparing job cost reports, making agendas, and maintaining and updating websites related to the project.

Although the PA's primary responsibility will be to the project manager, he or she will provide a variety of administrative support functions to the project team. A typical job description for a PA might consist of the following:

- Assist in the development of the project work plan.
- Compose, revise, and edit a variety of routine correspondence, reports, technical charts, tables, and other specialized materials, ranging from routine to complex.
- Produce materials to promote the project, including brochures, newsletters, and flyers.
- Prepare minutes of team meetings.
- Arrange appointments for the project manager, receive visitors, and screen calls.
- Maintain office systems, such as a filing system for project-related documents.
- Collect financial, statistical, and specialized data from multiple sources for the project team.
- Assist in solving complex problems by consulting with team members, including senior management.
- Provide logistical support.

Again, this is only a partial list. The PA may need to assume additional support functions, since each project is as unique as the project team.

It is important to remember that you may be assigned to serve as a PA on a project in addition to your other ongoing duties. Learning how to juggle the two roles can present some unique challenges. The ability to manage your time, work, and resources, as discussed in Chapter 3, is essential in order to find a balance when working in this type of environment.

Figure 9-2 Traits of a project manager.

Top 10 Project Manager Qualities	
✓	Communication
✓	Organization
✓	Competent
✓	Integrity
✓	Delegation
✓	Enthusiasm
✓	Visionary
✓	Team Building
✓	Problem Solving
✓	Flexible

Building the Project Team

The project team is critical to the success of the project. In selecting the team, the project manager must determine if the skills of each potential team member will match the project. It is important to have the right people working on the right projects. The project manager may prepare checklists to ensure that each member of the project team has the skills and abilities to reach the targets of the project. Getting the right balance of skills, knowledge, and ability is difficult but essential for the smooth implementation of a project plan.

When the team is assembled, the background and benefits of the project will be explained. This will establish the foundation for execution of the project plan. It is important that all members of the team fully support the overall project as well as the methods for its implementation. All team members need to be flexible, and the team leader needs to set reasonable and realistic expectations.

The importance of good communication among team members cannot be underestimated. The project manager is ultimately responsible for the way in which information and updates are communicated and for creating an environment in which members feel free to share their ideas. Everyone has a preferred approach to communicating, so it is important, where possible, to accommodate and adapt to these preferences. This will make team members more comfortable and more confident in their abilities. Whatever method of communication is chosen, it should be easily accessible to ensure that team members always have the most up-to-date information.

In addition, the project leader must provide encouragement and **motivation**. Being overly critical will have a negative effect and discourage team members from fulfilling the requirements of the project. The project leader should also schedule meetings, either face-to-face or online, so that team members can ask questions and set action lists. Problems can also be addressed and resolved during these routine meetings.

Finally, the team needs to trust the project manager. They need to have confidence that the project manager will lead the team effectively, and they need to know they can come to the project manager with questions and concerns. Team members will also look to the leader to set the tone for how the team will function. It is very difficult to solve problems in a distrustful environment. By the same token, when team members trust each other they are much more likely to work well together and accomplish their goals.

CERTIFICATIONS & CREDENTIALS

Certification requirements for project management professionals as set forth by the PMI are globally recognized as providing the standard for knowledge and skills in this growing field. Project assistants may consider securing certifications and/or credentials offered by PMI to boost career opportunities in this area.

PMI states the following regarding their certification standards: "PMI is one of the world's leading not-for-profit membership associations for the project management profession, with more than 650,000 members and credential holders in more than 185 countries. Our worldwide advocacy for project management is supported by our globally-recognized standards and credentials, our extensive research program, and our professional development opportunities" ("About Us," *Project Management Institute*, www.pmi.org/About-Us.aspx). PMI was the first organization to offer certification for project managers. It currently offers certification in the following areas:

Certified Associate in Project Management (CAPM)® This is an entry-level certification for someone who is new to project management but who wants to embark on a career in this field. Certification eligibility for each credential is based on several factors such as project management experience and education. To formalize the process, an exam is usually required to obtain this certification. Generally speaking, to be eligible to write the exam, you are required to demonstrate that you have either approximately 1500 hours of experience related to project management or 20 to 25 hours of in-class project management education.

Project Management Professional (PMP)® This certification attests to the ability to lead projects and teams. To obtain this certification, a candidate normally requires several years of practical experience in project management.

Program Management Professional (PgMP)® This is an advanced certification for project managers who have handled multiple projects to satisfy organizational goals.

Self-Check

1. Name three recommended skills for a project manager.
2. Name two tasks a project assistant will perform.

Professionals often use terminology that is unique to their area of expertise. The field of project management has its own specialized terminology. Familiarizing yourself with these terms will help you to communicate more effectively when you are assigned to a special project.

1. **Acceptance.** The formal process of accepting delivery of a product or intermediate project deliverable after having assured that it meets the stated requirements.

2. **Acquisition.** The obtaining under contract of supplies and services to meet the needs of a project.

3. **Assumptions.** Factors that, for planning purposes, are considered to be true, real, or certain. Assumptions affect all aspects of project planning, and are part of the progressive elaboration of the project. Project teams frequently identify, document, and validate assumptions as part of their planning process. Assumptions generally involve a degree of risk.

4. **Baseline.** A formally approved version of the project schedule and/or budget that is used as the benchmark for comparing future progress as the project is completed. A baseline cannot be changed without going through a change approval process. Usually used with a modifier (e.g. cost baseline, schedule baseline, performance measurement baseline).

5. **Chain.** A series of elements joined together in sequence, such as a logical series of activities or occurrences.

6. **Deficiency.** All or part of an item that does not comply with its governing requirements or specifications.

7. **Deliverable.** Any measurable, tangible, verifiable item that must be produced to complete the project. Often used more narrowly in reference to an external deliverable, which is a deliverable that is subject to approval by the project sponsor or customer.

8. **Forecast at Completion ("FAC").** Scheduled cost for a task.

9. **Gantt Chart.** A graphic display of schedule related information created by Henry Gantt. In the typical Gantt Chart, activities are listed down the left side of the chart, dates are shown across the top, and planned activity durations are shown as date-placed horizontal bars. Also called a "bar chart."

10. **Hand-Over.** A process of transfer of responsibility for all or part of a project or its deliverables. Typically, this takes place at the end of a project or a major part thereof. See also Completion and Project Close-out.

11. **Key.** In project management, typically means an item that is a deciding factor, i.e. is critical, instrumental or central to arriving at some determination.

12. **Medium Term.** Anything occurring over or involving an intermediate period of time, i.e., between long term and short term.

PMI Agile Certified Practitioner (PMI-ACP)™

This certification is awarded to professionals who possess the demonstrated technique of developing and delivering incremental components of business functionality, product development, or process design.

PMI Risk Management Professional (PMI-RMP)®

This certification recognizes the professional manager's unique expertise and competency in assessing and identifying project risks, mitigating threats, and capitalizing on opportunities, while still possessing a baseline knowledge and practical application in all areas of project management.

PMI Scheduling Professional (PMI-SP)®

This certification recognizes the professional manager's unique expertise and competence to develop and maintain project schedules, while still possessing baseline knowledge skills in all areas of project management.

This list is just an example of some of the certifications available to project managers. There are a number of other institutions, each with its own curriculum and requirements, that offer project management credentials.

PROJECT MANAGEMENT TOOLS

As with any task or responsibility, in project management a variety of tools can be used to maximize success. One of the duties of the project manager is to determine, in collaboration with the project team, which tools will be most effective.

Tool Categories

According to Project Management Tips, a collaborative blog located at www.pmtips.net offering advice on a number of project management topics, there are three categories of tools that can be used during a project: individual, collaborative, and integrated:

1. *Individual.* These are tools individual members on the program team will use. An individual tool could be something as basic as a task manager program or a spreadsheet stored on an individual's computer or device.

2. *Collaborative.* These are tools that more than one person on the team can access and contribute to, such as a document made available on an intranet site. Another example might be a wiki that team members can use to resolve a challenge they are facing.

3. *Integrated.* This is a tool that can take data from different sources and make it available in one place. Calendars and instant messaging systems are examples of integrated tools.

Project Management Software and Apps

Because special projects often depend on many different people, departments, and outcomes, they can be complex. Project software can help in managing some of these factors. For example, project management software can determine which events depend on one another, how exactly they depend on each other, and what happens if things change or go wrong.

There are many different types of project management software—even the definition of it varies widely—and what software your organization will use is likely to depend substantially on the size and scope of the project. Some types of project management software are designed to help organize a project from start to finish. Software is also available that provides task and resource management, tracking, and outcome report standards.

If your organization decides to invest in project management software, there are a few formats in which it can be obtained.

Desktop A desktop package typically gives the most responsive and graphically intense **interface**. Desktop project management applications typically store their data in a file. Although some versions offer the ability to collaborate with other users, the desktop format does limit collaboration significantly. Some desktop programs permit users to store their data in a central database. Multiple users can then share file-based project plans or data. Microsoft Project (see Figure 9-3) is an example of this type of software.

When using desktop project management software, it is important to keep the version current. All users should regularly obtain software updates.

Client Server Server-based collaborative project management applications are also available. These are designed to support multiple users who are working on different parts of a project. Server-based project management systems hold data centrally and can also incorporate collaboration tools so that users can share knowledge and

Figure 9-3 Screen capture of Microsoft Project.

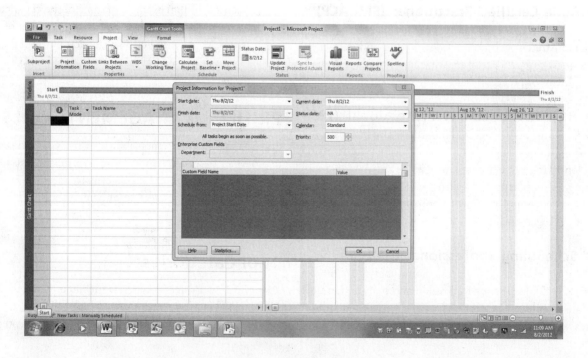

expertise. Microsoft Project is also available as a server-based application.

With client server software you are in control of updates, and you can cut ties with the provider if you do not need upgrades or technical support. A drawback to server-based products is that they usually cost more than desktop software; licensing fees are often charged on an annual basis.

Web-based Project management software can be obtained as a web application. Web-based software is accessed through an intranet or extranet, or the internet itself, using a web browser. Users can access the application from a computer or mobile device without needing to install the program on their computers. They will always have the most recent version as the provider will automatically update it. One of the greatest advantages of web-based programs is that they support multiple users. A drawback to this type of software is that, unlike a desktop application, the software is not available when the user is not online.

PROBLEM SOLVING & DECISION MAKING

In a perfect world, problems get solved with little to no effort. The project team (see Figure 9-4) must work together to solve problems quickly and efficiently. When a problem occurs, people on the team need to take ownership of it by involving those individuals most familiar with it. This will promote prompt resolution. When the problem is defined and all options are weighed, a solution can often be found. Here are some basic guidelines to follow

Figure 9-4 A project management team.

when problem solving collaboratively within the project team:

- Define the problem. What prevents this aspect of the project plan from working?
- Identify alternatives. Consider a variety of solutions.
- Avoid blaming. Focus on solutions, not blame.
- Be creative. Encourage a different approach.

QUESTIONS FOR STUDY AND REVIEW

1. What is the difference between a project and ongoing work?
2. What title are administrative assistants often given for their support role in project management?
3. What does PMI stand for?
4. Describe the initiation phase of project management.
5. List two types of plans developed in the planning phase.
6. Identify staffing and development responsibilities of the project manager.
7. List two certifications available through the Project Management Institute.
8. Describe the three categories of tools used during a project.
9. Identify one of the benefits of using desktop-, server-, or web-based software for project management.
10. Identify a disadvantage of using desktop-, server-, or web-based software for project management.
11. Suggest three important considerations a project manager should take into account when building a project team.
12. Explain what happens during the execution phase of a project.
13. Define the following project management terms:
   acquisition
   chain
   deliverable

EVERYDAY ETHICS

The Presentation

You have been working at a construction firm for three years as an administrative assistant. Two months ago you were asked to assume the role of project assistant on a new project proposal. This new responsibility has required you to work closely with a new sales manager, Maureen Frances. Ms. Frances is responsible for putting the initial proposal together for the large project, which if successful will generate a significant profit for the company. You are nearing the end stage of the proposal preparation; a meeting has been set to present the proposal to the senior management team for final endorsement next week. Ms. Frances has asked you to take the information she has gathered so far and create a slide show to "wow" the senior team.

Following Ms. Frances's instructions you placed significant key points from the feasibility study, including the financial analysis and the risk management analysis, into the slide show. The day before the presentation Ms. Frances asked to review your slide show. After viewing it she thanked you and appeared pleased with the work you did.

Today Ms. Frances presented the slide show to the senior team and received full endorsement to move forward with the proposed project. You should be happy, as this means you will continue on as the project assistant and receive higher pay, but you are not. Your concerns are based on the presentation Ms. Frances gave. Many of your slides involving the potential risks of the project were either removed from the presentation or changed to make the project more attractive to the senior team. You believe the senior team did not receive the full information necessary to make an informed decision.

- Should you ask Ms. Frances about the altered slides? If yes, how will you approach her? If no, what are the possible consequences of your silence?

- Should you speak to the senior team members about what happened? Why? Or why not?

- Do you have any other choices in this situation?

Problem Solving

1. You have been working on a new project team for the last couple of weeks, and you find you are often the liaison between the project manager and the client. When you communicate with the client you feel you get vague instructions, and several times the client has changed his requirements. Today, the project manager has asked you to contact the client to set up a face-to-face meeting in one week's time with the project team to discuss the status of the project. The status update meeting is a periodic meeting that offers team members an opportunity to address issues and concerns. How will you address your concerns about the client's vague instructions and unexpected requests for changes?

2. The project manager, Raymond William, has asked you to call two subcontractors to set up a meeting for tomorrow morning to discuss some urgent work to be completed, as the project has come to a standstill. You make the necessary calls, and both of the contractors tell you that they will consider a meeting only after they have received some key pieces of information. You agree to forward these documents to them electronically very shortly. Unfortunately, you have been very busy today, as a computer emergency took up a lot of your time and your son came home from school sick. It is now 4 p.m. and you haven't sent the information to the contractors. Is there anything you can do now to fix the situation?

3. You are approaching the midway point of a project, and the date of the next status meeting is fast approaching. You have almost everything you need to put the status report together for the stakeholders. You are working with five members of the team. Four of them have been wonderful about sending you updates, but one team member, Christopher Raymondi, is consistently behind schedule. The team uses web-based software so that everyone can see when a task has been completed. You have repeatedly reminded Christopher that he needs to send you timely updates. Each time he promises he will be more punctual in sending you the updates. Still, you feel you are spending a lot of your energy in following up with Christopher, and his updates still come in late despite your best efforts. Is there anything you can do?

Special Reports

1. Working in groups of two or three think of a time you have been part of a project team. In your groups discuss the following:
   a. the main objective of the project
   b. the project outcome
   c. what was positive about the experience
   d. what was negative about the experience

   Report your findings to the class.

2. Interview a project manager asking the following questions:
   a. Describe the qualities you need in your project assistant.
   b. How would you recommend someone gain experience in project management?

   Prepare a memo to your instructor sharing your findings.

3. Review Brian K. Willard's descriptions of nine projects in his article "Project Success and Failures," at http://www.maxwideman.com/guests/metrics/failures.htm. Select three descriptions, and prepare a brief report for your instructor explaining why you believe these are examples of success or failure. Be sure to provide evidence to support your opinion.

PRODUCTION CHALLENGES

9-A Assigning Duties and Tasks

Supplies needed:

- *Project Responsibilities, Form 9-A, page 404*

Read over the checklist presented on Form 9-A. Several duties and responsibilities are listed on this form. You are to decide who is responsible for each task listed, the project manager or the project assistant. If you believe both are responsible, place a check in the "both" column and provide a rationale for your choice in the comments section on the form. If you think someone other than you or the project manager is responsible, place a check mark in the "other" column and again provide a reason for your decision.

9-B Determining Resources

Supplies needed:

- *Determining Software Resources for Project Management, Form 9-B, page 405*
- *Access to the internet*

Your supervisor, Patricia Johnson, has just given you a "wish list" (provided on Form 9-B) detailing her requirements for project management software. Ideally, she would like to have you provide three top choices that are web based. Then she will consult with her team and make a decision based on your findings. This is a significant task as you know the success of a project can be compromised if the wrong tools are used.

After conducting some research online and comparing the wish list, you are ready to pick three potential prospects. Complete Form 9-B using the instructions and requirements outlined. Hand in your completed form to your instructor for evaluation.

9-C Project Problems

Supplies needed:

- *Project Management Challenges, Form 9-C, page 406*

Working in small groups, discuss the three problem scenarios presented on Form 9-C. As a group, brainstorm and determine how your team would approach solving the problems, and identify any resources required.

Hand in one form on behalf of the team with all the members' names clearly identified.

Weblinks

Project Management Institute
www.pmi.org
This site provides information about globally recognized standards for the profession of project management.

Project Management Tips
www.pmtips.net
This site provides tips and tricks for project management practitioners.

Project Management Podcast
www.project-management-podcast.com
This site provides downloadable podcasts on a variety of topics related to project management.

Project Connections
www.projectconnections.com
This site offers a variety of articles related to project management.

Major Projects Management Office
www.mpmo-bggp.gc.ca /index-eng.php
This is a Canadian government website detailing major project proposals submitted to the federal government.

Business Balls
www.businessballs.com
This site provides free information on tools, processes, plans, and planning tips for project management

Chapter 10
Information Management

Learning Outcomes

After completion of this chapter, the student will be able to:

1 Describe what is involved in maintaining effective and efficient information systems in a professional business environment.

2 Explain how governmental laws have affected the management of information in Canadian businesses.

3 Describe the process of organizing information for both visible and electronic filing systems.

4 Explain the benefits and downsides of using electronic files.

5 Explain the options available for storing information.

6 Identify the factors that govern retentions and transfers of records.

7 Understand the four classifications of records for retention.

8 Index and alphabetize names for the alphabetic filing system.

9 Prepare cross-reference cards for alphabetic filing.

10 Compare alphabetic, subject, geographic, and numeric filing systems.

11 Determine the correct folders in which to place electronic documents.

12 Review and assess an online test related to Canada's privacy laws for electronic documents.

Filing is one segment of a broad office function called **information management**. Filing involves classifying, arranging, and storing materials according to a systematic plan for quick reference, for preservation, and—most important of all—for retrieving an item readily when it is required. It is not how fast you file a document but rather how fast you find a document that is important. This chapter will provide effective filing procedures that will help you be an efficient manager of information.

Managing information can involve both paper and, increasingly, electronic files. In fact, technology has made it possible for some offices to maintain records without ever printing a paper copy. An effective administrative assistant, however, will be skilled in handling paper and electronic information.

PROTECTING INFORMATION

Information is one of the most valuable resources of any business. It is important to protect this information from abuse and misuse. This can range from sharing personal information about employees to exposing corporate plans and budgets. As an administrative assistant, you are responsible for protecting information according to company policy as well as government legislation.

Cathy Marcucci
Clerk II

Halton Healthcare Services—Oakville-Trafalgar Hospital
Oakville, Ontario

College Graduation:
Medical Office Administration Diploma
Sheridan College—Institute of Technology and Advanced Learning
Brampton, Ontario

2011

"Work hard, and I promise it will all pay off in the end."

Cathy had her first job as an administrative assistant right out of high school. She followed that up with an entry-level job at another company, and she then worked her way through the ranks from administrative assistant, to sales rep, to AutoCAD operator. But, after taking a break from work to raise her family, she decided to combine her natural affinity for office administration with an interest in healthcare and went back to school to study Medical Office Administration.

After a placement at Oakville-Trafalgar Hospital, she started in a position with the diagnostic imaging department. The best part of her job is the variety of work. Her role changes each day as she takes her turn with eight-hour shifts in front-line reception, report distribution, image library, phone reception, booking, or clerical support. Diagnostic imaging includes MRIs, mammography, ultrasound, radiology, and other modalities, so Cathy must be familiar with numerous policies, practices, and terminologies.

With this kind of change in the daily job routine, Cathy must call on all of her communication skills—interacting with patients, doctors, technicians, and fellow clerks—in person, over the phone, with email, and through the overhead paging system. The hospital environment also requires the use of extensive databases and specialized software such as MEDItech and Electronic Medical Records.

Sometimes, in addition to her general administrative roles, she helps the transcriptionists with inputting of cardiology reports, a specialized task she enjoys—and does well, since she types well over 100 words per minute.

Since working in a hospital, Cathy has discovered that knowing sign language would be a great asset for communicating with hearing-impaired patients, and she wishes she had obtained her CPR certification—also a useful skill in the healthcare environment.

While working hard is Cathy's main piece of advice, she also recommends that students get involved in the various opportunities available in the college setting. Cathy herself volunteered as a scribe at the Mississauga Summit and helped to create Sheridan's first Medical Office Administration portfolio; she won the Julie Lang Award for Volunteerism and High Academic Achievement. Cathy now works on a contract basis as a field placement coordinator for the Medical and Executive Office Administration program at the college.

The Canadian government has legislated the *Access to Information Act*, and some Canadian provinces and territories have legislated a *Freedom of Information and Protection of Privacy Act*. This legislation has motivated public and private organizations and business to:

- establish formal information management systems
- set up policies and procedures based on the legislation
- institute training programs to ensure staff familiarity with the new policies

This legislation establishes records management as a priority function in the office.

Privacy Legislation

The Government of Canada has legislated protection of information through two privacy laws: the *Privacy Act* and the *Personal Information Protection and Electronic Documents Act* (*PIPEDA*).

The *Privacy Act* primarily deals with personal information the government has collected about its citizens. It ensures that all Canadians have access to their personal information and provides for privacy, ethical handling, and correction by the individual if necessary. *PIPEDA* has been fully in effect since 2004. It legislates the use of personal information for all commercial activities in Canada. It sets strict laws regarding what information a business can collect about its customers, how long it can keep that information, how it can use that information, and how it can share that information with others.

The purpose of *PIPEDA* is to help businesses manage personal information and, at the same time, allow individuals to protect their personal information. A description of this legislation and how it affects Canadian businesses can be found at www.priv.gc.ca.

Not only is information protected under federal government legislation, but also some provinces and territories of Canada have legislation that affects privacy and access to information. Where the federal government deems that a province or territory does not have fully adequate privacy legislation, *PIPEDA* applies.

Access to Information Guidelines

The *Access to Information Act* gives Canadians the right to obtain copies of federal government records. These records could be in any format, including letters, emails, photographs, audio and video recordings, and the like. The premise of the act is that government information should be made available to the public.

For some Canadian businesses, these laws have meant a heavier workload and new procedures for handling information, both paper and electronic. These laws have forced the cautious handling and protection of customer/client information.

Self-Check

1. Define the word *filing*.

2. What two Government of Canada privacy laws legislate protection of information?

3. When does *PIPEDA* take precedence over province or territory legislation?

ORGANIZING INFORMATION

Information management involves much more than placing a sheet of paper in a folder. The administrative assistant's role in filing involves:

- Setting up both electronic and paper systems so they are synchronized and systematized. This means that they will work together and that they will follow a solid set of rules and procedures.
- Preparing paper and electronic documents for filing.
- Managing and maintaining the systems. This is a very responsible job that can be difficult.

Among many other tasks, administrative assistants must ensure each staff member follows strict procedures for filing, retrieval, and replacement of files. Especially with electronic systems, people tend to make multiple copies and file the documents in numerous places, except the one place you are expecting to find the document.

Managing information is a very comprehensive responsibility and involves a critical set of procedures for the efficient and effective office.

Preparation for Visible Filing

What is **visible filing**? Visible filing is simply the most current word used to describe paper filing. This section will provide an overview of visible filing, but most activities we do in paper filing are possible and even more efficient in electronic filing.

Paper records are often very untidy and disorganized. We have all seen stuffed and worn file folders crammed into overcrowded cabinets. These same files often have handwritten labels, no **charge-out** system, and redundant information. No wonder filing is the task least enjoyed by many administrative assistants. However, by following the procedures suggested here, filing can become efficient, effective, and satisfying. The procedures to follow, before placing a paper inside a file folder, are:

1. reviewing
2. indexing
3. coding
4. cross-referencing
5. sorting

Reviewing Review each document before you determine how to file it. Follow these guidelines:

- Check papers that are stapled together, and decide if they should be filed together.
- Staple together related papers where one document refers to the other.
- Remove paper clips and extra staples.
- Keep the routing slip with the appropriate documents. You may need to determine later to whom the document was circulated.
- Determine if documents are duplicates and should be **delete**d/destroyed or filed.

Indexing **Indexing** is thinking about how you will file each paper. It is the mental process of determining the key word or number under which a paper will be filed. Careful indexing is the most important part of the process of filing papers. The key word can be a name, a number, a subject, or a geographic location. For example, if you wanted to file a document where the name is *Mr. Benjamin Ross*, you would determine that the most important word for filing is *Ross*.

When you are filing correspondence by name, scan the correspondence to decide which name to use.

Note:

1. Incoming letters are often called for by the name of the organization appearing in the letterhead, so index them by that name.

2. Outgoing letters are often called for by the name of the organization appearing in the inside address, so index them by that name.

To learn how to index for the variety of names you will encounter, follow the standardized indexing rules presented later in this chapter under "Alphabetic Filing Rules."

Coding
After you decide how a paper should be filed, mark the indexing caption on the paper. This process is called **coding**. To code by name, underline the name with a coloured pencil.

In the following three examples, the key words have been bolded and the number of indexing units has been identified. The order in which to consider the units for filing is shown with a number above the unit. The first unit or the most important word in the sequence has been underlined.

(3rd) (2nd) (1st)

■ Mr. **Benjamin** <u>**Ross**</u> = 3 indexing units

(1st) (2nd) (3rd)

■ <u>**National**</u> **Geographic Photography** = 3 indexing units

(1st) (2nd) (3rd)

■ <u>**Ontario**</u> **Publishers** Ltd. = 3 indexing units

The code on the paper should be complete enough that you can return the paper to the same folder each time it has been removed. As you study the indexing rules, you will learn how to determine the order of units within a name.

Cross-Referencing
When a document is apt to be called for by two different names at different times, you should be able to locate it by looking under either name. To make this possible, file the document according to the name by which it is most likely to be requested. Also prepare a reference to it by a second name. This is referred to as **cross-referencing**.

The purpose of cross-referencing is to send you to the correct file and eliminate filing similar documents in more than one place. An electronic or paper card filing system is an effective way to manage cross-referencing.

To make a cross-reference card, use a card of the same size as the primary card in the file but use a different colour. Notice in Figure 10-1 the two cards prepared for Maclean Hunter Limited. The information printed below SEE on the cross-reference card is the same caption as that on the primary card.

Avoid preparing unnecessary cross-references, but if you are in doubt, make one: it may help you locate a paper

Figure 10-1 Primary card; cross-reference card.

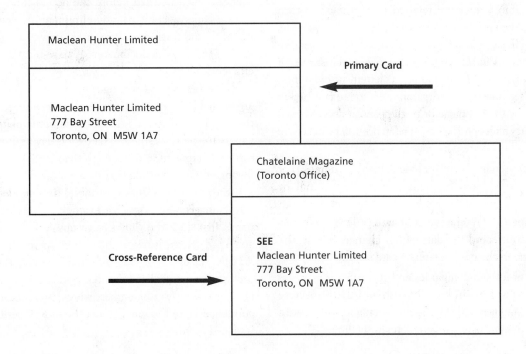

when you need it. There are various situations in which cross-referencing is necessary. Consider the following:

1. Correspondence pertaining to individuals may be filed by subject (for example, Temporary Employees) instead of by the name of the employee.

2. It may be difficult to determine the individual's surname. Consider names like Abdalla Mohammed, Chen Yu, or Kent Ross. What are the surnames?

For the example of Kent Ross, if the surname is Ross, the correct file will read *Ross, Kent*, and the cross-reference card will read:
Kent Ross
SEE Ross Kent

3. The names of married women can be confusing to file and may need support from cross-referencing. For example:

Written or Indexed	Name before Marriage (if she uses her maiden name as her surname)	Name after Marriage (if she marries Robert Whyte and adopts his surname)	
As Written	Ms. Heather Ross	Mrs. Heather Whyte	Mrs. Robert Whyte
As Indexed	Ross Heather Ms.	Whyte Heather Mrs.	Whyte Robert Mrs.

A cross-reference will be necessary for two of the three cases. Most commonly, correspondence would be filed under either Ross Heather Ms. or Whyte Heather Mrs. Only one file should be set up to hold the documents. One primary card will be needed, but two cross-reference cards will be needed for the card file.

4. Subdivisions of a parent company are filed under the name used on their letterhead; they are not filed under the parent company name. To avoid confusion, file correctly under the name of the subdivision, but prepare a cross-reference for the name of the parent company. For example, a subdivision business called Pizza Town with a parent company called Pizza Enterprises would have the correspondence filed as Pizza Town, but a cross-reference card for Pizza Enterprises would send the records manager to the Pizza Town file.

5. Some organizations are referred to by their acronym because they are better known that way—for example, IAAP (International Association of Administrative Professionals) and CNIB (Canadian National Institute for the Blind). Check the organization's letterhead or business card to see how the organization refers to itself. Whether you file by the full name or by the popular abbreviation, *consistency must prevail*. A cross-reference will be necessary to keep all the correspondence in the same file.

6. A business name may include several surnames. For Baines, Jones, and Samuelson, file the original by Baines and cross-reference Jones and Samuelson.

7. A company may change its name. File by the new name, and record the date of the change. Retain the old name in the cross-reference card system.

8. Names of foreign companies and government agencies are often written in both English and the respective foreign language. File by the English name, and make a cross-reference card with the foreign spelling.

9. A foreign company is handled differently than a foreign government. For a foreign company, file the documents by the name as it is written on the letterhead or business card and make a cross-reference card under the English translation.

10. When confusion exists concerning a filing rule, alleviate the confusion by making a cross-reference. A cross-reference will send the reader to the correct file.

11. When a department is renamed because of restructuring within the organization, internal correspondence filed by department name will be affected. File the correspondence by the new name, and create a cross-reference card under the old name.

Sorting Sorting is prearranging papers in the same order that they will be filed before the actual filing begins. By sorting paper documents, you eliminate unnecessary shifting back and forth from drawer to drawer or from shelf to shelf as you file the documents. As a result, you work more efficiently.

Portable vertical sorting trays with dividers and guides are available in a variety of sizes. Use a sorting tray to hold the papers until you file them. If you accumulate a stack of papers in the to-be-filed basket each day and do not have sorting equipment, request it. In the meantime, use the following efficient method of sorting manually.

Sitting at your desk or a table, first divide the papers into manageable groups. For example, if you are sorting by name, first stack the papers in groups A–E, F–J, K–P, Q–T, and U–Z. Next, arrange the papers in the first group in A, B, C, D, and E stacks, and then assemble the papers in each stack in alphabetical order. Sort the remaining groups in the same way. Remember, where two pieces of correspondence share the same name, the most recent document is placed on top.

Figure 10-2 Automated sorting system.

Where there is a very large amount of paper filing to handle, automated sorting systems are available.

See Figure 10-2 for an example of an automated sorting system.

Techniques for Putting Away Papers

One of the steps of filing is the placing of papers in folders. Allow at least 30 minutes a day in your schedule for this activity.

Many administrative assistants rate filing as their most disliked task. When unfiled papers stack up, a simple task becomes a burden. You will spend more time locating a paper in an unarranged stack than in one that is properly organized. Note also that you run the risk of losing papers when they are disorganized. It is crucial that you keep up with filing on a daily basis.

In any new office job, you will be placing and locating materials in files that were maintained by your predecessor. Do not try to reorganize the files in your office until you are familiar with what they contain. Allow yourself several months to learn the system. In the meantime, become thoroughly familiar with the contents of the files. Write down your suggestions for improving the filing system.

The following are very important practices for putting away papers. If your office is not currently doing them, implement them as quickly as possible.

- Always file most recent correspondence at the front of the file (on top).
- When a file folder is held horizontally, the top edges of the documents inside that folder should all be on the left side and the documents should face the front of the folder so that the stapled edge is located in the right upper corner.

Charge-Out Methods

Charge-out methods do not apply to electronic filing. In fact, one of the advantages of electronic systems is that when you retrieve a document from the filing system, you just take an electronic copy. This means, of course, that there is never any reason to return the document to the folder, since the original never left the folder.

However, paper filing is a very different story. Since materials are kept in active files for use, effective charge-out methods must be followed if you are to keep track of materials that have been borrowed from the files and are to be returned.

Charge-out procedures can be electronically controlled. This reduces the time spent searching for files. Software can provide the location of a file and determine whether it is in the filing system or has been charged out.

Manual charge-out systems are very popular. A manual system uses special cards, folders, and pressboard guides with the word "OUT" printed on the tabs to substitute for papers and folders that have been taken from the files. When only a few sheets of paper are removed from the files, an **out guide** is placed inside the folder; when the entire folder is removed, an **out folder** is substituted. If new documents must be filed after the original folder has been removed, the out folder will hold the documents until the original is returned.

Charge-out guides have printed lines for writing a description of the materials removed, the name of the person who has taken the file or the materials, and the date the materials were taken.

The method you use for keeping track of materials removed from the files you maintain will depend on what works best in your organization. Here are some suggestions:

- When important documents are removed from the files, and there is no electronic copy, make a paper copy. Everyone occasionally loses or misplaces documents; this happens to even the most organized people.
- If time permits, you or other administrative assistants who are trained in the charge-out procedures should handle all the removals and returns of materials. When other employees attempt to remove and return the files on their own, charge-out and refiling procedures are not completed, and files go missing.

- When it's not possible for the administrative assistants to control all the charge-outs and returns of files, train all the staff on the charge-out system. Be sure to let them know how important this is to the smooth operation of the business.

Self-Check

1. List four features of the administrative assistant's role in filing.

2. List, in the order in which they will be carried out, the steps in preparing paper records for filing.

3. Why is it important to sort paper documents before putting them away?

4. What is the major advantage of using charge-out methods in your filing system?

Organization of Electronic Files

Because most organizations depend heavily on electronic filing methods as well as paper filing methods, it is essential that the administrative assistant have an effective and efficient means of filing and locating documents on the office network and on removable storage.

In some ways, the electronic system works much like the paper system. Put simply, in the paper system we have cabinets that contain folders that contain files that contain documents. Refer to Figure 10-3 for a photo of electronic folders and files.

In an electronic system, we have **directories** that contain folders that contain files that contain documents. A directory is a section of the network that is allotted to certain people for their files. Having your own directory is like having your own filing cabinet.

When using the office network, certain directories will be allotted for your use. In these directories, you can create folders as you need to open them. Other directories will be available for you to access and read but not to alter, while still other directories will be completely off limits for your use. This is comparable to confidential paper files.

You will need to set up and maintain an organized system for both your removable media as well as the office network. Removable storage comes in many forms. Popular forms for storing information include **pen drives**, flash

Figure 10-3 Electronic folders and files.

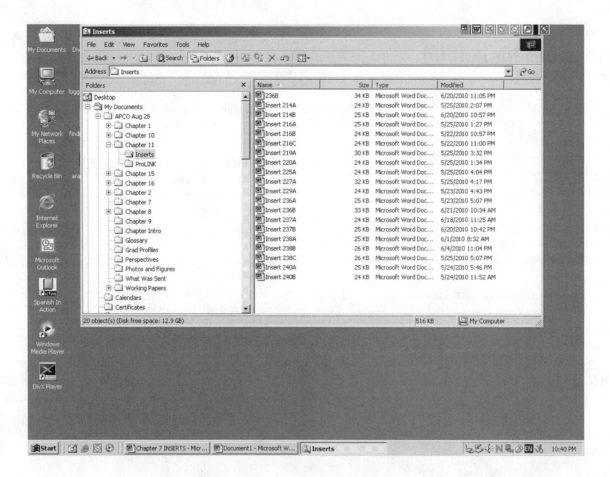

Figure 10-4 Popular removable storage media.

cards, CDs, and portable hard drives. Refer to Figure 10-4 for a photo of popular removable storage media. Removable storage is used for either a primary means of electronic storage or as a backup for documents stored on the office network.

Be sure to label the outside of your removable media stating what directories they contain. Some offices assign different media for each member of the staff for different topics such as expense accounts, budgets, or correspondence for the month of February.

When labelling your directories either on the network or on removable media, be sure to use descriptive words so that you can return to the directory, folder, or file at a later date and know exactly what to find there. As well, it is essential to be consistent with your labelling. If you identify your letters as "Correspondence—February" on one folder, don't label the next directory as "Corr—March." Consistency in labelling is an important key to locating information efficiently.

Benefits and Drawbacks of Electronic Filing

Electronic filing is seen as an efficient and effective way of managing information. However, it has both benefits and drawbacks.

Benefits The fact that documents take up much less space is a major advantage. No large and awkward metal filing cabinets are required to house electronic documents compared to the systems used to house bulky paper files. In addition, offices can conserve paper and avoid unnecessary printing.

Speed of accessing information is greatly increased by using electronic systems.

The fact that files can be accessed by any authorized person using an internet connection, from just about any location, at any time of the day or night, has given office professionals the flexibility they need to be competitive in business.

Drawbacks Because documents are easily accessible to many people through the office network, a number of different authorized people can access the same **e-file**, take a copy, and then file it into another system. The problem increases when people edit the original document to suit their own purposes, resulting in confusion as to which is the original document and how many edited versions are filed outside the main system.

Just as consistent labelling of directories is important, consistent naming of electronic records is essential for timely retrieval. Management would be wise to ensure that employees receive training in electronic file management to avoid "lost" records.

Other drawbacks like easy manipulation of documents and unethical distribution also exist. Better controls for electronic filing continue to develop.

Electronic filing can be expensive. If your office doesn't already have a scanner, one will need to be purchased. You may also have to upgrade your computer system to handle the increased storage demands.

Self-Check

1. Define *directory* as it relates to electronic files.
2. Why is it important that employees be trained in electronic file management?

ORDERING SUPPLIES ONLINE

Products for both visible and electronic filing should make your systems more organized, efficient, effective, and interesting. There are numerous products, styles, sizes, and shapes available to make a filing system work well for the organization. Many products will be available at the local stationery store: however, to get the greatest variety in products, use e-commerce—shop online through the internet. The catalogue will be dynamic with pictures and descriptions, and the prices displayed will be up-to-date

Examples of online shopping sites that offer the latest products in both visible and electronic filing supplies are:

- www.basics.ca
- www.staples.ca
- www.officedepot.ca
- www.ronensystems.com
- www.ebay.ca

The following is a brief discussion of some basic items that are essential to manage your records. Once you have the basics, you will need to enhance and improve on what you have.

Supplies for Visible Filing

Guides Dividers in conventional filing drawers are called guides. They serve as signposts, separating the filing space into labelled sections. Guides also help to support the folders in an upright position.

Guides will have a tab projecting from the edge. Tabs are available in a variety of sizes and colours. While you can purchase blank tabs in order to customize your system, you can also purchase tabs that list the days of the week, the names of the months, or alphabetic letters.

Guides for open-shelf filing differ from guides for vertical file drawers. Figure 10-5 shows open-shelf filing. Note that the tabs on the guides are along the side and not on the top, as they would be on vertical files.

Folders Folders are the containers for holding the correspondence and other paper. Since folders tend to take a lot of abuse, they are constructed of a heavy paper. They can be purchased in a variety of colours, sizes, and weights.

The tabs on the folders also come in a variety of places and sizes. Figure 10-6 shows some of the possible tab cuts.

All folders should have creases at the bottom. The creases are called *scores*. When the folder begins to fill with correspondence, the score allows you to fit more documents in the folder without damaging the papers.

Expandable folders are available for oversized files. The folders shown in Figure 10-7 have a gusset instead of a score; gussets allow a folder to expand more than a conventional folder.

Suspension, or hanging, folders are popular for active files. Figure 10-8 shows a suspension folder with label. Hanging folders are suspended by extensions at their top edges across a metal frame within the file drawer, which

Figure 10-5 An administrative assistant locates a file in an open-shelf filing system.

Figure 10-6 Variety of tab cuts.

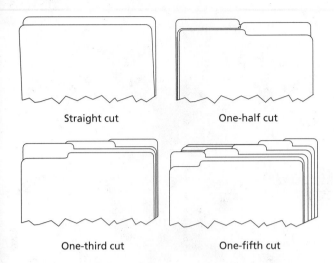

Straight cut   One-half cut

One-third cut   One-fifth cut

Figure 10-8 Hanging file folder.

means they don't rest on the bottom of the cabinet. Materials filed in suspension folders are easily accessible because the folders open wide and slide smoothly on the hanger rail. Attachable tabs are inserted into slots at the top of the folders and are used in place of conventional guides and tabs.

Refer forward to Figure 10-17 for an illustration of guides and folders within an alphabetic system.

Labels Labels help us find our way through the file cabinet. Each folder and each guide needs a label. Labels come in a variety of sizes, shapes, and colours so you can customize your filing system to meet the needs of your organization. Colours should not be used at random. Use colours to represent a topic or the status of a file.

Figure 10-7 Expandable folders.

Labels can be purchased either on a continuous strip or on flat sheets, which work well with a printer. They are self-adhesive and pressure sensitive.

If the labels can be read from both sides, such as with open files, be sure that both sides of your label bear accurate and attractive information.

Key the names on your labels in the indexed order. Use an easy-to-read font and do not use all capital letters. Words keyed in all capital letters are sometimes more difficult to read. Above all, remember to be consistent with labelling through your system.

The captions on the labels of your files should resemble an aligned list of names as shown in Figure 10-9.

Label drawers or sections of files with either open or closed notations. A closed notation indicates the entire span of the contents. A typical example of a closed notation would be:

Correspondence

A–H

A typical example of an open notation would be:

Correspondence

Figure 10-9 Aligned labels on folder tabs.

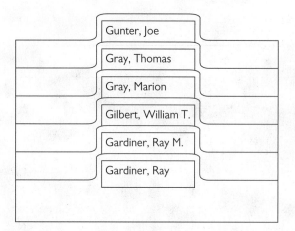

Gunter, Joe
Gray, Thomas
Gray, Marion
Gilbert, William T.
Gardiner, Ray M.
Gardiner, Ray

Figure 10-10 Vertical filing cabinet.

Supplies for Electronic Filing

One of the advantages of electronic filing is that very few supplies are needed. Depending on the requirements of your office, you will need a supply of pen drives, CDs, or an external hard drive. Each medium has a different storage capacity.

All media require adhesive labels of varying sizes. The label should reflect the contents of the information stored on the disk.

vertical filing cabinet shown in Figure 10-10 and the lateral filing cabinet shown in Figure 10-11. The type you choose will depend on your office space available and your personal preference.

Lateral files save space because 25 to 50 percent less aisle space is needed to pull out a lateral file drawer than is needed to pull out a vertical file drawer.

Cabinets may be used as single units or may be grouped together to serve as area dividers. They can be adapted to store almost any kind of record such as disks, letters, legal documents, or cards.

Check the cabinets available at the websites listed in the "Ordering Supplies Online" section earlier in this chapter.

Self-Check

1. List three types of supplies required for visible filing systems.

2. How should you key names on file folder and guide labels?

3. List the supplies needed for electronic filing.

Figure 10-11 Lateral filing cabinet.

STORING INFORMATION

Paper correspondence is usually filed in drawers. Information printed on cards is filed in a variety of ways—in drawers, in trays, on wheels, in panels—to make it easily accessible to the operator. Some filing units are automated, so that the operator can bring the files or cards within easy reach by pressing a button.

Storing Visible Documents

Paper correspondence is usually filed vertically, standing upright and supported by guides and folders in file drawers. The two types of popular filing cabinets for paper are the

Figure 10-12 Wire organizer.

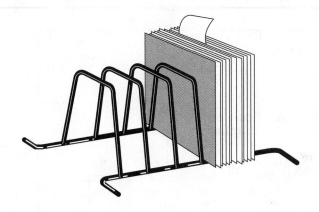

Figure 10-13 Storage case for CD-ROMs.

One type of lateral file is open-shelf. This type is used to save floor space, filing and retrieval time, and initial installation costs. For open-shelf filing, the tabs project from the side of the folder. For an illustration of open-shelf filing, refer back to Figure 10-5.

Lateral files are equipped to handle either regular or suspension folders. The folders may be arranged either side by side or from front to back. The tabs are at the top of the guides, and the folders are arranged in closed drawers.

A popular device designed to hold files upright inside the filing drawer is the wire organizer. See Figure 10-12. With the wire organizer, folders may be placed directly into the file drawer without any suspension folders being used. Folders remain upright, and space is saved. Time is also saved, since duplicate labels for the hanging folders are not needed.

Automated filing equipment is available for both visible card files and folder files. This equipment is constructed so that an operator can bring a shelf of folders, or cards assembled in trays, within easy reach by pushing a button.

Storing Electronic Media

Flash drives and CD-ROMs are not very susceptible to changes such as temperature fluctuations within the surrounding environment.

Refer to the photo of CD-ROM storage shown in Figure 10-13. Cases designed for CD-ROM storage help to keep this mass media organized within a very limited space.

Manufacturers produce a variety of cases to suit your filing requirements. Check the internet websites provided in the "Ordering Supplies Online" section of this chapter to gain a good sense of what is available.

All critical information needs to be backed up for safety. The backup copy may be kept on another removable

medium or on the computer system. Whatever you decide, store the original and the copy away from each other so that the same accident will not destroy both copies.

Storing Business Contact Information

Most business professionals keep their own list of contacts. They develop an electronic database from all the business cards they collect from clients, customers, agents, competitors, et cetera. Executives will either maintain their own database or ask for help from the administrative assistant. Often professionals store a contact list within their email account to ensure easy access for ongoing contact. Microsoft Outlook is one of many software programs used today to store and organize basic contact information.

The database should consist of the client's name, title, company, geographical address, email address, and telephone and fax numbers.

Administrative assistants often collect all client information into one database and make it accessible to all employees. The database will only be effective if it is frequently updated.

Some businesses choose to store business contact information using a manual system known as a Rolodex. A Rolodex is rotating device that holds index cards; each card lists one business contact. Index cards can be removed or added as needed.

Figure 10-14
Sample information for the Quality Flooring Company illustrates a character, a field, a record, a file, and a database.

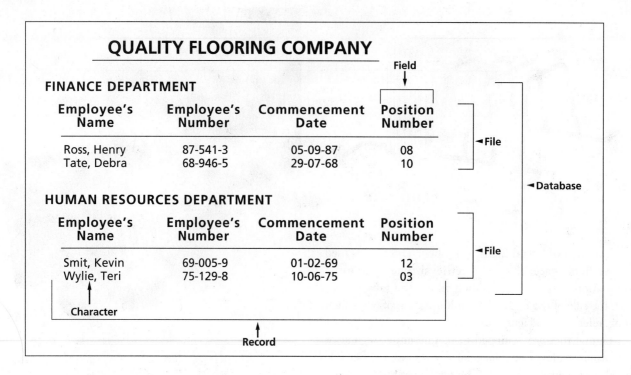

Electronic Databases

Computer records lend themselves perfectly to storing and sorting lists of just about anything, including records on employees, projects, products inventory, and lists of paper files and descriptions of their contents. A variety of computer software is available for creating databases.

Please refer to the database illustrated in Figure 10-14 while you read the following information:

- A name or number, such as a family name, postal code, email address, or telephone number, is called a *field*.

- The complete information about one person or one item is called a *record*. An example of a record would be all the information about Henry Ross.

- A collection of records is called a *file*. An example of a file would be all the records of employees in the finance department.

- A *database* is a set of logically related files. An example would be all the department files for a company.

Please refer to Figure 10-15 for an illustration of an electronic database.

Figure 10-15 Electronic database.

$0.00	$2.07	$2.00	$1.50	$0.00	$0.90	8.97	5720.79	6.47	16.52	14.21	30.73	33.69	$1,010.80
$2.50	$3.77	$2.50	$1.00	$1.40	$0.00	15.17	5735.96	11.2	17.00	14.02	31.02	32.55	$976.43
$1.50	$9.07	$3.50	$0.00	$0.70	$0.30	33.07	5768.73	15.1	17.65	14.09	31.74	33.15	$994.37
$9.00	$10.47	$0.50	$1.50	$1.40	$0.00	46.87	5815.60	22.9	18.14	14.38	32.52	34.08	$1,022.43
$2.50	$4.44	$2.00	$1.50	$3.15	$0.00	33.84	5849.44	13.6	17.49	14.39	31.88	33.58	$1,007.52
$5.50	$13.72	$1.50	$0.50	$4.20	$0.90	44.57	5893.11	26.3	17.76	14.34	32.10	33.45	$1,003.55
$2.00	$4.72	$2.50	$0.00	$1.05	$0.00	37.27	5930.38	10.3	16.40	15.13	31.52	33.09	$992.62
$2.00	$1.56	$0.00	$0.00	$0.35	$0.60	10.51	5940.29	4.51	16.16	16.23	31.39	31.51	$945.38
$1.00	$4.00	$0.00	$1.00	$1.05	$0.00	14.05	5954.34	7.05	16.08	15.27	31.35	29.91	$897.27
$3.50	$13.42	$7.50	$0.50	$0.70	$0.30	48.07	6002.11	25.9	16.85	15.71	32.56	31.06	$931.67
$8.00	$8.23	$4.00	$2.50	$1.05	$0.00	42.68	6044.79	23.8	17.44	15.65	33.09	32.04	$961.09
$4.00	$7.90	$2.00	$1.25	$4.20	$0.30	43.95	6088.44	19.7	17.12	16.17	33.28	32.28	$968.37
$3.00	$6.78	$2.50	$2.50	$1.05	$0.00	44.63	6133.07	15.8	16.78	16.94	33.72	32.34	$970.29
$2.00	$6.20	$1.50	$1.50	$0.70	$0.00	36.50	6169.57	11.9	15.31	17.55	32.87	31.79	$953.70
$1.00	$1.26	$0.00	$0.25	$0.35	$0.00	10.96	6180.53	2.86	15.06	17.95	33.01	30.95	$928.44
$0.00	$3.83	$1.50	$2.00	$1.40	$0.90	18.63	6198.26	9.63	14.95	18.31	33.26	30.91	$927.25
$8.50	$9.74	$3.00	$0.00	$1.40	$0.00	42.44	6240.70	22.6	15.49	18.44	33.93	31.78	$953.46
$3.50	$9.17	$2.00	$1.50	$1.40	$1.20	41.87	6281.37	18.8	15.19	18.38	33.57	32.81	$984.22
$3.00	$9.73	$5.50	$0.50	$5.25	$0.00	49.78	6331.15	24	15.94	18.77	34.71	33.70	$1,011.02
$4.00	$11.00	$3.00	$2.00	$21.00	$0.00	72.20	6403.35	41	16.99	19.70	36.68	34.91	$1,047.20
$1.00	$7.12	$1.00	$1.50	$3.50	$0.00	40.52	6443.87	14.1	17.26	19.65	36.91	34.83	$1,044.93

Electronic databases are essential to the efficiency of a professional office. Accessing information through a database saves a lot of time. Remember that having the ability to locate information gives you a professional advantage over people who don't have these skills. Take every opportunity to learn how to use the electronic databases in the office.

Figure 10-16 MS Outlook Contacts list.

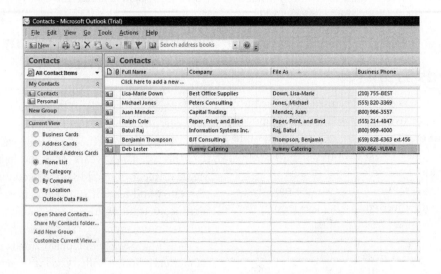

Self-Check

1. What is an advantage of using lateral filing cabinets?

2. Why is it important to back up important electronic records? Where should the backup records be stored?

RETAINING AND TRANSFERRING RECORDS

When the file cabinets or your removable electronic storage systems become full of files, what do you do? Should you destroy them? Should you transfer them to another location? These decisions cannot be made at random. Records retention and transfer is strictly governed by the policies of both your organization and your government.

Paper Records Retention

The following factors determine how long records must be preserved:

1. the nature of an organization's business operations

2. provincial statutes of limitations

3. regulations or statutes of the federal government

Each province has its own statutes of limitations, specifying the time after which a record cannot be used as evidence in the courts. An organization is subject to the statutes of limitations of the province in which it operates. Among the records affected by provincial statutes of limitations are written contracts, injury claims, and accident reports.

Banking records, records of employees' taxes, and aircraft operation and maintenance records are examples of records covered by the federal government's regulations and statutes.

Determining which records to keep and for how long is a critical function. An administrative assistant should not dispose of any records or papers from the files without a clear knowledge of retention legislation.

Record Classification for Retention

According to the Vital Records Protection website at www.vitalrecordsprotection.org, records are classified based on their importance and retention practices. Consider the following:

- **Vital records** are records that must be maintained forever by an organization. They can include articles of incorporation, mortgage records, minutes of meetings, and insurance policies. These records should always be considered active as they are irreplaceable. Vital records usually account for 3 percent of records maintained by an organization.

- **Important records** are records that are very important to the business; they should be retained for five to seven years. These can include financial statements, cancelled cheques, and inventory records. These documents can be replicated, but doing so would require a very costly and involved process.

- **Useful records** are items that are usually retained for one to two years within the organization. These can include correspondence, employment applications, and petty cash vouchers.

- **Nonessential records** are items that have only an immediate need to the organization such as telephone messages, and some emails.

These are some general considerations. It is essential to familiarize yourself with your organization's rules for maintaining records. Check before disposing of any record if you are unsure.

Paper Records Transfer

The most accessible file space should be used for active files; this means that the less active papers will have to be moved from time to time in order to free up the most accessible space for the current papers. Organizations use two methods of transfer: perpetual and periodic. Paper storage can consume a great deal of space. When the inactive records are transferred, they are either moved to a back room or a storage site away from the office.

Perpetual Method *Perpetual* transfer is a method of continually transferring files to inactive storage as a project or case is completed. It is highly applicable for records kept by organizations that handle projects or cases, such as legal firms or construction companies. All the records for one project or case are transferred at the time it is completed.

Periodic Method The *periodic* method provides for transferring files to inactive storage at predetermined intervals, such as six months, one year, or 18 months. The inactive files are transferred to the storage centre, leaving more space to house the active documents.

Electronic Records Retention

Like paper records, inactive electronic records are transferred into storage. This process is called **archiving** and usually involves moving records from the computer system onto CD-ROMs. Both the perpetual and periodic transfer methods apply to electronic files.

Records managers are expected to retain and protect electronic records in the same way they do paper records. According to Canadian federal law, all business records should be kept for a minimum of six years. However, company policy could dictate a longer period.

Government policy affecting electronic records also stipulates that records must be easily converted into a readable format. This means that if you change your software application, you must ensure that related documents less than six years old can still be quickly accessed and clearly read. With the rapid upgrades in technology, it is a challenge to ensure that yesterday's technology and software are kept available and in operating condition in the event you are expected to produce readable documents compatible to the old system.

When government officials request documents, they must be available immediately. This is another good reason

why maintaining and managing a highly organized electronic filing system is essential.

Maintaining Records in Medical and Legal Offices

Rules for regulating standards for medical records are similar across Canada. The College of Physicians and Surgeons governing a jurisdiction ultimately sets the standard. Generally, medical records are to be maintained for a period of ten years after the last entry. Electronic Medical Records, or EMRs, are becoming the standard for data entry and records management in healthcare settings. Significant training in software usage is required to effectively maintain an EMR.

The Law Society of Upper Canada publishes guidelines for lawyers to follow called *Guide to Retention and Destruction of Closed Client Files. The Guide* provides recommendations for retention of files based on the nature of the documents and the case. The guidelines also provide information on the contents of a client file, organization of the file, and closing a file.

---

pro-Link
Paper Preference

For years we've been told that offices would become paperless. It's as if the Paperless Office has become our professional destiny, our professional duty. But only in some office tasks are we seeing less use of paper, while in others we are seeing a greater use of paper.

We use less paper when we:

■ use electronic calendars

■ send attachments on email

■ leave voice mail messages

■ take notes on a keyboard

■ store files electronically

But some offices are becoming more paper dependent. You see this when people:

■ insist on working from tangible records

■ don't trust the electronic system and want records backed up on paper

■ print their email messages and place them into paper files

With the proliferation of communication, offices that like to print their documents have more to print than ever before. So, it's unlikely that paper suppliers and photocopier vendors have much to fear in the near future.

Self-Check

1. List three factors that determine how long records must be preserved.

2. Which transfer methods apply to the archiving of paper records? electronic records?

3. List four ways in which records can be classified for retention purposes.

4. Where can you find out more information on record retention in a medical or legal office?

ALPHABETIC FILING PROCEDURES

All filing systems are based on the alphabet. The main filing systems are alphabetic, geographic, subject, and numeric.

The *geographic* system is arranged alphabetically, but geographic locations, such as provinces and cities, provide the primary subdivisions.

The primary subdivisions in a *subject* filing system are the functions of the organization; the topics in the subject system are filed alphabetically.

The *numeric* system is an indirect system. Each person (or topic) is assigned a number, such as a Social Insurance Number. The information is filed in sequence by number, but an alphabetic index of the individuals (or topics) to whom numbers have been assigned is also maintained. Several combinations of subject and numeric filing systems have been devised.

The *alphabetic* system is the arrangement of names or other captions in order from A to Z. Organizations do not follow identical filing rules; however, with few exceptions the names are usually indexed according to the rules presented and explained in the next section of this chapter. (Variations in the rules are explained at the end of this chapter.)

To set up the simplest alphabetic system in strict sequential order for filing correspondence in regular folders, you need:

- primary guides
- individual name folders
- miscellaneous folders
- special guides
- colour coding (optional)

Primary Guides

Primary guides divide a file into alphabetic sections. A guide is placed at the beginning of each section. Guides direct the eye to the section of the file in which the folder being sought is located.

Guides are not needed with hanging folders, as the folders are supported on a metal frame and the guide tabs are attached directly to the folders. When guides are used, the correspondence is filed in either individual or miscellaneous folders placed behind the guides. Normally miscellaneous items are placed at the end.

Individual Name Folders

When you accumulate at least five items for one correspondent, or when you determine from the current letter that much communication will take place between the correspondent and your manager, prepare an individual folder with the full name of the correspondent keyed in indexed order in the caption.

Arrange individual folders in alphabetical order immediately following the appropriate primary guide, as shown in Figure 10-17. File correspondence within individual folders in chronological order, so that the correspondence bearing the most recent date is placed at the front of the folder.

Miscellaneous Folders

For every primary guide in your file, there should be a miscellaneous folder with a caption corresponding to the caption on the primary guide. Miscellaneous folders belong *behind* individual folders. File in the miscellaneous folders the papers to and from all correspondents for whom you do not have individual name folders.

Within a miscellaneous folder, arrange the papers in alphabetical order by name. When you have two or more papers for one correspondent, arrange them in chronological order, so that the one with the most recent date will be in front of the others. Staple related papers together to increase the ease of locating them.

Special Guides

Special guides direct the eye to individual folders that are used frequently. Special guides are also used for subdivisions of the alphabet or to mark the section of a file containing individual folders for several correspondents with the same surname, such as Smith.

Colour Coding

Colour coding can be applied to any filing system—alphabetic, numeric, geographic, subject, or chronological.

Colour coding is popular because:

1. It provides easy identification for sorting, filing, and finding.

2. It confirms that the folders have been filed in the right places.

Figure 10-17 Arrangement of guides and folders in alphabetic filing system.

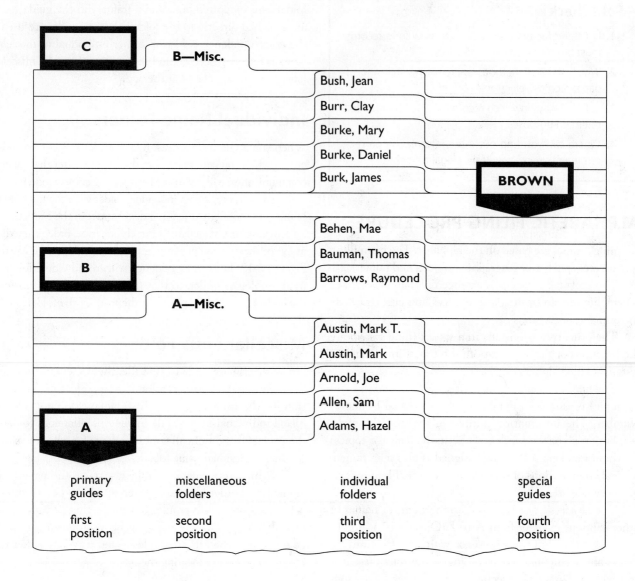

primary guides	miscellaneous folders	individual folders	special guides
first position	second position	third position	fourth position

All types of filing supplies are available in a variety of colours. If you develop your own filing system, you should use colour. First determine how you are going to use colour, and then be consistent in following your plan.

Self-Check

1. What are the four main filing systems?
2. Where would you place a miscellaneous folder in a particular alphabetic section of a visible file system?
3. List two advantages of colour coding your filing system.

ALPHABETIC FILING RULES

Standardization of alphabetic filing rules is very important because it allows office procedures to be consistent and efficient. In 1960, the Association of Records Managers and Administrators (ARMA) recognized the need for standardization and so published the first standardized rules for alphabetic filing. Although the association still refers to itself as ARMA, it has expanded its role to include training, publications, and development of ethics and standardization of the most sophisticated records management systems. The full name for ARMA is now the Association for Information Management Professionals. However, because the name ARMA is so highly respected and recognized, it's likely that the ARMA acronym will continue to be used for years to come. The best way to contact ARMA is through its website at www.arma.org.

The alphabetic filing rules presented in this chapter are based on standardized and simplified rules suggested by ARMA and adapted to meet Canadian needs.

Order of Filing Units

Before you begin any filing process, it is important that you understand the following three terms:

Unit Each part of a name that is used to determine the filing order is called a *unit*. For example, the name *Steven Andrew Watson* has three units: *Steven, Andrew, Watson*. The business name *The Wacky Wig Boutique* has four units: *The, Wacky, Wig, Boutique*.

Indexing Names are not always filed in the same way they are written. In preparation for alphabetic filing, the format and order of a name is often altered. This process of arranging units of a name in order for filing purposes is referred to as *indexing*. An example of indexing is where *Steven Andrew Watson* has his name indexed as *Watson Steven Andrew*. Indexing always precedes alphabetizing.

Alphabetizing Placing names in an A-to-Z sequence is considered alphabetizing. This process is necessary to maintain an alphabetic filing system. For example, placing the name *Adamson* before the name *Boulton* is alphabetizing.

This process appears relatively simple; however, because the English language is made up of words from other languages, word derivatives, prefixes, suffixes, compound words, and other combinations, the filing process may become complicated and inconsistent unless rules are applied.

Before working with the rules, there are some basic principles to remember:

1. Alphabetize by comparing names unit by unit and letter by letter. When first units are identical, move on to compare the second units; when second units are identical, compare third units; and so on. For example, in comparing the following indexed names you would need to make the distinction in the third unit, since the first and second units are identical.

Unit 1	Unit 2	Unit 3
Black	Jeff	Peter
Black	Jeff	Robert

2. Nothing comes before something. Thus, in comparing the following indexed names, you would file *Ross William* first, since the first two units are identical, and *Ross William* does not have a third unit. Nothing is filed before something (*Robert*).

Unit 1	Unit 2	Unit 3
Ross	William	
Ross	William	Robert

Another example of this principle would be

Unit 1	Unit 2	Unit 3
Chatham	Bus	Depot
Chatham	Business	College

In this case, *Bus* would come before *Business* under the principle that nothing comes before something.

3. All punctuation marks should be ignored when indexing. Examples of punctuation marks found in names include periods, quotation marks, apostrophes, hyphens, dashes, and accent marks. Where words have been separated by a hyphen or dash, consider them together as one indexing unit.

4. When the name of a person or business is known in more than one format, file it in the way that it is written on letterhead and business cards. Then prepare a cross-reference. Refer to the discussion on cross-referencing in this chapter for further details on this process.

Rule 1—Basic Names

A. Names of People Names of individuals are transposed. The surname is the first filing unit, followed by the first name or initial, and then the middle name or initial. If it is difficult to determine the surname, consider the last name as the surname. Because nothing comes before something, initials (such as M) are filed before a name (such as Martha) that begins with the same letter.

Example of Rule 1A

AS WRITTEN	AS FILED		
	Unit 1	Unit 2	Unit 3
M Appleton	Appleton	M	
Martha Appleton	Appleton	Martha	
Martin A Appleton	Appleton	Martin	A
Benjamin Frank	Frank	Benjamin	
Abdulla Mohammed	Mohammed	Abdulla	

B. Names of Businesses Names of businesses should be indexed in the order they are written by the business. Therefore, a surname in a business is not necessarily the first unit. Always use the business's letterhead or business card as your guide, or telephone the business receptionist to confirm the correct name of the business.

Example of Rule 1B

AS WRITTEN	AS FILED		
Ben Frank Submersibles	Ben	Frank	Submersibles
Donald Chow Services	Donald	Chow	Services
Ice Delights	Ice	Delights	
Stony Plain Restaurant	Stony	Plain	Restaurant
Tim Tucker Trucking	Tim	Tucker	Trucking

Rule 2—Symbols and Minor Words

Symbols should be indexed in the way they are pronounced. Examples of such symbols include:

AS WRITTEN	AS INDEXED
$	dollar/s
#	pound or number
&	and
%	percent
+	plus

Minor words include conjunctions, articles, and prepositions. Examples of these minor words are:

CONJUNCTIONS	ARTICLES	PREPOSITIONS	
and	the	on/off	in/out
or/nor	a/an	at	by
but		with	of

Each is considered as a separate indexing unit and is not moved in the indexing process. "The" is the only exception. When the word "The" appears as the first word in a business name, it is considered as the last indexing unit.

Example of Rule 2

AS WRITTEN	AS FILED		
	Unit 1	Unit 2	Unit 3
A Catered Affair	A	Catered	Affair
Bailey & Shaw	Bailey	And	Shaw
$ Store	Dollar	Store	
Dots and Spots	Dots	And	Spots
Lacy of Linwood	Lacy	Of	Linwood
Million $ Baby	Million	Dollar	Baby
Play the Game	Play	The	Game
Service +	Service	Plus	
The Sock Shop	Sock	Shop	The

Rule 3—Punctuation

A. Names of People Both given and surnames are sometimes hyphenated. In these cases, ignore the hyphen and write the two words together as one indexing unit.

Example of Rule 3A

AS WRITTEN	AS FILED		
	Unit 1	Unit 2	Unit 3
Irene Dale-Scott	DaleScott	Irene	
Irene Dale Scott	Scott	Irene	Dale
Laura Lee Wilkes	Wilkes	Laura	Lee
Laura-LeeWilkes	Wilkes	LauraLee	

B. Names of Businesses Ignore all punctuation marks. Where a hyphen separates two words, disregard the hyphen and index the two words as one unit.

Examples of Rule 3B

AS WRITTEN	AS FILED			
	Unit 1	Unit 2	Unit 3	Unit 4
Fab-Abs Gym	FabAbs	Gym		
Lotta Dots!	Lotta	Dots		
Marty Allen's Beauty Salon	Marty	Allens	Beauty	Salon
Mr. Lube	Mr	Lube		
When (Pink) Pigs Fly!	When	Pink	Pigs	Fly
Who's Coming?	Whos	Coming		

Rule 4—Abbreviations and Single Letters

A. Names of People Abbreviated and shortened personal names are indexed as they are written. Do not spell out the short form of the name.

Example of Rule 4A

AS WRITTEN	AS FILED		
	Unit 1	Unit 2	Unit 3
Ed Kaye	Kaye	Ed	
Edward G. Kaye	Kaye	Edward	G
Geo. Little	Little	Geo	
Bob N. Ross	Ross	Bob	N
Robt. Ross	Ross	Robt	

B. Names of Businesses When abbreviations and single letters are used in business names, they should be filed as they are written. They are spelled out only when the business writes them that way on letterhead or business cards. Check to see if initials are separated by spaces. If they are separated, then each initial is a separate indexing unit. It does not matter if initials are separated by periods because punctuation is ignored. If the letters are separated by periods but without spaces, the letters will be considered as one indexing unit. Television and radio station letters are indexed together as one unit.

Example of Rule 4B

AS WRITTEN	AS FILED			
	Unit 1	Unit 2	Unit 3	Unit 4
A B C Moving	A	B	C	Moving
AT&T Wireless	ATandT	Wireless		
C.P. Bell Travel Co.	CP	Bell	Travel	Co
CROC Radio	CROC	Radio		
MSS Inc.	MSS	Inc		

Rule 5—Titles and Suffixes

A. Names of People Titles (Dr., Ms., Sir, Sheikh, Mayor, Senator) are written before a person's name. Make the title the last indexing unit. The exception to this rule is religious or royal titles that are followed by only one name. In this case, index them exactly as written.

Suffixes (MBA, Ph.D., Sr., II) are written after a person's name. Keep them in place and use them as indexing units. Disregard punctuation.

Example of Rule 5A

AS WRITTEN	AS FILED			
	Unit 1	Unit 2	Unit 3	Unit 4
Sister Mary Adamson	Adamson	Mary	Sister	
Sheikh Mohammed Ahmed	Ahmed	Mohammed	Sheikh	
Daniel Hart II	Hart	Daniel	II	
Daniel Hart III	Hart	Daniel	III	
Daniel Hart CPS	Hart	Daniel	CPS	
Dr. Phil Hart, MD	Hart	Phil	MD	Dr
Reverend Edward Kaye	Kaye	Edward	Reverend	
Mother Theresa	Mother	Theresa		
Queen Elizabeth	Queen	Elizabeth		
Mayor Joseph Reimer	Reimer	Joseph	Mayor	
Joseph Reimer, Sr.	Reimer	Joseph	Sr	
General Newton Ross, MBA	Ross	Newton	MBA	General
Sister Mary	Sister	Mary		
Ms. Eleanor Vaugh, B.Ed.	Vaugh	Eleanor	BEd	Ms
Ms. Eleanor Vaugh	Vaugh	Eleanor	Ms	

B. Names of Businesses This rule is simple to apply. Write the titles and degrees in the order they appear.

Example of Rule 5B

AS WRITTEN	AS FILED			
	Unit 1	Unit 2	Unit 3	Unit 4
Sister Sara Sue Sweets	Sister	Sara	Sue	Sweets
Dr. Phil Dentistry	Dr	Phil	Dentistry	
King Edward Hotel	King	Edward	Hotel	

Rule 6—Prefixes

Prefixes such as De, Des, Du, El, La, Les, Mac, Mc, O', Van, Vonder, St., and the like are indexed with the name that follows the prefix. It does not matter if there is a space between the prefix and the following name. They still become one unit.

When a large number of names begin with a particular prefix, the trend is to treat that prefix as a separate group and to file the prefix group preceding the basic listing; for example, *Mac* and *Mc* may be filed before the other M names.

Example of Rule 6

AS WRITTEN	AS FILED		
	Unit 1	Unit 2	Unit 3
Jose El Toro	ElToro	Jose	
Louis O'Connor	OConnor	Louis	
A.R. MacNaughton	MacNaughton	A	R
A.R. McNitt	McNitt	A	R
Louis St. Denis	StDenis	Louis	
Michelle Ste. Denis	SteDenis	Michelle	
Adam Vandermallie	Vandermallie	Adam	
John Vander Mallie	VanderMallie	John	
Ray L. Van der Mallie	VanderMallie	Ray	L

Rule 7—Numbers

For names containing numerals, observe the following guidelines:

■ Names using either Arabic numerals (e.g., 7, 54) or Roman numerals (e.g., IV, X) are filed in ascending (lowest to highest) order before the alphabetic characters. Arabic numerals are filed before Roman numerals. So the ordering is Arabic numerals, then Roman numerals, and finally alphabetic characters.

■ When a number is spelled out, such as twelve, it is treated as an alphabetic unit. So 100 would precede twelve.

- When a digit is used in an ordinal number, such as 1st, 2nd, or 3rd, ignore the suffix (st, nd, rd, or th) and index only the number itself. Therefore, 1st is indexed as 1, 2nd is indexed as 2, 3rd as 3, 4th as 4, and so on.

- When a number contains a hyphen, in most cases the hyphen should be ignored. For instance, 8-1 Convenience Store would be filed under 81 Convenience Store. See, however, the next bullet point for an exception to this guideline.

- Where a number is hyphenated to show a range of numbers—for example, 1–100 Corner Dollar Store—only the number before the hyphen (in this example, the number "1") is considered. The number that follows the hyphen (again, in this case the number "100") is ignored. If the hyphen replaces the word "to," then you know this rule applies.

- When a numeral is separated from a word by a hyphen, as in 2-Much Fun Shoppe, the hyphen is ignored and the numeral joins the word to become one unit— 2Much Fun Shop.

- When a number is spelled out and hyphenated— for example, Seventy-Seven Sunset Shop—the hyphen is ignored, and the two numbers become one unit—SeventySeven.

Example of Rule 7

AS WRITTEN	AS FILED			
	Unit 1	Unit 2	Unit 3	Unit 4
1–2 Corner Dollar Store	1	Corner	Dollar	Store
1st Street Bistro	1	Street	Bistro	
4-By-4 Sales	4By4	Sales		
8-1 Convenience Store	81	Convenience	Store	
XVIII Century Costumes	XVIII	Century	Costumes	
XXI Century Designs	XXI	Century	Designs	
AA Advertising	AA	Advertising		
Fat Fred's 50s Club	Fat	Freds	50s	Club
Forty-Two Club	FortyTwo	Club		
One-Hour Cleaners	One	Hour	Cleaners	
Salon on 5th	Salon	On	5	
Salon on 7th	Salon	On	7	

Rule 8—Organizations and Institutions

Examples of names that fit this category are unions and associations, financial institutions, hospitals and care homes, clubs, schools, hotels, magazines and newspapers, and religious and charitable organizations.

Index the names of institutions and organizations just as you would any business name (see Rule 1B). Remember to confirm the names of institutions or organizations by checking their letterhead or business cards.

Example of Rule 8

AS WRITTEN	AS FILED			
	Unit 1	Unit 2	Unit 3	Unit 4
4-H Club	4H	Club		
Alvin Buckwold Sanatorium	Alvin	Buckwold	Sanatorium	
Chinese Baptist Church	Chinese	Baptist	Church	
Edmonton Journal	Edmonton	Journal		
Habitat for Humanity	Habitat	For	Humanity	
Jewish Historical Society	Jewish	Historical	Society	
Ramada Hotel	Ramada	Hotel		
Rashid Mohammed Mosque	Rashid	Mohammed	Mosque	
Royal Bank of Canada	Royal	Bank	Of	Canada
Saskatoon Convalescent Home	Saskatoon	Convalescent	Home	
Toronto Sick Children's Hospital	Toronto	Sick	Childrens	Hospital
United Grain Growers	United	Grain	Growers	
United Way	United	Way		
University of New Brunswick	University	Of	New	Brunswick
The Vancouver Philharmonic Orchestra	Vancouver	Philharmonic	Orchestra	The

Rule 9—Identical Names for People or Businesses

At times, two or more names will be identical. In such cases, use the geographical address to determine the filing order. Consider the following elements in this order:

- **City/municipality name**—When the names are the same, compare the names of the cities/municipalities.

- **Province/territory/state name**—When the cities/municipalities have the same name, compare the names of the provinces/territories/states.

- **Street name**—When the names of the provinces/territories/states are the same, compare the street names. File street names as they are written following the same principles learned in the rules for filing business names. Remember that numerals written as digits come before the alphabetic numbers (22 Street, Second

Avenue). Remember that numerals are considered in ascending order (22 Street, 43 Avenue). Compass directions (North, SE, Southwest) are indexed as they are written.

- **Building number and name**—When the street names are the same, compare the building names or numbers. This refers to buildings of all sizes (houses, apartment blocks, business towers, and the like). Always try to compare building numbers; but when a building's number is unknown, you will have to use the building's name for the comparison. As always, numerals come before words. Remember that numbers are placed in ascending order before words (11 Saskatoon Drive, 22 Saskatchewan Crescent, Sampson Medical Building). Postal codes and zip codes are always ignored.

Example of Rule 9

NAMES AND ADDRESSES	UNIT COMPARED
General Assurance Agency **Milton,** Ontario	City/municipality
General Assurance Agency **Toronto,** Ontario	
Top Travel Vancouver, **British Columbia**	Province/territory/state
Top Travel Vancouver, **Washington**	
Kids' Korner 222 – **5th Avenue** Halifax, Nova Scotia	**Street**
Kids' Korner **4 Baxter Avenue** Halifax, Nova Scotia	
Classique Coffee Café **11 Deer Foot Trail** Calgary, Alberta	**Building number or name**
Classique Coffee Café **55 Deer Foot Trail** Calgary, Alberta	
Classique Coffee Café **Calgary Investment Building** Deer Foot Trail Calgary, Alberta	

Rule 10—Government Names

A. Provincial/Territorial/Municipal The first indexing unit should be the province/territory or municipality that has control over the government department. The next indexing unit is that of the most distinctive name in the department, agency, or ministry.

When the name includes "Department of," "City of," or similar, consider each word as a separate indexing unit.

Indexing government names can be a confusing task if you aren't sure which level of government has jurisdiction over the department. When in doubt, check the local telephone directory's government listings. (Example of Rule 10A is at the bottom of the page.)

B. Federal When the jurisdiction is the federal government, the first two indexing units will be *Canada Government*. (Example of Rule 10B is on the next page.)

C. International When filing the names of foreign governments, always use the English spelling of the country name as the first unit. The next units will include the most distinctive name of the department; then bureau, commission, or board. (Example of Rule 10C is on the next page.)

Variations in Alphabetic Filing Rules

Because conflicts in alphabetic indexing have existed for many years and continue to exist, you need to be aware of the conflicts as well as the standardized rules. When you report for a new work assignment, you will have to retrieve papers that have been filed by someone else. Furthermore, the organization for which you work may have its own rules for indexing and alphabetizing. If so, learn them and apply them, so that the files you maintain will be consistent with the other files in the organization.

Watch for the following variations in indexing and alphabetizing names of individuals:

1. The hyphenated surname of an individual might be treated as separate units rather than as one filing unit.

Example of Rule 10A

AS WRITTEN	Under Jurisdiction of	AS FILED				
		Unit 1	Unit 2	Unit 3	Unit 4	Unit 5
Department of Bylaw Services Winnipeg, Manitoba	**City**	Winnipeg	Bylaw	Services	Department	Of
Department of Social Services Whitehorse, Yukon Territory	**Territory**	Yukon	Social	Services	Department	Of

Example of Rule 10B

AS WRITTEN	Under Jurisdiction of	AS FILED					
		Unit 1	Unit 2	Unit 3	Unit 4	Unit 5	Unit 6
Health Canada	**Country**	Canada	Government	Health	Department	Of	
National Defence	**Country**	Canada	Government	National	Defence	Department	Of

Example of Rule 10C

AS WRITTEN	Under Jurisdiction of	AS FILED			
		Unit 1	Unit 2	Unit 3	Unit 4
Ministry of Tourism Bahamas	Foreign Government	Bahamas	Tourism	Ministry	Of
Industrial Development Commission Netherlands	Foreign Government	Netherlands	Industrial	Development	Commission

2. Names beginning with *Mac* and *Mc* might be filed before names beginning with M.

3. A nickname used in the signature might be filed under the true given name, such as *Lawrence* instead of the nickname *Larry*.

4. Numeric seniority designations, such as II and III, might be filed as spelled out rather than in numeric sequence; also *Sr.* might be filed before *Jr.*

5. The name of a married woman might be filed under her husband's name instead of her own name.

There are many variations in the alphabetic filing rules for business establishments, institutions, and other group names. Watch for the following variations:

1. Each part of a hyphenated business name made up of surnames might be indexed as a separate filing unit, instead of the hyphenated name being treated as one filing unit.

2. Geographic names beginning with prefixes might be filed as two separate units rather than one.

3. Words involving more than one compass point (northeast, northwest, southeast, and southwest, and their variations) might be treated as two words instead of being indexed as written in the company name.

4. Geographic names that are spelled as either one or two English words—such as *Mountain View* and *Mountainview*—might be filed inconsistently, with the result that papers pertaining to one business establishment are filed in two different places.

5. Names beginning with numbers expressed in figures, as opposed to being written out, might be filed in regular alphabetical sequence with all the numbers spelled out in full rather than filed in strict numeric sequence preceding the entire alphabetic file.

6. The *s* following an apostrophe might be disregarded, so that the word is indexed without the *s*.

Self-Check

1. What services does ARMA's expanded role encompass?

2. Define *unit, indexing*, and *alphabetizing*.

3. What is the first filing unit in a personal name?

4. What is the filing rule regarding punctuation in names? abbreviations?

5. List three variations in indexing and alphabetizing names of individuals that you might find from one organization to another.

OTHER FILING SYSTEMS

Alphabetic filing is a *direct* system for finding filed documents. A document's indexed name, if known, can be located easily by going *directly* to the files, looking through the alphabetized folders for the folder with the appropriate caption, and retrieving the document from this folder. Most offices dealing with individuals and companies use some form of alphabetic name system for filing papers. There are, however, other filing systems that may be more useful for particular types of businesses.

Subject Filing

With *subject filing*, records are arranged by topics rather than by personal, business, or organization name.

A furniture manufacturer might want to keep documents dealing with tables, chairs, sofas, and beds in separate file folders. In this case, these topics or *subject* headings would be written (coded) on the appropriate documents, and the papers would be put away in folders bearing the same captions.

Care should be taken to choose subject headings that are specific enough that documents are likely to be requested by these headings. A major subject heading should be subdivided into more specific headings if this will make for faster and easier location of papers. If a document deals with more than one subject, cross-reference sheets or photocopies should be placed in the other subject folders.

There are two methods of subject filing. These are:

1. the encyclopedic system
2. the dictionary system

The *encyclopedic system* is used for both small- and large-volume filing. In this system the major topic is broken down into related subheadings, and folders appear behind each subheading. An example might be:

BEVERAGES	(MAJOR TOPIC)
Coffees	(Subtopic)
■ Decaffeinated	(Folder)
■ Gourmet	(Folder)
FOOD	(MAJOR TOPIC)
Breads	(Subtopic)
■ White	(Folder)
■ Brown	(Folder)
■ Rye	(Folder)
Vegetables	(Subtopic)
■ Potatoes	(Folder)
■ Tomatoes	(Folder)

The dictionary system is not effective where a large volume of files exists. Topics are filed alphabetically, with no grouping by related topics—hence the term *dictionary system*. An example might be:

FOOD	(MAJOR TOPIC)
Brown Bread	(Folder)
Potatoes	(Folder)
Rye Bread	(Folder)
Tea	(Folder)
Tomatoes	(Folder)

Subject filing requires the records manager to refer to an index or list of topics before searching for a folder; for this reason, it is considered an indirect access system. The list is called a **relative index**.

The relative index is an alphabetic listing of all topics that appear in the system. Before returning a folder to the system or searching for a folder, the records manager consults the index to establish which topic the folder is kept under. Refer to Figure 10-18 for an example of a relative index.

Geographic Filing

A real estate company may wish to keep its records of houses for sale arranged by street names and numbers. A large organization with many branch offices across the country may wish to file its records by branch office location. A company that does work internationally may choose to file its records by country name. The arrangement of files by location is called *geographic filing*.

In geographic filing, the largest locations—street, city, province/territory, or country—are used as main divisions, arranged alphabetically by guides. Individual document folders pertaining to these main divisions are arranged behind the division guides, also alphabetically. The system can be as simple or as complex as desired. To meet the needs of customers, office supply companies maintain a wide variety of prearranged geographic, subject, and alphabetic filing systems with guides.

Geographic filing is usually a direct filing system. If the name under which the document is filed is known, the document can easily be retrieved by going directly to the files and looking for it in alphabetic order behind the appropriate guide. However, a geographic system in which an index must be consulted before a file can be located is an indirect filing system.

Geographic filing may use either the encyclopedic or the dictionary system (as explained in the section "Subject Filing"). Which one is used will be determined by the volume of topics.

Figure 10-18 Relative index.

RELATIVE INDEX FOR RECREATION TOPICS	
TOPIC OF FOLDER	**REFER TO THE GUIDE ENTITLED**
Bait	Fishing
Boating Registration	Fishing
Competitive Swimming Rules	Swimming
Court Fees	Tennis
Cycle Helmets	Cycling
Golf Clubs	Golfing
Knot Types	Sailing
Mountain Bikes	Cycling
Racquets	Tennis
Reflective Clothing	Running
Shin Splint	Injury
Sun Stroke	Injury
Tacking	Sailing
Tred-Fast	Athletic Shoes

How a geographic system is divided will depend on the company. One company might find it convenient to use guides with the names of provinces/territories and then further subdivide the filing system by city names. Another company, if it operates in only one city, might use guides that divide the city by districts. They would then further subdivide the filing system by street names. A company that works internationally might divide the filing system by country and then possibly subdivide by city.

Numeric Filing

Numeric filing is an *indirect* method of storing records. In numeric filing, even if you know the name, subject, or geographic heading of a document, you cannot simply go to the files and find it in its alphabetic order. In numeric filing, each document is given a number and put in a folder with that number on the label. The numbered folders are arranged in the files in sequential order. Refer to Figure 10-19.

To find a document filed under a numeric system, you must first consult an alphabetic index to determine the number assigned to that particular document. The index will be kept on a computer database that may be in card format. The index will relate alphabetized file names to their file numbers.

Retrieving and updating information in a numeric system is extremely quick. The computerized database shows the number that has been assigned to the file. It may also

Figure 10-19 Numeric filing arrangement.

show other helpful information such as postal and email addresses, telephone and fax numbers, and the date the file was created.

Once the file has been recorded on the database, the new folder is placed numerically in the filing system. The number of the file is coded on all documents that go in this folder. Inside the folder, the documents are filed chronologically, with the most current document on top.

While numeric filing may seem cumbersome, it has many advantages over straight alphabetic filing. Three of these are:

1. **Time.** Once filed, document folders are faster and eas-ier to find if they are arranged in numeric rather than alphabetic sequence.

2. **Filing Expandability.** In an A–Z alphabetic system, if the B section becomes overcrowded, all sections behind it must be moved to accommodate the overflow. In a

numeric system, because each new name gets the next available number, the file folder is simply added to the end of the files; this does not disarrange the previous file folders.

3. **Privacy of Files.** Numeric filing protects the privacy of files, because numbers rather than names are printed on the file folder labels.

Self-Check

1. Why is alphabetic filing considered a *direct* system?
2. In what order are records arranged in subject filing?
3. Is geographic filing a *direct* or *indirect* method of filing? Explain.
4. List three advantages of using a *numeric* filing system.

ETHICAL ISSUES IN RECORDS MANAGEMENT

In recent years, it has been quite common to hear news reports of unethical behaviour in the workplace and in records management in particular. Loss of important documents, discovery of confidential or personal information stored in unsecured areas, and disposal of sensitive information in regular garbage without being shredded or otherwise made inaccessible are issues that have made headline news.

Employers are expected to be aware of various laws and principles that promote the rights of their employees and customers. The person responsible for managing the company's records must be knowledgeable about laws pertaining to the confidentiality and security of employee and customer records. Some of the issues related to ethical principles of records management are:

■ confidentiality of personal information

■ security of physical equipment such as desktop and laptop computers, as well as paper file cabinets and portable storage media such as USB flash drives

■ validity of information

■ disposal of records

■ improper use of personal identification numbers (PINs) that intentionally or unintentionally allows unauthorized persons (other employees, internet users, or internet hackers) access to confidential or personal information

As an office professional, you should be aware that customer and employee records and emails, as well as other correspondence, are often used as legal documents, and that legal actions may be taken if records are not handled in a safe and secure manner.

INTERNATIONAL STANDARDS IN RECORDS MANAGEMENT

Standards create a professional environment of "best practice" procedures. The International Organization for Standardization (ISO) is a global network that identifies what international standards are required by businesses and government, develops them in partnership with the sectors that will put them to use, adopts them through procedures based on national input, and delivers them to be implemented worldwide.

The ISO is recognized worldwide for establishing the baseline for excellence in records management programs. The ISO states that records management includes:

■ setting policies and standards

■ assigning responsibilities and authorities

■ establishing and sharing procedures and guidelines

■ providing a range of services relating to the management and use of records

■ designing, implementing, and administering specialized systems for managing records

■ integrating records management into business systems and processes

More information on the ISO can be found at their website, www.iso.org.

QUESTIONS FOR STUDY AND REVIEW

1. List four information management responsibilities that an administrative assistant may have.

2. Explain the purpose of the federal *Access to Information Act.*

3. Explain the purpose of the federal *Personal Information Protection and Electronic Documents Act* (*PIPEDA*).

4. What is the meaning of the term *visible filing*?

5. List the five steps involved in getting related papers ready for filing.

6. Before you put papers away, you review them. State four things you look for when you review the documents.

7. What is indexing? What is coding?

8. Explain how a cross-reference can be helpful in locating a paper in the files.

9. Name five situations in which cross-references would be needed for locating materials from the files.

10. Describe the proper way to place paper documents in a folder.

11. Why do charge-out procedures not apply to electronic documents?

12. Describe an effective charge-out method for visible files.

13. How is the filing system organized with electronic files?

14. State three benefits and three drawbacks to having an electronic filing system.

15. Explain the difference between a guide and a folder.

16. What are the most common supplies needed for electronic filing?

17. What is the difference between vertical and lateral filing cabinets?

18. What is the purpose of a wire organizer in a filing cabinet?

19. What is the most efficient way to store business contact information?

20. What is a field? a record? a file? a database?

21. State three factors that determine how long records must be retained.

22. Define the following terms: *perpetual transfer method* and *periodic transfer method*.

23. Why are primary guides used in an alphabetic visible filing system?

24. What should be filed in miscellaneous folders?

25. Describe the proper arrangement of papers within a miscellaneous folder.

26. How are electronic files archived?

27. What does government legislation say about retaining electronic records?

28. Why was ARMA established?

29. In filing rules, what is the meaning of the rule "nothing comes before something"?

30. How are two identical names for different people filed in an alphabetic system?

31. Compare the encyclopedic system and the dictionary system of subject filing.

32. What is the purpose of a relative index for subject filing?

33. In geographic filing, what is the first indexing unit?

34. Why is the numeric filing system an indirect system?

35. A paper that is urgently needed is missing from the correct file folder. Describe the steps you will take to locate it.

EVERYDAY ETHICS

Financial Records

Lyndsay has recently started working for a small office supply company as an administrative assistant. One of her key responsibilities is updating and maintaining a number of records for the organization. It is nearing year end, which means financial records need to be prepared for the accountant to submit a summary of business activity to Revenue Canada. Today, Lyndsay called you on her lunch break; she sounded very upset and didn't know what to do. Her immediate supervisor, Mr. Brown, had asked her to omit some expense reports for the accountant.

Lyndsay realizes this omission could have some serious consequences for the company and possibly for herself. Lyndsay doesn't know what to do. She has just started this job and has told you how much she needs it. She thinks she should ignore Mr. Brown's request and submit all of the expense reports to the accountant—without telling Mr. Brown

■ Is this the best course of action for Lyndsay? Why or why not?

■ How would you recommend Lyndsay handle this situation?

Problem Solving

1. You work with three administrative assistants in a publishing company. You share a centralized paper filing system for the business files. To stay organized you spend at least 20 minutes each day filing, as does your co-worker Inga. Unfortunately, your other co-worker, Ashley, hates to file and rarely does any filing; instead, she puts the files in a pile on her desk. Often when you are searching for a file you can't find it in the file system, but eventually you locate it on Ashley's desk. You are getting increasingly frustrated with having to search for missing files, since this wastes a considerable amount of time. How should you address this issue?

2. You are convinced that your predecessor made up his or her own filing rules. You have been working for three weeks, and you are having difficulty finding anything your predecessor filed. Your office supervisor has asked you to redo the files and to set up your own system. You are eager to set up a better filing system, but this is the peak season for your department. It will be at least two more months before you have time to redo the files. What can you do in the meantime?

3. You have set up an electronic filing system for your office, complete with directories and folders. At numerous staff meetings you have asked the managers in your organization to please file their completed proposals into the correct folders that you have set up. However, whenever you have to search for a proposal, you rarely find it in the correct folder or even in the correct directory. What ideas do you have for solving this problem?

Special Reports

1. Use the Yellow Pages to find the name of a business that is listed two ways. How would you cross-reference it? Using the illustration given in Figure 10-1, prepare two filing cards. On one 7.6 cm × 12.7 cm card, key the name as you would file it. On the other card, prepare the cross-reference.

2. Visit three websites that sell filing supplies and equipment online. Select five items that you would need in order to set up a filing system. Prepare a brief report for your instructor comparing the products and the prices listed on the three websites. Be sure to state the website addresses and names. Use an electronic spreadsheet to display your information.

PRODUCTION CHALLENGES

10-A Indexing and Filing Names

Supplies needed:

- *35 7.6 cm × 12.7 cm cards*
- *Set of alphabetic guides, A to Z*
- *Answer Sheet for 10-A, Form 10-A, page 407*

You have many names, addresses, and telephone numbers stored on cards. Since the cards are worn and inconsistent, you have decided to make new cards. The names, addresses, and telephone numbers are computer stored. You have requested a new computer printout of address labels for all your cards. Key the names in indexing order at the top of each card. In the upper-right corner of each card, key the corresponding number for each name. (You will need the number to record and check your answers.) The first day you work on this project you key 35 cards.

After you have keyed Cards 1 to 35, separate the cards into five groups, arrange the cards in alphabetical order, and file them in correct sequence. Complete Answer Sheet for 10-A and check your answers.

Do NOT remove the 35 cards from your file. In Production Challenges 10-B and 10-C you will add more cards to your file.

Here are the names for Cards 1 to 35:

1. James R. Larsen
2. Bob O'Donald
3. Helen Vandermallie
4. Martha Odell-Ryan
5. Sister Catherine
6. George Harris, Ph.D.
7. Mrs. Georgia Harris
8. Father Jenkins
9. Ty Chen
10. Martha Odellman
11. Allens Swap Shop
12. J. T. Larson
13. Herbert Vander Mallie
14. George Harris, M.D.
15. Mary Allen's Beauty Shop
16. Marshall Field & Company
17. Georgia Harris
18. Allens' Print Shop
19. Trans-Continent Truckers
20. George Harris
21. James Larson
22. Hubert Vander Mallie
23. George E. Harris
24. Cayuga Industries
25. North East Fuel Supply
26. AAA Batteries
27. CHAM Radio
28. Higgins Cleaners
29. Electronics Laboratory, General Electric Company
30. Niagara Office Supply
31. Over-30 Club
32. Prince Arthur's Hair Styling
33. C & H Television Repair
34. First Baptist Church
35. Hotel Isabella

10-B Indexing and Filing Names

Supplies needed:

- *35 7.6 cm × 12.7 cm cards*
- *The card file prepared in 10-A*
- *Answer Sheet for 10-B, Form10-B, page 408*

The next time you work on your filing project, you key 35 more names in indexing order on cards. (Be sure to key the corresponding number on each card so that you can record and check your answers.)

Here are the 35 names:

36. James Danforth, Jr.
37. Burns Travel Agency
38. Strathcona County Water Department
39. Norton R. Henson
40. Sister Marie O'Doul
41. The Lone Ranger Riding Supplies
42. The Jefferson Party House
43. El Rancho Inn
44. Cecil Young-Jones
45. RCT Manufacturers
46. Administrative Management Society
47. Hotel Baker
48. Triple-Star Enterprises
49. Miss Robert's Charm School
50. Acadia University, Wolfville, Nova Scotia
51. Bob Guerin
52. William T. Au
53. Thomas Kaplan, M.D.
54. Irene McGregor
55. Arthur P. Van der Linden
56. Ontario Municipal Board
57. John Wilkins Supply Corp.
58. Southwestern Distributors
59. Department of Employment and Immigration
60. Four Corners Answering Service
61. Reliable Answering Service
62. Montgomery Ward & Co.
63. South East Pipeline
64. Webbers' Home for the Aged
65. People's Republic of China
66. Prince Albert Printing Co.
67. The Mercantile Bank of Canada
68. Aero Bolt and Screw Co., Montreal
69. Strong Memorial Hospital
70. Surv-Ur-Self Pastries, Inc.

After you key the names on the cards, separate the cards into five groups, arrange the cards in alphabetical order, and file them with the 35 cards you filed in 10-A. Complete Answer Sheet for 10-B and check your answers.

Next, prepare for Finding Test No. 1, which will be distributed by the instructor. If you had a card filed incorrectly, find out why. Before you take Finding Test No. 1, be sure that all 70 cards are arranged in correct alphabetical order.

When you have completed Finding Test No. 1, you are ready for 10-C. Leave the 70 cards in your file in order.

10-C Indexing and Filing Names

Supplies needed:

- *43 7.6 cm × 12.7 cm cards*
- *The card file prepared in 10-A and 10-B*
- *Answer Sheet for 10-C, Form 10-C, page 409*

You key 40 names in indexing order to complete your list of names. Here are the names:

71. Jason Wayne Suppliers
72. Prudential Assurance Co. Ltd., Winnipeg, Manitoba
73. Prince Charles Tea Shoppe
74. Federal Department of Consumer and Corporate Affairs
75. Hank Christian
76. East Avenue Baptist Church
77. CKY Television
78. Maudeen Livingston
79. Jim Waldrop
80. Department of Highways Alberta
81. The Royal Inn
82. Human Rights Commission, British Columbia
83. Ellen Jan Elgin
84. Robert E. Kramer, D.V.M.
85. Robert E. Kramer
86. United Hauling, Ltd.
87. Prince James Portraiture
88. Harold Roberson
89. London-Canada Insurance Co., Toronto, Ontario
90. The Royal Bank of Canada, 2411 Bellrose Drive, St. Albert, Alberta
91. Harold O. Roberson
92. Maverick
93. Mrs. Maudeen Livingston
94. George Zimmer Corporation
95. Simon Fraser University
96. Rain or Shine Boot Shoppe
97. M. T. Torres
98. Marion Burnett
99. Harold Robertson
100. John R. de Work
101. Del Monte Properties
102. Mason-Dixon Consultants

103. Robert E. Kramer, M.D.

104. La Belle Arti Furniture Manufacturing

105. Camp Edwards

106. Northern Alberta Pipeline

107. Frank T. Forthright

108. Bill Carter Petroleum Corporation

109. London & Midland General Insurance Co., London, Ontario

110. George Johnston Museum, Teslin, Yukon Territory

You anticipate that you may have difficulty finding cards 71, 75, and 79, because they could be called for by different names. Therefore, make cross-reference cards for them. In the upper-right corner of each cross-reference card, key 71X, 75X, and 79X, respectively.

After you have keyed all the names on the cards, including the cross-reference cards, separate the cards into five groups, arrange the cards in alphabetical order, and file them with the 70 cards you filed in 10-A and 10-B. Complete Answer Sheet for 10-C and check your answers.

Next, prepare for Finding Test No. 2, which will be distributed by the instructor. If you had a card filed incorrectly, find out why. Before you take Finding Test No. 2, be sure that all the cards are arranged in correct alphabetical order.

10-D Setting Up E-Folders and E-Files

Supplies needed:

• *List of Electronic Folders and Files, Form 10-D, page 410*

You have neglected your electronic filing for the past week. Thirteen electronic documents you've created for Mr. Wilson are not yet in folders. The following list gives the document names that you have given to each document. Determine into which electronic folder you should place each document.

1. Minutes November 10

2. Sales Training

3. Annual Leave Request Wilson

4. Guest Speakers October Conference

5. Northwest Budget 20XX

6. Agenda December 7

7. Minutes December 7

8. Halifax Appliance Manufacturers

9. Annual Leave Request Levine

10. Invitations November Sales Seminar

11. Vancouver Better Homes Builders

12. Agenda November 10

13. Records Management Training

10-E Taking the Privacy Test

Supplies needed:

• *Plain paper*

Mr. Wilson has concerns about how the Canadian privacy laws relate to the electronic documents at Millennium Appliances. He wants all the administrative staff to receive training. He asks you to visit the *PIPEDA* site at www.priv.gc.ca, view the video related to Canada's private sector privacy laws, take the online test, and report back to him. He asks you to:

■ make a list of all the questions asked on the test and the correct answers

■ comment in writing on the effectiveness of the video and test as training tools for the Millennium administrative staff

Prepare your responses on plain paper or in an email message to Mr. Wilson.

Weblinks

ARMA International
www.arma.org
This site of the Association for Information Management Professionals includes a list of local chapters, upcoming conferences, and other useful information including a download of disaster recovery plans and forms.

Filing Systems Online
www.filingsystems.com
This site contains information on records management products.

Vital Records Protection
www.vitalrecordsprotection.org
This site provides information on records protection. A variety of articles are available for reference, and relevant links are provided to assist with understanding how to manage business information.

Managing Information
www.managinginformation.com
Managing Information magazine's website includes past issues and many articles pertaining to information management.

Privacy Legislation
www.priv.gc.ca
This site contains a description of privacy legislation and how it affects Canadian businesses.

Kardex Systems, Inc.
www.kardex.com
Kardex is an information and materials management company; its site includes a section on office systems and products.

The Law Society of Upper Canada

http://www.lsuc.on.ca/

This site provides guidelines for lawyers on records management.

The Canadian Medical Protective Association

www.cmpa.org

This site publishes information on how to set up and maintain electronic medical records.

International Organization for Standardization (ISO)

www.iso.org

ISO's website provides information about the organization, membership, their strategies and policies, and the scope of their authority in implementing ISO standards.

Rolodex

www.ideafinder.com/history/inventions/rolodex.htm

This site provides a history of the Rolodex card filing system and a link to the official Rolodex website.

Chapter 11

Front-Line Reception

Learning Outcomes

After completion of this chapter, the student will be able to:

1 Demonstrate communication skills needed for effective use of the telephone.

2 Describe the procedures for answering, transferring, conferencing, and screening office calls.

3 Describe the procedures for placing and receiving long-distance calls.

4 Provide guidelines for scheduling and cancelling office appointments.

5 Explain advantages and drawbacks of using an electronic calendar system in the office.

6 Explain techniques for keeping a well-ordered appointment book.

7 Demonstrate how to handle difficult and/or abusive customers.

8 Discuss the function of the Better Business Bureau.

9 Complete telephone message taking.

10 Search a local telephone directory for information related to telephone services and efficiencies.

11 Plan, enter, and adjust appointments in either an electronic calendar or a paper calendar.

This is where it often begins—a job as a receptionist. Many office professionals start here. This can be an entry-level position and a way to get your foot in the door of a company.

Although a receptionist's job may be viewed as entry level and it may command a lower salary than most other office professionals, this job, without doubt, is one of the most important jobs in the whole company. Companies need to be very selective when hiring a receptionist, since it is the receptionist who makes the first impression, the most important impression, with the client.

As an administrative assistant, communicating with people by telephone, fax, email, or in person, you represent the organization. To people who deal only with you, you are the organization. The first impression and the lasting impression that you make with your voice, your appearance, and your expressions must be favourable. You create the atmosphere by the way you respond to people within and outside your organization.

Large organizations have public relations departments that devote themselves full-time to creating and maintaining a favourable image of the organization. But public relations do not begin and end with a public relations department. Good public relations are every employee's responsibility. Every employee who deals with people from outside the organization is engaged in public relations.

Some of the important aspects of public relations discussed in this chapter are using the telephone effectively, making appointments, receiving visitors, and handling difficult customers. A lot of attention is being given to electronic assistants, also called **virtual receptionists**, who

Devika Bala
Administrative/Planning Assistant, Planning & Redevelopment

Royal Victoria Regional Health Centre
Barrie, Ontario

College Graduation:
Office Administration—Medical
Georgian College
Barrie, Ontario
2011

"The bottom line is positive attitude, aptitude, and being polite and professional."

Devika Bala's career took a turn after she lost her job as a purchasing manager for an automotive company in Vaughan, Ontario. The company went bankrupt, and Devika was forced to re-examine her career options. She says she was always interested in the medical field, so she took advantage of the Ontario government's Second Career program to study medical office administration.

In her role as an administrative/planning assistant, Devika carries out a range of tasks, including administrative duties such as transcribing and filing, planning meetings, maintaining calendars, preparing agendas and minutes, tracking expenses and purchased equipment, managing project databases, organizing workshops and training sessions, and assisting with patients.

Devika also provides backup to the senior medical administrative assistant, which requires her to perform several specialized tasks. In this role, she is responsible for welcoming new doctors, organizing meetings for the medical advisory committee, and explaining hospital admission procedures to new staff. Devika says that she greets new doctors when they arrive, gives them a brief tour of the hospital, and sees that they are paired with an existing physician in the same work area.

Serving as the front-line person for incoming staff means Devika needs to demonstrate strong communication and interpersonal skills. She says that because people are often used to their own way of doing things, she needs to be very clear with her messaging to establish hospital procedures and policies. Although Devika admits that she finds public speaking to be one of her more challenging duties, she also feels her role as a greeter can be rewarding, as it allows her to meet new faces and interesting personalities.

With such a busy workload, Devika says she manages her responsibilities by arranging her tasks on a daily basis. However, she also admits it can be difficult to balance work life and home life. To manage, she tries to put a clear divide between the two. "When you are at work, you put your full mind to work, and when you are at home, you put your full mind to your family," she says.

Her advice to future graduates of administrative assistant programs is to persevere and stay positive. Devika says that her education played a huge part in her career success and that it enabled her to gain valuable skills needed to stand out in a highly competitive field. She's also working toward becoming a manager, and is currently enrolled in a bachelor of health administration program through Athabasca University. "Work hard at school, as every bit counts," she says. "The bottom line is positive attitude, aptitude, and being polite and professional."

perform these tasks at a fraction of the cost of having a true receptionist.

VIRTUAL RECEPTIONIST

Does the idea of a virtual receptionist (VR) make you worry about your future career? Stop worrying!

Companies that hire receptionists know the value of personal customer service—a service that can best be offered by human beings. Companies that insist on having an individual receptionist are intent on establishing and maintaining good relationships with clients. They will hire you because you can outperform a machine.

What Can a VR Do?

The virtual receptionist is an electronic assistant. It's a clever high-tech tool and a telephone application that performs many functions traditionally carried out by administrative assistants. Can an electronic assistant do more than a human office professional? No, it can't—but it can look after some of the routine receptionist tasks. An electronic assistant can:

- answer the telephone with an upbeat greeting
- set up a conference call
- store and forward faxes
- forward calls

- respond to simple verbal commands
- schedule appointments
- record the caller's information such as name and telephone number
- receive incoming calls while the user is checking messages
- store hundreds of names, telephone and fax numbers, and email addresses

Most of these systems are entirely voice-driven, meaning the user does not have to touch the keypad. As well, the VR has almost a human touch—it uses naturally spoken phrases like "Oh, hi," "How are you?" and "I'm back."

Who Uses a VR?

Small to midsize companies often use a virtual receptionist. These companies:

- look for cost efficiencies
- look for an effective way to handle receptionist responsibilities
- have service-oriented businesses
- have managers that spend considerable time out of the office
- want to be responsive to their customers
- want to portray an image of professionalism
- sometimes want to give the impression of being a larger company than they actually are
- do not want their customers to feel they are being processed by a machine

Electronic assistants should be a receptionist's tool, not a receptionist's competition. Learn how to use this tool to your best advantage. Take pride in the public relations role of your job and the personality you can inject into it.

Self-Check

1. List four duties a VR can perform.

EFFECTIVE USE OF THE TELEPHONE

Effective telephone techniques involve placing and receiving local and long-distance calls in the most efficient and cost-effective way. Talking with your friends over the telephone does not prepare you for handling business calls. When it is your responsibility to handle business calls, it is important to learn and remember effective techniques, and to apply them consistently. Observe the techniques other professionals use when they call you or when they answer your call. Can those techniques be improved? If so, apply the improvements to your own calls.

Practising Telephone Communication Skills

Speaking clearly, using correct grammar, and listening actively are essential skills in communicating successfully and in projecting a professional image, and this is especially true in telephone communications.

Speak Clearly Whether you are making or receiving telephone calls, it is important to remember that your voice projects an image of your company. Your tone of voice, volume, and inflection are as important as the words you say when communicating via telephone. Because you cannot rely on nonverbal expressions such as body language and facial gestures to help convey a message, you must rely on your voice to convey a professional image of your company. Speaking clearly with a positive tone is essential to good communication. The image you project with your voice is determined by the following elements:

1. **Volume.** Speak as though you are talking to someone across the desk from you. Of course, if the person is having difficulty hearing you, you will have to adjust your speech volume to the appropriate level.

2. **Rate of Speed.** Speak distinctly and at a rate that is not too slow and yet not too rushed. If you speak rapidly, your words may be jumbled and the caller may ask you to repeat the information. Avoid speaking rapidly when answering the telephone. Because you use the company's greeting often, you may have a tendency to speak rapidly. Answer as if you were voicing the greeting for the first time; speaking at a controlled rate will enable you to appear confident and poised.

3. **Inflection.** Be aware of your voice tone. Vary it to show expression; avoid speaking in a monotone voice. Using inflection in your voice brings out the meaning of what you say and emphasizes important points in the conversation.

4. **Quality.** Smile when answering the telephone or when engaged in a telephone conversation. You don't need to paste on a giant clown smile! A slight uplifting of the corners of your mouth will ensure that you don't sound as if you are frowning or angry at the world. A voice that conveys a smile will project an image of a courteous and enthusiastic worker who is ready and willing to help— a professional image.

Use Correct Pronunciation and Grammar

Pronunciation means saying each word correctly, clearly, and distinctly by moving your lips, tongue, and jaw freely.

Speaking clearly and distinctly is especially important when communicating with people whose first language is not English and who may have difficulty interpreting run-together words. For example, avoid common grammatical errors such as:

"wouldja" for "would you"

"wanna" for "want to"

"gimme" for "give me"

"innerview" for "interview"

Using correct grammar is important both in projecting a professional image and in ensuring the message is conveyed correctly. Incorrect grammar includes both poor sentence structure and the use of jargon, technical terms, or local sayings that people not familiar with a particular culture, industry, or geographical region may fail to understand. Can you imagine the confusion that might result if you refer to an ordinary happening as a "run-of-the-mill" occurrence when talking to an international caller from a country where English is not spoken? If the caller is too "polite" to ask for clarification, the communication breakdown may have a negative impact on your organization.

Listen Actively Effective listening is active rather than passive. In passive listening, you absorb the information given. If the speaker provides a clear message and makes it interesting enough to keep your attention, you will probably get most of what the caller intended to communicate. In contrast, *active listening* requires you to understand the message from the caller's point of view. Hearing what the speaker says is easy, but active listening is hard work.

Improve your active listening skills when communicating via telephone by practising the following:

■ Give the caller your complete attention; concentrate on what is being said.

■ Avoid letting your mind wander.

■ Do not interrupt the speaker unless the conversation is wandering aimlessly. If this happens, ask direct, open-ended questions to bring the speaker back on track and to gather more information.

■ Listen objectively; try to put yourself in the speaker's shoes.

■ Wait until the speaker has finished before formulating a response. Thinking about what you will say in response to the speaker will result in a loss of concentration.

■ Paraphrase your understanding of the message to ensure accurate communication.

■ Jot down key points in the conversation.

■ Avoid distractions such as using the keyboard while listening to the speaker.

Effective telephone practice also involves using telephone technology, such as voice mail, call forwarding, or conference calling to the best advantage of both the customer and the company.

Using Voice Mail

Voice mail is a computer-based system that processes both incoming and outgoing telephone calls. Special computer chips and software convert the caller's voice into a digital recording that is stored in the computer. Some organizations offer a single in-box feature that will allow you to process voice mail messages from an Outlook email in-box in order to review and respond to the message accordingly. The recording can then be retrieved at any time for playback.

Voice mail can help in the following ways:

1. Voice mail ensures that no telephone calls are missed.

2. Messages can be sent to voice mail systems regardless of time zones or work schedules.

3. Recorded messages can be left for people calling in with an access code. For example, if you are out of the office and want to leave details about a scheduled meeting, give those people who are invited your access code and leave a descriptive voice mail message.

4. Voice mail allows messages to be recorded and saved in a mailbox.

5. A voice mail system can also forward messages to another location and/or to other office members.

6. Voice mail messages can be sent to a number of people at the same time.

7. Voice mail can serve as an automated telephone operator by answering your calls with a personal recording.

When it is used correctly, voice mail can eliminate the annoying practice of **telephone tag**. It does, however, have its disadvantages:

1. Callers are often forced to listen to long, annoying messages.

2. Callers often prefer to initially talk to a person rather than leave a recorded message.

3. Recipients may not check their mailboxes regularly.

4. Recipients may not know that a message is waiting unless the system has a signalling feature.

5. Recipients may use voice mail to filter their incoming calls so they don't have to speak to people they wish to avoid.

Telephone companies provide voice mail systems with many sophisticated voice mail features. For example, your local telephone company may provide voice mail services in several different languages. With such features, voice mail can help employers handle language diversity in their workforce and help workers and customers access the company's voice mail without encountering a language barrier.

Although voice mail lacks the richness of direct communication, there are some fundamental practices you can follow that can help to improve voice mail interactions.

As a recipient of voice mail messages:

- Change the message and date of your greeting on a daily basis. Doing so provides the caller with information that you are, in fact, accessing your voice mail system regularly.

- Record an appropriate announcement on your greeting message when leaving for vacation or other extended periods of time to let the caller know you will not be checking your voice mail for incoming messages.

- Provide clear instructions for your callers. If you wish to direct your callers to someone else in your organization, provide specific instructions in your recorded message.

As a caller, when you must leave a message for someone else:

- Speak clearly, concisely, and politely.

- Avoid leaving a lengthy message.

---

pro-Link
Voice Mail Jail

Voice mail is both a productivity enhancer and a potential problem! Many companies establish voice mail policies to ask the fundamental question, "Do our customers really want to use voice mail in order to contact us?" Consider these concepts:

- Customers may be uncomfortable speaking to a computer—many are!
- Be sure your customers don't experience voice mail jail. This is where the customer is trapped in the voice mail with no option of getting out and speaking to a person.
- Callers hear the same message each time they call you—keep your greeting messages short.
- Allow customers to choose an option at any time rather than force them to listen to an entire list of choices first.
- Research tells us that customers prefer to have contact with a person first—the person can then ask if the customer wants to be connected to the voice mail system.

What's your experience with voice mail?

- Be aware of your tone of voice and the impression that you will leave in your message.

- State your message, your name, and your telephone number clearly and at a slow enough pace for transcription.

- Specify the action you want to occur.

- Indicate when you will be available to receive a return call.

- Leave key pieces of information; if you think it would be helpful, restate your name and phone number at the end of your message.

The features and functions of voice mail systems are improving rapidly. Unless used correctly, however, voice mail systems can be annoying and frustrating for callers, which may have a negative impact on the organization. It is essential that organizations employ efficient procedures when using voice mail. The following three practices will help minimize caller frustration:

1. Provide an opportunity for the caller to speak to a representative of the company at any time during the caller's voice mail interaction. This is often achieved by implementing what is known as a *zero out* option: the caller may press zero at any time during the call to speak to a live representative.

2. Introduce a company policy for responding to voice mail promptly and efficiently. This will resolve the problem of messages not being collected or not being answered.

3. Ensure that all staff are fully trained to use the voice mail message system. When a system fails to meet its objectives, it is often because of inadequate staff training.

Self-Check

1. Describe four elements of speaking clearly that can help project a professional image.
2. What is active listening?
3. What are four disadvantages of voice mail?

Answering the Telephone

Every time you answer the telephone or leave a voice mail message, you are projecting the image of your organization. To the caller, you *are* the organization. You must rely on your voice to project a pleasant, businesslike attitude and to give the caller your full attention (see Figure 11-1). Be aware of your tone of voice; vary it to be expressive. Both what you say and how you say it are important. Treat every call as if it were the only call of the day.

Figure 11-1 A smile in your telephone voice will help project a pleasant, businesslike attitude.

Using Automatic Answering Services The front-line reception of many companies is often an automated answering system rather than a live receptionist. These can be sophisticated telephone systems that handle incoming calls with efficiency and effectiveness. They are known as Interactive Voice Response (IVR) systems.

IVR services can be programmed to:

- prompt the caller through a menu of options to acquire information or leave messages
- play a variety of announcements
- respond after a predefined number of rings
- respond between specific times of the day
- repeat messages based on the length of time the caller has been on hold

IVR systems should not be confused with voice mail. Reaching a voice mail box is just an option that the IVR menu allows the caller to select.

Administrative assistants are often called on to help optimize their office's IVR system. If this becomes your responsibility, it will be helpful to involve your local telephone service provider or IVR manufacturer to help you design scripts and procedures that most appropriately represent your company.

Answering Promptly Answer the telephone by the first or second ring. Leaving the telephone to ring five or six times may convey an image of inefficiency. However, don't lift the receiver and let the caller wait while you finish a conversation with someone else—this is unprofessional and rude.

In order for the caller to understand you clearly, speak directly into the mouthpiece in a normal, conversational tone and volume, which will make your voice sound pleasant to the listener.

Identifying Yourself Let the caller know that he or she has reached the right office. If the incoming call is answered by a receptionist, he or she will say, "Good morning (or Good afternoon), Millennium Appliances." When the receptionist transfers the call to you, you can say, "Mr. Jamison's office, Linda McElroy speaking," or "Advertising Department, Linda McElroy speaking." Your manager may tell you specifically how to answer the telephone. If not, be sure to ask. Never answer a business telephone with "hello." "Hello" is considered far too casual for the business office.

It is courteous to let the caller know who you are. To identify yourself, use both your first and last names. A courtesy title—Miss, Mrs., Ms., Mr.—is not usually necessary; however, follow the procedure that is expected in your organization.

When telephone calls come directly to your phone, first let the callers know they have reached the right organization; then add the identification for the particular telephone you are answering, and give your name. For example: "Millennium Appliances, Finance Office, Louisa speaking."

As an administrative assistant, you may not receive your manager's calls. Most managers have telephone numbers that ring directly through to their offices.

When you answer the telephone for more than one manager, create a system to code each station or line on your telephone so that you can give proper identification for each person whose calls you are taking. When you answer a telephone call for a colleague, answer it in a similarly courteous manner, but use your name to let the caller know who is speaking. For example, "Brent Napier's desk, Linda Lewis speaking."

Being Courteous A greeting such as "good morning" or "good afternoon" is a courtesy when answering the telephone. Such greetings are also helpful because often callers do not hear the name of the organization if it is the first set of words spoken when a telephone is answered.

When you must leave the line to obtain information, explain why and how long it will take. Give the caller a choice. Ask whether:

1. the caller would prefer to wait
2. the caller would prefer that you return the call shortly

If the caller chooses to wait, avoid keeping him or her waiting for more than two minutes. When you return to the caller who is on hold, be sure to thank the caller for waiting.

During telephone conversations use "please," "thank you," and other courteous phrases. At appropriate times, use the caller's name.

If you discover that neither you nor your manager can help the caller, redirect the call to someone who can. Do not leave the caller stranded by saying that your department cannot handle the issue. Make a special effort to be helpful, and give the caller the name and number of the appropriate person. Let the caller know when you are looking up a number. It's your job to be helpful.

When the caller has dialled the wrong number, be especially courteous. Callers often reach a wrong number because they have looked at the wrong number on a list of frequently called numbers. The caller may be one of your current or future customers.

The person who initiates a telephone call should terminate it. However, you can bring the call to an end by thanking the person for calling or suggesting that you will give the message to your manager, or whatever is appropriate. When you initiate the call, let the other person know that you are going to leave the line. Do not end abruptly. You may close with "good-bye" or "bye." "Bye-bye" is too familiar, so avoid it.

Taking Messages
Keep a small notebook, a pen, and a pad of telephone message blanks by the telephone. Spare yourself the embarrassment of asking a caller to wait while you look for something to write with. Taking telephone messages may seem like a simple task. However, handling this task inefficiently wastes time and may cause loss of customer goodwill and business.

There are seven essential elements in a complete telephone message:

1. The date and time of call. The time of the call is important; for instance, if your manager talked with the caller at lunch, the manager needs to know if the call was made before or after lunch.

2. The complete name of the caller, spelled correctly. Remember that your manager does not know every Lawrence or Pierre who calls. If you do not know how to spell the caller's name, ask him or her to spell it for you.

3. The telephone number with area code. Some callers will say your manager or the person for whom this call is intended has the number. You can simply explain you would like to save your manager the time it would take to look up the number. Larger cities have more than one area code. For example, Toronto metropolitan area codes include 416, 647, and 905.

4. The name of the business that the caller represents.

5. All pertinent information to help the person for whom the call was intended know what to expect when returning the call.

6. Your initials. If you are the only person taking messages, initialling the form is not necessary. If several people are taking messages, it is helpful to the person receiving the messages to know who took the message should there be any questions regarding the call.

7. Always restate the message to ensure both yourself and the caller that you have recorded it accurately and entirely.

When you must record the name and the number so someone can return the call, write it on a telephone message form as the caller gives you the information. A typical message form is illustrated in Figure 11-2. All of the information on the message form is important; do not skip any part.

Explaining Your Manager's Absence Be careful how you explain your manager's absence from the office. Simply say, "Susan is away from her desk right now. May I ask her to call you?" or "Susan is not in her office at the moment. Would you care to speak to someone else?" or

Figure 11-2 A completed telephone message form.

A completed telephone message form showing:

Message For:		Urgent ☐

For K. Macri
Date 2/24/0x   Time 2:15

Message From:

Mr. Fred Dahl
Of Inkwell
Phone 845-555-9518

AREA CODE	NUMBER	EXTENSION
Called while you were out ☑		Please call ☑
Stopped to see you ☐		Will call you back ☐
Returned your call ☐		Wishes to see you ☐

Message
Follow-up on estimate

Signed LTC

"She is not here at the moment. May I help you?" *Avoid* statements such as these:

- "She's playing golf this afternoon."
- "Susan is in Ottawa."
- "She is at a doctor's appointment."
- "She's still out for lunch."
- "She's tied up."
- "She has not come in yet."
- "Susan is in a meeting."

The "in a meeting" explanation has been overused and could be perceived as an excuse to avoid your call. When it is in fact true, state it in a sincere tone and suggest a time you expect the manager to be available.

Transferring Calls Nothing is more frustrating than to be transferred from one department to another two to three times during one phone call. Transferring calls properly not only involves knowing how to use the transfer feature on your telephone but also knowing who performs various functions within your company. The following suggestions can help you to increase your efficiency in transferring calls:

- Explain to the caller that you are going to transfer the call to someone else who will handle the call. For example, you might say, "Mr. Jenkins in our accounting department will be able to help you rather than Miss Truong in this department. May I transfer your call to him?"
- Be sure you transfer the call to the right person. Knowing "who does what" will ensure you know the appropriate person to handle a transfer call. Never transfer a call on the **speculation** that the person to whom you are transferring the call might be helpful.
- Never say, "I will transfer you; if I should lose you, Mr. Brighton's number is 531-6088." Say, "For your reference, Mr. Brighton's number is 531-6088. I will transfer you now." Give the caller the name and the telephone number of the person to whom he or she is being transferred, so the caller can place the call again if he or she is disconnected as you transfer the call.
- If your department cannot handle the request and you do not know who should handle it, tell the caller so. For example, you might say, "I don't know the answer to your question; I will be happy to make some inquiries. May I call you back in half an hour?" Another approach is to say, "I need to find out who has that information. May I call you back in half an hour?" Be sure to follow through on your promise.
- Limit transfers as much as possible. Callers often find themselves being transferred three or four times. Imagine how frustrating this must be for them each

time they have to repeat their story. In addition, three or four people will have been interrupted by calls they cannot handle. When these callers reach you, stop the runaround. Offer to locate someone who *can* help.

Answering a Second Telephone If two telephones ring at the same time, answer one and ask the caller if you may be excused to answer the other telephone. For example, "ABC Company. This is Shandra. I have another call coming in. May I put you on hold?" Do not leave the line until the caller agrees. Press the hold button and answer the second call. Then you might say: "ABC Company. This is Shandra. I am on another line. May I put you on hold?" When you return to the line of the first caller, say, "Thank you for holding, How may I direct your call?"

or

"Thank you for holding. How may I help you?"

What you need to do to answer multiple calls depends on whether the calls are local or long distance.

If the second call is a local one, you may ask the caller to hold or you may offer to return the call. Briefly explain why. If the second caller agrees to hold, press the hold button and return to the first caller. If the second caller agrees to be called back, hang up the second telephone and return to the first caller. As soon as this conversation ends, dial the second caller.

When the second call is a long-distance call, do not offer to call back. Either ask someone else to take the call or explain to the long-distance caller that you interrupted a local call on another line in order to answer. Excuse yourself long enough to get back to the first caller to say, "I will be with you in a minute." Complete the long-distance call as quickly as possible. Try not to keep the first caller waiting more than a minute. When you get back to the first caller, apologize for the delay and thank the caller for waiting. Use these same methods if you are talking on the telephone when the second telephone rings.

Knowing When to Answer In most organizations, managers answer their own telephone when they are in the office. Alternatively, you may be expected to take all telephone calls and immediately put them through to your manager.

Know when to answer the telephone. For example, if you are not responsible for answering all of your manager's calls, be sure to answer your manager's telephone when a client or colleague is in his/her office. It would be inappropriate for your manager to have to interrupt a conversation with another person, regardless of who the person is, to answer the telephone.

Don't ask your manager to take a telephone call when she or he has a visitor, unless you have been given specific instructions to interrupt if a particular call comes in. Let the caller know that your manager is not available at the moment and ask, "May I have Ms. Yee return your call?" Be sure to get the caller's name and number. Tell the caller your manager is not free to receive a telephone call *before* you ask who is calling. If you ask who is calling before you let the caller know that your manager is not available, you may give the caller the impression that your manager doesn't want to speak to him or her specifically.

Not all managers refrain from accepting calls when visitors are in the office. Again, it is best to clarify the desired procedures for different office personnel.

Distributing Messages
Distribute telephone messages to office personnel as soon as the messages are received. If your manager is trying to work without interruption, he or she may wish you to send the message electronically. The plan your manager has for handling messages and returning calls will depend on individual schedules, preferences, and workload.

If you receive calls from people who have previously called and left messages with your manager but their calls haven't been returned, simply say, "I will be sure the message is delivered." That's all you can guarantee. Do not say your manager will return the calls. It is up to your manager to decide which calls are of high (or low) priority.

When you place a message on someone's desk, put it in a designated location or in a location that will not be covered by papers and overlooked.

If your manager needs to review materials from files before returning a call, locate the materials and clip the telephone message to them.

When members of your management team are not available to take calls, don't just take messages—take initiative! Many telephone requests can be satisfied by you or by other employees.

Screening Calls
Many people on management teams have such heavy demands on their time that they want their calls to be screened.

If you must screen calls, probe courteously for information. Either respond to the caller yourself or determine what the caller's request is, and refer the call to someone else who can help.

When **screening** calls, you are attempting to find out who is calling and what the caller wants. You might say, "May I tell Mr. Morton who is calling, please?" You should never ask a caller bluntly, "Who is calling?" or "Who is this?" To find out what the caller wants, you might say, "May I tell Mr. Morton what you are calling about, please?"

Screening calls:

1. saves your manager time

2. ensures someone addresses the caller's request

All incoming calls should be handled by someone in the office. The more knowledge you have about the organization, the easier your job of screening calls will be. Never end the

call by saying, "I don't know" and leave the caller wondering what to do next. If you really don't know the answer, you might say, "I don't know the answer to your question, but I will ask Ms. Blanco," or "I will need to find out that information. May I call you back in about ten minutes?" If you really don't know, it's your responsibility as a receptionist to find out or to solicit the assistance of someone who does know.

Conference Calling
A conference call takes place when three or more telephone stations are connected across a network that supports the conversation. Conference calls can be initiated by:

1. using the "conference" feature on most business telephone sets

2. using a temporary pass code created by a telephone company

3. using specialized software like Skype, which permits up to 25 users to participate in a conference call via the internet

With the first option, you use the convenient conference feature that most business telephone sets have. You dial a number and ask the receiver of the call to hold while you conference another person into the call. You simply put the first caller on hold, press the conference button, and dial the second number. When the second caller is connected, you release the hold button to include the first person who has been waiting. A three-way conversation is now possible.

With the second option, the telephone company sets up a pass code and temporary number information that participants call into. This is an automatic process and does not require the intervention of an operator.

With the third option, the host would set up a contact list for the conference group and then call the group when ready. A computer or mobile device is needed to use this option.

No special equipment is needed for conference calls. However, specially designed speaker/microphone conference sets, designed for boardroom use, may be used to enhance the clarity of the conference stations.

Self-Check

1. Is it appropriate to end a business call with "bye"? Why or why not?

2. List the seven essential elements of a complete telephone message.

3. What should you do to avoid unnecessary telephone call transfers?

4. Why should you avoid saying that your manager *will* return the call?

5. What two purposes does screening calls serve?

6. Describe the main features of a conference call.

Using Telephone Directories

The most efficient way to locate telephone numbers and addresses is to access the information electronically from a database. The organization where you work will likely have a shared database with client information that can be accessed by all employees. If not, taking on the creation of such a database is an excellent opportunity for you to show initiative.

The website www.Canada411.ca is an excellent resource for checking telephone numbers and addresses of individuals as well as businesses. At this site, you can perform a search that covers just your local area, or you can perform a much broader search to include international communities. Other sites are available that perform the same or similar services; however, Canada 411 produces quick and effective results.

International telephone directories can be accessed by using the website http://www.infobel.com. Directories are arranged by continents and then by country.

If you prefer to use paper directories, local telephone books are made available through the local telephone service provider. Directories for other geographic areas may be obtained by contacting the telephone company that publishes that directory. Libraries also carry copies of directories for other cities and, in some libraries, for other countries as well.

An alphabetic directory contains the name, address, and telephone number of every subscriber in the local calling area with the exception of unlisted numbers. Names of individuals and organizations are listed in alphabetical order. In most Canadian city directories, the municipal, provincial, and federal government listings are found in a section separate from the alphabetic listings.

Goods and services are arranged by subject in the classified directory called the Yellow Pages. Listings under each subject are then arranged in alphabetical order. To use the Yellow Pages, think of all the possible ways the reference you are seeking might be listed, and search first for the most likely classification. Some Yellow Pages directories offer a quick reference section at the beginning of the book; this can save you a lot of time.

The **Talking Yellow Pages** is a service that helps the general public locate business information. It has business information stored in voice mailboxes, and callers access the information in the mailboxes by following numeric instructions. To use the Talking Yellow Pages, simply dial the appropriate access numbers listed in the front of your Yellow Pages.

As an administrative assistant, you should be skilled at using the alphabetic and classified sections of public telephone directories, and you should be thoroughly familiar with telephoning procedures described in the introductory section of your local directory.

Paper-based directories have their place in the office. However, they are increasingly more awkward, slower to use, and take up more space than the more common electronic directories. Most offices use a combination of both paper-based and computer-based systems. In this case, create efficiencies whenever possible. For example, stop looking up frequently called numbers in your paper-based system—start using your electronic system. Code new numbers into your electronic telephone database. When you are given an unlisted number, be sure to record it in your electronic telephone database since you will not be able to locate it in a paper-based directory.

Organizations generally provide their employees with an electronic or hard copy of their staff directory for calling other employees within the organization. An organization's directory will include, for example, the telephone numbers of its branch offices, plants, and distribution centres. Both computer-based and hard-copy directories must be updated as staff and telephone assignments change. It is most likely that the task of updating the office directory will be the responsibility of the administrative assistant. If the responsibility is not assigned to anyone in particular, take this opportunity to demonstrate your initiative, and offer to update the directory.

Placing Local Calls

Before you place a call, assemble all the materials that you may need to reference during the conversation. Jot down the questions you want to ask and the comments you want to make. Be sure you have the correct number and name of the person with whom you wish to speak.

If the first person you reach is the receptionist, give the extension number of the person you are calling. If you don't know the extension number, give the receptionist the person's name and department.

When the person answers the telephone, identify yourself immediately. Use an appropriate identification, such as, "Good morning, this is Linda McElroy, Executive Assistant of Millennium Appliances. May I speak to Ms. Delacroix, please?"

Managers often place their own calls, but at times you will be expected to get a caller on the line for your manager. When you are placing a call for your manager, make sure she or he is ready to talk before you get the other person on the line. It's inconsiderate to call someone and then ask him or her to wait while you search for the person who asked you to place the call. Your conversation might go something like this:

> Hello, Ms. La Roué. This is Linda McElroy calling. I'm executive assistant to Mr. Wilson of Millennium Appliances. Mr. Wilson would like to speak with you about the gas range order for Labrador. Is it convenient for you to take Mr. Wilson's call at this time? Thank you, Ms. La Roué. I'll put Mr. Wilson through now. One moment please.

Placing Domestic Long-Distance Calls

Long-distance calls are all calls placed outside the local calling area. Domestic long-distance calls are those placed outside your local area but still inside Canada. Canada is divided into numerous areas identified by three-digit codes called **area codes**. Although area codes are necessary for dialling all domestic long-distance calls, they are also necessary for making local calls within certain major metropolitan areas. For example, within the greater city of Toronto, instead of dialling the familiar seven digits to make a local call, you must prefix the seven digits with either 416 or 647 to form what is known as a local ten-digit number. See Figure 11-3 for the Canadian numbering plan.

The number of Canadian area codes in use in Canada increases as the number of telephone numbers in use increases. If you have difficulty finding an area code, just dial the operator and ask for the correct area code.

Long-distance calls may be placed either directly or with operator assistance.

Direct-Distance Dialling (DDD)
Whenever possible, dial your number directly without the assistance of the operator. The cost of making a direct call is lower than that of an operator-assisted call.

To make a direct long-distance call, in Canada dial the access code 1, the area code of the geographic location you are calling, and the seven-digit local number.

Operator-Assisted Dialling
Remember that of all the services offered by telephone companies, those requiring the intervention of a live telephone operator are the most costly. Therefore, you should always try to use automated services and avoid operator assistance whenever possible.

When would you need the operator to assist you with making long-distance calls? There are a variety of instances. These might include:

- You are having difficulty getting through to the destination.
- You wish to reverse the charges.
- You wish to bill a third party. Third-party billing means you don't want the charges to be applied to the telephone from which you are calling or to the destination telephone. Rather, you wish to have the charges billed to another telephone number, for example, often your home or business telephone number.

To place long-distance calls in Canada requiring operator assistance, use the **zero-plus dialling** method. Simply dial 0, then the area code, and the seven-digit local number.

Figure 11-3 Canadian telephone area code map.

After you have dialled the complete number, a short automated process will start during which you will have the choice of entering your calling card number or speaking to a *live* operator for assistance in placing your call.

Many long-distance telephone companies have introduced a computerized operator. If you are placing a long-distance call and wish to use a special service such as reversing the charges, dial 0, the area code, and the local number. A computer-controlled voice will ask you which service you want, and then ask you to state your name clearly. When the call is placed, the computer-controlled voice system announces your name and the fact that you wish to reverse the charges or activate one of the other special services available. When you wish to reverse the charges, the person on the receiving end will accept or refuse the charges either by keying in a response on the telephone pad or by responding to questions with a simple "yes" or "no." All of this takes place without the intervention of a live operator.

Calling Cards

Telephone **calling cards** are sometimes given to employees for expense purposes. These employees are expected to use calling cards when they travel, rather than claiming each individual long-distance telephone call on their expense accounts. Telephone calling cards may or may not require the assistance of an operator. Most pay phones are equipped with a magnetic strip reader to accommodate telephone calling cards. When you use a calling card for placing a call, the charge is automatically billed to your personal or business account. Some service providers add a surcharge to the cost of each call that is made using your calling card. The information stored on the card includes a coded account number.

Prepaid calling cards are set up in the same way as direct debit cards. The magnetic strip on the back of a prepaid card stores the original purchase value of the card and updates (debits) that amount each time a call is made. Pay telephone equipment can read and update a prepaid calling card as the call progresses. Prepaid cards are available in different denominations; you can purchase cards with values of $5, $10, or $20, for example.

Long-Distance Directory Assistance

If you want to call long distance but you don't know the number of the party you want to reach, you need to access long-distance directory assistance. Similar to accessing directory assistance for local calls, dial 1, the area code of the geographic location you want, and 555-1212. You will reach the information operator or the automated directory system for the area you wish to call. First provide the name of the city or town you want and then the name of the person or business. Write down the number that is given to you and hang up. Then dial 1, the area code, and the seven-digit number provided by the operator. This same procedure is used whether you are dialling inside or outside your own area code.

Time Zones in Canada

The Canadian provinces and territories are divided into six time zones:

1. Newfoundland
2. Atlantic
3. Eastern
4. Central
5. Mountain
6. Pacific

From east to west, the time in each zone is one hour earlier than the time in the adjacent zone. The only exception is the Newfoundland time zone, which is only half an hour ahead of the Atlantic time zone. The time and location where the call originates determine what long-distance rates apply.

During Daylight Saving Time (DST), clocks are turned forward one hour in each Canadian province except for Saskatchewan, which remains on Standard Time year round. For most time zones, DST begins at 2 a.m. on the second Sunday of March. DST ends and reverts back to Standard Time at 2 a.m. on the first Sunday of November. An easy way to remember how to set your clock is, "Spring forward, and fall back." Check your local media for the actual dates to set your clock each year.

When you are placing a long-distance call, know the time zone of the city you are calling. For instance, when it is 3:30 p.m. in Victoria, British Columbia, you can expect that offices in Quebec City will be closed. When it is 5:00 pm in Quebec City, offices on the West Coast will still be open. Time zones around the world are explained in the following section and are illustrated in Figure 11-4.

Time Zones around the World

The world is divided into 24 time zones, which are based on degrees of longitude. The zones are one hour apart in time. Greenwich, England, is recognized as the prime meridian of longitude; in other words, standard time is calculated from Greenwich. Basically, each time zone covers 15 degrees of longitude; however, the time zone lines bend to accommodate local geographic regions.

The Greenwich zone is called the *zero zone*, because the difference between standard time and Greenwich Mean Time is zero. A number representing the number of hours by which the standard time of the zone differs from Greenwich Mean Time in turn designates each of the zones.

Zones in west longitude are numbered in sequence from 1 to 12 and labelled *minus*; zones in east longitude are numbered 1 to 12 and labelled *plus*. In each zone the zone number is applied to the standard time (Greenwich Mean Time) in accordance with its plus or minus sign to obtain the time in that particular zone. For example, Toronto is in the -5 zone, as shown in Figure 11-4. When it is 0600 Greenwich Mean Time, subtract five hours to determine that it is 0100 in Toronto. Moscow is in the $+3$ zone.

Figure 11-4 Standard time zone chart of the world.

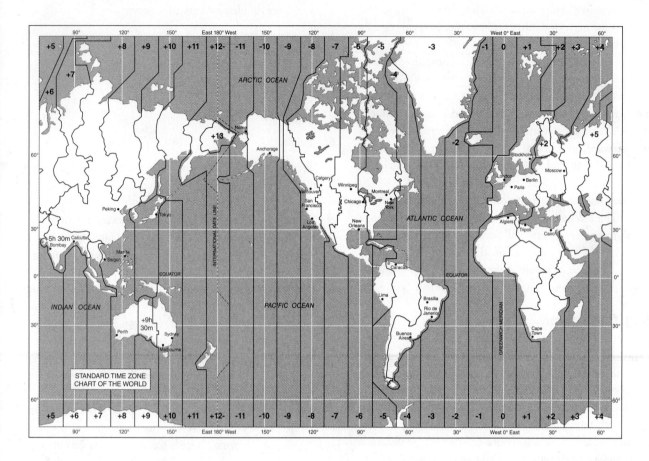

When it is 0600 Greenwich Mean Time, add three hours to determine that it is 0900 in Moscow.

The International Date Line is in the twelfth zone. It coincides with the 180th meridian, except that it zigzags so that all of Asia lies to the west of it and all of North America—including the Aleutian Islands—to the east of it. The 180th meridian divides the twelfth zone; therefore, the half in east longitude is *minus* 12 and the half in west longitude is *plus* 12. Each calendar day begins at the International Date Line. When crossing the International Date Line in a westerly direction, *advance* the date by one day; when crossing it in an easterly direction, set the date *back* one day.

The best way to determine times in cities around the globe is to check the world clock through the internet. This can be accessed at www.timeanddate.com/worldclock. Figure 11-5 compares the times of major cities around the world.

Placing International Calls

Making calls to the United States, Puerto Rico, the Virgin Islands, Bermuda, and other Caribbean Islands is like making long-distance calls within Canada. Each of these places has an assigned three-digit area code. Placing a long-distance call to Puerto Rico would require you to dial 1 + 809 (the area code for Puerto Rico) + the local number.

You can dial directly to most foreign countries. For example, to dial directly to a telephone number in Tokyo, Japan, you would dial 011 + 81 + 3 + the local number. The international long-distance access number 011 will direct your call out of Canada; the code for the country being called—Japan in this case—is 81. The routing code will direct your call to the region or city that you want to reach—in this case 3 for Tokyo—and then the local number. Local numbers in Tokyo have four digits. International country and routing codes are given in many local telephone directories.

If you require operator assistance with your international call, dial 01 + the country code + the routing code + the local number. For example, if you want to dial a number in Weymouth, in the county of Dorset, England, the procedure would be 01 + 44 + 1385 + the local number. At this point the operator will intercept, asking you what assistance you require. The routing code—1385, in this case—will direct your call to the region in Dorset.

What Can Go Wrong? Telephones are easy to use, but people may tend to panic when an international call does

Figure 11-5 Understanding international time changes.

City	Calculating Time in the International Location	Time
Sydney	GMT + 10 *Standard Time*	Saturday 1010
Hong Kong	GMT + 8 *Standard Time*	Saturday 0810
Moscow	GMT + 4 *Daylight Saving Time*	Saturday 0410
Greenwich	0	Saturday 0010 *(10 minutes after midnight)*
Toronto	GMT − 4 *Daylight Saving Time*	Friday 2010
Vancouver	GMT − 7 *Daylight Saving Time*	Friday 1710
Honolulu	GMT − 10 *Standard Time*	Friday 1410

not go through immediately. You may ask yourself questions such as:

- Why is there no answer at the company I am calling?

  (Perhaps the difference in time zones means that it is after hours in the location you are calling. . . . Perhaps the country you are calling is observing a national holiday or has a midday extended siesta built into the workday.)

- What do I do now that an unexpected person is answering the phone in a language I don't understand?

  (Perhaps you should hang up and dial using an international operator who is trained in the language. . . . Perhaps you can ask to speak to someone who speaks English.)

- Why did someone in Saskatoon answer the phone when I was dialling Auckland, New Zealand?

  (Perhaps the area code is incorrect, or perhaps the country code wasn't dialled.)

When making international calls, be sure to check the following:

- the correct format for dialling the international number
- international holidays
- time zone differences
- language barriers

TELEPHONE EQUIPMENT

The telephone is a valuable tool for conducting business. It is therefore is imperative for the administrative assistant to become familiar with the telephone equipment used in his or her office. Refer back to Chapter 6 for an overview of various types of telephone equipment features.

Self-Check

1. Your manager has asked you to call a client with whom he wishes to speak. Why is it important to make sure your manager is ready to take the call before you get the other person on the line?
2. Give examples of materials you should gather in preparation for making a telephone call.
3. Describe direct distance dialling (DDD).
4. What series of numbers should you dial when placing a domestic DDD call?
5. What are two reasons to seek the assistance of an operator when making a long-distance call?

MAKING APPOINTMENTS

Who makes appointments for managers? Both managers and their administrative assistants make these appointments. The freedom that an administrative assistant is given in making appointments will depend on the manager's preference and on the assistant's astuteness in scheduling.

The trick with scheduling is to keep the appointment calendar up-to-the-minute to avoid conflicts.

Scheduling Appointments

Use good judgment in scheduling appointments. Begin by learning:

1. Your manager's preference for scheduling appointments. For example, she may want to schedule out-of-office appointments for the mornings only, or no appointments after 3 p.m.

2. Which appointments your manager considers priority: perhaps those that are made by her president, her lawyer, or her husband.

3. What your manager considers is an optimum length of time for an appointment. Learning this will help you schedule a busy day for your manager. It will also enable you to further assist your manager in conducting efficient appointments by setting appropriate appointment finishing times.

Guidelines for Scheduling Appointments Here are some simple guidelines you can apply when scheduling your own appointments or those for management:

1. Avoid scheduling too many appointments on the manager's first day back after being out of the office for several days.

2. Avoid crowding a schedule with appointments the day before a trip. Preparation for the trip has priority.

3. Allow plenty of time before and after a top-priority meeting.

4. Avoid scheduling an appointment in another location too soon after a meeting that may run overtime.

5. Schedule free time between appointments. This gives people a chance to make telephone calls, answer email, sign letters, think about the next meeting, or just take a needed break.

6. Schedule appointments with others with whom your manager has a close working relationship late in the afternoon. These appointments are easy to shift when your manager is not keeping to the schedule.

7. When someone requests an appointment, suggest specific times, giving the person a chance to select a time from at least two choices.

8. When you are arranging an appointment for a short period of time, let the person know the length of the appointment. For example, say tactfully, "Your appointment is from noon until 12:15."

9. When you arrange for an unexpected visitor to see your manager right away, let the visitor know if your manager has only a few minutes to spare. For example, you

might say, "Ms. Campbell has another commitment in ten minutes. However, she can see you for a few minutes before then if that's acceptable to you. Shall I show you to her office?"

10. Arrange appointments in another part of the city for first thing in the morning or late in the afternoon so that the manager can go directly from home to the early-morning appointment or not return to the office after a late-afternoon appointment.

Appointments Made by Telephone or Email When someone telephones or emails your office requesting an appointment, determine the purpose of the appointment. Then decide who the best person is for the caller to see. Set the appointment, confirm the date, day, and time, and enter these details into the calendar.

If your office is located in a difficult-to-find location, ask callers if they need directions. And, of course, always get the telephone numbers and email addresses of the callers in the event that you have to change the details of the meeting.

Tell callers that if there are any changes in the arrangements, you will contact them with the new information. Confirm appointments with the manager and then contact the callers either through email or by telephone if the manager is unable to keep the appointment or if other details such as location or time must be changed. Many receptionists for doctors and dentists confirm every patient's appointment. Although this seems an onerous task, it ensures that the patient doesn't miss an appointment and leave a gap in the doctor's schedule.

Appointments Made Online by Clients Some organizations are integrating online web-based tools that allow clients to book their own appointments using preset parameters. Websites such as www.appointmentsonline.ca offer this capability. The software can be synchronized with other software such as Outlook to manage the schedule effectively. This ensures the appointment scheduling is ultimately managed by the organization.

Using Electronic Calendars

If your workplace has an integrated electronic network, you will use the computer to schedule appointments for management as well as your own appointments. The e-calendar system, such as the popular Microsoft® Outlook, is an excellent time-saver when used to check and organize calendars, find the common availability of a number of people and schedule all of them into a conference, cancel appointments, and create up-to-the-minute schedules. This system is a receptionist's super tool. (See Figure 11-6.)

Advantages of Electronic Calendars There are many benefits to using electronic calendar systems. Here is a list of some of the advantages of using a networked

Figure 11-6 Electronic calendar displayed on computer screen showing daily and monthly views.

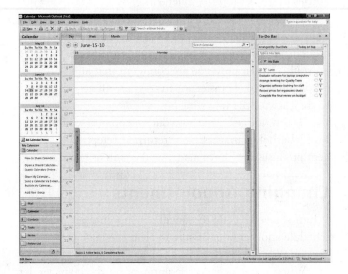 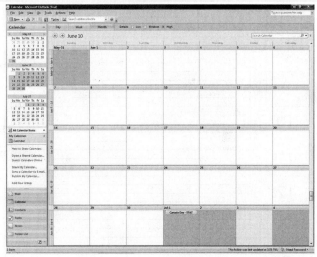

electronic calendar system as opposed to using a traditional paper calendar system.

1. Electronic calendars can be set to remind you of your upcoming meetings.

2. They will produce a list of appointments as well as electronic to do lists.

3. You can key a full set of details regarding each meeting because you are not working in the small blocks of space found in traditional paper calendars.

4. Using the electronic calendar makes cancelling or editing the details of an appointment very simple.

5. When you set up a meeting in your electronic calendar, the software gives you the flexibility of creating an invitation list and automatically sending an email asking each invitee to decline or accept the meeting. If they accept, the meeting is automatically entered into their electronic calendar. When they accept or decline, a message is automatically sent back to you giving the status of their attendance.

6. With Windows™ software, you can exit the electronic calendar and then enter other application software without having to close down applications.

For these reasons, the electronic calendar is always convenient to use as long as you have access to a computer system. For people who spend considerable time out of their office, at meetings, or travelling, a smartphone or a mobile device may be the answer (see Chapter 6).

Drawbacks of Electronic Calendars
The advantages of using e-calendars far outweigh the drawbacks. But here are two things to be aware of.

1. Unless you have reliable and exclusive access to a laptop computer or smartphone, you will need to back up your electronic calendar with a paper calendar. Being

at a meeting without your electronic calendar will be unproductive when you can't refer to dates and times.

2. Many people are remiss at keeping their e-calendars up to date. This is frustrating for the receptionist trying to electronically schedule a meeting that includes these people.

Using Paper Calendars

A wide selection of paper calendars is available at stationery stores. They are made in a variety of sizes; some provide a page for each month, others a page for each week or a page for each day. Office professionals will have their own preference when choosing the right appointment calendar. Preferences are usually based on ease of use, portability, and the number of appointments a person has to make each day.

People who make commitments months in advance may prefer a full month displayed on one page, with small insert calendars for the preceding and following months. With a monthly calendar, they can review engagements without flipping through a lot of pages. People who make several appointments in one day may prefer a daily appointment calendar like the one shown in Figure 11-7. In this sample, each day is divided into 30-minute segments with the time printed in the left column.

Making Entries in Calendars

All appointments (even regularly scheduled meetings)—whether they are made by telephone, fax, email, or in person—should be entered into the calendar. When the days are very busy—and they will be—it is easy to forget even a regularly scheduled meeting. Be consistent and prompt in recording all appointments and commitments.

Figure 11-7 Daily appointment calendar.

DATE		Monday, December 9, 20--
8	00 15 30 45	
9	00 15 30 45	Call for hotel reservation R. C. Thompson ABC Corp.
10	00 15 30 45	Manager's Staff Meeting
11	00 15 30 45	Explore procedure changes Ruth Raires, Ads
12	00 15 30 45	
1	00 15 30 45	Interview Applicant- Jane Allright
2	00 15 30 45	Assemble forms Leo Society Forms Design
3	00 15 30 45	Interview Applicant- Louisse Petruzza
4	00 15 30 45	Complete Proposal Meet Jass Hunter - Airport
5	00 15 30 45	
6	00 15 30 45	AMA Meeting

It's much easier to cancel or edit the details of an appointment when you are using an electronic calendar. Enter appointments in pencil when you are using a desk calendar. Even the firmest commitments can change suddenly. In the paper calendar, draw a diagonal line through each entry once the conference is held or the task is completed; this way, you will know whether items have been completed or not.

Because professional commitments are often made outside the office—at social or recreational events such as games of golf—it is imperative for people making these commitments to relay the information back to the office so that administrative assistants can make the appropriate entries into calendars. Where a person carries a PDA, the appointment can be entered even between holes of golf; however, people are less likely to take paper appointment calendars to social and recreational events.

Administrative assistants should try to spend a few minutes with management each morning to discuss the work scheduled for the day. As a general procedure, ask management to send you a voice mail or email, or even leave a brief note on your desk, each time they make an appointment that has not been recorded electronically.

As you read incoming mail, watch for announcements of meetings that managers will be expected to attend or

might want to attend. Call attention to them, and make entries in the appropriate calendars.

At the end of the day, check the manager's calendar against yours to make sure you have all the correct and comprehensive appointment information. Never turn the page on your calendar until you are confident that all items have been completed. Transfer any items that still need attention to the page for the following business day.

When you are clearing your calendar, if you are not sure whether managers have returned telephone calls or kept promises they have made, send emails as reminders.

Changing Appointments

When someone calls to cancel an appointment, offer to schedule another one. Be sure to clear the manager's calendar and your own of the cancelled appointment.

When you cancel an appointment for the manager, let the person whose appointment is being cancelled know as soon as possible. Use the following guidelines for changing or cancelling an appointment:

1. Express regret on the manager's behalf.
2. Mention that the appointment must be changed.
3. State a reason in general terms.
4. Offer to schedule another appointment.

Think twice about what explanation you will give for the change. Be diplomatic and discreet when you change the appointment. For example, "Ms. Park will be out of town. She is expected back next week. Would you like an appointment for Tuesday?" Don't discuss where she is going or what she will be doing but, as it is Ms. Park who wants to reschedule the appointment, it is appropriate to provide a little more information in terms of the reason why she is requesting the change.

Listing Appointments

Some managers prefer to have a separate list of appointments for each day. If so, near the end of each day, prepare your manager's list of appointments for the next business day in a form he or she prefers. Keep a duplicate copy on your desk. If you are using a computer to keep the appointment calendar, a printout may be sufficient (see Figure 11-8).

Self-Check

1. What three pieces of information about your manager will help you in scheduling his or her appointments?
2. List four guidelines that will help you to schedule appointments effectively.
3. When would it be more appropriate for a manager to use a monthly rather than a daily calendar?

Figure 11-8 List of appointments.

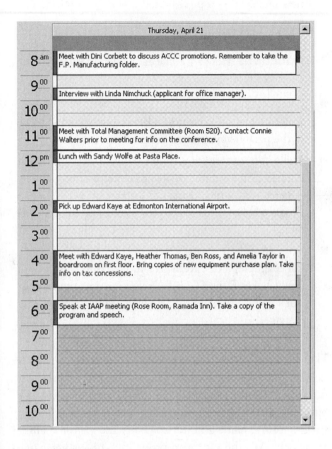

Thursday, April 21

8 am — Meet with Dini Corbett to discuss ACCC promotions. Remember to take the F.P. Manufacturing folder.

9 00 — Interview with Linda Nimchuck (applicant for office manager).

10 00

11 00 — Meet with Total Management Committee (Room 520). Contact Connie Walters prior to meeting for info on the conference.

12 pm — Lunch with Sandy Wolfe at Pasta Place.

1 00

2 00 — Pick up Edward Kaye at Edmonton International Airport.

3 00

4 00 — Meet with Edward Kaye, Heather Thomas, Ben Ross, and Amelia Taylor in boardroom on first floor. Bring copies of new equipment purchase plan. Take info on tax concessions.

5 00

6 00 — Speak at IAAP meeting (Rose Room, Ramada Inn). Take a copy of the program and speech.

7 00

8 00

9 00

10 00

RECEIVING VISITORS

Receiving office visitors is a responsibility that requires office professionals to be courteous, gracious, and diplomatic. In your contact with visitors, make a special effort to represent your organization favourably. Your responsibility is threefold:

1. to carry out your manager's wishes

2. to present a positive image for yourself, your manager, and the organization

3. to help visitors, within the policy limitations of the organization, to accomplish their purposes for coming to your office

In some organizations, the administrative assistant is also the receptionist and the first person the visitor speaks with. Large organizations may have a reception area where all visitors check in with the receptionist. The receptionist then calls the appropriate person to announce the visitor's arrival. Either the receptionist escorts the visitor to the appropriate office, or the person whom the visitor is seeing comes to the reception area to welcome the visitor.

Whatever the setup, the receptionist usually receives visitors before they are admitted to the manager's office.

This is a very important part of your work. Never regard a person's visit as an interruption. The customer is the reason you have a job!

Find out the manager's policy for seeing visitors. You need to know whom management prefers *not* to see and where you should direct these visitors. The company policy could be to arrange for *all* visitors to see someone within the organization for at least a few minutes.

By turning away visitors, you may be damaging good relationships that already exist or preventing good ones from developing. When you are uncertain what to do, it's best to make an appointment for the visitor.

Good Morning!—Greeting Visitors

Visitors are influenced by their first impressions of the office and the receptionist. A favourable first impression, coupled with your courteous efforts to make visitors feel welcome, will create a receptive climate. The visitor's first impression should be that of an efficient receptionist working in a well-organized office.

As a person who welcomes the public, you should look like you belong in a professional office setting. Many offices have a casual environment, but they still want to convey a business-like atmosphere to the public. Your clothing, hairstyle, accessories, and demeanour should convey the message that you are a professional representing the organization where you work. The way you dress should make you feel at ease in the presence of executives and visitors, who are usually well dressed.

Immediate Attention It's your job to make all visitors, whether they have appointments or not, feel at ease. When visitors come to your office, you should greet them the minute they arrive. As a visitor approaches your desk, look at the person directly, smile, and speak immediately. Nobody likes to be ignored, even for a few seconds. To continue keying or reading until you reach the end of the line or paragraph is extremely rude. To continue chatting with another employee is inexcusable.

Put your materials out of sight of glancing eyes, but do so discreetly. If you keep confidential materials that you are working on in a folder, you can subtly close the folder as a visitor nears your desk.

If you are talking on the telephone, the visitor probably will hesitate before approaching your desk. Acknowledge visitors by nodding and smiling so they know you are aware of their presence.

Greet an office visitor formally by saying, "Good morning" or "Good afternoon." "Hello" or "hi" are too casual for most offices. Use the visitor's name whenever you know it. The greeting may go something like this: "Good morning, Mr. Oliver. I'm Chris Rogers, Mr. Sung's assistant. Mr. Sung is expecting you." If you don't know the visitor's name, don't guess it. Introduce yourself and ask how you may be of assistance.

Most business visitors will introduce themselves immediately and give you a business card. As soon as a stranger does this, repeat the visitor's name, introduce yourself, and add whatever statement is appropriate. For example, "Mr. Sung is expecting you" or "May I help you?"

- lists of names, addresses, and company affiliations of new members of a professional group, or anything else that is related to the purpose of the meeting

Introductions Here are some easy guidelines for making introductions in the office.

- Gender and age have nothing to do with whose name you state first. In a business relationship, state the name of the person you want to honour first.
- Make the introduction sound natural. Just state their names. For example, "Mrs. Kensington, this is Mr. Adams." Or simply, "Mrs. Kensington . . . Mr. Adams." Reserve "May I introduce" or "May I present" for formal affairs and for very distinguished people.
- You can add the person's business after his or her name. For example, "Mrs. Kensington, this is Mr. Adams of Great Lakes EnviroTech." Or you can just use the visitor's name and hand the visitor's business card to your manager.

The Visitor Who Has an Appointment A visitor is a guest. Make the visitor feel welcome. Indicate to the visitor where to leave a coat, boots, or hat. Collect the visitor's business card. The business card will indicate the correct spelling of the name and the company the visitor is affiliated with. Ask the visitor to pronounce his or her name if it is difficult for you to pronounce. Escort the visitor to the correct office, and make the introduction. Pronounce the visitor's name and your manager's name distinctly when you introduce them. A sample introduction might be, "Mr. Sung, this is Mrs. Haines of R.C. Products." Give the business card to your manager and then leave.

If the manager knows the visitor, you can be less formal. As soon as the manager is free, you can invite the visitor to go in.

Invite visitors who must wait to have a seat. Keep current magazines, the morning paper, and other interesting reading material nearby so that visitors who must wait for any length of time can read. You are not expected to entertain the visitor by carrying on a conversation while the visitor is waiting. You should continue with your work.

A visitor who arrives early should expect to wait until the time of the appointment. As soon as the manager is free, tell the manager that the visitor has arrived, and ask if he or she is ready to see the visitor.

A visitor who has an appointment should not be kept waiting. Remember, the visitor's time is valuable. Asking the visitor to wait more than a few minutes is inconsiderate. Nevertheless, a busy executive may have difficulty keeping to an appointment schedule. This happens even when the manager and the administrative assistant are making a real

The atmosphere in most organizations is informal enough that employees refer to managers by their first name. Regardless of the informality of your relationship, it may be most appropriate to use your manager's last name in the presence of guests, especially international visitors. With experience you will determine how to address management in the presence of guests.

Advance Preparation Will the meeting require materials from the files—correspondence and records? If so, locate them prior to the meeting.

You may have to compile data or collect information from other departments. Make sure you give the manager any information you have compiled well enough in advance of the meeting so that it can be reviewed adequately before the meeting. Anticipate any other items that will be needed during the meeting and have them ready. These materials might include:

- notes taken during previous meetings
- brochures to be distributed
- presentations to supplement a speech

effort to keep appointments on time. But you can't plan for everything. A previous visitor may take twice the expected time, or a high-level executive may drop by unexpectedly. When this occurs, the visitor with the next appointment often has to wait. In addition to making the visitor feel welcome and comfortable, you should assure the visitor that the wait shouldn't take too long.

The real test of how well you carry out your role as office host lies in how you act when the wait is long. Don't let your actions reveal that the day is hectic. When emergencies occur or the day is not going smoothly, slow down, put some of your work on tomorrow's list, and approach visitors in a very relaxed manner. Give each visitor the impression that your priority at that moment is to meet the visitor's needs. Your relaxed manner (or tension) will be contagious.

Be cautious when you state the reasons for a delay. You can apologize and say that all appointments are running behind schedule, but do not explain why. Avoid statements referring to important business, problems, or inefficiency. The visitor is concerned about his or her own schedule and wants to know how long the wait will be. If you know that the manager is involved in a long meeting, tell the visitor approximately how long he or she will have to wait. The visitor may decide to postpone the appointment.

Don't forget about the visitor. If you can judge that a conference is ending, indicate to the visitor who is waiting that it is ending. If a visitor whose appointment is delayed cannot wait any longer, offer to make another appointment. Remember, this visitor has been inconvenienced and deserves special attention.

Staff Visitors A difficult part of every manager's job is maintaining good communication with the employees. Whatever a manager's efforts to establish an easy, two-way flow of communication, breakdowns occur and misunderstandings arise. This is one reason why many executives maintain an "open door" policy for seeing personnel.

According to office protocol, a meeting between a subordinate and a superior is held in the superior's office. Arrange for employees who report to your manager to meet in your manager's office or in a local conference room. When your manager's superior requests a conference, the implied message is that your manager will go to the superior's office unless a specific statement is made to the contrary concerning the place of the meeting.

Excuse Me—Interrupting a Meeting

Until you know differently, expect that the manager does not want to be interrupted while someone is in his or her office. Most executives discourage interruptions while they are in conference. The interruptions an executive *will* tolerate are governed by the executive's judgment and personality.

You must arrive at a clear understanding with the manager regarding what conditions are important enough to justify your interrupting a meeting. At times the manager may ask you to interrupt—say, when an important telephone call comes in. At other times, the manager may indicate that there should be no interruptions at all. When you are left to your own judgment and do not know what to do, do not interrupt. An intrusion detracts from the flow of the meeting.

Clearly establish which method the manager prefers you to follow when you must deliver an urgent message. The following method is often used: the administrative assistant keys the message, quietly enters the executive's office, hands the message to the executive or places it face down on the desk, and leaves unless an immediate response from the manager is necessary.

To keep telephone interruptions to a minimum during meetings, the manager should forward calls to voice mail or to the receptionist's telephone line.

When you receive an urgent telephone call for the manager, write the name of the person calling and the purpose of the call, hand the note to the manager, and wait for instructions. The executive will either give you a message or take the call.

When you receive a telephone call for a visitor, offer to take a message or to give the visitor the number so that the visitor can return the call. Add your name and the time at the bottom of the message. If the caller insists on speaking to the visitor, interrupt the meeting, and let the visitor know. As you enter the office or conference room, apologize for the interruption. Tell the visitor who is calling, and ask if the visitor would like to take the call at your desk. When several visitors are in the room, key the message, walk in and hand it to the right person, and wait for the reply. If the visitor wishes to return the call at a later time, be sure to get the caller's correct telephone number.

It's Over!—Terminating a Meeting

Arrange with the manager how you should assist in terminating a meeting.

On those days when the manager's appointment schedule is crowded, watch the time, and tactfully interrupt a conference following predetermined guidelines you have arranged with your manager. One appointment that runs overtime on a busy day can throw all the other appointments off schedule, inconveniencing many callers and giving the impression of inefficient planning. At the manager's request, you may have to interrupt a meeting in order to inform and dismiss visitors who overstay their allotted time.

When a second visitor arrives promptly for an appointment, and someone is in the manager's office, if it is appropriate to interrupt, you might:

1. Send a text message to the manager's cell phone.

2. Enter the manager's office, apologize for the interruption, and give the manager the visitor's name on a slip of paper to indicate that the visitor has arrived. Say nothing more and exit the office.

3. Enter the manager's office and say, "Excuse me. Your three o'clock appointment is here. May I tell her when you can see her?"

4. Call the manager on the telephone, especially if you think he or she does not want to rush the first visitor.

5. Send the manager a priority message that will flash or signal on the computer screen.

Your interruption, either in person, by telephone, or by computer, may be all that is needed to prompt the visitor to leave. If not, it will be adequate to enable the manager to terminate the conversation.

What should you do when the manager does not have another appointment, but the visitor stays and stays, taking up the manager's time unnecessarily?

Managers are busy people who need to get on with their responsibilities. Most executives are skilled at terminating office visits. They thank the visitor for coming, stand, tactfully make statements that let the visitor know the conference is over, and lead the visitor to the door. At times, however, they rely on administrative assistants to rescue them from persistent visitors.

Be sure you understand what the manager expects you to do when he or she is having difficulty dismissing a visitor. How does the manager want to be interrupted?

Between the two of you, figure out a tactful and effective way to interrupt and end unwanted or prolonged meetings. Will it be:

■ a note you quietly hand to the manager?

■ a telephone call you make to your manager's office?

■ an announcement you make at the manager's office door?

■ a message you flash on the manager's computer screen that will help end the appointment?

Visitors without Appointments

Be just as pleasant to the unexpected visitor as you are to one who has an appointment. Never judge a visitor by appearance. Appearance is not indicative of a person's contribution to the organization. Whether the visitor is a member of the family, a friend, or a business associate, always invite the visitor to be seated. If the manager is already engaged with another appointment, you could say, "Mrs. Kensington has someone in her office, but I'll let her know you are here." Key a note and take it to the manager, or call her on the telephone. Friends or family members may prefer to wait without interrupting your manager, but business associates are trying to keep up with a busy schedule and may prefer to come back later, leave a message with you, or leave an email or voice mail message on the manager's system.

If you interrupt your manager to tell him or her there is an unexpected visitor, the manager may step out of the office briefly to speak to this person. But if the visitor is kept waiting, reassure the visitor by saying something like, "She knows you are here. It shouldn't be long."

Visitors may come to your office and decide not to wait when they discover the manager is not immediately available. Always offer to help the person yourself. If you cannot be of assistance, give the visitor the option of leaving a message or making an appointment to see the manager.

When a sales representative calls unexpectedly, find out the purpose of the call to determine if:

1. the sales representative should see someone else

2. you should offer to make an appointment for the sales representative

3. you should tell the representative the manager is not interested in the product or service

If the manager is no longer involved in purchasing the representative's products or services, give him or her the new contact information if you have it available. Write the name, title, and location of the person you have referenced on a sheet of paper and give this to the representative. Be courteous in explaining to the sales representative how to reach that person's office. However, due to increased security practices in most public and commercial places of business, visitors will no longer be able to wander freely about the office. There will probably be a procedure for allowing an unknown visitor on the premises. Some offices simply require the visitor to wear an identification badge; others will require the visitor to be escorted to employees' locations. Make yourself familiar with the current security procedures in your office.

When you know your company won't want this representative's particular product or service, graciously tell the sales representative. The representative may still want to convince the manager of the need for the product or service. Invite the sales representative to leave a business card and literature about the product or service, and offer to contact the sales representative if the manager is interested in learning more about the product.

Remember that your job is to make friends for the organization. Give a reason, at least in general terms, before you say "no." Visitors who are turned away should feel that they have been dealt with fairly.

Organizations have definite policies, too, about dealing with **solicitors**. Know what the policies are. If you have been given the authority to handle solicitors, do so assertively but always with courtesy.

Sorry—Refusing Appointments

Many managers plan blocks of time in which they hope to work without interruption. At other times an executive will be forced by the pressure of a deadline to work full-time on a task that must be completed.

During periods when the manager is not seeing anyone, simply state that the manager cannot fit anything more into today's schedule, and then centre the discussion on future arrangements. Indicate when the manager will have time to see the visitor and invite the visitor to make an appointment.

Self-Check

1. How can you tactfully keep confidential materials out of sight of a visitor who approaches your desk?

2. Give an example of how you might show initiative in helping your manager prepare for a meeting.

3. How should you treat a visitor who

   (a) arrives early for an appointment?

   (b) does not have an appointment?

4. Explain how you might assist your manager to terminate a meeting when a visitor outstays the allotted time.

5. What should you do when you are speaking with a customer on the telephone and a visitor approaches your desk?

HANDLING DIFFICULT CUSTOMERS

Every administrative assistant will handle difficult customers or clients at some time in his or her career. Although this situation is undesirable, by handling it professionally you will benefit both your company and the customer.

What can you do when a customer is aggressive or rude? It's a difficult question to address, especially when the answer is, "It depends!" The first decisions you must make will be based on whether the difficult person actually is a customer and whether the difficulty is based on dissatisfaction with your company's actions, and whether there is personal abuse involved. Clearly, if someone who is *not* a customer is personally abusive toward you, then civil action might be in order. However, here the discussion differentiates only between

customers calling on the telephone and those visiting your office. The reaction and response to both is similar, the main difference being that you are dealing face-to-face with the visitor but are removed from the physical presence of a caller.

Difficult Callers

Difficult customers who call to voice their problems on the telephone are arguably easier to handle, the important difference being that there is no immediate and physical presence. These circumstances better allow you to maintain composure. You may even be able to read the procedural script that deals with difficult telephone callers in your office procedures manual—if it has been developed.

Fundamentally, difficult customers who call in should be handled in much the same way as those who appear in your office, at the counter, or in the showroom; that is, with diplomacy, respect, and the help of the points outlined in the "Tips for Success" section on page 216.

Unwanted Visitors

How do you deal with a visitor who is obnoxious or one who makes you feel threatened? Many office buildings have security 24 hours per day. If this is the case in your organization, you would call security to have the individual removed. Dealing with unwanted visitors is something you need to discuss with your office team. Your colleagues may be able to provide names of people who have an abusive history with your office and are, therefore, not welcome. Your company may have an organizational policy for handling unwanted visitors. If so, follow it. If no policy exists, your office team should draft a policy and submit it to management for approval. Every organization wants to provide excellent customer service, but customer abuse toward employees should never be tolerated.

Complaining Customers

One unhappy customer may lead to two unhappy customers may lead to three unhappy customers . . . and so on. When you fail to convert a complaining customer into a contented one, you risk losing more than just one customer. You risk losing all the existing customers as well as potential customers as a result of the influence of one unhappy customer. The receptionist must be skilled at handling difficult people.

Ultimately, what you *don't* want is for your customers to go so far as to file an official complaint such as those submitted to the Better Business Bureau (BBB). There are 20 voluntary self-regulated Better Business Bureaus across Canada. Their objective is to promote and cultivate the highest ethical relationship between businesses and the public. The BBB can share with you reliability reports of businesses that are ethical and reliable; it can provide consumer tips, and it can provide information to consumers before they buy a good or service. It also investigates and exposes fraud against consumers and businesses, arbitrates disputes, and may report on cases of complaints made by both customers and its voluntary business members. While the BBB has no legal jurisdiction, its network and reporting processes may influence customers' and suppliers' behaviour across the country. Any negative exposure with the BBB may result in a loss of business for your company as customers leave and look for alternatives.

What you *do* want is to be able to offer advice and a solution in order to resolve the customer's problem. Remember, an unhappy customer who is allowing you to resolve his or her problem is actually giving you and your organization another chance to make things right. View this as an opportunity.

When dealing with unhappy customers, these simple principles will help you stay objective and better enable you to successfully resolve any problem:

- Don't get emotionally involved in the problem.
- Don't get defensive or aggressive—it never works.
- Provide solutions, not excuses.
- Customers are *not* always right, but don't tell them this.
- All customers have a right to be heard.
- Allowing a customer to abuse you is not acceptable.
- Promising action *without* action will lead to a customer service disaster.
- "Sorry" without corrective action is just an empty word.
- Preventing problems is easier than resolving them.

Abusive Customers

Abuse from customers can come in several forms. For example, a customer might attempt verbal abuse such as swearing, shouting, or even threatening employees. Physical abuse also takes place in offices where customers get angry enough to push people or throw items.

As an administrative assistant, you are expected to be diplomatic, courteous, and to treat all colleagues and customers with respect. However, under no circumstances should you tolerate abuse. Model professional behaviour for people who are being abusive toward you. The best way to do this is to treat others with dignity and respect and in the way you would like to be treated in return. If a customer continues to be abusive, remain professional and courteous, but take control of the situation. If you have exhausted your diplomacy your next steps might be:

- Call your supervisor for assistance to deal with the abusive customer.
- Ask the customer to leave the premises and state that you will deal with him or her when calmed down.

- In extreme cases, tell the customer that his or her actions are not acceptable and you will call security.

Tips for Success

The following are tips for turning an undesirable situation into one that is satisfactory to both parties:

1. **Listen to the customer.** Listen to the spoken words, but also listen to the unspoken—that is, to the tone of voice and the body language. Often there is more information in what customers *don't* say than what they do say. Does the body language indicate anger or frustration? Has the customer omitted an important step in the process he or she is complaining about? If so, is there a reason for this omission?

   Listen quietly and carefully as the customer explains the source of distress. Take notes if necessary and ask questions to ensure clarity.

2. **Apologize if it is appropriate to do so.** Remember that customers are not always right, especially in situations where they have been dishonest or unethical. Where the company is not at fault, an apology might be phrased this way: "We apologize for any inconvenience our company may have caused. However, [company name] has done everything possible to provide you with a quality product [or service]."

   If your company has not performed to the highest of standards, a full apology is in order. Remember to use your tone of voice and your body language to reinforce the sincerity of your message.

3. **Show empathy and understanding.** Demonstrate that you have listened carefully and that you understand the customer's reason for distress. Paraphrasing the customer's story may be helpful. Example: "I understand how frustrated you must feel after receiving no response to your voice mail message."

4. **Promise follow-up.** Commit to assisting the person yourself or to having someone else take action. Tell the customer exactly what your action plan will be and when she or he can expect to hear from you. If you do not know what action is necessary, commit to finding out and to calling the customer within a specified time. Then check with the customer to see if your action plan has his or her approval.

5. **Follow through.** Carry out the action plan just as you promised you would. Be certain to keep the customer informed of your progress.

6. **Use common courtesies.** Learn the customer's name and use it along with the appropriate courtesy title (Mrs., Ms., Mr., Dr.). Be sure your tone of voice and body language always convey a positive and sincere message. Most important, do not reciprocate the aggression. It is easy

to become defensive and annoyed at a customer who is complaining about your service or product. However, do not personalize the comments of a distressed customer. If you feel the situation is beyond your control and you have been unable to deal effectively with this individual, contact your supervisor for support.

If you follow these basic rules, a more satisfactory situation should result.

MANAGING DIVERSE SITUATIONS

Visitors and Language Barriers

Encounters with visitors can also be challenging if they do not speak your language and you do not speak theirs. Listen actively—you will have to listen more carefully to a visitor who is not fluent in the English language. Do not interpret and finish the sentence that the visitor is trying to say. Instead, paraphrase after your visitor has finished speaking to ensure understanding of what was said. Be patient. Just remember, the visitor's English may be a lot better than your Arabic, Japanese, German, or Spanish!

When they do not speak English at all, attempt to determine the native language of the visitors. The names of many languages are often recognizable in both English and the mother tongue. If you do not recognize the visitors' language, asking a one-word question ("Arabic?" for example), will likely get a response that you can understand. If the visitors do not speak Arabic, it is highly likely that they will recognize what you are asking and respond with the name of their language in a one-word answer.

If you do recognize the language and know someone in your area who speaks it, ask the visitors to take a seat (this may be done with hand motions). Then call the person who can speak with them, explain the situation, and ask if he or she would please assist you in helping the visitors by translating.

Don't assume the visitors do not *understand* your language. Ask. Many times a person can understand a language but not speak it. If your visitors understand English, you will be able to explain to them that you are going to ask a co-worker to translate.

Either way, display a positive attitude toward these visitors. Be careful what you say, verbally and nonverbally. Nonverbal communication can be as effective as voice in showing your interest and desire to help. Coming to your office can be a frustrating experience for those visitors, and your courtesy and understanding will contribute to their favourable impression of your company.

Visitors with Special Needs

Today's businesses deal with a diverse clientele, and you are likely to encounter a number of visitors with special needs, visible and invisible. Be observant of visitors with special needs, and make them as comfortable as possible. If appropriate, offer to help; don't wait to be asked. Here are examples of ways in which you can demonstrate courtesy toward, and show consideration for, those visitors.

1. Hold open doors (if the door does not have buttons that automatically open) for someone who uses a wheelchair or for someone who has difficulty walking.

2. Make special arrangements to accommodate the needs of all participants of a meeting. Before booking meetings, ask whether special arrangements will be needed. If a visitor requires wheelchair access, ensure the meeting is booked in a room that has an adequate door opening to accommodate the wheelchair. If an interpreter is needed by a participant, arrange for one. Vegetarians will be appreciative of your efforts in meeting their dietary requirements by providing a choice of nonmeat dishes at luncheon meetings.

3. Promote the acquisition of at least one telephone that is fitted with technology to aid the hearing impaired, and ensure that it is located in an area accessible to visitors but that will not compromise the confidentiality of your company. You can direct visitors who are hearing impaired to this telephone if they wish to make a call.

4. Encourage basic audio aids that will accommodate the needs of visitors who are sight impaired. If your office is accessed by elevator, point out to your employer the benefits of having the elevator equipped with audio signals, audible inside and outside the elevator, to signal each floor.

5. Show courtesy by facing the visitor with a hearing impairment when talking to him or her. This will help the visitor who lip-reads to compensate for the hearing difficulty. Speak up, and enunciate your words carefully.

6. Place a sign in both English and Braille next to a bell if visitors are expected to ring for service. If you do business with a large number of people who share a common language, include the message written in their language as well.

7. Post signs in the reception area to inform visitors of special accommodations that can be made. This will advise of services such as employees who speak languages other than English or who know sign language.

8. Familiarize yourself with the location of wheelchair-accessible restaurants, full-service gas stations, and other businesses in your area that accommodate special needs. Visitors will often ask you questions if they are unfamiliar with the area. Your knowledge and helpfulness will ensure that both you and your employer are perceived as a respectful and customer-oriented organization.

9. Arrange to have a supply of juice and liquids that can be made available to visitors with medical considerations

such as diabetes. This small consideration will reap rewards in terms of goodwill if a visitor experiences sudden low blood sugar levels that require immediate attention while visiting your offices.

As you see, some accommodations for special needs that can be implemented by you, simply by your consideration and actions, can increase your visitors' comfort and satisfaction. Other accommodations are outside your control and will require your employer to become involved; they may even require small financial expenditures. Be proactive in getting your employer involved. Impress them with your understanding of the benefits the company will accrue when it is recognized for its commitment to meeting the diverse needs of *all* its customers.

Your courteous manner and commitment to meeting customer needs will show visitors that your company is caring and wanting to help in any way it can. The benefits will far outweigh the costs of having a sign printed or of purchasing a telephone.

Self-Check

1. What is the main objective of the Better Business Bureau (BBB)?
2. List several principles to help you stay objective when dealing with an unhappy customer.
3. How might you handle the situation if a visitor arrives who does not speak your language?
4. In addition to the examples given, list two ways you might accommodate a visitor with special needs.

ETHICS AND VISITORS

You will often have the opportunity to chat with visitors while they are waiting for your manager or another staff member. Remember to treat visitors in a fair, courteous, and respectful manner, while upholding the principles of the organization. Here are some guidelines to follow when dealing with waiting visitors:

- Avoid sharing confidential information about products, office gossip, and company successes or problems. Customers will sometimes ask questions of a confidential nature to gather information that may help them get ahead of any competition.

- Treat each visitor equally. When two or more visitors appear, use the "first come, first served" rule. Acknowledge both visitors, but invite the second visitor to have a seat while you help the first.

- Avoid asking questions of a personal nature. A visitor may be offended by questions that appear to be prying into his or her personal life. Don't discuss family, children, religion, or politics.

- Do not assume that a visitor is from a particular foreign country, or from a foreign country at all, based on a stereotypical perception such as the colour of a person's skin. The visitor may very well be a Canadian who has lived in Canada for his or her entire life. You should never ask or make reference to a person's country of birth.

When handling visitors, keep in mind your organization's code of ethics as well as your own values.

QUESTIONS FOR STUDY AND REVIEW

1. Compare and contrast the role of a virtual receptionist to a "live" receptionist in a small company.
2. List three situations where a virtual receptionist would be more advantageous to a company than a "live" receptionist.
3. Name six ways that voice mail can enable the administrative assistant to become more efficient in the office.
4. Does voice mail eliminate telephone tag? Why or why not?
5. State five ways that voice mail interactions may be improved.
6. Discuss two disadvantages of voice mail.
7. Offer three guidelines for adopting voice mail to ensure that it will be effective and efficient in the office.
8. Describe five guidelines for answering a business telephone.
9. State the exact words you would use for answering William Wilson's telephone.
10. Explain why it is important to record the time of the call when you are writing a telephone message.
11. State five comments you should avoid saying when you take calls for an absent manager.
12. State four guidelines for transferring a call to another telephone.
13. Describe what to do when two telephones ring at the same time and you are the only person in the office.
14. Under what conditions would you interrupt your manager to take a telephone call while a visitor is in your manager's office?
15. What do the letters IVR represent?

16. If a manager is trying to work without interruption, how should you get a telephone message to her/him?

17. Why do many managers want their calls screened?

18. Name a Canadian website that acts as a directory for Canadian telephone numbers.

19. How are government offices listed in a telephone directory?

20. How are the Yellow Pages arranged?

21. Explain how you would make a direct long-distance call to another city.

22. Explain the purpose of zero-plus dialling.

23. State reasons why telephone calling cards would be given to employees.

24. Explain how to obtain long-distance directory assistance.

25. How does Daylight Saving Time affect the administrative assistant's work?

26. Where is the International Date Line? What happens when you cross it in an easterly direction? What happens when you cross it in a westerly direction?

27. Describe how to place an overseas call when no operator assistance is required. Then describe how to place an overseas call for which operator assistance is required.

28. Suggest how you can tactfully let people know that their appointments are for a short segment of time.

29. Suggest how the administrative assistant can avoid scheduling conflicts in granting appointments.

30. State reasons why it is essential to record the telephone number of a person who has requested or confirmed an appointment.

31. Describe five advantages of using an electronic calendar.

32. Describe two drawbacks of using an electronic calendar.

33. What guidelines should you follow when you must cancel an appointment because the manager cannot keep it?

34. What are the administrative assistant's main responsibilities as they relate to receiving office callers?

35. Explain what is meant by giving a caller immediate attention when you are keying or talking on the telephone.

36. Describe the administrative assistant's role in making a caller who must wait feel comfortable.

37. What should you say if a caller who has an appointment cannot wait and tells you he or she must leave?

38. Explain the basic guidelines for making introductions in business.

39. Why do some managers have an "open door" policy for seeing personnel?

40. Suggest two ways to help an executive terminate a conference when he or she does not have another appointment soon.

41. What would you do if each of the following visitors did not have an appointment: the CEO of your company; the manager's spouse; the manager's former college friend from out of town; a sales representative your manager wants to keep in touch with but cannot see right now; a salesperson representing a product your company does not need; a person soliciting funds; and an aggressive and abusive person?

42. Explain why a customer complaint might be detrimental to your organization.

43. State five actions that work when dealing with complaining customers.

44. Explain what to do when a customer becomes abusive and you have exhausted your diplomacy.

45. Explain six successful tips for dealing with a customer who believes she has received an inferior product from your company.

EVERYDAY ETHICS

Lying on the Job

You are a single parent, working as the receptionist for a fast-paced and aggressive law firm in Toronto. The firm maintains an impersonal work environment, in which relationships are "strictly business" between the administrative assistants and the lawyers. You are very efficient in keeping track of the lawyers, their whereabouts, and the cases they are working on. They rely on you to give out only information that assists them and not to jeopardize any personal or professional situations.

Kristin is an exceptionally busy lawyer with a heavy caseload. When she is unprepared to meet her clients, she asks you to give them false information, saying she is out of town or in court. Kristin is only one of many lawyers that expect your help in this way. If you refused to cooperate, you would be dismissed from your position.

When her husband calls, she expects you to continue with the same routine, saying she is in court or out of town for the day. You've been giving him false information for several years. Recently, you have begun suspecting that Kristin is having an intimate relationship with one of the other lawyers. When her husband calls, you give the standard excuse but are uncomfortable doing so because you suspect she is spending social time with her colleague.

- Why do you think you feel uncomfortable about this new situation?
- Could you have avoided this situation in the first place?
- What is the best course of action you can take?

Problem Solving

1. During your first job performance appraisal, you were criticized for the way you answer the telephone. You have been asking the caller to state the purpose of the call before you say whether or not your manager is in the office. After you find out who the caller is and the purpose of the call, you say, "Mrs. Burke is not in her office" or "Mrs. Burke is in a meeting." It is true that Mrs. Burke is not in her office when you say this, but apparently the callers are not convinced. What can you do to improve rapport with the callers?

2. You know that your manager, Mr. Perkins, is expecting an important long-distance call. He called Mike Brendl at 9:30 a.m., and he is expecting Mr. Brendl to return his call. At 4:30 p.m., Mr. Perkins was called to the president's office. A few minutes later, Mr. Brendl calls. You feel that you should not interrupt Mr. Perkins in the president's office. You do not know whether Mr. Perkins will return to his desk before 5 p.m. What should you do? Do you have any alternatives?

3. Recently Mrs. Garson has made three appointments with your employer, Mr. Stoney. Each time she has cancelled the appointment the day before—once because she was ill, another time because of bad weather, and the last time because she was too busy to keep the appointment. The last time she cancelled the appointment, Mr. Stoney said emphatically, "Please do not grant her another appointment!" This morning Mrs. Garson called requesting another appointment. You told her that Mr. Stoney could not work in another appointment this week and that he would be out of town the following week. Mrs. Garson is furious and insists on talking with Mr. Stoney. What should you do? What will you say to Mrs. Garson?

4. Your manager, Mr. Harper, had a serious heart attack in his office late Tuesday afternoon. Today you are cancelling his appointments for the remainder of this week and next week. You are explaining that the appointments will be rescheduled with someone else. What can you ask in order to judge the urgency of each appointment? How much information can you give about Mr. Harper's illness? What can you say?

Special Reports

1. Use the Yellow Pages of your local telephone directory to determine how the following are classified: educational services (public schools, private schools, colleges, and universities); food catering services; medical doctors (general practitioners and specialists); furniture for an office; office stationery; office computers; and airlines. Prepare a list and submit it to your instructor.

2. Have you ever done any kind of office work? If so, recall what you observed about how office visitors were received in the organization where you worked. Did the organization have a receptionist? Were the visitors escorted or directed to the offices of those with whom they had appointments? Were the salespeople's calls restricted? If so, how? What was the visitor's first contact with the administrative assistant? Jot down what you recall, and share your ideas with the class. If you have never worked in an office, ask an administrative assistant you know about how visitors are received in the organization in which he or she works.

3. In groups of two or three classmates discuss positive and negative experiences you have encountered when calling an office for an appointment. Make a list of the positive points and the negative points and share it with the rest of the class.

4. Locate a business in your community that uses online appointment booking for its clients. In a memo to your instructor describe the features of this online booking format.

PRODUCTION CHALLENGES

11-A Receiving Telephone Calls

Supplies needed:

• *Forms 11-A-1, 11-A-2, 11-A-3, and 11-A-4, page 411*

When your managers are in their offices, they answer their own telephones. Today, August 11, Mr. Wilson, Jack Rush, and Sid Levine are not in their offices. You receive the following telephone calls:

9:15 a.m.—for Jack Rush from Archie Sellars, 683-4750. He wants to know if parts are available for an electric range, Model 1621. Please return his call.

10:30 a.m.—for Sid Levine from Al Wilcox, 442-8761, about a printing order Sid Levine placed with him. Urgent. Please call.

11:00 a.m.—for Mr. Wilson from Bob Arnett, 366-8184, a speaker for the November Sales Seminar. He has a business conflict and cannot attend the seminar on Wednesday. Please call.

11:15 a.m.—for Mr. Wilson from the Human Resources Department, Extension 5738, asking, "When can Mr. Wilson see an applicant?" Please call.

Complete the telephone message blanks for each of the telephone messages you received today. Indicate the sense of urgency and therefore priority implied in each message.

11-B Placing Telephone Calls

Supplies needed:

- *Forms 11-B-1 and 11-B-2, page 412*

Mr. Wilson asked you to place some telephone calls. Here is Mr. Wilson's conversation with you:

"Mr. Arnett, who was scheduled to speak at the November Sales Seminar on Wednesday, November 12, at 10 a.m., cannot attend the Sales Seminar on Wednesday. He has an important business conflict. He is substituting for his manager, who had a heart attack and will not return to work for at least six months. Mr. Arnett must be in his Burlington office on November 12. He can attend the seminar on Monday and Tuesday."

"Find a speaker who can trade times with Mr. Arnett. Call James Epstein in Winnipeg, at 690-8699, who is scheduled to talk at 2 p.m. on Monday. If he can't do it, ask Ruth Agway in Vancouver, at 487-3232, who is scheduled to speak at 11 a.m. on Monday. Another possibility is Ray Morris from Margate, in England. Mr. Morris is a special guest on a panel on Tuesday afternoon. He may wish to stay over and speak in place of Mr. Arnett before flying back to England. Mr. Morris's number in England is 01843-386126."

"Be sure to call Mr. Arnett and tell him what arrangements you have made."

"Be sure to make the proper notations in the official copy of the program. It is necessary to write a confirmation letter to the person whose time is changed."

Note: When you called Mr. Epstein, he said he could not attend the seminar on Wednesday.

Before you place any calls, use a page or two in your telephone notebook to plan your calls. Record all essential information, such as names, telephone numbers, dates, and times of day. Also jot down reminders about what you need to do after you have found someone who can trade times to speak with Mr. Arnett.

11-C Telephone Services

Supplies needed:

- *A local telephone directory*
- *Questions on Telephone Services, Forms 11-C-1 and 11-C-2, pages 413 and 414*

Use a local telephone directory to complete the questions on pages 413 and 414.

11-D Keying Messages

Supplies needed:

- *Plain paper*

Mr. Wilson has a very busy week full of meetings with an international delegation that is visiting to discuss a new line of home furnishings. The delegates are:

Mr. Abdalla from Egypt

Mrs. Yoko from Japan

Mr. Schneider from Germany

Ms. O'Neil from Ireland

Throughout the week, you have a number of requests to interrupt the meetings. In each case, you key a message. Depending on the situation, you might take the message into the meeting and leave it with the appropriate person, or you might send a text message to his or her cell phone. Regardless, you key the text. If you want to give the guest a return telephone number, be sure to provide the international access code, country code, and city code when appropriate. Key messages for the following situations:

1. Tuesday, March 11 at 11:30 a.m.—You receive a call from Mrs. Yoko's son in Tokyo saying he needs to speak to his mother. When you tell him that she is engaged in a meeting, he says that his call is urgent and relates to his father's health. The telephone number that shows on your electronic message system is 4314545.

2. Thursday, March 13 at 8:30 a.m.—You receive a call from the local Air Canada office regarding Ms. O'Neil's flight home to Dublin. Apparently, the flight has been cancelled and Air Canada is trying to reschedule people onto different flights. They are offering a flight out of Toronto tomorrow departing at 6:30 a.m. Because you know that she has an 8:00 a.m. meeting tomorrow, you suggested to the Air Canada agent that she needed a later flight. There is nothing available until Saturday evening at 8:30 p.m. The flight on Friday is direct, but the flight on Saturday goes to London where Ms. O'Neil will have to transfer to British Airways.

3. Thursday, March 13 at 12 noon—You receive a call from a Mr. Mohammed of North Africa Home Design in Cairo. This is the same company where Mr. Abdalla is the regional sales manager. He insists on telling Mr. Abdalla some very good news regarding a successful sale to one of the company's clients. He wants to talk to Mr. Abdalla immediately. The number showing on your electronic message is 1224557.

4. Friday, March 14 at 11:30 a.m.—A call is received, but you cannot understand the caller very well. He has a strong German accent. You believe he is requesting information regarding Mr. Schneider's flight arrangements. He has called twice leaving urgent messages. He tells you his number is 1445577.

11-E Scheduling Appointments

Supplies needed:

- *Mr. Wilson's appointment calendar, Form 11-E-1, page 415*

- *Administrative assistant's appointment calendar, Form 11-E-2, page 415*
- *Plain paper*

If you have access to an electronic calendar, perform the following challenge electronically. Otherwise, use the paper forms provided.

Mr. Wilson has been scheduling his own appointments. He uses a monthly paper calendar and crowds the appointments into the spaces. During a discussion with Mr. Wilson on Friday, he asked you to schedule his appointments for him.

You decided to use electronic appointment calendars—one for Mr. Wilson and one for yourself. Mr. Wilson has no appointments scheduled for Monday and only one for Tuesday. He has the following appointments for Wednesday, August 6, entered in his monthly calendar:

- 10 a.m. Pete Rollins, sales representative for Home Gadgets, Inc., 416-741-2408
- 9 a.m. Agnes Smith, sales representative for Small Home Appliances, Inc., 905-681-5432
- 11 a.m. Joanna Hansen, Manager of the Eastern Region of Millennium Appliances, Inc., and J. R. Rush, Assistant Vice-President of Marketing, Eastern Region
- 3 p.m. Charlene Azam, Assistant Vice-President of Marketing, Western Region, to review marketing plans for fall
- 12 noon Lunch with Ms. Hansen and Mr. Rush

You transfer these appointments to Mr. Wilson's daily calendar and yours.

On Tuesday, August 5, you receive the following telephone calls concerning appointments:

1. From Linda Yee, Assistant Vice-President of Marketing, Midwestern Region, saying that she must attend a funeral out of town on Wednesday. She has an appointment on Wednesday at 3 p.m. with O. C. Conners, President of Mapledale Homes, Inc., 905-872-1411. She asks if Mr. Wilson can see Mr. Conners for her at 3 p.m.

Here is your response: "I'll try. Mr. Wilson has an appointment with Ms. Azam at 3 p.m. I'll see if I can move Ms. Azam's appointment to 2 p.m. I'll call you and let you know."

Later you call Mrs. Yee and confirm that Mr. Wilson will see Mr. Conners at 3 p.m.

2. From Pete Rollins's assistant, saying that Mr. Rollins had an automobile accident, is hospitalized, and obviously cannot keep his appointment.

3. From Ray Rogers, Co-Chairman of the Eastern Region Sales Seminar, asking for an appointment on Wednesday to review plans for the November seminar. You suggest 10 a.m., and Mr. Rogers accepts.

4. From the Human Resources Department, asking Mr. Wilson to see a job applicant. You try to postpone this appointment, but the Human Resources Department insists that Mr. Wilson will want to meet this applicant while he is in the building on Wednesday. You schedule an appointment for Bill Horvath at 4 p.m.

Before leaving the office on Tuesday, you key Mr. Wilson's appointment schedule for Wednesday, August 6.

On Wednesday at 10:05 a.m., Jason Rhodes, a college friend from out of town, comes to the office for a brief visit with Mr. Wilson. You say you will schedule him for a few minutes between appointments at 10:45 a.m.

On his way to lunch, Mr. Wilson asks you to call the Lakeside Restaurant to tell the manager how many will be in his dinner party Wednesday evening. (Be sure to enter this in the reminder section of your calendar.)

Weblinks

Intelligent Office
www.intelligentoffice.com
This is the site of a company that offers virtual business assistance throughout North America. Informative videos explain how Intelligent Office works to provide remote reception and a complete line of administrative assistant services to the businessperson on the go who does not need on-site office assistance.

Telephone Etiquette
www.careerknowhow.com/ask_sue/officephon.htm
A weekly column about professionalism, etiquette, and problems in the workplace is featured on this site.

Canadian Telephone Directories
www.Canada411.ca
Finding the names and addresses of people and businesses in Canada is made easy with this website. It offers over 12 million listings, including postal codes, toll-free numbers, Yellow Pages, and City Guides in Canada.

Infobel
www.infobel.com
This is a site providing information on telephone directories worldwide.

Day-Timer
www.daytimer.com
This site includes Day-Timer's product information as well as articles with time management tips.

World Clock
www.timeanddate.com/worldclock
The World Clock site allows you to determine the time in cities around the world.

Booking Calendar.com
www.bookingcalendar.com
On this site you will find one of many online calendar services that are offered for a fee as an alternative to application software such as Microsoft® Outlook.

Chapter 12

Travel Arrangements

Learning Outcomes

After completion of this chapter, the student will be able to:

1 List the travel services provided by the internet and travel agencies.

2 Indicate the information needed before contacting a travel agent about a proposed trip.

3 Describe the advantages of making online airline reservations.

4 Explain how jet lag can affect a business trip.

5 Read the 24-hour clock.

6 Describe the procedures for making flight, car, and hotel reservations.

7 Discuss the requirements for acquiring passports, visas, and immunizations.

8 Describe the implications for the traveller of the need for increased security in airports.

9 Discuss the differences in the status of women in business in different cultures.

10 Prepare travel itineraries.

11 Make an airline reservation.

12 Prepare a travel fund advance.

13 Prepare a travel expense voucher.

14 Research destination countries and compile information that the traveller should know before departing.

Anyone who works as an administrative assistant can expect to make travel arrangements. If you work for a manager who travels, you should become thoroughly familiar with the organization's travel policies. Know what travel accommodations are available and how to schedule them to meet your manager's preferences. Your responsibilities also will include ensuring that procedures are followed and office tasks are completed while the manager is away.

PLANNING THE TRIP

Before you proceed to make travel arrangements, ask questions about the policies and procedures followed within the organization. For example:

- Who is responsible for making travel arrangements?
- Do designated administrative assistants handle the travel arrangements for all the executives of the organization?

- If the services of a travel agency are used, which agency?

- Are the executives expected to fly business class or economy class?

- What is the policy concerning the use of private cars and car rental services?

- Does the organization have a preference for a particular airline?

- If so, what are the policies for using it?

- How are payments for reservations handled?

- What is the procedure for getting a cash advance for a traveller?

As soon as you have answers to a few of these questions, you will know whether to turn the arrangements over to someone else or make them yourself. Regardless of who makes the arrangements, try to request all reservations far enough in advance to ensure that you obtain the travel arrangements and accommodations desired.

Internet Travel Services

Using the internet to make airline bookings is efficient and accurate. The internet offers an abundance of information that will help the administrative assistant plan business trips. By searching the **website** of a travel service company, the administrative assistant may access information regarding:

- passports

- visas

- tourism

- flight schedules

- latest pricing

- telephone numbers
- travel tips
- email, fax, and postal mailing addresses

When reservations are made through the internet, as in Figure 12-1, the subscriber pays for the tickets with a credit card number. In addition to providing a confirmation number that can be printed directly from the computer, the internet travel service faxes or emails a ticket voucher containing trip details to the subscriber. This documentation replaces the traditional paper ticket when the traveller checks in at the airport.

Travel Agencies

You will definitely appreciate the services of a travel agent when you make arrangements for international travel; you will find that working through a travel agent is the easiest and best way to make arrangements for domestic travel as well. Many agencies guarantee 24-hour telephone access to travellers who run into problems such as flight delays or cancellations during the trip.

Travel agents receive their commissions from the airlines, hotels, and other organizations whose services they sell. Some agencies also charge your company a small fee for service.

The local travel agencies are listed in the classified section of the telephone directory. If you are concerned about finding a reputable travel agency, call the Better Business Bureau or the Alliance of Canadian Travel Associations (ACTA) in Ottawa, or check the internet for a listing of ACTA members. ACTA's membership includes travel agents in all major Canadian cities. ACTA has high

Figure 12-1 Administrative assistant accessing travel information.

standards and a rigorous code of ethics; the group's members are reliable and efficient.

Most travel agents are approved by the International Air Transportation Association (IATA). IATA is a conglomerate of international airlines. It allows travel agencies that meet its stringent requirements to use its insignia. An agency seeking IATA's approval must have a solid reputation, as well as the financial backing to ensure its own stability.

Travel agencies use the internet to maintain up-to-the-minute information on all airline schedules and hotel accommodations. Because of their experience and business connections, travel agents can obtain information quickly; and they often find availability and better prices than most people who do their own bookings.

The travel agent represents *all* the transportation lines, hotels, and motels, not just certain ones. You, of course, must provide the travel agent with all the details needed. When planning a trip, try to deal with only one person at the agency, and rely on that person to prepare the complete package.

The travel agent will make out the itinerary, secure tickets, make hotel reservations, arrange for car rental, and perform other services related to the trip.

For international travel, travel agents will provide information on the need for visas and how they can be obtained, how much luggage is allowed, luggage size restrictions, the countries being visited, the local currency, and the regulations for bringing foreign purchases through Canadian Customs.

They do not give advice on immunizations. That advice should be obtained through your local health authority.

Trip Information Needed

As soon as the manager mentions a trip, start compiling information. Before you contact a travel agent or a carrier, compile the details concerning:

1. the destination
2. intermediate stops, outward and inward bound
3. date of departure and date of return
4. date and time of the first business appointment and the time needed between arrival and the appointment
5. preferred time of day for travel
6. method of travel—air, rail, automobile
7. type of service—business class, economy class
8. preferred service provider (i.e., airline)
9. preferred seat selection (aisle? window? front of the airplane?)

10. special accommodations (extra legroom, wheelchair access, dietary restrictions)

11. hotel preference or the desired location of the hotel within the city

12. hotel amenities required (conference facilities, wireless internet, multimedia equipment)

13. need for transportation at the destination or at intermediate stops

14. make or size of the car preferred if car rental is involved

For use in planning future trips, maintain a folder labelled Trip Preferences. When your employer returns from a trip, make comments about the transportation and hotel accommodations on a copy of the agenda for the trip. In this folder, keep the manager's comments, and all other information that will help you recall preferences when you are planning another trip to the same city or part of the country. If you plan trips for more than one manager, maintain a Trip Preferences folder for each one.

pro-Link
Trusting Travel

Dreaming of faraway places? Cruising the internet to make your arrangements to visit them? It's interesting to know that only a small percentage of businesses rely on booking travel arrangements through the internet. Why?

■ Many offices don't trust the internet for something as important as booking flights and hotels.

■ It's easier to make a single telephone call to a travel agent and let the agent do the rest of the work.

The reluctance by businesses to use the internet for travel arrangements is not likely to change dramatically until airlines and hotels offer greater incentives, such as reduced prices, to internet bookers.

Self-Check

1. When air reservations are made by an organization via the internet, how is payment made?

2. List five pieces of information an administrative assistant must have before contacting a travel agent to make a reservation.

ARRANGING THE TRAVEL

Making transportation arrangements for international travel is similar to making transportation arrangements for domestic travel. However, an additional factor to take into account when planning international travel is the effect of a long trip through different time zones. International travellers commonly suffer from **jet lag**, the disruption of the body's natural rhythm that comes from high-speed jet travel. Effects (such as fatigue and irritability) and severity vary with individuals, directions travelled, and the number of time zones crossed. Many, but not all, people report that easterly travel makes adjustment more difficult. The important thing to remember is that international travel is both physically and mentally wearing on the traveller. When planning an overseas trip, allow an adequate rest period following arrival in the country you are visiting and following the return home.

To make travel arrangements with ease, you should know about air travel services and other types of transportation, including car rental services; how to make hotel

reservations; how to obtain **passports** and **visas**; and what is involved in meeting immunization requirements.

Air Travel

Because many managers are required to fly to meetings in different cities, you need to be well informed about air travel services.

Sources of Air Travel Information You can obtain air travel information about a specific trip by telephoning a local travel agent or airline. However, all this information is easily accessible on the internet.

As well, the Canadian Transportation Agency has made available a number of free brochures of information about air travel.

Types of Flights Flights that encounter the fewest delays and inconveniences are considered to be the most desirable. When making travel arrangements, consider the flights available in this order:

1. a **nonstop flight**, which is uninterrupted from point of departure to destination

2. a **direct flight**, on which, regardless of the number of stops en route, the passenger remains on the same plane from departure to destination

3. a **connecting flight** with another flight of the same airline

4. a connecting flight with another flight of another airline

When a passenger changes aircraft without changing airlines, the gate for the connecting flight should be near the deplaning gate. The distance between the boarding gates of two different airlines at a major airport can be great, and walking or being shuttled from one gate to another is time-consuming. If the first flight is delayed, the passenger may not have enough time to get to the connecting flight.

Because delays cannot be predicted, use wise judgment when making reservations; if the traveller must make a connection, allow adequate time between the flights. Remember that many airports have more than one terminal and that some cities have two airports. A connection between two different terminals or airports in the same city can take two hours, or even longer. Think of the activities involved: deplaning, getting transportation to the second airport, and locating and boarding the next flight.

Commuter flights are short direct flights between two neighbouring cities. These neighbouring cities need not be in the same province, but they must be close enough that significant numbers of travellers use the service as a convenience. There are commuter services between Vancouver and Victoria, Edmonton and Calgary, Toronto and Ottawa, and various other Canadian cities. Many business travellers rely on commuter flights to meet with clients or colleagues in neighbouring cities and even to go to work each day. These flights leave frequently—often every hour. Although reservations are recommended, they are often not required because of the frequent schedules.

Classes of Service
The services passengers receive aboard the plane—especially where they sit and the food and beverages served—are purchased by class of service. The basic classes of service are business class and economy class. The priority services for business-class travelling include expeditious check-in and boarding as well as additional comfort and service during the flight.

Airlines sometimes refer to business-class service as first-class service. When an airline offers both first-class and business-class service on the same flight, the first-class service offers even greater seating comfort, at a proportionately greater cost. Some airlines, particularly on international flights, include extra-wide seats that recline fully into beds for their first-class passengers.

Some organizations require their executives to fly *business class*, because it is considered more prestigious and because it provides greater comfort such as wider seats with more legroom and working room—an important consideration on long flights. Other organizations, for obvious financial reasons, require their executives to fly *economy class*, the most popular class of airline tickets. Disadvantages of economy-class air travel include longer check-in lines at airports, crowded cabins, and limited food service. The obvious advantage of economy-class travel is the cheaper ticket cost.

Figure 12-2 First-class airline cabin seating.

Flight Reservations
You can make a flight reservation yourself through the internet or by simply telephoning the airline reservations office. You can pay for your tickets by providing a credit card number and then receive them through email, through regular mail, or at the airport reservations desk.

Most airlines no longer prepare paper tickets; instead, digital tickets (e-tickets) are provided. The system now works like this:

- Book the reservation over the telephone or internet.

- Use a credit card or charge account to pay for the tickets.

- Receive a faxed or emailed itinerary and confirmation from the airline carrier.

- An electronic boarding pass can be accessed online anytime within the 24-hour period prior to departure. Timelines will vary depending on whether the flight booked is domestic or international. Be sure to confirm electronic boarding pass requirements at the time of booking. You print your pass and proceed to the gate.

- Many airlines are offering a mobile device boarding pass option. When the electronic boarding pass is issued, it can be saved as a PDF file to the traveller's smartphone or tablet, which can then be scanned at the gate. Ensure the airline has a mobile scanner with which to scan your device appropriately.

Before you contact the airline reservations office, collect all the trip information you need for making a flight reservation. The reservations agent will be using a computer system that stores all the reservations. The agent will establish whether the space you want is available. If it is, make the reservation during the initial contact. When the traveller does not know the return date, purchase an **open ticket**. As soon as the traveller knows the return date, call the agent and make the return reservation.

If space is not available on the flight you want, proceed with alternative plans. Inquire about earlier and later flights with the same airline and with other airlines. If you can't select an alternative flight, ask that the manager's name be placed on a waiting list in case there is a cancellation on the flight desired.

Reconfirmation of airline reservations is required on international flights. The traveller should reconfirm reservations for each leg of the trip.

Making Online Reservations

Booking the airline reservations online can be very efficient for the office assistant. The assistant can access the availability of flights in minutes. Alternative schedules can be printed and then compared and selected by the travellers. Keep in mind that executive travel and flight plans change frequently and rapidly. While the administrative assistant can save time and make changes promptly online, travel agents are more up to the minute on price and schedule changes that may have occurred since the reservation was made.

Many executives like to make their own reservations. In this case, the assistant should train the executives on how to access flight information and book flights online. This way the traveller can quickly change plans without getting the assistant involved.

Cost of Tickets and Payment

While fares for all scheduled intra-Canadian airline flights are deregulated, the National Transportation Agency of Canada still evaluates tariffs and monitors competitive economy fares between Canadian destinations. International fares are regulated by IATA based on bilateral agreements between international carriers. Fares may vary minimally between Canadian airline companies. However, one company may offer a seat sale or an excursion fare.

In order to compete, some smaller airline companies offer **no-frills flights** for reduced prices. No-frills flights usually do not offer the in-flight cabin services of flight attendants, and passengers are required to provide their own food and drink. Even larger Canadian airlines such as Air Canada no longer provide meals to economy travellers on many of their domestic routes. Economy passengers on other routes may have the option to *purchase* prepackaged food from the airline during the flight. All travellers should check on the availability of food services before embarking on lengthy flights. All airlines include food and beverage service on their international flights.

Most airlines today offer travel incentives to their customers. Travellers who become members of an airline's travel plan earn points each time they fly. Points are earned in relation to the distance flown and class of service purchased. They can be redeemed for free travel with the airline or one of its partner airlines at a later date. Points are earned in the name of the traveller rather than the organization and are often influential in the traveller's choice of airline carrier. Air Canada's travel plan is Aeroplan, and members can use accumulated points for future travel with Air Canada or one of its partners, including international airlines such as Lufthansa and Air New Zealand.

Another way to save money is to make reservations well in advance of travel, since costs of remaining seats tend to rise as seats are sold for particular flights. While booking in advance can save the organization money, spontaneous travel plans are more common for business travellers. When a passenger must change travel plans or cancel a reservation, the passenger should call the nearest reservations office of the airline at once. Unused airline tickets and unused portions are sometimes redeemable where full fares have been paid. When discounted tickets are involved, there is a penalty for making changes or cancelling reservations. Penalties vary between airlines and with the type of ticket purchased. Refund regulations should be investigated at the time of booking.

Reading the 24-Hour Clock

For air travel, the times shown are based on the 24-hour clock. This is to eliminate confusion between a.m. and p.m. Under this system, time begins at one minute past midnight (0001) and continues through the next 24 hours to midnight (2400). (See Figure 12-3.)

Ground Transportation

Airports are usually located from 6 to 30 (or more) kilometres from cities; for that reason, one or more types of ground transportation—airport limousine, taxi, shuttle bus, and car rental—are available at all airports.

The distance and direction of the airport, the travel time needed, the types of ground transportation available,

Figure 12-3 Time conversion for the 24-hour clock.

1:00 a.m.	=	0100	1:00 p.m.	=	1300
2:00 a.m.	=	0200	2:00 p.m.	=	1400
3:00 a.m.	=	0300	3:00 p.m.	=	1500
4:00 a.m.	=	0400	4:00 p.m.	=	1600
5:00 a.m.	=	0500	5:00 p.m.	=	1700
6:00 a.m.	=	0600	6:00 p.m.	=	1800
7:00 a.m.	=	0700	7:00 p.m.	=	1900
8:00 a.m.	=	0800	8:00 p.m.	=	2000
9:00 a.m.	=	0900	9:00 p.m.	=	2100
10:00 a.m.	=	1000	10:00 p.m.	=	2200
11:00 a.m.	=	1100	11:00 p.m.	=	2300
Noon	=	1200	Midnight	=	2400

and approximate costs are all listed in the Official Airlines Guide (OAG) for most destination cities.

To determine what arrangements to make for ground transportation, ask the airline reservations agent or your travel agent.

Limousines and shuttle buses operate on a regular basis between the airport and downtown hotels. They leave the designated hotels in time to get the passengers to the airport for departing flights, and they meet incoming flights.

Air taxi is a helicopter or small airplane service available at some airports. Helicopters operate between two airports of a destination city, between an airport and downtown heliports, and/or between the destination airport and an airport not served by jet aircraft. Compared to other types of transportation, air taxi service is expensive, but it saves time.

A traveller who must make a connecting flight at a different airport may need air taxi service in order to make the connection. On domestic flights, avoid scheduling a connecting flight that involves a second airport. When people travel abroad, they may have to make a connection involving two airports, because the traveller's incoming flight may arrive at one airport and the international flight may depart at another. Before making a reservation for air taxi service, find out about airport limousine or bus shuttle service between the terminals serving the airports involved.

Car Rental Services

The best way to arrange for car rental is either to telephone the local office of the car rental agency or to contact the agency online.

The largest car rental agencies offer both domestic and international car rental services, publish worldwide directories of their services, provide a toll-free number for making reservations, and have a website with reservation facilities.

When you are making arrangements for car rental, specify the following:

- city, date, and time
- size of the car desired
- location where the car is to be picked up
- name of the person who will pick up the car
- location where the car is to be left
- length of time the car will be used
- the method of payment for the charges
- request for map with directions from car rental centre to destination

A car can be picked up at the rental agency right at the airport. All the traveller has to do on arrival is go to the airport car rental office, state that there has been a reservation, present a driver's licence, and complete arrangements for payment of the charges.

Charges incurred are payable at the completion of the rental, but the arrangements for payment must be made in advance. Major credit cards are accepted. At the time you are making the reservation, be prepared to give the account number and the expiry date of the credit card to be used for payment. Your organization may have arrangements with car rental agencies entitling you to a discount.

Self-Check

1. What is jet lag?
2. What is a nonstop flight? a direct flight?
3. Distinguish between business-class and economy-class airline tickets.
4. What is an e-ticket?
5. Why is it important to cancel airline reservations as soon as you know your manager will not be travelling?

Hotel Reservations

Many hotels provide a toll-free number for making reservations. You can obtain the toll-free number for the hotel by calling 1-800-555-1212.

If you are not familiar with the hotels in the destination city, contact a local travel agent. Most international accommodation information changes so rapidly that agents consult online computer information, which is updated frequently. Many of the larger hotels and resorts have their own websites, so it's very possible to access this information and make your own reservations. Most hotel and resort websites provide online booking services and toll-free telephone numbers. There are also many discount travel sites that offer significant reductions in accommodation cost.

Always ask for a confirmation of a hotel reservation. When the operator gives you a confirmation number or an electronic confirmation note, be sure to attach it to the itinerary so that the traveller will have it if there is any question about the reservation.

Hotels require a deposit when you request that a room be held for late arrival. A room that is being held for a possible late arrival is called a *guaranteed* reservation. Make the request and provide a credit card number as a deposit if there is the slightest chance that your manager might arrive late. Late arrival varies between 4 p.m. and 6 p.m. Major credit cards are accepted by hotels, and providing the credit card information simplifies the process of making a deposit for a guaranteed room reservation. The benefit of a guaranteed reservation is that your manager can be assured of a room regardless of the arrival time. However, if travel plans change and the guaranteed reservation is not cancelled before a specified time on the arrival date (e.g., 6 p.m.), the cost of the room will be billed to the credit card number, and the authorized owner of the card will be required to pay the cost.

Passports

A passport is a travel document, given to citizens by their own government, granting permission to leave the country and to travel in certain specified foreign countries. A passport serves as proof of citizenship and identity in a foreign country. It asks other countries to allow the bearer of the passport free passage within their borders. It entitles the bearer to the protection of her or his own country and that of the countries visited. Any Canadian citizen who goes abroad must carry a Canadian passport.

Canadians citizens travelling by *air* to the United States are required to present a valid passport; a NEXUS card is also acceptable when used at a NEXUS kiosk. This card is issued to applicants who pass rigorous security checks and is approved by both countries. It is intended to expedite border crossings. Crossings by land or sea require a passport to cross the Canada–US border effective June 1, 2009, according to the Canada Border Services website, http://www.cbsa-asfc.gc.ca/menu-eng.html.

To apply for a passport, a person must complete an application form. The passport application is available free of charge at any post office or passport office and at most travel agencies. The Passport Office is an agency of the Government of Canada. Along with the completed application, the applicant must submit (1) two identical passport photos taken within the previous 12 months and certified on the back by an eligible guarantor and (2) an *original* document as proof of Canadian citizenship. A photocopy of a birth certificate is not acceptable. Payment must be submitted with the application form and must be made in the form of cash, money order, or a certified cheque made payable to the Receiver General of Canada.

Passport applications may be made in person at a regional office or can be submitted through the mail; processing time is longer in the latter case. If a passport is urgently required, processing can be expedited at an extra cost when presented in person.

Under current regulations, a Canadian passport is valid for five years and may not be renewed or extended. This timeline, however, will change with the introduction of the **electronic passport (e-passport)**, scheduled to be available in 2013. With the e-passport, adults will select either a five- or ten-year passport time limit. Children's e-passports will be limited to five years. An electronic chip will be embedded into the back of the e-passport. The chip will contain information that is currently located on page 2 of the paper passport: the holder's date of birth, sex, place of birth, and signature, as well as the passport's date of issue, date of expiry, and issuing authority.

The e-passport is designed to reduce tampering. Border crossings are equipped with an e-passport reader in order to scan the chip on the e-passport. According to the Passport Canada website, over 95 countries have been using e-passports with no reported chip failures.

Visas

Many countries require foreign travellers to hold a visa. A visa is a stamped permit to travel within a given country for a specified length of time. It is granted by the foreign country's government and is usually stamped or attached inside the passport. However, some countries provide loose visa documents so that the visa can be removed when travelling to uncooperative countries.

Foreign Affairs and International Trade Canada (DFAIT) maintains a website that contains information for Canadians who travel abroad. It promotes different cultures and values worldwide. The website can be located at www.international.gc.ca/index.aspx. It includes a link to Canadian government offices abroad where you can get up-to-date visa information. The site also gives current travel updates on conditions of foreign destinations, political unrest, threatened security and health conditions, entry requirements, and consular contact numbers. Information that pertains to foreign countries, including visa requirements, is subject to change. Well in advance of the departure date, a traveller should check passport and visa requirements with the consulates of the countries to be visited. Most countries require the Canadian passport to be valid for a specified period of time past the scheduled departure date from that country. The traveller should obtain the necessary visas before going abroad. Visas are obtained through consulates and embassies located in Canada. Most foreign consular representatives are located in principal Canadian cities, particularly Ottawa, Toronto, and Vancouver. The addresses of foreign consulates in Canada may be obtained by consulting the DFAIT through its website, www.dfait-maeci.gc.ca. This comprehensive website includes an inquiry service. If you wish to contact Canadian embassies and consulates abroad, these can be searched by location or city at http://travel.gc.ca/assistance/embassies.

The traveller must send his or her passport to each consulate involved to obtain visas. The time (and level of patience) it takes to process a visa after it reaches a consulate office varies between one day and three weeks. Allow plenty of time and use prepaid courier services whenever possible. Some travel agents are experienced in obtaining visas; but, because the process is usually straightforward, you should not need to rely on travel agents.

Immunization Requirements

The International Health Regulations adopted by the World Health Organization (WHO) stipulate that certain vaccinations may be required as a condition of entry to any country. The WHO recommends that all travellers whether domestic or international should be up to date with routine immunizations. The WHO sends communiqués to local health departments advising them of required and recommended **immunization** for travellers. Additional information on major health risks to travellers to various countries can also be found on their website at www.who.int/ith/en.

For travel to many countries, an International Certificate of Vaccination is not required. If you need one, you can obtain it from the local health clinic. The form must be stamped by the clinic where the vaccinations are administered.

Refer to your local health authority well in advance of trips to developing countries. Canadian websites that contain information related to immunization requirements are the Public Health Agency of Canada, under "Travel Health," at www.travelhealth.gc.ca and Health Canada at www.hc-sc.gc.ca.

Carry-On Luggage

Airlines differ with regard to their regulations for carry-on luggage. Policies may vary concerning

- the number of pieces allowed
- the size of the carry-on
- the weight of the carry-on

Travellers are generally allowed only one or two pieces of carry-on luggage. All pieces must be small enough to fit under the seat or in the overhead cabinets of the aircraft.

Carry-on luggage is scanned as it passes through security. The Canadian Air Transport Security Authority (CATSA) provides detailed information on carry-on baggage limitations as well as specific information on what items are considered unacceptable to pack. If any suspicious items show up on the scan, the luggage is checked by hand. It is forbidden to carry any items deemed to be potentially dangerous. More information can be obtained by visiting www.catsa.gc.ca.

Security

All travellers, both national and international, should be aware of security issues. Many airports now use full body scans to look for concealed weapons or objects. For the administrative assistant who makes travel arrangements and who helps the executive prepare for the trip, here are some factors to consider:

- Travel to and through some countries can put Canadians at risk. When booking flights, choose flights that are reputable and ones that avoid countries that are unfriendly to Westerners.
- Location is a critical consideration when booking hotels. Be certain that you book reputable hotels in safe locations.
- Security at airports is very heavy. Executives who travel should expect to have their notebook computers, pocket organizers, pagers, cell phones, and briefcases thoroughly examined before they board a flight.
- Prescriptions and over-the-counter drugs that are legal in Canada (e.g., codeine) may be restricted in other countries. Keep the original prescription and the original container while the medication is being taken and even after the treatment is finished since traces of certain medications can still be detectable in the system for a period of time.
- Batteries in the travellers' notebook computers and pocket organizers should be charged. With increased airport security, people carrying electronic devices may be asked to start these machines to prove they are truly business tools and not explosive devices.
- Many airports insist on jackets and shoes being removed as travellers pass through security.
- Some countries deny entry to travellers whose passports indicate travel in countries on their "uncooperative list" within a certain period of time. Travellers should check to see if restrictions apply between countries they intend to visit.
- Travellers should expect to answer questions about why they are travelling to certain countries. Is it for business? If so, what business?
- Travellers should carry their passports and their immunization cards (in some countries) since government officials can request these at any time.
- Gifts for clients should not be wrapped prior to boarding the flight. Airport security can insist that you unwrap all parcels for inspection.
- Travellers should expect to be frisked by security officers if any level of metal registers as the traveller passes through the metal detection gate.
- Increased security at airports throughout the world often results in longer delays in boarding airplanes than in the past. Take this into consideration when determining how early to arrive at the airport.
- Travellers should never carry any device or substance that security will deem as dangerous. If found in your

carry-on luggage, these items may be confiscated and charges could be laid.

To avoid any unnecessary risks, check the Foreign Affairs and International Trade Canada website prior to the trip. Give this website address and the Canadian Embassy coordinates for the foreign country to the executive before the trip.

Self-Check

1. **(a)** How would you make a guaranteed hotel reservation?

   (b) What is the benefit of having one?

2. State the two options for time limits on Canadian electronic passports for adults.

3. What document(s) do you need to show to travel from Canada to the United States by air? by land?

FOLLOWING THROUGH

While administrative assistants can rely on a travel agent when planning a trip, they are directly responsible for checking the completeness and accuracy of the final arrangements.

Prior to the Trip

Just before the manager leaves on a business trip, your main responsibilities may include checking the tickets, getting money for the trip, preparing the itinerary, assembling materials for the trip, arranging to have new business cards made, and getting instructions about special responsibilities you will have in your manager's absence.

Checking the Tickets Obtain the tickets in enough time to check them carefully. First compare the information on the tickets with what your manager requested; then thoroughly check each item on the tickets with the itinerary. The information on the tickets and the travel portion of the itinerary should be identical.

Getting Money for the Trip Credit cards such as American Express, Visa, and MasterCard make it possible to travel without carrying large sums of money. Most people rely on credit cards while travelling.

To cover the expenses of the trip, however, some travellers prefer cash. In this case, many organizations will provide a cash advance to employees who travel. If this is the policy in your organization, complete the required form, and obtain the cash. Figure 12-4 shows a **travel fund advance** form. Although forms vary, it is important on all forms to fill all appropriate blanks with accurate information. This will help avoid delays in receiving the travel advance.

Whether you are obtaining cash from a bank or from the cashier of your organization, get some small bills to be used for tips.

Most business travellers take limited cash and carry their Visa, MasterCard, or American Express credit cards. Cash in the foreign country's local currency is readily available through automatic teller machines found in most international hotels.

Occasionally, managers prefer to carry traveller's cheques instead of cash, but this is rare for business trips. A company cannot supply traveller's cheques to its executives because traveller's cheques must be signed at the time they are purchased by the person who is to use them.

Understanding Per Diems One of the first things you will need to understand is the **per diem rate**. *Per diem* is a Latin term meaning per day. It means an amount of money, determined by the company, that it will pay per day for expenses to an employee who must travel for business. There is usually a meal per diem and sometimes an accommodation per diem.

In-Canada travel will have different rates than international travel. International rates are often determined by rates suggested by the Treasury Board Secretariat. For information on international travel rates, refer to www.tbs-sct.gc.ca.

The Treasury Board Secretariat publishes the rates that Canadian government employees are reimbursed for their expenses when travelling abroad. They must publish this because they are accountable to the Canadian taxpayer. Many nongovernmental Canadian organizations use these published rates as their own policy within their organizations. Travel expense policies vary greatly among nongovernmental organizations. Some companies allow travellers to claim more than the per diem if receipts can be provided, while other companies expect their travellers to cover their own expenses beyond the per diems allowed.

As an administrative assistant, be sure to check out your company's per diem rates and policies before you make travel arrangements.

Preparing the Itinerary Usually, an **itinerary** is a combined travel/appointment schedule. However, the travel itinerary and the schedule of confirmed appointments can also be prepared as two separate lists. An itinerary shows when, where, and how the traveller will go. It should include:

- the day
- the date
- the local time of departure and arrival
- the name of the airport
- the flight numbers

Figure 12-4 Travel fund advance.

TRAVEL FUND ADVANCE

Please forward completed forms to: Accounting Department
Millennium Appliances
3431 Bloor Street
Toronto, ON   M8X 1G4

Tel (416) 795-2893   Fax (416) 795-3982

Name of Employee Requesting Advance: *Iain Brown*

Date of Request: *25 March, 20xx*

Employee Number: *784244*

Destination: *Vancouver, B.C.*

Reason for Travel: *Meetings with sales staff & clients*

Departure Date: *5 April, 20xx*   Return Date: *7 April, 20xx*

Date Advance Required: *3 April, 20xx*

Amount Requested:

Accommodation	(Refer to Policy 430)	$ *475.00*
Meals	(Refer to Policy 431)	$ *120.00*
Transportation	(Refer to Policy 432)	$ *100.00*
TOTAL REQUESTED		$ *695.00*

Preferred Method of Payment/Distribution   √ Company Cheque _____Traveller's Cheque

Balance Outstanding (Includes this request) $ *0*

L. Phillips   G.M./Marketing   26 March, 20XX

Authorization   Date of Authorization
(as per Schedule of Authorities)

Approval Limits

$3000	*-Manager*
$10 000	*-Director*
$10 000+	*-President*

- the place of departure and arrival
- the name of the hotel for each overnight stay on the trip

The itinerary should also include details about confirmed appointments. Examples of such details might be:

- the names and titles of the people the traveller will see.
- personal notes about people the traveller may see. These comments are intended to aid conversation and familiarity. They may include reminders about family members, recent achievements or personal interests.
- the dates and times of the appointments.
- the purpose of the appointments.
- software and/or documents required for the appointments.

These details are illustrated in the itinerary in Figure 12-5.

As soon as the travel and hotel accommodations and the appointments have been confirmed, you can prepare the final itinerary. Make a step-by-step plan that is so complete that the manager will know where to go, when, and what materials will be needed by referring to the itinerary.

Preparing an itinerary is time-consuming because you need information from several different sources. Arrange the papers relating to hotels and appointments in chronological order. Give the itinerary an appropriate heading. Use the days and dates as the major divisions, and list the entries under each division in order according to time. Check the final itinerary more than once to make sure it is 100 percent correct.

Prepare the itinerary in the style your manager prefers. However, if the travel agent has already prepared a detailed itinerary, instead of rekeying it to add the appointments, prepare a separate schedule of appointments.

Just prior to departure, when all the details have been finalized, send an electronic copy of the itinerary to the traveller and the traveller's superior. Keep a copy in the office information system as a record.

Assembling Materials for the Trip As you make arrangements for the trip, you should compile a complete list of items the manager will need on the trip. After you have assembled the items that will be needed, your last-minute responsibilities will include numbering them in the order in which they will be used and checking them off your list as you stack them to go in the briefcase.

Many people travel with a laptop computer, as shown in Figure 12-6. If a laptop computer is one of the items the manager will be taking, make sure he or she takes a fully charged spare battery, a flash drive or CDs, and current data for en route work.

Place the papers for each appointment in separate envelopes or folders. Number each envelope in consecutive order to match the order of appointments. If you use folders, fasten the materials in the folders.

Make two copies of the list you have compiled of items your manager must take. Staple the list inside Folder #1, or attach it to Envelope #1. Keep one copy for yourself.

Getting Special Instructions Take notes if the manager gives instructions about what to do in her or his absence. Find out about mail that should be forwarded, materials to be sent to meetings the manager cannot attend, and any special responsibilities you must handle in the manager's absence. Be sure you understand how to follow through on important correspondence and telephone calls.

Printing Business Cards If your manager is travelling to a foreign country, have new business cards printed before the business trip. One side should contain the usual information in English; the reverse side should be printed in the foreign language. Foreign business contacts will view this as a courteous gesture.

During the Manager's Absence

While your manager is away, work at the same pace as you normally work. This is an excellent opportunity to work on assignments you may have put off.

Managers will use the internet to access their email while they are away from the office in order to keep up with information and work. They will telephone the office regularly to keep in touch. Be ready to report on significant events, important mail, and telephone calls. In your notebook, make a summary of what you should discuss. If the manager keeps in touch with the office through email, you can provide this information on a daily basis and get the manager's feedback immediately.

Many organizations use an email provider such as Microsoft Outlook that includes an "out-of-office" feature. This feature can be set to alert senders of incoming emails that the recipient is out of the office for a specified time. It will be your responsibility to ensure that this feature is activated on your manager's email system so that emailers will be aware of the reason their correspondence may not be answered as promptly as it otherwise would be.

Plan your schedule so you can spend the first day the manager is back in the office following through on work generated by the trip.

When the manager is away, you will have added responsibilities and may need to allow extra time to handle them. For example, you will want to read the manager's email, postal mail, and faxes to determine if any of the information is urgent and needs to be handled by the acting

Figure 12-5 Itinerary.

ITINERARY FOR IAIN BROWN

Toronto—Vancouver—Toronto
April 5—April 7, 20XX

Monday, April 5

0905	Depart Toronto Pearson International Airport for Vancouver on AC167.
1030	Arrive Vancouver International Airport.
	Reservations are at the Westin Bayshore. Hotel confirmation attached.
1230	Lunch with Benjamin Edwards and Bob Ross at Olives Restaurant in the Westin Bayshore.
1430	Conference with Sales Team, Vancouver Branch. The meeting is scheduled to be in the Pacific Room, 2nd floor.

Tuesday, April 6

1000	Meet with William Mack, Manager Victoria Sales Branch.
	Mr. Mack will meet you in the lobby of your hotel.
1300	Lunch with Christine Bollen, Editor of Sales Unlimited magazine.
1930	Dinner with Sandy Wolfe, President of Avanti Products, at the Pines Restaurant in the Westin Bayshore.

Wednesday, April 7

0730	Depart Vancouver International Airport for Toronto on AC443.
1710	Arrive Toronto Pearson International Airport.

HAVE A PRODUCTIVE TRIP!

Note: All times are shown as local times.

Figure 12-6 Working en route with a wireless laptop computer.

manager or by you. Save some time for communicating with the person who has been designated to act in the manager's role. Offer your assistance if you can perform any of these responsibilities.

Try to keep the manager's calendar free of appointments for the first day following the trip. Before the manager returns, key a summary of the appointments you have made. Indicate the date, names, and purpose of each appointment. If the manager uses an electronic calendar, there should be no need to key a list of appointments; the software gives a clear picture of appointments and can print a summary.

After the Manager Returns

Your activities on the manager's first day back after a trip will centre on briefing the manager on what happened during the trip, following up with correspondence, assembling receipts for the expense report, and filing materials your manager brings back.

Report the most significant happenings first. Put the following items on your manager's desk: correspondence that arrived in your manager's absence, arranged in folders as explained in Chapter 8; the summary of appointments; a summary of important telephone calls that were not left on voice mail; and a list of who came to the office to see the manager.

Early in the day, call attention to anything that requires immediate action.

Review your list of the materials the traveller took on the trip that must be returned to the files. Locate these materials and file them. Also file materials your manager acquired during the trip. This includes business cards that have been collected. Copies of materials from the files that your manager took on the trip can be disposed of. First, however, check carefully for notes that may have been made on them.

Discuss the trip with your manager. Record any problems encountered with hotels, car rentals, or other arrangements so that you may avoid such problems in the future. Likewise, note particularly good service your manager received. This will be valuable information to consider in the future when opportunities to use those same services arise.

Write messages of gratitude to people who hosted your manager. Offer your support to complete reports related to the trip. Of course, one of the most important responsibilities is to collect receipts and prepare the expense account.

Travel Expense Voucher If you are not sure about your company's policy with regard to expense claims, consult a policy manual so that your work on the voucher is accurate. Completeness and accuracy are the two necessary ingredients for ensuring a quick return of funds owing to the traveller.

Refer to Figure 12-7 for a sample **travel expense voucher**. Note that all expenses must have the approval of a senior employee. Although these forms vary from company to company, most require at least the following information:

- the date the expense was incurred
- the location where the expense was incurred
- the cost of transportation
- the cost of the hotel where the traveller stayed
- the cost and explanation of other business expenses that relate to the trip (including telephone calls, laundry services, or a necessary business item that was purchased)
- the cost of company-related entertaining
- the cost of meals
- the amount of any travel fund advance that may have been received prior to the trip. This amount is deducted from the amount the employee will now receive from the company.

It is common practice for organizations to arrange and pay in advance for air transportation. For convenience, these

Figure 12-7 Travel expense voucher.

TRAVEL EXPENSE VOUCHER

NAME: *Iain Brown* PIN: *784244*
TITLE: *Sales Manager* DATE: *10 April, 20xx*

CONTROL #: _____

Date	Location	Work Order	Transport*	Hotel	Other	Entertain	Meals	Total	Explain Other, Entertain & Meals
05 April	Vancouver		55.00	185.00		70.00	— / 19.00	329.00	Taxi airport – hotel / Lunch with Edwards & Ross
06 April	Vancouver			185.00		125.00	11.00 / —	321.00	Lunch with Bollen / Dinner with Wolfe
07 April	Vancouver		55.00				11.00 / —	66.00	Taxi hotel – airport
07 April	Toronto				45.00		— / —	45.00	Airport parking / 3 days at $15.00
EXPENSE TOTAL			110.00	370.00	45.00	195.00	41.00	761.00	
LESS: CASH ADVANCES								695.00	
BALANCE CLAIMED OR RETURNED								66.00	

LEGEND
* Include vehicle from Side 2 (if applicable)
** Enter on Side 2
*** Distribute on Side 2

CERTIFICATION OF EXPENSES
I certify that I have incurred these expenses.

I. Brown _____ *10 April, 20xx*
Employees Signature Date

AUDIT

Checked by _____ Date _____

APPROVAL OF EXPENSES
K. Winters
Payment Approved by
V.P. Sales
Title
16 April, 20xx
Date

---

arrangements are made through the organization's associate travel agent. In such cases, the cost of air transportation will not appear on the traveller's travel expense voucher.

Remember that most claimed expenses must be verified by receipts and must not exceed costs specified by company policy.

These forms are completed by anyone who has a legitimate company expense. This may include any level of employee. If the travel expense voucher form is stored on your computer, you can key the information. If not, it is acceptable to submit these documents in handwritten form.

ETHICAL ISSUES IN REPORTING TRAVEL EXPENSES

Employers expect employees to operate in accordance with the highest attainable standards of ethical business conduct. They also expect employees to take action against improper conduct by reporting it if they are aware of it.

When an employee demonstrates **unethical** behaviour, it may begin with peer pressure or a supervisor's direct request to violate the company's code of ethics. Consider the situation of Nada, who routinely assisted in the preparation of travel expense reports. What began as a one-time request from her supervisor to "pad" expenses became a mountain of bogus entries. Once found out, Nada was terminated.

Although companies have their own policies, there may be grey areas in expense regulations that often lead employees to "fudge" the numbers in their favour. What if you are asked to falsify an expense report for your manager? You have several options: (1) inform your manager you feel it is wrong to inflate the numbers and ask for his or her support in your decision; (2) report the request to your ethics officer or a human resources representative before you do anything; (3) honour the request, but inform your superior you will not do it again; or (4) comply with your manager's request.

Employees are expected to follow the travel expense policies to ensure honest and efficient use of company funds. If you prepare travel expense records or certify the accuracy of information in such records, you must be diligent in ensuring the accuracy and integrity of this information.

CULTURE AND INTERNATIONAL TRAVEL

Customs vary widely from one country to another, and understanding and observing these cultural variables is critical to a traveller's success. Helping your manager learn something about the culture of a country before doing business there will enhance the chances of a successful outcome and help him or her develop prosperous, long-term relationships.

1. Research national holidays and important events in the country your manager will be visiting. Then she or he can show respect for those occasions by honouring customs and restrictions associated with special events and holidays.

2. Help your manager learn a few foreign words and phrases such as *Hello, How are you? Please, Thank you,* *Goodbye, It was a pleasure to meet you.* Books on language translations of common terms are readily available for purchase in many bookstores.

3. Learn to correctly spell and pronounce the names of your hosts and business associates, and ensure your manager does too. Both your efforts will be appreciated and accepted as a gesture of respect for and acceptance of their culture.

4. Research the local habits and restrictions of countries your manager will be visiting. For example, did you know it is unacceptable in some countries for women to appear in public without shoulders and knees covered, even for casual events? Are you aware that while a gift wrapped in red might be well received in Denmark where red is seen as a positive colour, the same wrapping might offend the recipient in an African country where red represents witchcraft and death? Your manager will appreciate it if you inform her or him of any pertinent information you learn in this area.

Self Check

1. Why is it important to help your manager learn a little about the culture of a country before she or he leaves to conduct business there?

2. Describe two customs of foreign countries which are not normally practised in Canada.

QUESTIONS FOR STUDY AND REVIEW

1. Organizations have definite policies concerning executive travel. Name some areas in which you would expect policies to be clearly stated.

2. How can access to the internet help the administrative assistant make travel arrangements?

3. How are travel agents paid?

4. What services will a travel agent perform for domestic travel? for international travel?

5. What information relating to a trip should an administrative assistant compile before contacting a travel agency or carrier?

6. Distinguish between the following:
   a. nonstop flight
   b. direct flight
   c. connecting flight
   d. commuter flight

7. Explain how jet lag can affect travellers and how this relates to business trips.

8. If the flight space a traveller desires is not available, explain how to proceed to make alternative plans.

9. What is meant by reconfirmation of an airline reservation? When is it necessary?

10. Using the 24-hour clock, write 6 a.m., 2 p.m., 9 p.m., noon, and midnight.

11. What ground transportation is available at airports?

12. What is an air taxi? What is a heliport?

13. What information should an administrative assistant compile before making arrangements for car rental?

14. Suggest two ways to make hotel reservations.

15. Why should an administrative assistant always ask for a written confirmation of a hotel reservation?

16. What is a passport? Who can issue a passport? What is an e-passport?

17. List the items that must be submitted along with a passport application.

18. What is a visa? Who can issue a visa?

19. How would an administrative assistant obtain information that the World Health Organization produces about immunization requirements?

20. State two factors to consider when packing carry-on luggage.

21. List three security precautions that travellers should be aware of before catching air flights.

22. After all the planning and reservations have been completed, what are an administrative assistant's main responsibilities just prior to the manager's departure on a business trip?

23. How can an administrative assistant avoid delays in receiving a travel advance?

24. What is a travel per diem? Who determines the amount? Where could you find guidelines for overseas travel per diems?

25. What information should be included in an itinerary?

26. Explain how an administrative assistant's time can be used efficiently during the manager's absence.

27. What are the administrative assistant's main responsibilities pertaining to the trip after the manager's return?

28. State four ways you could help your manager learn about the culture of a foreign country prior to a business trip to this country.

EVERYDAY ETHICS

Exaggerated Expenses

You work for Craig, the executive director of Power Product Corporation. Craig has just returned from a two-week business trip to Asia and has handed you a stack of receipts to organize. It's your responsibility to prepare Craig's travel expense voucher.

You sort through the receipts and find some that you doubt can be considered as business expenses. These include bar expenses, tickets for sightseeing trips, and an expensive amethyst necklace purchased in Canada prior to the trip. You separate these receipts from the others and broach the issue with Craig. Craig insists that these entertainment and gift expenses are a necessary part of doing business in Asia. The necklace, he explains, was given as a corporate gift to the Asian client. He tells you to put these expenses under the entertainment column on the expense form. According to Craig, the trip cost him a lot of personal money and he is in a hurry to get reimbursed.

He doesn't want the hassle of having to explain his expenses to the vice-president who must approve his expenses. So he instructs you to hide the words "amethyst necklace" and write "company gift" in its place. His tone edges on being aggressive. You are uncomfortable with this but feel convinced that these expenses are just a part of corporate life. You treat the expenses as Craig has requested. Craig signs the expenses and you send them to the office of the vice-president for approval.

Then it happens! The day after you submit the expenses, Craig's wife appears at the office wearing a dazzling amethyst necklace.

■ Whose actions have been unethical?

■ What do you say to Craig?

■ Should you contact the administrative assistant in the vice-president's office and request that the expenses be returned to you?

■ What will you do when Craig submits the next bogus expense claim?

■ Will your work on the expense claim reflect poorly on you or on Craig?

■ Is there a chance you will lose your job?

Problem Solving

1. The manager is planning a business trip to one of the organization's branches located across the country. At the time that the manager asked you to make a reservation for him, all the tickets had been sold for the date he requested; his name was placed on a waiting list for both directions of the trip. Today you checked with the airline and found that space is available to the destination city at the time your manager requested but that he still would have to be on a waiting list for the return trip. Should you accept the reservation to the destination city? Explain.

2. When the office manager, Mrs. Orlando, arrived in Saskatoon, she could not find her luggage. Her notes for the talk that she is to give at the conference are in her suitcase. Another copy of the notes is in Mrs. Orlando's desk at the office. She calls you at home on Saturday morning and asks you to go to the office, find the notes, and get them to her. How will you get the notes to her? What suggestions would you make about packing notes for future talks?

3. You work for three executives. Two of them are planning to attend a national management conference in Toronto, and you have made travel reservations for them. Now the third executive has decided to attend the conference. He has asked you to make travel reservations for him for the

same time the other two executives are travelling. You call the airline. A reservation is not available at that time. What should you do while you are talking with the reservations agent?

4. This was the first time you made travel arrangements for your manager, and your manager had the following problems on his trip. How would you prevent these problems from reoccurring on the next trip?

   a. The hotel room was guaranteed for arrival, but a nonsmoking room was not requested. Because of a large convention being held at the hotel, your manager could not get a nonsmoking room when he arrived.

   b. Although you told your manager that a car had been rented, the rental agency did not have a reservation. Your manager could not rent the type of car that he prefers.

   c. A schedule of appointments was not included in the travel file given to your manager.

Special Reports

1. Find a local airline schedule on the internet. Select the departure city and a destination city. List the schedules of service available between these two cities.

2. Research the following foreign locations: Berlin, Germany; Beijing, China; and Bangkok, Thailand. For each location, obtain the latest information and prepare a report on one of the following topics:

   a. visa regulations and where they can be obtained

   b. immunization requirements

   c. ground transportation to and from the local airport

   d. recommendations for city transportation

3. Search the internet for information on current airline fares. Compare the fares of two airlines travelling between Calgary and Vancouver. Then compare the fares for the same airlines travelling between Halifax and Montreal.

4. Use the internet to research the status of working women in China, Saudi Arabia, Russia, Cuba, and England. Explain how their work status compares to that of Canadian women. Prepare a keyed report for your instructor and present your findings to your class through computer software.

PRODUCTION CHALLENGES

12-A Preparing an Itinerary

Supplies needed:

- *Notes on Mr. Wilson's Trip to Midwestern Region, Form 12-A, pages 416 and 417*

- *Plain paper*

William Wilson, Vice-President of Marketing at Millennium Appliances, Inc., will make a business trip to the Midwestern Region during the week of September 11 to 14. He will visit the Midwestern Regional Sales Office of Millennium Appliances in Regina and the Millennium Appliances manufacturing plant in Winnipeg. He will speak to the Sales Management Club at Red River College.

Prepare Mr. Wilson's itinerary.

12-B Making an Airline Reservation

Supplies needed:

- *Plain paper*

Mr. Wilson asked you to make an airline reservation for him from Toronto to Vancouver on Tuesday, October 10. Since Mr. Wilson does not know how much time he will spend in Vancouver, you are to request an open return ticket.

You know that Mr. Wilson prefers to travel in the morning and that he prefers an aisle seat on nonstop and direct flights.

You call the airlines. A nonstop flight is not available. You make a reservation for him with Air Canada. Flight AC895 leaves Toronto at 1005, arrives in Winnipeg at 1210, leaves Winnipeg at 1230, and will arrive in Vancouver at 1345. He will be on the same airplane for the entire trip. His tickets will be ready at the counter.

Key Mr. Wilson a note giving him complete information about the airline reservations.

12-C Preparing a Travel Fund Advance

Supplies needed:

- *Millennium Travel Fund Advance, Form 12-C, page 418*

Mr. Wilson has requested an advance for his trip to Vancouver. The purpose of this trip is to visit Ms. Singe, Sales Manager. Together they will attend the annual Sales Strategies Seminar. Mr. Wilson will require the advance the day before his departure. He prefers to receive it in the form of a company cheque. The per diem rate is $180.00 for his accommodation and $50.00 for his meals. He estimates that he will remain in Vancouver for three days. The airline tickets will be prepaid by the company; therefore, Mr. Wilson will not be required to claim this as a personal expense. His employee number is 847254. Complete the form using your most legible handwriting.

12-D Preparing an Open Itinerary

Supplies needed:

- *Plain paper*

Although you do not have complete information for Mr. Wilson's trip to Vancouver, you still need to prepare an itinerary. Use the information provided in 12-B, Making an Airline Reservation, and 12-C, Preparing a Travel Fund Advance, to complete the best open itinerary possible. Do not use the information from 12-E, Preparing a Travel Expense Voucher, since this information is unknown prior to the trip. You will be booking the Westin Bayshore for Mr. Wilson for Tuesday, Wednesday, and Thursday evenings.

12-E Preparing a Travel Expense Voucher

Supplies needed:

- *Millennium Travel Expense Voucher, Form 12-E, page 419*

Mr. Wilson returned from Vancouver on Friday, October 13. He has requested that you complete a travel expense voucher on his behalf. He has provided receipts for all his expenses. The receipts give you the following information:

- He stayed at the Westin Bayshore using the full per diem rate each evening.

- Meals for each day were:

Tuesday	–	Dinner =	$25.62
Wednesday	–	Breakfast =	$10.50
		Lunch =	$15.10
		Dinner =	$21.10
Thursday	–	Breakfast =	$10.50
		Lunch =	$14.18
		Dinner =	$25.80
Friday	–	Breakfast =	$12.10

- Please note—charge the per diem amount for the two full days but only the actual expenses incurred for Tuesday and Friday.

- Millennium Appliances has prepaid Mr. Wilson's airfare through its associated travel agent; therefore, this expense will not show up on the travel expense voucher.

- On the day Mr. Wilson arrived in Vancouver, he hired a taxi. The fare was $52.00. The day he left Vancouver he again hired a taxi, for $56.50.

- On Wednesday he rented a car for three days. His receipt shows a total charge of $187.83.

- He had one miscellaneous receipt showing a charge of $50.35 for a portfolio purchased on Wednesday.

- One receipt showed an entertainment expense of $135.50. This was incurred on Thursday, when he bought theatre tickets for Mr. and Mrs. Singe.

First, refer to the information in 12-C, Preparing a Travel Fund Advance. Then, using your most legible handwriting, complete the Travel Expense Voucher, Form 12-E, page 419.

12-F Planning an International Business Trip

Supplies needed:

- *Plain paper*
- *Internet access*
- *Directions*

Mr. Wilson has asked you to plan his international business trip. He is making a presentation in Mexico City and Guadalajara one month from today. His first presentation will be in Mexico City.

1. Mr. Wilson needs reservations at the Hilton Hotel in each of the two cities he is visiting. Reservations will be for one week at each hotel. He has asked you to determine specific information about these two cities. Your findings must include the following:

    a. travel times

    b. time zone changes

    c. travel documents needed

    d. medical requirements

    e. airlines to use

    f. approximate cost for transportation and lodging

    g. nearest Canadian Embassy location

    h. international country and city telephone codes

    i. average weather temperatures

    j. holidays during his stay

2. To assist him in understanding the hosts' cultural and business practices, Mr. Wilson asked you to research the following:

    a. greetings, handling of introductions, using appropriate titles, exchange of business cards, and any other important points of business etiquette

    b. gift giving for the hosts

    c. the hosts' work-hour practices

    d. the hosts' attitudes toward time in general

    e. nonverbal communication patterns as they relate to the hosts

    f. the country's currency and exchange rates

    g. letter-writing styles

3. Because you are already working on completing a large project, you have asked one of the assistants in your work group to help gather this information.

4. Summarize your team's findings in a memo to your instructor.

5. Be prepared to present your findings to the class.

12–G Keying Vacation Requests

Supplies needed:

- *Vacation Requests, Form 12-G, page 420*
- *Plain paper*

It's Monday, May 12. Mr. Wilson has asked you to key a list of the department's employees and their vacation requests in chronological order. He explains that he has not yet scheduled two weeks of his vacation, and that he has a policy of not taking a vacation when any of the assistant vice-presidents of marketing are on vacation. He said a chronological list will quickly point out the weeks when he should be in the office.

You set up and key the vacation information from Form 12-G. You send it to him electronically as an attachment to an email message.

Weblinks

Expedia.ca
www.expedia.ca
This Canadian travel site lists airlines, hotels, and car rentals, as well as travel news and advice.

Travelocity.ca
www.travelocity.ca
This Canadian travel site lists airlines, hotels, car rentals, European and Canadian rail information, as well as travel news and advice.

Discover Canada
www.angelfire.com/hi/Rahasia/3can.html
This site lists Canada's provincial tourist bureaus.

World Time Zones
www.worldtimeserver.com
World Time Server provides current local times anywhere in the world.

Treasury Board of Canada Secretariat
www.tbs-sct.gc.ca
This site provides information about the financial management of Canada's affairs and the departments that manage the wealth. This is the location for finding the Treasury Board's Travel Directive for allowable hospitality rates for government employees travelling within and outside Canada.

Converting Currencies
www.xe.com/ucc
There are many sites that convert worldwide currencies. This particular site is easy to use and works with the most current conversion rates.

Passport Canada
http://www.ppt.gc.ca/index.aspx
This site provides up-to-date information on the requirements for obtaining a passport in Canada

The International Business Etiquette Internet Source Book
http://www.paulinetang.com/images/3752_e.pdf
Learn about doing business in many other countries and cultures by accessing the links on this informative site.

WorldWeb Travel Guide
www.worldweb.com
This comprehensive online travel and tourism guide provides resources for travel to destinations worldwide.

World Health Organization
www.who.int/ith/en
This site is a valuable resource for people seeking information on health risks to travellers to various countries. Comprehensive information on health statistics in countries throughout the world is also provided.

Foreign Affairs and International Trade Canada
www.travel.gc.ca
This site provides information and assistance for Canadians travelling abroad, including a traveller's checklist, reports on safety and health issues in various countries, and a list of Canadian government offices abroad.

www.international.gc.ca/international/index.aspx
This site provides easy-to-access travel reports and warnings on various countries, contact information for Canadian embassies and consulates abroad, passport information, and numerous other links to valuable information for international travellers.

http://www.international.gc.ca/international/index.aspx?view=d
This direct link to Foreign Affairs and International Trade Canada safe-travel publications for the Canadian public who are travelling abroad is a wealth of information. Of particular interest are publications in the general category, such as those for women travelling alone, Canadians who hold dual citizenship, and traveller's checklists. Publications related to specific countries and situations are also available for downloading.

Chapter 13
Meetings and Conferences

Learning Outcomes

After completion of this chapter, the student will be able to:

1 Describe the preparation and arrangements needed for informal and formal meetings.

2 Prepare notices and agendas for meetings.

3 Compose and key minutes of a meeting.

4 Hold a team meeting that requires the use of an agenda, nominal group voting, a meeting log, brainstorming, and cause-and-effect diagrams.

5 Describe poor meeting behaviours, and provide solutions and strategies for dealing with them.

6 Identify the benefits of virtual meetings.

7 Discuss forms of teleconferencing that are used to conduct meetings and conferences.

8 Locate an appropriate conference speaker, prepare a speaker's biography, and plan the expenses involved in using the speaker's services.

9 Research the internet for information on conference speakers and how to plan conferences.

An administrative assistant may be responsible for arranging a wide range of meetings, from small informal meetings to large **conferences**. They may be conducted face-to-face in a boardroom, or remotely, using virtual conferencing. This job may involve handling all the preliminary activities—arranging the meeting **venue** and time, inviting the participants, preparing the **agenda**, assembling materials needed during the meeting, and arranging for food and accommodation—as well as follow-up activities such as transcribing the minutes and reminding your manager to carry out the commitments made during the meeting.

In addition to handling the preliminary activities and the follow-up, the administrative assistant is often expected to participate during the meeting, making valuable contributions to the decision-making process.

An office that is skilled in teamwork has learned that conducting meetings effectively involves having input from all team members associated with the meeting agenda. It is vital to remember that each team member has something important to contribute. The extent of the contribution will be based on the participant's experience and expertise.

BUSINESS MEETINGS

Meetings will range from informal meetings in your manager's office to formal meetings for boards of directors in large conference rooms. Depending on the formality, you may be responsible for any or all of the following:

- arranging the date and time
- reserving the meeting room
- sending notices
- preparing the agenda

Laura McArthur
Program Assistant

Georgian College
Barrie, Ontario

College Graduation:
Office Administration—Executive
Georgian College
Barrie, Ontario

2011

"Prioritizing and reviewing my goals for work and home help me to achieve balance and stay on track."

Laura McArthur's ability to adapt and respond to the unexpected has been instrumental in shaping her career path. After the school she worked at for 15 years closed, Laura found herself coping with the upheaval by returning to college and launching a new career. "I wanted to find a career that would survive the ups and downs of the economy," she says. Her office administration program at Georgian College led to an on-campus placement, which in turn led to the position she holds today—a position she loves.

That willingness to respond positively to surprises serves Laura well in her role as a program assistant, where one of her most challenging tasks is scheduling meetings and other events. Not only does she have to set the time, invite attendees, arrange for transportation, order catering, and plan the event—she also has to do it while taking everyone's schedules (and the unexpected) into account.

"There are many details beyond anyone's control to consider in creating schedules that satisfy those involved," she says. "Time management, prioritizing while multitasking, and maintaining a friendly, calm disposition are essential skills needed to undertake this task."

When an event or meeting is planned, Laura needs to step in early to arrange the booking, invites, and catering. She points out that with catering, she needs to check with attendees for food allergies, and then she needs to be prepared to

address those needs. "Being aware of details like these ahead of time makes the process more professional," she says.

However, no matter how much planning she does, Laura still has to be prepared for the unexpected, such as the timing of meetings. "Estimating the timeline of a meeting is difficult, because covering the necessary items can work out differently on paper than it does in practice," she warns. "Everyone has a tight schedule, and meetings that become lengthy can wreak havoc with the rest of the day, which can adversely affect attendance at other meetings."

To help stay organized, Laura relies on Microsoft Office, which enables her to book internal meeting rooms and catering, and send invites with an auto accept/decline feature that automatically records the event on an attendee's calendar. She says the training she received on MS Office for office administration was essential, preparing her to multitask in a fast-paced environment while still meeting deadlines.

Despite the challenges her job presents, Laura says she is rewarded by the interpersonal opportunities she experiences by being a front-line person in the office. "I really enjoy my role in facilitating the opportunity for postsecondary education for students with learning challenges, and the contact this provides me with students and staff," she says. "Since I was a student so recently myself, I can empathize and support students with a greater understanding."

- planning for supplies, equipment, and software
- planning for food and refreshments
- assembling materials
- attending the meeting
- handling telephone interruptions
- recording the meeting
- following up
- preparing and editing minutes

This chapter, as well as other chapters in this book, will help to prepare you for all your meeting and conference responsibilities.

Creating an Action Checklist

How will you ensure that you remember all the necessary steps and that you are organized? It is best to work from an action checklist. You may require more than one checklist if you have a lot of responsibilities for the meeting or conference. The following checklist is just a guide—you will have to customize your own list for your own purposes:

- Find a common date and time when key members can attend.
- Book conference room.
- Invite members to the meeting.

- Confirm attendance of members.
- Prepare an agenda.
- Send the agenda to participants at least two days ahead of the meeting.
- Ensure the facilities are adequate and in good working order for the meeting (chairs, presentation equipment, computer, tape recorder, etc.).
- Prepare materials.
- Order food and/or refreshments.
- Forward telephone calls to voice mail.

Arranging the Date and Time

Arranging meetings of several people is easy if:

- The meeting participants use electronic calendars and keep them up to date.
- The calendars are not classified as private and, therefore, are available to other people on the office network.

When you have electronic access to other people's calendars, let the software find a time when all the participants are free, schedule the meeting, and then send the information about the meeting to the participants by email.

Using the telephone to find a convenient time for all the participants to meet is too time-consuming. If you are working with desk calendars, always enter meetings in pencil. They are likely to change!

Another option once you have isolated a few possible meeting times is to use scheduling polling software such as Doodle®. Such programs allow you to survey the group with suggested times for a meeting. Each group member selects a preferred meeting time, and the most commonly selected time is then chosen for the meeting. This provides everyone with an opportunity to have input.

Executives Scheduling Their Own Appointments

Many executives schedule all their own appointments, while others prefer that the administrative assistant schedule all the appointments. Still others prefer a combination. Because many executives travel and do much of their work outside the office, the tendency is for executives to make some of their own appointments, while, back in the office, the administrative assistant is also making appointments for the executive. It is imperative that the schedule is kept accurate and current. Otherwise, there will be duplication of bookings.

When you are arranging a meeting for eight or ten executives, you probably will not find a time when all of them are free, unless you book well in advance. Schedule the meeting for a time when most of them—especially the principal members—can attend. At an executive level,

corporate politics often determine attendance. Notify all participants of the time and place of the meeting. Any executive who has a time conflict must decide how to resolve it.

As soon as you confirm the date and time of the meeting, reserve a conference room.

Reserving the Meeting Room

Reserve a room as soon as you know the date and time for the meeting. It's best to know the location when you send out the meeting invitations. The type of conference room needed will depend on the equipment required for the presentations, the size of the group, and the activities that will take place during the meeting. For example, specially equipped rooms are needed for a videoconference, a computer presentation, or an interactive whiteboard presentation. The right equipment is very important since it will greatly enhance a presentation at a meeting. (See Figure 13-1.)

The size of the room will depend on how many people are planning to attend. You can estimate this by checking the list of expected participants. As well, the space required will depend on the activities planned during the meeting. Will the participants remain seated, or will they move around during the meeting?

Figure 13-1 An interactive whiteboard acts as an effective presentation tool during a meeting.

Whenever possible, make a special effort to inspect the room in advance. Before you determine which room is right, ask the following questions:

- Will the participants remain in the same room for refreshment or lunch breaks?
- Will the team be required to perform some physical routines, or will the members remain seated throughout the meeting?
- Will the team need to break out into smaller rooms?
- Will special equipment requiring significant space be used?
- Will the meeting be an audioconference or **videoconference**?
- Will there be a guest speaker? Does the speaker have special requirements for the room?

In order to get the best room, reservations are often made far in advance of a meeting date. Be alert to any changes in meeting dates, times, and rooms. If changes occur, follow up immediately. Several days before the meeting, confirm the room reservation. Remember that change happens all the time. Keep on top of it. Otherwise you may be left without a good room after all your preparation and attention to detail.

If the meeting or conference has been arranged in an external facility such as a hotel or conference centre, become familiar with the terms and conditions of your booking agreement—particularly the cancellation and refund policy.

Sending Notices

Business professionals are busy people, so it's important to announce meetings as soon as possible. Most participants have heavy schedules and prefer plenty of advance notice.

As soon as you have established a date, times, and venue, send out the notices by email. Refer to Figure 13-2 for an example of a meeting notice that shows essential information.

When composing notices, always specify:

- the purpose of the meeting
- time
- date
- venue
- deadline for accepting agenda items
- action to take if member will attend
- action to take if member cannot attend

Participants for a meeting are sometimes asked to submit topics for the agenda. Requests for items should be made early enough that the administrative assistant has time to prepare a final agenda based on the replies received. Clearly state the deadline for the latest time you will accept agenda items.

Figure 13-2 Notice of meeting.

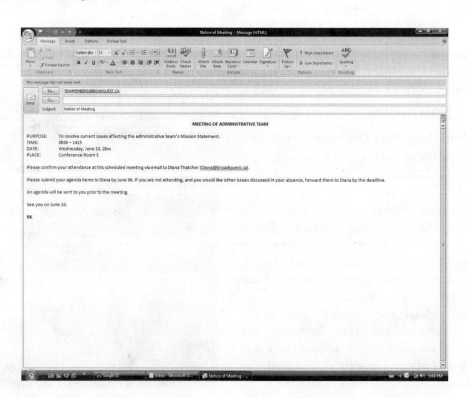

Preparing the Agenda

Chairpersons or team leaders follow prepared agendas as they conduct meetings. Preparing the agenda is the responsibility of the administrative assistant.

An agenda is a list of topics to be taken up and acted upon during a meeting. It is arranged in the order in which the topics will be discussed. Refer to Figure 13-3 for a sample agenda.

Use the following list of topics as a guideline in preparing an agenda for a *formal meeting*:

1. call to order by presiding officer
2. roll call—either oral or checked by the secretary
3. approval, amendment, or correction of minutes of previous meeting
4. reading of correspondence
5. reports (in this order):
   - officers
   - standing committees
   - special committees
6. unfinished business from previous meetings
7. new business

Figure 13-3 Agenda.

AGENDA

MEETING NO. 4
QUALITY CONFERENCE COMMITTEE

Date:	Wednesday, June 10, 20—
Time:	1500–1630
Place:	Conference Room 3
Chairperson:	Jeffrey Keaton
Recorder:	Gina Darroch
Committee Members:	Jodi Alford, Satvinder Bhardwaj, Allan Kohut, Kenneth Skoye, Benjamin Ross, Brian Van Bij, Marian Weston, Edward Woods

TIME	TOPIC	MEMBER RESPONSIBLE
1500	Adoption of Minutes from Meeting No. 3	J. Keaton
1510	Facilities Report	B. Van Bij
1525	Registration Report	A. Kohut
1540	Budget Report	S. Bhardwaj
1555	Public Relations Report	B. Ross
1610	Other Business	J. Keaton
1625	Adjournment	J. Keaton

8. appointment of committee

9. nomination and election of officers—once a year

10. announcements, including the date of the next meeting

11. adjournment

Use the following list of topics as a guideline in preparing an agenda for an *informal meeting*:

1. check-ins or warm-ups (optional)

2. review goals of agenda or purpose of meeting

3. review roles of members (optional)

4. review ground rules (optional)

5. discuss issues listed on agenda

6. review follow-up actions that members have committed to

7. closure

8. determine date and time for next meeting if necessary.

If you are responsible for preparing the agenda, key it and send it out as an email attachment. Even for a very informal office meeting, an agenda should be distributed to all the members. Send the agenda early enough that the members receive it several days before the meeting. They will need time to prepare for the meeting. The more prepared people are, the more productive the meeting will be.

Planning for Supplies, Equipment, and Software

The list of meeting supplies and equipment will be different for every meeting. How many supplies and the type of equipment necessary will depend on the type of meeting, the style of presentations to be given, and the guests who have been invited. The following is a general checklist for any meeting:

❑ notebook computer for presentation hook-up or for note taking

❑ computer presentations stored on hard drive and removable media as a backup

❑ professional presentation software, such as MS PowerPoint or Presentations from Corel, loaded on the hard drive or available via the internet

❑ data projector

❑ laser pointer for presentations

❑ projection screen

❑ digital video disc player (DVD)

❑ remote control for DVD or computer

❑ overhead projector

❑ transparent sheets for overhead projector

❑ spare bulb for overhead projector

❑ coloured markers for overhead transparencies

❑ flip chart tripod or support for paper block

❑ flip chart paper

❑ adhesive tape or putty to suspend flip chart paper around the meeting room

❑ coloured markers for flip chart paper

❑ name tents or tags, and a marker to write the names

❑ scissors

❑ whiteboard markers and eraser

❑ writing block for each participant

❑ writing pen or pencil for each participant

❑ telephone message pad and pen next to meeting room telephone

❑ promotional items such as lapel pins, key tags, or pens with company logo

❑ enough chairs for all participants

Planning Refreshments and Food

At many meetings there will be international guests and members of various religions and cultures. There may also be vegetarians and people with special-needs diets. So it's important to include a variety of foods and beverages if you wish to ensure the comfort of all participants.

If you schedule a luncheon or dinner meeting at a hotel or restaurant, call the banquet or convention manager to help you with the refreshment and lunch requirements. Inquire about food options and costs. You may have to guarantee a minimum number of attendees.

Participants perform at their best when their energy is high. For that reason, it is important to provide beverages and often food at meetings. The types of beverages will depend on the participants and on the time of day. Some beverage guidelines follow:

Beverages

■ North Americans are, in general, health conscious. Keep this in mind when arranging the menu.

■ Most participants enjoy coffee and tea regardless of the hour. Supply some decaffeinated coffee and herbal teas for those who cannot tolerate caffeine.

■ Juices are popular at morning meetings. Supply both sweetened and unsweetened juices. Many people avoid excess sugar intake.

■ Participants at afternoon breaks often enjoy juice or soft drinks. Remember to provide both regular and unsweetened varieties.

■ Bottled mineral water is appreciated at both morning and afternoon meetings. In this case, smaller is better. Larger bottles are awkward to handle and inappropriate.

- During a lunch meeting, all of the above choices are acceptable, as is milk. Low-fat white milk (*not* skim) is the safest choice.
- The key is to provide some variety. At the very minimum, provide coffee and juices for any of the meeting breaks.
- At each break, you can expect that participants will consume one or two beverages.
- Ensure that fresh water and glasses are available throughout the meeting.

The break should bring renewed energy and relieve stress caused by the meeting. Therefore, supply light foods that provide energy. Some food guidelines follow:

Food

- Some participants will have special-needs diets (such as no meat, low-calorie, low-sugar, or low-cholesterol). Don't wait for a participant to identify this ahead of time. Plan enough variety to accommodate differences.
- Never make pork the only food option. For religious reasons, many people do not eat any form of pork.
- Participants enjoy fruit and muffins for morning breaks.
- Order food in small, manageable pieces. People generally converse during breaks, and most find that small sandwiches or fruit sections are easiest to handle.
- If you want the participants to maintain a high level of energy, stay away from heavy desserts or starchy foods.

Assembling Materials

Before a meeting, assemble the materials that will be needed during the meeting. Arrange them in a folder in the order in which they will be required. For a formal meeting, you will need:

- extra copies of the agenda
- minutes of previous meetings
- a list of standing committees
- a list of special committees
- a list of action items that have not yet been completed by members
- documents related to the agenda items
- copies of materials that have been prepared for distribution

If possible, prior to the meeting, send out all these documents to the participants through email attachments or make them available through a secure online filing sharing program. This gives the participants an opportunity to review them and print their own copies before the meeting.

Even if you distribute all the documents available prior to the meeting, you will still need to bring extra copies of them to the meeting. It's highly unlikely that all members will remember to bring their copies.

Certain supporting materials may be called for during the meeting that you did not expect. If your electronic and paper filing systems are in good order, you should be able to retrieve these materials without too much difficulty. If unexpected materials are needed and the meeting is being held in another city, your manager should be able to contact you by telephone or email and have you fax or email the documents to the meeting.

Self-Check

1. What is an agenda?
2. What are three factors that you should consider when determining the supplies and equipment needed for a meeting?
3. Why is it important to send copies of all meeting documents to participants prior to a meeting?

Recording the Meeting

When the meeting is more formal, it is usually recorded and later keyed into minutes. As an administrative assistant, you may be assigned the task of recording and transcribing the minutes of a business meeting. Although your office may provide an informal setting, your manager may be the chairperson of a committee where the meetings follow very formal rules. Senior administrators are often members of charitable organizations, hospital boards, and community service organizations.

Your manager may need your assistance in preparing a record of the meeting, especially if the manager's role on the board is that of corporate secretary.

Using a Voice Recorder A voice recorder is used to obtain a **verbatim** record of a meeting for the purpose of:

- preparing a verbatim transcript
- assisting the administrative assistant in writing accurate minutes
- securing a record of discussions on controversial topics

Audio recordings may be made on digital recorders, on microcassettes, or on software designed for recording meetings, such as Soniclear. Keep each recording until the minutes have been approved, or for a longer time when the topics are controversial or may become controversial. Some groups save the minutes in a digital file permanently. Check the company and government policy before erasing the file

Although audio recordings are very useful, you still need to be aware of what information is not being recorded and, when necessary, take notes. For instance, when a chairperson acknowledges a speaker, the chairperson does not always call the speaker's name. Likewise, a chairperson does not always restate a motion as it is being voted upon. An audio recording may not indicate who made and who seconded a motion. When one of the participants is reading from distributed materials, the section to which the speaker is referring is not always clear from the recording. Use your notes to supplement the recording.

The best way to take notes at a meeting is with a notebook computer.

Using a Laptop Computer Most meetings do not require a verbatim transcript. In this case, the best practice is to key notes onto a laptop computer during the meeting. Your job of transcribing your notes into minutes will be mostly complete when you leave the meeting. All that will be required is some reformatting and editing. Refer to Figure 13-4, which shows a laptop computer being used during a meeting.

During a meeting, a computer can be used for more than recording notes. A laptop computer may operate independently but may also be connected online to the office network. The online connection gives the ability to access information that may be needed to make informed decisions during the meeting. Refer to Figure 13-5, which shows a mobile computer device being used to access company resources, such as the intranet.

Figure 13-4 Laptop computer used during a meeting.

Figure 13-5 Wireless access for digital devices is essential for many meetings.

Tips for Successful Note Taking Taking notes at a meeting can be a challenging assignment. Here are some tips for successful note taking.

- Before the meeting, study the minutes of similar meetings. Become familiar with the format used.

- Prior to the meeting, create a template with as much information as possible. During the meeting, have the template on the screen of your laptop computer so you can add information as the meeting progresses.

- Sit near the chairperson so you can assist each other.

- Ask the chairperson to see that you get a copy of all materials read or discussed. These materials are a part of the record and should be attached to the minutes. Do not wait until the end of the meeting to collect them.

- Arrange a signal, such as slightly raising your hand, with the chairperson to let him or her know that you need assistance in getting details.

- Before the meeting begins, record the name of the group, date, time, and place of the meeting. Also record the names of those people in attendance and those who are absent.

- When the previous minutes are corrected, draw a line through the words to be deleted and write in the words to be substituted or added. The action of correcting the minutes of the previous meeting should be described in the new minutes of the current meeting.

- Indicate in your notes the names of people making motions.

- Record the exact words of people who ask that their views be made a part of the record.

- Listen to the informal discussion that sometimes follows the adoption of a main motion. This discussion centres on implementation of the action—the details about who will do what, when, and how. Record each detail as it is suggested. After a detail is agreed upon, write "agreed" beside it. Each of these items must be followed up. Be sure to take notes on any obligations your manager assumes during the meeting.

- While a committee is being appointed, record the name of the committee, the full names of the members, and who accepted the position of chairperson.

- When officers are elected, record their names and their respective offices.

- Record the place, date, and time of the next meeting.

- Write the time of **adjournment**.

- As soon as the meeting adjourns, verify any points about which you are doubtful. You may need to ask about a person's title, the full name of a product or a place, the correctness of a technical term, or any small details you need in order to prepare complete minutes.

Following Up

Immediately after a meeting, prepare a to do list of all the actions you need to take. Some items might include:

- Make entries in the calendars for deadlines on work to be completed.

- Send materials through email to members who were absent.

- Prepare a list to remind your manager of his or her obligations.

- Enter the time of the next meeting in the calendars.

- Make edits to the minutes of the previous meeting.

- Complete the minutes.

- Arrange for equipment to be returned.

- Book a room and equipment for the next meeting.

All distributed materials that were introduced and discussed are a part of the minutes and should be referred to in the minutes and attached to them. Everyone who was present already has a copy, but you have the added task of mailing copies to members who were absent. To simplify your own work and to extend a courtesy to those who were absent, also mail copies of any materials distributed but not discussed.

Put a copy of everything—agenda, resolutions, reports, and so on—in an electronic or paper folder, ready to be used as a reference while you are preparing the minutes.

Keep in mind that the record of a meeting must be meaningful in the future to those who were not present. The record must show that the decisions made actually were carried out.

To ensure that there is an understanding of what was agreed upon, and to provide a complete record of transactions, the chairperson writes a memo to all members involved in follow-up actions. The chairperson also sends letters of congratulations to newly elected officers—even if these members were present at the meeting.

Preparing Minutes

Given adequate information, you can prepare minutes without having attended the meeting yourself. If your manager is recording secretary for a civic or professional organization, the manager will probably do one of the following:

- give you a recording of the meeting and expect you to transcribe it into minutes

- give you detailed written notes and expect you to turn them into minutes

- give you an electronic copy of the minutes that have already been roughly keyed and ask you to edit and improve on the format

If you wonder why preparing minutes for a civic or professional organization is a part of your job, remember that being an active participant in these organizations may be part of your manager's job. Corporations, institutions such as universities and hospitals, and various types of businesses encourage managers to participate in civic and professional organizations. As the administrative assistant, you provide essential support to the manager's role.

Key the minutes immediately following the meeting. Ask questions while the meeting is fresh in your manager's mind. If you recorded the minutes of the meeting yourself, you will be able to organize the motions and amendments and summarize the discussion much faster if you do these things soon after the meeting.

Before you prepare a final version, key a rough draft of the minutes, double-spaced, and submit it to your manager for approval. Then submit the final copy to the organization's secretary or presiding officer for signature.

Your purpose in preparing the minutes is to:

1. include all the essential information as a record that will be meaningful to others in the future

2. make it easy for the reader to locate information

Refer to Figure 13-6 for a sample of meeting minutes.

Informal Meeting When a meeting has been conducted informally, there will be no motions and no voting. Instead, agreement may be made by consent. In this case, include the essential facts in the minutes. For an informal meeting include:

- the purpose of the meeting
- date and time
- location
- who attended and who was absent
- summary of discussion and decisions
- summary of the follow-up

Formal Meeting For formal meetings, use the following as a guide:

1. Either single- or double-space minutes.

2. In all capital letters, key a heading that fully identifies the meeting: MINUTES OF THE PROGRAM PLANNING COMMITTEE, XYZ SOCIETY. Key the date as a subheading a double-space below the heading. Repeat the date on each page. If the group holds special meetings, the subheading could read: "Special Meeting, October 22, 20–."

3. Use the past tense, and write complete sentences. In the opening paragraph, state the name of the group, where the meeting was held, both the time and the date, who presided, and whether the meeting was regular or special. When the meeting was "called" (that is, when it was "special"), add the purpose of the meeting, since it was called for an express purpose.

4. State whether the minutes of the previous meeting (mention its date) were "approved as read," "approved as corrected," or dispensed with.

5. Use side headings or marginal captions to help the reader locate items. The agenda will be helpful in organizing the minutes.

6. Mention all reports presented by officers, standing committees, and special committees in the order they were presented, and tell what actions were taken. Usually a member of a group moves that the report be accepted; when it is, this action should be reported in the minutes.

7. To make each distributed report a part of the official record, refer to each one in the appropriate section of the minutes. You could say, "The attached report on Revised Plans for Issuing Supplies was distributed by Tamara Yee, Chairperson of the Committee on Reducing Office Costs." In the same paragraph, state who made the motion and the action taken.

8. Key verbatim all reports read orally and treat them as quoted material; that is, indent five spaces from the left and the right. This way, the format will reflect the origin of the material. If a report that was read is lengthy and in a form that can be copied, you can say, for example, that "the report on Downtime for Reproduction Equipment, presented by Norman Hanover, was copied and is attached."

9. Treat each main motion (and the amendments related to it, if any) as a separate item. Be sure to include in the minutes all motions made and how they were disposed of. State each motion verbatim, along with who made it, that it was seconded, whether it was adopted or defeated, and the votes cast for and against it. For some groups, also include the name of the person who seconded the motion.

10. When a motion has been made from the floor, you can begin the paragraph by saying, "Lillie Williamson moved [not made a motion] that . . . ," or "It was moved by Lillie Williamson and seconded by Raj Falfer that . . . ."

11. When a motion is amended, give the history of the motion in the minutes. First, state the motion, who made it, and that it was seconded. Next, take up the amendments in the same order as they were made. State each amendment verbatim, who made it, that it was seconded, and the votes cast for and against it.

12. The debate concerning a motion does not have to be included; nevertheless, reasons for a decision are often helpful to the current officers and to others in the future. Therefore, discussion can be included in the minutes. Summarize the debate in broad, concise terms. Try to include all the main ideas—both pros and cons—but don't overload the minutes with who said what.

13. Motions should appear in the minutes in the same order that they were taken up during the meeting. Minutes shift abruptly from one topic to another. Just separate them with side headings, or triple-space between them when you use marginal captions.

14. An agenda item that has been taken up but not completed becomes unfinished business on the agenda of the next meeting; therefore, indicate with some detail any information that will be helpful when this item is taken up again.

Figure 13-6 Minutes.

MINUTES OF THE EXECUTIVE TEAM OF CONTINENTAL TECHNOLOGY INC.
Meeting No. 9 - July 8, 20--

The Executive Team of Continental Technology Inc. met in a regular session at 1030, Wednesday, July 8, 20--, in Conference Room 3. The following members were

PRESENT:	Verna Chiasson	(Quality Advisor)
	Penny Handfield	(Guidance Team)
	Maurice Ingram	(Team Member)
	Daniel Lawrence	(Team Member)
	Laura Milton	(Team Leader)
	Betty Noble	(Guidance Team)
	Paul Noel	(Team Member)
	Gregory Patrick	(Recorder)
	Dana Rahn	(Facilitator)
	Michelle Savard	(Team Member)
	Gayle Schmitt	(Team Member)
	Mike Sherman	(Team Member)
ABSENT:	Wendy Scarth	(Team Member)

Maurice Ingram moved to approve as read the minutes of meeting no. 8. This motion was seconded by Mike Sherman. The following topics were then discussed:

REDUCTION IN ADMINISTRATIVE COSTS: The ideas presented at the June 10 meeting for cutting administrative costs were revised and the following decisions were made:

Travel. Effective August 1, 20--, all executives of Continental Technology will no longer travel Executive Class; economy fare only will be paid by the company, with the exception of Executive Class fares approved by the Vice-President. Where Continental executives are taking major clients on business trips, the Executive Class will automatically be approved by the Vice-President.

Sales Incentive Trips. The consensus was that the yearly sales incentive trips, given to sales executives reaching their quotas, should be shortened in length. The trips will be shortened from one week to four days. As well, these trips will no longer be to extremely distant points; they will now be to warm weather North American resorts. It was felt that this would reduce both the air fare and accommodation charges considerably. This will be effective May of next year.

EMPLOYEE EVALUATIONS: Laura Milton circulated copies of a new Employee Performance Evaluation which has been designed to follow ISO 9001:2005 principles. The Executive Team voted unanimously in favour of using the new form beginning September 1.

ANNOUNCEMENTS: **Catalogue.** A new product catalogue will be available July 25. Copies can be obtained by calling Betty Noble.

New Team Member. Wendy Scarth joined the team as of July 1. However, she is currently on a training course and was absent from meeting No. 9. Wendy works in the Marketing Department and was previously employed by CanTech in Montreal.

Next Meeting. The 10th regular meeting will be held in Conference Room 3 at 1030 on Thursday, August 15, 20--.

ADJOURNMENT: The meeting was adjourned at 1145.

July 10, 20xx	*G. Patrick*
Date	Gregory Patrick, Secretary

15. Group announcements near the end under the heading "Announcements." Some of the announcements may have been made at the beginning of the meeting or during it, but they can be grouped together.

16. Include the time, place, and date of the next meeting, and the time of adjournment.

17. Minutes that are to be read aloud are signed by the secretary; minutes that are to be distributed are signed by both the chairperson and the secretary.

18. Provide a place for the signature and the date of approval, such as

_____	_____
Date	Secretary

OR

_____	_____
Date	Chairperson
_____	_____
Date	Secretary

19. Arrange the file copy of the minutes in chronological order. Arrange all attachments in the order they were introduced in the minutes.

Correcting Minutes Once minutes are signed and distributed to members, some members may request amendments. These requests usually take place over email immediately after the minutes have been distributed. If they are not urgent, they wait and take place at the next meeting.

When minutes have been corrected or amended, the changes should be recorded in two places:

1. as an insertion in the minutes being corrected
2. in paragraph form in the new minutes of the meeting during which the changes were made

To show corrections and additions in the file copy of the minutes being corrected, add words in longhand and delete by drawing lines through words. You want the changes to be obvious. Enter the date of the meeting at which the changes were made.

Never rekey minutes to correct them. Make the changes so anyone reading the minutes can tell what corrections and additions were made and when they were made.

Minutes that are distributed are usually approved at the start of the next meeting. However, sometimes the approval of minutes is dispensed with, and then several sets are approved at a later meeting. The place provided for the date of approval appears at the end of the minutes. To be able to tell at a glance which minutes have been approved, write "Approved" and the date of approval at the top of the first page of the file copy immediately after the meeting where the minutes were approved.

TEAM MEETINGS

The team concept of meetings focuses on equal participation. Each participant's input is considered to be as significant as that of all other participants, from the janitor to the chief executive officer of the company. The team concept is effective because each member is empowered to participate, regardless of his or her organizational status.

Teams make decisions at their level of authority. If a decision must be made at a higher level of authority, the team forwards a recommendation to management.

Because team meetings encourage all participants to express their views, conflict and team dynamic challenges may occur. Please refer to Chapter 1 under the section "Nonproductive Behaviours" to learn how to work through challenges at meetings.

Preparation for the Meeting

A meeting that follows team techniques requires the same preparation as any other meeting—a convenient time is established, people are invited, and an agenda is prepared and delivered to participants prior to the meeting.

When team techniques are followed, careful attention is given to issues that arise even at the preliminary stages.

- Choosing an appropriate time is important. You want the attendance and full attention of every team member.

- The people who form the team may be from all levels of the organization. All people who are involved in the issue that will be discussed at the meeting must be invited.

- All team members carry equal status. No one person is allowed to dominate the meeting. Refer to the section "Roles of the Participants" for an understanding of each team member's responsibilities.

The agenda is much like that of a more traditional meeting. However, agenda items are sometimes determined in the meeting, so agenda topics may be very general. Refer to Figure 13-7 and an earlier section in this chapter, "Preparing the Agenda."

Figure 13-7 Agenda for a team meeting.

AGENDA

MEETING NO. 1
ADMINISTRATIVE TEAM

Date:	Wednesday, June 10, 20—
Time:	0830–1130
Place:	Conference Room 3
Leader/Facilitator:	Jeffrey Keaton
Recorder:	Gina Darroch
Guidance Team:	Kenneth Skoye, Donna Welch
Team Members:	Jodi Alford, Satvinder Bhardwaj, Chris Dennison, Allan Kohut, Benjamin Ross, Brian Van Bij, Marian Weston

TIME	ACTIVITY	LEAD PERSON
0830	Check in	Jeffrey
0845	Brainstorm issues affecting Admin Team	Jeffrey
0930	Use NGT to vote on issues	Benjamin
0945	Refreshment break	
1000	Discuss priority issues and make recommendations	Jeffrey
1100	Discuss any other business (AOB)	Jeffrey
1115	Review *"Next steps"*	Gina
1130	Bring closure • *Determine time and date for next meeting*	Jeffrey

Separate from the agenda, design a page for participants to take more detailed notes during the meeting. This meeting log helps the recorder and team members to stay focused during the meeting and to later recall their perception of topics and decisions. Refer to Figure 13-8 for a sample meeting log. Often, a meeting log can be used in place of more formal minutes. A complete copy of the meeting log may serve as the record of the meeting.

Roles of the Participants

Part of the team philosophy is to get input from people who are actually working within the process. In other words, the people who know the most about a topic should be at the meeting to discuss it and to make wise recommendations and decisions about it.

Each role in the team is equally important. The following briefly discusses the roles of team participants.

1. **Team Leader.** The team leader acts as a chairperson, directing the meeting, moving from one topic to the next, and keeping on schedule.

2. **Guidance Team.** The guidance team should consist of two or more people who are very familiar with the organization. Because of work constraints and time pressures, the guidance team may send only one member to a meeting. Often these people hold management positions; this enables them to provide information that other members

Figure 13-8 Meeting log.

MEETING LOG

MEETING OF: _Administrative Team_

LOCATION: _Conference Room 3_	DATE: _June 10, 20—_ TIME: _0830_
MEMBERS PRESENT: _J. Alford, S. Bhardwaj, G. Darroch, J. Keaton, A. Kohut, B. Ross, M. Weston_	**MEMBERS ABSENT:** _D. Welch, C. Dennison, B. Van Bÿ, K. Skoye_

ISSUES DISCUSSED	RECORD OF DISCUSSION
ISSUE NO. 1 **Topic =** _Dissatisfaction of customers due to delayed billing._	— _equip. downtime is high_ — _messages on telephone not working_ — _competition is high-tech_ — _paperwork is slow from sales staff_ — _work flow is between buildings_
Follow-up = 1. _Gina Darroch will set up meeting with Info. Systems manager._ 2. _Ben Ross will discuss paperwork with Peter._	**Recommendation/s =** 1. _upgrade hardware & software_ 2. _make paperwork easier for sales staff_
ISSUE NO. 2 **Topic =**	
Follow-up =	**Recommendation/s =**
ISSUE NO. 3 **Topic =**	
Follow-up =	**Recommendation/s =**

may be unaware of and that will be helpful when team decisions are made. The guidance members should be people who have the authority to make changes and the clout to put decisions into practice.

3. **Project Team Members.** All members who will take part in the discussions and vote on issues are considered project team members. This includes the team leader, but it does not include the guidance team. The votes of the project team members are critical to the decision-making process.

4. **Facilitator.** The team leader often carries both the roles of team leader and facilitator. When there are enough staff members available or when any type of disagreement or friction is expected at a meeting, it is important to have a separate person act as facilitator. The facilitator's responsibility is to make the meeting process flow with ease. The facilitator will ask the participants questions to help clarify their ideas.

The facilitator structures the comments into a simple list, a flowchart, or a cause-and-effect diagram. (Refer to the section "Brainstorming" for more information on cause-and-effect diagrams.) These visual aids make the participants aware of comments that have been presented.

The facilitator's task is a demanding one; therefore, he or she will often ask a team member to assist by recording the comments on a flip chart or erasable board.

The facilitator must be completely nonbiased about the topics being discussed. For that reason, the facilitator is often a person from a different department who has no stake in the direction the team takes. The facilitator does not vote.

5. **Recorder.** The recorder's task is to prepare minutes. Topics discussed, decisions, and follow-up actions to be taken must be a part of the minutes. The recorder is also responsible for forming the priority list of issues after the participants have voted.

The task of recording is often rotated among team members so that no one team member always has the additional responsibility of taking notes at each meeting. When a team member has the responsibility of taking notes, the attention needed for the task often eliminates her or him from part of the meeting discussion.

This task is made infinitely easier by the use of a notebook computer at the meeting. A further explanation of this process is found in the section "Nominal Group Technique."

Off to a Good Start

With the team process, considerable effort is applied to making meetings productive. Therefore, it's very important to get the meeting off to a good start.

1. **The team leader starts early.** He or she should arrive before any of the other participants in order to write the agenda in a place that is visible to all members. A flip chart or an erasable board works well.

If house rules have been established at a prior meeting, the leader will want to place these rules in a visible location.

The leader should make sure the room configuration is conducive to team participation. Do the chairs and tables need to be arranged in a circle? Is there an area for the coffee and juice containers? Does the coffee pot need to be plugged in?

As each member arrives, the team leader should give him or her a warm welcome in order to establish a friendly environment for sharing information and ideas.

2. **The meeting begins and ends as scheduled.** Do not wait for late arrivals. People appreciate a team leader who starts and ends a meeting on time. Once late arrivals learn that the meetings begin exactly on schedule, they will try harder to be on time.

3. **Warm-up.** If the members do not know each other, the team leader should start the meeting by having all people introduce themselves. This can be considered part of the meeting warm-up. There are many activities that the leader can initiate for team warm-ups. If the members of the team already know each other, the warm-up can be dispensed with.

4. **Check-in.** "Checking in" is an opportunity for each team member to express his or her present state of mind to the whole team. It is not necessary for everyone to check in; however, most people cannot simply switch off their feelings and become active participants. When possible, it is best to check in with the team. Checking in may sound something like this.

   ■ "I've been looking forward to getting some of these issues resolved, so I'm very happy to have been invited to this meeting."

   ■ "My desk is loaded with work and I have a paper due for my night school class. If I seem a little stressed, that's why."

   ■ "I've just had a super weekend; my energy has returned and I'm ready to participate."

5. **Agree on the goals.** Once the check-in is complete—that is, once all those who wish to check in have done so—the team leader should review the agenda.

6. **Review the roles of the team.** At the first meeting, the roles of the team leader, guidance team, quality advisor, facilitator, and project team members should be reviewed by the team leader. Of course, this will be

necessary only for the first or second meeting. Once the team members have exercised their roles, they will know what is expected of them.

7. **Establish the house rules.** The next step toward a successful project is establishing the house rules, also referred to as the "ground rules." The team should suggest and agree on some general house or ground rules before the meeting progresses. When these rules are not adhered to, any team member may point this out and bring the meeting back on track. Suggestions for house rules might be as follows:

- Everyone will be given an equal opportunity to speak.
- Any person wishing to speak must raise his or her hand.
- Criticize only the issue, not the person with the issue.
- Side conversations are not allowed.
- Each person must focus on the speaker.
- Expect unfinished business.
- The meeting will begin and finish on schedule.
- Everyone will focus on the topic and will not interrupt the team's work for outside reasons.
- No negative body language is allowed.

Brainstorming

If the agenda is general and the team is expected to provide the issues for discussion, the next step is team brainstorming. Even if the topics for discussion have been predetermined, brainstorming is a useful tool to apply now. Brainstorming will help the team develop many ideas in as short a time as possible.

Brainstorming may be carried out in one of two ways: structured or unstructured.

1. **Structured.** The structured method works well if the point is to avoid having one or two people dominate the meeting. It also works to encourage more introverted members to share their ideas.

   When structured brainstorming is used, every person is given a turn to express opinions, concerns, or ideas. The opportunity to speak rotates among the participants; people wishing to express their ideas must wait their turn. The rotation of ideas will be repeated until all ideas have been expressed. As each member states a problem he or she would like to deal with at the meeting, that person should also state why it should be considered an issue.

   During the rotation, any member may forfeit the opportunity to share an idea.

Each of these ideas must be recorded by the facilitator (or the facilitator's assistant) and by the person responsible for preparing the minutes or the meeting log.

2. **Unstructured.** The unstructured method of brainstorming has a freer atmosphere; participants are allowed to express their ideas as they think of them. No rotation or waiting for turns is involved. Although this creates a very relaxed atmosphere in which to brainstorm, the problem of domination by one or two members may arise.

Whether the atmosphere is structured or unstructured, the facilitator will work hard to make the ideas clear and relevant and to balance the participation. All ideas must be recorded where the participants can view them. As well, all team members must agree on the wording.

The recorder remains busy during the brainstorming session, documenting all the issues that the team has identified. These problems are then prioritized by the group according to their importance.

Nominal Group Technique

Once the problems have all been listed, and assuming there are no duplicate problems, the team should establish by vote which issues are most important and need immediate attention.

To ensure that the most vocal or persuasive participants do not dominate the proceedings, the Nominal Group Technique (NGT) should be applied. Without NGT, concerns raised by less forceful participants might never be worked on and resolved.

The recorder should prepare a form similar to the one in Figure 13-9. With this form, each participant can vote on each problem separately. Weighting is based on the following:

3 = This problem is of high priority and should be dealt with now.

2 = This problem is of medium priority and should be dealt with as soon as possible.

1 = This problem is of low priority and should be dealt with when possible.

0 = This problem does not affect me or my work.

Once the voting on issues is complete, the importance of the issues is calculated. The weighting on each listed problem illustrates which issues the team wishes to discuss and resolve first. The recorder should sort these weightings on the computer and provide all team members with the revised list. Refer to Figures 13-9 and 13-10, where NGT has helped the team to reach a **consensus**.

Figure 13-9 Voting sheet.

VOTING SHEET FOR NOMINAL GROUP TECHNIQUE					
ITEM NO.	ISSUES FOR DISCUSSION	TOTAL VOTES			
		3	2	1	0
1.	Ticketing of cars parked in the south lot				
2.	New payment schedule for per diem expenses				
3.	Criteria for Employee of the Month award				
4.	Lack of nutritious food in the staff cafeteria				
5.	Purchase of more voice mailboxes				
6.	Upgrading of fax machine				
7.	Purchase of a colour photocopier for the Reprographics Department				
8.	Extension of office network				
9.	Further leadership training for administrative assistants				
10.	Dissatisfaction of customers due to delayed billing				

REMEMBER:
3 = This problem is of high priority and should be dealt with now.
2 = This problem is of medium priority and should be dealt with as soon as possible.
1 = This problem is of low priority and should be dealt with when possible.
0 = This problem does not affect me or my work.

Discussion and Solution

The problems that receive the highest priority under NGT are discussed and resolved first. To encourage brainstorming, the facilitator might now draw a cause-and-effect diagram.

The cause-and-effect diagram is often referred to as a fishbone diagram (see Figure 13-11). The lines on the diagram (which appear as fishbones) represent the causes of the problem. The facilitator usually starts with four to six major categories such as the ones shown in Figure 13-11 (Equipment and Software, Procedures, People, External Sources). These major categories help to get the team thinking. The participants add to the diagram by suggesting more specific causes that fit under these major categories. It is important to use as few words as possible but to make the causes very clear.

The rectangle on the right of the diagram (the fish's "head") represents the effect, or the major problem. The effect has been brought on by the causes (bones).

A structured or unstructured brainstorming technique can be used to fill the diagram with all the possible causes of the problem.

Once all the causes have been identified, the team leader leads a discussion in which solutions are sought.

The team leader will probably ask the team members why each of the causes happens. No doubt this will encourage discussion.

During the discussion and solution phase, the team must remain respectful of the house rules. Any infraction of the rules should be brought to the attention of the team.

Team members may use their meeting logs to write personal notes, while the designated recorder makes a more detailed record of important discussion points, solutions, recommendations, and planned follow-up. The meeting log will form the official record of the meeting.

Closure

Although discussion of the topics has now concluded, it is important to spend a few minutes debriefing. The debriefing session allows participants to express their feelings. Each participant is invited to **debrief**, or "check out"; however, it is not required.

During the debriefing phase, you might hear comments such as the following:

- "I feel this was a successful meeting today. The candour of the participants was very helpful in reaching decisions."

- "I feel some scepticism at the decisions made today; however, I am willing to work with these new ideas."

- "Because I'm tired, I was ready to check out some time ago. Although it seemed a long meeting, plenty was accomplished."

Figure 13-10 Issues have been placed in order of priority.

ITEM NO.	ISSUES FOR DISCUSSION	TOTAL VOTES				WEIGHTED AVERAGE
		3	2	1	0	
10.	Dissatisfaction of customers due to delayed billing	14	1	0	0	2.9
8.	Extension of office network	12	2	1	0	2.7
2.	New payment schedule for per diem expenses	12	1	1	1	2.6
6.	Upgrading of fax machine	12	1	1	1	2.6
5.	Purchase of more voice mailboxes	10	3	2	0	2.5
3.	Criteria for Employee of the Month award	10	2	3	0	2.4
9.	Further leadership training for administrative assistants	9	3	3	0	2.4
7.	Purchase of a colour photocopier for the Repro. Dept.	5	8	1	1	2.1
1.	Ticketing of cars parked in the south lot	7	3	4	1	2.0
4.	Lack of nutritious food in the staff cafeteria	0	3	9	3	1.0

VOTING SHEET FOR NOMINAL GROUP TECHNIQUE

REMEMBER:

3 = This problem is of high priority and should be dealt with now.

2 = This problem is of medium priority and should be dealt with as soon as possible.

1 = This problem is of low priority and should be dealt with when possible.

0 = This problem does not affect me or my work.

CALCULATION OF WEIGHTED AVERAGE:

(3 x No. of Votes in Priority 3)

Plus (2 x No. of Votes in Priority 2)

Plus (No. of Votes in Priority 1)

Divide the sum by total number of votes on the problem.

Figure 13-11 Cause-and-effect diagram.

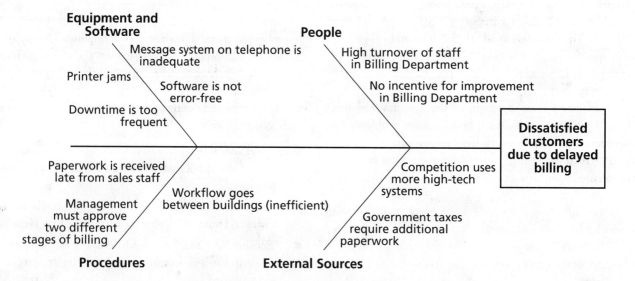

MEETING DYNAMICS

One of the many roles of the office professional is to attend and contribute to meetings. However, many administrative assistants are taking a more active role by leading and facilitating meetings. This means they have to become comfortable with meeting dynamics or the interplay that happens between meeting participants. Please refer to Chapter 1, under the sections "Be a Team Player" and "Nonproductive Behaviours," for discussions of interpersonal relations in the office. Many of the behaviours described in Chapter 1 become very obvious at meetings. In addition, some unique behaviours occur at meetings.

Poor Body Language

Nowhere is it easier to see body language in action than at a meeting. In a meeting environment, participants may sit for long periods of time in close proximity. So it's easy to get your message across to others without even opening your mouth. Common negative body language messages found at meetings will include:

- I am bored.
- You are wrong.
- I'm too busy to be here.
- I need to get out of here.
- I don't want to be here.
- Your comments are not important.
- Your comments are foolish.
- I'm frustrated.
- I don't agree with you.

Always Late

When a meeting is called for 0800, it means being in the correct meeting room, having your coat off, being seated, and being prepared to start at 0800. It doesn't mean flying through the meeting room door at 0810, and making loud apologies for your busy schedule and late arrival.

Although people know this, many continually show up late and interrupt the meeting with their arrival. The message that they are giving to the other participants is that their work is more important—more important than the meeting and more important than the work of the other participants.

Never Prepared

What is more frustrating than participants who attend meetings without being prepared? This may include:

- not completing the activities you have agreed to at the previous meeting
- not reading the agenda before the meeting
- not preparing handouts for your presentation
- not reading background documents that have been sent to you prior to the meeting

This lack of preparation is completely unfair to the other participants.

Not Participating

Preparing for a meeting is work. Attending a meeting is work. Following up from a meeting is work. The person who comes to a meeting expecting to get a break or socialize is doing a disservice to the other members.

Some people are masters at avoiding meeting follow-up. When they leave the meeting, everyone else has an action list to follow, but they leave without a follow-up list of activities.

During the meeting, they may offer verbal suggestions or advice; but they do not offer to prepare background reports, statistics, or any concrete evidence of work. Some nonparticipants remain completely quiet at meetings and simply occupy the chair.

Being Rude

Rudeness comes in many forms at a meeting. Rudeness might include:

- speaking over the top of other participants
- not listening to others
- ignoring the ideas of other people

- discounting the ideas of others
- speaking directly to one person and shutting out a third party (This is often done through body language, not responding to the third person's attempts to get into the conversation, and not making eye contact with them.)
- coming late to a meeting
- holding side conversations
- reading or working on unrelated materials during the meeting
- using vulgar language or stories to make a point
- rushing to finish the meeting regardless of where you are on the agenda and regardless of what you have not yet accomplished

Creating Solutions

The study of meeting dynamics is fascinating, and the list of nonproductive behaviours found at meetings could be very long. Meeting dynamics make leading a meeting a difficult challenge. However, there are some strategies a meeting facilitator or leader can take that will help solve some of the difficulties. Here are some suggestions:

- Rely on the ground rules. The ground rules are created at the first meeting of the team. The team members create them, so they are likely to buy into them. When a member's behaviour does not follow the ground rules, stop the meeting momentarily, point to the rule, and ask the member to get back on track.
- Start the meeting on time every time. It doesn't matter if only half the members are there. Move ahead. Once members see that the leader is serious about getting started on time, they will make a greater effort to be ready on time.
- Don't stop the meeting when people arrive late with loud interruptions. You can acknowledge them with a facial gesture, but do not let the flow of the meeting be interrupted.
- The leader should speak privately to errant members at the break or after the meeting. A one-on-one private conversation about poor behaviour will be more effective than challenging the person head-on during the meeting in front of the other members.
- Sticking to an agenda, and using printed time charts and action plans that are on display at every meeting will help to remind and encourage people about their needed activities and their deadlines.
- The team leader or facilitator can discourage poor behaviour and encourage productive behaviour by managing the input during the meeting. A diplomatic and assertive request for participation or for productive team behaviour can be very effective.
- Be sure that the team leader has the respect of the team members. If the team members have selected the leader, there will be a greater chance for respect and better behaviour at the meetings.
- Pay attention to what is said after the meeting. Don't get involved in side meetings held outside the main meeting, or criticism of the leader or decisions made inside the meeting; but be aware of what is taking place outside the walls of the meeting.
- Strive for consensus by the team members. If all the team members are in agreement or at least can support recommendations made by the team, the behaviour will be productive.
- Meetings should be enjoyable as well as productive. Humour and fun should be mandatory at meetings.

Self-Check

1. Identify one way to increase the likelihood of the team leader having the respect of all team members.
2. What should the facilitator do when people arrive late for the meeting?

VIRTUAL MEETINGS VIA HIGH-TECH

Many companies use telecommunications in the office to conduct virtual meetings, including teleconferences, web conferences, and videoconferences. These forms of meetings reduce travel costs and losses in productivity that result from time spent away from the office.

Service providers and technology vendors support their customers with the latest virtual conference tools to ensure the greatest possibility of success. They may provide complimentary training on the virtual meeting service, live help during the teleconference, or a **hotline** into their technical support facility.

Before selecting a virtual meeting, spend some time to consider your real needs. If simple communication is all that you require, then a teleconference is the least complicated and most cost-effective approach. If your virtual meeting necessitates the sharing or presenting of data and other material, then **web conferencing** will meet your needs. In Chapter 7 web conferencing is covered from a technical requirement standpoint.

Teleconferences

Teleconferences, also known as **conference calls**, are telecommunication-based meetings that use ordinary telephone lines to bring together three or more people at various locations. Teleconference services offered by your local telephone company can connect dozens of people to the same call. They can involve local, national, or international calls. Office professionals will often find themselves arranging or participating in teleconferences.

Many business telephones have a simple conference function that allows the conference coordinator to dial up participants and put them into the conference call. This does not require operator assistance. The conference coordinator may control the teleconference from a touch-tone telephone using commands on the keypad. There are no additional fees except for the "collective" cost per minute of conference.

However, for more complex teleconferencing, the traditional process of contacting your local service provider to reserve a common **bridge** or dial-in number for participants is probably the safest method. There are a number of somewhat inflexible conditions that surround these reserved teleconferences such as a predetermined number of lines for participants and a fixed length of conference time; and there is invariably a charge for services.

To ensure a successful teleconference, always remember that you are part of a meeting involving many people. Here are some specific teleconferencing suggestions:

- If you are a single participant at your location during a teleconference, use a lightweight headset consisting of earphones and a built-in microphone. The headset allows you to move around the room with both hands free as you take notes or search through documents.

- Identify yourself when speaking, and direct your questions or comments to people by name.

- Remember that comments not specifically directed to an individual will be perceived as intended for the entire group.

- Speak naturally as you would during any telephone call, but pause for others to comment.

Web Conferences

Web conferences allow participants to be online in real time via the internet. Using your PC and web-conferencing application software, often found in your web browser, you can establish an inexpensive and reliable way to share information, software applications, PowerPoint presentations, or anything running on your PC with others in online meetings.

As the coordinator, you can guide participants through the conference, enabling them to see what you display on your PC screen.

Coordinating a conference call to coincide with a web conference may enhance web conferencing and encourage those without the benefit of a PC to participate.

Videoconferences

Videoconferences can be an important vehicle for collaborative office communication. They allow participants in scattered geographic locations to see and hear one another on computer or television monitors by way of images transmitted over special telephone lines or satellite.

Videoconferences typically cost 20 to 50 percent less than face-to-face meetings, but they remain the most expensive form of virtual meetings.

It's very popular for people to hold meetings through their computers, just using their screens and keyboards. By simply downloading software from the internet, participants can engage in real-time keyed conversations. Audio and video options are available as long as the participants have the right multimedia software, a computer microphone and speaker, and a simple web camera placed near the screen. The cost is minimal, the procedure is simple, and the result is highly effective.

---

pro-Link
Warm Up with an Icebreaker

When people come to meetings, their minds are busy with other priorities, deadlines, and pressures that they bring with them to the meeting. That's why a meeting facilitator will often use a simple exercise at the start of the meeting to help get people focused. These exercises are often called Icebreakers or Warm-Ups. These same activities, when used at the end of meetings, are called Cool-Downs. Here's an example:

Select comic strips from the newspaper. Cut out each frame in the strip. Place all of the frames into a large container. When the meeting begins, ask each participant to take one frame out of the container. Start the clock! The participants must find the other frames that belong to the same comic strip. Once all the frames have been located, they must be ordered chronologically so that the comic strip can be read correctly. If the facilitator wants the participants to work in groups, it's an easy way for groups to be formed. Participants have actively moved about, they may have met new people, laughed at the comic strip, and now are ready to start the meeting.

Figure 13-12 Virtual meetings type and use.

Type of Virtual Meeting	Use of Meeting
Teleconference	A conference using ordinary telephone lines and sets, with three or more participants. Teleconferences are used for local, national, or international voice conferencing wherever there is a telephone service. They are "verbal only" and may be both impromptu and informal meetings.
Web Conference	A conference of two or more people at different workstations connected to the Internet. Participants may share documents, applications such as PowerPoint, and video images. It may be used in conjunction with a teleconference to enhance participation. Web conferences are inexpensive and reliable.
Videoconference	Videoconference facilities using special telecommunication lines or satellite services are often set up and administered by third party specialists. This type of virtual meeting may be made to a corporate wide audience or to a smaller, more focused audience in a single office. Videoconferences provide the best quality of all virtual conferences but remain the most expensive and require the participant to have special skills and coordination in order to effectively participate.

Self-Check

1. Describe two ways in which teleconferences can be arranged.
2. Describe two ways that your PC can assist you in running a web conference.

ETHICAL BEHAVIOUR IN MEETINGS

As you know, ethics is a system of deciding what is morally right in a given situation. You may find yourself in situations where you might not want to tell the truth to avoid hurting someone's feelings. For instance, imagine you are a new participant in a team meeting. After the meeting, the facilitator asks you if you enjoyed the meeting and learned a lot of helpful information. In fact, you were really bored and already knew everything discussed. Is it wrong to say, "Oh, yes, I really enjoyed the meeting," to avoid hurting the facilitator's feelings? It would be an outright lie. You may want to learn to sidestep a question or issue without being brutally honest when it is simply a matter of avoiding hurting someone's feelings. Your response to the facilitator could be, "I really did find several points you made interesting and helpful."

What if, however, the situation has damaging consequences? For instance, while attending your manager's presentation, you notice certain figures in the sales report have been changed to report higher sales. After the meeting, you question him about it; and he tells you he increased the figures because the department is under pressure to increase sales. If you do not report this behaviour and he does it again, he can say you helped him change the figures because you did not report it the first time you noticed it.

You have the responsibility to do the right thing based on your own values, and you should report any unethical behaviour from the beginning. By doing so, you will be following your company's code of ethics. Adhering to ethical behaviour in meetings, as well as in any personal interaction, involves making choices that will build positive qualities—trust and credibility.

INTERNATIONAL CONFERENCING

As global communications become more commonplace, you may find yourself helping your manager prepare for an international meeting or conference. In addition to your usual responsibilities in making routine meeting arrangements, you might also find yourself responsible for other aspects of planning. Examples might include:

- arranging hotels and transportation
- tracking and handling finances and payments, including exchange rates
- arranging interpreters
- arranging business cards, printed in both English and the language of the host country
- providing protocol advice to your manager
- making security arrangements
- researching the names of major political leaders, sports figures, and other celebrities
- compiling a dossier on the host country, including information on business philosophy, social customs, and seasonal climate

The following guidelines will help you to deal effectively with cultural and language differences during your consultations with people from the country to which your manager will be travelling:

- Learn courtesy greetings in the language of that country. A simple "Good morning," "Thank you," and "Goodbye" in that language at the beginning and end of a telephone call will make a favourable impression.

- Educate yourself as to the geography and transportation systems of the country so that you will be somewhat familiar with distances, terrain, and mode of transportation when discussing meeting locations and time schedules with your counterpart in the country being visited.

- Gather information on major landmarks and their histories in the host country. This will enable you to make informed decisions when collaborating with your counterpart in preparing a schedule of meetings and activities for your manager during his visit.

- Determine the preferred times for calling to discuss your manager's pending visit, and make an effort to adhere to those preferences.

- Become familiar with the religious beliefs, social customs, business philosophy, and family structure of the country where the meeting is to be held. This will ensure that you do not unintentionally give offence during consultations.

As you research communication and cultural barriers that may arise between cultures, keep an ongoing file of pertinent information. Realize, though, that the information will have to be updated from time to time. You will give yourself an edge as you plan or progress through your career and gain the reputation of an "expert" in international conferencing protocol.

QUESTIONS FOR STUDY AND REVIEW

1. Why should you create an action checklist before making arrangements for a meeting or conference?

2. List ten examples of actions that might appear on a meeting checklist.

3. How can the computer be helpful in arranging the date and time for meetings?

4. When both the administrative assistant and the executive are booking meetings for the executive, what can an administrative assistant do to prevent double-booking an executive's time?

5. What information does an administrative assistant need before he or she can schedule a conference room for a meeting of a few executives?

6. What information should be included in a meeting notice?

7. What items might appear on an agenda for a formal meeting?

8. What items might appear on an agenda for an informal meeting?

9. List 15 supplies or pieces of equipment that may be required for a meeting.

10. State five guidelines to follow when ordering beverages for a meeting. State five guidelines to follow when ordering food for a meeting.

11. What supporting materials will be required for a formal meeting?

12. What is a *verbatim* transcript?

13. How is a notebook computer useful at meetings?

14. List ten tips for successful note taking during a meeting.

15. What are some of the actions that might appear on your to do list following a meeting?

16. Why might you have to prepare minutes for an organization you don't work for?

17. What would you include on the minutes of an informal meeting?

18. What would you include on the minutes of a formal meeting?

19. Corrections and additions (or deletions) to minutes should be recorded in two places. Where should these changes be recorded?

20. How is a team meeting different from a formal meeting?

21. What is the purpose of a meeting log?

22. What is the role of the team leader at a meeting?

23. What is the role of the facilitator at a meeting?

24. What is the purpose of a warm-up at a team meeting?

25. What is the purpose of a check-in at a team meeting?

26. State five house rules you believe would help make team meetings more productive.

27. Differentiate between structured and unstructured brainstorming.

28. Explain how the Nominal Group Technique is used when an issue must be voted on.

29. What is the purpose of a cause-and-effect diagram?

30. How does debriefing take place at a team meeting?

31. What is the meaning of "meeting dynamics"?

32. Describe five poor behaviours that are often witnessed at meetings.

33. Describe seven strategies that a team can use to avoid and handle poor behaviour.

34. What is the meaning of a *virtual* meeting?

35. Suggest two advantages in holding virtual meetings instead of face-to-face meetings.

EVERYDAY ETHICS

Cove or Conference?

You work in the Public Relations Department of the Southern Saskatchewan Petroleum Institute (SSPI). SSPI has paid your expenses to attend a business conference in Halifax where you are representing the company. Your participation includes leading a one-hour seminar in public relations issues for Canadian petroleum companies. You spent one full weekend preparing your materials and making sure that you would represent your company in the very best way possible.

Then you travelled to Halifax after working hours on a Tuesday evening. Your presentation was held on the first day of the two-day conference. You performed in an excellent fashion, and you know that positive reports will get back to your management team in Regina.

You are expected to attend other people's seminars on the second day—but in your judgment there appears to be nothing of interest for SSPI. However, there is a full-day tour available from the hotel lobby that takes tourists to Peggy's Cove and to other tourist points in Halifax. You have never been to Halifax and have always wanted to see Peggy's Cove. You feel you "deserve" the time off in lieu of all the personal time you put into preparation for the conference. Instead of attending the second-day seminars, you board the tourist bus. Edward Graham, a business associate, sees you leaving on the bus.

■ What are your next steps?

Problem Solving

1. You arranged an all-day meeting for a group of 25 executives within your office and national branch offices. You have planned and arranged the location, agenda, and meals for this meeting. Everything is going well until lunchtime. Five executives had requested a vegetarian lunch, but when lunch arrives from the caterers none of the meals are vegetarian. Everyone is ready to eat, but there are no meals for the five executives. What should you do?

2. Your manager, Ms. Corona, is giving a talk at a national conference in a large city at 1400 tomorrow afternoon. As soon as she arrived at her destination, she called you to say that she does not have the PowerPoint presentation she needs to illustrate her talk. "Can you find a copy of it?" she inquires. She is certain that the hotel where she is speaking has a business centre with internet. You commit to following through. It is now 1530. What will you do?

3. Your manager, Lee Chung, is the chairperson of a regional group of office managers. The group meets once a month. Today you keyed and duplicated the minutes of the January meeting. Mr. Chung is leaving the office to attend the February meeting, and he plans to take the minutes of the January meeting with him for distribution. As you are looking over the notes of the January meeting, you discover that you omitted a motion that had been voted upon. Mr. Chung does not have time for you to rekey the minutes and duplicate them. Should Mr. Chung take the minutes you have prepared? How can the correction be made?

Special Reports

1. Interview an administrative assistant, in person or by email, who is responsible for preparing minutes of meetings. Find out how the minutes are prepared (from written notes, a recording, etc.). Ask your interviewee to share five tips for minute preparation. Prepare a report for your instructor detailing your findings.

2. The Olympics is held every four years. This international sporting celebration is a mammoth event to organize. It requires a lot of time and money but mostly a team of highly skilled people to manage the event.

   a. Locate the website for the next Olympic Games.

   b. Consider that you are working with the Olympic organizing team. You have been assigned as the team leader for managing one particular sporting event. Select one of the activities from those listed on the site. Then become familiar with this activity through internet research.

   c. Make a comprehensive list of all the sub-teams that you, as the team leader, will form to take care of all aspects of this sporting event. For example, if you have chosen downhill skiing as your sporting event, you might form a sub-team for housing the athletes, another sub-team for transporting the athletes, and so on. Be as thorough as possible.

   d. Now select one of your sub-teams and brainstorm all the potential barriers/problems that you will have to avoid. For example, if your sub-team is Transportation for the Downhill Skiers, one of your potential barriers might be lack of suitable racks to carry the skis on the bus. Again, make your list exhaustive.

   You do not have to write paragraphs. This is a "thinking" exercise. Use enumerations and bullets for your two lists. There are no right and wrong answers. Instead, this is a brainstorming exercise and a chance for you to think through the complexities of organizing a major event.

3. You have been asked to arrange a workshop for your classmates on career planning to be held at your campus in one month. This will be a three-hour workshop. Research event planning online and prepare an event-planning checklist that includes all of the items to consider when arranging this type of event. Hand in the checklist to your instructor for feedback.

PRODUCTION CHALLENGES

13-A Composing, Faxing, and Emailing a Notice of Meeting

Supplies needed:

- *Fax transmittal forms 13-A-1 and 13-A-2, pages 421 to 422*
- *Plain paper*

The current date is September 3. Mr. Wilson has called a meeting of the Executive Committee of the November Sales Seminar, and he has asked you to send the notices. The meeting will be held in Mr. Wilson's office at Millennium Appliances, Inc., at 1700 on Wednesday, September 10. The purpose of the meeting is to finalize plans for the November Sales Seminar. The names and contact numbers for the Executive Committee members follow. You know that all the members have email, but you don't have all the correct addresses in your file. Where you have an email address for the member, write the message as an email. If you have no email address, fax the notice.

Mr. Wilson needs to know if each committee member can attend the September 10 meeting, if he/she has a report to make, and if he or she thinks that an October meeting of the Executive Committee will be necessary. Ask all members to email their responses to Mr. Wilson's address, which is wwilson@millennium.ca.

Mr. Michael Wong
Electronic Systems

Fax: 905-322-7043
Tel: 905-322-5839

Mr. Jasim Mohammed
CanTech Industries
Fax: 705-428-3390
Tel: 705-429-7192

Ms. Louise Witherspoon
City Centre Appliances
Fax: 298-781-7498
Tel: 298-781-6735
Email: louisew@cca.com.ca

Ms. Dimitra Theodorakopoulos
Seneca College of Applied Arts and Technology
Fax: 416-366-9811
Tel: 416-366-9981
Email: dimitrat@senecac.on.ca

13-B Composing and Keying Minutes

Supplies needed:

- *Notes on September 10 Meeting of the Executive Committee for the November Sales Seminar, Form 13-B, pages 423 to 424*
- *Plain paper*

Mr. Wilson put his notes for the September 10 meeting of the Executive Committee of the November Sales Seminar in your in-basket. The following note was attached: "Please compose and key these minutes."

13-C Holding a Team Meeting

Supplies needed:

- *Voting Sheet, Form 13-C-1, page 425*
- *Meeting Log, Form 13-C-2, page 426*
- *Cause-and-Effect Diagrams, Forms 13-C-3, 13-C-4, and 13-C-5 pages 427 to 429*
- *Plain paper*

Mr. Wilson asks you to hold a team meeting. The purpose of the meeting is to discuss and make recommendations on the following three issues:

1. Sales brochures are being prepared from an external source. It seems as though there is a problem with the communications between Millennium Appliances and the print shop, since the finished brochure has not matched the intended design on the last two orders.

2. Some employees are abusing the summer working hours. These hours allow employees to begin work at 0700 and finish at 1500. However, reports are being received that employees are not arriving until 0730 or 0745 but are still taking the privilege of leaving at 1500.

3. We are currently placing employee training information on the bulletin board in the staff room. However, a number of employees report that they have not seen the brochures, either because they do not read the bulletin board or because the training information is being removed by other employees. Of course, Millennium Appliances wishes to give all employees an equal opportunity to apply for training courses.

Form a team that includes a team leader, recorder, facilitator, guidance team, quality advisor, and other team members. The person on the team who is most knowledgeable about NGT should act as the quality advisor to guide the team members through the correct steps.

The team leader will prepare an agenda on plain paper. The meeting is to be held in Conference Room C at 1030 on June 31, 20—. The meeting will continue until 1430. The team leader should remember to include coffee breaks and lunch on the agenda. The team leader must make sure to get an agenda to each team member prior to the meeting.

The team leader should conduct the meeting according to the information in the section "Team Meetings."

The recorder would normally list the issues on the voting sheet, and supply all team members with the form.

However, since the three issues are listed here and each team member already has a form (Form 13-C-1), the team leader may instruct the team to write the issues onto their forms. The facilitator should ensure that all team members understand the issues and that they record the issues on the voting sheet using the same wording.

The team leader will instruct the team members to vote on the priority of the issues. Each team member may use a vote of 3, 2, or 1 on each issue. (A team member may choose to give all of the issues the same weighting.)

The facilitator will then calculate the votes and announce the priority in which the issues will be discussed.

All members will use the meeting log (Form 13-C-2) to take notes and record special comments during the meeting. The recorder must be especially astute to record the details of the discussion, since he or she will use these notes to prepare the minutes after the meeting.

The team leader and facilitator will lead the team members through the cause-and-effect diagrams (Forms 13-C-3, 13-C-4, and 13-C-5), starting with the top-priority issue. The facilitator may wish to use a blackboard or overhead transparency to guide this discussion. The team members should follow along by filling in their own cause-and-effect diagrams. Recommendations to improve the current problems must be made by the group and recorded on the meeting log.

When the team leader has guided the meeting through closure, the recorder will prepare the minutes on plain paper, using the format shown in Figure 13-6, page 253.

13-D Event Management

Supplies needed:

- *Plain paper*

You are all currently working on a team with the goal of improving customer relationship management within Millennium Appliances. Mr. Wilson has asked your team to organize a seminar for the company.

For the seminar, the team has decided to bring in an expert guest speaker. You search the internet and find sites that give profiles of speakers who will travel to your city to work with your team. One such site that you have located is www.leadingauthorities.com.

Prepare a three-paragraph biography about the speaker you have chosen that you could use to convince Mr. Wilson to give you approval to book this expert for your upcoming seminar.

Then create a document that will capture a list of all your potential expenses for hiring the guest speaker. In your document, list all the potential expenses, a justification for each expense, and your educated estimate of each expense. Don't forget to consider the following in your list of potential expenses:

- services
- travel
- accommodation
- meals
- products

- shipping
- transportation
- equipment and supplies
- rentals and leases
- communication
- miscellaneous
- gifts

Weblinks

Make Meetings Work
www.meetingwizard.org
Here you will find information on how to hold effective meetings, schedule meetings, create agendas, take minutes, and much more.

www.effectivemeetings.com
This site offers hands-on meeting advice for every possible situation. It includes a special section where the "Meeting Guru" solves dilemmas.

Canadian Association of Professional Speakers (CAPS)
www.canadianspeakers.org
This site is the number one internet resource for the Canadian speaking industry. It includes a bulletin board for CAPS members.

Business Etiquette
http://mannersandcareer.learnhub.com
Learnhub.com provides numerous tips on a variety of business etiquette topics.

https://courseware.e-education.psu.edu/resources/Videoconf_etiquette4.pdf
This site provides information on videoconferencing etiquette.

Chapter 14
Business Communication

Learning Outcomes

After completion of this chapter, the student will be able to:

1 Describe ways to improve verbal communication.

2 Explain appropriate nonverbal communication that relates to image, personal space, eye contact, posture, and facial expressions.

3 Demonstrate ways to improve your listening skills.

4 Demonstrate methods of giving and receiving constructive feedback.

5 Discuss ways to be comfortable and effective when giving oral presentations.

6 Explain methods for preventing presentation hazards.

7 Describe the qualities of an effective business letter.

8 Compare the techniques for writing favourable and persuasive letters, and letters of disappointment.

9 Differentiate between full-block and modified-block letter styles.

10 Discuss the following types of reports: letter, email memorandum, informal, and formal.

11 Differentiate between in-text citations, references, and bibliographies.

12 Use the internet in the reference list of a formal report.

13 Compare formal reports written in inductive, deductive, and chronological arrangements.

14 Correctly address envelopes for international correspondence.

15 Identify differences in writing styles among international companies.

16 Write and key a letter of request.

17 Key the final draft of a manuscript for corrected copy.

Effective communication is the responsibility of every person in an organization. As organizations increase their dependence on computers and other electronic equipment, the volume of work that everyone is expected to manage increases. This greater amount of responsibility is accompanied by increased communications, both electronic and personal. As an administrative assistant, you will become involved in both interpersonal and written communications that require skills in both electronic and personal domains.

Sandra Whan
Assistant Director
Eastern Regional Medical Education
Program (ERMEP)

College Graduation:
Office Administration—Executive
Algonquin College Heritage Institute
Perth, Ontario

2004

As a result of downsizing in the manufacturing company she worked for, Sandra went from holding a position as a receptionist to driving a forklift to running large machinery and packaging inventory items. Feeling that factory work was not for her, she decided to return to school. Although Sandra had 14 years of office experience, she knew she was lacking in some areas, and she was certain that attending an office administration program would help her gain the skills and confidence required to work in an administrative position. She was right!

Following graduation, Sandra volunteered as administrative coordinator for the Friends of Murphy's Point Provincial Park and worked part-time as administrative assistant at her "alma mater," Algonquin College Heritage Institute. These experiences added to her skill set and led her to her current position with ERMEP where she handles the administrative duties of the program in addition to sourcing work placements for third and fourth year university medical students. Researching through the internet helps Sandra handle her other responsibilities of arranging transportation and accommodations for the students and locating preceptors (doctors) to host them.

"My most challenging responsibility is to make sure that my customers are 100 percent satisfied with my efforts."

Using computer software is key to managing her busy workload. Sandra maintains an Access database of the preceptors and keeps the budget on track with Excel spreadsheet. She also uses the Microsoft calendar feature and spends time at the end of each day planning for the next day. She says, "That way when I arrive at work in the morning, I know what needs to be done." Email has proven to be the most effective means of communicating with the medical students as their schedules are hectic, but Sandra still uses the "good old" telephone to communicate with most of her contacts.

Sandra's ambition is to be very successful at anything she does and to climb the ladder of success to become executive director in both her career and her personal business as a Mary Kay consultant. Sandra says, "Someday, I would like to be a motivational speaker to help others, to guide and teach them to achieve their careers and dreams."

INTERPERSONAL COMMUNICATION

The term **interpersonal communication** refers to personal interactions between individuals or members of a group. Whether you are discussing with a co-worker the implementation of a new filing system or conversing with your friend about anxiety over an upcoming job interview, you are engaging in interpersonal communication. This communication includes the use of verbal (words and voice), nonverbal (body language, image), and listening skills; and its effectiveness depends on the level to which those skills have been developed.

Various studies tell us that in a conversation or verbal exchange:

Words are 7–10% effective.

Tone of voice is 38–40% effective.

Nonverbal clues are 45–50% effective.

How effective your communication is depends as much on how you say something as on what you say. Also, whether your message is understood depends on the method of communication you choose to use to deliver it.

VERBAL COMMUNICATION

Verbal communication can mean a telephone conversation, a voice mail message, a formal meeting, or even an informal chat with a co-worker at lunch. Much of the communication in the office is verbal, and the degree to which communication occurs depends on the skills of the individuals involved in the interchange. The most effective verbal communication takes place in a comfortable atmosphere and on a one-to-one basis. Effective verbal skills can be learned. Strive to continually improve those skills by following these guidelines:

- **Listen and watch for verbal and nonverbal feedback.** Many factors affect how someone reacts to what you are saying. Among them is past experience—what happened to that person in a similar situation.

- **Choose your words carefully when the topic you are discussing is sensitive or controversial.** You may wish to withhold your opinion entirely if you know your view will offend the listener, put the listener on the defensive, or force the listener to disagree with you.

- **Encourage the other person to talk: communication should be two-way.** Communication will be open and honest if the person trusts you; it will be restricted if the person does not.

- **Give the other person your undivided attention.** Performing another task while you are talking is distracting and rude. This is equally important whether you are talking face-to-face or over the telephone.

- **Avoid talking incessantly.** Pause often to give your listener an opportunity to respond.

- **Summarize the important points in logical order and give the listener a chance to ask questions at the end of a conversation.** Communication does not take place until the listener truly understands what you are saying.

You can improve your own speech patterns by being aware of any negative habits you may have developed. For example, do you say "uh," or "you know" when you are talking? Those or similar repetitive phrases can be quite distracting to the listener. A person once said, "I counted 104 'uhs' in another person's message." It is doubtful whether the listener heard any of the intended message through the "noise" of the repetitive phrase. "You know what I mean?" is an example of another habit that detracts from the intended message being sent. Be careful not to pick up those and other similar habits that you find distracting in others.

In order to convey the clearest message possible, be aware of the tone and volume of your voice when speaking. Consider the following:

- Slow your speech. When you talk fast, you may appear to be nervous and unsure of yourself.

- Don't talk in a monotone. Inflection helps convey meaning. When you want to make a point or emphasize something, put a dip in your voice by lowering it briefly. Raising your voice slightly at the end of a statement makes it a question.

- Don't speak loudly. If you are standing close to someone, keep your volume down. Increase your volume depending on the distance between you and the person. Don't, however, speak so softly that your listener has to ask you to repeat what you are saying.

- Speak clearly. Don't mumble. When you hear "huh?" or "pardon?" that is a warning you are not speaking clearly.

- Use the correct pronunciation. Misuse occurs from hearing words mispronounced by others so often that we begin to mispronounce them ourselves. Have you heard "candidate" mispronounced "cannidate"? or "especially" mispronounced "expecially"? Pay particular attention to correct pronunciation; common misuse or mispronunciation neither makes the habit acceptable in business nor conveys a professional image.

- Use the right word. If you aren't sure of a word's meaning, don't use it.

Self-Check

1. What skills are included in interpersonal communication?

2. Discuss three guidelines for improving verbal communication.

3. How can you use your voice to improve the clarity of the message being sent?

NONVERBAL COMMUNICATION

Most people are skilled at communicating a message without speaking even one word. Our facial expressions, our body gestures, and the way we dress often express our feelings and opinions better than our spoken words. Make certain, however, that the person with whom you are communicating doesn't misinterpret what are often seen as subtle nonverbal cues. It is imperative that your actions convey a clear meaning—that is, the meaning you intend. Verbal communication can be completely discredited by the nonverbal kind. The following are some of the ways through which people interpret nonverbal messages:

Image

It is no surprise that the way we dress sends a message to customers and colleagues. Accurate or not, people do form immediate perceptions of your professionalism, your competence, your credibility, and your ability based on your personal appearance. Promotions may be granted or denied on the basis of appearance.

Conservative dress conveys the message that you are a professional and want to be taken seriously. While formal dress is still adhered to in some organizations, especially for top management, the trend, overall, is toward more relaxed business attire. Many highly professional companies consider business-casual clothing to be quite appropriate. Take your cue from the other workers you see in the office, or ask if there is an official dress code. When in doubt, dress up rather than down.

The location of the office, the style of management, organizational culture, and the type of industry you work in will all dictate the level of professional dress that is required. If you work in an organization whose clientele consists of trendsetters, you will likely find the dress code to be cutting-edge stylish but professional. On the other hand, a high-profile corporate law firm will likely require employees to dress in a more formal manner in keeping with their corporate clientele. Consider your customers. In our multicultural society, customers come from varied cultural backgrounds, and the image you convey through your appearance should be one that will avoid offending all visitors.

Regardless of the casualness of the office environment, do not confuse social dress with business dress. You might wear a cropped top or an open, revealing neckline to a party, but it would be inappropriate in the workplace for both male and female workers.

Not only clothing but accessories, too, help to create an image of you as a professional. Large, dangling jewellery and multiple visible body piercings should be avoided at the office unless you are working in a jewellery store or body piercing parlour where you are expected to promote the product by wearing samples! Likewise, excessive makeup has its place in theatre but conveys an unprofessional image in the office environment. As with clothing, wearing accessories conservatively will portray a professional image to both your customers and your supervisors.

It is common practice among many Canadian offices to designate Friday as **casual day**. This policy allows employees to dress in a casual style that is still attractive and presentable. However, customers and clients may be unaware of this convention and receive the incorrect message that the office is less than professional. You might consider taking the initiative to create an attractive, tasteful sign explaining "casual day," and getting permission to post it in a public area to attract clients' attention.

Be conservative in using perfumes, colognes, and scented products! Many Canadian offices and buildings have banned the use of scents altogether because of increased allergic reactions to ingredients used in the manufacture of many of the products. Ask about the policy in the office or building where you work and adhere to any restrictions that are in place.

Personal Space

Canadians, like all other nationalities, have expectations about their **personal space**. Personal space refers to the distance apart from another at which one person feels comfortable talking. People who stand too close are viewed as aggressive or perhaps overly friendly; people who stand too far away may be seen as aloof. Always be considerate, and do not violate another's personal space.

People's perception of personal space varies among cultures. We live in a multicultural society, and it is important to understand the difference between our perception of personal space and that of a co-worker from another culture. We should not assume someone is being rude because their communicating distance is shorter or longer than we are used to.

Eye Contact

It takes confidence to look directly into someone's eyes when you are speaking to them. Eyes are one of our most important nonverbal language tools—we use them to read the other person's body language and, in turn, they give off our own nonverbal messages. In Canadian culture, direct eye contact tells the receiver that you are interested and listening. In other cultures, direct eye contact can make a person feel uncomfortable or even threatened. Avoid prolonged eye contact in such instances, but bear in mind that a total lack of eye contact can send a message of disinterest or even arrogance.

If you find it impossible to look someone directly in the eye, try looking at a facial feature near the eyes; for example, the nose. This will give the appearance of making eye contact and may prevent that person's interpreting your discomfort as a sign of shiftiness or dishonesty.

Posture

Your posture, the way you stand, sit, and walk, tells others a story and can convey your level of confidence. By leaning toward someone, you show attentiveness; likewise, leaning away can show lack of interest and some level of reserve.

When you hunch your shoulders and keep your head down, it appears you have low **self-confidence**. When you puff yourself up, you may be showing aggression. When you cross your legs and arms, you may be perceived as being closed to the ideas of the person with whom you are communicating; uncrossed legs and arms may lead him or her to believe you are more open to the conversation.

Remember that your posture may not be telling the story you intend to tell, so be cautious about how your posture is perceived. A relaxed body posture will help you appear and feel more relaxed and confident.

Facial Expressions

The face is the most expressive part of the body. It is capable of many expressions that reflect our attitudes and emotions. In fact, the face speaks a universal language. Many cultures share the same expressions of happiness, fear, anger, or sadness. Others interpret your meanings from your facial expressions. You can reverse a misrepresentation of appearing aloof, disapproving, or disinterested by simply smiling. Your smile is the strongest tool you have. It can help you appear warm, open, friendly, and confident. Be aware of the impact this powerful nonverbal tool can have.

Because nonverbal language is far more powerful than verbal communication, it is imperative that you pay attention to the messages your body language sends. Smiling, making eye contact, using open gestures, and using good posture can project self-confidence. Being aware of your body language can help you send a consistent message.

Self-Check

1. Why is it important to dress appropriately in the workplace? What is considered appropriate dress?
2. In addition to your clothes, how do other aspects of the image you present contribute to a client's or supervisor's perception of you?
3. What does one's posture say about a person? Give examples.

LISTENING

Few people listen as attentively as they are capable of doing, and those who do have trained themselves to listen. Real listening is an active process. Being an active listener:

- shows the other person you care and want to understand
- shows the other person you are receptive to him or her talking to you

- fosters more meaningful, more helpful, closer relationships
- may reduce prejudice or negative assumptions about others because you get to know them better
- encourages others to view you as an enjoyable conversationalist and to open up more

Recognize that good listening skills can be learned, and adopt a plan for improving your listening skills. Tips to help you improve in this area include the following:

- Give your full attention to the person who is speaking. Concentrate on what is being said and on grasping the meaning of what is said. Avoid saying you understand when you do not.
- Become aware of your listening barriers, such as allowing your mind to wander, planning on what you are going to say next, or being close-minded about what is being said.
- Let the speaker finish before you begin to speak.
- Actively listen to what the speaker is saying.
- Repeat information (paraphrase) to ensure complete understanding. Ask questions if you are not sure you understand what the speaker has said.
- Take notes and confirm that what you understand is what was meant. Listen for key ideas.
- Don't judge until you fully comprehend what the other person is saying.
- Give feedback. Sit up straight and have good eye contact with the speaker. Nod your head now and then to show you understand. When appropriate, smile, frown, laugh, or be silent. These clues help the speaker know you are listening.

Self-Check

1. List four benefits to being an active listener.
2. What are three listening barriers you should avoid?

CONSTRUCTIVE FEEDBACK

One of the best skills an administrative assistant can possess is the ability to give and receive constructive feedback without sounding or appearing to be critical. Giving and receiving constructive feedback requires diplomacy, as well as sensitivity to the needs of other people. It also requires a high degree of professionalism, maturity, and experience.

Giving Feedback

If you are inexperienced in giving constructive feedback, the following tips will help you to be more effective:

1. If you make a practice of giving positive feedback when appropriate and on a regular basis, the negative feedback will be easier for the listener to accept. Your comments will be more credible if the listener is accustomed to receiving your positive feedback.

2. Phrase your comments as constructive feedback and not as criticism. Be certain to include what the listener has done well and what you see as areas of improvement. Ask the recipient for an opinion on how to improve matters. Perhaps the person will have a better solution than your own.

3. Be certain to describe the context of the problem. Always review the actions that led up to the problem. Just commenting on the problem without providing the details that surround it will lead to confusion and possibly no resolution.

4. Provide constructive feedback only when *you* are capable of doing so. If you are carrying around *personal baggage*, or if your emotions are running high, your chances of being effective are minimal.

5. Provide constructive feedback only when the listener is capable of receiving it. If it is obvious that the recipient is suffering from low self-esteem, perhaps offering friendly assistance is more appropriate than offering constructive feedback at this particular time.

6. Provide the correct environment. Never offer constructive feedback to an individual when there is an audience present. Show respect for the receiver by creating a confidential atmosphere.

7. Describe the facts; do not generalize or exaggerate. If the person has been late five times for your ten team meetings, say, "You have been late five times," not "You are late all the time." Ask yourself if your data are accurate. What you don't know for certain should not be promoted as fact.

8. Don't be judgmental. Comments such as "That's the worst report I've ever read" tend to belittle others. If your intent is to elicit a mature response, use discretion in how you choose your words. A better comment would be this: "I have detected five typographical errors and two missing sections in your report."

9. Don't state your impression of the person; instead, describe the problematic actions of that person. For example, if you say, "You are lazy," you are likely to receive an angry response. But if you say, "You have not completed your last three reports on time," you may get a more cooperative response.

10. Do not be a conduit for other people. Speak only for yourself. Comments such as "Everyone is concerned about . . ." are unjust. Rather, say "I feel concerned when you. . . ."

11. Don't ask the listener a question about her or his behaviour. Instead, state a fact. If you ask, "Have you been late for the last five meetings?" you are inviting defensive behaviour and encouraging the listener to lie for the sake of self-preservation. Simply state: "I have observed that you were late for the last five meetings."

12. Use a strategy that expresses how the person's actions make you feel, and ask for the person's feedback. Examples:

    ■ I have observed that you have been late for the last five meetings."

    ■ "When you are late, I feel disappointed because your input at the meetings is valuable."

13. Allow the receiver to comment, and leave the door open for a discussion.

    ■ I would appreciate it if you would attend every meeting on time because, as your team leader, I am depending on your commitment."

    ■ "How do you feel about this?"

    Then discuss alternatives and a possible compromise.

Receiving Feedback

When your supervisor is giving the feedback, there is no guarantee that it will be positive or constructive. The following tips are designed to help you work through an uncomfortable situation:

1. Attempt to relax. An employee who is being criticized for perceived lack of performance often finds this advice very difficult to follow. Remember to breathe deeply. When we become tense, we often breathe shallowly; when we do that, we aren't providing our body with the oxygen it needs to perform at its best.

2. As your supervisor is explaining the problem, listen very carefully. Take notes if possible and appropriate.

3. To clarify the situation, ask your supervisor questions that will help you to understand her or his point of view.

4. If you agree that you have mishandled a piece of work, apologize. Also, acknowledge valid points that are made by your supervisor.

5. Remember, if you feel uncomfortable with your supervisor's comments, you can ask for time before

responding. You might say, for example, "Thank you for explaining this; however, I feel uncomfortable with this situation. I'd appreciate some time to think about your comments. May we continue discussing this tomorrow?" Use this time to speak to a mentor and, if necessary, to collect facts. Be certain that you have regained your composure before meeting with your supervisor. This is preferable to responding in a way you will later regret.

PUBLIC SPEAKING

Be at Ease in the Spotlight

Speaking to an audience is the number one phobia for many people. Some speakers can learn to overcome this fear simply with practice, while others have a great deal of difficulty conquering the phobia. What works for one speaker does not work for another. Here are some useful suggestions that may help.

- Don't rush to the presentation. Give yourself plenty of time to travel to the location, find the room, and set up. You will need time to lay out your handouts, set up the computer and/or projector, flip charts, pens, et cetera.

- Know your topic inside out and become passionate about it. Your passion should override your nervousness.

- Stand behind a podium if possible. This barrier will help to hide shaky legs and hands.

- Prepare excellent visual aids. These will impress your audience and act as a guide to you for your presentation.

- Prior to the presentation, psych yourself up. Use music and relaxation exercises, and think of the best highlights of your presentation.

Given time and practice, most people can improve their verbal presentation skills so they can offer informative and entertaining presentations.

Avoid Anxiety

A great presentation requires a lot of planning and organizing of details. Whether you are giving the presentation or it's your responsibility to introduce or host the speaker, you want everything to go without a single hitch. But the chances are that something may go wrong, especially if you believe in Murphy's Law: "Anything that can go wrong, will."

With some serious attention to detail and thoughtful preparation, you can improve the odds. Here are some points to prevent presentation anxiety.

- If you are introducing the speaker, be sure you have adequate and accurate information to introduce that person.

- Be certain that the speaker arrives in plenty of time. This may include changing air flights or picking up the speaker at the airport. If there is plenty of time, there is reduced panic and pressure for both the speaker and the organizer.

- Most presentations require technical equipment, and technical equipment leaves plenty of opportunity for mishap. That's why it's imperative to have a backup plan whenever technical equipment is involved. For example, if a speaker is using a computer presentation, you should prepare overhead transparencies and arrange for an overhead projector and extra bulb—just in case! Does the microphone work? How does it work? Does the speaker need a mobile microphone? Does the speaker need a remote control for the computer projector? If you are uncertain about the technical setup, learn all you can about the equipment ahead of time; or you might arrange to have a technician in the room prior to the presentation.

---

pro-Link
Presentation Jitters

What will happen if you forget your words in the middle of an oral presentation? Will you stammer and stutter? Will you look foolish in front of the audience? These are common concerns that presenters often face. Here are some tips to prevent you from becoming speechless.

- Use your computer presentation or overhead transparencies as your guide. These visual aids are not intended just for the audience; they are also for you.

- Keep a set of notes, just in case you need them. If you do, the worst thing that can happen is that you have to read your notes. You will find comfort in knowing you have notes to rely on.

- Know your topic so well that you are the expert—and, better, get passionate about the topic so you are the passionate expert.

- Ask yourself what is making you so nervous that you are drawing a blank. If it's a particular person in the audience, stop looking at him or her. Your eyes can glance around the entire room and still avoid a particular person or location.

- If your presentations are usually peppered by pause words such as "um" and "ah," it may be a habit you need to break. Try attending public speaking classes.

- When you book the presentation room, if you are not familiar with it, visit the room to be certain it will accommodate the presenter, the audience, and the equipment.

- Rooms are full of surprises! You can never depend on the condition that the last group left it in. Chairs and tables may need to be rearranged. Flip chart paper and pens may need to be replaced. Where is the switch that dims the lights? Where is the switch that lowers the projection screen?

- Know the audience. Anticipate their needs, concerns, interests, and questions. If you don't do this research ahead of the presentation, you may be opening up yourself or the speaker to a potentially embarrassing situation. Not all audiences are patient and polite.

- If you are the presenter, know where your presentation can be shortened. Presentations often have a delayed start. If you need to stretch your presentation, some well-prepared questions for the audience will extend the presentation without too much extra work.

Self-Check

1. Compare constructive feedback with criticism.
2. How can you prepare yourself for a successful presentation?

ETHICS IN PUBLIC SPEAKING

When you speak to an audience, your audience must believe you to be credible, truthful, and qualified. Every statement you make, each figure you show, and each conclusion you draw must be supported by fact or based on credible information. Your audience will be attentive to your presentation, so ensure that your research has been thorough and that you are presenting accurate information. Use only information that you can confirm should someone question it.

What happens if inaccurate or incomplete information is presented? Consider the case of Olivia. As guest speaker at a workshop, she presented information that she had researched. After she spoke, several participants came to her and said they were familiar with the research behind the topic she had presented and were offended that she had not given appropriate credit for the material. Olivia apologized for not identifying the source. Even though this error was not intentional, it may affect her future presentations with this group; her apology may not have been enough to rebuild her credibility.

Always give credit where credit is due, whether presented in oral or written form.

WRITTEN COMMUNICATION

Excellent writing skills are among the most important skills you can possess. The business letter is one of the main vehicles for transmitting messages between the organization and its customers. You need to develop techniques that enable you to write well, just as you would use effective techniques in developing interpersonal communication skills.

BUSINESS LETTERS

The business letter is still the main vehicle for transmitting official messages to and from customers. An administrative assistant skilled in composing letters may write replies and originate correspondence.

The letters an administrative assistant writes fall into two categories:

1. those the administrative assistant writes for the signature of another person
2. those the administrative assistant writes as a correspondent for the organization

Whether letter writing becomes one of your major responsibilities will depend on the letter-writing talent you exhibit and on your manager's willingness to delegate the responsibility. Let the manager know that you are interested in writing letters, and give the manager a chance to see what you can do. Occasionally, answer a letter that has just arrived in the incoming mail. Key a draft of your letter, attaching it to the letter you are answering, and put it on the manager's desk in the stack of incoming mail. Be certain not to delay the usual letter-answering process by hanging on to the incoming letter too long.

By relieving the manager of the task of dealing with correspondence, you are increasing your value to the organization; you are also augmenting your routine duties with a challenging and creative administrative responsibility.

Effective Communication

Writing business letters is a significant endeavour (see Figure 14-1). Think of the business letter as your organization's representative, going out alone to do a job. Keep in mind that communication does not take place until the reader comprehends and responds to the message. Realize that the effectiveness of each letter you write depends on how well you have equipped it to accomplish its task. As you compose a letter, ask yourself this question: Will the letter

Figure 14-1 Excellent communication is necessary in both electronic and personal formats.

get the results I am seeking? Although you may learn many guidelines for writing letters, recognize the significance of giving more thought to reactions and to anticipated results than to rigid procedures for writing letters.

The person who writes outstanding business letters has learned to concentrate, weigh each word, anticipate the reader's reaction, and carefully organize every piece of correspondence to accomplish its purpose.

An effective business letter contains the essential facts. The words have been chosen precisely, and the sentences are grammatically correct and carefully structured. The letter indicates that the writer knows business procedures and policies and thinks logically. It delivers the message the sender intended.

Letters that convey a favourable message are organized differently from letters that convey an unfavourable message, and persuasive letters are organized in still another way. The basic principles for organizing different classes of letters are discussed as separate topics in this chapter. Certain qualities, however, are common to all effective letters. Incorporate these qualities in all the letters you write.

QUALITIES OF EFFECTIVE LETTERS

An effective business letter:

1. centres on a single purpose
2. focuses on the reader
3. conveys a meaningful message completely, correctly, coherently, concisely, clearly, and courteously
4. reflects a positive, sincere, and appropriate tone
5. uses natural, vivid, and varied language

Know Your Purpose

The purpose of a letter may be to inform, to create understanding and acceptance of an idea, to stimulate thought, or to get action.

Isolate the main purpose of the letter you are writing and develop your message around it. Make other points secondary to the main purpose; give the secondary points a subordinate position. Use one letter to do the job when you possibly can, but do not overwork your letter. Sometimes you will need a series of letters to accomplish one purpose. Unrelated topics that require answers should be presented in separate letters.

Focus on the Reader

Keep in mind at all times that you are writing for the reader. Know who your audience is, and show consideration for that person. You can do this by putting the reader's needs first, emphasizing words and ideas that will be meaningful and of interest to the reader.

Try to put yourself in the reader's place. Get to know the reader through the letters in your correspondence files, and try to visualize the reader in the reader's type of business. When you are persuading readers to accept ideas or to carry out suggested actions, remember that self-interest is a potent force. In your letter, show the same interest in the reader's needs that you would if you were talking in your office or over the telephone.

Convey a Meaningful Message

To ensure that your message will be meaningful to the reader, check it for completeness, correctness, **coherence**, conciseness, clarity, and courtesy (sometimes called the six C's of business writing).

Completeness If you are responding to a letter, in order for your reply to be complete you must answer all the questions the reader asked or discuss all the subtopics mentioned in the reader's letter. When you are making a request, ask all the questions for which you need answers. When you are originating correspondence, always anticipate the background information the reader will need in order to grasp the full meaning of the message. Also, anticipate the questions the reader will have when reading your letter; include the response to these anticipated questions.

Correctness Correctness means accuracy in every detail: accurate facts and figures in the content, perfect spelling of every word, flawless grammar and punctuation in every sentence, an absence of typographical errors, and an esthetically pleasing arrangement of the letter on the page. Inaccurate facts will confuse, and possibly irritate, the reader. Furthermore, they will likely delay the response. Always try to eliminate the confusion and extra correspondence generated by inaccurate, incomplete, or vague information.

You could contend that a letter containing misspellings and incorrect grammar and punctuation can still be meaningful, and you would be correct. However, inaccuracy of any kind reveals carelessness. A customer would be justified in wondering whether an organization that carelessly misspells the customer's name and omits essential punctuation would be equally careless in manufacturing its products or rendering its service. Just as the sales representative must make a good first impression, so must your letter. The only contact the reader has with your organization may be by letter. Give all the letters you send out a chance to make that all-important first impression. Do this by displaying them in an attractive professional **format** and by ensuring that they are correct in every detail.

Coherence

Coherence Coherence refers to the arrangement of words and ideas in logical order. Words and ideas must be arranged so that they flow naturally within each sentence, within each main paragraph, and in the transitional paragraphs that hold an entire communication together. A coherent communication is woven together so carefully that the reader is always sure of the relationship of the words and ideas. Numerous writing guidelines exist. See the following list of some of the more important guidelines for achieving coherence in writing:

1. **Put modifiers next to the words they modify.**

   WRONG: The rough draft was mailed on May 9 that contains the original specifications in plenty of time for you to revise it.

   RIGHT: The rough draft that contains the original specifications was mailed on May 9, in plenty of time for you to revise it.

2. **Express parallel ideas in parallel form.**

   WRONG: Mary's additional responsibilities this year have been writing letters and to handle travel arrangements.

   RIGHT: Mary's additional responsibilities this year have been writing letters and handling travel arrangements.

3. **Complete comparisons (or eliminate the comparison).**

   WRONG: The prices of the new homes in the Lakeside Addition are much higher than the Southside Addition.

   RIGHT: The prices of the new homes in the Lakeside Addition are much higher than the prices of those in the Southside Addition.

4. **Connect an agent to the right word.**

   WRONG: Before seeking applications for the position, a detailed job description should be written.

   RIGHT: Before seeking applications for the position, you should write a detailed job description.

5. **Place a pronoun close to a definite antecedent.**

   WRONG: Jason and Steve went squirrel hunting, but they were unable to find any.

   RIGHT: Jason and Steve went hunting for squirrels, but they were unable to find any.

6. **Use conjunctions in pairs to connect coordinate ideas.**

   WRONG: Mr. Arnett hoped to be transferred to Victoria or that he would remain in Halifax.

   RIGHT: Mr. Arnett hoped either to be transferred to Victoria or to remain in Halifax.

7. **Hold the same point of view.**

   WRONG: You either may deliver the claim papers to our branch office in Prince Albert, or they may be mailed to our home office in Regina.

   RIGHT: You may either deliver the claim papers to our branch office in Prince Albert or mail them to our home office in Regina.

Conciseness

Conciseness To write **concise** messages, use all the necessary words, but no more. Send the reader a complete message, but avoid obscuring the thought with needless words. To distinguish between completeness and a profusion of words, watch for irrelevant details, obvious information, and unnecessary repetition of words and ideas, and then eliminate them.

Concise is not the same as *brief*. When you concentrate on brevity, you run the risk of writing a message that is incomplete or curt, or both. A good approach is to write the full message and then stop. Notice the contrast in the following paragraphs:

Wordy: Should any premium that becomes due not be paid before the expiration of the grace period, which in reference to the above-noted premium will be June 15, 20—, said premium automatically will be charged as a loan against the policy in accordance with the automatic premium loan provision contained in your policy.

Concise: If this premium is not paid before the end of the grace period, which is June 15, 20—, it will be automatically charged as a loan against your policy.

Sentences can become loaded with words and phrases that add nothing to the message. Wordiness detracts from the message by slowing down the reader. To write concise sentences, study your phrases and omit the needless words. Compare the phrases in the "wordy" list to the words and phrases in the "concise" list:

Wordy	Concise
A cheque in the amount of	A cheque for
At the present time	Now
During the year 1812	In 1812
For the purpose of providing	To provide
In accordance with your request	As requested
Make an inquiry regarding	Inquire about

Wordiness also results from the inclusion of expressions—often called *trite expressions*—that convey no meaning. They are obstacles to concise writing because they are used in place of meaningful words.

For example:

1. **Trite:** It is as plain as the nose on your face.

   Better: It is obvious.

2. **Trite:** Our staff meets once in a blue moon.

   Better: Our staff meets infrequently.

Clarity Clarity in writing cannot be isolated entirely from completeness, correctness, coherence, and conciseness, but it does involve an added dimension: choice of words. Words have different meanings to different people. Therefore, you must choose words that will have the intended meaning for the reader.

To write a message that can be understood is not enough. You must write a message *that cannot be misunderstood*. Assume that if the message can be misunderstood, it will be; then make an effort to eliminate any chance of misunderstanding. This will force you to learn the precise meanings of words, to use familiar words, to explain technical words, and to avoid colloquialisms, slang, and coined phrases.

Words are symbols; they are tools of thought. Your goal is to choose words that will penetrate the reader's mind and create there the image you want. To do this, you need a vocabulary large enough that you can select the word that will convey your precise meaning. You must understand both the denotation and the connotation of the words you use. *Denotation* is the explicit dictionary meaning of a word. The suggested idea or overtone that a word acquires through association, in addition to its explicit meaning, is called its *connotation*. Avoid any word with a connotation that would be distasteful to the reader.

Write to express an idea, not to impress the reader with your vocabulary. This involves choosing words that

are familiar to the reader. Avoid **colloquialisms**, slang, and coined phrases because they may not be familiar. The reader may not know the meaning you give a word or phrase, and may have no way of checking on the meaning you intend.

Use a technical term when it conveys the meaning better than any other word, but write so skilfully that the reader grasps the meaning of the technical term. First use the term; then explain it either in a phrase or in a subsequent sentence or paragraph. The following illustrations of this approach are from newspapers; however, the same techniques for using technical terms well can be applied in writing business letters:

1. **Descriptive Phrase** A hypersonic plane *capable of flying 8000 km an hour* was envisioned by the president of the corporation.

2. **Phrase Set Off by Commas** On Friday, the country's largest banks boosted to 11 percent their prime, or *minimum*, lending rates to large corporations, making the higher charge almost industry-wide.

3. **Phrase Set Off by Dashes** The minister underwent a tracheotomy—*a windpipe incision*—yesterday to aid his breathing.

4. **Subsequent Sentence** A total of five companies competed for the contract to install a local area network (LAN). A LAN is a system for communicating electronically among a number of PCs located within close proximity.

Courtesy Your attitude toward the reader will have a noticeable effect on the tone of the letter. Even though your attitude is not described in the letter, it has a way of creeping in. Therefore, regardless of your feelings toward the reader, show consideration and courtesy by using words like *please* and *thank you*. Consider how different the following sentences might appear to the receiver. In the first, you are giving an order; in the second, you are asking.

You must tear along the above perforation and keep this portion for your records.

Please tear along the above perforation and keep this portion for your records.

Self-Check

1. What are the six C's of business writing?

Establish an Appropriate Tone

Your attitude toward the reader will have a noticeable effect on the tone of the letter. Even though your attitude is not described in the letter, it has a way of creeping in.

Therefore, to set the appropriate tone, examine your feelings toward the reader. Show consideration for the reader. Reflect a sincere attitude.

The tone of each letter must be appropriate for the given situation. Whenever it is appropriate, write informally and radiate a warm, friendly tone. Be courteous and tactful. Do not write sentences or inject words that you will later regret.

One way to achieve tact in business letters is to replace negative words and phrases with words and phrases that are positive in tone. Watch for negative words; do not let them creep into your writing. Compare the tone in the phrases below. The italicized words in the left column are negative in tone. They have been omitted from the phrases in the right column.

Negative	Positive
We are disappointed at your *failure* to include	We had hoped to receive your report
If you would *take the trouble to*	Please
You are probably *ignorant* of the fact	Perhaps you did not know
It is *not* possible for us to	We are unable to
We *must* ask that you send us	Please send us

Develop an Interesting Style

Writing style is a distinctive way of expressing ideas. Develop your own style. Give your letters personality. Be natural. Sound like yourself in your letters. Write as naturally as you talk—not exactly as you talk, but with the same naturalness. Trade in stilted and time-worn phrases for natural ones. Compare the phrases in the following list:

Stilted and Time-Worn	Natural
As per our telephone conversation	By telephone
At an early date	(Refer to a definite date.)
Enclosed please find	Enclosed is
This will acknowledge receipt of your letter	(Refer to the letter by date.)
Under separate cover	Separately

To make your letters vivid, choose words that give life to what you say. For example:

- Use active verbs, except when you want the statement to be impersonal.

- Make the subject of the sentence a person or a thing.
- Use specific, meaningful words. Use general or abstract words only when a concept has not yet been reduced to specific terms.
- Use familiar words and phrases in place of the unfamiliar.
- Use short words instead of long words. Here are some examples of short words that can be substituted for multisyllabic words:

Multisyllabic	One Syllable
endeavour	try
interrogate	ask
demonstrate	show
encounter	meet
purchase	buy
obtain	get

For variety, mix simple sentences with compound and complex ones. Choose the type of sentence that will most effectively convey the idea.

Increase Readability

Careful writing will contribute to the readability of your message. To increase readability, control the length of the sentences and the arrangement of the letter on the page. Below are some suggestions for increasing readability.

Sentence Length To change the pace and to increase reader interest, vary the length of your sentences. Write some short sentences and a few long ones. Short sentences are emphatic, but too many short sentences make the letter seem choppy and elementary. A few long sentences are effective, but too many of them will cause the reader to lose interest and will make the letter harder to understand.

Authorities who have studied sentence patterns have found that copy with sentences averaging 17 words in length is highly readable. For business letters, write sentences that average between 17 and 20 words in length. Do not attempt to limit the length of your sentences to 17 or 20 words; be concerned only about the *average* length of all the sentences in one message. Most word processing software programs have a **grammar check** feature that will send a message when the sentence is too long or incomplete.

Arrangement Arrange the letter on the page so that it is easy to read. Keep the paragraphs short. Try to condense the opening paragraph into four keyed lines or less. A one-sentence opening paragraph in a business letter is permissible.

Divide the rest of the letter at the logical points—that is, at the places where there is a change in thought. However, if a paragraph develops into more than seven or eight keyed lines, divide it into two paragraphs. Tie the letter together by arranging the ideas in logical order so that one idea naturally follows another.

If possible, vary the arrangement so that all the paragraphs are not the same length. End with a short paragraph. The end of the letter, like the opening, is a place for emphasis.

BASIC LETTER-WRITING PRINCIPLES

Most business letters fall into one of three distinct classifications. These are:

1. a favourable message
2. a disappointing message
3. a persuasive message

An effective letter must be planned. The classification of a letter provides clues for organizing it.

In order to supply a "yes" or "no" response, give an explanation, or speak convincingly, you must know what the organization's policies are concerning the topic being discussed. You must be absolutely sure that your reply reflects the current policy, not one followed at an earlier time or one that is being considered but has not yet been approved. If in doubt about a policy, always check to make certain your reply falls within the current policy guidelines of the organization. Correspondents who make statements that are not supported by, or are in disagreement with, the organization's policies can find themselves in embarrassing predicaments.

Incorporate the basic writing principles discussed here in your business letters. Use them as general outlines for organizing favourable, disappointing, and persuasive messages. You should not follow these principles rigidly; you should use them only as guides. You must alter them to fit each individual case and vary them to emphasize the specific purpose. You will find the favourable letter the easiest to write, for you know at the time you are composing the letter that the reader will be receptive to what you say.

Favourable Letters

Replies that carry a "yes" message, requests that you anticipate will be granted without persuasion, and goodwill letters are classified as favourable. You can use the following guidelines for writing all favourable letters:

1. Begin favourable letters directly with a favourable statement. Do not waste words getting the letter started.
2. Make sure the content is complete, correct, and clear.
3. Use a tone that reflects consideration for the reader.

4. When you finish the message, either stop or write an appropriate closing paragraph. Not all favourable letters need a specially prepared closing paragraph. Include one only when it improves the tone of the letter enough to warrant the time you spend composing it.

Replies When you are writing a reply, establish in the opening that you are doing what the reader has asked you to do. State this in the first sentence, preferably in the first main clause. For example:

Your antique eight-day clock, which arrived this week, can be repaired and adjusted to keep accurate time. It has been carefully inspected by our service department.

When you are sending something, say so in the opening lines. Thus:

All 16 rugs that you ordered are on their way. Riverton Truck Lines should deliver them to you on or before March 27.

When you are partially complying with a request, establish in the opening sentence what you are doing; then use the rest of the letter to explain why you are complying with only part of the request.

Do not restate the obvious. "We have received your letter . . . ," "This is an answer to . . . ," "I am writing this letter to tell you . . . ," and "This will acknowledge receipt of your report . . ." are not effective openings.

Check carefully that your reply is complete, correct, and clear. If the reader asked questions, answer every question, whether it was direct or implied. Whenever possible, make one letter do the job.

Some replies should end when the explanation is finished. When you write a closing paragraph, always end confidently. Avoid statements such as "I hope that I have answered your questions," or "I trust that this is the information you are asking for." An expression of willingness to comply, when it is used, is much more appropriate in the closing than in the opening. At times an expression of willingness to comply can be used to avoid the possibility of sounding curt.

All replies should be prompt; delay is disappointing and detracts from a favourable situation.

Direct Requests When you write a request that you anticipate will be granted without persuasion, make your major request in the first line of the letter. Do not hint; write directly. For example:

Please send me a copy of your booklet, "Tips for Successful Management of a Word Processing Centre," which you offered to those of us who participated in the word processing seminar you conducted in Quebec City on May 15.

If you use a subject line in your letter, do not depend on it to introduce the topic in the body of the letter. Instead, write the letter as though you had not used the subject line.

When you must ask questions, include all the questions to which you want answers, and arrange them in logical order. Word your questions to get the information you want. Do not imply that a yes-or-no answer will be adequate when you need a more complete answer. If you have a series of questions, number them so that they can be read quickly. Numbering them will also increase your chances of getting answers to all of them.

Provide the reader with an adequate explanation. If the explanation applies to the request as a whole rather than to a specific question, put it in a separate paragraph either before or after the questions. If, however, the explanation applies to a specific question, put the explanation close to the question it relates to.

When you are asking for confidential information, state that the information will be handled confidentially. Here are two examples:

> We shall appreciate your answering these questions and supplying any other confidential information concerning Mr. Green's managerial qualifications.

> All the information you supply us will be kept confidential.

Your title, plus a statement within the letter, should show that you have a right to be making a confidential inquiry.

In the closing paragraph, express gratitude cordially in first person, future tense: "I would appreciate . . ." or "I would be grateful. . . ." Avoid thanking the reader in advance. It is appropriate to express thanks only after someone has complied with a request. Set a deadline if it is appropriate or if it will expedite the reply. Note the following closing paragraph:

> The 20— directory of the Bridge City Chapter of IAAP is ready to go to press, and we want to include your name on the Education Committee. Please let me know by July 16 that we can count on you to serve on the Education Committee.

Special Goodwill Letters Thank-you notes expressing appreciation for a favour or for special cooperation, congratulatory notes to a business associate on a promotion or to an employee on an important anniversary with the organization, and a welcoming note to a newcomer are examples of goodwill letters. These letters should be concise, appropriate in tone, and timely.

The letter must convey that the sender delighted in writing it. The most important single element common to all goodwill letters is timeliness: they must arrive promptly. (Timeliness and appropriate tone are also the two important elements of sympathy letters.) The following letter was used to congratulate a business associate on an important promotion:

> How exciting to read about your promotion in this morning's edition of the Edmonton Journal. Congratulations! Those of us who have worked closely with you know how much you deserve this promotion to executive vice-president. Best wishes for your continued success!

Repetitive Favourable Replies Save yourself writing time by speeding up the way you handle favourable messages. When giving the same response over and over, stop composing individual letters. The method you choose for replying will depend on the number of replies and the equipment and personnel available. Consider the following ideas:

1. When you are mailing a catalogue or literature about your products or services, either send it without a letter or enclose a preprinted letter. Make a note on the request that the literature was mailed.

2. Use a form letter, but print it individually for each recipient. Prepare the form letter (primary document) on your word processor. Then merge the date, inside address, salutation, and any other variable information with the primary document. Each form letter will have the appearance of a unique document.

3. Prepare and store form paragraphs. At the time you are answering the letter, compose only the opening and closing paragraphs. Then merge these new paragraphs with the stored paragraphs.

4. Macro functions may be used with word processing software so that merging and printing a letter is a very quick and efficient process. The macro function allows you to program a series of instructions and store them under a single command. The instructions can then be carried out with a few simple keystrokes.

Letters of Disappointment

The letter of disappointment requires a lot of planning. More words are needed to say "no" than to say "yes."

Use the opening paragraph to reflect a pleasant, cooperative attitude. Perhaps you can agree with the reader on something. Begin closely enough to the subject of the letter for the reader to know that you are answering her or his letter. It often helps to think of a general statement you can use to begin the letter. Never state the refusal in the opening; but at the same time, avoid giving the impression that the answer is favourable. Also, avoid recalling dissatisfaction or stating dissatisfaction any more than is absolutely necessary.

If you are complying with a part of what was requested, either start with a discussion about what you are doing to comply, or include this discussion in the first paragraph.

The opening paragraph, or *buffer paragraph*, should lead naturally into the second paragraph. Your opening paragraph will not be effective if it is not a natural transition to the main content of the letter.

Your explanation should be courteous and convincing. Give at least one reason for the disappointing news before you actually state it. Whenever you can, ferret out reasons that are for the benefit of someone other than yourself or your organization. Make the disappointing news a logical outcome of the reasons you have presented.

Phrase explanations in impersonal terms. For example, say "Your order was incomplete," instead of "You failed to state the size of the sweaters you ordered."

To avoid delaying the disappointing news too long, do not give *all* of the reasons first; provide some of these afterwards. To improve the tone, subordinate the disappointing news; put it in the middle of a paragraph and in a dependent clause. For example: . . . *which we have not stocked for two years*, or . . . *that are commercially unsuccessful.*

When you are refusing a request, avoid leaving any room for doubt about the refusal. Do not apologize for the refusal. Eliminate negative words and phrases such as *impossible, must refuse,* and *very sorry to tell you that we cannot.* State what you *can* do instead of what you *cannot* do.

If you can suggest an alternative plan, do so at the end of your letter; then provide the reader with information on how to take up the suggestion. Otherwise, use an ending (often unrelated to the problem discussed in the letter) that will provide a pleasant tone.

The following three paragraphs are excerpts from a reply received by a teacher who had requested copies of teaching materials used in office administration courses. The first excerpt contains:

■ a general opening statement

■ an agreement with the reader

■ a partial compliance

You can provide your office administration students additional employment opportunities by offering a specialized program for students interested in becoming executive assistants. I am sending you the associate degree requirements for the executive assistant program at our college and a list of the topics covered and the textbooks used in each of four specialized executive assistant courses.

The second excerpt contains:

■ a courteous explanation

■ a reason for being refused

■ subordinated refusal

■ additional reasons

The students purchase kits of practice materials that I have prepared for use in the executive assistant courses. Since I am planning to publish these

materials, I cannot release them at this time. As the students use the materials in each kit, I make the essential revisions and hope to publish these materials, along with teaching suggestions, in the form in which I actually used them in my classes.*

The third excerpt provides a pleasant ending:

By all means, submit your proposal for an executive assistant program for approval. If you have specific questions that I might be able to answer about the development of your program, please write to me again.

Persuasive Letters

Persuasive letters are used for selling products, services, and ideas. The informative office memorandum should also be persuasive; that is, it should persuade the recipients to accept the ideas or changes mentioned in the memorandum. When you write a job application letter, be persuasive; after all, you are selling your qualifications for a job.

Letters selling ideas can follow the same plan as a sales presentation:

1. gain the reader's attention and interest

2. create a desire

3. convince

4. stimulate action

Instead of beginning a persuasive letter directly, use the opening statements to get the reader interested in what you are saying. Wait until the second paragraph to start explaining your proposal. In the opening paragraph, avoid:

1. using a question that can be answered obviously "yes" or "no"

2. depending on an explanation to arouse interest

3. using obvious flattery to win the reader's attention

Use facts to convince. Give the necessary details to show that your request deserves to be considered and acted upon. Do not phrase the explicit request until most of the reasons leading up to it have been stated. When you do make the request, state it directly; do not hint.

Maintain a tone of positive confidence. Do not apologize for your request, and do not supply excuses that the reader can use to refuse the request. When a negative element is involved, discuss it as a part of the explanation. Omitting any necessary part of an explanation usually results in additional correspondence and delay.

Close the letter by expressing appreciation and by restating the action you want the reader to take. Establish your appreciation cordially in first person, future tense. The recipient, having finished reading the letter, should know what is expected, how to do it, and the reasons for prompt action. If you have discussed these points at various places throughout the letter, you may need to summarize them in the closing. Discard generalities such as "early reply" and "at your convenience"; cleverly suggest a deadline.

The following four excerpts are from a persuasive letter about new parking procedures. Before the Miller Company purchased the parking lots, the employees parked on these same lots and paid high daily or weekly rates. Employees could park on any lot where they could find a space. In the letter, the Miller Company is asking each employee to cooperate by using the parking lot designated for him or her. The approach here is to point out the advantages that will accrue to each employee.

The first excerpt is designed to:

■ **gain attention and interest**

  Beginning Monday, June 1, you may park your car near the main office of Miller Company. The company has purchased seven parking areas near the main office to provide ample parking space for Miller employees.

The second excerpt is written to:

■ **create a desire to cooperate**

  To assure each of you a parking space near the building entrance close to your work area, we have assigned employee parking by departments. The parking areas have been designated by numbers, and parking area stickers have been distributed to the department heads.

The third excerpt will:

■ **provide ample facts**

■ **make desired action clear**

  To obtain entry and to park your car in a company area, obtain a sticker from your supervisor and display it on the lower-left side of the windshield of your car.

The fourth and final excerpt will:

■ **explain the benefit of action**

  Using designated parking areas should result in a smooth flow of traffic around the main office of Miller Company and enable you to enter and leave your area with ease.

CORRESPONDENCE FOR THE MANAGER'S SIGNATURE

Writing letters for another person's signature requires a special skill. It is not an easy assignment because the letter must sound as though the person signing the letter actually wrote it.

The letter that is the easiest to write for another person's signature is the letter report setting forth a series of facts. This is because the personality of the writer is not so apparent in factual reports. If the message is lengthy, another way to carry out the assignment is to write an informal report, to be accompanied by a covering letter actually written by the person over whose signature the information is transmitted.

When you have the assignment of writing letters for someone else's signature, study previous letters to become thoroughly familiar with vocabulary and style. Where possible use the same phrases; use the same salutation and complimentary close; and organize the letters in the same way. "Lift" paragraphs, making appropriate changes, from similar letters the originator has written. When feasible, prepare a draft of the letter and ask the originator to review it and make changes before you key the letter in final form. Be tactful; do not advertise that you are writing letters for someone else's signature.

CORRESPONDENCE FOR THE ASSISTANT'S SIGNATURE

From the first day on your job, you may be writing correspondence for your manager. As the need arises, you will write correspondence for your own signature.

Correspondence to the Manager

It is often more appropriate and more prudent to communicate by recorded memorandum than by speaking. It is useful when the corresponding party is absent or when a record of the event may be referenced at a later time. The memorandum is also a means of collecting independent or unrelated information that comes into the office, such as time-sensitive messages or schedule changes.

Use the electronic mailbox, voice mail, or a written memorandum to give your manager a reminder, a message, or an update on a particular transaction. Keep each reminder, message, or update separate so that your manager may dispose of it as soon as he or she has acted upon it. Be certain to date each of these pieces of information and to record the time. Your name or initials should always be given as a part of the information.

If the information is a telephone message, key the message on a message form. For instance, you might relay a telephone message as follows:

  Clyde Barker said that he cancelled the Thursday meeting of the Progress Club because two members of the group cannot attend. He has rescheduled the meeting for Tuesday, June 4, at noon in the Chamber of Commerce dining room. He is expecting you there. I made these changes in your appointment calendar.

Often when someone comes to the office but does not see your manager, you will receive information that you should pass on to your manager. For example:

Mr. Roberts from the facilities department delivered the extra table for your conference room this morning. The table was too large for the space in which it must fit. Mr. Roberts has returned the table to the warehouse and will deliver a smaller table tomorrow morning.

If your manager asks to be reminded of work that he or she must get done, write a memorandum something like this:

The report for the District 9 sales conference must be ready by November 19. You asked me to remind you to get started on this report at least one week in advance of the time you must present the report. Copies of the report for the previous period and the report for the corresponding period last year are attached.

To a letter that cannot be answered until additional information is received, attach a memorandum that calls attention to what is needed. State what you have done, if anything, to obtain the information. Do not write the obvious. Your message might be stated in this way:

As soon as I read this letter, I called Ms. Vance and requested the number of overtime hours worked by her department during the past year. Ms. Vance promised to have this figure ready for you by Friday. I believe this is the only additional figure you need to reply to Mr. Cummins's request.

Correspondence with Others

In carrying out your daily work, you may find yourself writing letters that you sign yourself concerning such things as appointments, requests, orders, routine replies, acknowledgments, transmittals, delays, and follow-ups. Use the title "Administrative Assistant to" followed by your manager's name. For your **courtesy title**, use Ms., Miss, Mrs., or Mr. Use appropriate courtesy titles when you are addressing others. Ms. is a female courtesy title that does not denote marital status. Use Ms. for women who prefer it and for women who do not indicate a preference. When a woman specifies her courtesy title, add it to your address list and use it. Do *not* use Ms. when a woman has given you another courtesy title.

Appointments Appointments are requested, granted, confirmed, changed, cancelled, and sometimes refused as a part of regular business procedure. Typically, appointments are handled entirely by fax, telephone, email, or voice mail. However, there are occasions where letters are required.

Letters concerning appointments should follow the same guidelines used when appointments are arranged by telephone:

1. Refer to the purpose of the appointment.
2. Clearly set forth the date, day, time, and place.
3. Request a confirmation of the appointment when it is applicable.

When postponing or cancelling an appointment for an indefinite period of time, always express regret and suggest some provision for a future appointment. When you are postponing the appointment, suggest another specific date, and ask for a confirmation. The following examples illustrate different situations that arise when appointments are handled by letter:

■ **appointment requested; time suggested**

Mr. Robert Arnet will be on the West Coast during the week of July 17. He is scheduled to be in Nanaimo on Thursday, July 21, and Friday, July 22.

Mr. Arnet asked me to set up an appointment with you concerning the production problems you described in your letter of July 7. Will it be convenient for you to meet with Mr. Arnet on Thursday afternoon, July 21, at 2 p.m.?

Sincerely yours,

Ms. Karen O'Brien

Administrative Assistant to Mr. Arnet

■ **appointment granted; time suggested**

Mr. Harrison will be glad to talk with you while you are in Charlottetown during the week of January 24. Will Wednesday, January 26, at 3 p.m. be convenient for you?

Mr. Harrison is looking forward to seeing you again and to hearing about the plans you have outlined for the Ritter project.

■ **appointment confirmed**

Mr. Hanson will be expecting you on Thursday, May 15, between 10:30 a.m. and 11:15 a.m. in his office, Room 783, to discuss the need for improved shipping containers.

■ **appointment confirmed in manager's absence**

Before Ms. Wilcox left on an out-of-town trip, she asked me to tell you that she will return on Thursday, June 12, in time to meet with you to discuss the need for temporary help in your area.

■ **change of appointment**

Ms. Thompson has been called out of town on business and regrets that she must postpone your appointment with her for 9 a.m., Thursday, July 16. Ms. Thompson will be back in the office on Monday. She suggested Tuesday, July 21, from 9 a.m. until 10 a.m. as a time when she could see you.

Please let me know if July 21 will be satisfactory. When you arrive, come directly to the fourteenth floor and ask the receptionist for Ms. Thompson.

■ **cancellation of appointment**

Mr. Darnell was suddenly called to our Edmonton office because of the tornado damage to our plant there. He regrets that he cannot keep his appointment with you for Thursday, July 29, at 3 p.m.

When Mr. Darnell returns, I will contact you in order to arrange another appointment that will be mutually convenient.

Routine Requests, Inquiries, and Orders
Use the suggestions presented earlier for writing favourable letters as a guide for writing routine requests and inquiries. Expect that the reply to your letter will be favourable. State the request or inquiry directly, include only essential information, and create a pleasant tone. These letters will be short. If the letter seems curt because it is too brief, add a sentence or two to improve the tone. Observe how these points are achieved in the following excerpts from letters:

■ **request for a publication**

Please send me a copy of your booklet, "21 Ideas: Tested Methods to Improve Packing, Shipping, and Mail Room Operations." We are continually searching for methods to improve our mailing operations. We look forward to receiving your booklet.

■ **request for information**

Mr. R. T. Wilson is interested in obtaining information about the notebook computer you have made available to your employees. Please send me the brand name of the computer and the name and address of the company that manufactures it.

■ **inquiry**

Ms. Jane Williams would like to purchase 125 copies of a booklet recently published by your organization, "Tips on Using Word Processing for Desktop Publishing." Is this booklet available in quantity? If so, what is the charge for 125 copies?

Orders are usually submitted on an order form. If you do not have an order form, include the essential information in a letter. Be sure to give the order number, quantity, an adequate description, the unit price, and the total price. When you are ordering several items, tabulate the information for easy reading. If you do not enclose a cheque, state how payment will be made.

Routine Replies
When a response is favourable, state it in the opening sentence. If you are declining a request, give at least one reason before you state the refusal. The message of a favourable reply carries a favourable tone; for this reason, even a brief message is effective. In a reply that may be disappointing to the recipient, add a sentence or a paragraph to cushion or soften the message.

When the reply concerns a meeting, repeat the date, day, time, and place. Following are some examples of routine replies:

■ **favourable reply about meeting**

You can count on Mr. Stephens to attend the Area 5 Board of Directors meeting to be held on Friday, March 24, at the Four Points Hotel, Kitchener, Ontario. Mr. Stephens plans to arrive Thursday night and expects to be present at the 7:30 a.m. breakfast meeting on Friday.

■ **favourable reply; material sent**

We welcome the opportunity to furnish you with the Right-Way teaching aids you requested. The material will be shipped to you from our Winnipeg warehouse. If we may be of further help in your in-service office course, please let us know.

■ **request temporarily declined**

Because of the heavy demand for the booklet "Guidelines for Today's Consumer," our supply is exhausted. This booklet is being updated and will be reprinted in quantity. I have made a record of your request for eight copies of "Guidelines for Today's Consumer" and will forward them to you as soon as they are available. We appreciate your interest in this publication. If we can be of service to you in any other way, please let us know.

Acknowledgments
Most acknowledgments either state or imply that another communication will follow. The administrative assistant often has the responsibility of writing acknowledgments when the manager is away from the office for an extended period of time.

Acknowledge correspondence promptly—preferably on the same day it is received. Be cautious about giving away business secrets; make statements about your manager's absence in general terms. Avoid making promises or commitments your manager cannot keep or would prefer not to keep. Make copies of the letters you refer to others and of the letters you forward to your manager.

What you say in an acknowledgment depends on what you are doing about the correspondence. You can acknowledge the letter without answering it, supply the answer yourself, say that you are referring the letter to someone else for reply, or let the reader know that you are forwarding the letter to your manager for reply.

Other uses of acknowledgments are to let the sender know that important business papers have arrived and to confirm an order when the recipient is not expecting immediate shipment.

Following are examples of the many ways acknowledgment letters can be used:

■ **acknowledgment; letter not answered**

Mr. Martin will be out of town on business for the next two weeks. Your letter, which arrived this morning, will be given to Mr. Martin for his attention on June 3, the date he is expected to return to his office.

■ **acknowledgment; letter answered**

Mr. Argyle has set aside every Wednesday afternoon to talk with sales representatives. Mr. Argyle is out of town on business, but he plans to return to the office on Friday of this week. He will be glad to see you any Wednesday afternoon that is convenient for you. Please telephone, fax, or write me to set up a definite appointment.

■ **acknowledgment; letter referred**

Your letter, outlining the difficulties with the equipment you recently purchased from us, arrived today. Mr. Chung will be out of the office for an indefinite period of time. In his absence, Mr. Walter Barbato, Equipment Specialist, is handling all of Mr. Chung's correspondence concerning equipment. I have referred your letter to Mr. Barbato, and you should hear from him soon. If you wish to call Mr. Barbato, his telephone number is 705-555-3501; his fax number is 705-555-3741.

■ **acknowledgment; letter forwarded**

Ms. Anderson is away on vacation. Since I do not know the title of her talk to be given at the Third Annual Conference of Fashion Designers, and because your letter seems urgent, I forwarded it to Ms. Anderson via fax. You should hear from her before your April 10 deadline.

■ **acknowledgment of business papers**

Today we received the Substitution of Trustee and the Notice of Default in the case of Hamilton Life Insurance Company v. John R. Hilton, along with your confirmation of recording them. Thank you for recording these documents and returning them to us.

Covering Letters

Covering letters are actually letters of transmittal. For a detailed discussion of how to write letters of transmittal, refer to the section "Writing the Letter of Transmittal" in this chapter.

A covering letter may be brief. It should, however, state what is being transmitted and whom it is from. The covering letter often mentions a focal point or a major highlight of the attached report. Here is an example of a short covering letter.

■ **covering letter**

Here is your copy of the report "Ten Years Ahead." Mr. Daigle asked me to send each member of the Camp Warwa Committee a copy of this completed report. He requested that all members take special note of the section on fiscal restraint.

Notices of Delay

Because success in business depends on quality of service as well as quality of products, you may be asked to notify a customer whose delivery of merchandise will be delayed. In the letter, include an explanation for the delay, and tell the customer what he or she wants to know most—when the merchandise can be expected. Do *not* promise delivery by a date that your organization cannot meet. The following is an excerpt from a letter sent when the delay was only 24 hours:

■ **notice of delay**

Your printing order for 20 000 customer order forms was promised for shipment today. Unfortunately, because of a breakdown in equipment and the additional delay of obtaining a part for the machine from Dartmouth, we are 24 hours behind in our printing schedule. Our machine is operating this morning. We will ship your order forms tomorrow.

Follow-Up Letters

Write a follow-up letter when you have not received something promised or due, or when you have not received a reply to a letter after a certain period of time. Keep a careful record of missing enclosures and other items promised, and write follow-up letters to obtain them. See Chapter 8 for additional suggestions concerning missing enclosures. Write follow-up letters also as reminders.

Be specific about what is being requested. If you are referring to an unanswered letter, send a duplicate of it. Avoid making the reader feel at fault. Notice the core content of the follow-up letters below:

■ **follow-up letter; missing enclosure**

In your letter of May 16 to Mr. Balint, you said you were enclosing a biographical sketch to be used in the brochure for the 47th Annual Conference of RNA. However, your biographical sketch was not enclosed with your letter. Since the conference brochure must be printed by May 22, will you please send your biographical sketch in the next mail?

- **follow-up letter; order not received**

  On March 12 we ordered 25 copies of your book, Management Under Stress. We have not received the books or an acknowledgment of the order. Since we need these books for a seminar that begins two weeks from today, please ship us 25 copies of Management Under Stress immediately. Mail the invoice to Mr. Arthur Shepherd, Director of Education, who will forward it to the accounting department for payment.

- **reminder**

  Ms. Yates plans to use your report on basic changes in inventory control when she meets with the Executive Committee on March 16. This note is a reminder that Ms. Yates should have the report on March 14 in order to become thoroughly familiar with it before her presentation on March 16.

- **reminder; lapse of time**

  We have not received your expense report covering the period from October 1 to October 31. As you know, we cannot reimburse any of the sales representatives until all the expense reports for October are approved by the comptroller. Apparently your October report has gone astray. Please mail us another copy.

- **reminder to confirm**

  This note is to confirm our meeting, Friday, May 31, at noon in the Chamber of Commerce dining room for the purpose of discussing membership activities in the Lethbridge Chapter of CMA for the coming year.

Appreciation Letters Many opportunities arise in business for expressing appreciation. Do not neglect to write thank-you letters. Be prompt in sending them, for they lose their effectiveness if delayed.

To let the reader know that the letter was written especially for him or her, be specific, as illustrated below:

- **thank-you letter**

  Thank you for sending your proposal for needed changes in the contract with dealers. Ms. Wilroy asked me to express her appreciation to you. Your proposal arrived in time for Ms. Wilroy to present your ideas to the Executive Committee, which meets this Thursday.

LETTER FORMATS

With the efficiency of email messages, fewer formal letters are being prepared. Further, unless the letter is very formal, contemporary letters usually adopt a basic style. The most popular and recognized formats are the full-block and modified-block letter styles. However, there are many acceptable formats for letters. When you are new to an office position, begin by following the letter style already used in the office. Once you have established some credibility, you may want to introduce one of the following styles.

Full-Block Letter Style

Figure 14-2 illustrates a full-block letter style. Note that:

- Every single line from the date to the initials begins at the left margin.
- Paragraphs are single-spaced.
- A double space separates paragraphs.

Figure 14-2 has used two-point punctuation (also commonly known as mixed or closed punctuation). This popular punctuation style uses only a colon after the salutation, a comma after the complimentary close, and no other punctuation at the ends of lines outside the body. These are general guidelines; spacing format will vary depending on software and templates used.

Modified-Block Letter Style

Figure 14-3 illustrates a modified-block letter. Note that the format is the same as the full-block style with the exception that:

- The date, complimentary closing, and signature lines begin at the centre and are keyed to the right of centre.
- Although not shown in Figure 14-3, the paragraphs are sometimes indented. However, the preference is to block them at the left.

Self-Check

1. What is the difference between full-block letter format and modified-block format?

CLASSIFICATION OF REPORTS

Reports are used in business primarily:

1. to inform
2. to provide decisions and recommendations

Figure 14-2 Full-block letter style with two-point punctuation.

MILLENNIUM APPLIANCES

3431 Bloor Street, Toronto, ON M8X 1G4
(Tel) 416-795-2893 (Fax) 416-795-3982
www.millennium.ca

05 September 20XX

Samuel Jenkins
Director of Architecture and Design
Abbotsford Contemporary Housing
1000 Mountain View Street
Abbotsford, BC V2T 1W1

Dear Sam:

We were very pleased to read about your recent promotion to Director of Architecture and Design, for Abbotsford Contemporary Housing. No doubt, you will add to the already dynamic team that Abbotsford has been building for the past three years.

Call me once you get settled into your new position. We should have lunch together and discuss a potential business partnership where Millennium Appliances, Inc., can supply you with top-of-the-line home appliances at a wholesale price. Millennium's quality appliances would work well with the very attractive contemporary designs you are putting on your new housing. I am enclosing our latest brochure showing our new kitchen appliances.

Again, congratulations on your promotion and good luck with your new challenges. I look forward to hearing from you.

Sincerely,

Charlene Azam
Assistant Vice-President of Marketing
Western Region

lr

Enclosure

Some reports are prepared merely to keep a record. Much reporting consists of presenting data in statistical form. For the data to be meaningful to the reader, however, someone who understands them must interpret them to determine what they mean and to express their meaning in clear language. Consequently, reports are written for the reader's benefit.

Reports can be classified in many ways. Some reports are classified on the basis of function, others on the basis of form.

Reports that inform without giving conclusions and recommendations are called *informational reports*. Examples of informational reports are personnel booklets on employee benefits and progress reports on the construction of a new building.

Reports that present an analysis and/or interpretation of data, and that perhaps recommend action as well, are called *analytical reports*. Market surveys and analyses of business conditions are examples of analytical reports.

Figure 14-3 Modified-block letter style.

MILLENNIUM APPLIANCES

**3431 BLOOR STREET, TORONTO, ON M8X 1G4
(TEL) 416-795-2893 (FAX) 416-795-3982
www.millennium.ca**

05 September 20XX

Samuel Jenkins
Director of Architecture and Design
Abbotsford Contemporary Housing
1000 Mountain View Street
Abbotsford, BC V2T 1W1

Dear Sam:

We are pleased that everything is going well in your new position as Director of Architecture and Design. Your leadership is no doubt adding value to the creative team of architects at Abbotsford.

We would like to thank you for your time and the information that you shared with us last Thursday, when you visited our Saskatoon engineering plant. Our production engineers were able to take immediate benefit of the innovative ideas you introduced. From the results of the ideas they have implemented to date, Millennium has saved 12 percent in process costs and a further 17 percent in delivery costs.

Based on these outstanding cost savings, we would like to formally invite you to our strategic planning session on 05 November. Our concept is to invite you as a consultant and provide you with an honorarium and an out-of-pocket expense account. Kindly let me know if you are able to participate.

Again, our thanks for your contribution to the Saskatoon engineering plant. I look forward to a positive response to our invitation.

Sincerely,

Charlene Azam
Assistant Vice-President of Marketing
Western Region

Some reports are specialized. The annual reports of corporations are financial reports to the shareholders; but, in addition, these annual reports perform a significant public relations function.

Reports vary in size from a short, one-page memorandum to enough pages to make a thick book. Reports also vary in writing style and format. Some are formal; others are informal. Whether a report is formal or informal depends on the relationship between the reader and the originator, the purpose of the report, and its length. Informal reports, in contrast to formal reports, do not always follow a prescribed format.

As an administrative assistant, you should first learn about the format and organization of reports. Eventually you will compose reports.

INFORMAL REPORTS

An informal report may take the form of:

1. a letter

2. a short internal report

3. an email memorandum report

Letter Reports

Letter reports are used as both internal and external means of communicating information, analyses of data, and recommendations. They are printed on letterhead stationery, and their layout is the same as that of a letter. They are single-spaced. Letter reports may contain all the parts of a business letter, but sometimes the inside address and the complimentary close are omitted. Letter reports are signed. The name of the originator is keyed at the end of the report, with adequate space allowed for the signature. Reference initials appear on the letter report in the same position as on a letter.

Letter reports differ from business letters in two main ways:

1. Headings are often inserted in the letter report to guide the reader to the different points covered in the report.

2. Tables are often used to summarize data.

Much of the content of a report is factual. The facts should be presented objectively; they should be written without being filtered or influenced by the writer. An objective presentation is stripped of all statements indicating personal opinions or impressions. To achieve objectivity, the writer presents the facts in the third person. However, a letter report can contain some statements written in the first and second person—for example, "I interviewed the managers of the Southern, Western, and Midwestern regions," or "Having studied the facts gleaned from these three managers and presented here, will you approve the recommendations contained in this report?"

A **subject line** may be used; if it is, it should appear immediately preceding the body of the report to serve as a title for the text of the report. Double-space before and after the subject line. The subject line may begin flush with the left margin.

The headings within a letter report may be either centred or left-aligned. For emphasis, they should be underscored, keyed in bold, or placed in all capitals. Triple-space before a heading; double-space after a heading. At least two lines of text should appear after a heading near the bottom of the page. At times you may have to leave additional white space at the bottom of a page to avoid separating a heading from its text.

Formal tables have titles, called *captions* or *headings*. If more than one formal table appears in the same letter report, the tables should be numbered. The table number, such as TABLE III, may be keyed in either capital or lowercase letters, but the title of the table should be in all-capitals. Sometimes a subtitle is also used. Key a subtitle in lowercase letters with the first letter of each main word capitalized. The table number, main title, and subtitle should be centred. See Figure 14-4.

Arrange the data in the table in columns under appropriate headings. It will often be necessary to show the source of a table. Key the source a double-space below the last line of the table.

When a letter report contains tables, spend some time planning the layout of the letter. Observe the following two rules for inserting tables:

1. When possible, an entire table should appear on the same page.

2. A table should be introduced in the text before it appears.

Figure 14-4 Numbered table with subtitle.

TABLE III			
COMPARISON OF DISTRICT SALES			
Information Technology			
DISTRICT	DOLLARS THIS YEAR	DOLLARS LAST YEAR	DOLLARS INCREASE/DECREASE
Northern	300 000	350 000	(50 000)
Western	560 000	500 000	60 000
Eastern	725 000	700 000	25 000
Southern	300 000	345 000	(45 000)

Use 2.5 cm margins for letter reports. Key the second and subsequent pages on plain paper of the same quality and colour as the letterhead. Key a heading on each additional page, using a form acceptable for the heading of the second page of a letter. Indicate the subject of the report, the page number, and the date.

Short Internal Reports

Short reports used within an organization may be written in an informal style. The tone as well as the organization of the report is informal; thus, first-, second- and third-person writing may be used in combination, and the report may be organized in a variety of ways. Informal reports differ from formal reports in length and purpose; however, the text of an informal report can contain the same divisions as the text of a formal report. Usually the preliminary pages used in formal reports—letter of transmittal, cover, title page, letter of authorization, table of contents, list of illustrations, and other items—are not included.

An informal report should have a title and contain at least the following three divisions:

1. an introduction, in which the authorization for the report, its purpose, and the procedures and limitations for compiling the data are stated

2. a presentation of facts, if the purpose of the report is informational; or, if the report is analytical, a presentation of facts *plus* an analysis of them

3. a summary, which may or may not include conclusions and recommendations

A detailed explanation of these divisions is given in the section concerning the divisions of a formal report (see "Organizing the Report").

Informal reports are printed on good-quality plain paper, 21.5 cm × 28 cm. They may be single- or double-spaced, depending on how the reports will be used. The margins are even—2.5 cm on the right and left—because the reports are not bound.

Headings and tables are used to speed up the reader's comprehension of the report. The suggestions given for incorporating tables in letter reports may also be followed when tables are inserted in the text of informal reports. You have more leeway in incorporating tables in informal reports than you do in letter reports. If the tables are long, you can key each table on a separate page and then insert these pages, properly numbered, at the appropriate places in the report. Doing this will save time you otherwise would spend planning the text so that each inserted table comes at the logical point in the text and also fits on the page.

Informal reports often follow a deductive arrangement of ideas. In the basic format of the deductive arrangement, the conclusions and recommendations are presented first and the supporting facts are presented last. In many ways, the deductive arrangement is the reverse of the logical arrangement, which is the standard format for a formal report. The ideas in an informal report, however, can be organized according to either the deductive or the inductive (logical) arrangement. Refer to page 302 for a discussion of deductive and inductive arrangements.

Email Reports

The email report has largely replaced the traditional informal memorandum report as a means of internal communication. Email is always less formal than letter reports and can be written using a combination of first, second, and third person. Inherently, email has TO, FROM, DATE (automatically stamped), and SUBJECT headings, which in the past distinguished the memorandum from other forms of informal reports.

Because email is a computer-based document-distribution service, memoranda and documents are quickly copied from one computer to another. The growth, speed, and convenience of this medium require the user to exercise caution and forethought before communicating. Many unintentional problems occur as a result of overuse and inappropriate length of messages, failure to credit the original author of text, impulsive or inappropriate use, and simple poor communication.

The administrative assistant should compose email with the same diligence as traditional memoranda in an effort to avoid many of the common problems associated with office email. Pay special attention to the following guidelines for using email:

■ **Become familiar with the email application.** Learn to use all features including those that provide security and confidentiality.

■ **Check punctuation and spelling.** Do not distribute an email document without proofreading for spelling and grammatical errors.

■ **Ensure confidentiality.** Obtain permission of others before forwarding confidential content.

■ **Don't assume privacy.** Emails are not secure. A good rule of thumb is that you should not send anything by email that you would not want posted—with your signature—on the company bulletin board.

■ **Special formatting.** Avoid the use of special **fonts,** *italics,* or bold type. Special characters are often read as emphasis and could be misinterpreted as adding an aggressive tone to your communication.

- **Include a salutation.** If you would normally address a person as Ms. or Mr., use "Dear Mr. Jones" or "Mr. Jones" as your salutation. If you would normally address the recipient of the email by his or first name, you may use "Dear Ann" or "Ann."

- **Use a meaningful subject line.** Recipients scan subject lines to determine the level of priority the email should be given. "Change in Policy" will not deliver as much impact as "Change in Vacation Policy."

- **Keep each email to one subject.** If you have two concerns to discuss, send two emails to ensure that one won't get overlooked or ignored.

- **Flag an email as important only if it is.** If you use the email feature to flag all mail you send as priority, you run the chance of having all of your mail handled as unimportant since recipients will not take the top-priority notice seriously.

- **Copy only people who really need the information.** Don't reply to all. Reply to only the individual(s) who should receive the information, especially if the information should be kept private.

- **Avoid inappropriate language.** Use courtesy and tact just as you would in regular postal mail. Do not use swearing or offensive language. In some companies, email administrators are assigned the responsibility to check emails. You could be risking your job if you write something inappropriate.

- **Do not open suspicious email.** If the subject says, "YOU HAVE WON THE LATVIAN LOTTERY," don't believe it! Either delete the message without opening it; or if you are doubtful, inform your email administrator so it can be dealt with properly. The message will likely contain a virus that, if opened, could harm your computer.

FORMAL REPORTS

The format and writing style of a report are determined largely by its purpose and length. Reports moving upward to top management are more likely to be formal than reports moving horizontally between departments. Long reports are easier for the reader to follow when they are arranged according to a prescribed format. For this reason, formal reports, which tend to be long, usually follow a prescribed format. Note here that any report can be presented formally or informally, depending on the preferences of the originator. The following discussion includes guidelines for preparing a formal report and for the proper arrangement of its parts, as well as suggestions for composing formal reports. Keep in mind as you review the guidelines provided in this chapter

that many companies will have their own format that they will want you to follow. Some organizations prepare a style guide for all employees to follow when composing a report.

Guidelines for Formatting

Your first encounter with a formal report will be when you key it. Someone else may compose the report, but it will be your responsibility to prepare in final form nearly all—if not all—parts of the text. You may also perform some of the necessary research for the report.

The material may not resemble a report when the originator first hands it to you. Take time before you begin the report to plan the layout and to itemize what is to be included in the final report.

Preliminary Steps Read enough of the report to understand its overall plan. Check all of the following items carefully:

- headings
- tables
- graphics
- accuracy of data
- possible inconsistencies

Ask questions such as these:

- Does the draft contain all the headings that are to be used in the final copy?
- Are the headings correctly related to one another?
- Are headings at each level constructed in a parallel fashion?

An oversight concerning a heading usually results in the need to reformat more than one page. To avoid an oversight, list the headings in outline form and consider how they relate to one another. Headings of the same level should be of equal importance.

To achieve parallel structure, notice the parts of speech used in the headings. If one secondary heading begins with a present participle (an "–ing" word), *every* secondary heading must begin with a present participle. If one subheading under a topic is a noun phrase, *every* subheading under this topic must be a noun phrase. However, subheadings under a given topic need to be parallel *only to each other*—not to subheadings used elsewhere in the report.

Before you begin, decide which tables should be inserted on the same page as the text that refers to them, and which should appear on "stand-alone" pages.

Determine whether any graphics (charts, illustrations, drawings, or photos) are being prepared for inclusion in the report. If there are, how many, and where will they be inserted? All visual materials are treated as belonging to the numbered pages and should be numbered. Allow for them as you number the pages of the text. Make a list of them so that you will not overlook a page that is to be inserted as the report is being assembled.

If you have any doubt about the accuracy of the data in either the tables or the text, get verification. Statistical analyses in the text are often based on data provided in tables and charts; this means that one wrong figure in the basic data can affect several pages of analysis.

Word choice and format should be consistent throughout a formal report. Inconsistencies often occur when more than one person is responsible for the writing of the report, and because a number of formats are acceptable. Be alert to shifts from one acceptable format to another. Select a standard style and be consistent throughout the report. Be alert, too, for poor grammar.

Margins The margins of a report should be uniform after the report is bound. Allow 2.5 cm margins, exclusive of the part of the page used for binding. Leave extra white space at the top of the first text page. Twelve or so blank lines is the suggested amount.

Always begin a new major section on a new page unless the report is too lengthy. In this case, be certain to number all the sections.

Before you begin, you need to know how the report will be bound. For most reports, a binding allowance of 1.3 cm is adequate. If the report is to be bound at the left, use a 3.8 cm left margin, unless you have determined that it should be more. If the report is to be bound at the top, allow at least a 3.8 cm top margin. Also keep in mind that when the report is bound at the left, the margin allowance for binding affects all centred headings. Of course, when word processing is used, the software automatically adjusts for this.

Spacing Formal reports may be either double- or single-spaced, depending on how the report is to be used and the preference of the author. Reports that are reproduced in quantity are often single-spaced and printed on both sides of the page to save paper and filing space. Reports to be mailed are often single-spaced and printed on both sides of the paper to save mailing costs. A periodic report should be prepared with the same format—including the same spacing—that was used in previous reports.

Double-spacing should be used between the paragraphs of single-spaced material. Single-spacing is used in double-spaced reports to display a list of items.

Even when the report text is double-spaced, single-space the following:

1. Quoted material of more than three lines.

2. An enumeration that occupies two or more lines. Double-space between the items.

3. A bibliographical entry that occupies two or more lines. Double-space between the entries.

4. A two-line notation below a table indicating the source of the data, even when the table is double-spaced.

5. Tables that have headings, unless the table is very short or appears on a page by itself and needs to be expanded to fill the page.

6. A title in the table of contents, in a list of tables, or elsewhere. Exceptions to this guideline are the main title of the report, a chapter, or major section, where the heading is too long to occupy one line.

Paragraph Indention Indent the paragraphs of a double-spaced report either five or ten spaces to indicate where they begin. Five-space indention is most common.

Since paragraphs in single-spaced reports are separated by double-spacing, paragraph indention in single-spaced reports is optional.

Subject Headings Headings and subheadings are used to show the reader the organization of the report. They point the reader to where the reader has been and is going. A good heading should indicate clearly the content below it. Headings enable the reader to locate specific sections of the report and to read or reread only those portions of the report that supply the information the reader is seeking.

The form and location of a heading should make its relative importance clear at a glance. Headings for all divisions of equal rank must be in the same format and occupy the same location on the page. Each heading must either be in a different form or occupy a different location than its superior (of which it is a part) and than its inferiors (which are its subdivisions).

Centred headings are superior to side headings in the same format. "All-caps" headings are superior to those with lowercase letters. Headings appearing above the text are superior to those starting on the same line as the text.

Headings should not be depended on as the sole transitional elements in a text. If all the headings were removed, the report should still flow easily from one section to the next.

Here are examples and explanations of headings most frequently used:

FIRST-LEVEL HEADINGS

The title of the report is the first-level heading. Since there is only one title, this heading should be written at the highest level, and no other heading should be written in the same form.

Second-Level Headings

Second-level headings are used to indicate the major divisions of a report. They are centred horizontally. The first and last words are always capitalized. So is the first letter of every other word, unless it is an article, or a preposition of four letters or less. The heading is usually underscored and/or printed in bold type. There should always be at least two second-level headings.

Third-Level Headings

Third-level headings are used as subdivisions under second-level headings. They are usually formatted exactly like second-level headings, except that they are placed tight against the left margin. See Figure 14-10 for an example of the first page of a formal report using first-, second-, and third-level headings.

Fourth-Level Headings. For further breakdown, fourth-degree headings are used. These are placed at the beginning of the paragraph on the same line as the text. They may be written in the same form as the second- and third-level headings. They should be separated from the paragraph by a period, and they should be underscored or printed in bold. They are often called run-in headings.

Fifth-level headings can be handled as a part of the first sentence of the first paragraph about each separate topic, as illustrated by this sentence. The key words at the beginning of the sentence are underscored or printed in bold, but the sentence is written as a regular sentence. Only the first letter of the first word is capitalized.

When any level of heading is used (that is, beyond the first-level or title heading), there must be at least two headings. If a section of a report contains only one heading and does not logically divide into two parts, write the entire section without subdivisions. Each section of a report is subdivided independently of the other sections; that is, third-level headings can be used in one section without being used in the others; fourth- and fifth-level headings can be used only where they are needed.

Two headings should not appear in a report without intervening text. Often, the discussion between headings of different degrees is a transitional paragraph that tells the reader what to expect next. Transitional paragraphs may be written last; for that reason they are sometimes forgotten. When you are studying the layout of the report and find a heading that is immediately followed by another without intervening text, ask the originator to add the essential paragraphs. Or, better, compose them yourself and submit them for approval.

Page Numbers

Number the pages of the report consecutively with Arabic numbers from the first page of the introduction through the last page of the supplementary sections. Examples of supplementary sections include appendices and reference pages. Number the pages in the preliminary section with small Roman numerals.

All pages of separate tables and graphic illustrations are counted and should be numbered when it is possible and attractive to do so. More than likely, the report will be collated and bound by someone who is not familiar with the report. Numbering all the pages is a guard against omitting and misplacing pages.

In the preliminary section, count the title page as *i*; but do not print the number. Number the remaining preliminary pages *ii*, *iii*, *iv*, and so on; centre these numbers horizontally 2.5 cm from the bottom of the page.

When a report is reproduced on both sides of the paper (*duplexed*) and bound on the left, it is best to centre page numbers at the bottom of each page. If page numbers appear at the top right on odd-numbered pages, they should appear at the top left on even-numbered pages. When you choose to alternate the page numbers from left to right, remember that this will also alternate the running heads. A running head is a heading printed at the top of each page.

Tables

Tables should be inserted in the text immediately following the paragraph in which reference is made to the table. A paragraph should not be divided by a table. A table less than one page in length should not be spread over two pages.

If there is no room on the page for the table to follow the paragraph referring to it, continue the text to the *next* page and insert the table immediately following the *next* paragraph.

A table that requires a full page should follow the page on which the reference to it is made. You can save time and avoid a last-minute rush by printing each table that almost fills a page on a separate sheet of paper. Following are the reasons why:

1. Tables are usually prepared before the report is written. You can prepare many of the tables in final form while you are working on drafts of the report. If you are not sure of the order of the tables at the time you are preparing them, you can number them before you print the final draft.

2. Preparing the text is faster when tables are not inserted on the page with the text.

3. Tables, because they consist of numbers and headings, can be keyed by someone else on different software and still harmonize with the prepared text.

All the tables in the report do not have to conform to the same spacing. That being said, tables usually are single-spaced. Treat each table independently, displaying the data in the most readable and attractive manner possible. A table may be landscaped (placed broadside on the page). When it is, the page should be numbered in the usual way, and the table should be inserted with the top at the left edge of the report.

Tables should be numbered or lettered consecutively throughout a report. When there are many tables, Arabic numbers are preferable to Roman numerals because the higher Roman numerals can be difficult to read. Key the table number, such as Table III or TABLE 3, in either lowercase or uppercase letters. Centre it horizontally above the title of the table. Key the title in all-caps above the column headings. If the title contains a subtitle, key the subtitle below the title. The guidelines for arranging titles, subtitles, column headings, and sources in a letter report apply to all formal tables. By using shading and double-lines, and by changing the width of lines, you can create attractive tables.

Quotations Short direct quotations of three lines or fewer should be enclosed in double quotation marks and incorporated into the text. The lines should extend from margin to margin. See the following example:

> *The study concluded that "most customers preferred to deal directly with a company representative" (Lyons, 2009, p. 74). This conclusion supports our recommendation to hire additional support staff.*

Direct quotations longer than three lines should be set off from the text, indented five spaces from both the left and right margins, and single-spaced. A quotation that is set off from the text is not enclosed in quotation marks. Refer to the following example:

> *Lyons (2009) surveyed corporate clients from several different industries to determine their preferences regarding customer service. He arrived at the following conclusion:*
>
> > *Regardless of their industry, most customers preferred to deal directly with a company representative. Survey respondents indicated that they were able to resolve their problems effectively and efficiently when customer service representatives replied to phone and email requests within three hours. (p. 74)*

To indicate a quotation within a quotation, use single quotation marks if the quoted material is enclosed in double quotation marks. However, where quoted material has been set off from the text (and thus is not enclosed in quotation marks) use double quotation marks to indicate a quotation within a quotation.

Occasionally words are omitted from quoted material. This is permitted if the original meaning is not changed. An omission less than one paragraph in length is indicated by an ellipsis, which is three periods in a row. An ellipsis may be "open" (spaces between the periods), or "tight" (no spaces). However, there is always a space *before* and *after* an ellipsis.

Documentation Documentation is used to:

- give credit to the source of ideas quoted directly or indirectly or paraphrased
- enable the reader to locate the quoted material
- lend authority to a statement not generally accepted

In business and scientific reports, citations are often placed within the text. This is known as in-text citation. Do one of the following:

1. State the facts as naturally as you would if you were presenting them orally.

2. Use the author's name or some other reference to the source at the logical point in the sentence, followed by the documentation in parentheses.

3. Give the citation at the end of the sentence—either state the author, date, and page number in parentheses or refer to a reference list, arranged alphabetically, at the end of the report.

At times you will need to refer to a source named in your reference list. There are many acceptable ways to credit sources. One effective approach, using MLA style, is to state the author's surname and the page in the source from which the reference is taken. The following is an example of a quotation where the source is given credit.

> *"People from other nations may be more attentive listeners" (Smithson 337).*

This tells the reader that the quotation was extracted from page 337 of Smithson's book, which is listed in the works cited list.

Business reports often use APA style to **cite** sources. When using APA style for in-text citations, you should list, in parentheses, the author's surname, the date of publication, and the page number for the quotation you have used. The following is an example of an in-text citation using APA style:

> *"This technique can be difficult for people to learn, because proper resources may not be available" (Smith, 2010, p. 207).*

If you wish to refer to an author directly by name before quoting him or her, the date of publication should follow the author's name:

> *According to Smith (2010), "Some people had trouble following the instructions, which prevented them from succeeding" (p. 207).*

These parenthetical citations let the reader know that the quotations are from a work by Smith, published in 2010, which is listed in the references list at the end of the report. Refer to Chapter 4 for more information on both MLA and APA styles.

Preliminary Sections

Key and assemble the preliminaries of the report after you have completed the text of the report. Among the items placed in the preliminary section of a report are the following:

- letter of transmittal
- cover
- title page

- executive summary or **synopsis**
- acknowledgments
- table of contents
- list of tables
- list of illustrations

Examples of some preliminary pages are shown in Figures 14-5, 14-6, and 14-7.

Supplementary Sections

Materials that add to the report but do not belong in its text are placed in supplementary sections. The pages of the supplements are numbered as a continuation of the page numbers used in the report text. There are any number of sources that explain how to format supplement pages. If you need more detail than provided here, consult a current office reference manual or internet reference source such as *The Research Guide for Students*.

References All sources used in preparing the business report are listed in the **references**, also called the works cited list or **bibliography** in academic reports. References you have cited in the text (see the section "Documentation," above) will necessarily appear in the references list, but, in

Figure 14-6 Table of contents.

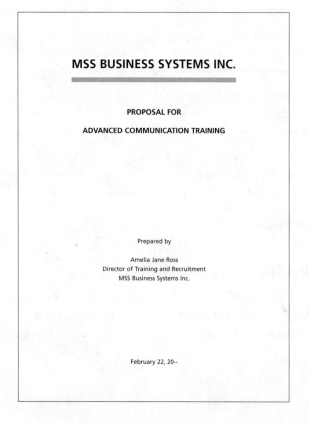

Figure 14-5 Sample title page.

MSS BUSINESS SYSTEMS INC.

PROPOSAL FOR

ADVANCED COMMUNICATION TRAINING

Prepared by

Amelia Jane Ross
Director of Training and Recruitment
MSS Business Systems Inc.

February 22, 20--

Figure 14-7 List of tables.

addition to those references, all work that you read but did not use directly in your report should also be listed. The reference list should include all references for information and ideas consulted in the preparation of your report. A report based entirely on the organization's own data (as numerous business reports are) would not have a reference list.

Materials obtained from the internet should be noted in the list of references. However, material found on the internet is more "temporary" than that found in traditional publications such as books and should be cited with the date that you last accessed the information. Refer to the internet entry on the example of an APA-style reference page, Figure 14-8.

The reference page appears at the end of the manuscript on a separate page or pages. Entries are listed alphabetically by the author's last name. Page numbers for reference entries are included only if the material cited is part of a larger publication, such as a book or journal. Figure 14-8.

As more graduate administrative assistants apply their skills to productive office work, traditional titles and headings for the supplementary sections are blending with those from the academic world. Though the titles and headings of supplemental pages may differ, the purpose remains to give credit to the authors of material from which you derived your information or ideas.

Appendix Supporting data that the reader will refer to while reading the report should be incorporated as part of the text; any additional supporting data should be placed in a supplementary section, called an *appendix*, at the end of the report. Examples of items placed in the appendix are:

- a copy of a questionnaire used in an investigation
- sample forms and letters
- detailed summaries of data
- graphs and charts

Not all reports contain appendices. When only one item is appended, its title is APPENDIX. If more than one item is appended, each item should be numbered or lettered under its own heading: APPENDIX A, APPENDIX B, APPENDIX C, and so on.

The appendix begins with a cover sheet stating the appendix number and the contents of the appendix. (See Figure 14-9.)

Figure 14-8 References.

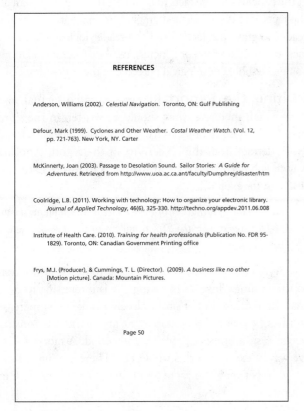

Figure 14-9 Appendix cover sheet.

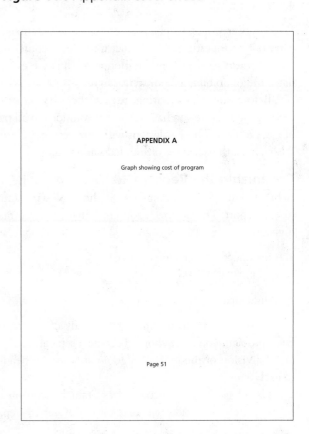

The appendices are the final items of the report. They follow the references. Each appendix, along with the page number on which it begins, is listed in the table of contents. (See Figure 14-6.)

Guidelines for Composing

Your first step in preparing a formal report should be to study the purpose of the report to determine precisely what the expected outcome is. You should be able to state the purpose of a report in one clear sentence.

Next, list the problems that must be solved in order to achieve the purpose of the report. The answers to the problems to be solved will become the main text, or body, of the report.

Do your research thoroughly and accurately. The content presented in the body of the report will be the result of one of the following:

- an analysis of data on the organization's operations
- secondary research, which is information gleaned from published sources
- primary research

The methods of primary research are

1. observation
2. questionnaire
3. interview
4. experimentation

In other words, to obtain your facts you may need to carry out an investigation, conduct interviews, confer with a few authorities, send out questionnaires, analyze existing data, and/or do bibliographical research.

Before you begin writing, review the purpose of the report to make sure you have arrived at solutions to all parts of the problem. Those solutions will form your conclusion. Also, check the accuracy of your facts and figures.

Organizing the Report Give your report a title that is broad enough to encompass all the topics presented in the report. Divide the report into at least three main divisions:

1. introduction (see Figure 14-10)
2. body
3. summary

Next, prepare an outline for the body of the report. Each problem you solve should become a separate division or subdivision of the body. Assign an appropriate heading to each one.

Use a logical arrangement of ideas. State the problem and how the study was conducted. Take the reader step by step, in

Figure 14-10 Introduction to a formal report.

logical order, through all the procedures you followed to arrive at the conclusion. Use facts to convince the reader. Present all the facts, and use tables and graphics to make it easy for the reader to grasp the facts. Lead the reader logically from the facts to the conclusion or conclusions. Any recommendations you make should be a logical outcome of the conclusions.

Writing the Report Reports must be factual and impersonal; therefore, they should be written in the third person. Strive for objectivity. Do not let "we," "I," and "you" detract from the objectivity of the report. Another way to achieve objectivity in writing is to report statistical findings, for example:

Sales in the first quarter of 20— were $77.9 million, a gain of 15 percent over the $67.8 million in the previous year's first quarter.

Avoid using words or phrases that reflect your reaction to the findings. Instead of saying, "It is interesting to note that the increase in net profit closely parallels the increase in sales," make a direct statement about the relationship between sales and net profit for the period. A more objective way of expressing this would be, "There is a direct relationship between the increase in sales and the increase in net profit."

Write as much of the report as possible in the present tense. A combination of past and present tenses may be used. The discussion about how the study, investigation, or analysis was conducted should be expressed in past tense to show the reader that the work is completed, not still in progress. Some business reports must be expressed in the past tense because the facts reported were true only on a given day or for a definite period. Examples of such reports are accounting reports, such as the balance sheet and the profit-and-loss statement.

When describing conditions that definitely have changed since the day the facts were collected, use the past tense. Use the present tense to describe conditions that to a large extent will still exist after the report is finished.

Write first the part of the report that is easiest for you to compose. Consider each main division and each subdivision as a separate topic. Most of the time, you can develop these topics in any order.

Before you begin developing a topic, carefully check all the facts and figures related to that topic. Next list your subtopics in the order that you will present them. Also prepare the tables and graphics you will use to illustrate the topic you are writing about. Carefully label all the columns of your tables and graphics. You can work from a draft or a sketch while these graphic illustrations are being prepared in final form, but keep copies of the illustrations in front of you as you write.

The graphic illustrations belong in the text of the report. Introduce the reader to each illustration before it appears by referring to it in the report. You may want to assign numbers to tables and letters to graphics in order to avoid confusion.

After you introduce a table or graphic, take the reader completely through it, to help the reader understand exactly what is being illustrated. Avoid constructions such as "Table 3 shows . . ." or "Chart 4 illustrates. . . ." Instead, begin sentences with the subject of the table or chart. Example: "A sharp increase in computer sales is illustrated in Chart 4."

Avoid beginning sentences with "There. . . ." You can strengthen the report by placing the key word of the topic being discussed in a prominent position at the beginning of the sentence. For example: "Telecommunications has made global business a reality."

Write your report so that the reader can grasp the important facts from the written copy without having to study the graphic illustrations. The reader should not have to read the headings to understand the topic.

A well-written report will be clear and meaningful even when all the headings and illustrations have been removed.

Interpret data at appropriate points so that they will be meaningful to the reader. Tell the reader what the facts mean in a natural, logical way. For the most significant data, give both the figures and percentages, or other computations.

By interpreting the data you will be presenting a picture, not just a string of facts and figures. Present the data to the reader step by step in the same logical order you followed when analyzing them.

Summarize your facts in the final section of the report. If you provided a summary sentence or paragraph as you developed each main topic, restate the content of the interim summaries in the last section of the report. Do not include new facts or new interpretations in the summary section. The conclusions and recommendations, if you write them, belong in the summary section and should be the logical outcome of the facts presented in the report. Make sure the recommendations are based on the conclusions. At the time you are given the assignment, establish whether you are expected to include recommendations. Sometimes when an executive assigns a report to a writer, the executive prefers to write the recommendations.

Usually more than one solution exists for a business problem. In the summary section, present all the alternatives. Present the most feasible alternative first; then present the others in any order, or in decreasing order of feasibility.

If you require a synopsis at the beginning of the report, write a synopsis and place it in the preliminary section of the report immediately preceding the first page of the text. When you include a synopsis, do not change the summary section; both belong in the report.

The introduction to the report may be written either first or last. The introduction should be brief. Subheadings are optional. Write the purpose of the report and the authorization in the opening paragraph without a heading other than the title of the report. In the paragraphs that follow, describe the methods of collecting the data and the scope and limitations of the study. Using the outline of the text of the report, list the topics in a paragraph in the same order in which they will be discussed in the report.

Read the entire report through from beginning to end at one sitting to examine how all the parts relate to one another. Do you need to add transitional paragraphs or sentences? Transitional paragraphs are guideposts that introduce what is coming next. They give direction to the reader. They may be written after the draft of the report proper is finished; in fact, it often saves time to write them last, because you can compose them more easily when you know precisely what you are introducing.

Writing the Letter of Transmittal The purposes of the letter of transmittal are to:

1. transmit the report
2. refer to the authorization (or request)

The letter of transmittal should indicate why the report was written; for that reason, the subject of the report, the authorization or request, and the date of the authorization or request should be included. These facts can be stated in the opening of the letter. Refer to the following three examples:

1. Here is the report on internet, television, and radio advertising possibilities that you requested on June 24.

2. In accordance with the authorization given in your letter of May 11, 20—, I have completed the branch plant location survey of Windsor, Ontario, and I am submitting a detailed report of my findings.

3. Following the instructions contained in your letters of July 2, 20—, and August 22, 20—, I am submitting the data you will need for selecting a brand of car to replace the two-year-old models now in the sales fleet.

The letter of transmittal should be factual. It should be written in a direct style because the main message is a positive one. Do not use the letter of transmittal to persuade the reader to accept your conclusions, and do not use it to defend your findings.

You may write in an informal style, using first person, even if the letter accompanies a report written entirely in the third person. You may use the past tense in the letter to show that the report is completed, thus:

I presented the analysis of the compact cars first because of the cost savings. In the second section of the report, I have made a detailed comparison between compact and medium-sized cars.

Letters of transmittal are usually short. Even so, they can also serve the following purposes:

1. show the purpose of the investigation and of the report

2. indicate how the facts were collected

3. give significant findings

4. orient the reader to the report

5. state the scope and the limitations of the report

6. point out special problems or special considerations

7. mention whether the report marks the completion of the investigation or is a progress report

8. state conclusions if it is feasible to do so

9. call attention to another study or investigation that is needed

Arranging the Report Reports may be arranged according to any of the following styles: inductive, deductive, or chronological.

The **inductive** arrangement is used when a report is lengthy, when it is difficult to understand, or when the reader must be convinced of something. The arrangement of ideas is in a logical order. The reader is taken step by step through all phases necessary to arrive at the conclusion. The inductive arrangement is the approach that was described in the preceding discussions on organizing and writing reports.

The **deductive** arrangement is used when the writer knows that the reader will be receptive to the findings in the report. Executives prefer reports organized by the deductive arrangement because they are easy to read. Because the significant findings appear at the beginning, the executive can read the first part only, or the first part plus selections from the supporting data.

The content of a report is the same whether it is arranged inductively or deductively; only the arrangement of ideas differs. The elements in a deductive arrangement are usually presented as follows:

1. an introduction, which includes the purpose of the report, the authorization, and how the study was conducted

2. a summary of the findings and conclusions

3. the recommendations, if any are given

4. the supporting data

Variations of this outline may be used.

Some reports consist mainly of historical background to a problem. When you must refer to situations that occurred at different times over an extended period, the best way to organize the report may be according to the time sequence, using the dates as the subheadings. **Chronological** reports are easy to write but difficult for the reader to comprehend. The chronological arrangement does not help the reader see how the parts of the report relate to the problem. For this reason, do not use the chronological arrangement when you can organize the data inductively or deductively.

ETHICS IN WRITING

Many businesses today have a written code of ethics that encompasses everything from ethics in business practices to ethics in receiving and writing email. Whether or not your employer operates under a *written* code of ethics, use the following guidelines to ethical standards in your writing:

- Make certain the information included in your writing is correct. Verify that your source is a credible one.

- Keep confidential information away from prying eyes. Place sensitive information in a folder when you are not working on it rather than just in your in-basket or on your desk where others might read it.

- Make certain the information you write is your own. Always give credit where credit is due when you use others' work.

- Never violate copyright laws. A copyright identifies the legal right of authors or artists to protect their work against unauthorized reproduction. Make certain you have the permission to use copyrighted material before you copy it.

Maintain integrity in your communications. Everyone in the organization is accountable for their actions, including you as an administrative assistant. Never agree to cover for someone else's mistake that might compromise your position. Make certain that you know where the information you work with comes from, and keep supporting documents should you be asked to justify or verify information.

INTERNATIONAL CORRESPONDENCE

You cannot assume that all the rules you have learned about business writing in Canada apply to other countries. Just as you must recognize the differences in cultures, you must recognize and adjust to the differences in rules for writing in those cultures. With the globalization of our economy, your learning must include international information to build your skills in this area.

Addressing Envelopes

When addressing envelopes to countries outside Canada, type the entire address in all capital letters. The postal delivery zone should be included with the city, when required. The country name must be typed in English, in all capital letters, and as the only information on the last line. Do not abbreviate the name of the country. For example:

> MR THOMAS CLARK
> 117 RUSSELL DRIVE
> LONDON W1P6HQ
> ENGLAND

Correspondence being sent to the United States will have *UNITED STATES OF AMERICA* as the last line of the address.

Writing Letters

Many Canadian companies have offices or plants outside Canada or do business with international companies, and it is highly likely you will encounter letters from outside the country. Letters from abroad may be translated to English before being sent to your company. The wording may differ greatly from what you have learned in this chapter or in a Business Communications class. For instance, the usual format for a letter written in Canada that gives bad news to the reader would begin with a neutral first paragraph that softens the blow by reviewing the facts leading to the bad news; then there would be an expression of the bad news; finally, a polite closing would be included to maintain rapport with the reader. In Germany, however, the buffer might be omitted, going right to the bad news. In Latin America, the letter might avoid the bad news altogether. In Japan, the letter may present the bad news so politely that someone from Canada wouldn't even recognize it.

Be aware that misunderstandings are possible, not only in the different writing styles but also in the translation from one language to another. It is sometimes difficult for translators to find the words to exactly describe a sentiment being expressed by the writer, and the message delivered may not be exactly as intended. The more opportunities you have to read and analyze business letters from abroad, the more you will become familiar with the differences in style and wording. Here is a beginning sentence from the translation of a Spanish letter into English.

> *I am grateful for the opportunity to write to you to offer you my catalogue. . . .*

If you received this business letter from someone in Canada, you might consider the language flowery and wordy." We would say, "Thank you for requesting our catalogue. . . ." Yet again, if the letter came from Germany, the writer would likely be more straightforward and say, for example, "We are enclosing our catalogue. . . ."

Your acceptance of cultural diversity should extend to business letters from abroad. Be patient, tolerant, and understanding, and remember the sender's culture is different from your own. This difference may be reflected in both the writing and formatting of the correspondence.

QUESTIONS FOR STUDY AND REVIEW

1. Describe five guidelines for giving constructive feedback and five guidelines for receiving feedback.

2. Explain five guidelines for coping with the fear of giving oral presentations.

3. Discuss seven methods for preventing the anxiety caused by presentation hazards.

4. What nonverbal messages are conveyed through the way you dress and the amount of personal space you allow other people?

5. Describe how eye contact can make the receiver feel comfortable or uncomfortable.

6. Discuss how posture can send a message of interest or disinterest.

7. Why are facial expressions considered a universal language?

8. Suggest four ways to improve listening skills.

9. Suggest how an administrative assistant can take initiative in answering correspondence.

10. List the qualities common to all effective letters.

11. When the writer is originating correspondence, what guidelines should be used to check the completeness of the message?

12. What is achieved through coherence in a communication?

13. Compare conciseness with brevity.

14. Compare connotation and denotation.

15. Summarize the techniques for using technical words effectively in business letters.

16. State the requirement for an effective opening sentence in a favourable reply.

17. What can the writer say to let the reader know that confidential information will be handled properly?

18. What is the most important single element common to all goodwill letters?

19. Describe the opening paragraph of a letter with disappointing information.

20. When should the request be stated in a persuasive letter? How should the request be phrased?

21. Assume that you have been given the assignment of writing letters for a manager's signature. What can you do to make your composition sound as though the letter were written by the manager?

22. Contrast the following letter styles: full-block and modified-block.

23. What are the primary uses of business reports?

24. What determines whether a report is formal or informal?

25. Where should the source of data contained in a table be indicated?

26. List three guidelines for email report preparation.

27. State three reasons why reports are often single-spaced.

28. What guidelines concerning parallel structure should you follow when composing headings?

29. Explain the main differences between fourth- and fifth-level headings.

30. What guidelines should be followed for keying direct quotations of fewer than three printed lines? What are the guidelines for more than three printed lines?

31. Describe the ordering of the supplementary sections in the report.

32. What are the differences between in-text citation and a reference page?

33. What is the difference between works cited/references and bibliography pages for academic reports?

34. State the guidelines a report writer should follow to help the reader understand the tables, charts, and graphs used in a report.

35. Compare the inductive and deductive arrangements of reports.

EVERYDAY ETHICS

The Blender

Your supervisor, Mr. Sims, Vice-President of Sales, has been away for three weeks on vacation and still has another week to go. You have been able to keep up with replying to a variety of inquiries, when needed, on behalf of Mr. Sims. Today, you receive a letter of complaint from a customer named Ms. Jans about a blender she recently purchased at one of your company's stores. The customer tried to return the blender to the location where she purchased it, but the store manager would not accept the return and told the customer that there was nothing wrong with the blender. In frustration, the customer has written to your office looking for resolution. Ms Jans's complaint is that the blender does not crush ice as she had expected.

You believe this can be quickly resolved by offering to replace the blender Ms. Jans bought with another model your company sells. In fact, your company sells three different models, each with its own unique specifications. It is a very busy day, but you want to prove to Mr. Sims that you can resolve any issue. Without confirming the specifications of the alternative blender, you draft a letter to Ms. Jans offering her the exchange. You mail the letter today.

■ What are the potential problems with your action?

Problem Solving

1. You are eager to write letters, and the manager needs help to keep up with the correspondence. This morning as you processed the mail, you selected six letters that you believed you could answer satisfactorily and put them in your desk drawer. At about 11 a.m. a customer called the manager and asked if he had received the letter that the customer had written to him. Your manager asked you about the customer's letter. You had to admit that you were attempting to

answer it. What did you do wrong? What would be a better plan for getting an opportunity to write letters?

2. The manager, Kathy Shapiro, left you an email with an attachment. Her email asks you to have 12 copies of the attached report ready for 8:30 a.m. tomorrow. The report needs to be edited, and tables need to be inserted. The tables are computer printouts that have been left on your desk. Kathy is out of the office for the day. With your normal daily workload—opening the mail, answering the telephone and email, and handling clients—you cannot complete the report before tomorrow morning. What should you do?

Special Reports

1. Obtain information about two similar office products that you have seen advertised in an office technology magazine or on the internet. Develop and write an informal report comparing the two products. Present both the final report and your rough development work to your instructor.

2. Imagine that you are employed in a professional office where the office manager is out of town for two weeks. Before she left, she asked you to acknowledge every fax that is addressed to her. However, you are not to answer the faxes; simply acknowledge them. Draft a fax message you can use as a guide for acknowledging the office manager's faxes in her absence.

3. Consider the excerpts from (i) a letter of disappointment and (ii) a persuasive letter on pp. 283–284. Rekey these excerpts and identify the component parts according to headings in the text. For example, which sentence or phrase is the "general opening statement"? Which is the "subordinated refusal"?

PRODUCTION CHALLENGES

Challenge A: Writing a Letter of Request

Supplies needed:
- *Current issues of newspapers/journals*
- *Plain paper*

You want to know more about desktop publishing. Search the current issues of journals or newspapers for advertisements about desktop publishing equipment and/or software. Write a letter to a vendor of desktop publishing software requesting information. Submit the letter to your instructor.

Challenge B: Preparing the Final Draft of a Manuscript

Supplies needed:
- *Draft for Work Improvement Methods, pages 430 to 433*
- *Plain paper*

Linda Yee is preparing an article on work improvement methods for publication in the company magazine. Key the manuscript in Form 14-B in final format using edits indicated to make changes. Watch for all formatting, grammatical, and spelling errors. Use double-spacing; print one copy for Mrs. Yee's files. Note: More error and formatting corrections are required than those indicated by Mrs. Yee, and you are responsible for making the article error-free.

Challenge C: Correcting a Letter

Supplies needed:
- *Letter for Correction, Form 14-C, page 434*
- *Common Proofreaders' Marks, page 453*

You were experimenting with your new software and quickly keyed a letter. You were not pleased with what you printed and decided to mark the corrections with your pen. The letter you keyed is Form 14-C. Mark the corrections needed using your pen and the Common Proofreaders' Marks.

Weblinks

Grammar Slammer
http://englishplus.com/grammar
This site contains a number of links to English grammar and composition reference materials.

Elements of Style
www.bartleby.com/141
Peruse William Strunk's classic reference book for writers, *The Elements of Style*.

Letter Writing Resources
www.writinghelp-central.com/letter-writing.html
This site includes information on letter formats and specific-purpose letters, and provides tips on effective letter writing.

A Research Guide for Students
www.aresearchguide.com
This site provides all the necessary tools to do research and to present your findings.

Listen with Your Eyes
http://humanresources.about.com/od/interpersonalcommunicatio1/a/nonverbal_com.htm

Here you will find articles on nonverbal communication and links to other sites with similar topics.

Intelligent Editing
http://www.intelligentediting.com/writingastyleguide.aspx
This site provides practical information on how to design a style guide for your organization.

Dress for Work Success: A Business Casual Dress Code
http://humanresources.about.com/od/workrelationships/a/dress_code.htm
Visit this site for a practical guide to business casual dressing at work.

Chapter 15

Office Commerce and Record Keeping

Learning Outcomes

After completion of this chapter, the student will be able to:

1 Describe the concept of e-commerce.

2 State the two areas of particular concern for e-commerce legislation.

3 Define the following: (a) cheque, (b) certified cheque, (c) bank draft, (d) bank money order, (e) traveller's cheque.

4 Explain the difference between a "payee" and a "drawer."

5 Prepare cheques.

6 Describe how to stop payment on a cheque.

7 Compare a restrictive endorsement, a blank endorsement, and a full endorsement.

8 Reconcile a bank statement.

9 Key a bank reconciliation statement.

10 List the standard procedures for keeping a petty cash fund.

11 Make out petty cash vouchers.

12 Prepare a petty cash report.

13 Describe payroll processing requirements.

14 Explain the administrative professional's role in budget preparation.

15 Report on the use of technology in commercial banking practices.

16 Research the Federal Privacy Commissioner's website in order to answer a legal privacy issue.

Handling office commerce is one of the more typical duties of the administrative assistant who works for a private company or for a small professional office such as a doctor's or dentist's office. This part of the job includes handling banking transactions, payments received, bank deposits, and cheques, and preparing bank reconciliations.

In large organizations, there is usually a department designed for the purpose of handling these commercial activities. Depending on the nature of the business, this department may be called the finance department, accounts payable department, accounts receivable department, or simply the administration department. All incoming cash and cheques are forwarded to that department. After invoices and statements are approved for payment, they are forwarded to the same department for payment.

Funds may be transferred electronically or by cheque, but both small private companies and larger organizations alike are moving toward establishing **electronic funds**

Margo Firman
Acting Superintendent—RCMP Administration

Royal Canadian Mounted Police Department
Regional Municipality of Wood Buffalo

College Graduation:
Office Administration Program
Keyano College
Fort McMurray, Alberta
1996

The Regional Municipality of Wood Buffalo is one of the fastest-growing municipal regions in the country as a result of local economic expansion in the oil sands sector. Such changes demand increases in government and services, something that Margo Firman has experienced firsthand.

Margo is the municipality's office supervisor for the RCMP detachment based in Fort McMurray. Her current role has expanded to include that of Acting Superintendent—RCMP Administration, a position created in 2003 in response to increased administrative and operational needs within the department.

Margo's new role is one with greater responsibility and authority for decision making. This includes leading and managing departmental resources to support delivery of policing services within approved budgets and policies. She researches and implements alternative methods of providing best-value service, which includes exploring funding and resource options, assessing risk, and conducting internal audits to verify management and service-delivery quality. In her role as Acting Superintendent, Margo provides a link between the RCMP and the municipality; as a member of the department's senior leadership team, she works to ensure compliance with contractual requirements and to ensure effective delivery of RCMP programs and services.

Margo's most challenging responsibilities are related to coordination of the municipality's current multiyear capital construction project to build a new facility to house the RCMP in Fort McMurray. Her ability to organize and manage multiple projects has allowed Margo to develop her leadership and management skills and to have an impact on the whole organization.

She continues to enhance her management skills from her job and continues to take courses that will help her achieve her goals. She is a great example of her own advice to future graduates: "Recognize and develop your strengths, have the courage to dare to take risks, and maximize your potential." Like Wood Buffalo, Margo's career is sure to continue to grow.

transfer (**EFT**) as an efficient and cost-effective method of moving money between accounts electronically. Electronic funds transfer is just one facet of e-commerce (synonymous with e-business) that is broadly defined on Canada Revenue Agency's website as the delivery of information, products, services, or payments by telephone, computer, or other automated media.

The agency's definition includes a broad range of business transactions that use electronic equipment to conduct trade. In fact, it covers any business transaction that may use the telephone, fax, automatic teller machine, credit card, or debit card, or involve a government service, business over the internet, or banking.

This chapter will introduce e-commerce from a banking perspective, as well as provide traditional banking and record-keeping functions essential to the professional administrative assistant.

THE E-EFFECT

These days we don't have to take our goods to market or demonstrate our services to conduct business. In fact, we hardly ever see real money—hard cash—the essence of our business.

E-Commerce

A major step in the evolution of business is the concept of exchanging goods or money (commerce) as a result of advanced (electronic) technology. Electronic commerce, or **e-commerce**, is simply an applied term for electronic file transfer, although e-commerce is also a broader concept. E-commerce may be considered as electronic file transfer between businesses or between businesses and their customers, but in each case it's a different application.

Business to business (B2B) transactions typically use private telecommunication networks. These networks were originally built to automate and speed up the exchange of data and information between companies that regularly did business together. Banks are a typical example of this type of exchange. Banks have been using **electronic data interchange (EDI)** for many years, exchanging account information and adjusting balances based on any number of activities. Despite being relatively unknown, EDI still forms the basis of most e-commerce transactions on the internet. It provides a standard exchange of business data from one computer to another computer. Documents exchanged in the EDI process contain the same information that you would expect to find in bank transaction, catalogue, payment system, or shipping information.

The internet has become the network of choice for business to customer (B2C) transactions. Consider Canadian Tire at www.canadiantire.com, one of the thousands of businesses that provide e-shopping opportunities around the globe. The company offers a wide selection of hardware and household items in addition to building and garden materials. Customers can use the internet to virtually shop their local store by browsing Canadian Tire's online catalogue, loading a virtual shopping cart, and choosing to pay by several methods. Delivery is scheduled, and you may sit back and wait for your goods. Personal banking, stock trading, and tracking a package with Canada Post are other examples of the way both businesses and consumers engage in e-commerce.

E-commerce is increasing in popularity for several reasons:

- It increases productivity.
- It improves internal business processes.
- It improves the relationship between business partners and the company.
- It increases sales.
- It reduces the cost of doing business. Sending orders and account information across a network is cheaper, faster, and more convenient than traditional methods of doing business.

Privacy When establishing e-commerce business facilities, it is prudent to study correspondents' privacy policy to be sure it agrees that customers' sensitive information will never be shared or sent over the internet without being encrypted. Many organizations subscribe to a certificate process for improved privacy and security. One form of certification confirms the identity of the internet user. This form of personal certification is used when you send personal information over the web to another user who needs to verify your identity. Other website certificates ensure that the website is bona fide and trustworthy. It is wise to check the certificates not only of websites that will receive your sensitive information but also those that deliver information—you need to know that such information comes from a known and reliable source. Many organizations supporting trustworthy websites subscribe to a third-party certification process that requires them to provide a safe, legal, and ethical internet environment. See, for example, Trust Worthy Website Certification, www.speedyadverts.com/html/trust_worthy.html.

Legislative Protection Through legislation, the government is supporting the reduction and control of e-commerce abuse in Canada. All regulations and laws that affect traditional business apply equally to those that practise e-business. However, certain business practices in the areas of consumer protection and privacy are of special interest. A working group committed to consumers, businesses, and government protection has developed a set of guiding principles for e-business. The principles call for:

1. clear disclosure of a business's identity, the goods and services it offers, and the terms and conditions of sale
2. a transparent transaction confirmation process
3. payment security
4. protection of personal data
5. restriction of unsolicited commercial email (spam)
6. a fair balance of liability in the event of transaction problems
7. timely and affordable means of complaint handling and redress
8. effective consumer education

See Industry Canada's site at www.ic.gc.ca/epic/site/ic1.nsf/en/home for research and information on consumer protection in electronic commerce.

Similarly, the government is acting to protect personal information with the *Personal Information Protection and Electronic Documents Act (PIPEDA)*, which deals with the issues of collection and disclosure of personal information, and the protection of information and privacy. The act generally considers email addresses as protected personal information. For reference and research, visit the Office of the Privacy Commissioner of Canada at www.priv.gc.ca.

Web-Banking

Most chartered banks offer business banking, investing, and insurance facilities to their customers on the internet. **Web-banking** provides easy management of banking transactions online wherever you have access to the internet. Primary functions of such services enable business customers to make electronic transfers between accounts and get real-time information on balances and transactions. Accounts may be viewed and manipulated "on screen" just as you might with more traditional methods of banking.

Establishment of a web-banking account is achieved by first visiting the company's bank to provide a company profile and, perhaps, to acquire software that is loaded to your PC or computer network. This software will allow you to make the connection with the company's bank and its accounts. In some cases, downloading the software may provide the connection. In either case, web-banking should be established with the assistance of a commercial banking expert at your company's bank.

Access to your web-banking services will depend upon the bank with which your company is partnered, and your company's unique identification and password. A unique password can be established for each authorized user of the business account. Commercial banking services are comprehensive but varied in their design. An example of commercial services may be found at the following website: www.tdcommercialbanking.com/index.jsp.

Mobile Banking

As a variation to web-banking most banks offer **mobile banking** also known as m-banking. Most chartered banks offer customers with smartphones, tablets, and PDAs access to banking services similar to web-based banking.

Automated Teller Machines

A gain in efficiency is often accompanied by a loss of personal contact. This is true of the teller service provided by the **automated teller machine (ATM)**. The customer's contact is entirely with the ATM and not with a bank employee. ATMs, located in banks and on just about every street corner, enable customers to obtain cash, make deposits, check the status of their accounts, transfer money between accounts, and pay bills. A simplified version of the ATM is the cash machine, which enables customers to check the balance of their accounts and obtain cash. Cash machines are often located in shopping malls, supermarkets, and gas stations to provide instant access to cash. To access the ATM or cash machine, the customer simply activates the machine with a magnetically coded card and enters a personal identification number (PIN) for access to the account. ATMs may be used in conjunction with web-banking accounts for access to information and cash.

Direct Payroll Deposit

Direct payroll deposit enables an organization to pay its employees without writing cheques. Instead, the organization furnishes the bank with a description of all payroll disbursements to be made to employees. The bank credits the account of each employee with his or her net pay and withdraws the amount from the account of the employer. The employer then sends a statement to the employee. The statement, often produced by a third party, shows gross payment, types and amounts of deductions, and the net payment. Usually, an organization makes arrangements for direct payroll deposit with several banks.

Preauthorized Payment

Another type of automated transfer of funds is the preauthorized payment. A preauthorized payment transfers funds from one account to another within the same financial institution. For example, a customer can arrange payment from a company chequing account to a loan account on a regular basis. In the office, preauthorized payments may be useful for repaying business loans or petty cash accounts.

Self-Check

1. Define the term *e-commerce*.
2. What types of issues does the *Personal Information Protection and Electronic Documents Act* (*PIPEDA*) deal with?
3. How does direct payroll deposit work?
4. Why would a business use preauthorized payments in its banking?

NON-ELECTRONIC TRANSFERS

Traditional banking services continue to play a major role in office commerce. Customers buy goods with cash, cheques arrive in the mail, employees need petty cash, and some suppliers may not have access to an e-banking service—but they need to deal through a company bank account somehow.

A company establishes a corporate account at a bank as a convenient means of transferring funds. In addition to the electronic transfer, a more traditional non-electronic instrument used for transferring funds is the ordinary cheque, which is defined as *a written order of a depositor upon a commercial bank to pay to the order of a designated party or to a bearer a specified sum of money on demand.*

The cheque is, in fact, a written contract between two parties in a financial transaction. The major benefits of using a traditional cheque are that the cheque is portable and that neither party needs an active computer network in order to initiate the transaction—the written cheque is simply handed over.

The parties to a cheque are the *drawer*, the person who draws the cheque on her or his account, the *drawee*, the bank upon which the cheque is drawn, and the *payee*, the person to whom payment is made. (See Figure 15-1.)

At the time that the depositor opens a chequing account, the depositor places on file with the bank a signature card showing her or his authorized signature. A depositor should always use that authorized signature when signing cheques. If you are to sign cheques for the organization where you work, your manager will ask the bank to honour your signature. You will be asked to fill out a signature card, thereby placing your authorized signature on file with the bank.

Figure 15-1 Cheque with notations.

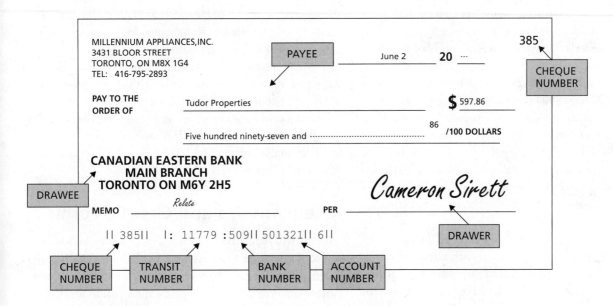

In addition to the ordinary cheque, the following are other non-electronic methods used to transfer funds:

- certified cheque
- bank draft
- money order
- traveller's cheque

Certified Cheque

A *certified cheque* guarantees payment to the payee by the drawee bank. To obtain certification, the depositor completes the cheque in the usual way and then takes it to the bank where the depositor has an account. After ascertaining that sufficient funds are in the depositor's account to cover the amount of the cheque, an officer of the bank stamps CERTIFIED, accepted, or guaranteed across the face of the cheque, signs her or his official name, dates the cheque, and immediately charges it to the depositor's account. The "acceptance" written across the face of the cheque is the bank's acknowledgment of its obligation to pay when the cheque is presented for payment. The drawer of a certified cheque cannot stop payment on it.

A depositor whose financial status is unknown to the payee can use a certified cheque as a means of payment. Certified cheques are commonly used when large amounts of money are involved. A certified cheque is required in certain business transactions, such as the purchase of real estate.

If a certified cheque is not sent to the payee, it should be deposited back to the depositor's bank account. This is because a certified cheque has effectively been withdrawn from the depositor's account upon acceptance and a reversal must be made to keep the account in order. A certified cheque should never be destroyed.

Bank Draft

A *bank draft* is a cheque drawn by a bank on its own funds (or credit) in another bank. The draft is made payable to a third party, who upon endorsing it may cash it at the bank on which it is drawn.

A bank draft can be used to transfer money to another person or organization in another geographic location. A bank draft payable in foreign currency may be purchased.

The process of obtaining a bank draft is quite easy. Simply provide the desired amount of money in the form of cash, a personal cheque, or a business cheque made payable to the bank. The bank will additionally charge a nominal administration fee. In exchange, you will receive a bank draft made payable to the person or organization specified as payee.

Money Order

A *money order* may be obtained from a bank. The service is used mainly by people without chequing accounts to send relatively small amounts of money through the mail.

A bank money order is negotiable, and requires the endorsement of the payee to transfer it. It may be cashed at any bank. The fee for obtaining a money order is nominal. The amount for which a single money order may be written is limited, but the number of money orders that may be issued to the same person to be sent to one payee is not restricted.

Traveller's Cheque

Most banks, trust companies, and select Canada Post locations, as well as travel-related companies and online affiliates, sell **traveller's cheques**. Some examples of issuers of traveller's cheques are American Express, Visa, and Thomas Cook. Most traveller's cheques are sold in denominations of $20, $50, $100, and $500 (Canadian). They are also available in many foreign currencies. Costs vary, but it would be safe to estimate a purchase cost of approximately 1 percent of the face value of the total purchase. There is no time limit on their validity. A traveller who plans an extended stay in a foreign country may find it economically worthwhile to purchase some traveller's cheques in the currency of that particular country.

Traveller's cheques may be purchased in person or online. When purchased in person, each cheque must be signed in the presence of an agent from whom the cheques are being purchased. When purchased online together with foreign currency, the maximum value must not exceed $1000. Orders made in this way must be delivered to your home or office where signature endorsements of the traveller's cheques will be made. Online purchase of traveller's cheques can only be made with a major credit card. The purchaser's signature on each cheque is her or his identification and protection. The purchaser can cash a traveller's cheque at a hotel or bank, at other places of business, or at an office that represents the traveller's cheques he or she is carrying (such as a Thomas Cook or American Express office).

Traveller's cheques are numbered serially. When you purchase traveller's cheques, you should prepare a list of the serial numbers on the cheques in duplicate—one for your files and the other for the traveller to carry, preferably in a place separate from the traveller's cheques.

When traveller's cheques are lost or stolen, the owner can usually obtain a refund immediately by contacting a representative office of the company whose cheques were purchased.

Self-Check

1. What are two advantages of the traditional cheque?
2. Who are the three parties to a cheque?
3. Besides the traditional cheque, list four other non-electronic methods used to transfer funds.
4. How does a certified cheque differ from a traditional cheque?
5. How would you obtain a bank draft?
6. How many times must the purchaser's signature appear on a *traveller's cheque*?

WRITING CHEQUES

Blank cheques are assembled in various forms, but the information to be entered in the cheque does not vary. Follow standard rules for writing cheques.

Many organizations use computers to prepare cheques. Cheques may also be prepared with a cheque-writing machine, a computer and printer, or a pen. Some businesses use cheque-writing machines as a safety measure against possible alteration of cheques. Others make use of commercially available software for cheque writing such as Intuit's Quicken or Simply Accounting.

Chequebooks and Cheque Forms

A bank will supply books of single cheques, as well as large books with three cheques to a page. One type has the cheque stub attached to each cheque; another type comes with a separate book for recording information about each cheque written.

Although banks will supply depositors with cheques, an organization may wish to use its own printed forms, called *voucher cheques*. The form of voucher cheques varies. When cheques are written by the computer, attached to the voucher cheque is a perforated form, called a *stub*, for recording the details of the cheque, such as gross payment, type and amount of deductions, and net payment. Some cheques are unbound in multiple copy packs. All cheques must bear a unique sequence number for identification and processing.

Rules for Writing Cheques

Follow these rules when you are writing cheques with a printer or a pen:

1. Make sure that sufficient funds are in the account to cover the cheque and bring the chequebook balance up to date.

2. If you are preparing cheques by computer printer, use a dark-colour ink cartridge whenever possible. If you are preparing cheques by hand, use a pen. (Faintly printed figures and letters are easy to alter; so are handwritten ones.)

3. If the cheque is in a chequebook that contains a stub record, number the stub to agree with the number on the cheque being written.

4. Complete each stub or voucher statement as you write a cheque. Fill in the stub before you write the cheque. When you are paying two invoices with one cheque, show each separately on the stub or voucher statement.

5. Date the cheque as of the day it is being written. Cheques may be dated on Sundays and holidays. Postdating a

cheque in anticipation of having additional funds in the bank by the date entered on the cheque could result in an overdraft, because the payee might present the cheque before the date shown and may even be paid. Postdating a cheque is permissible, but doing so should be avoided to protect the financial reputation of the organization. (If you receive a cheque that is not dated, write in the date on which you received it.)

6. Write the name of the payee in full without a title—such as Ms., Mrs., Miss, Mr., or Dr.—preceding the name. If the payee is serving as treasurer or chairperson, or in some other capacity, include the official title following her or his name to indicate that the payee is not receiving the money personally. Begin the name at the extreme left.

7. Before entering the amount, verify that the amount of the payment is correct.

8. Take precautions to protect the cheque against alteration. Enter the figures first, placing them as close to the dollar sign and to each other as possible. For even amounts, be sure to fill in the cents space with xx ("xx/100"). Notice how the figures are written in the cheque in Figure 15-2.

9. Enter the same amount in words. Capitalize only the first word. Begin the words close to the left margin and fill in the space following the words with dashes or a wavy line. Express cents as a fraction of 100. Write large amounts with the fewest number of words. For example, $4365.73 may be written in the following two ways, but the second example occupies the least space:

> *Four thousand three hundred sixty-five and 73/100.....
> ....Dollars*
>
> *Forty-three hundred sixty-five and 73/100............
> ....Dollars*

10. Verify that the amount expressed in words agrees with the amount expressed in figures. When the figures and words do not agree, the bank may choose to not cash the cheque.

11. If you make a mistake, do not erase or cross out the error. Although some people cross out, correct, and initial their errors, it is better to write "VOID" across the face of the cheque and the stub. File the voided cheque in numerical order with the cancelled cheques from the bank. Never destroy a voided business cheque.

12. If your manager is an authorized signatory, present the completed cheques to your manager for signing. Your manager should sign them in ink. Be prepared to disclose the original invoices and your calculations including applicable discounts.

Stop-Payment Notification

At the request of the drawer, a bank will stop payment on a cheque at any time until it has cleared the bank upon which it is drawn. Stopping payment is a safety measure that should be taken when a cheque has been lost or stolen; it may also be taken when a cheque is written for an incorrect amount, when certain conditions of an agreement have not been met, or for other reasons.

As an administrative assistant, you may stop payment of a cheque signed by your manager. To do so, first call the bank or access web-banking and request that payment be stopped. Give the names of the drawer and the payee, the date, number, and amount of the cheque, and the reason why payment must be stopped.

The bank will request a written confirmation of the verbal order to stop payment. The bank will ask you either to complete a stop-payment form or to write a letter of confirmation and fax it immediately.

Figure 15-2 Keyed entries on cheques.

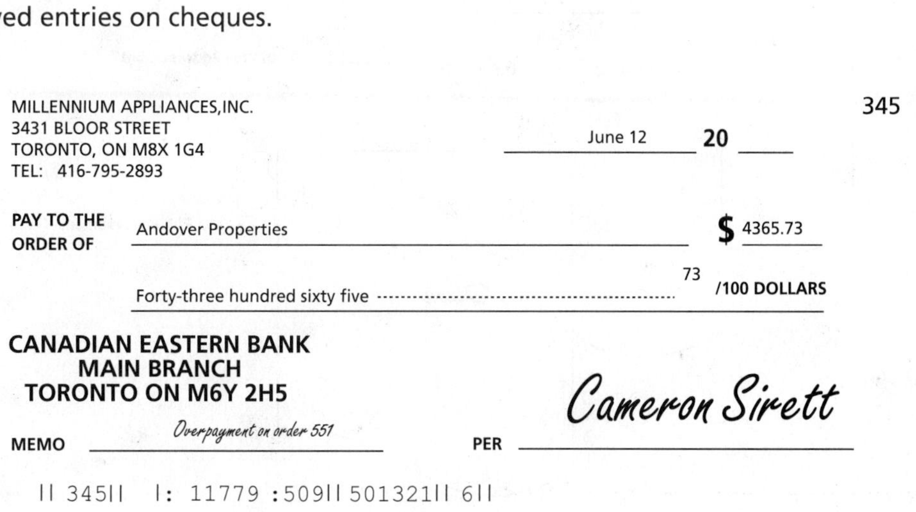

MILLENNIUM APPLIANCES, INC.
3431 BLOOR STREET
TORONTO, ON M8X 1G4
TEL: 416-795-2893

345

June 12 **20** _____

PAY TO THE ORDER OF Andover Properties   **$** 4365.73

Forty-three hundred sixty five .... 73 **/100 DOLLARS**

**CANADIAN EASTERN BANK
MAIN BRANCH
TORONTO ON M6Y 2H5**

Cameron Sirett

MEMO   *Overpayment on order 551*   PER _____

II 345II I: 11779 :509II 50132III 6II

When you are certain that payment has been stopped, write "stopped payment" across the stub of the cheque and add the amount to the current chequebook balance. Later, if the cheque is returned to you, mark it void and file it with the cancelled cheques. Depending on the circumstances, you may need to write a replacement for the cheque on which you stopped payment. There is often a charge for this bank service.

Cash Withdrawals

A depositor can withdraw funds from her or his personal chequing account by writing the word "Cash" on the line provided for the name of the payee, filling in the amount, and signing the cheque. However, since a cheque written in this way is highly negotiable, a depositor should fill in the cheque only when actually at the teller's window ready to receive the money.

One of your responsibilities may be to obtain cash from your manager's personal chequing account. If your manager hands you a cheque made payable to "Cash," be especially careful with it. Anyone who comes in possession of it can cash it.

Handle cash as inconspicuously as possible. Put the cash you obtain for your manager in a sealed envelope. Always keep cash that you obtain for others separate from your own funds.

ENDORSING CHEQUES

A cheque presented for cash or deposit must be signed (endorsed) by the payee on the reverse side of the cheque—preferably at the left end. A bank will accept for deposit cheques that have been endorsed by a representative of the payee. The endorsement may be made with a rubber stamp, or it may be handwritten in ink.

The payee should sign her or his name exactly as the payee's name is carried on the bank account. If the payee's name is written differently on the face of the cheque, it should be endorsed twice—first as it is written and then exactly as the payee's account is carried.

Endorsements are of three types: restrictive, blank, and full. See Figure 15-3.

Restrictive Endorsement

A restrictive endorsement limits the use of a cheque to the purpose stated in the endorsement. Words such as "For deposit only" or "Pay to" are written before the organization's name or the depositor's signature. As a result, further endorsement of the cheque is restricted. A restrictive endorsement should be used when deposits are sent to the bank by mail.

Since most organizations deposit all the cheques they receive, the restrictive endorsement is the most widely used on business cheques. On cheques to be deposited, the endorsement can be made by a rubber stamp. As the endorsement merely transfers the cheque to the depositor's account, a handwritten signature is not usually needed.

Blank Endorsement

A blank endorsement consists only of the signature of the payee. Because a cheque endorsed in blank is payable to the bearer, the holder should use a blank endorsement only

Figure 15-3 Endorsements.

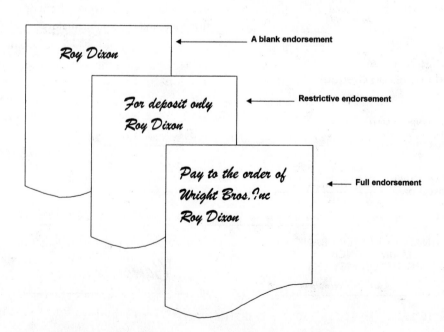

Roy Dixon ← A blank endorsement

For deposit only
Roy Dixon ← Restrictive endorsement

Pay to the order of
Wright Bros. Inc
Roy Dixon ← Full endorsement

when he or she is at the bank depositing or cashing the cheque.

Full Endorsement

A full endorsement transfers a cheque to a specified person or organization. "Pay to the order of" followed by the name of the person or organization to whom the cheque is being transferred is written on the cheque preceding the signature of the endorser.

When a cheque that has been received is forwarded to another person or organization, a full endorsement should be used to ensure that only the specified payee can transfer or cash it. To further negotiate the cheque, the endorsee must sign it.

MAKING DEPOSITS

While web-banking is taking care of day-to-day transfers between accounts and information on balances and transactions, businesses still need to deposit money into their accounts. Many organizations use e-commerce applications, which accept electronic deposits from customers, but cash deposits remain an administrative function of many retail-oriented and small businesses.

If making cash deposits is one of your administrative functions, make them regularly. In between times, keep cash and cheques in a secure place.

Present coins, paper currency (bills), cheques, traveller's cheques, money orders, and bank drafts to the bank teller for deposit, along with a deposit slip in duplicate listing what is being deposited.

Preparing Items for Deposit

Use coin wrappers supplied by the bank to package a large number of coins in rolls. Write the account name on the outside of each roll. The numbers of coins that can be packaged in different rolls are shown in this table:

Coin	Number in Roll	Value of Roll
Pennies	50	$0.50
Nickels	40	$2.00
Dimes	50	$5.00
Quarters	40	$10.00
One Dollar	25	$25.00
Two Dollars	25	$50.00

Put coins insufficient for a roll in a sealed envelope on which you have written the account name and the total value of the coins enclosed.

Stack bills face up according to denomination, and then enclose them in bill wrappers supplied by the bank. Write the account name on each wrapper.

Stack bills of varying denominations face up with the largest denomination on top and the lowest on the bottom. Place a rubber band around them.

Examine each cheque to determine that the amount of the cheque is correct, that the amount written in figures agrees with the amount written in words, and that the cheque is properly signed and not postdated.

Ascertain that the cheques are correctly endorsed either by a rubber-stamp endorsement or by a handwritten signature. Group together all cheques drawn on a given bank. Endorse money orders and bank drafts as though they were cheques.

If you are depositing returned traveller's cheques, write the traveller's name as payee on each cheque, and have the traveller countersign each one. If the traveller has accepted a traveller's cheque from someone else, enter the traveller's name on the cheque as a payee. Endorse traveller's cheques on the back.

Preparing the Deposit Slip

Keep on hand a supply of deposit slips, which are obtainable from the bank. These are often available as multiple-copy sets encoded with the depositor's account number.

Key the current date, the name exactly as it appears in the account, and the address. Add the account number if it is not already on the deposit slip. Some banks require a separate listing of coins and paper currency. See the sample deposit slip in Figure 15-4.

List each cheque by the drawer's name or the drawee's name. Use whatever system works best for your record-keeping purposes. Whichever you use, be consistent. When you cannot list all the cheques on one deposit slip, either staple two deposit slips together, or show on the deposit slip the total of the cheques being deposited and attach a separate list of the cheques. Present the cheques to the bank teller in the order in which you list them.

List a money order as "money order." List a traveller's cheque as "traveller's cheque."

Make sure that the total shown on the deposit slip is correct.

Depositing after Hours

Some organizations that collect cash and cheques after the close of banking hours use the night depository. For this purpose, the bank provides the depositor with a bag with a lock. The depositor places the deposit and deposit slip in the bag, locks it, and takes it to the bank at any

Figure 15-4 Deposit slip.

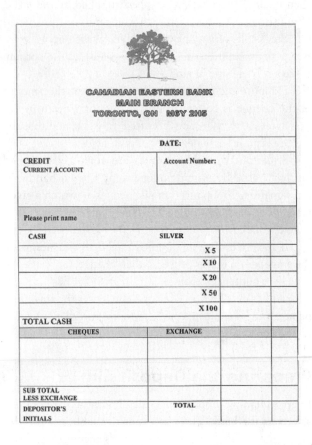

CANADIAN EASTERN BANK
MAIN BRANCH
TORONTO, ON   M6Y 2H5

DATE:

CREDIT CURRENT ACCOUNT	Account Number:		

Please print name

CASH	SILVER		
	X 5		
	X 10		
	X 20		
	X 50		
	X 100		
TOTAL CASH			
CHEQUES	EXCHANGE		
SUB TOTAL LESS EXCHANGE			
DEPOSITOR'S INITIALS	TOTAL		

time during the night. From the outside of the bank, the depositor drops the bag through a slot that leads into the vault. The next day the deposit is completed in one of two ways:

1. The bank teller unlocks the bag and makes the deposit.
2. The bank leaves the bag locked until the depositor arrives to make the deposit in person.

Self-Check

1. How might you protect a cheque you are issuing against alteration?
2. Give three reasons why you would stop payment on a cheque.
3. How should the payee endorse a cheque for deposit when the name on the cheque is written differently than the name on the bank account?
4. Outline how you would make a deposit to a bank after hours.

RECONCILING THE BANK STATEMENT WITH THE CHEQUEBOOK BALANCE

Each month, the bank issues a current bank statement to the depositor. If requested, the bank will also return all cancelled cheques that coincide with the current bank statement (see Figure 15-5). The cancelled cheques are the ones that have been paid by the bank. The statement shows the previous month's balance, deposits made, cheques paid, bank charges, and the ending balance.

Reconcile the bank statement with the chequebook balance as soon as you receive the bank statement and the cancelled cheques. Compare the final balance on the statement with the balance in the chequebook, and then account for the difference. Usually the two balances do not agree, because some cheques that have been written have not been presented for payment, deposits made since the date on the statement are not listed, and automatic subtractions and/or additions may have been made by the bank. For example, if there is a service charge for the account, the bank will deduct the charge. If monthly rental payments or other types of income are deposited directly to the account, the amounts will be added to the statement.

To make the reconciliation statement, assemble:

1. the current bank statement and cancelled cheques
2. the bank reconciliation statement for the previous month
3. duplicate deposit slips representing the deposits made since the last one listed on the previous month's reconciliation statement
4. the chequebook or cheque register

Adopt a Consistent Method

Use the same method each month to prepare the reconciliation statement. By working systematically and checking carefully, you should get the bank balance and the chequebook balance to agree on your first attempt. Here are the steps:

1. While the cancelled cheques are still in the order in which they are listed on the statement, compare the amount of each cheque with the amount on the bank statement. When they agree, make a light pencil mark near the amount on the cheque and by the corresponding amount on the bank statement.
2. Compare the deposit slips with the bank statement to locate any deposits that have not been credited on the

Figure 15-5 Bank statement.

Carter Enterprises
P.O. Box 782
Station A
Toronto ON M6Y 2J6

CANADIAN EASTERN BANK
MAIN BRANCH, TORONTO

Account Number: 820116742

CODE	DESCRIPTION	DEBIT	CREDIT	DATE	BALANCE
	Balance Brought Forward				4 061.74
CH	Cheque #66	26.17		04/11	4 035.57
LN	Loan Payment	500.20		04/11	3 535.37
MB	From Bank 2749-11		2 500.00	06/11	6 035.37
NS	Cheque Return NSF	200.36			5 835.01
SC	Service Charge	10.00		06/11	5 825.01
DC	Other Charges—Cheque Print	23.00		07/11	5 802.01
IB	Inter-Bank Transfer		8 274.92	09/11	14 076.93
DD	Direct Deposit		624.25	12/11	14 701.18
CH	Cheque #67	490.00		15/11	14 211.18
CH	Cheque #68	762.60		15/11	13 448.58
INC	Interest		56.07	17/11	13 504.65
DS	Chargeable Service—Insurance	79.64		18/11	13 425.01
SC	Service Charge	3.50		18/11	13 421.51
CH	Cheque #71	4 270.50		20/11	9 151.01
CH	Cheque #72	100.00		21/11	9 051.01
DD	Direct Deposit		272.82	23/11	9 323.83
DC	Other Charges—Cheque Back Fee	5.00		29/11	9 318.83
IND	Interest	21.00		30/11	9 297.83
	TOTAL BALANCE FORWARD	6 491.97	11 728.06		9 297.83

statement. As you make this comparison, place a light pencil mark on the deposit slip and by the corresponding amount on the statement.

3. Arrange the cancelled cheques in numerical sequence.

4. Compare the cancelled cheques with the chequebook stubs (or entries in the cheque register). If the amount on the cheque agrees with the amount on the stub or in the register, make a distinctive mark on the stub (or in the register) to show that the cheque has been paid. Next, make a distinctive pencil mark on the cheque—possibly in the upper left corner—to indicate that the cheque stub or register entry has been marked. (Marking the cheque is particularly helpful when several cheques have been paid to the same payee for similar amounts.)

5. On the bank reconciliation statement for the previous month, place a check mark by the outstanding cheques that have now been paid. Doing this will ensure that you locate any cheque from the previous month that still is outstanding. (Make a note on your to do list to follow up on any cheque that has not cleared through the bank within a few weeks of issue.)

6. Prepare the bank reconciliation statement. Either complete the form on the back of the bank statement or key the reconciliation statement on plain paper.

7. Make the adjustments that should be made in the chequebook or register, such as subtracting a service charge or adding interest earned.

8. Mark the cheque stub or cheque register to indicate agreement with the bank statement balance.

Prepare the Reconciliation Statement

To prepare a bank reconciliation statement similar to the one shown in Figure 15-6, proceed in this way:

1. Key an appropriate heading, including the company name, the name of the form (bank reconciliation), and the date.

2. Enter the chequebook balance and the bank statement balance across the top of the page. In the example, Figure 15-6, the chequebook balance is given as $9401.42.

3. List any credits to the account that may have been deposited automatically or without your knowledge. An example of an automatic credit is interest earned on your account. Add the credit to your chequebook balance.

4. List and add to the bank statement balance all deposits to the account that are not shown on the previous month's statement. In Figure 15-6, a deposit of $149.00

Figure 15-6 Bank reconciliation statement.

BANK RECONCILIATION Carter Enterprises December 1, 20xx					
CHEQUEBOOK BALANCE		$9401.42	BANK STATEMENT BALANCE		$9297.83

ADD:
  Interest Earned
	$56.07	$56.07
		$9457.49
			ADD:
			  Deposit of *11/30*
					$149.00
					$9446.83

DEDUCT:
  NSF Cheque Plus Service Charge
  Cheque Printing Charge
  Interest Charge
  Cheque Back Fee
  Service Charge
	$210.36
	23.00
	21.00
	5.00
	3.50
		$262.86
		$9194.63
			DEDUCT:
			  Outstanding Cheques
			  No. 69
			  No. 70
				$180.00
				72.20
					$252.20
					$9194.63

was made on November 30. This deposit does not appear on the previous bank statement.

5. List, add, and finally deduct the total of all bank charges from your adjusted chequebook balance. These charges would appear on the previous month's statement. Service charges and nonsufficient cheque charges, also known as NSF, are examples of these deductions.

6. Deduct the sum of all outstanding cheques from the adjusted bank statement balance.

7. Show both the adjusted chequebook balance and the adjusted bank statement balance. They should be equal.

Search for Errors

If the adjusted bank statement balance and the adjusted chequebook balance do not agree, first find out how much you're "out" by and look for that figure. Then, check the reconciliation statement. Are the figures accurate? Have you added when you should have subtracted?

Next, look for omissions of cheques and/or deposits. Have all the cheques written been subtracted from the chequebook balance? Have all the cheques that have not cleared through the bank been listed as outstanding cheques on the reconciliation statement? Have all the deposits been included on the reconciliation statement?

If you still have not located the error, check for an arithmetical mistake in the cheque stubs. When you find one, mark the correction in two places. On the stub where the error occurs, write "Should be" followed by the correct amount. Make the compensating adjustment at the bottom of the last stub used or in the first blank line of the cheque register.

File Cancelled Cheques

Organizations that are committed to web-banking often do not request the return of their cancelled cheques. Instead, they rely on the virtual bank statement for reconciliation. For those that prefer the security of possession of the cancelled cheques, they do offer legal and tangible evidence of payment.

The system you use for filing cheques will be governed by the frequency with which you must refer to them. File the current bank reconciliation statement so that it will be accessible next month. File statements in chronological order, placing the most recent in front. You can either keep the cancelled cheques inside the folded bank statements or file the cheques separately in numerical order.

The retention period for the cheques and the method of disposing of them will be determined by the organization's policy. The person in your organization who is responsible for records retention will provide you with information about destroying cheques. Records retention was discussed in Chapter 10.

KEEPING RECORDS

Most organizations keep their accounting records on computer. Accounting is a separate business function, performed by accountants; record keeping occurs wherever a record originates. Consequently, office professionals maintain and assist with various financial records. Some administrative assistants, especially those who work for owners of small businesses, help their managers with personal business records.

You can expect to be responsible for a petty cash fund. You may be asked to keep a record of office supplies on hand or to assist with payroll records.

Petty Cash Fund

When the amount of an office expenditure is small and payment should be made immediately, it may be more convenient to make the payment by cash than by cheque. To provide cash to pay for incidental items, such as ad hoc courier service, postage due on packages, or emergency purchases of office supplies, organizations establish a petty cash fund. These funds usually range from $20 to $100 or more, depending on the cash needs for a period of time—perhaps a month. Even though the petty cash is used to make miscellaneous payments, it must still be accounted for.

Generally, the administrative assistant is responsible for handling the petty cash fund. When you are the one who keeps track of petty cash, observe the following standard procedures:

1. Keep the cash and the completed vouchers (see Figure 15-7) in a box or an envelope, and put them in a safe place. They should be in a locked desk drawer or file or in an office safe. Balance the petty cash record at least once a week. If the cash and vouchers are left unlocked, balance the record at the end of each day.
2. Prepare a petty cash voucher for each expenditure you make. The voucher, which is a receipt, should show the amount paid, the date to whom the payment was made, the purpose of the payment, the expense category to which the payment will be charged, and the signature or initials of the person authorizing payment. Some organizations also require the signature or initials of the person receiving payment. Unless the accounting department stipulates that the vouchers be machine printed, write them, using a pen; this way, you complete the voucher quickly at the time you are making the payment and without interrupting work you may have in the printer.
3. Keep an accurate petty cash record, using either a petty cash book or a distribution sheet or envelope (see Figure 15-8). For each payment from the petty cash fund, enter the date, the amount, the voucher number, and an explanation in the petty cash report (see Figure 15-9). Total expenditures plus cash on hand should equal the original amount of the petty cash fund.

   Some petty cash books provide columns for expense categories; others do not. The columns and the appropriate headings for the petty cash record can be printed on a sheet of paper or a manila envelope. Accounting departments often supply manila envelopes imprinted with columns and headings for the petty cash record, including columns for the distribution of payments.

   A petty cash record with columns for the distribution of payments is shown in Figure 15-8. Posting the expenditures to the columns provided for each predetermined expense category simplifies preparing the summary of expenditures when you need to replenish the petty cash fund.

Figure 15-7 Petty cash voucher.

Amount: *$4.96* Voucher No.: *170*

PETTY CASH VOUCHER

For: *Pencils*
Paid to: *Ben Ross*
Charge to: *Supplies*
Date: *June 9, 20xx*
Approved by: *E. Miller*
Comments: *For stock replenishment*

pro-Link
Fraud Filter

Fraud in the office can be an expensive proposition for any organization. According to the Association of Certified Fraud Examiners (ACFE), small business is the most vulnerable to three main types of fraud and abuse: misappropriation, fraudulent statements, and bribery and corruption.

Here are some preventative tips for *your* office:

- Designate a front-line receptionist to open the mail and systematically list all cheques before passing them on to the accounting department.
- Develop cheque-signing limits. For example, the administrative assistant may sign for $100, the manager $1000, the executive $10 000, et cetera.
- Pay attention to your bookkeeping practices. Have your work periodically reviewed by a colleague as a "sanity" check.
- Establish a dual signature practice for cheques, but do not sign cheques in advance of your absence.
- If you are about to ask someone new to handle the accounts, make sure the person is in good standing with the company—not just qualified to do the work.
- Create an office atmosphere that encourages everyone to be honest and on the lookout for fraud. Each employee has a vested interest in the well-being of the company.

Can you think of more?

Figure 15-8 Petty cash envelope.

PETTY CASH ENVELOPE													
Petty Cash Fund		Date	No.	Explanation	Distribution of Payments								
Received	Paid Out				Supplies		Post		Misc.		Del.		Tele.
	4 08	May 3	161	Tape & liquid ppr	4	08							
	8 50	May 3	162	Telepost									8 50
	3 90	May 4	163	Stamps			3	90					
	3 84	May 10	164	Reg. Mail			3	84					
	2 87	May 15	165	Cleaning Supplies					2	87			
	2 50	May 18	166	Flower Delivery							2	50	
	3 64	May 27	167	File Labels	3	64							
	2 79	June 4	168	Reg. Mail			2	79					
	2 75	June 8	169	Messenger							2	75	
	4 96	June 9	170	Pencils	4	96							
	3 75	June 12	171	Parcel Delivery							3	75	
	43 58			Totals	12	68	10	53	2	87	9	00	8 50

4. Replenish the petty cash fund soon enough to keep an adequate supply of cash on hand. In some organizations, petty cash is replenished at a predetermined time—for instance, when only one-fourth of the cash is on hand. In other organizations, replenishing the petty cash fund is left to the judgment of the office professional responsible for maintaining the fund.

5. To replenish the petty cash fund, balance the petty cash record, formally request a cheque for the amount needed, and prepare the petty cash report.

Begin by balancing the petty cash record: count the cash on hand, total the columns of the petty cash record, determine the amount needed to replenish the petty cash fund to the original amount, and enter the balance in the petty cash record. Verify that the cash on hand plus the total amount of the vouchers equals the original amount of the fund. Also, add the totals of the distribution of payment columns as a check that the total amount distributed equals the total amount spent. In the illustration in Figure 15-9, the original petty cash fund was $50. Total expenditures were $43.58; the balance is $6.42. The cash on hand should be $6.42. The amount of the cheque written to replenish the fund should be $43.58.

Request the amount needed to replenish the petty cash fund to its original amount, unless you have been authorized to decrease or increase the fund. In some organizations, the person in charge of the fund is expected to write the cheque. If you write the cheque, make it payable to "Petty Cash," and present it to the person who is authorized to sign it.

With the request for cash, submit the records called for by the accounting department. When the accounting department supplies a petty cash distribution envelope, the usual procedure is to submit the envelope with the supporting vouchers enclosed. Before you release an envelope, make a copy for your files. If you keep a petty cash book, submit a petty cash report similar to the one shown in Figure 15-9. Attach the petty cash vouchers.

6. Cash the cheque. Enter the amount and the date in the Received column of the petty cash record. If you are using a new petty cash distribution envelope, transfer the balance of the old envelope to the Received column of the new petty cash envelope, together with the amount of new cash received.

Payroll Processing

In a small business you may be responsible for processing payroll for team members and for yourself. In larger organizations a payroll or accounting department would oversee

Figure 15-9 Petty cash report.

MEMORANDUM

TO: Tyler Rivest
        Accounting

FROM: Belinda Nixon
        Research and Development

DATE: June 13, 20--

SUBJECT: **PETTY CASH REPORT**

The following report is a summary of petty cash paid out from May 3, 20-- until
June 12, 20--.

Petty Cash Report
June 13, 20--

Opening Balance		$50.00
Expenditures		
Supplies	$12.68	
Postage	10.53	
Delivery	9.00	
Telepost	8.50	
Miscellaneous	2.87	43.58
Closing Balance		$ 6.42

Please issue a cheque for $43.58 to replenish the petty cash fund to the original amount
of $50.00. Eleven petty cash vouchers are attached.

bn

Attachments (11)

this function. Even with a payroll department you may still be required to track hours worked and submit reports based on any changes in hours.

If you are expected to complete payroll you need to be aware of legal requirements and regulations set forth by the federal and provincial governments, as accurate payroll records must be maintained by all businesses. Here are some key points to keep in mind:

1. Calculation of earnings and deductions must be made for each payment processed.

2. For each employee, three mandatory deductions must be recorded: Canada Pension Plan or Quebec Pension Plan, employment insurance (EI), and income tax.

3. Each employee must receive a statement detailing earnings and deductions. This statement will show gross pay, which is the total amount earned before any deductions are made, and the net pay, which is earnings after deductions are made.

4. On a monthly basis, prepare and remit payment to Canada Revenue Agency (CRA), specifically the

Receiver General, for the three mandatory deductions. There are variations in the remittance schedule depending on the organization; some organizations remit on a quarterly basis.

Revenue Canada provides several online tools showing calculation tables for the mandatory deductions. See www.cra.gc.ca for more specific information.

Several payroll software packages are also available to assist with accurate payroll preparation.

Office Supplies on Hand

Administrative assistants should replenish their office supplies during the time of day or week that they are the least busy. Yet they need to plan well enough that they are not searching for supplies when pressed for time to complete a rush job. Sometimes an administrative assistant is responsible for stocking office supplies for an entire floor or a department. Inventory control is essential to maintain a constant supply of needed materials. To manage this, you need a record, preferably kept in longhand, of supplies on hand.

An easy way to determine supplies needed is to keep an inventory of each item on a 10.2 cm × 15.2 cm card. These cards, when completed, are known as perpetual inventory cards. When you check supplies out of the main supply department or order them directly, enter the amount of each item received on its card, and then add the amount to the figure in the balance column. When you take supplies from the supply cabinet or shelf, enter the amount in the checked-out column, and then subtract the amount to show the new balance. Encourage others who check out supplies to follow the same procedure. See Chapter 3 for guidelines on ordering supplies.

By looking at the perpetual inventory cards, you can decide:

1. whether or not the item you need is on hand in sufficient quantity
2. when it is time to order additional supplies

Self-Check

1. Why do some companies prefer to have all the cancelled cheques in their possession?
2. When would a company's petty cash fund be used?
3. How is a petty cash voucher used? Explain.
4. What are the three mandatory deductions required by law when preparing payroll?
5. List two decisions you could make easily with the help of accurate perpetual inventory cards.

BUDGET PREPARATION

A **budget** is a yearly plan a business uses to determine revenue and expenses. This document is critical for planning for future growth and development. Businesses take the compilation of an annual budget very seriously. In large organizations each department may have a portion of the budget they are required to complete. An administrative assistant will assist with the budget process by gathering and recording financial data from sources such as monthly financial statements, expense reports, and income summaries. Here are some helpful guidelines to consider if you are preparing the budget documents:

1. Use a reliable template to confirm all areas of the budget are identified and addressed.
2. Ensure data is entered correctly. An error will affect the entire budgetary outcome.
3. Take time to readjust your figures when necessary.
4. Obtain input from all departments involved in the budget process.

ETHICS IN ACCOUNTING PROCEDURES

You may remember hearing news items about the financial collapses of well-known companies without warning, often companies with spotless reputations and histories of positive financial reports. What went wrong? The inevitable question is, "Where were the auditors and the accountants as these financial statements of well-being were released?" The problem often appears to be one of a lack of ethics. Could the financial troubles have been hidden deliberately to ensure strong investor support or to maintain a strong presence in the industry? Were they the result of fraud or embezzlement? The unfortunate result is that investors lost millions of dollars, and our trust in those involved in accounting practices was shaken.

Ethics can be taught and learned. In 2003, the Association of Certified Public Accountants incorporated a requirement that to maintain a license to practice, CPAs are required to take an ethics course once every three years.

Because of the high cost of dishonesty, you must be a person others see as having high values. You must be a person who would not compromise those values, especially when working in the accounting area and even at the request of your manager or supervisor. High ethical standards are required in every phase of the administrative assistant's job.

INTERNATIONAL CURRENCY EXCHANGE

With international business travel so commonplace, it is very possible that you will be required to provide current currency exchange rates when your manager travels abroad. You might have to arrange to exchange Canadian money into a foreign currency before your manager leaves—and back into Canadian money when your manager returns from the trip abroad.

You can check the current exchange rate for any country's currency in a number of ways. You could search the internet, contact your local bank, or check the newspaper. If your airport handles international flights, you will likely find a company there that exchanges currency. Likewise, destination airports handling international flights will usually have currency exchange companies on site.

A word of caution. Canadian currency can be easily exchanged in Western countries. However, smaller countries or those in the Far East and Middle East will not necessarily deal in Canadian currency exchange. It is very important to research the destination country to confirm that Canadian currency is accepted at exchange centres. If in doubt, exchange currency before your manager leaves Canada. Always arrange for your manager to have small amounts of local currency upon arrival in another country to cover such things as transportation and food.

Credit cards are widely accepted throughout the world. Charges are made in the currency of the country where the purchase is made and converted to Canadian currency when it appears on your credit card statement.

QUESTIONS FOR STUDY AND REVIEW

1. What do the letters EFT represent?
2. What are the two main broad categories of e-commerce?
3. Explain three reasons why the popularity of e-commerce is increasing.
4. What is a cheque?
5. Explain how an administrative assistant can obtain a certified cheque for his or her manager.
6. How does a bank draft differ from an ordinary cheque?
7. Summarize the rules that should be followed when writing cheques.
8. Describe the steps an administrative assistant would need to take to stop payment on a cheque.
9. Why should cheques made payable to the order of Cash be given special protection?
10. When should each of the following endorsements be used: blank, full, restrictive?
11. An administrative assistant or other representative of an organization can endorse the organization's cheques that are being deposited. Explain a time-saving way to make endorsements.
12. Describe how to prepare coins for deposit. Describe how to prepare a large number of bills for deposit.
13. How should money orders and bank drafts be endorsed?
14. Explain how an endorsement should be made on unused traveller's cheques.
15. State how to list cheques on a deposit slip.
16. What are the two plans for completing the deposit when the night depository is used?
17. What information is needed for making a bank reconciliation statement?
18. Why do the bank statement balance and the chequebook balance seldom agree?
19. Summarize the steps involved in making a bank reconciliation statement.
20. When your bank reconciliation statement does not balance, how should you proceed to locate errors?
21. What should be done with cancelled cheques?
22. What is the purpose of the petty cash fund?
23. How can you be sure you have kept an accurate petty cash record?
24. When you replenish the petty cash fund, how do you determine the amount of money to request?
25. Where can you locate information to calculate mandatory payroll deductions?
26. To show the distribution of expenditures, why should you use categories predetermined by the accounting department rather than your own?

EVERYDAY ETHICS

Sales at Any Cost?

Call centres have often been compared to pressure cookers; calls are monitored for proper conduct, speed, and accuracy, as well as quota. At the Barkley Trust Bank's Call Centre (BTBC), the operators, or associates as they are called, are not only expected to handle the incoming and outgoing calls but also to "upsell" the client caller with other products such as investment accounts, mutual funds, or insurance coverage. The bonus is good but high pressure is always on!

One of BTBC's associates, Tammy, is determined to exceed her quota but seems to be experiencing only "high-maintenance" calls today—complaints! By chance, she picked up her headset this morning to hear Bob telling a customer that he was not able to talk to the customer's business associate about bank products because he was too busy dealing with other business.

Tammy didn't say a word. She quietly noted the associate's details and decided then and there that if Bob couldn't be bothered to take this opportunity to sell something, then she would! After all, any sale generated from any customer is revenue for BTBC. She rationalized that it doesn't matter which associate or by which method the associate gets the sale—a sale is a sale! Right?

- What's the main issue in this case?
- What principle, if any, was violated?
- Do you agree with Tammy's assessment of the situation?

Problem Solving

1. You mail a deposit to the bank almost every business day. Normally, the deposit envelope has a place on the envelope for your company name and account number; a deposit slip is also included in the envelope. Today you received a blank envelope from the bank, but the deposit slip was missing. What should you do?

2. You work for an investor. Your responsibilities include keeping a record of money received and writing cheques for expenses. When you reconciled the bank statement for March, you had a difference of $550 between the chequebook balance and the bank statement balance. The bank statement was $550 more. You rechecked every entry. You finally remembered that your manager had recently purchased a house to rent and had instructed the renter to mail the rent cheque to the bank. You went through the cheques and other items returned from the bank. There was a deposit slip for $550. What entry should you make in the chequebook?

3. When you reconciled the balance of the bank statement for September with the chequebook balance, the bank statement balance exceeded the chequebook balance by $1100, a difference for which you had difficulty accounting. You finally discovered that this was the amount of a cheque issued for supplies that were never delivered. The cheque was returned to you by the vendor. What adjustments, if any, would you make to the chequebook balance side of the bank reconciliation statement?

Special Reports

1. Search the internet and locate three providers of computerized payroll software. Create a table comparing the features of each product and write a brief recommendation for the software you would choose providing a rationale for your answer. Submit the table and your written recommendation to your instructor.

2. Interview two administrative assistants to find out how involved they are with banking procedures. Do they do all of the banking? How do they perform the banking tasks, in person or online? How do they maintain their banking records? Identify any challenges they experience with banking procedures. Prepare a brief report and present it to your instructor or your class.

3. Visit a local chartered bank branch and find out about business banking services offered at this branch. Prepare a brief report outlining the key business services offered at this bank and present it to your class or instructor.

PRODUCTION CHALLENGES

15-A Making Deposits
Supplies needed:

- *Deposit slip, Form 15-A-1, page 435*
- *Cheque Register, Form 15-A-2, page 436*

Sid Levine is in charge of registration for the November Sales Seminar, and you are assisting him.

On Tuesday, November 4, you received cheques from four registrants as follows:

Leroy McGovern, $75.00

Janet Temple, $75.00

Kevin Smythe, $75.00

Laura Cole, $75.00

Make out a deposit slip for the November Sales Seminar account (by William Wilson) for November 4. The account number is 09-04156. Also, record the amount of the deposit in the cheque register, and show the balance. The account has a balance of $360.27.

During the week, you received cheques from the registrants for the following amounts:

Nov. 5	$1500.00	20 registrants
Nov. 6	$3000.00	40 registrants
Nov. 7	$2250.00	30 registrants

On Monday, November 10, the first day of the seminar, eight more people registered; the total amount of cheques was $600.00.

Assume that you made out daily deposit slips, took the deposit slips and the cheques to the bank, and entered the daily amounts in the cheque register. (In an actual situation, you would also make out a receipt and a name tag for each registrant.)

15-B Writing Cheques

Supplies needed:

- *Blank cheques, Forms 15-B-1 through 15-B-12, pages 437 to 442*

- *Cheque Register used in 15-A*

On Thursday, November 13, the November Sales Seminar is over, and you are writing the cheques for the expenses incurred because of the seminar. Mr. Wilson signed the signature card at the bank for the November Sales Seminar account, so he must sign the cheques.

Prepare cheques for the following expenses:

- Parker's Restaurant for banquet, $1224.00

- A & R Breakfast House for Tuesday's breakfast, $510.00

- Jane's Pancake House for Wednesday's breakfast, $450.00

- BJ Florist, $96.00

- Ramco Signs, $78.25

- Al's Print Shop, $1700.00

- City Equipment Rental, $25.00

- William Wilson, reimbursement for postage, $60.00

- Parker's Hostess Service, for coffee and rolls at morning and afternoon breaks, $300.45

- Louise Barclay, keynote speaker, $500.00

- Raymond Clevenger, banquet speaker, $500.00

15-C Reconciling the Bank Statement

Supplies needed:

- *Cheque Register used in 15-A and 15-B*

- *Bank Statement, Form 15-C, page 443*

- *Plain paper*

On November 26, you received the bank statement for the November Sales Seminar account. On November 23, you received a cheque from Al's Print Shop for $170.00 as a 10 percent discount for paying promptly. You mailed this cheque to the bank, but it is not shown on the bank statement.

Reconcile the bank statement with the cheque register for the November Sales Seminar. Key the bank reconciliation statement.

15-D Handling Petty Cash

Supplies needed:

- *Petty Cash Envelope, Form 15-D-1, page 444*

- *Petty Cash Vouchers, Forms 15-D-2 through 15-D-13, pages 445 to 447*

- *Plain paper*

Martin Kline, who had been handling petty cash transactions for the Marketing Department, was transferred to another division, and you were asked to handle petty cash.

You started with a clean petty cash envelope. The balance in the fund was $100.00. Write $100.00 in the Received column.

You paid out cash for the following items:

- December 1, paid Stationery Store $5.12 for a special drawing pen.

- December 3, paid $5.55 to the post office for stamps.

- December 3, paid $7.16 to post office for postage and insurance for a package.

- December 4, paid City Taxi $10.25 to deliver a package to Airlift Freight office.

- December 5, paid Williams Drugstore $12.58 for two magazines for the reception area.

- December 8, paid BJ Florist $18.50 for plant for Mr. Wilson's office.

- December 8, paid Williams Drugstore $4.56 for fertilizer tablets for plants at the office.

- December 9, paid Rapid Courier $19.50 to deliver a telegram.

- December 9, paid Meyers Stationery Store $5.63 for a set of markers.

Your cash fund is getting low. Record the totals for the Paid Out column and the Distribution of Payment columns. Carry the balance forward to the Received column, but label it as "Balance." On plain paper, key a petty cash report and ask for enough money to bring the petty cash fund balance back to $100.00. Attach the petty cash vouchers to the report. You are authorized to sign the vouchers.

15-E Checking on Privacy

Supplies needed:

- *Plain paper*
- *Access to the internet*

There have been customer complaints of rudeness toward them by Sid Levine, the AVP of Marketing for the Northwestern region. William Wilson has asked you to confidentially record all customer-related calls from Sid Levine so that he may judge how improper the calls really are. You are not comfortable with this request and feel that it may violate Sid's privacy rights.

William empathized with your concerns and suggested that you research the issue and provide a brief report of your findings before you record Sid's calls.

Go to the Federal Privacy Commissioner's website at www.priv.gc.ca to determine whether it is illegal for you to record Sid Levine's calls without his consent.

Write a brief one-page report of your findings for William Wilson.

Weblinks

Bank of Montreal
www.bmo.ca
Bank of Montreal's main site provides links to all of its services, initiatives, and economic reports.

RBC Financial Group
www.royalbank.ca
RBC's main site offers access to personal, business, and corporate products and services, plus a wide variety of topics from international trade to starting a business.

TD Canada Trust
www.tdcanadatrust.com
TD Canada Trust's main site offers access to a wide range of banking, investment, insurance, and small business products, services, and information. It also offers brokerage services through its partner, TD Waterhouse.

Federal Privacy Commissioner
http://www.priv.gc.ca/index_e.asp
See the guide for businesses and organizations concerning the *Personal Information Protection and Electronic Documents Act* (*PIPEDA*). Valuable resources are available for individuals and businesses.

Office of Consumer Affairs of Industry Canada
www.ic.gc.ca/epic/site/ic1.nsf/en/home
Read "Internet Business Guide" and the "Canadian Code of Practice for Consumer Protection in Electronic Commerce."

Scotiabank
www.scotiabank.ca
Scotiabank's main site provides interest rates, personal and business banking services, and economic reports.

E-Commerce Guide
www.ecommerce-guide.com
E-commerce business owners are offered e-commerce news, hardware and software reviews and tutorials, online business solutions, and much more.

Trust Worthy Website Certification
www.speedyadverts.com/html/trust_worthy.html
Find out about the third-party certification process that requires organizations supporting websites to provide a safe, legal, ethical internet environment.

Canadian Marketing Association
www.the-cma.org
The Canadian Marketing Association is the industry's leading advocate on legislative affairs; electronic commerce is one of the many areas for which it develops self-regulatory policies.

Universal Currency Converter
www.xe.com/ucc
Convert world currencies quickly and easily using up-to-the minute currency rates.

Chapter 16
Employment Strategies

Learning Outcomes

After completion of this chapter, the student will be able to:

1 Describe the role played by the Conference Board of Canada in helping people to be employable.

2 Suggest methods for locating employment opportunities.

3 Inventory job qualifications.

4 Conduct a thorough and effective job campaign.

5 Prepare a personal résumé that gets attention.

6 Prepare an effective letter of application.

7 Complete an employment application form.

8 Develop a portfolio that illustrates accomplishments and skills.

9 Prepare for and participate in a successful job interview.

10 Answer behavioural descriptive interview questions.

11 Analyze interview experiences.

12 Prepare employment follow-up letters such as thank-you, reminder, inquiry, and acceptance and refusal letters.

13 Use the internet as a valuable job search and recruitment tool.

14 Prepare a résumé for electronic scanning.

Very few administrative assistants' positions are protected from corporate restructuring and job layoffs. Therefore, it is important to be sure you are very employable and that you know how to drive an effective job campaign.

Job number one is to prepare yourself with the right skills, the skills that will make you the most marketable. Then you can search for a job that matches your qualifications, personality, and interests. Your administrative career should be rewarding not only monetarily but also in terms of job satisfaction and opportunities for promotion.

The first part of your job campaign should be your decision about where you want to work—the geographic area and the type of business. Unless you have specialized in the legal or medical field, do not limit yourself to seeking a job in a specific department, such as human resources, accounting, or sales. Remain open to opportunities; often, getting your foot in the door is the first step to gaining experience and eventually getting the position you really want.

Your office technology skills are transferable. Often the same basic skills are required in different departments; therefore, never limit your opportunities by expressing interest in working only for one department—instead, express interest in working for the organization. Let the interviewer know you are flexible and willing to adjust to the needs of the organization. The interviewer will strive to match you to a position that will maximize your talents.

Graduate Profile

Tracy Lynn Staunton
Call Taker/Order Entry

Clarke Transport Inc.

College Graduation:
Office Administration Executive
Georgian College
Barrie, Ontario
2010

"I feel that I'm doing something good in this position. I'm making a difference because our pickups ensure that freight is getting all over the country to where it needs to be."

Tracy has spent almost two decades working in customer service and retail; after completing a college program in the early 1990s, she had a few short-term jobs that involved office administration skills. Eventually, when she couldn't find a full-time office job, she took a position with a major convenience store chain. This turned into a 12-year career in retail. She continued to hope, however, to find a position in office administration. When she applied for an administrative position at a major company, she lost out to a candidate with more recent experience and skills. The woman in the human resources department encouraged her to go back to school to update her skills.

After graduating from Georgian College, it still took time for Tracy to find a full-time job. It was frustrating, as she saw other classmates get jobs. Some even had jobs before they completed the program. But Tracy persevered and signed up with a temp agency that specialized in office administration.

Eventually, Tracy obtained a temporary position in the billing department of Clarke Transport Inc. This placement led to the offer of a permanent position in the same department; she was soon offered an even better position in the customer service department.

As a call taker, Tracy's primary responsibility is to take calls from Clarke's customers who want to arrange pickup times for their freight. Sounds easy, right? But moving freight across the country is a major job. There are three call takers who share the job of taking requests for transport, and they must receive and review a constant flow of phone calls, faxes, and email messages over the course of the business day. Tracy also manages the pickups for a regular client and coordinates with third-party companies to arrange transport outside of Clarke's service areas.

Tracy's day is filled with time-sensitive tasks, and she overlaps her workday with her co-workers so that customer requests are processed from 7 a.m. to 6 p.m. The phones get very busy in the afternoons, and it's difficult to get away to complete other tasks.

But organization and follow-through are must-haves—using standard Microsoft Office programs, as well as the AS400 system for tracking and the Routronics dispatch system, Tracy must make sure all the information is in the right place so that the trucks are in the right place at the right time, the shipper's freight is ready to go, and the billing department can do its job!

When information is missing, Tracy must contact the shipper to track it down. Most of her communication, around 70 percent, is over the phone, and the rest is via email (especially with co-workers) and fax.

The best part of her job is her work environment: "I love the atmosphere of teamwork here at Clarke; everyone is supportive and is always willing to help me with this ever-changing industry." Because she is still new to her job, Tracy is grateful that her supervisor and co-workers are generous with their time when she has questions or needs training.

Right now, Tracy's co-workers handle the calls from French-speaking customers, but Tracy would like to upgrade her language skills. She regrets not taking her French classes more seriously in school: "If I knew then what I know now! A lot of positions I came across while job hunting were asking for bilingual applicants, and those were the times I very much wished I had stayed with French."

While the road to postgraduation employment was a little rocky, Tracy urges future graduates not to get discouraged. It's important to start your job search early, even before your course is completed. Then, consider registering with a temp agency—it may lead to a great job, as it did for Tracy, but even if it doesn't, it will add valuable work experience to your résumé.

Start your job campaign several months before graduation. As soon as you decide where you want to work, make a job prospect list using the sources listed in this chapter. Next, prepare your self-appraisal inventory and your résumé, write your application letter, and make a list of the qualifications you plan to stress during job interviews. After you launch your job campaign, keep searching until you find the right job for you.

EMPLOYABILITY SKILLS
Ready for Work

Your main goal as a student is to gain employment skills that will earn you job satisfaction as well as a good income. Once you earn that job, you will need skills to help you keep your job and then to progress in your career. So exactly what skills will make you desirable in the workplace?

Although each job in the workplace requires some unique skills, most jobs require a common set of skills. Every job requires a worker who can, among other things, think and solve problems, work with others, demonstrate positive attitudes, communicate effectively, and act responsibly. As a student, you have to become a graduate with a package of skills that will give you the leading edge in the job market.

You should continuously be looking for ways to improve your own employability skills. Fortunately for you, there is a website where information about these important skills is published. The address is www.conferenceboard.ca/education.

Conference Board of Canada

You've graduated from your program at college, but are you ready to be employed? The Conference Board of Canada is a not-for-profit Canadian organization. It is an expert organization at conducting and publishing research. Every year the Conference Board hosts conferences and holds leadership development programs. It has among its members representatives from Canadian private industry and business, the military, government, and education.

One of the Conference Board's mandates is to act as an advisory board to guide the education sector in preparing students to be productive members of the Canadian workforce. Both educators and employers respect the Conference Board of Canada, and documents that it publishes on the topic of employability skills are highly regarded.

So it is important to be familiar with the most current *Employability Skills 2000+* publication that lists skills needed to enter and progress in the workforce. Please refer to Figure 16-1. The Conference Board breaks these skills into the following three categories:

- **Fundamental Skills.** These are the basic skills needed to prepare people to progress at work.
- **Personal Management Skills.** These skills relate to attitudes and behaviours that help a person to develop in the workplace.
- **Teamwork Skills.** This category relates to the importance of being able to work with others and contribute positively to a team.

LOCATING JOB PROSPECTS

Some of the sources for job prospects are the internet, college placement offices, the Yellow Pages, job fairs, private and public employment agencies, government service announcements, chambers of commerce, the newspapers, and your network of friends and associates.

Use all of these sources, not just one, to find job leads. Once you begin your job campaign, keep it going. Be persistent in checking up and following through on what is available for someone with your qualifications and interests. It has been said looking for a job is a full-time job.

Networking

Put in simple terms, **networking** means exchanging information. Information is the most powerful asset a business professional can have. If you have information and are willing to share it, you will be viewed as a valuable person to have on staff.

During the job hunt, networking is an essential step toward gaining successful employment. Sharing employment information with a network of people is probably one of the most effective methods of obtaining employment. As a student, you can begin to build your network by attending functions such as career fairs, where prospective employers will be available to meet students. Attend and participate in seminars and other functions where office administrators and assistants will be present. By expressing your keen desire for employment and by leaving a positive impression, you will be increasing your opportunity to learn about possible employment prospects.

The early stages of forming a network should include discussing your employment goal with your instructors and with business friends of the family. Tell your neighbours, relatives, and business contacts that you are actively seeking employment and that you would appreciate their help in finding out about job openings.

When your contacts give you job leads, follow through on them or they will not share with you additional leads. Then let the person who told you about the lead know the results. This is a simple courtesy and a way of thanking this person for his or her assistance.

Figure 16-1 Conference Board of Canada document: *Employability Skills 2000+.*

Employability Skills 2000+

The skills you need to enter, stay in, and progress in the world of work—whether you work on your own or as a part of a team.

These skills can also be applied and used beyond the workplace in a range of daily activities.

Fundamental Skills	Personal Management Skills	Teamwork Skills
The skills needed as a base for further development	The personal skills, attitudes and behaviours that drive one's potential for growth	The skills and attributes needed to contribute productively

You will be better prepared to progress in the world of work when you can:

Communicate
- read and understand information presented in a variety of forms (e.g., words, graphs, charts, diagrams)
- write and speak so others pay attention and understand
- listen and ask questions to understand and appreciate the points of view of others
- share information using a range of information and communications technologies (e.g., voice, e-mail, computers)
- use relevant scientific, technological and mathematical knowledge and skills to explain or clarify ideas

Manage Information
- locate, gather and organize information using appropriate technology and information systems
- access, analyze and apply knowledge and skills from various disciplines (e.g., the arts, languages, science, technology, mathematics, social sciences, and the humanities)

Use Numbers
- decide what needs to be measured or calculated
- observe and record data using appropriate methods, tools and technology
- make estimates and verify calculations

Think & Solve Problems
- assess situations and identify problems
- seek different points of view and evaluate them based on facts
- recognize the human, interpersonal, technical, scientific and mathematical dimensions of a problem
- identify the root cause of a problem
- be creative and innovative in exploring possible solutions
- readily use science, technology and mathematics as ways to think, gain and share knowledge, solve problems and make decisions
- evaluate solutions to make recommendations or decisions
- implement solutions
- check to see if a solution works, and act on opportunities for improvement

You will be able to offer yourself greater possibilities for achievement when you can:

Demonstrate Positive Attitudes & Behaviours
- feel good about yourself and be confident
- deal with people, problems and situations with honesty, integrity and personal ethics
- recognize your own and other people's good efforts
- take care of your personal health
- show interest, initiative and effort

Be Responsible
- set goals and priorities balancing work and personal life
- plan and manage time, money and other resources to achieve goals
- assess, weigh and manage risk
- be accountable for your actions and the actions of your group
- be socially responsible and contribute to your community

Be Adaptable
- work independently or as a part of a team
- carry out multiple tasks or projects
- be innovative and resourceful: identify and suggest alternative ways to achieve goals and get the job done
- be open and respond constructively to change
- learn from your mistakes and accept feedback
- cope with uncertainty

Learn Continuously
- be willing to continuously learn and grow
- assess personal strengths and areas for development
- set your own learning goals
- identify and access learning sources and opportunities
- plan for and achieve your learning goals

Work Safely
- be aware of personal and group health and safety practices and procedures, and act in accordance with these

You will be better prepared to add value to the outcomes of a task, project or team when you can:

Work with Others
- understand and work within the dynamics of a group
- ensure that a team's purpose and objectives are clear
- be flexible: respect, be open to and supportive of the thoughts, opinions and contributions of others in a group
- recognize and respect people's diversity, individual differences and perspectives
- accept and provide feedback in a constructive and considerate manner
- contribute to a team by sharing information and expertise
- lead or support when appropriate, motivating a group for high performance
- understand the role of conflict in a group to reach solutions
- manage and resolve conflict when appropriate

Participate in Projects & Tasks
- plan, design or carry out a project or task from start to finish with well-defined objectives and outcomes
- develop a plan, seek feedback, test, revise and implement
- work to agreed quality standards and specifications
- select and use appropriate tools and technology for a task or project
- adapt to changing requirements and information
- continuously monitor the success of a project or task and identify ways to improve

The Conference Board of Canada

255 Smyth Road, Ottawa
ON K1H 8M7 Canada
Tel. (613) 526-3280
Fax (613) 526-4857
Internet: www.conferenceboard.ca/education

Remember that networking is an *exchange* of information, not a one-way effort. The more information you give, the more information you usually get back.

To be a good networker you must be a good listener. By applying your best listening skills you will collect accurate information. This, in the long run, may save you time and effort in your job search.

By listening to the needs of other networkers, you will be able to offer them greater assistance. In this way, you will be viewed as a valuable network partner. As previously stated, the more information you provide others, the more people will reciprocate.

Networking is a developed skill that will help you enhance your life and your career. It will increase your ability to be employed and to advance.

The following are suggestions for improving your networking skills:

1. If you have recently been employed, choose a corporate **mentor**. A corporate mentor usually holds a position at a higher level than yours. This person can offer you information and advice about the organization and give you career direction. For more information about mentors, refer to the section "Learn from a Mentor," on page 367 in Chapter 17.

2. Never limit your contacts by missing an opportunity to meet new people. Your network may include business associates, friends, neighbours, past graduates from your college, relatives, and many other groups of people. A network should become a vast chain of information. The more effort you put into networking, the more the network will expand, and the greater your chances of career success will be.

3. Make yourself visible. Becoming a leader of a professional organization or volunteering to serve on a committee will open networking doors.

4. If you haven't already, purchase a telephone message machine or sign up for a voice mail plan. Missed messages may mean lost contacts.

5. Increase your reading of business materials. Remember that information is power, and reading will build your information base.

6. Develop an organized database of your contacts. A computer database will be invaluable as the number of contacts expands. You will want to keep a current record of:

   ■ names
   ■ addresses
   ■ telephone and fax numbers, and email addresses
   ■ places of employment

   ■ job titles
   ■ personal information that will assist your communications with your contacts

7. Be a giver and not just a taker. Business organizations attempt to hire candidates with a reputation for being contributors to the team, not people who are self-serving. Therefore, don't provide information to your network contacts only because you think you will get some in return.

College Placement Office

Most postsecondary institutions have a placement office to provide their graduates with assistance in making contacts for jobs. At the beginning of your job campaign, register with the placement office at your college. Complete the application form, and provide a résumé, transcript, and any other information required to place your name on the active file with the placement office. Your credentials, when kept in an active file, are available to employers on request.

The placement director and counsellors keep up to date on employment opportunities. Often the placement director arranges for company representatives to conduct interviews on campus. The placement director maintains a list of job openings prepared from the requests of human resources managers, who call the placement office in search of prospective employees.

Watch for the announcement of forthcoming campus interviews at your school, and call the placement office to schedule interviews for jobs you are interested in. Campus interviews are discussed later in this chapter.

Get acquainted with the placement director and counsellors. Schedule an appointment with a counsellor to talk about your specific interests, to ask questions, and to seek guidance. Whether your job hunt is simple and quickly successful or difficult and protracted, you will need all the contacts you can get.

Job Fairs

Look for and attend job fairs. Job fairs are often hosted at community centres and colleges. This will be an opportunity for you to meet face-to-face with prospective employers. Many employers will conduct a brief interview during the fair, and this is your opportunity to shine. Be sure to bring several copies of your résumé, and dress as if you were going on an interview.

The job fair will help you to determine if you are a good fit for an organization, as many prospective employers hand out brochures or flyers detailing what they have to offer and who would make a good candidate. Take time to read the information so that if you do get called for interview you will have a good understanding of your potential employer.

Job fairs may also be specific to certain fields. For instance, some may be intended only for legal administrative assistants; others may be for medical administrative assistants. This helps you to tailor your search.

Business News Items

Read the business news in the newspaper or the online edition of papers in the city where you plan to seek employment before you apply for jobs. Search for news about established organizations that are relocating their offices in your city or opening a branch, established organizations in your city that are moving their offices to new buildings or expanding at their present sites, newly formed organizations, and companies that are merging. Any changes within organizations may indicate career opportunities.

When you find a news item of interest to you, clip it and save it. It should provide you with the complete name, the type of operation, the location, and possibly the opening date of a new office.

The number of administrative assistants who move to another city when an organization relocates is small compared to the number of executives who transfer to the new location. Therefore, you can expect that any organization that has relocated its offices to another city will be hiring administrative assistants.

Direct Application

Often, the best jobs are not advertised. Many organizations prefer to select their employees from applicants who have taken the initiative to come to them seeking employment.

Do not wait for a job to come to you; it probably will not. Take the initiative to search for a job. Decide where you want to work, and apply. Call the organization and arrange an appointment with the person in charge of hiring office staff.

Be optimistic. Some of the organizations on your prospective list may not be seeking administrative assistants at this time, but an impressive application and interview may put you in line for a future opportunity. If an opening for the job you are seeking does not currently exist, ask the human resources manager to place your application on file.

If you decide you want to work for a particular business but do not have a specific company in mind, refer to the Yellow Pages, which provides a list of local businesses. For example, if you are interested in working for an advertising company, look up "Advertising"; there you will find the names and addresses of the local advertising companies.

Self-Check

1. List four sources you might check for job prospects.
2. Why is networking so important in your job hunt?
3. List five ways to improve your networking skills.
4. Why would you expect an organization that has just relocated to your city to be hiring administrative assistants?
5. Explain what "do not wait for a job to come to you" means.

Federal Government

The federal government of Canada makes employment information readily available to the public. Human Resources and Skills Development Canada (HRSDC), an agency of the Canadian federal government, is responsible for helping Canadians locate employment, engage in training, and develop their careers. HRSDC's comprehensive website, www.hrsdc.gc.ca/en/home.shtml, has an excellent job-search facility for both employers and job seekers.

Accessing Service Canada's "Training and Careers" page, http://www.jobsetc.gc.ca/eng/, allows you to refine your job search and select the region, type of work, and the kind of company or government agency you are interested in working for. As well, it lists Service Centre locations across Canada where you can get personal service in locating employment. The internet and personal services are free to any job seeker and to any employer.

Canadian citizens are given preference when applying for federal government positions in Canada.

Employment Agencies

Employment agencies are a very good source for locating job opportunities. Employment agencies keep information regarding available employment confidential until a candidate is tested, interviewed, and judged as suitable for the position.

Private employment agencies usually give excellent service. They administer tests, scrutinize the appearance of the applicants, conduct thorough interviews, and carry out a complete job hunt for each applicant. Private employment agencies make a sincere effort to refer applicants to jobs for which they are qualified and which they are likely to accept.

Most employment agencies do not charge the applicant a fee for the agency's services. They do, however, charge the employer a **markup**. Once the agency has tested, selected, and placed the applicant, the employer pays the agency a rate. When the work is temporary and the worker is being paid by the hour, the agency collects the markup from the employer and pays the employee a portion of this.

It is unethical for Canadian employment agencies to restrict the applicant's right to hold contracts with other employment agencies. More than one contract means you may work for more than one personnel agency at the same time. This should provide more opportunities for work.

Newspaper Advertisements

The career sections and help-wanted columns of newspapers are valuable sources for job openings. In these, the jobs will be listed under a variety of headings, such as:

- administrative assistant
- office professional
- medical office assistant
- legal administrative assistant
- secretary
- executive secretary
- executive assistant
- secretary-receptionist

By studying career sections and help-wanted ads, you will gain valuable information concerning trends in employment opportunities, salary ranges, and qualifications required. Study the ads in newspapers early in your job campaign.

When you answer a help-wanted ad, be prompt. Reply the same day, if possible. Remember that newspapers are widely read and that looking in them for available jobs requires less effort than other search techniques. It follows that the competition will be very high for jobs posted in newspapers.

Follow instructions. If a telephone number is given, call for an appointment. If a post office box number is given, submit your résumé. Many advertisements request that applicants submit résumés by mail, by fax, or by email and clearly state that they do not want applicants to call. If this is the case, follow the instructions. You risk irritating the employer if you ignore the request for no telephone calls. Of course, it's always more proactive and shows a sense of initiative to telephone the employer and to drop off your résumé in person. These techniques should be part of your strategy unless the employer has requested otherwise.

Always study the advertisement carefully to determine all the stated qualifications and then submit an application letter and résumé showing that you meet all the qualifications for the job. Do not overlook any of them. Follow the suggestions for writing a solicited application letter

discussed in the section "Application/Cover Letters" later in this chapter. See Figure 16-2 for sample online job ads.

Blind Advertisements Newspaper recruitment advertisements either give the name and address of a company or person to contact, or are **blind advertisements** giving a post office box number or a telephone number. When blind ads are used in a legitimate fashion, it is generally because the organization wishes to avoid receiving large numbers of résumés from unqualified applicants. For example, if the local NHL hockey team requires an office professional and advertises its name in the newspaper, it will get a flood of applicants, many of whom are unqualified but apply because of their desire to work for celebrities. A simple advertisement that lists the responsibilities of the position, the desired qualifications, and a post office box number is more likely to attract those who are legitimately interested in performing the advertised responsibilities.

Scrutinize blind advertisements carefully. Sometimes they are used for purposes other than recruitment for employment, such as preparing a mailing list of prospective purchasers. If you receive a telephone call in response to a reply to a blind advertisement, ask for the name of the company, and ask some questions about the job during the telephone conversation to be sure the job advertised is legitimate.

Prospects in Another Geographic Area

The best way to locate job opportunities in a different city or country is to get proactive on the internet. Websites such as www.jobstreet.com, which lists jobs in Asia, or www.jobsetc. gc.ca, which lists information about jobs in Canada, are just two of the many excellent sites that can help you get started. Another underestimated, overlooked source of employment is known as the **hidden job market**. This is a virtual market of unadvertised opportunities in which you have to find the employer rather than where employers find you through employment agencies. Finding opportunities in the hidden job market requires determination and a good network. The Government of Canada, recognizing the significance of this market, has published a guide to it, "Access the Hidden Job Market," at http://www.jobsetc.gc.ca/pieces.jsp?category_id=298. Here job seekers may learn strategies and develop skills to explore this market.

Once you've located employment opportunities that interest you, follow through with your résumé and application letter. Be assertive! The opportunity to work abroad or even in another Canadian city will make your résumé more powerful, increase your future potential, and bring you self-satisfaction and personal growth.

Figure 16-2 Sample online job ads.

Office/Clerical Help Wanted

EXECUTIVE ASSISTANT TO THE CITY ENGINEER

Engineering is one of the city's major departments. As Department Head, the City Engineer requires an administrative assistant who has excellent communication and critical thinking skills, is a team player, and who can give support by performing technical and administrative tasks quickly and accurately. The successful candidate will have been trained in ISO 9001 and will have demonstrated commitment to its philosophy.

Duties include preparing for and arranging meetings, taking minutes, composing correspondence, and assisting the City Engineer with administrative tasks. The ability to train junior office workers and to be an office team leader are desirable. There is frequent contact with private executives, professionals, and senior government officials. The diverse duties and responsibilities of this position allow considerable latitude for personal initiative and growth.

The successful applicant will have achieved a postsecondary diploma in office administration and will have superior word processing, database management, spreadsheet, and desktop publishing skills. A university degree would be an asset.

Salary will be commensurate with training and experience. A full benefit package is offered.

Please call (506) 363-1893 for an appointment.

RECEPTIONIST/BOOKKEEPER We need an enthusiastic, energetic, and organized assistant to perform general office duties. Experience and training in electronic bookkeeping is required. Bring your résumé to 1609 Northfield Rd.

C.A. FIRM Small C.A. firm requires an enthusiastic graduate of an office administration program to key correspondence and financial statements on word-processing and spreadsheeting software. Candidate must be able to assume general office duties, and work well in a team. Salary negotiable. To apply please call Mrs. L. Rossin at 869-0020.

OFFICE ASSISTANT Required by small sales office. Responsibilities include bookkeeping, payroll, and keying. Applicants must have Microsoft skills (Word, Excel, Outlook, Access), good organizational skills, and the ability to work with minimum supervision. Reply to P.O. Box 654.

WORD PROCESSING Trained and experienced people needed for temp. and perm. positions. Please contact J. Johnson, 598-2306.

Other ways to locate job opportunities in other geographic locations are:

- Conduct research on the internet by city name or by company name.
- Ask the career counsellor in your college to help you. The career counsellor will have lots of useful information and tips on how to secure employment and where to look for it.
- Inquire at the local public library for the telephone directory and newspapers for the city where you want to work.
- Write, email, or fax the chamber of commerce in the desired geographic area.

Your career counsellor will have the most recent copy of *Career Options*, a publication from the Canadian Association of Career Educators and Employers. This valuable publication can be found online at www.cacee .com. It offers much useful information regarding your career search and industry profiles, and it also provides a directory of employers interested in hiring college graduates.

Tell your college career counsellor your employment goal, and ask for suggestions. Ask the counsellor to contact the career counsellor at a college in the area where you plan to relocate, in order to find out about work prospects for administrative assistants there.

The telephone directory for the city where you want to relocate will be an excellent source of information. Many telephone directories can be found online; however, you may have to subscribe to them. Large public libraries have telephone directories from all the major cities in Canada. They will have the directories either in paper version or online. Public libraries also subscribe to many newspapers from other cities.

Find out what your public library has on file. The librarian will answer your specific questions concerning what telephone directories and newspapers are available. You can also obtain the addresses of a few companies from the librarian by telephone.

When you write to a chamber of commerce, state your employment goal, and ask about opportunities in your field in the geographic area. If the chamber of commerce sends you a list of prospective employers, realize that the list is limited to chamber of commerce members.

Self-Check

1. Who pays employment agencies for their services?
2. Why is it beneficial to study the career sections and help-wanted ads in newspapers even if you are not currently seeking employment?
3. What is a blind advertisement?
4. Explain what is meant by the *hidden job market*.
5. Give three suggestions of ways to locate job opportunities in other geographic locations.

BOUNCING BACK

As a result of organizational **downsizing** or **rightsizing,** being overqualified, being made **redundant, company merger,** or **company takeover**, you've been fired or laid off. Now what? Should you get depressed, angry, or emotional? Go ahead. Allow yourself to vent, but keep it short and keep it private. Most people who have been released from their employment go through various emotional stages, but how they handle it will make a difference as to when they are ready to jump back into the job market.

Eligible for Employment

These ideas, if applied, will help to move you back to gainful employment.

1. Learn from the experience. Ask yourself why you are in this position. What responsibility is yours? Did you do something to invoke this? What can you learn from this? What will you do differently next time?

2. Cut out the "If only I had," "I should have," "I could have," phrases. The truth is that you didn't. That was then. This is now. Develop the attitude of putting the past behind you and moving forward with a new experience under your belt.

3. Develop the attitude that when one door closes others open.

4. Look at the job market as a challenge that you are ready to accept. Take the challenge and prepare yourself to win.

5. Draw up an action plan that includes actions and dates to accomplish them. Stick to the plan.

6. Consider other types of work. This is an opportunity to start fresh.

7. Dress and act the part. Don't run your job campaign at home in your pyjamas. Get up at the same time every day, and prepare yourself in the same way as you did when you were employed. Take care of yourself.

8. Consider joining a health club to keep fit. Having a healthy body makes it easier to have a healthy mind.

9. Build a budget. If you are without a regular cheque, you will need to fall back on your reserves, so you will need to spend them wisely.

10. Inquire through your provincial and federal government agencies to see what financial or training assistance is available during the time you are searching for work.

11. Use the time away from work to upgrade your employment skills. Get certification for your upgrading so that you can present this to potential employers.

12. Most of all, don't become discouraged. Get a friend or mentor to help keep you focused and on track with your action plan.

APPLYING FOR JOBS

The résumé, the application letter, and the job interview are the applicant's direct contacts with prospective employers. The following discussion will provide you with methods of making all three more persuasive and effective.

Résumés

A résumé is a tool that you use to sell yourself to the right employer. It is a reflection of who you are. It is not a document that rambles on about your qualifications and experience. It must be

- well written,
- well presented, and
- well organized.

An excellent résumé can be your passport to success.

A résumé, sometimes called a **curriculum vitae** or CV, is a summary of an applicant's qualifications for the job being sought. Your résumé should answer questions concerning:

1. who you are
2. the type of job you are seeking
3. the qualifications you have to offer
4. the experience you have to offer

Note that the proper way to spell *résumé* is with two accents.

Résumé Styles All résumés should be personalized; however, there are two recommended formats that offer an attractive and easy-to-read document to the potential employer. The styles and benefits of these résumés are listed below.

Chronological Résumé The chronological format arranges your work experience, education, and personal history so that the most recent information is first. The chronological résumé has many advantages: it is the preferred résumé for employers because it is easy to follow and shows exactly what the applicant has done, not what the applicant thinks he or she can do. This is certainly the résumé format of choice, especially when the applicant has an impressive work or educational history. This résumé works well for recent graduates because it emphasizes their education and also identifies previous work experience responsibilities that relate to the job being sought. The chronological résumé is most often the style preferred by employers. It is featured in Figure 16-3.

Functional Résumé The functional résumé is designed to point to the applicant's skills, abilities, and accomplishments. If you have never been employed, the functional résumé will work well. A functional résumé will give you an opportunity to point out leadership and organizational experience indicating that you will be a productive employee. A person who has not been employed but has acquired comparable work experience through volunteering and day-to-day living can also prepare a functional résumé. In this style of résumé, the experience section is organized by functions, without reference to the time of the performance or to an organization. Refer to the example in Figure 16-4.

Purpose of the Résumé The purpose of a résumé is to obtain an interview. It should be personally delivered, emailed, or faxed with a one-page application, or cover, letter. As soon as your résumé opens the door for a job interview, it has served its function. Whether or not you are offered the job will depend on your qualifications and how well you project your knowledge, abilities, and personality during the interview.

Administrative assistants with excellent skills in communication, organizing and planning, information technology, and public relations are in demand in Canada. An attractive, informative, and accurate résumé that accents these skills will be partially responsible for getting you the employment you desire.

You will deliver a résumé to the place of employment when you apply for work. Take additional résumés with you to the job interview. Hand one to the interviewer(s) at the beginning of the interview so that it may be referred to during the interview. By bringing along extra copies of your résumé, you indicate to the interviewer that you are organized and well prepared.

Self-Appraisal Inventory As a preliminary step to preparing a résumé, decide exactly what your qualifications are. Prepare a detailed inventory of your educational background, work experience, and personal qualities and interests so that you will know exactly what assets you have to offer an employer.

To prepare your inventory chart, record all the data you think might help you in your job search. Use separate sheets of paper to list your skills, education, work history, interests, and personal qualities. Include everything as you make your list; record the items in any order, and then rearrange them later, deleting any that may not be relevant to the work you want.

Under Skills, list the highlights of your abilities that are the most essential for the specific job for which you are applying.

Under Education, list the following:

1. the postsecondary institute(s) attended, date(s) of graduation, and degree(s), diploma(s), or certificate(s) attained
2. the high school you attended, and the dates
3. any special courses that may support your employment hunt
4. your skills, including computer and software training, and the ability to operate any additional equipment
5. school activities that suggest organizational, team, and leadership skills

Under Work History, list all your jobs, including part-time, summer, and volunteer work. Do not exclude jobs that were not office jobs. For each job, give the name and address of the organization, your job title, the details of your responsibilities, and the dates of your employment.

Under Interests, list your hobbies and special talents, and the ways you spend your leisure time.

Under Personal Qualities, list your strengths, such as initiative, leadership, ability to organize, and willingness to learn and participate in a team. Discuss these when you write your application letter.

Figure 16-3 Résumé.

Ms. Dini Lawrence

101 Keele Street
Toronto, ON M3P1K1
Tel: 416-555-1329   Fax: 416-555-2390   Email: dini@z-wave.ca

OBJECTIVE

To work as an office professional with a progressive and innovative organization.

SKILLS

With over seven years of professional office experience and an Office Administration diploma from the Southern Alberta Institute of Technology, I have learned to be technically efficient in the office. My human relations skills include leadership and cooperation, as well as loyalty and dedication.

EDUCATION
1999–2001

Southern Alberta Institute of Technology
Office Administration Diploma
Calgary

- Honours Diploma Received
- Keying Achieved = 70 words per minute
- **Software Training**
  - Word
  - Excel
  - Peoplesoft
  - PowerPoint
  - Simply Accounting
  - Access
  - Project
  - Visio
  - Publisher

- **Application Courses Completed**
  - Document Processing
  - Marketing
  - Project Management
  - Business Law
  - Meetings and Conferences
  - Professional Development
  - Office Procedures
  - Report Writing
  - Advanced Keying
  - Records Management
  - Office Supervision
  - Public Relations
  - Advanced Business
  - Communications

- **School Activities**
  - President of the Office Administration Society
  - Chairperson of the Graduation Planning Committee
  - Participant in Charity Fundraising

1997–1998

Career College
Customer Service Specialist
Saskatoon
- Honours Certificate

Figure 16-3 *Continued.*

<u>WORK HISTORY</u>

2002–2010   **Administrative Assistant**
                      Coron Industries
                      Calgary

- **Responsibilities**
  - coordinating ISO 9000 procedures
  - supervising junior staff
  - keying correspondence using word processing software
  - organizing budgets on electronic spreadsheet
  - composing routine correspondence
  - making travel arrangements
  - arranging meetings and conferences
  - researching potential client markets
  - managing electronic databases
  - performing reception duties
  - designing sales brochures using desktop publishing software

July 1995–   **Sales Assistant**
September 1996   Image Plus
(part-time)   Calgary

- **Responsibilities**
  - assisting customers
  - handling cash
  - logging financial transactions into computer system
  - answering telephone inquiries
  - participating in training programs

<u>INTERESTS AND ACTIVITIES</u>

I enjoy playing tennis, cycling, reading, and attending theatre events.

July 2004   • member of International Association of Administrative Professionals
October 2003   • volunteer for Special Olympics

<u>REFERENCES</u>

Mr. Elton Margate	Mr. Richard Fenwick	Ms. Sharon Mott
Director Quality Control	Program Head	Manager
Coron Industries	Office Administration	Image Plus
1601 5 Avenue SW	SAIT	237 4 Avenue SW
Calgary, AB T2P 4C8	1301 16th Avenue NW	Calgary AB T2P 4P3
Tel 403-555-5489	Calgary, AB T2M 0L4	Tel 403-555-5877
Fax 403-555-9008	Tel 403-555-8581	Fax 403-555-4455
Email: emargate@caron.net	Fax 403-555-8940	Email: sharonmott@image.com
	Email: richard.fenwick@sait.ab.ca	

Figure 16-4 Functional résumé.

Ken Moss, B.B.A.

11654–160 Avenue
Edmonton, AB T6M 0R5
Tel: 403-555-1111   Fax: 403-555-2222
Email: kenmoss@b-wave.ca

QUALIFICATIONS

- Business professional with superior organizational skills
- Excellent academic credentials in Business Administration
- Excellent communicator with fluency in English and French
- Consistently promoted to positions of increased responsibility
- Proven leadership in managing office employees and conducting presentations

SELECTED ACCOMPLISHMENTS

- Exceeded sales quotas for four consecutive years in MSS Corporation
- Launched mega products for Canadian region of MSS Corporation
- Improved sales team performance by 25 percent in Image Canada Co.

PROFESSIONAL EXPERIENCE

Business Analysis

- Collected and organized account data from multiple sources
- Used database applications to prepare financial reports
- Presented findings and recommendations to senior staff

Management

- Guided the activities of front-line reception staff
- Resolved complaints from customers
- Interacted with administrative staff and senior management

EMPLOYMENT HISTORY

Image One Ltd., Fredericton, NB
Supervisor of Accounts, 2003–2005

Canada First Inc., Toronto, ON
Office Manager, 2001–2003

EDUCATION

Northern Alberta Institute of Technology, Edmonton, AB
Bachelor of Applied Business Administration—Accounting, 2001

Northern Lights College, Fort Nelson, BC
Diploma in Office Administration, 1999

Points of Emphasis Organize your résumé so that the interviewers will grasp your most important qualifications if they read only the first line of each section of your résumé. Prepare a one-page résumé, or put the most essential data on the first page.

Many authorities on résumés emphasize preparing a brief résumé. Although some advocate a one-page résumé, this is rarely enough space to include the critical facts. As your experience and education expand, so must your résumé. Most applicants for clerical work should have résumés no longer than two pages.

Indicate the type of position you are seeking in the Objective or Goal section.

Decide whether your work experience or your education will be most persuasive, and then place that section immediately after the Objective.

To highlight your education, list your most recent postsecondary attendance first; after that, list the other schools you attended in reverse chronological order. It is helpful to display key courses that relate to the employment opportunity. For the administrative assistant, this means software or skills-oriented courses.

Be consistent; just as you listed your education, arrange your work experience by listing the most recent employment first, followed by other employment in reverse chronological order.

Suggested Outline for a Chronological Résumé
The résumés of two applicants should not be identical, but good résumés do tend to follow a recognizable pattern. Plan your résumé so that it presents all your qualifications and highlights your strongest points.

A résumé is a list. It is not necessary to write complete sentences. Use lists to describe duties or skills; but remember to be consistent. A common error in résumés is the use of inconsistent verbs.

Following is an example of an *inconsistent list*:
Responsibilities

- Keying documents
- Manage electronic databases
- Planned meetings and conferences

Following is an example of a *consistent list:*
Responsibilities

- Keying documents
- Managing electronic databases
- Planning meetings and conferences

Avoid using "I." A résumé contains facts only. Statements that reveal philosophy or opinion may be used in the application letter but not in the résumé. The suggestions that follow are illustrated in Figure 16-3.

Heading In the heading, include your name, postal address, telephone number, fax number, email address, and website address if applicable. If you have a temporary address, provide a permanent mailing address to ensure that you receive any documentation sent to you. Use a telephone number that has an answering system so you will not miss any important calls from potential employers.

Objective or Goal This section may be referred to as either Objective or Goal. State the type of position you are seeking and the name of the organization with which you are seeking employment. Write the full name of the organization. Using the name of the company in the résumé shows that the résumé was prepared exclusively for that company.

Skills Use a brief sentence or two to give the reader a snapshot of your best skills that will enable you to perform the job with excellence.

Education The following information should be included in this section:

1. List the date, name, and city of each postsecondary institute and high school attended. Place the most recent college first. If you are still attending college, write *Expected Graduation Date (or EGD) April 20xx.*

2. For each entry, indicate your major area of study, stating the degree, diploma, or certificate obtained.

3. List your skills. Indicate your keying speed only if it is applicable and impressive.

4. List the different types of software you have experience using.

5. List courses you took that you believe will be helpful to you on the job. List them by name, not number.

6. Add school activities that reflect your organizational, leadership, and team skills.

Experience In reverse order, list your employment experience. If your work experience has been limited, include part-time, summer, and volunteer work, even when the work was unrelated to office work. Employers place value on experience that is common to all jobs, such as carrying out instructions, being prompt and dependable, working cooperatively with others, and accepting responsibility.

Use a separate entry for each job, and arrange the entries in reverse chronological order. Give the beginning and ending dates (months and years), the name of the employer, the city in which the organization is located, the position held, and the specific responsibilities performed. If the job was part-time or voluntary, place this information under the date. To indicate that you are currently working, simply write the commencement date followed by a hyphen.

Interests and Activities Because the human rights codes relating to equal opportunity employment make it illegal for an employer to discriminate on the basis of age, sex, colour, marital status, religion, place of origin, race, or creed, you are not required to include personal data.

However, where you believe that certain personal data may be to your benefit, you should include them.

In this section you may add whatever you believe will support your application, such as honours received, extracurricular activities, hobbies and sports you enjoy, and professional associations you belong to.

References The question of whether or not to include references is often raised. Employers know that applicants list as references those persons who will give the applicant favourable recommendations. Many employers check with the persons who are listed as references; some do not.

Some résumés say, "References available upon request." Others go ahead and include the references. The people you select for your references must be people who will give you very positive reports. They should provide the pulling power you need to get the job. So why not include your references directly on your résumé? This is a way of encouraging the prospective employer to contact these people. Employers are busy people; by including the references on the résumé, you save the employer the effort and time of having to contact you again in order to make your references available. The best advice, then, is to include references with the résumé. You may wish to include references with some résumés and not with others. In this case, key your references on a separate page and treat them as a separate section. This way, you can choose to include the references or not.

For references, give two or more former employers or instructors who can provide a specific evaluation of your competence, work habits, and attitude toward work. If you include a character reference, do not give the name of a relative. Prior to using the references on your resume, ask permission of each person you want to include.

For each reference, give the full name, position held, and complete address, including the postal code. Also include telephone and fax numbers and email addresses. Use a courtesy title before each name. The position held is significant because it will indicate the person's association with you. The person you want to use as a reference may now be retired or may have moved to a different company. If that person's former title is important to your résumé, write, for example:

Mrs. Christine Blackwell
(Former) Director of Finances

or

Mrs. Christine Blackwell
(Retired) Director of Finance

When you succeed in getting a job, send your references a thank-you message expressing your appreciation for their assistance. Thank-you letters are discussed in more detail later in this chapter under "Follow-Up Correspondence."

Appearance of the Résumé Remember that the résumé is a specimen of your work. Use appropriate word processing or desktop publishing software features so that your résumé will be a higher-quality document.

Print your résumé with a laser printer on 21.5 cm × 28 cm bond paper. High-quality white paper is very acceptable. Many applicants choose a high-quality lightly coloured paper in order to attract attention to the résumé.

The rule, however, is to be conservative. Never use a bright or pastel shade that will detract from the conservative appearance.

Give the résumé plenty of white space using margins of approximately 2.5 cm. The size of margins will actually depend on the setup and on the usual requirement to fit the résumé on two pages. To avoid a crowded look, use ample white space before and after headings and between entries. Too much white space, however, will suggest inefficient planning.

Print the main heading at the top of the first page. It should be centred, and it should be highlighted in such a way that it is eye-catching and easy to read. Suggestions are to use bold, enlarged, or italic print. Boxes or lines used in this area will enhance the appearance.

Remember the "be conservative" rule. Using too many enhancements will detract from the qualifications your résumé is trying to present.

Side headings should be emphasized but should not detract from the main titles. To this end, use a combination of capital letters, underlining, and bold or italic print. However, be moderate; you do not want to reduce the importance of the main heading.

The second page will require a running head. It should consist of a brief title and the page number.

You must get your résumé noticed in the pile that will be received by the recruiter. Hundreds of résumés might be received for one attractive job opportunity. A recruiter will often ask an administrative assistant to sort out the résumés that do not meet the job requirements or that appear unsuitable. When in doubt about a particular résumé, the administrative assistant will probably cut it from the "suitable" pile. These unsuitable résumés will never reach the desk of the recruiter. Follow these simple rules to be sure your résumé is not filtered out:

■ Clearly state your skills that meet the key requirements of the job.

■ Carefully follow instructions. Give precisely what is requested. If the ad states that the company wishes to have résumés dropped off in person, then drop yours off in person.

- Many ads request that applicants not telephone the company. This request must be respected.

- Concentrate on every detail. A good administrative assistant will catch the smallest error when scrutinizing the résumés. Any typographical or spelling error will mean immediate rejection. No employer will want to interview an applicant for an administrative assistant's position who allows errors in a document as important as a résumé. For that reason, don't rely only on the **spell-check** feature to proofread your document. Manually proofread the document as well. When you are finished, do it again and again. Then have another person with good spelling ability read it for you.

Put yourself in the position of the person who must sort through and filter out the résumés, and then in the position of the recruiter. Make their jobs easier by making your résumé attractive, applicable, easy to understand, and flawless. If you follow these suggestions, your chances of receiving an interview will be better.

Faxing Your Résumé
You've spent hours printing your résumé on bond paper of perfect quality and colour, and perhaps have even used coloured ink for just the right amount of accent. After all that perfection and care, your prospective employer has asked you to fax it. What a disappointment! The employer is about to get the "grey" version. Although faxing does take away from the professional image of the document, it does have the advantage of expediency. Employers request that résumés be faxed in order to save time. If you are requested to fax your résumé, consider the following:

- A faxed résumé will probably not be confidential. In fact, several people may see it before the designated receiver collects it. You may be able to avoid this disclosure by telephoning the recipient just prior to sending the fax and asking him or her to collect the faxed document.

- A faxed résumé should always include a cover letter, just like the résumé you mail or hand deliver.

- If your résumé is attractive enough to earn you points, mail an original in addition to sending the fax.

Emailing Your Résumé
Emailing your résumé and cover letter might be preferable to faxing it. Emailing has the advantage over faxing of keeping the document relatively confidential. However, it does not guarantee that the document will look more attractive. Although the document may look perfect on your screen, it may not have exactly the same format on the recipient's screen or printer.

If you email your résumé, also send a backup copy in the postal mail.

Although emailing your résumé is a good option, some employers may not want to receive your résumé as an email attachment. This is due to the **proliferation** of computer viruses spread by opening attachments. If the employer has not requested your résumé be sent as an email attachment and you choose to send it that way, know that the receiver may decide not to open it.

Résumé Reminders Before submitting your résumé, use the following checklist to ensure that your document will work for you. Remember that any poor work may cause an employer to send your résumé to **File 13**!

Appearance:

- ❏ The spacing is attractive.
- ❏ You have plenty of white space.
- ❏ You have used quality paper that is white or of a conservative colour.
- ❏ Excessive enhancements have been avoided.
- ❏ A proportional font has been used.
- ❏ Your format is consistent throughout.
- ❏ Your headings are emphasized.
- ❏ Your information is in point form and uses bullets.
- ❏ You have followed the format described in this textbook.
- ❏ Your résumé is free of creases or folds.

Content:

- ❏ Résumé headings shown in this textbook have been used.
- ❏ Your résumé emphasizes skills and mastery of software.
- ❏ Your résumé shows your most recent education first.
- ❏ Your résumé shows your most recent work experience first.
- ❏ You included references on the bottom of your résumé, or you prepared a reference sheet that includes three or four former employers and/or educators.
- ❏ Your references are complete (courtesy titles, working titles, company names, full addresses, telephone and fax numbers, and email addresses).
- ❏ The people given as your references will actually promote your chances of gaining employment.

Accuracy:

- ❏ There are absolutely no typographical errors in your résumé. It has been proofread repeatedly by you and by someone else who gave you constructive feedback.

- You have used the spell-check function to ensure your résumé is free of spelling errors.
- You have checked your résumé for spelling errors that the spell-check function would not detect.
- Your lists are consistent in wording as well as in format.
- You have stated your expected date of graduation if you have not already graduated.

Other:

- Your résumé has been delivered in an appropriate way.
- Your résumé has been delivered on time.

Self-Check

1. What questions should your résumé answer?
2. Which is the preferred résumé format? Why?
3. Under what circumstances does the functional résumé work particularly well?
4. In what order would you list your employment experience on your résumé? your education?
5. Should you include personal data such as interests and activities on your résumé? Explain.
6. List four rules to follow in preparing your résumé to be certain it will not be filtered out of the job competition.
7. If you submit your résumé by fax or email, should you send a hard copy of your résumé by postal mail as well? Why or why not?

Application/Cover Letters

An application letter is a sales letter that is selling a product. The product is you. Write an application letter as a covering letter for your résumé. The main purpose of an application letter is to introduce your résumé in the hope of obtaining an interview.

Application letters are either prospecting or solicited. A **prospecting letter** is written by an applicant who does not know if a job opening exists. It is written to express the applicant's interest in working for a particular organization, to call attention to the applicant's qualifications, and to inquire about the possibility of a job opening. A **solicited letter** is written in response to an announcement that a job opening exists. The announcement might be made through an ad in the newspaper, placed with a private employment agency, sent to the placement office of a school, or disseminated through other sources. As a college graduate, write prospecting application letters; don't wait until you know that a specific job opening exists.

The Prospecting Letter A prospecting letter represents your initial effort at locating an employer seeking the qualifications you have to offer and at convincing the employer to consider your qualifications. You increase your application letter's chances of gaining attention when you submit a résumé along with it. Let the reader know what qualifications you possess so that he or she can compare them with the requirements of the jobs available within the organization.

Organize your prospecting application letter around the steps of a sales presentation:

1. Use an opening that gets the reader's attention and arouses interest in knowing more about your qualifications.
2. Emphasize facts that will convince the prospective employer that you possess qualifications that match the requirements of a job he or she is trying to fill.
3. Make a brief reference to the résumé you are enclosing.
4. Use a closing that requests action, which in most application letters is a request for an interview.

These points are illustrated in the application letter in Figure 16-5.

The Solicited Letter When you hear or read about a job opening, write a solicited (invited) letter.

A solicited application letter can be more specific than a prospecting letter because the applicant knows that a particular job opening exists. Use the first paragraph to refer to the job and to reveal how you found out about it. Include a reference to the source. Request in the opening paragraph that you be considered for the job. Write a persuasive letter in such a way that you discuss the requirements mentioned in the announcement, and show how you meet these qualifications.

Enclose a résumé and refer to it in the letter. In the résumé, cover all the qualifications and key words mentioned in the announcement, and include others that may contribute to your getting the job.

Close the letter by requesting action, which usually is a request for an interview where you can discuss your qualifications for the position.

For example, to respond to a job advertisement that says the successful incumbent will need office technology skills, you could write:

Please consider the enclosed résumé as an application for the position of Administrative Assistant as advertised in the May 14 issue of the Cape Breton Post. *I recently earned an honours diploma for Office Technology. Through my studies I mastered numerous office skills, including the use of word processing, desktop publishing, and database management software packages. Because I*

Figure 16-5 Prospecting letter of application.

Ms. Dini Lawrence

101 Keele Street
Toronto, ON M3P1K1
Tel: 416-555-1329 Fax: 416-555-2390 Email: dini@z-wave.ca

20 May 20xx

Mr. William Wilson
Vice-President of Marketing
Millennium Appliances, Inc.
3431 Bloor Street
Toronto, ON M8X 1G4

Dear Mr. Wilson:

Re: *Administrative Assistant Position*

During my two years of study in the Office Administration Program at the Southern Alberta Institute of Technology (SAIT), my goal was to become qualified to work as an administrative assistant for a progressive and rapidly growing company. Because Millennium Appliances has the reputation for being an innovative organization I have a keen desire to join your team.

In April of 1999, I graduated from SAIT, became successfully employed in Calgary, and have recently relocated to Toronto with the desire to become an employee of your company.

The skills and knowledge attained at SAIT and through industry have prepared me to be both effective and efficient as an administrative assistant. Because I key at a rate of 70 words per minute and have excellent communication, word processing, and desktop publishing skills, I can prepare accurate and attractive business communication with ease. As well, studies and experience in supervision of junior office staff have taught me the importance of cooperation and strong leadership. My knowledge and practice of public relations, conference and travel arrangements, and electronic database management enable me to perform a variety of tasks in a busy executive office. A résumé has been enclosed for your further information.

At your convenience, I would appreciate an appointment to discuss my qualifications for an administrative assistant position with Millennium Appliances, Inc. I look forward to your response.

Sincerely,

D. Lawrence.

Ms. Dini Lawrence

Enclosure

am an energetic graduate who is willing to learn, I am confident I could contribute to your team.

I would welcome an opportunity to further discuss my qualifications for the position. Please contact me at your earliest convenience. I can be reached by telephone at 306-456-7890. I look forward to hearing your positive response.

Appearance of the Application Letter

Key your application letter on good bond paper 21.5 cm × 28 cm in size. Use plain paper that matches the quality and shade of the paper used for your résumé. Include your personalized letterhead above the date. Since your application letter could get separated from your résumé, put your complete mailing address on both the letter and the résumé.

Address the letter to a specific person, if possible. Make an effort to find out the name of the employer to whom the letter should be addressed. This information can be obtained with a single telephone call to the company.

Limit your letter to one page. Since you have organized all your facts in the accompanying résumé, you can limit your application letter to three or four well-written paragraphs. Most letter styles are acceptable. The key factors in appearance are:

- Keep the font and format conservative.
- Keep the appearance professional.
- Keep the information balanced on the page.

Application/Cover Letter Reminders

A cover letter is the window to your résumé, so it's critical that your cover letter gives the best view of your skills. Consider your application letter as one of your marketing tools. The following checklist will help you create an application letter that works for you.

Appearance:

- ❑ The letter is keyed.
- ❑ You have used high-quality bond paper.
- ❑ Your paper and font match those of the résumé.
- ❑ Your cover letter is stapled to the top of your résumé.
- ❑ The documents have been placed in an envelope large enough that they lie flat without folding.

Content:

- ❑ You have opened with an attention-getting statement.
- ❑ You have demonstrated knowledge of the company.
- ❑ Your letter complimented the company.
- ❑ Key words have been included that were used in the job posting.
- ❑ You have described what would make you valuable to the company.

- ❑ Your background has been summarized.
- ❑ You closed with a call to action.
- ❑ The letter is short.
- ❑ The letter is simple.
- ❑ The letter sounds sincere.
- ❑ The letter sounds enthusiastic.

Accuracy:

- ❑ You have proofread the letter several times for typos, grammar, spelling, punctuation, and content.
- ❑ Another reliable person has proofread it and given you feedback on it.
- ❑ The letterhead contains the correct information (full address, telephone and fax numbers, and email address).

Application Forms

During your job campaign, you will be asked to complete application forms. When a company requests that you complete an application form, do so. Your résumé does not substitute for a completed application form. Be sure to complete each section of the application. If a question on the application form does not apply to you, write "Not Applicable" or "Does Not Apply" in the blank. If a question calls for salary expected and you do not want to state a figure, write "Open to Negotiation," which means you would prefer to discuss salary once an offer of employment is made. If you leave the answer blank, the employer may assume:

- You were careless and missed the question.
- You did not understand the question.

Either of these assumptions will eliminate your form from the stack of successful applications.

Each organization designs its own form for employee recruitment in order to include the specific questions it wants applicants to answer. Nevertheless, most application forms are similar.

Supplying information on the application forms you are requested to complete is a significant part of your job campaign. Follow the instructions carefully, and supply the information exactly as it is called for. If the instruction reads, "Please print," do so. Your printing and handwriting must be legible. After all, you want it to stand out in the pile.

Prepare your answers before you write or key on the application form. When you do this, your form will appear neat and organized. A completed application form becomes a part of the permanent record of the applicant who is hired.

Be prepared to complete the application. Do you:

- have a pen?
- know the current date?

- have the names, titles, addresses, telephone and fax numbers, and email addresses for your references?
- have the dates of previous employment?
- have a list of your volunteer activities and the associations you belong to?
- have the dates you attended high school and postsecondary institutions?
- know your social insurance number?
- know the exact title of the job you are applying for?

Complete the form as requested even if you have your résumé with you. In this case, staple a copy of your résumé to the back of the application form

Portfolios

A portfolio is one of best marketing tools you can have on a job interview. It is a collection of samples of your best work and should include only perfect work; nothing less than perfect is acceptable.

A portfolio is often presented in electronic form. An **e-portfolio** should contain the same documents as a hard-copy portfolio; however, the documents will be stored on a personal website or arranged in an electronic folder. An e-portfolio requires the applicant to take a notebook computer to the interview. An advantage of the e-portfolio is the ease of sending it to or leaving it with an employer. Note that due to the spread of computer viruses, many employers may not want to open a folder of materials that is sent as an email attachment. In this case, storing an e-portfolio on a personal website and providing a **hyperlink** from the email to the website would be preferable.

When a hard-copy portfolio is used, no writing of any kind should appear on the documents.

Regardless of whether the portfolio is presented on paper or electronically, it should contain samples of your original work and be highly organized. One suggestion is to organize it into sections such as:

- correspondence
- spreadsheets
- tables
- graphics
- minutes of meetings
- reports
- newsletters or advertisements
- website developments
- documents demonstrating knowledge of specialized areas, such as legal or medical office administration

It should also contain:

- your transcript of marks (but only if it is impressive)
- letter/s of reference
- certificates and diplomas earned

When using an e-portfolio, transcripts, letters of reference, certificates, and diplomas should be scanned and stored electronically.

All portfolios must be well organized. To give the hard-copy portfolio an organized appearance, use a table of contents, dividers, and title pages. Protect all documents by placing them in plastic sleeves. Then package all of the work into an attractive leather or simulated leather case with rings to hold the pages. Do not use a binder, since it doesn't have the professional appearance you need. Keep your e-portfolio organized by using web page links or electronic folders with titles that accurately reflect the contents.

During the interview, find an appropriate opportunity to introduce the portfolio and discuss your work with the interviewer. Remember that the portfolio is not intended to be an information tool. It is a sales tool and the product it is promoting is you!

Self-Check

1. What is a prospecting application letter? a solicited application letter?

2. List three key factors to consider as you improve the appearance of your application letter.

3. What assumptions might the prospective employer make when you leave sections of the application form blank?

4. How is a portfolio considered a marketing tool?

5. List four guidelines to help give your portfolio an organized appearance.

Job Interviews

A job interview gives you the opportunity to convince a prospective employer that you can make a real contribution to the organization. An interviewer can judge your basic qualifications by studying your transcript, application letter, résumé, test results, and completed application form. During the interview, the interviewer will evaluate your personality, attitudes, professional appearance, and ability to communicate (see Figure 16-6). An impressive college record and evidence that you possess the necessary office technology skills are pluses, but your success in landing the job you want will hinge on the way you project yourself during the interview.

Figure 16-6 Interviewer and applicant.

Remember that the purpose of the job interview is twofold:

1. to give the interviewer an opportunity to evaluate the applicant
2. to give the applicant a chance to evaluate the job and the organization

The interview is not just for the benefit of the employer. It should be mutually beneficial.

Sometimes getting an interview is extremely difficult. If getting an interview seems impossible, don't get discouraged: this difficulty may reflect the competition for jobs in your area.

Try to schedule several interviews with organizations that you believe will offer the type of work you are seeking. Don't set your expectations on one particular job. Becoming overly anxious about getting a particular job can create unnecessary tension. Nevertheless, you should enter each interview with the attitude that the job you are applying for is precisely the one you want. As you learn more about the job, it may *become* the job you want.

Before the Interview Prepare thoroughly for each interview. Your preparation should include:

- researching the organization where you have scheduled the interview
- taking a practice run to the location of the interview
- learning what the current salaries are for administrative assistants in the community
- summarizing your own qualifications
- deciding which qualifications to emphasize
- anticipating the interviewer's questions
- formulating your answers to the interviewer's questions
- choosing clothes appropriate for the interview
- scheduling ample time for personal grooming

Research Researching the organization is crucial. The following are effective research methods:

- using the internet to study the organization
- exploring the organization in the reference section of the library
- reading the organization's most recent annual report
- calling the organization's receptionist and requesting information.

Learn all you can about the organization. Research:

- the organization's products or services
- how profitable the organization is
- the number of employees the organization has
- how long the organization has been operating
- the extent of the company's operations
- any recent expansion the company may have experienced
- any mergers or name changes the company has undergone
- the company's competitive standing in the industry
- the organization's hiring practices

Many applicants do poorly during an interview because they lack knowledge about the organization. The interviewer will tell you about the organization and its employment opportunities, but you will be able to converse with more ease and ask pertinent questions if you have researched the organization. Lack of knowledge could be viewed by the interviewer as lack of interest in the organization. Prepare thoroughly; show your interest in the organization through your knowledge about it.

Anticipate Questions Think about what you have to offer and the qualifications you want to emphasize. Review your résumé before you go to the interview. The interviewer will expect you to discuss your job objective and why you feel qualified for it. You should be prepared to talk about yourself in an organized way without hesitation.

Anticipate the questions the interviewer will ask, and know what your answers will be. In an attempt to determine if you can handle the job, the employer may ask:

1. What do you know about this company?
2. What do you know about the position you are applying for?
3. We are looking for someone with extensive experience. Your résumé indicates limited experience as an office professional. How do you expect to compensate for your lack of experience?
4. Why do you think you might like to work for this organization?

5. What do you expect to be doing five years from now?

6. Why did you choose a career as an administrative assistant?

7. Relating to the responsibilities described in the advertisement for this position, what strengths will you bring to our office?

8. Relating to the responsibilities described in the advertisement for this position, what responsibilities do you believe will be your greatest challenges? How do you expect to meet these challenges?

9. How do you rate the education you received? Why?

10. Throughout your training to be an administrative assistant, what courses did you enjoy the most? the least? Why?

At the outset of the interview, you may be asked some general questions relating to your personal interests, or you may be asked to give your opinion about the latest current events. Some interviewers begin with questions that they think will put the applicant at ease. Answer all questions thoroughly but without rambling. Consider your answers to all questions seriously; the interviewer is searching for qualified employees who will stay with the organization if they are hired.

To gain insight into your personality and to check on your attitude, the interviewer may ask questions such as these:

1. Tell me about yourself.

2. If we asked your friends or colleagues to describe you with three words, what words would they use?

3. Give an example of how you have displayed initiative.

4. Do you prefer working within a team or by yourself? Explain.

5. How do you spend your leisure time?

6. What personality characteristics do you think are essential for the job you are seeking?

7. How do you accept criticism?

8. Provide an example of a time when you were criticized.

9. Describe the best/worst employer/teacher you have ever had.

10. Explain a stressful situation you encountered, and describe how you handled it.

Unethical Questions Interviewers who want information on marital status, age, smoking habits, physical disabilities, race, ancestry, or place of origin must phrase their inquiries very carefully. Many questions relating to these topics are unethical. Basing employment decisions on these factors is usually illegal.

Although most organizations fall under provincial human rights jurisdiction, some are under federal human rights jurisdiction. Those that are federally governed include all federal government departments, federal Crown corporations, federally chartered banks, and national interest organizations (such as transportation and communication companies). Most other organizations fall under provincial human rights authority. Some businesses are subject to both federal and provincial human rights acts. Human rights legislation is subject to change.

If you have concerns about your human rights as they relate to your job search, your best course of action is to contact both the Human Rights Commission for your province and the federal Human Rights Commission.

The Canadian Human Rights Commission website at www.chrc-ccdp.ca discusses employment equity, harassment in the workplace, sexual discrimination, and many other topics. Refer to Figure 16-7 for a chart developed by the commission, "Prohibited Grounds of Discrimination in Canada."

Ask Intelligent Questions An interviewer will expect you to ask questions too. Some interviews lend themselves to the applicant asking questions periodically throughout the interview, while other interviews give the applicant an opportunity at the end of the interview to ask questions. Your research prior to the interview should help you generate a list of appropriate questions. State that you have researched the company website and that you prepared a few questions. Choose a selection of questions, key them on your crib sheet, take the sheet to the interview, and refer to it. The following is a list of good questions to ask on an interview:

■ To whom would I report? To how many people would I report?

■ What personal qualities improve the likelihood for success in this position?

■ What is the organization's mission?

■ What are the major barriers for this organization to fulfill its mission?

■ I read in the . . . that you are expanding your . . . division. How would that affect the position I am applying for?

■ Does the organization have a human resource development program?

■ What is the organization's plan to increase revenues or capacities?

■ How would you describe the corporate culture of this organization?

Figure 16-7 Prohibited grounds of discrimination chart.

Prohibited Grounds	Federal	British Columbia	Alberta	Saskatchewan	Manitoba	Ontario	Quebec	New Brunswick	Prince Edward Island	Nova Scotia	Newfoundland	Northwest Territories	Nunavut	Yukon
Race or colour	•	•	•	•	•	•	•	•	•	•	•	•	•	•
Religion or creed	•	•	•	•	•	•	•	•	•	•	•	•	•	•
Age	•	19-65	18+	18-64	•	18-65	•	•	•	•	19-65	•	•	•
Gender (incl. pregnancy or childbirth)	•	•	•[2]	•	•[3]	•[2,4]	•[2]	•[2]	•	•	•	•	•	•
Marital status	•	•	•	•	•	•	•[6]	•	•	•	•	•	•	•
Physical/Mental handicap or disability	•	•	•	•	•	•	•	•	•	•	•	•	•	•
Sexual orientation	•	•	•	•	•	•	•	•	•	•	•[5]	•	•	•
National or ethnic origin (incl. linguistic background)	•		•	•[7]	•	•[8]	•	•	•	•	•	•[7]	•[7]	•
Family status	•	•	•	•[9]	•	•	•[6]	•	•	•[9]	•			
Dependence on alcohol or drug	•	•[5]	•[5]	•[5]	•[5]	•[5]	•	•[5,10]	•[5]	•[10]	•[5]			
Ancestry or place of origin		•	•	•	•	•		•				•		•
Political belief		•				•			•	•	•			•
Based on association				•	•	•			•	•	•		•	•
Pardoned conviction	•					•	•					•	•	
Record of criminal conviction		•					•						•	
Source of income			•	•[11]	•		•	•	•	•	•			•
Assignment, attachment or seizure of pay						•					•			
Social condition/origin						•	•				•	•	•	
Language						•[5]	•	•				•		•

Harassment on any of the prohibited grounds is considered a form of discrimination.

Threatening, intimidating or discriminating against someone who has filed a complaint, or hampering a complaint investigation, is a violation of provincial human rights codes, and at the federal level is a criminal offence.

* Any limitation, exclusion, denial or preference may be permitted if a bona fide occupational requirement can be demonstrated.

1) also refers to perceived race
2) includes transgenderism
3) includes gender-determined characteristics
4) Ontario accepts complaints based on a policy related to female genital mutilation
5) complaints accepted based on policy
6) Quebec uses the term civil status
7) defined as nationality
8) Ontario's Code includes both ethnic origin and citizenship
9) defined as being in a parent-child relationship
10) previous dependence only
11) defined as receipt of public assistance

Self-Check

1. What are two purposes of the job interview?
2. List seven topics you should research about the prospective employer before your interview.
3. List six questions the interviewer may ask in order to determine if you can handle the job.
4. List six questions the interviewer may ask to gain insight into your personality and attitude.
5. Think of three questions you should *not* ask at a job interview.

Your Appearance Makes a Statement Although first impressions rarely win jobs, your appearance—your clothes, hair, shoes, cosmetics, and jewellery—can certainly cost you the job before you ever open your mouth.

Your goal is to look the part of a business professional. Your appearance should make the statement that you are a professional and that you want to be taken seriously. This is true even in companies that have a dress-down policy. Companies that encourage their employees to dress casually still expect applicants to dress and act professionally on the interview. Once they are successful and join the staff, they may adopt the dress code of the company.

Spend the extra time it takes to look well groomed. Dress conservatively since you want the interviewer to focus on your answers without being distracted by your appearance. By applying the following guidelines to your

Did you know that the Canadian Human Rights Commission (CHRC) advises employers how to conduct job interviews without violating the law? Their guidelines for screening and selection are comprehensive, but these few examples are for *your* record:

- **Gender:** CHRC says avoid asking males or females to complete different applications, and don't ask about pregnancy or childbearing plans.
  You may ask the applicant if attendance requirements can be met.
- **Marital Status:** CHRC says avoid asking the applicant whether they are married, single, divorced, or whether an applicant's spouse is employed or subject to transfer.
  You may ask if there are any circumstances that might prevent minimum service commitment.
- **Race or Colour:** CHRC says avoid any inquiry into race or colour, including colour of eyes, skin, or hair.
- **Height and Weight:** CHRC says that the employer can make no inquiry unless there is evidence it is for genuine occupational requirements.
- **Photographs:** CHRC says avoid asking for a photograph of the applicant before the interview. Photographs for security passes or company files can be taken after successful selection.

interview preparation, you may be able to convey the proper message:

- Your hair should be neat and away from your face.
- If you wear cosmetics, apply them sparingly.
- Your nails should be well manicured and clean.
- Your jewellery should be simple, minimal, and complementary. Since you don't know the nature of the interviewer, it is best to play it safe and wear limited and conservative jewellery.
- Your professional attire should include a suit jacket.
- Your clothing should not be revealing; skirts should be of a comfortable length and blouses should never reveal cleavage or camisole.
- Shoes should be clean, polished, and conventional.
- White blouses or shirts must be very white. Cuffs or collars that have a grey appearance are a sign that grooming is less than perfect.
- Ties should complement a suit rather than be flamboyant.
- Cologne should be avoided. A fragrance that is attractive to you could be offensive to another person.

- For men, the most appropriate choice of colour is a variation of black, navy, brown, or grey. Acceptable business clothing for women tends to be more colourful than that of their male counterparts, although it still must be conservative.

Whatever you decide will be your image for an interview, consider the strong nonverbal message that your image will send. Clearly there are things to avoid wearing for an interview, including the following:

- extreme colours of nail polish
- capris, leggings, or jean pants
- strapless dresses (if you wear a dress, consider wearing a jacket with it)
- a garment with a low neckline, see-through fabric, or midriff-baring top

Business Professional versus Business Casual When attending an interview, business professional is always the right choice. This means wearing a matching suit—a skirt and jacket or pants and jacket—to the interview. Business casual is more relaxed: you may choose to wear a non-matching jacket and skirt or pants. Remember, though, that this business casual look is only appropriate on the job, after you have been hired, not during the interview itself. Some organizations have dress-down days, and it is important you understand the guidelines your company sets for these days.

Be Punctual Know the exact location of the interview. Plan to arrive 10 to 15 minutes early, so you can avoid rushing before the interview. You can undermine yourself before the interview by becoming stressed because you did not allow yourself enough time. A few days before the interview, travel to the office, and time yourself. On the actual day of the interview, allow more time than is needed to get there.

Never schedule two interviews for the same morning or afternoon. You have no control over the length of the interview, and you will not feel at ease if you are concerned about time.

Park in a location where you do not risk getting a ticket; the last thing you need to worry about is your car.

What to Take to the Interview For the interview, you will want to have important materials on hand; but you will not want to be encumbered with items you do not need.

You should avoid bringing the following items to an interview. (Although it seems like common sense not to bring them, many employers report that applicants often do.)

- Never bring packages. Avoid shopping immediately before an interview, unless you can leave all the packages in your car.

- Women should never carry a large purse. A small hand-bag with only necessary items will not distract from a professional appearance.

- Men and women should never carry a briefcase that is oversized or resembles a schoolbag. Keep everything neat and simple and nondistracting.

- Most important of all, never bring another person. Naturally you wouldn't bring another person into the interview; but a number of applicants make plans to meet friends or relatives immediately after the interview.

The applicant needs to concentrate on the interview, not on the friends or relatives waiting in the lobby or reception area. In particular, don't bring children, since their behaviour may cause you to worry. Demonstrate that you are an independent person; arrive alone and leave alone.

Here's what you *should* take to the interview.

- Your portfolio, if prepared to a professional standard, will be one of the best sales tools you have. Bring it to the interview and look for the perfect opportunity to walk through it with the interviewer.

- Always bring along a pen and paper to write down important facts you learn during the interview. Your pen should be attractive and in good condition. One that has been chewed or runs out of ink will give a poor impression.

- Bring along extra copies of your résumé. Offer copies to the interviewers just as the interview is ready to start. This demonstrates your preparation. You will also need a copy for yourself to refer to throughout the interview.

- If references do not appear on your résumé, you should bring a list of three or more references that includes names, titles, company names, company addresses, company telephone and fax numbers, and email addresses. This should be attractively keyed on a single sheet. Be prepared to leave this sheet with the interviewer.

- It is very acceptable to prepare a crib sheet and bring it along to the interview. On the crib sheet, you can list the responsibilities of the job; and for each one, cite specific examples of how you have demonstrated competence. Also, on this crib sheet, key any questions you have prepared. Don't be afraid to refer to this sheet during the interview. The sheet should appear neat and organized and, of course, should be keyed.

- With desktop publishing, you can prepare personal business cards that are professional-looking when printed on cardstock. Or, for a nominal charge, you can have a professional printer produce a small number of business cards. The applicant who leaves a business card leaves a professional statement.

During the Interview Be courteous, confident, and composed. As you approach the interviewer, smile, greet the interviewer by name, and introduce yourself. Give the interviewer a firm handshake. This will express your confidence. Try to relax. You will probably feel a little nervous because the interview is important to you. If you feel nervous, don't call attention to your nervousness by twisting your hair, tapping your foot, thumping on the table, sitting on the edge of the chair, talking too rapidly, or showing other outward signs.

There may be one interviewer or a panel of interviewers. The interviewers have a job to perform; they must match an applicant to the requirements of the job to be filled.

The initial interview will probably last 30 minutes or more. A good interviewer will allow the interviewee to talk throughout most of the interview.

Some interviewers break the interview into the following segments:

1. getting acquainted
2. presenting the organization's opportunities
3. evaluating the applicant
4. answering the applicant's questions

When you are asked a question, give a full answer, not simply a yes or no. The interviewer will use a question or a comment to introduce a subject you are expected to discuss. Look the interviewer in the eye, and answer all questions frankly. Be deliberate; don't start talking before the interviewer completes the question. Avoid talking too much; keep to the point. Don't attempt to answer a question you do not understand. Either restate the question as you understand it or ask the interviewer to clarify it.

While you are talking, keep your goal in mind, which is to promote yourself. Use every opportunity to emphasize your good points and to relate them to what you can do for the organization. To sound sincere, present facts, not your opinion, about yourself. Don't criticize yourself, and never make derogatory remarks about an instructor or a former employer.

As you are talking, the interviewer will evaluate your mental and physical alertness, your ability to communicate, your attitude toward life and toward the organization, and your enthusiasm for work. Some interviewers will give tests in order to evaluate your skill level.

As discussed in the section "Before the Interview," you should prepare questions to ask at the interview.

What about Salary? At the initial interview, your first questions should not concern salary or benefits. The questions of salary can be an issue that many find difficult to address, but it is a necessary part of the job-searching process. You may wish to address salary closer to the end of the interview or choose to reserve these questions until you are offered the job. Many employers appreciate knowing whether the salary they are offering is suitable to a candidate, thus avoiding the waste of valuable time and resources. If the interviewer asks you about your expected salary, be prepared to state a range. Remember that the figure the interviewer is likely to remember and focus on is the low end of your range.

If you have prepared a personal budget and have researched office salaries in your location, you will know what an appropriate starting salary is for this employment opportunity.

Remember that although salary is often a negotiable item, these negotiations must be handled with diplomacy. Although job satisfaction will be achieved mostly through obtaining a challenging and responsible position, don't sell yourself short when salary is discussed. If you have earned postsecondary credentials, you have gained bargaining power.

Closing the Interview
Watch for cues that the interview is coming to an end. The interviewer may thank you for coming, suggest that you schedule a time to take employment tests, invite you to arrange for a second interview, stand up, tell you that you will hear by a certain date if the organization is interested in your application, or offer you a job.

A good closure to an interview would include the following actions:

- Firmly shaking hands.
- Restating your interest in the position. Example: "I hope you will consider me for the job. I feel confident I would make a positive contribution to your organization."
- Checking the follow-up procedure that will be employed by the organization. Example: "When might I expect to hear from you? If I don't hear from you by that date, may I call you?"
- Leaving a business card.

If you are offered the job, you are not expected to accept it on the spot. You are making a long-term commitment, and you should be sure that it is the job you want. The interviewer would prefer that you give it enough thought to be absolutely certain. You may accept at once if you have no doubts about it. Otherwise, tactfully say that you would like time to consider it. Ask if you can let the interviewer know in a day or two or at some definite time you can agree upon.

You cannot always accurately judge how you are being rated by an interviewer. Interviewers who rely on the second interview for making a decision are noncommittal during the initial interview. Appear interested and confident as the interview draws to a close. Always express appreciation to the interviewer before leaving.

After the Interview
Make each interview a learning experience. Ask yourself the following questions to improve your self-promotion techniques:

- ❏ What points did I make that seemed to interest the interviewer?
- ❏ Did I present my qualifications well?
- ❏ Did I overlook any qualifications that are pertinent to the job?
- ❏ Did I learn all I need to know about the job, or did I forget or hesitate to ask about factors that are important to me?
- ❏ Did I talk too much? too little?
- ❏ Did I interview the employer rather than permit the employer to interview me?
- ❏ How can I improve my next interview?

The Campus Interview
Many organizations actively recruit postsecondary graduates. Your career counselling office will set up appointments for students nearing graduation to be interviewed by representatives from these companies. These interviews often occur right on the campus.

Stress your strong points; listen attentively; in response to the interviewer's questions, relate how you meet the qualifications for the job; project your personality; and ask relevant questions.

Don't expect that because the interview is held on campus that it means you should dress casually. Give the interviewer a chance to see how you would look on the job if the interviewer hired you. You must look mature and capable of accepting responsibility. The interviewer will be comparing your appearance with that of administrative assistants who already work for the organization, not with the appearance of other college students.

If, as a result of the campus interview, you are invited for a second interview or to take tests, be sure to get the address of the building where you are to go. Write down the date, time, address, and name of the person who will meet with you.

Testing
The placement director and your instructors may know which organizations in your area give tests. If you apply for a job with an organization that administers tests, be prepared to take at least a word processing production test or a keying test. They could test your skill on any software application, or they could test your ability to compose correspondence.

Many tests have time limits. Listen carefully to the instructions you receive. If you do not clearly understand what you are expected to do, ask questions. You will be expected to perform at speed levels determined by the organization administering the tests. Test papers are usually evaluated by degree of accuracy.

Personality tests and mental ability tests are popular. It is not possible to prepare for these. The goal of these examinations is to determine which applicants will work well with existing staff members, which applicants will most likely share the company's goals, and which applicants have potential leadership skills.

The Second Interview You may be invited for more than one interview. During the initial interview, members of the interview team will screen the interviewees. If tests are given as part of the screening, it will probably be the human resources department that administers them and evaluates the results.

A procedure commonly used is this. When human resources staff members discover applicants they are willing to recommend as candidates for specific jobs, they arrange interviews for the applicants with the actual employers. When you are told that you will be interviewed by the person who will be your manager if you are hired, you will know that your chances of getting the job are increasing. The final selection will be made by the person for whom the administrative assistant will work.

The second interview provides you with an opportunity to promote yourself to the person for whom you would work. Emphasize your strong points. Be as relaxed and natural as possible, so that the interviewer can detect your true personality. Ask questions about the scope of the job and about the responsibilities that the person performing it would have. Listen carefully, and answer the questions you are asked. When you know you want the job, say so. The interviewer is not just searching for a qualified applicant; the interviewer is searching for a person who is definitely interested in working for the organization.

Self-Check

1. How should you dress for an interview with a company whose dress code for employees is casual?

2. List three precautions you can take to ensure you are not late for an interview.

3. List six guidelines you should follow during an interview to leave a favourable impression.

4. What would be an acceptable response if you are offered a job at the end of the interview?

5. How should you dress for an interview conducted on your campus by external recruiters?

Behavioural Descriptive Interviews

An applicant can prepare thoroughly for an interview; however, it is impossible to anticipate all possible interview scenarios. Behavioural descriptive interview questions are commonly used by recruiters to sort facts from exaggerations. These interviews use a "domino" questioning technique, in which each question leads to the next and probes deeper into an experience or scenario described by the applicant. A typical set of behavioural interview questions is:

1. Describe a situation where you were a team leader in a professional environment and conflict arose within the team.

2. What did you do to resolve this conflict?

3. What did you learn from this experience?

4. Since the conflict, how have you applied what you learned?

5. Who has benefited from your ability to resolve conflict?

Some applicants feel threatened and almost interrogated by the probing nature of these questions. However, these questions, if presented in a diplomatic manner, are highly successful in determining the best candidate. Because many people embellish their résumés and then perform well at exaggerating their talents during the interview, the best candidate is not always selected for the job.

Behavioural descriptive questions are not difficult to answer if the candidate has the experience the recruiter is seeking. If you are asked a behavioural descriptive question and simply don't have the experience necessary to answer the question, be honest. The best policy is to tell the interviewer that you have no experience in this particular area. If you have related experience, ask the recruiter if you might refer to a similar situation in a different type of environment.

Follow-Up Correspondence

The letters essential for continuing and finalizing a job campaign fall into five categories: thank-you, reminder, inquiry, job acceptance, and job refusal. Key follow-up letters on the same quality paper you used for the résumé; be sure to include your return address, telephone and fax numbers, and email address. Check them carefully for accuracy. Be sure that the company's name and the interviewer's name are spelled correctly.

All of the letters can be sent as email messages, but your choice to use this method will depend on the formality of the situation. Most employers are interested in quick and to-the-point communication, so email is very appropriate. However, where the environment is very formal, a letter on bond paper may be necessary.

Thank-You Writing a thank-you letter following a job interview is not a requirement but a courtesy. Always write a thank-you letter and send it immediately after the interview. If you want the job for which you were interviewed, you can use a thank-you letter to do far more than express appreciation to the interviewer. Not everyone writes thank-you letters; consequently, when your thank-you letter arrives at the interviewer's desk, it will single you out from other applicants and call attention once more to your application. See Figure 16-8 for a sample of a standard thank-you letter for mailing, faxing, or delivering in person. See Figure 16-9 for a sample of an email thank-you letter.

Reminders When you do not receive a response to an application or are told that your application has been placed on file, write a message after a few weeks have elapsed to remind the human resources manager that you still are interested. You will find reminder messages especially helpful when you plan to move from one region of Canada to another and make inquiries about jobs months in advance of your availability for employment.

Inquiries Following a job interview, you can write a letter of inquiry or make a telephone call if you have not heard anything by the time the human resources manager said you would receive a reply. Be patient. Wait a day or two beyond the time you are expecting a reply and, if you do not hear, telephone or write to inquire. If you are told that the job has not been filled, indicate that you definitely are interested.

Figure 16-8 Thank-you letter.

Ms. Dini Lawrence
101 Keele Street
Toronto, ON M3P1K1
Tel: 416-555-1329   Fax: 416-555-2390   Email: dini@z-wave.ca

February 11, 20xx

Mr. William Wilson
Vice-President of Marketing
Millennium Appliances, Inc.
3431 Bloor Street
Toronto, ON M8X 1G4

Dear Mr. Wilson:

Speaking with you yesterday afternoon about the responsibilities of an administrative assistant with Millennium Appliances Company convinced me that this is exactly the position I am seeking.

The time and information you shared with me discussing employment opportunities and management policies of Millennium Appliances was certainly appreciated. Thank you.

I feel confident I can meet the requirements of the available position and am looking forward to hearing a positive response from you.

Sincerely,

D. Lawrence.

Ms. Dini Lawrence

Figure 16-9 Sample email thank-you letter.

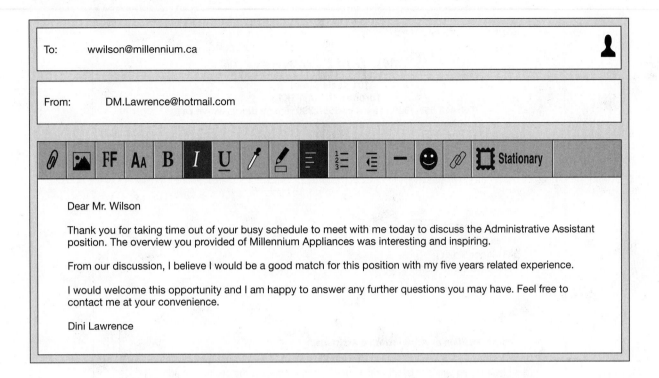

To: wwilson@millennium.ca

From: DM.Lawrence@hotmail.com

Dear Mr. Wilson

Thank you for taking time out of your busy schedule to meet with me today to discuss the Administrative Assistant position. The overview you provided of Millennium Appliances was interesting and inspiring.

From our discussion, I believe I would be a good match for this position with my five years related experience.

I would welcome this opportunity and I am happy to answer any further questions you may have. Feel free to contact me at your convenience.

Dini Lawrence

Job Acceptance Even when you accept a job offer during an interview or over the telephone, follow up with an email or a letter. You will probably receive a letter offering you a job and suggesting that you call to accept. Respond by telephone, but also send a letter to leave no doubt about your acceptance. The letter offering you the job, plus your written response, should contain all the elements of a contract and, as such, constitute a contract.

In the opening, accept the job enthusiastically. Mention the specific job being accepted. If you have received a form for supplying additional information, complete it, enclose it, and refer to it in your letter. Repeat the report-to-work instructions, giving the date, time, and place. In either the beginning or the closing, express appreciation. Keep a copy of the letter of offer and your reply. Please refer to Figure 16-10 for an example of a job acceptance letter.

Job Refusal If you conduct a thorough job campaign, you may be offered more than one job. In this case, you will have to refuse all but one offer. What a good problem to have!

Be as prompt in refusing as possible. If you have already accepted a job, refuse the second offer at once. This is a courtesy you owe the person who must search elsewhere to fill the job offered to you.

Since your letter will be disappointing to the reader, you should organize it in the same way you organize other letters of disappointment. Begin by making a favourable statement concerning your contact with the interviewer or about the organization. Express appreciation for the job offer at either the beginning or the end of the letter. Include at least one reason for refusing the job offer. State the refusal tactfully, but make it clear that you are refusing. By making a definite statement about already having accepted a job or about your continuing to search for a particular job, you will be refusing the offer without making a negative statement. Close with a pleasant comment.

Don't burn your bridges—you may want to work for the organization at some point in the future. Check your letter to make sure that the attitude reflected by your statements does not close the door for you. In Figure 16-11, the writer shows appreciation and says that she would be interested in a more senior position.

Self-Check

1. List the five categories of letters essential in continuing and finalizing your job campaign.

2. Suggest two factors to be considered when you prepare a job refusal letter.

Figure 16-10 Job acceptance letter.

Ms. Dini Lawrence

101 Keele Street
Toronto, ON M3P1K1
Tel: 416-555-1329   Fax: 416-555-2390   Email: dini@z-wave.ca

June 1, 20xx

Mr. William
Vice-President of Marketing
Millennium Appliances, Inc.
3431 Bloor Street
Toronto, ON M8X 1G4

Dear Mr. Wilson:

Subject: Position as Administrative Assistant

As I expressed over the telephone, I am delighted to accept the position of administrative assistant in the Marketing Department of Millennium Appliances.

Enclosed are the forms you requested I complete after our conference last week.

I appreciate the opportunity to join your team and am eager to commence work on Monday, June 16. Again, thank you for offering me the opportunity to work with Millennium Appliances.

Sincerely,

D. Lawrence.

Ms. Dini Lawrence

Enclosures

Figure 16-11 Job refusal letter.

Ms. Sabrina Tang

1010 Carlton Avenue, Toronto, ON   M4W 1R1
Tel: 416-555-1111   Fax: 416-555-3333   E-mail: stang@home.com

05 September 20xx

Mr. Jeremy Davis
Public Relations Manager
Telus Corporation
1111 Bloor Street East
Toronto, ON M4W 3R3

Dear Mr. Davis:

Subject: Receptionist Position

Thank you for the job offer to become receptionist in the Public Relations Division of Telus Corporation. However, as I mentioned at the time of the interview, I am seeking a position as an administrative assistant. Another company in the city has offered me this level of employment and I have accepted it.

Mr. Davis, I appreciate the offer to work for your company and the interest you have shown in me. In the future, if a more senior position becomes available, I would be very interested in working for Telus Corporation.

Yours truly,

Sabrina Tang

Sabrina Tang

ELECTRONIC JOB SEARCH

The internet has become a popular tool for searching for available employment and for posting résumés for potential employers to view. Yet another innovation is the computer-scanned résumé; with current technology, specially prepared résumés get the attention of a computer before they attract the attention of an employer.

Using the Internet

The computer is a valuable job-searching tool. Searching the internet for job opportunities will not eliminate the need to practise traditional job-hunting techniques, but it will add another dimension to your job search.

Job announcement databases are available for browsing. By browsing through websites, you will reach many online Canadian job-search facilities. Here are a few web locations:

- www.monster.ca
- www.workingincanada.gc.ca
- www.jobshark.ca
- www.workopolis.ca

In the highly competitive search for work, the internet is an important job market. The internet may be used for job searching, but it is also useful for sending your résumé to one of the online career services. The online career service will ask you to either complete the online résumé builder form or to send a copy of your résumé.

Your résumé information now becomes a part of a database that is accessible to employers looking for employees with the right skills. Any reputable online career service keeps confidential the personal portion of your résumé (name, addresses, and contact numbers). When an employer believes that your credentials match a job opportunity available, the employer will offer to purchase your name and contact numbers. With your permission, the online career service will release the header to the paying customer—the potential employer.

Electronically Scanned Résumés

A growing number of companies are relying on the services of executive search firms who use electronic scanning systems to digitally scan, store, and track résumés and covering letters. In fact, with current scanning technology, hundreds of résumés can be scanned in only a few minutes. When recruiters wish to retrieve or **short list** a group of appropriate candidates, they supply key words that are essential for the right applicant. These key words will identify expertise, experience, and education. For example, they might include such words as *bilingual*, *entrepreneur*, *desktop publishing*, *total quality management*, *supervisor*, and *teams*. The computer software scans the database, and within minutes a list of applicants whose résumés match the stated criteria is brought to the screen.

Refer to Figure 16-12 for an example of a partial résumé that has been prepared for electronic scanning.

Electronically scanned résumés save the recruiter a large amount of time. However, even a résumé with extensive credentials may go unnoticed if the scanner cannot identify them. Many scanning programs make mistakes when reading words or special characters. To ensure that all the information on your résumé is collected by the electronic system, follow these tips to make sure your résumé is scan friendly:

1. Do not use italics. Instead, use a standard typeface.
2. Do not bold any text.
3. Do not underline or use graphic lines.
4. Do not use indents or centering.
5. Describe your personal traits in nouns, not verbs.
6. Use the key words found in the job ad.
7. Use straightforward words to describe your experience.
8. Use multiple pages if necessary. Unlike humans, computers do not tire of reading.
9. Use common résumé headings such as Objective, Education, Experience, and Interests.
10. Do not print your résumé on coloured paper.
11. Increase your lists of key words. Include specific software names such as Microsoft Word.

One advantage of an electronic scanning system is that electronic storage takes so much less space than paper storage. This means that résumés may be kept on file for an extended period of time.

If applicants are not aware of the electronic scanning process and submit attractive yet traditionally formatted résumés, they may not be identified by the computer, no matter how outstanding. The best approach when you do not know whether electronic or human screening will be used is to submit two résumés. The résumé intended for human scrutiny should be printed on attractive paper, using highlighting features, graphic lines, and so on. Place a removable note on the nicely formatted résumé that states "Visual Résumé." Place another removable note on the résumé destined for electronic scanning that says "Scannable Résumé." The reason you have included two résumés should be briefly explained in your cover letter.

Self-Check

1. How does an online career service work?
2. List an advantage for employers that an electronic scanning system for résumés would have over hard copies.

ETHICAL ISSUES IN THE JOB SEARCH

As you know, many businesses adopt a formal document called a code of ethics that states the primary values and ethical rules they expect all employees to follow. Naturally, they expect prospective employees to hold similar values in terms of their job search as they would exhibit in the workplace.

Suppose you read an employment ad and you believe you are capable of doing the job. However, the ad mentions the need for specific experience. Although you do not have experience in the area mentioned in the ad, you feel you can do the job. After all, you believe you are a quick learner. The action you choose will determine your success. Based on your values and beliefs, study the following options:

■ Option 1: Move to the next employment ad. Because you don't have the required experience, you don't qualify for the position.

■ Option 2: Create false experiences and apply for the position. You can just make something up. After all, the last company you worked for isn't in business anymore.

■ Option 3: Take a chance and apply for the position. In the interview process, you can emphasize you have related skills and share how you can apply those skills to the position.

Figure 16-12 Partial résumé prepared for electronic scanning.

Ms. Kimberly Wong
10507 53 Avenue NW
Edmonton AB T6H 0R6
Tel 403-478-1320
Fax 403-478-2398
E-mail: kimwong@netcom.ca

OBJECTIVE
To earn the position of administrative assistant with a company that has a progressive
team spirit.

EDUCATION
September 1996 to April 1998
Southern Alberta Institute of Technology
Office Administration Program
Calgary
Honours Diploma
Keying 70 words per minute
Microsoft Word
PowerPoint
Excel
President Office Administration Society
Team Leader Graduation Planning Committee
Leader Charity Fundraising

EXPERIENCE
May 1999 to September 2002
Administrative Assistant
Coron Industries
Calgary
Supervisor of junior staff
Coordinator of budget
Coordinator of conferences and seminars
Designer of brochures and newsletters
Coordinator ISO 9001

May 1998 to May 1999
Administrative Assistant
Image Publishers
Calgary
Supervisor of reception desk
Coordinator of media

Let's consider the options above. In the first option, you may be missing a great opportunity. Although you lack the specified experience, you may have related skills that would be acceptable to the employer. You can proceed as Option 3 shows. The worst that can happen is that your résumé would be rejected. The best that can happen is the prospective employer will see your potential and decide experience is not as important as initiative.

In Option 2, you are the loser. Adding false or misrepresenting information is never a good idea. Misrepresentation of information has a way of "snowballing." If you are hired and cannot perform the duties that your résumé indicated you could, you will lose the respect of your manager and co-workers—and possibly your job.

INTERNATIONAL EMPLOYMENT

Working overseas can be an exciting option. The potential benefits to working abroad are many, including lucrative salaries, tax exemptions, overseas service premiums, free housing, completion bonuses, forty days or more of annual vacation time, international travel, and education allowances for dependents.

The range of international employment opportunities available is broader than most Canadians expect. Staffing requirements in the overseas job market are as diverse as in the domestic Canadian market. Highly skilled administrative assistants are in great demand, particularly if they communicate fluently in the English language, which is considered the international language of business.

The curriculum vitae (CV) or international-style résumé is used in overseas job hunting. The standard CV is between four and eight pages long and may contain a personal information section, references, detailed information on all former positions held, a list of memberships in professional organizations, overseas living and working experience, publication credits, and detailed education information. It should also include a recent picture. You will be required to present copies of all diplomas, certificates, transcripts, and a copy of your passport as the selection process progresses. Before hiring, countries may require results of medical examinations and chest x-rays, and proof of up-to-date immunizations as required by that country. Many countries also require certificates of good conduct, which you may request from your local court and police authorities. The certificate of good conduct certifies that you do not have a criminal record.

You should be aware that companies and organizations outside Canada do not fall under Canadian legal constraints as to what information they may require from a potential job candidate. Depending on the country in which you are seeking employment, you should be prepared to provide personal information such as pictures, marital status, date of birth, number of children, and other information that would be restricted by discrimination codes in Canada.

Research can be conducted easily on the internet by using a search engine such as Google to search for *international résumé, international curriculum vitae*, or similar topics.

Interviews conducted for international employment may not follow the same process as in Canada. For example, you may find that you are asked questions of a personal nature—about family, marital status, and health. Restrictions on questions that can be asked will vary with the country's policies guarding personal information and human rights issues. Even within the same country, company interviewing policies may vary, within the guidelines set down by that country. Researching the internet for information on the recruitment and interview process before the event will minimize the chances that you will be unprepared for differences from what you would encounter in Canada.

QUESTIONS FOR STUDY AND REVIEW

1. What is the name of the document published by the Conference Board of Canada that lists skills needed to enter the Canadian workforce? Where on the internet could you find that document?

2. Explain the meaning of the term *networking*. State ways you could network to improve your opportunity for employment.

3. What services are generally available to the postsecondary graduate through the school's placement office?

4. Explain how business news items can be a valuable source of job prospects.

5. What is the advantage of searching for job openings that are not advertised?

6. How can you find out about and apply for a position with the Government of Canada?

7. Compare the services of government and private employment agencies.

8. How does answering a newspaper advertisement for a job differ from using other means of seeking employment?

9. Why might a company place a blind job advertisement in the newspaper?

10. Name the principal sources of information for seeking employment in another geographic area.

11. Provide ten tips that would help you re-enter the workforce once you have been laid off from your employment.

12. What is the meaning of the term *curriculum vitae*?

13. What is the main purpose of a résumé?

14. Suggest why a prospective employer would be interested in information about an applicant's work experience unrelated to office work.

15. Should you include the names of references on your résumé? Explain.

16. What is the purpose of the application letter?

17. How does the purpose of the solicited application letter differ from the purpose of the prospecting application letter?

18. Why would an organization request that an applicant fill out its application form when the applicant has already submitted a résumé?

19. If a question on an application form asks what salary you are expecting, how should you complete this question?

20. State six guidelines for being prepared to complete a job application form.

21. Describe the contents of a portfolio you would show on an interview.

22. What information about an applicant can an interviewer glean from a personal interview that cannot be learned from the applicant's résumé or transcript?

23. Recommend ten guidelines for personal grooming in preparation for an interview.

24. List four items that should not be taken to the interview. List six items that *should* be taken to an interview.

25. Suggest three appropriate questions for the applicant to ask at the interview.

26. At what stage in an interview should salary range be discussed?

27. How will you know when the interview is over?

28. State four guidelines for effective closure to a job interview.

29. What is the purpose of behavioural descriptive interviews?

30. If you do not have the experience to answer a behavioural descriptive interview question, how should you respond?

31. Explain how the purpose of the second interview differs from the purpose of the initial interview.

32. List two advantages of writing a thank-you letter following a job interview.

33. Why should you write a job acceptance letter in addition to accepting a job by telephone?

34. How might the internet assist you in getting employment?

35. Give three reasons why companies might prefer electronically scanned résumés over the traditional method of screening résumés.

36. State eight guidelines for preparing a résumé to be electronically scanned.

37. Explain the procedure you should follow if you decide to send both a résumé for human screening and another one for electronic scanning.

EVERYDAY ETHICS

The Job Offer

Sandy recently had an interview for an administrative assistant position at a busy real estate office. This morning, she received a call from Ronn Edwards, the office manager of the real estate office, with a job offer. Sandy advised Ronn that she would need a day or two to think about the offer. Sandy didn't want to give an answer to Ronn because she had an interview later in the day at a municipal office in her town. She really wants the job with the municipality but doesn't want to ruin her chance at a job at the real estate office.

■ In your opinion, did Sandy handle this situation correctly?

■ If you knew Sandy, would you advise her to do anything differently? Why or why not?

Problem Solving

1. The interview has just begun, and you realize quickly that it is a behaviour descriptive interview. The interviewer has just asked you to describe a time when you were faced with a difficult situation and how you handled it. What example would you use in this case? What is the employer looking to find out about you through your answer?

2. A job announcement posted on the office technology bulletin board appeals to you. A variety of responsibilities are listed. You believe that you have the qualifications required for the job. The salary is excellent. The address of the company is local, but you have never heard of the company. You would like to know more about the company before you apply. You go to the library to find out about the company, but neither you nor the librarian who helps you can find out anything about the company. What can you do next to become informed about the company?

3. You have just sent your résumé by email and quickly realized you made a mistake in the years you stated you worked at your last job. Should you resend this résumé? Is this anything else you can or should do?

Special Reports

1. Research the internet for online career centres. Make a list of web pages, their addresses, and what they offer to the job seeker. Share this information with your fellow students through a class presentation.

2. Find an ad in a current newspaper that you are interested in answering. Write the opening paragraph of the letter you would send in response to the ad. Submit the paragraph to your instructor for approval.

3. Assume that you have been offered a job that you do not want to accept. Write a job refusal letter. Submit the letter to your instructor for approval.

4. Consider that you are applying for one of the positions posted in Figure 16-2. State which position you are applying for, and then prepare answers to all the questions posed in the subsection "Anticipate Questions" under the section called "Job Interviews" in this chapter.

5. Assume it has been one week since you had your interview for the job you applied for in question #4. The interviewer indicated she would be in touch within three to four days. Since you haven't heard back, you decide to write a follow-up email to determine the position status. Write the email message and submit it to your instructor for evaluation.

6. Working with a team of three or four members, research behaviour descriptive interview questions. As a team prepare a list of 20 questions. Then choose five of these questions to present to the class, and challenge your classmates to try to answer them through role-playing exercises. Hand in your group's list to your instructor.

PRODUCTION CHALLENGES

16-A Personal Inventory

Supplies needed:

- *Personal Inventory torm, Form 16-A, pages 448 and 449*

Completing a personal inventory is a useful step in developing a successful résumé. Attempt to make exhaustive lists when you work through the Personal Inventory form. Share the results of your form with a family member and again with a fellow student. These people will probably be able to help you add to your list. When your Personal Inventory form is complete, show it to your instructor.

16-B Visual Résumé and Scannable Résumé

Supplies needed:

- *Personal Inventory form, Form 16-A, completed in Production Challenge 16-A*
- *Plain bond paper*

Use the Personal Inventory form completed in Production Challenge 16-A and the information in this chapter to prepare an attractive résumé for human scanning. Then prepare one for electronic scanning. Write a cover letter for an unsolicited job for a position as an administrative assistant for Millennium Appliances. Your letter must explain why you are submitting two résumés.

16-C Your Job Campaign

Supplies needed:

- *Checklist for Your Job Campaign, Form 16-C-1, page 450*
- *Application for Employment, Form 16-C-2, pages 451 and 452*
- *Plain bond paper*

All 13 activities in this challenge are real. They provide guidelines for conducting your own job campaign.

Planning and conducting your own job campaign should be an exciting part of your office procedures course. Possessing office administration skills, knowledge of the business world, and a desire to work in an office are assets in your favour. However, the job market is competitive. To land the job you have prepared for, you must conduct a successful job campaign.

Start your job campaign at the beginning of the semester in which you are seeking full-time employment. Continue your job campaign throughout the semester or until you land a job.

Your instructor will assist you in planning your job campaign and will suggest the dates on which you should complete many of the job campaign activities. Enter the due dates on Form 16-C-1.

Job-Campaign Activities

1. Using the suggestions given in this chapter, prepare a self-appraisal inventory. Use Form 16-A. It should be helpful to you in determining which qualifications to emphasize during an interview and in preparing your résumé.

2. Look up a local corporation in a financial manual or directory available either at your school or in the public library. Prepare a concise report on the corporation, and submit the report to your instructor. Refer to Chapter 4 for information on financial publications.

3. Obtain literature that may be helpful to you in your job campaign from the placement office of your school. Read the literature, and then file it for ready reference in a job campaign file that you create.

4. Join a committee of peers to study employment opportunities for administrative assistants in your community. Separate committees should be organized on the basis of where the members of the class plan to seek employment—for instance, corporations, small companies, law firms, medical offices, hospitals, financial institutions, government offices, and other broad classifications. Consult several sources to study one organization. Obtain literature made available to prospective employees, ask corporations for annual reports and brochures, and confer with friends and former graduates who work in the various types of offices being studied. Share your findings with the members of your committee and other classmates.

5. Prepare for a job interview. Key a list of qualifications you plan to emphasize during the interview. Anticipate the questions you will be asked and list them. Also key a list of questions you may ask the interviewer. Submit a copy of your qualifications and of your questions to your instructor.

6. Prepare a résumé for employment with a specific organization. Use the example and suggested outline for preparing a résumé presented in this chapter. Submit your résumé to your instructor.

7. Write a prospecting job application letter (or a solicited one). Review the suggestions given in this chapter. Use the letter to sell yourself to a prospective employer.

8. As soon as your instructor returns your résumé, incorporate the suggestions that your instructor made, and print copies of your résumé for use in your job campaign. Take your résumé with you to your job interviews. If you mail a job application letter to a prospective employer, enclose a copy of your résumé.

9. Build a portfolio displaying samples of your perfect work. Remember that the portfolio must be organized with a table of contents. Tabs and dividers are also useful for keeping the portfolio organized. Review the discussion on portfolios in this chapter to see that you have included the correct items.

10. For several weeks, study the help-wanted ads in the newspaper published in the community in which you are seeking employment. Circle the ads that reflect employment opportunities for administrative assistants. Analyze the ads to obtain information about job trends, qualifications sought, salary, and so on. Put the help-wanted pages in your employment campaign portfolio.

11. Using the questions presented in this chapter, write an evaluation of your performance during an early job interview. Make suggestions that should be helpful to you during your next interview. List both what you think you did well and what you believe you should improve. Share what you have learned about job interviews with the members of your class.

12. To gain confidence in completing an application form neatly and accurately, complete the application form provided in Production Challenge 16-C, Form 16-C-2. Study the form carefully, and then write your answers in your most legible handwriting in the spaces provided. Key an application form when it is possible to do so.

13. When you accept a job, write a job acceptance letter. Submit a copy of your job acceptance letter (or your job refusal letter) to your instructor.

Weblinks

Job Opportunities

www.monster.ca
This popular Canadian site includes job postings; career, résumé, and interview information; access to jobs around the world; and much more.

www.workopolis.com/index.html
Workopolis is a large Canadian job site that includes job postings, resources, hints for researching companies and industries, and much more.

www.careerowl.ca
This leading-edge e-recruiting service brings post-secondary students, recent graduates, and employers together, matching job seekers with employers.

www.canadiancareers.com
Here is a comprehensive site providing career and employment information to Canadians. Explore careers, market yourself, find work, and review Canadian employment news. Links to many relevant sites are included.

www.jobstreet.com
This user-friendly site provides information on job opportunities throughout Asia.

www.jobsdb.com/default.htm
Here you will find numerous job opportunities in a number of international locations including Asia, Australia, and the United States.

Career Lab

www.careerlab.ca
This site offers information offers articles explaining how to manage challenges when job searching

Employability Skills

www.conferenceboard.ca/education
This Conference Board of Canada site provides information on the skills that make Canadians employable.

Canadian Association of Career Educators and Employers (CACEE)

www.cacee.com

This association provides information, advice, professional development opportunities, and other services to employers, career services professionals, and students. The publication *Career Options* is also available on this site.

Human Resources and Social Development Canada

www.hrsdc.gc.ca

This Government of Canada site provides employment-related information on services for individuals, businesses, and other organizations.

Canadian Human Rights Commission

www.chrc-ccdp.ca

This site deals with employment equity, workplace harassment, discrimination, and related topics.

Training and Careers

www.jobsetc.ca

Services Canada's online resource centre on training and careers in Canada includes links to regional service centres in your area where you can get personal help with your job search. The Career Navigator tool guides you through a number of quizzes to help you narrow down your abilities and interests and suggests occupations that match your profile. Statistics such as wages and employment prospects are available on various job categories. On this site you will also find the guide *Access the Hidden Job Market,* a discussion of unadvertised career opportunities.

How to Write an International Curriculum Vitae

www.cvtips.com/cv_international.html

In addition to providing useful information on how to write an international résumé or curriculum vitae, this site also provides tips on writing résumés for specific countries, since preferences among countries vary greatly.

Chapter 17
Professional Development

Learning Outcomes

After completion of this chapter, the student will be able to:

1   Describe the professional image of office workers that challenges old stereotypes.

2   Learn from a mentor.

3   Research the educational programs and certification offered by professional associations.

4   Describe the benefits of cross-training to both the organization and the employee.

5   Describe the qualities of a successful office supervisor.

6   Explain how the position of administrative assistant is excellent training for management.

7   Describe the expectations placed on office professionals in the contemporary office environment.

8   Discuss the benefits of an articulation agreement.

9   Develop a strategy for professional development.

In a common scenario for a Canadian family, both adults are wage earners *and* parents. Few adults can expect to work at a job for only a limited time and then be supported for the rest of their lives by other people. Typically, Canadian adults now plan to have more than one career, several jobs, greater responsibilities, and more years of work than any previous generation.

An administrative assistant's career is often a stepping-stone to other types of careers, including ones that involve supervision and management. Women and men who initially select a career as an administrative assistant should mentally prepare themselves for advancement, and for greater challenges and responsibilities.

The administrative assistant's role has become broader and more diversified, demanding thorough knowledge of computers and software, as well as strong problem-solving and critical thinking skills. Because this career requires people who have technical expertise as well as excellent human relations skills, it attracts competent people from both genders, various age groups, and diverse backgrounds.

ELIMINATE STEREOTYPES

The attitude that someone is "just a secretary" has no place in the contemporary office. This **stereotype** developed at a time when women were encouraged to "just get a job." It was perceived that serious positions in the workforce should be held by men, since men were to be providers for the family.

This scenario is, of course, no longer accurate or valid. The stereotype of an office worker who typed, filed, took shorthand, did only routine tasks, and was too emotional has been replaced by a new bold and professional image.

Professional Image

A professional image reflects:

■   an educated and skilled employee

■   a team player who is expected to contribute valuable ideas

Kim Blanchard
Administrative Assistant

Interprofessional Practice Department
Royal Victoria Regional Health Centre

College Graduation:
Office Administration Diploma—Medical
  (Honours)
Georgian College
Barrie, Ontario
2004

"Be flexible and ready for change at all times."

After graduating from Georgian College, Kim Blanchard interviewed with Royal Victoria and got the job. She's been with the health centre for over a decade, first with Occupational Health and Safety, and now with the interprofessional practice department.

Her job involves supporting a manager, director, and ten clinical educators, handling minutes, forms, and important hospital documents such as medical directives and policies and procedures. She also assists with student placements and organizes meetings and events. On a typical day, Kim completes a range of tasks from answering phones and answering inquires about her department's programs to attending meetings and assisting the team of educators with their work.

A hospital is a large and dynamic work environment—Royal Victoria has over 2000 employees and 1000 volunteers, and everyone's job is ultimately focused on patient care, even if it's behind the scenes. That's why Kim's biggest challenge is making sure everyone has what they need as quickly as possible. Administrative workspace is often limited in a hospital setting, but as Kim says, "If you are very organized, you can work in the tightest of spaces to make it work." Hospitals also

use specialized software, and Kim must keep up with advances and upgrades.

But working for a hospital is rewarding. "I love where and why we are here at RVH. I love the type of work I do and the people I work with on a daily basis." Only a portion of Kim's workplace communication is over email—the rest is on the phone, in meetings, and face-to-face in the busy healthcare environment.

Kim served as the president of the Barrie chapter of the International Association of Administrative Professionals (IAAP) and as chair of Georgian College's Office Administration Advisory Committee. In addition to her medical administration diploma, she has a diploma in legal office administration and two adult education credentials. With years of experience teaching adults, Kim has been teaching medical office admin courses at Georgian College for several years. After years of experience, her advice is to "look at change as growth not only for you, but for the benefit of everyone."

- a polished individual whose appearance and communication style are "professional"

- a person who can solve problems and integrate ideas

- a person who takes pride in each piece of work he or she produces

- an employee who works for the betterment of the organization and is not self-serving

- a person who takes pride in the career of administrative assistant and who has aspirations for the future

- an employee who manages assignments by applying quality standards

- an employee who is willing to work hard and accept new and more challenging responsibilities

The best way to eliminate the stereotypical view is for men and women in this profession to initiate the change

themselves. By living up to the new professional image of an administrative assistant, they will replace the old stereotype.

The best way to develop the professional image of an administrative assistant is to:

1. Set short- and long-term career goals that are obtainable.

2. Develop desired strategies for achieving these goals.

3. Set timelines for each step in the strategies.

4. Begin to carry out the steps immediately.

PREPARE FOR ADVANCEMENT

When you are comfortably settled in your first job, your initial reaction may be to take it easy. Don't coast. Many opportunities for advancement are available in business, but advancement comes only to those who are prepared to accept additional responsibilities.

Federal legislation that bars **discrimination** in employment on the basis of gender has opened up new opportunities for both men and women at the managerial level. Many organizations are committed to being **equal opportunity employers**.

Consequently, women have more opportunity for advancement today than ever before. Yet neither men nor women can advance to higher-level positions unless they are prepared to accept the responsibilities that go with those positions.

During your first year of employment, set a professional goal for yourself. Do you want to become an executive assistant, a supervisor, or a manager? Once you have decided on your goal, study and network to provide yourself with the background necessary to achieve that goal. Networking within your profession or organization will require you to join networking groups such as Business Network International Canada or your local chamber of commerce. Many personal performance and altruistic clubs and associations such as Toastmasters, Rotary Clubs, and the Progress Clubs welcome new members and usually provide a significant membership of experienced business people from whom you can learn.

To accomplish your goal, you may need support and resources from management. If so, select a person in management on whom you can rely for assistance and with whom you can develop a **mentor** relationship.

Learn from a Mentor

Mentors are people in your profession who are more senior than you. They understand the organization's policies, procedures, politics, and history, and they are willing to share useful advice with more junior members. They help people who are new to the organization or the profession to become successful. The mentor relationship often involves a young rookie and an office veteran. The rookie may have strong state-of-the-art technical skills, but the veteran knows the ropes.

Meetings with mentors and the information they share is confidential, since a mentor's advice is intended to show a junior member a shortcut to success. They welcome the questions of a junior staff member and see it as their responsibility to nurture younger people with potential for success.

People often consider their mentor as the most important person in their professional career.

How Do You Select a Mentor? A mentor has to be a person with whom you feel comfortable and who is pleased to answer your questions. The mentor has to consider the advice he or she gives you as confidential. As well, the mentor has to be someone who has the answers to your questions about:

- how the organization works
- how information flows in the office

- with whom to associate
- whom to avoid in the office
- how to avoid conflict
- how the organization selects people for promotion
- who holds the power to make decisions
- how to get your ideas noticed and accepted

Self-Check

1. Identify three ways you can begin to develop a professional image as an administrative assistant.
2. What does it mean to be an equal opportunity employer?
3. Why would you benefit by having a mentor?
4. List five topics on which a mentor might advise you.

Advance by Education

A college diploma or university degree is very useful in advancing to a higher-level office position. In fact, any additional education will prove helpful. When you have an efficient and effective performance record, additional education may provide the competitive edge you need to get ahead.

Many organizations offer in-house training. These courses usually are of short duration and do not carry college or university credit. Talk with your supervisor to find out what is available. Express an interest in taking courses that will help you perform your job or advance in your career. When you successfully complete enough courses, they will become an impressive part of your employment record and will support your efforts toward promotion.

If you are interested in obtaining a university degree, you may be able to use credits from courses you have already taken. Many colleges in Canada today have established **articulation agreements** with universities. Under these agreements, universities will grant substantial transfer credit from recognized office administration programs. The key benefit of this arrangement is that it reduces the time needed to obtain a degree. As well, you may be able take classes on a part-time basis while still staying employed—and thus continue to gain professional experience. Check with your college to find out what articulations may exist for your program.

Most large organizations have educational benefits. Some organizations will pay all or part of the tuition for job-related courses that are successfully completed. Ask your supervisor about educational benefits; express your interest in taking job-related courses. Consider courses in these areas:

- project management
- team building
- communication
- time management
- business administration
- software applications
- organizational behaviour
- office management
- social media and web development
- financial management
- supervision/management leadership

The emphasis in education today is on continuing education. By committing yourself to lifelong learning, you will be increasing your opportunities for promotion and enriching your personal life. Employees who believe in and practise continuous education are more likely to survive during periods of company **rightsizing** and **recession**.

As an administrative assistant, you choose either to have a job or to have a professional career. If you have a strong desire to advance and to earn a reputation for being a professional who contributes to the organization, you will seek ways to achieve professional recognition.

Join a Professional Association

Becoming a member of a professional association is an excellent way of gaining educational skills and new credentials in your field. A number of associations that promote office professionalism are available. The following discussion will identify three associations that offer credentials to office professionals willing to study and take the challenge.

If you are interested in joining or establishing a branch of one of these professional associations in your community, write or call the head office for information.

Association of Administrative Assistants (AAA) The Association of Administrative Assistants is a Canadian, chartered, nonprofit organization formed in 1951. The motto of the AAA is "Professionalism through Education." The association has the mandate of encouraging office professionals to upgrade skills and enhance professionalism. By helping members with skills, knowledge, and professional development, the AAA will meet its mission to enhance employment opportunities and contributions to the workplace and to the community.

It awards the designation of Qualified Administrative Assistant (QAA) to those who meet the criteria. A sample certificate is displayed in Figure 17-1. In order to achieve the QAA, office professionals must complete seven courses. These courses are offered at numerous Canadian universities and colleges. The program consists of three compulsory courses and four electives. The compulsory courses are:

- Business Administration
- Organizational Behaviour
- Effective Business English

Examples of elective courses are:

- Marketing
- Economics
- Human Resource Management
- Financial Accounting
- Psychology
- Commercial Law
- Principles and Practices of Supervision
- Interpersonal Communication
- Computer Technology

These courses help the participants to be valuable team members and to understand corporate initiatives. The QAA is a recognizable designation and identifies individuals as dedicated office professionals. Earning this designation

Figure 17-1 QAA certificate.

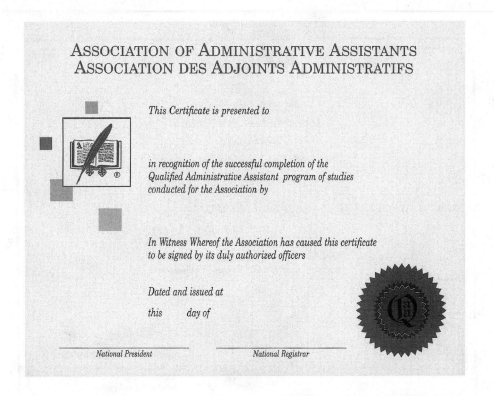

ASSOCIATION OF ADMINISTRATIVE ASSISTANTS
ASSOCIATION DES ADJOINTS ADMINISTRATIFS

This Certificate is presented to

*in recognition of the successful completion of the
Qualified Administrative Assistant program of studies
conducted for the Association by*

*In Witness Whereof the Association has caused this certificate
to be signed by its duly authorized officers*

Dated and issued at

this   day of

National President   *National Registrar*

will no doubt give an applicant a competitive edge when applying for more senior positions. To learn more about the Association of Administrative Assistants and the QAA certification, contact the association through its website at www.aaa.ca.

International Association of Administrative Professionals® (IAAP®)
IAAP is an association committed to advancing office professionals by promoting high standards and enhancing the image of the profession. This association provides resources and information to help its members enhance their skills, so they may contribute to their organizations in an even more effective manner. Not only does it work to improve the professional skills of its members, it also works to educate the public about the value of the office professional.

The educational program of IAAP includes workshops, seminars, and study courses on administrative topics. This proactive organization holds an international conference each year and publishes a popular magazine called *OfficePro*.

IAAP has two professional certification programs where successful candidates earn their Certified Professional Secretary® (CPS®) or the more advanced Certified Administrative Professional® (CAP®) rating. Refer to Figure 17-2 for an example of a CPS certification.

The CPS rating requires successful completion of a one-day exam covering the following areas:

- Office Systems and Technology
- Office Administration
- Management

The CAP rating is achieved after successful completion of the parts listed above plus an additional exam in

- Advanced Organizational Management

For more information about the IAAP and the CPS and CAP certifications, visit the association's website at www.iaap-hq.org.

Canadian Virtual Assistants Connection (CVAC)
A **virtual assistant**, or VA, is a self-employed professional offering administrative support to a variety of clients through his or her home office. The CVAC is a professional organization designed to bring together virtual assistants. Their goal is to provide a forum in which virtual assistants can network and share knowledge and skills. The CVAC offers professional development opportunities, and it also helps to connect virtual assistants with potential employers. Visit the organization's website at www.cvac.ca.

NALS—The Association for Legal Professionals
The Association for Legal Professionals provides a testing program and professional certification for legal administrative assistants. Part of its mandate is to offer continuing legal education training programs and

Figure 17-2 CPS® certificate.

International Association of
Administrative Professionals®
through its department the

Institute for Certification

certifies that the

Certified Professional Secretary®

rating has been awarded to

Pat Masters

March 2005 - March 2010

for having met the requirements and satisfactorily
completing an established program of examinations.

International President
International Association of
Administrative Professionals®

networking for its members. Office professionals who wish to demonstrate their commitment to and aptitude for the legal assistant profession are encouraged to take the examination leading to the basic certification of the legal professional, ALS®, previously known as Accredited Legal Secretary. Testing for the ALS certification covers the following topics:

- Written Communications
- Office Procedures and Legal Knowledge
- Ethics, Human Relations, and Judgment

NALS® also offers an advanced certification for legal professionals, the PLS, previously known as the Professional Legal Secretary®. The PLS® is a designation for lawyer's assistants who want to be identified as exceptional. This one-day, four-part exam includes questions on:

- Written Communication
- Office Procedures and Technology
- Ethics and Judgment
- Legal Knowledge and Skills

Those applicants who are successful in the examination will earn the PLS certification shown in Figure 17-3.

If you require more information, contact NALS® through its website at www.nals.org.

Self-Check

1. What is meant by *in-house training*?
2. What designation is awarded by the Association of Administrative Assistants (AAA)?
3. List two goals of the International Association of Administrative Professionals (IAAP).
4. What is the name of the magazine published by the IAAP?
5. Identify IAAP's two professional certification programs.
6. Name the association for virtual assistants.
7. What is the mandate of the Association for Legal Professionals (NALS)?
8. Which two designations can be earned through NALS?

Increase Technical Certification

Technical skills are some of the most highly valued skills of office professionals. By continuing to upgrade technical skills, office professionals can improve their résumés and increase their opportunities for employment and

Figure 17-3 PLS® certificate.

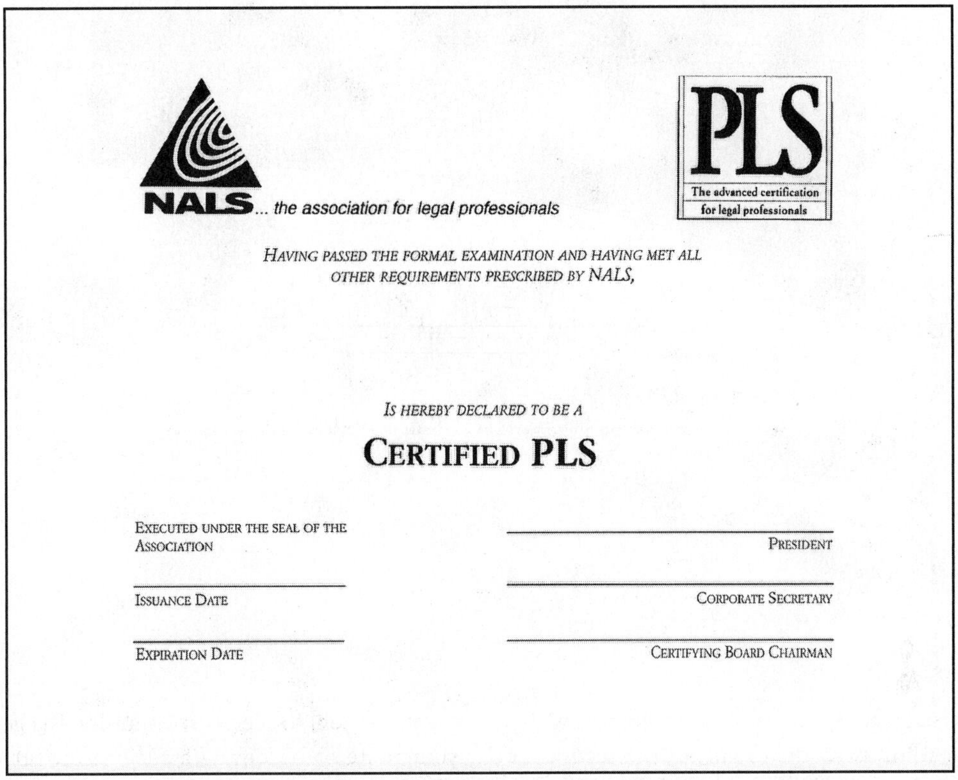

advancement. To validate technical skills, office professionals should earn certification from recognized programs.

One of the most recognized and popular types of technical certification is the Microsoft Office Specialist Certification (MOS) program. Candidates begin by selecting the Microsoft Office track and then the product for which they want certification. Then they select the appropriate level of expertise. Specialist certification is available for any of the following certification tracks:

- Office 2010 Editions
- Office 2007
- Office 2003

Although MOS certifications for Office 2013 products were not yet available at the time of the publication of this book, Microsoft will be offering them.

For each track there are core examinations and elective examinations available for the following products:

- Word
- Excel
- PowerPoint
- Access
- Outlook
- SharePoint
- Project, Managing Projects

Candidates can achieve certification at any of the following levels:

- Master
- Expert
- Specialist

If they require training before taking an exam, candidates can find training providers and approved courseware at www.microsoft.com/learning/en/us/certification/mos.aspx. Full details on the certifications are available at this same site. The certificate shown in Figure 17-4 is an example of the document awarded.

Cross-Train

Cross-training involves learning and performing the responsibilities of your co-workers. It is very valuable to the organization. When one employee is absent from work, other employees can simply fill in. However, it has even greater benefits to the person who has the initiative to learn how to perform other people's jobs. The more you know and the more you can do the more valuable to the organization you will be.

Figure 17-4 Microsoft Office User Specialist certificate.

The administrative assistant who is preparing for advancement, or who just wants to protect the security of his or her current job, should learn as many skills and gather as much information as possible.

Cross-training gives the administrative assistant the opportunity to:

- take on new technical and communication challenges
- learn more about the organization and the flow of work
- get more exposure by working with new people
- get acknowledgment from management

Cross-trained employees are more challenged, more knowledgeable, and more interesting, and generally happier.

Self-Check

1. Where might candidates for Microsoft certification receive training before taking the exam?
2. Why would an administrative assistant wish to cross-train?

BECOME A SUPERVISOR

Many administrative assistants step into the field of supervision without formal training for the new position. This acquired position is often the result of seniority, hard work, and success as an administrative assistant. But a supervisory job requires a different skill set from the administrative assistant's job, so specialized training is a genuine asset. On your route to becoming a supervisor, get as much supervisory training as possible.

What Does It Take?

One of the greatest assets of any good supervisor is effective human relations skills. Good human relations skills will enable you to direct the work of other employees and help them to feel personal satisfaction in their work. Experience in performing your own job, even when you perform it exceptionally well, is not enough to prepare you for leading others.

Being a good supervisor requires actual experience. You can *learn* to accept responsibility as a supervisor and to carry out your function effectively. You can learn from many sources that will be available to you, as well as from experience.

Through discussions with management, arrive at an understanding of what your supervisory responsibilities are and what authority you have for carrying them out. In addition, the people you supervise should be told what your role is.

Someone within the human resources department will discuss general policies with new employees and provide them with booklets dealing with employee rights and benefits. Nevertheless, one of your ongoing functions will be to interpret personnel policies to employees who have questions. Study the organization's policies until you can answer questions accurately and clearly. Keep your file on changes in policies and procedures up to date.

You can learn from your manager. Observe and recall supervisory principles and techniques that your manager uses successfully. Decide if you can apply them in your situation.

Get acquainted with other supervisors, and encourage them to share with you their ideas for handling supervisory problems. Be a good listener; learn the "why" as well as the "what" of the problems and solutions being discussed.

Improve your ability to communicate. Much of your success as a supervisor will depend on effective communication.

As a supervisor, self-appraisal is very important. Envision your total job, which could include staffing, planning, organizing, directing, coordinating, reporting, and budgeting. Frequently evaluate your own performance. Think in terms of what you did well and why. Recognize areas in which you need to improve. Concentrate on the skills that need improvement until you have accomplished greater expertise. As you improve, your confidence will increase.

Many books and magazine articles have been published on supervision, personnel management, business psychology, personal relations in business, motivation, communications, and so on. College courses are available on these same topics. Read materials and enroll in courses that will help you.

Technical know-how is an asset for a supervisor. However, the supervisor's role is to lead and guide. A good supervisor helps the *employees* become the technical experts, and relies on their expertise and recommendations to improve and enhance current processes.

You will be directing the work of people who are producing products and services; thus, it will be a benefit to learn about equipment, supplies, and methods that will enable employees to perform their jobs more economically and effectively. Keep up to date on the technical aspects of your job by reading periodicals on office products and methods and by making inquiries of suppliers. You can earn respect by being knowledgeable about the hardware and software your employees are using, and by empowering employees to make recommendations and decisions on matters that directly affect their work.

Along with your staff, examine methods to improve the work you are supervising. Brainstorm with your office team to find the best solutions for new procedures and new products. Based on the solutions determined by your team, make changes within the office. If the recommended changes are outside your realm of authority, you will need to get approval from management. Management will only accept your recommendations for improved products or procedures if your ideas will benefit the company and be cost effective. When you take your recommendations to management, be prepared to demonstrate their benefits and cost effectiveness.

How to Become the Office Manager

If you aspire to be an office manager, your chances of reaching your goal are much greater than those of your predecessors. In the past, an administrative assistant who reached a management position usually did so after many years of service. Today, more management positions are available to administrative assistants who have educational credentials, regardless of length of service.

Although an academic degree is not always required, the competition for management jobs is intense. If you are currently working toward a diploma in office technology, you may be interested in pursuing a bachelor's degree in business administration (BBA) as your next step.

There is no prescribed method or guaranteed success strategy for becoming a manager. Much of your success will be based on your ability to market your skills and to demonstrate competence in leadership. Volunteering to lead committees and projects is an excellent way to practise your leadership skills, demonstrate your commitment to the organization, learn more about the organization, and gain recognition as a potential manager.

Reading management journals and joining a management association are progressive steps toward a career in office management. Information about a variety of management societies is available on the internet. The BB&C Association Management Services is actually an *association of associations*. It was established to provide quality leadership and support for business associations. The association's website provides information on its services and benefits as well as a directory of Canadian business associations. If you are interested in joining a management/business association, you may wish to contact BB&C at www.bbandc.com.

The role of administrative assistant is excellent training for a managerial position. In fact, the administrative assistant is constantly making decisions and managing projects, people, and time. The following are examples of management responsibilities that the administrative assistant undertakes in a daily routine. Each of these functions is excellent preparation for advancement into a manager's position.

Manager of Communications One of the most important functions of the administrative assistant is to create and edit office documentation. As well, it is the administrative assistant who is the expert on communication equipment (computers, faxes, telephone systems, photocopiers, etc.) in the office.

Manager of Crises A skilled office professional will be able to remain calm, maintain office efficiency, and handle people with diplomacy even through an office crisis.

Manager of Records and Information Controlling paper and electronic files is usually the responsibility of the administrative assistant. The administrative assistant develops the system for organizing, finding, retrieving, and storing information.

Manager of Public Relations The administrative assistant is the first person in the organization that the public sees and to whom the public speaks. The image that administrative assistants project will reflect on the organization they represent. Administrative assistants must manage the reception area and the public.

Manager of Planning It is the administrative assistant who keeps track of meetings, schedules, deadlines, and the whereabouts of the office staff.

Manager of Policies and Procedures Office policies and procedures need to be interpreted, updated, and organized. Of course, the administrative assistant manages these responsibilities.

Manager of Inventory Maintaining control of inventory, ordering new stock, and selecting the best product for the best price are just some of the responsibilities of the administrative assistant in the role of inventory manager.

Self-Check

1. Identify ways in which you can evaluate your own performance as a supervisor.

2. How does an administrative assistant perform the functions of a manager of public relations? of communications?

CONTINUE TO DEVELOP PROFESSIONALLY

As you read this chapter, you may conclude that preparation for a successful career is endless. Your conclusion is correct.

Continue to increase both your general knowledge of office procedures and your special skills. The ability to relate well to customers, clients, and co-workers is essential (see Figure 17-5). A working knowledge of computer software—for word processing, spreadsheets, project management, graphics, desktop publishing, electronic messaging and calendaring, database management, and so on—is essential. Computer technology and software are changing

Figure 17-5 The ability to relate to clients and co-workers is essential for professional growth.

at a rapid pace. Develop an affinity for new equipment and learn the new applications.

To advance in your career, you need a broad, general education. An understanding of how to deal with all types of people and business and management concepts is a valuable asset. Organizations are looking for employees who are critical thinkers and problem solvers.

If you wish to advance professionally, make decisions and carry them out. Then take responsibility for both your successes and your failures. **Procrastination** and the inability to make decisions will be viewed as weaknesses and will prevent opportunities for promotion.

Contemporary Office Professional

In order to plan for your future professional development, you should understand what the **contemporary** office requires. Professionals in the contemporary office of the new millennium will:

- supervise people in nontraditional work styles that include flexible working hours in flexible locations

- use the most current office technology and high-tech communication

- rely almost exclusively on the office network and the internet to access and manage information

- make greater productivity their primary focus

- work effectively with people from diverse age groups and cultural and religious backgrounds

Involvement in professional organizations and lifelong education are the keys to keeping current and continuing to develop professionally.

How Do I Get Started?

To begin your path of professional development, you should:

- Subscribe to and read professional magazines.
- Listen to motivational or informational tapes while you drive to work.
- Read office bulletins and newsletters to remain up to date on corporate affairs.
- Attend seminars, conventions, conferences, and workshops to keep abreast of new technology and procedures.
- Volunteer to be a committee member or chairperson for special events.
- Apply or offer to work on special task forces.
- Request that you be placed on the office circulation list for all informational and professional materials.
- Make a point of meeting new people and listening to their ideas.
- Read the newspaper to follow local and foreign events.
- Travel to as many locations as possible.
- Visit libraries and make note of the many resources available to you.
- Make appointments with the corporate competition to learn more about other companies.
- Become aware of your company's policies.
- Make a point of watching documentaries on television and reading or studying new topics.
- Make learning a lifelong commitment.

Professional growth is stimulating. It has a motivating effect, and your reward will be a successful and enjoyable career.

COMMIT TO YOUR VALUES AND ETHICS

Values and ethics are central to any organization. Throughout this book, **ethical** issues have been discussed. Let's take a closer look at values.

Values can be defined as those things that are important to or valued by someone. Values are what people judge to be right. They are more than words—they are the moral, ethical, and professional attributes of **character**. When values are shared by all members of an organization, they are extraordinarily important tools for making judgments, assessing probable outcomes of contemplated actions, and choosing among alternatives. Perhaps more importantly, they put all employees on the same level with regard to what all employees as an organization consider important.

Values are the embodiment of what an organization stands for and should be the basis for the behaviour of its employees. However, employees, regardless of their position in the company, do not always share or internalize the organization's values. Obviously, this disconnect will be dysfunctional. Additionally, an organization may publish one set of values, perhaps in an effort to present a positive image, while the values that really guide organizational behaviour are very different. Disconnects may occur and may create problems. However, the central purpose of values remains. They state either an actual or an idealized set of criteria for evaluating options and deciding what is appropriate, while also taking into account other factors such as experience.

How do values relate to ethics? *Values* can help to determine what is right and what is wrong, and doing what is right or wrong is what is meant by *ethics*. To behave ethically is to behave in a manner consistent with what is right or moral. Part of the difficulty in deciding whether or not behaviour is ethical is in determining *what* is right or wrong.

Consider the values illustrated in the following cases and how those values lead to ethical or unethical decisions.

CASE A You unknowingly give a caller incorrect information by telephone.

Ethical: You realize your error and immediately call the person to apologize and correct the error.

Unethical: You realize your error but, because you don't want to admit you made a mistake, you decide not to call with the correct information. You tell yourself that maybe it won't matter.

The caller telephones to verify whether the information is correct because he or she is doubtful. You pretend you are unaware of the whole situation, including the previous call.

CASE B Your manager is out of the office today, and your workload is light and not urgent. You realize your co-worker is rushing to meet a tight deadline.

Ethical: You know you can postpone your work until tomorrow, and you offer to help the co-worker.

Unethical: You consider offering help; but instead, you decide to leave work early because, after all, you deserve some free time—and your manager will never know. Besides, your co-worker's workload is not your responsibility.

CASE C An administrative assistant with a hearing impairment has just joined your organization. You work in an open-concept office, and her desk is across the room. You occasionally need to communicate informally to each other across the room.

Ethical: You suggest ideas that would make it easier to communicate (e.g., arrange the desks so you face each other), and you encourage her ideas, too.

Unethical: When you need to catch her attention, you simply call her name. You feel she is not making an effort to be cooperative when she fails to respond.

CASE D Your manager asks you to alter expenses on her travel claim to include expenditures that did not really occur.

Ethical: You are apprehensive about upsetting your manager. However, you feel you cannot falsify the information. You tactfully advise your manager that the finance department will need receipts to substantiate all spending and you cannot agree to complete the claim without receipts to support the amounts.

Unethical: Although you know it is wrong, you agree to make the changes because you are applying for a promotion and want your manager to give you a good recommendation.

Actions based on strong personal values—integrity, honesty, loyalty, tolerance, respect, and accountability—are consistent with good business practices and will conform to your organization's code of ethics.

The influence of family, church, community, and school will determine your individual values as you develop. The organization, to a large extent, is dealing with individuals whose value base has been established already. While the internalized values of individuals are important, the organization has a major impact on the behaviour of its members and can have a positive or negative influence on their values. Staying committed to your values increases your satisfaction with your decisions and results.

How can you help to create an ethical climate? Be certain your pattern of behaviour aligns with your own values as well as your organization's. Increase your awareness of how to apply your organization's code of conduct. Through additional training, learn how to deal with situations with an ethical dimension and how to anticipate situations that involve your values and, ultimately, ethical choices.

QUESTIONS FOR STUDY AND REVIEW

1. Identify six qualities that help to make a professional image.
2. Explain the purpose of having a mentor.
3. Describe three qualities you should look for when selecting a mentor.
4. Name three associations that provide professional certification for administrative assistants. State the name of the particular certifications and how they can be achieved.
5. What is required for an office professional to gain Microsoft certification? List five areas of certification available.
6. Explain the meaning of *cross-training*.
7. Describe the advantages to the employee of cross-training. Describe the advantages to the organization.
8. Describe five activities that a supervisor should perform in order to be successful.
9. Describe five ways that the position of administrative assistant is excellent training for being a manager.
10. Identify the expectations that have already and will continue to be placed on office professionals.
11. Suggest ten ways to grow professionally once you are already employed.

EVERYDAY ETHICS

Climbing the Greasy Pole

You have been working for Bellco, the corporate insurance company, for six months. You realize that you have much to learn in regard to office politics, policies, and procedures, and simply how to get ahead.

One of the senior managers, Ken O'Mallie, has welcomed your questions on several occasions. In fact, a mentor relationship is clearly starting to form. Your co-workers, who have no mentors, have noticed that Ken appears to be nurturing your career. They are jealous.

Rumours have started about the amount of time you spend in Ken's office. The word is that you are trying to climb the greasy pole to success.

■ What should you do?

Problem Solving

1. You have been employed by a large organization as an administrative assistant for six years. You would like to specialize in project management. You have just found out about a four-day workshop on project management taking place in your city later in the month. You really see a future for yourself in this area, as well as a wonderful professional development opportunity. In order to complete this course you will need to take two days off work. How will you

approach your employer to secure the days off you need and also have them support your ambition? Draft a brief statement describing how you will sell your boss on this idea. What will you do if your boss turns you down?

2. You supervise a temporary employee, Karen, who assists you with your work. It is Friday afternoon, and she is keying a multipage report. Your manager is waiting for the report and intends to fax it to the head office as soon as it is finished. Karen volunteered to stay after 5 p.m. to finish the report; you leave. As soon as Karen finishes the report, she prints it, hands it to the manager, and leaves the office. Early Monday morning the manager calls you to her office to explain that she could not send the report because it contained errors. Could you have done something to prevent this?

3. You supervise two full-time office workers. One of them told you she was ill and asked to go home at noon. You insisted that deadlines had to be met and asked that she stay to finish her work if she possibly could. About 2 p.m. this employee passed out and had to be rushed to the hospital. You realize that you made a mistake. What can you do now? Suggest alternatives you could have pursued to get the employee's work finished.

4. You pride yourself on being very adept in your knowledge of many application software packages. In fact, many staff members, including your boss, come to you for help when they are experiencing challenges with software. Recently, a supervisory opportunity has become available in your department. You have applied and have been interviewed by a panel for this opportunity. You hope to hear back from the hiring committee in a few days. You know your performance is being evaluated closely by your boss and you know you can handle this new opportunity. In the last few days, however, your boss has been asking for a lot of computer assistance, so much so that you are falling behind on your duties. If you fall behind you may not get this new opportunity as your boss may not recommend you for the position. Is there anything you can do to keep harmony with your boss and at the same time not fall behind on your responsibilities?

Special Reports

1. Use the internet to locate articles and book reviews on either:
   - cross-training as a supervisor's motivation tool, or
   - the qualities of a great mentor.

   Write an abstract of your findings and document your sources.

2. Locate a university where an articulation agreement exists between an office administration program and a university. Read the articulation requirements for earning a degree and then create a list that includes the name of the degree, the number of degree credits needed, and the number of degree credits awarded with the office administration diploma. Share this list with your instructor.

3. Find articles and tips from current issues of *OfficePro* magazine that discuss professional growth. Summarize the tips into a brief report. Share this information with your instructor and other class members.

4. Use the internet to research two different professional organizations that you would like to join. Find the following information: how do you get membership, what can the organization do to further your career, and is there any certification available? Determine which organization you would prefer to join, and be able to support your decision. Prepare a chart where you can compare the two organizations. Present your findings to your class.

5. Develop a strategy for your own professional development. To do so, design an electronic spreadsheet that will capture the following information:
   - State your immediate career goal upon graduation.
   - State your career goal for the end of a five-year period.
   - Identify the gap between the two goals in terms of the experience, training, certification, human relations skills, and supervision/management leadership skills needed.
   - For each of the factors in the gap, describe your plan for achieving the necessary skills to close the gap.

6. Interview an office professional (in person or by email) who began his or her career as an administrative assistant and who has since moved into greater levels of responsibility. Find out the career path this individual took to get where he or she is now. In a brief report to be submitted to your instructor, outline your questions and the responses you received.

Weblinks

Professional Associations
www.aaa.ca
This website provides information about the Association of Administrative Assistants, its mission, and its certification.

www.iaap-hq.org
The International Association of Administrative Professionals (IAAP) has an extensive website with information about the organization, certification, benefits of membership, and its publication.

www.nals.org
The NALS® (Association for Legal Professionals) site offers information about the association, the benefits of membership, and certification.

www.cvac.ca
The Canadian Virtual Assistant Connection site is designed to bring Canadian VAs and worldwide clients together to network, learn, and benefit.

www.bbandc.com

If you are interested in joining a management/business association, visit this BB&C Association Management Services site.

Microsoft Office Specialist

www.microsoft.com/learning/mcp/officespecialist

This Microsoft site gives detailed information about what is involved in earning Microsoft Office Specialist certification.

Psychometrics—Online Testing

http://www.psychometrics.com/en-us/online-testing.htm

Perform online tests to learn about your career values, competencies, interests, and personality.

Canadian HR Reporter

www.hrreporter.com

This guide to human resources management offers current news, information on the latest trends and practices, expert advice, experience, and insights from HR practitioners, research, and resources.

Mentoring

http://humanresources.about.com/od/coachingmentoring/a/mentoring_boom.htm

This article discusses the benefits of a mentor relationship between baby boomers and young people just entering the job market. Links to other mentoring sites are provided.

www.quintcareers.com/mentor_value.html

This article offers information on the role of a mentor, finding a mentor, what to look for, and other important aspects of the mentoring process.

Working Papers

PERSONAL VALUES

Rank the following list of values by placing the number 1 next to the item you value the most, number 2 next to the item you value second, and so on. You will give the number 15 to the item you value the least. You must place a number beside each item and you cannot repeat any of the numbers between 1 and 15.

_____ Winning

_____ Health

_____ Education/Learning

_____ Safety

_____ Money

_____ Security

_____ Success

_____ Trust

_____ Power

_____ Honesty

_____ Fairness

_____ Relationships

_____ Recognition

_____ Truth

_____ Spirituality

Form 1-A

DIFFICULT PERSONALITIES

In the working environment, you will come in contact with a variety of people from diverse backgrounds. You may find that you will encounter people with whom it is difficult to interact effectively. Understanding how to cope with and handle challenging personalities is an essential tool for success.

Working in a group or individually review the table below and identify the difficult personality types described in the chapter. List the behaviours this type of individual may display and brainstorm for strategies to help manage each behaviour. Your goal should be to minimize the undesirable behaviour while maintaining a positive working relationship.

Personality	Behaviours	Strategies
Bully		
Gossip		
Know-It-All		
Backstabber		
Blamer		
Other		

Form 1-B

EXPLORING YOUR OWN CULTURAL BACKGROUND

One of the best ways to understand and appreciate various cultures starts with recognizing our own cultural beliefs and practices. Read each statement listed below and respond appropriately as it pertains to your own cultural practices. As an alternative you could also choose to interview a classmate to explore his or her cultural background. Share only what you feel comfortable telling your peers.

1. The traditions my family celebrates are:

_____

_____

_____

_____

2. My ethnicity is:

_____

_____

_____

3. In my family we speak the following languages:

_____

_____

_____

_____

4. In my family we practice these ceremonies:

_____

_____

_____

_____

5. In my family we recognize these symbols:

_____

_____

_____

_____

6. In my family we eat these foods:

_____

_____

_____

_____

Form 2-A

DAILY PLAN CHART

Activity	Description		Priority
A. Telephone Calls		**Phone #**	**1, 2, 3, 4**
B. Letters and Memos			
C. Other Tasks			

Priority Rank: Urgent = 1; Today = 2; Tomorrow = 3; This Week = 4

Form 3-A

TIME DISTRIBUTION CHART by Person

Date	Major Activities	Hours for Mr. Wilson	Hours for Ms. Azam	Hours for Mr. Levine	Hours for Mr. Rush	Hours for Mrs. Yee	Hours for the Group	My Own Hours	Total Hours
TOTAL									

Form 3-C-1

Notes on Time Spent During Week of May 19–23

Mon.
May 19

Processing postal mail	1 1/2 hrs
Answering email	1 hr
Handling telephone calls	1 3/4 hrs
Answering voice mail	3/4 hr
Revising draft of report for Ms. Azam	2 hrs
Filing	1/2 hr
Total	7 1/2 hrs

Tues.
May 20

Processing postal mail	1/2 hr
Answering email	1/2 hr
Handling telephone calls	1 hr
Answering voice mail	1 hr
Verifying statistical data using word processor (for Mr. Levine)	2 1/2 hrs
Revising draft for Ms. Azam	1 hr
Filing	1/2 hr
Replenishing office supplies	1/2 hr
Total	7 1/2 hrs

Wed.
May 21

Processing postal mail	1 hr
Answering email	1 hr
Handling telephone calls	1 1/2 hrs
Answering voice mail	1/2 hr
Filing	1/2 hr

Form 3-C-2

Receiving callers for Mr. Wilson	1/2 hr
Making final copy	
of report for Ms. Azam	2 hrs
Keying data for Mr. Wilson	1/2 hr
Total	7 1/2 hrs

Thurs. May 22

Processing postal mail	1 hr
Answering email	1 hr
Handling telephone calls	2 hrs
Answering voice mail	1/2 hr
Revising draft of a report for	
Mr. Wilson	2 hrs
Filing	1/2 hr
Receiving callers for Mr. Wilson	1/2 hr
Total	7 1/2 hrs

Fri. May 23

Processing postal mail	1 hr
Answering email	1 hr
Handling telephone calls	1 hr
Answering voice mail	1/2 hr
Drafting report for Ms. Azam	2 hrs
Preparing final copy of report	
for Mr. Levine	1 hr
Filing	1/2 hr
Planning work for following week	1/2 hr
Total	7 1/2 hrs

Form 3-C-2

MILLENNIUM REQUISITION FOR SUPPLIES

REQUESTED BY:		REQUISITION NO.:
LOCATION:		DATE:

QUANTITY	UNIT	DESCRIPTION

SIGNATURE:

Form 3-D-1

MILLENNIUM REQUISITION FOR SUPPLIES

REQUESTED BY:		REQUISITION NO.:
LOCATION:		DATE:

QUANTITY	UNIT	DESCRIPTION

SIGNATURE:

Form 3-D-2

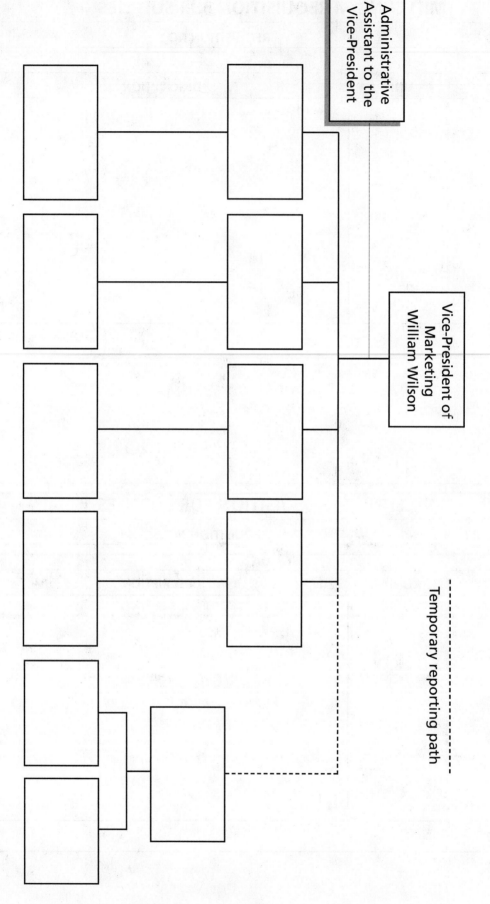

MILLENNIUM APPLIANCES, INC.
MARKETING DIVISION
REGIONAL ORGANIZATION CHART

Administrative
Assistant to the
Vice-President

Vice-President of
Marketing
William Wilson

- - - - - - - - - - - - - - - - - - - -
Temporary reporting path
- - - - - - - - - - - - - - - - - - - -

Form 5-B

ONLINE COPIER/PRINTER PROJECT

The pilot project established to assess the feasibility of using the "Dinero II" high-volume copier/printer on line as a productivity enhancement proved inconclusive. After months, less than 1/3 of the network users had responded to a user survey, providing too small a sample on which to base a sound evaluation.

- write out in full not 1/3

  The pilot project should be extended for another two months in order to solicit more responses from effected network users as there was sufficient evidence to show that the Dinero II will be both a productivity enhancement and cost effective. Further, a memo from Mr. Wilson should be sent directly to each user as an "incentive" to complete the survey.

- Start para. from "As there was . . .

effective, the pilot project . . .

  Doris Knight and Brian Webber suggested the concept of putting a high volume printer on-line forward in a June 21, 2005 memorandum addressed to the Administrative Director, Frank Bucks. In their three-part proposal, they firstly identified the current situation with regard to volume, accessibility, mean-time-to-failure (how many times it breaks down), and cost of ownership. The next part dealt with current and available technology. Its comparative evaluation demonstrated that not only was our current copier and remote printer inefficient, their cost exceeded that of a new, networked copier/printer. Finally, the memorandum compared three new copiers/printers for volume, cost effectiveness and connectability: the Diablo II was clearly surperior.

- Change "next" to "second" and "Its" to "Their"

Form 6-A

A photocopier/printer on-line, however, is a new concept and there is little evidence that network users would utilize the abundance of features and benefits available. There are certain things to consider before we go ahead with the purchase of the Dinero II, namely:

— Change "things" to "questions"

1.   Will the cost of connecting the Dinero II to the network invalidate the cost effective benefit that Knight and Webber proposed?

2.   Given the volume (speed) at which the Dinero II prints and the number of users who will have access on line, will we need to exmploy a new person to "collate" the potential flood of output from the printer?

3.   Given that both copying and printing will be committed to one machine, will copying interfere with the speed or quality of printing, and visa versa?

— Swap 1 & 4 and 2 & 3

4.   Do the majority of network uses need the features and benefits of a centralized, high volume, on-line copier/printer?

The vendor of the Dinero II is addressing questions 1 to 3. Question 4 was the subject of the survey in question.

— Catch the change in order

I have looked time and time again at the list of network users and have identified several classifications of users that would not be involved in the outcome of our project. There are those on the network who use only e-mail and calendaring. It is, therefore, my contention that we may yield better survey results if we selectively solicit only those with a steak in the outcome of the survey. In addition, I suggest that the scope of our survey be widened to include all stakeholders such as suppliers and the Information Technology, stationary supplies,

— Change "looked time and time again at" to "re-examined"

— Change "steak" for "personal investment"

Form 6-A

and mailroom staff. Perhaps this broader approach will identify redundant processes in the overall flow of paperwork from supplier to end-user.

The whole idea of cost-saving technology in our organization is sound, and I applaud the initiative of Knight and Webber, but the lack of response from our user community is deplorable. I recommend that:

1.   senior supervisors of each division immediately put forward names of two individuals from their division who would serve on a committee to review both the Dinero II and the overall process. This committee could take control and administer the survey and to figure out the results in order to compare it to our needs.

2.   a personal memo from Mr. Wilson to each network user be sent to make sure we get "participation" in the next printer/copier needs survey.

- Change "whole idea" to "concept"

- Change "take control and" to "further be responsible to"

- Change "make sure we get" to "encourage"

George Andrews
Procurement Officer

Form 6-A

In addition, please make the following global changes:

1. Capitalize Pilot Project throughout.

2. Change "Mr. Wilson" to "William Wilson" throughout.

3. Replace oblique (/) with "and."

4. The Dinero II is now superseded. Change "II" to "III."

Here are some other changes:

1. Bold the title.

2. Paragraph 1:

   a. Line 3 - change "six months" to "after <u>six</u> months"

   b. Add line 5 - "Twenty-seven percent is not good enough."

3. Paragraph 2:

   a. Line 1 - change "two" to "three."

4. Paragraph 3:

   a. Line 3 - change "Frank Bucks" to "Mary Gee."

5. Page 2. Enumerated paragraph 2:

   a. Replace "speed" (in parentheses) with "120 pages per minute."

6. Be sure to change the ordering in line "The vendor of the Dinero II . . ."

Form 6-A

MILLENNIUM APPLIANCES

3431 BLOOR STREET, TORONTO, ON M8X 1G4
www.millennium.ca

TO: William Wilson

FROM: George Andrews

DATE: September 31, 20XX

SUBJECT:

On-line Copier/Printer Project

Subject to m y report regarding the Online Copyer and Printer Project, I have to ask you to help me with implementing a better servay. I wood like you to instruct divissiun managers to select two people too serve on a comittee to reveiw the Dinaro II and the oveall prosess. Its important that we have imparsal people involved in the survey.

Secondly, I'd like to ask you if you would rite a personnel memo to every network user to make sure they partisipate in the next servay a little better. Last time we run the servay, we had less then one third of user partisipate.

Thank you four your cooperashun with this effort. If we suckseed, well have a lot to selebrate. It's become a real issue with the finance people.

Call me if you wood like to talk about this a little more I'll be inmy office on extenshon 23487 until 4 oclock every knight of this weak.

Form 6-B

IDENTIFYING APPROPRIATE/INAPPROPRIATE USE OF TECHNOLOGY

With new technological tools emerging at a never-ending pace, it is important for an office professional to be able recognize whether a tool is being used in an appropriate or inappropriate manner.

Review the examples below and determine whether they are appropriate or inappropriate uses of technology in the work environment. Place a check mark in the box corresponding to your answer. In the space provided explain your rationale.

		Appropriate	**Inappropriate**
1.	Saving and storing personal files on a company computer or network.	❑	❑

_____
_____
_____
_____

| 2. | Sending or receiving personal emails on a computer or device supplied by your employer. | ❑ | ❑ |

_____
_____
_____
_____

| 3. | An employer monitoring employees' work by using keystroke tracking software. | ❑ | ❑ |

_____
_____
_____
_____

| 4. | Using your breaks or lunchtime to surf the internet to access music downloads sites. | ❑ | ❑ |

_____
_____
_____
_____

Form 7-A

NOTES ON INCOMING MAIL FOR MONDAY, JULY 14

1. The July issue of <u>Sales and Marketing Management</u>.

2. A personal letter for Charlene Azam.

3. A complaint from a customer in the Midwestern Region. The white shade of the new dishwasher she had installed does not match her other white appliances.

4. A letter to Mr. Wilson asking him to speak at the International Conference of the Administrative Management Society.

5. A letter from Microwave Ovens, Inc. saying that the catalogue Mr. Wilson has requested is out of print and will be mailed as soon as it is off the press.

6. The July issue of <u>Management World</u>.

7. A memorandum from the Personnel Department on new personnel policies for Millennium Appliances, Inc.

8. A letter from the sales office in Edmonton, Alberta, saying that the demand for appliances in almond colour is twice as great as that for appliances in other colours. What can be done to increase the shipments of almond appliances?

9. The August issue of <u>Administrative Management</u>.

10. A letter from a customer in Vancouver complaining that the surface on the hood installed with her new electric range is peeling. Will Millennium Appliances replace the hood?

11. A sales letter from Microwave Ovens, Inc. on the new features of their latest microwave oven.

12. A letter from the manager of the Western Manufacturing Plant offering suggestions for speeding up delivery of appliances after they are manufactured.

13. A letter from the sales office in Fredericton saying that the demand for appliances in almond colour is twice as great as that for appliances in other colours. Send more almond appliances.

14. A letter from the Midwestern Manufacturing Plant saying that the parts ordered are not available and will have to be manufactured.

15. A letter from Maybelle Anderson giving the title of her talk for the November Sales Seminar.

16. A complaint from a customer in the Eastern Region. She is dissatisfied with her electric range, which is only two years old, because the element in the oven is burned out. Will Millennium Appliances replace the element?

17. A request from the executive vice-president asking for a comparative sales report for the past five years.

18. An expiration notice for <u>Administrative Management</u>.

19. A letter from the local Chamber of Commerce asking Mr. Wilson to serve as Chairperson of the Community Development Committee.

20. A letter from Jack Winfield cancelling the appointment he has with Mr. Wilson on Friday, August 22.

Form 8-A-1

MAIL-EXPECTED RECORD

EXPECTED FROM	DESCRIPTION OF DOCUMENT	DATE RECEIVED	FOLLOW-UP SENT

Form 8-A-2

TO DO
TODAY

Date _____ Completed ✔

_____ ☐

_____ ☐

_____ ☐

_____ ☐

_____ ☐

_____ ☐

_____ ☐

_____ ☐

_____ ☐

Form 8-A-3

ROUTING SLIP

SEQUENCE	TEAM MEMBER	DATE	INITIAL
	C. Azam		
	S. Levine		
	J. Rush		
	L. Yee		

This routing slip was initiated on _____

Please return to W. Wilson by _____

Form 8-A-4

ROUTING SLIP

SEQUENCE	TEAM MEMBER	DATE	INITIAL
	C. Azam		
	S. Levine		
	J. Rush		
	L. Yee		

This routing slip was initiated on _____

Please return to W. Wilson by _____

Form 8-A-5

ROUTING SLIP

SEQUENCE	TEAM MEMBER	DATE	INITIAL
	C. Azam		
	S. Levine		
	J. Rush		
	L. Yee		

This routing slip was initiated on _____

Please return to W. Wilson by _____

Form 8-A-6

ROUTING SLIP

SEQUENCE	TEAM MEMBER	DATE	INITIAL
	C. Azam		
	S. Levine		
	J. Rush		
	L. Yee		

This routing slip was initiated on _____

Please return to W. Wilson by _____

Form 8-A-7

POSTAL ADDRESSES

A. The following are the names and addresses of invitees to the reunion as Mr. Wilson can recall them. Key the full address for each invitee in the way it will appear on an envelope. Include the correct format and postal code.

1. Jeff Bacon
   P. O. Box 22
   Edmonton

2. Tony Spencer
   22 O'Donnell Avenue
   Etobicoke, Ontario

3. Tommy Kairnes
   General Delivery
   Destruction Bay

4. Bill Owens
   99 Portugal Cove Road
   St. John (or St. John's—Mr. Wilson couldn't remember.)

5. Roy Canteara
   RR4
   Dauphin, Manitoba

6. Martin Beard
   P. O. Box 330
   Elbow (or Eyebrow—Mr. Wilson couldn't remember.)
   S0H 1J0

B. Martin Beard would be the treasurer of the high school reunion. Mr. Wilson has asked you to determine the closest Postal Outlet to Martin's location for cash transfers. Provide the complete address of the Postal Outlet to Mr. Wilson in the form of a memo.

Form 8-B

POSTAL SERVICES

Instructions: *Use information collected from CP to answer the following questions.*

1. What is the fee to send a single letter by Priority Courier to a city in the next province or territory?

2. Describe the two pricing components of Business Reply Mail.

3. What is the cost to insure a $375 ring sent through the mail?

4. What are the three services for which CP will provide Registered Mail?

5. Using the internet and CP's website, identify three services that cannot be combined with Registered Mail.

6. If you're sending a letter to another Canadian location, and you want to register the letter, how much will the service cost? The letter weighs 35 g. You want to have a hard-copy signature receipt, which you request when you mail the letter.

7. What is the postal fee on a COD in Canada where the package is valued at $156.75?

8. If you want to send a postcard weighing less than 30 g from a Canadian location to Italy, how much postage will you have to pay?

9. For which services can you purchase COD?

10. If you sent a large Xpresspost item from Kelowna to Halifax COD, what would be the standard service delivery time?

Form 8-C

MAIL SERVICE OPTIONS

As an administrative assistant, you may be responsible for mail handling procedures. Listed below is a selection of mail service options available through Canada Post (CP); below that is a list of ten different items that you must prepare for mailing. For each item, determine which service method is most appropriate. Record your answers on Form 8-D-2, and submit your work to your instructor for evaluation.

Mail Service Options:

Lettermail

Xpresspost™

Priority Post Courier

Registered Mail

Admail

Mailing Items:

1. Business contract requiring the signature of a third party.

2. Invoice billing a customer for services provided by your company.

3. Brochure advertising your company services.

4. Bimonthly company newsletter that is addressed to employees.

5. A parcel, weighing 24 kg, containing 20 copies of the company's quarterly sales reports. The reports are needed for a meeting scheduled two days from today.

6. Passport application for your supervisor.

7. A letter requiring a signature of receipt.

8. A parcel containing a watch your supervisor left behind before leaving for a trip to Calgary. Your supervisor would like to receive the watch as soon as possible.

9. Flyer advertising your upcoming open house.

10. An ink cartridge that must be returned to the supplier because it is the wrong model.

Form 8-D-1

MAIL SERVICE SELECTIONS

Using the information provided on Form 8-D-1, complete the following chart, explaining why you chose each type of service:

Mailing Item	Service Selection	Reason
1.		
2.		
3.		
4.		
5.		
6.		
7.		
8.		
9.		
10.		

Form 8-D-2

PROJECT RESPONSIBILITIES

A project is a complex array of tasks and duties. In order to work effectively as a project assistant, it is essential to understand the roles of the manager and assistant.

Shown below is a checklist of many of the duties and tasks performed on a typical project. Read each task and determine who is responsible for the task: Project Manager (PM), Project Assistant (PA), both (B), or other (O). Place an X in the corresponding box for the responsible role. Use the comments section at the bottom of the page to explain your reasons for choosing "both" or "other."

Duties and Responsibilities	PM	PA	B	O
Creates and executes project work plan and revises as appropriate to meet challenges				
Manages project budget and accounting				
Prepares progress reports and financial reports on the project				
Analyzes project profitability and revenue margins				
Maintains office filing system and prepares minutes of meetings				
Exchanges correspondence associated with the project-related activities				
Manages day-to-day operational aspects of project				
Collects, registers, and maintains information on project-related activities				
Arranges appointments, receives visitors, and screens phone calls				
Ensures project documents are complete, current, and stored appropriately				
Reviews deliverables prepared by team before passing them on to client				

Comments:

DETERMINING SOFTWARE RESOURCES FOR PROJECT MANAGEMENT

The right choice in software will enable the project team to focus on the project tasks in an effective and efficient manner. Using the internet, research project management software and determine three top choices based on the features, ease of use, and system requirements. Complete the chart below, itemizing key details from your research.

Software	Features	Ease of Use	System Requirements
1.			
2.			
3.			

Form 9-B

PROJECT MANAGEMENT CHALLENGES

Consider the three project management scenarios described below. Working as a team brainstorm and come up with a solution to help resolve or prevent these common issues from occurring when managing projects.

Problem Scenario #1: **Your client does not like what you have created.**

Solution_____

_____

_____

Problem Scenario #2: **Your project does not start on time.**

Solution_____

_____

_____

Problem Scenario #3: **You are spending too much time problem solving after the project begins.**

Solution_____

_____

_____

Form 9-C

ANSWER SHEET FOR 10-A

A	B	C	D	E	F	G	H	I	J	K	L	M	N	O	P	Q	R	S	T	U	V	W	X	Y	Z

Form 10-A

ANSWER SHEET FOR 10-B

A | B | C | D | E | F | G | H | I | J | K | L | M | N | O | P | Q | R | S | T | U | V | W | X | Y | Z

ANSWER SHEET FOR 10-C

	A	B	C	D	E	F	G	H	I	J	K	L	M	N	O	P	Q	R	S	T	U	V	W	X	Y	Z

Form 10-C

ELECTRONIC FOLDERS AND FILES

Folders	Subfolders	Documents
Conferences	December	
	November	
	October	
Customers	Western Region	
	Eastern Region	
Marketing Dept Budgets		
Meetings	Agendas	
	Minutes	
Suppliers	Western Region	
	Eastern Region	
Training	Admin Staff	
	Managers	
Vacations	Admin Staff	
	Manager	

Form 10-D

Form 11-A-1

To _____

Date _____ Time _____

WHILE YOU WERE OUT

M _____

of _____

Phone No. _____ Ext. _____

TELEPHONED	PLEASE CALL
CAME TO SEE YOU	WILL CALL AGAIN
WANTS TO SEE YOU	URGENT
	RETURNED YOUR CALL

Message _____

_____

_____

Taken by _____

Form 11-A-1

Form 11-A-2

To _____

Date _____ Time _____

WHILE YOU WERE OUT

M _____

of _____

Phone No. _____ Ext. _____

TELEPHONED	PLEASE CALL
CAME TO SEE YOU	WILL CALL AGAIN
WANTS TO SEE YOU	URGENT
	RETURNED YOUR CALL

Message _____

_____

_____

Taken by _____

Form 11-A-2

Form 11-A-3

To _____

Date _____ Time _____

WHILE YOU WERE OUT

M _____

of _____

Phone No. _____ Ext. _____

TELEPHONED	PLEASE CALL
CAME TO SEE YOU	WILL CALL AGAIN
WANTS TO SEE YOU	URGENT
	RETURNED YOUR CALL

Message _____

_____

_____

Taken by _____

Form 11-A-3

Form 11-A-4

To _____

Date _____ Time _____

WHILE YOU WERE OUT

M _____

of _____

Phone No. _____ Ext. _____

TELEPHONED	PLEASE CALL
CAME TO SEE YOU	WILL CALL AGAIN
WANTS TO SEE YOU	URGENT
	RETURNED YOUR CALL

Message _____

_____

_____

Taken by _____

Form 11-A-4

TELEPHONE SERVICES

Instructions: Answer the following questions in the space provided. Research for all answers should be gathered from your local telephone directory.

1. List the following emergency numbers.

   a. fire _____

   b. police _____

   c. your doctor _____

   d. hospital closest to home _____

   e. ambulance _____

2. List the following general information numbers.

   a. gas trouble _____

   b. power trouble _____

   c. water trouble _____

   d. time _____

3. List the area codes for the following locations.

   a. Vancouver   g. Edmonton

   b. Calgary   h. Seattle

   c. Saskatoon   i. Ottawa

   d. Sault Ste. Marie   j. Yellowknife

   e. Montreal   k. Whitehorse

   f. Winnipeg   l. Halifax

4. In what part of the telephone directory do you find provincial government listings?

5. What is the telephone number for information on labour standards? (Clue: This deals with a provincial government department.)

6. If you wanted to inquire about obtaining a driver's examination, what number would you call? (Clue: This deals with a provincial government department.)

7. In what part of the telephone directory do you find federal government listings?

Form 11-C-1

8. If you wanted to receive information about filing your federal income tax return, what number would you call?

9. If you wanted to place a complaint with your local division of the Royal Canadian Mounted Police, what number would you call?

10. List the names and telephone numbers for two travel agencies in your town or city.

    a.

    b.

11. List the names and telephone numbers for two general contractors located in your town or city.

    a.

    b.

12. List the names and telephone numbers for two automobile dealers that sell Chevrolet cars in your town or city.

    a.

    b.

13. List the name, address, and telephone number for an office building located in your town or city.

14. List the name, address, and telephone number for a professional moving and storage company located in your town or city.

15. If you place a call when your local time is 1400, what time is it in the offices located in the following cities?

    a. Victoria   g. Halifax
    b. Ottawa   h. Miami
    c. Winnipeg   i. Los Angeles
    d. Montreal   j. Calgary
    e. Regina   k. Toronto
    f. Edmonton   l. Charlottetown

16. If all the offices referred to in Question 15 kept office hours of 0900 to 1630, which offices would be open when you placed your call at 1400 your local time?

Form 11-C-2

MR. WILSON'S CALENDAR	
DATE	
TIME	**APPOINTMENTS**
0800	
0820	
0840	
0900	
0920	
0940	
1000	
1020	
1040	
1100	
1120	
1140	
1200	
1220	
1240	
1300	
1320	
1340	
1400	
1420	
1440	
1500	
1520	
1540	
1600	
1620	
1640	
REMINDERS	

Form 11-E-1

ADMIN. ASSISTANT'S CALENDAR	
DATE	
TIME	**APPOINTMENTS**
0800	
0820	
0840	
0900	
0920	
0940	
1000	
1020	
1040	
1100	
1120	
1140	
1200	
1220	
1240	
1300	
1320	
1340	
1400	
1420	
1440	
1500	
1520	
1540	
1600	
1620	
1640	
REMINDERS	

Form 11-E-2

NOTES ON MR. WILSON'S TRIP TO MIDWESTERN REGION

Appointments:

Wednesday, September 13	At 2000, Mr. Wilson will give a presentation to the Sales Management Club, Red River College.
	From 1400 to 1600, Mr. Wilson will meet with Raymond Jones, Plant Manager, Midwestern Region.
Tuesday, September 12	From 1400 to 1500, Mr. Wilson will meet with James Tobacki, Manager of Refrigerator Sales, Midwestern Region.
	From 0900 to 1100, Mr. Wilson will meet with Art Jacobs, Manager of Small Appliance Sales, Midwestern Region.
	From 1530 to 1630, Mr. Wilson will meet with Agnes Vallesco, Manager of Electric Sales, Midwestern Region.

Luncheon and dinner engagements:

Tuesday, September 12	Mr. Wilson will have lunch at 1200 with Art Jacobs and John Reddin. Mr. Wilson will have dinner with Mr. and Mrs. Reddin in the Hilton Hotel Revolving Restaurant at 2000.
Wednesday, September 13	At 1200 Mr. Wilson will have lunch with Mr. Matlock and at 1900 he will have dinner at the Sales Management Club banquet at Red River College.

Hotel reservations:

Reservations have been confirmed for the Hilton Hotel in Regina for September 11 and 12. They have also been made for the Best Western Hotel in Winnipeg for September 13. (Hotel confirmations are in the envelope with the airline tickets.)

Travel plans:

Thursday, September 14	Leave Winnipeg Airport at 1130 on Air Canada Flight 192. Arrive in Toronto at 1440.
Monday, September 11	Leave Pearson Airport, Terminal 2, Toronto, at 1925, on Air Canada Flight 153. Arrive in Regina at 2045.
Wednesday, September 13	Leave Regina Airport on Air Canada Flight 160 at 0940. Arrive in Winnipeg at 1140.

Form 12-A

Additional notes:

John Reddin will pick up Mr. Wilson at his hotel on Tuesday morning at 0830 and drive him to the Midwestern Sales Office.

Complimentary limousine service is provided to and from the Regina Airport and downtown hotels.

Art Jacobs will drive Mr. Wilson back to his hotel after his meetings at the sales office on Tuesday.

Mabel Wiggins will meet Mr. Wilson at the Best Western Hotel at 1815 and drive him to Red River College for the Sales Management Club banquet. She will also drive him back to his hotel after his talk to the club.

Wilson will have to take a taxi from his hotel in Winnipeg to the airport to catch his flight to Toronto on Thursday.

A.C. Matlock, Vice-President in Charge of Manufacturing, Midwestern Region, will meet Mr. Wilson at the Winnipeg airport and take him to the plant for his meeting with Raymond Jones, Plant Manager. He will drive Mr. Wilson back to his hotel after the meeting.

Form 12-A

MILLENNIUM TRAVEL FUND ADVANCE

Please forward completed forms to:

Accounting Department
Millennium Appliances, Inc.
3431 Bloor Street
Toronto, ON M8X 1G4

Tel (416) 795-2893   Fax (416) 798-3982

Name of Employee Requesting Advance: _____

Date of Request: _____

Employee Number: _____

Destination: _____

Reason for Travel: _____

Departure Date: _____

Return Date: _____

Date Advance Required: _____

Amount Requested:

Accommodation   (Refer to Policy 430) $ _____

Meals   (Refer to Policy 431) $ _____

Transportation   (Refer to Policy 432) $ _____

TOTAL REQUESTED $ _____

Preferred Method of Payment/Distribution _____ Company Cheque _____ Traveller's Cheque

Balance Outstanding (includes this request) $ _____

_____

Authorization   **Date of Authorization**
(as per Schedule of Authorities)

Approval Limits

$ 3 000   - Manager
$10 000   - Director
$10 000+   - President

Form 12-C

MILLENNIUM TRAVEL EXPENSE VOUCHER

CONTROL #: _____

NAME: _____   PIN: _____

TITLE: _____   DATE: _____

Date	Location	Work Order	Transport*	Hotel	Other	Entertain	Meals	Total	Explain Other, Entertain & Meals

EXPENSE TOTAL

LESS: CASH ADVANCE

BALANCE CLAIMED OR RETURNED

LEGEND

*   Include vehicle from Side 2 (if applicable)

**   Enter on Side 2

*** Distribute on Side 2

APPROVAL OF EXPENSES

Payment Approved by

_____

Title

AUDIT

Checked by _____ Date _____

CERTIFICATION OF EXPENSES

I certify that I have incurred these expenses.

Employee's Signature _____ Date _____

Date _____

Form 12-E

Vacation Requests

Charlene Azam

    Mon., June 9 through Fri., June 13

    Mon, Aug. 18 through Fri., Aug. 22

    Mon., Dec. 22 through Tues., Dec. 30

Sid Levine

    Mon., July 7 through Fri., July 11

    Mon., Aug 18 through Fri., Aug 22

    Mon., Sept. 8 through Fri., Sept. 12

J.R. Rush

    Mon., Aug 25 through Fri., Aug 29

    Mon., Oct. 13 through Fri., Oct. 17

    Mon., Oct. 20 through Fri., Oct 24

Linda Yee

    Mon., Dec. 9 through Fri., Dec. 13

    Mon., Dec. 15 through Fri., Dec. 19

    Mon., Dec. 22 through Tues., Dec. 30

William Wilson

    Mon., July 14 through Fri., July 18

Form 12-G

FAX *from*

MILLENNIUM APPLIANCES

3431 BLOOR STREET, TORONTO, ON M8X 1G4
www.millennium.ca

Date _____

Time _____

Number of Pages _____
(including Cover Sheet)

To

Fax Number _____

Telephone Number _____

Name _____

Company _____

From

Name _____

Title _____

Message _____

_____

_____

_____

_____

_____

_____

_____

_____

_____

This fax contains confidential
information. If you are a recipient of
this fax but not identified in the
address, please treat this
communication as confidential and
deliver it to the addressee. If the
addressee is not known to you,
kindly inform the sender by collect
call as soon as possible. Thank you.

MA

Form 13-A-1

FAX *from*

MILLENNIUM APPLIANCES

3431 BLOOR STREET, TORONTO, ON M8X 1G4
www.millennium.ca

Date _____

Time _____

Number of Pages
(including Cover Sheet) _____

To

Fax Number _____

Telephone Number _____

Name _____

Company _____

From

Name _____

Title _____

Message _____

_____

_____

_____

_____

_____

_____

_____

This fax contains confidential
information. If you are a recipient of
this fax but not identified in the
address, please treat this
communication as confidential and
deliver it to the addressee. If the
addressee is not known to you,
kindly inform the sender by collect
call as soon as possible. Thank you.

MA

Form 13-A-2

Meeting of Executive Committee for
    November Sales Seminar
    Wednesday, Sept. 10, 1700 h
    W. Wilson's office
    Members present: M. Kornachi,
    J. Mohammed, L. Witherspoon

    Member absent: L. Theodorakopoulos

Announcement: Michael Kornachi has agreed to help
with the Nov. Sales Seminar. He will be responsible
for registration.

    The minutes of the August meeting of the
Executive Committee were distributed. One
correction was called for. Honorariums will be paid
to the keynote speaker and the banquet speaker but
not to the luncheon speakers. The minutes were
approved as corrected.

Jasim Mohammed proposed that the keynote
speaker and the banquet speaker each be paid an
honorarium of $500. Committee members agreed.

Form 13-B

Michael Kornachi reported that James Atwell, who is in charge of working with the hotel on setting up audiovisual equipment, is ill and has asked to be relieved of this responsibility. Whom shall we ask to do this? After some discussion, Jasim Mohammed volunteered for the job.

Louise Witherspoon reported that increased attendance at the seminar (over attendance of previous years) is anticipated. Therefore, some of the meeting rooms that have been assigned to the sectional meetings of the Nov. Sales Seminar may be too small. She raised the question, should we ask for larger rooms? The Executive Committee instructed her to check with the hotel to see if larger rooms are available and, if so, to make arrangements to shift the large sectional meetings to larger rooms. Be sure to give the information on room changes to A.C. Rothbaum, who is responsible for having the program printed. He needs the changes by Sept. 20.

Meeting adjourned, 1830 h

W. Wilson

Form 13-B

VOTING SHEET FOR NOMINAL GROUP TECHNIQUE

ITEM NO.	ISSUES FOR DISCUSSION	TOTAL VOTES				WEIGHTED AVERAGE
		3	2	1	0	

REMEMBER:

3 = This problem is of high priority and should be dealt with now.

2 = This problem is of medium priority and should be dealt with as soon as possible.

1 = This problem is of low priority and should be dealt with when possible.

0 = This problem does not affect me or my work.

Form 13-C-1

MEETING LOG

MEETING OF:

LOCATION:	DATE:	TIME:

MEMBERS PRESENT:	MEMBERS ABSENT:

ISSUES DISCUSSED	RECORD OF DISCUSSION

ISSUE NO. 1

Topic =

Follow-up =

Recommendation/s =

ISSUE NO. 2

Topic =

Follow-up =

Recommendation/s =

ISSUE NO. 3

Topic =

Follow-up =

Recommendation/s =

Form 13-C-2

CAUSE-AND-EFFECT DIAGRAM

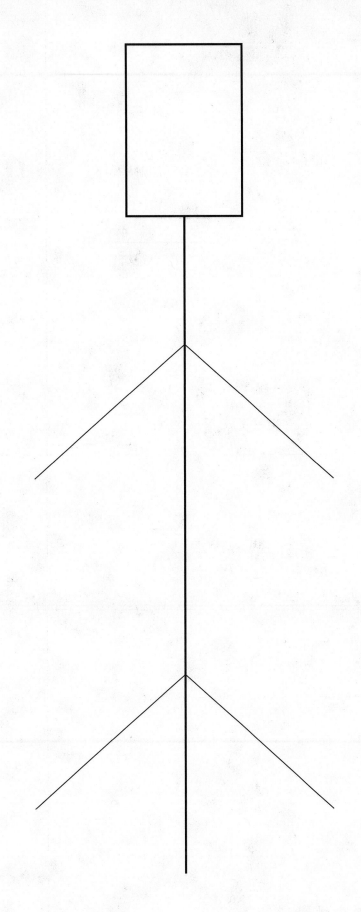

Form 13-C-3

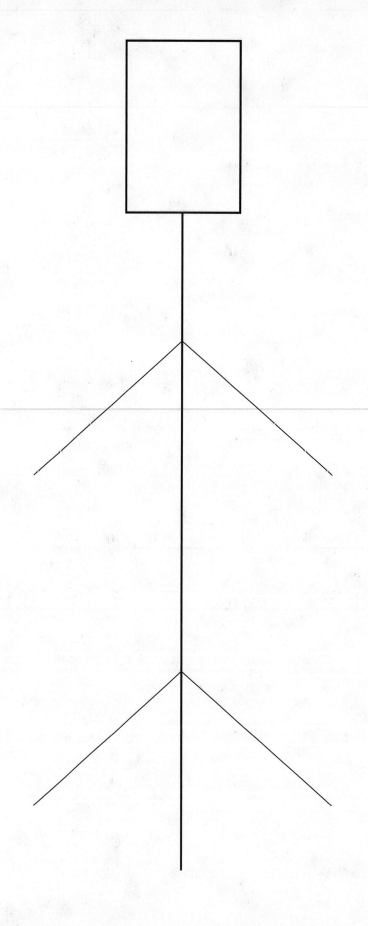

CAUSE-AND-EFFECT DIAGRAM

Form 13-C-4

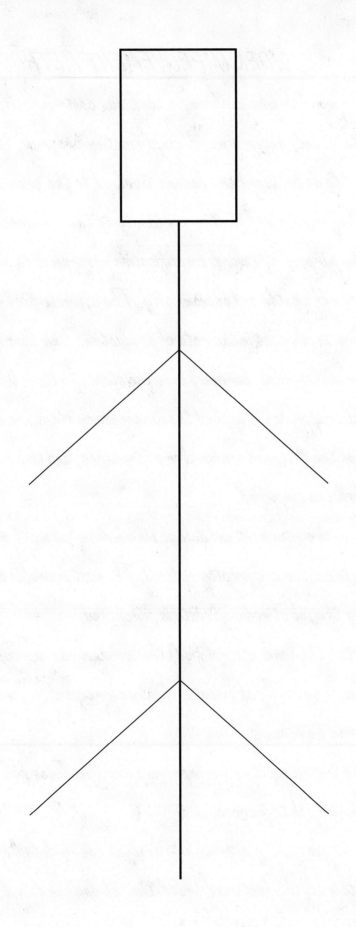

Form 13-C-5

WORK IMPROVEMENT METHODS

The worker who performs a task can contribute ideas for improving that task and, under a work simplification program, is encouraged and trained to do so. Workers become involved to the greatest extent in the aspect of work simplification pertaining to their respective tasks.

The purpose of a work simplification program is to enable workers to perform efficiently and economically. The ultimate goal is improved work, including an increase in the rate of production. This does not mean that the worker will speed up, hurrying thru the steps of a task. When the work simplification approach is applied the unnecessary steps are elimanated, other parts of the task are combined or rearranged, and the necessery parts of the task are simplified.

Excessive movement and delays which occur as work moves from 1 work station to another are greatly reduced. The most desirable equipment for performing the job at reduced costs is purchased. *[delete]*

After the task is simplified, the worker can improve the quality and increase the quantity of output without a corresponding increase in the amount of energy he expends. *[change to energy expended]*

The tested pattern for improving work includes five steps: *[four]*

1. Select a job to improve.

2. Use a questioning approach to analyze every detail of the job.

3. Obtain all the facts and break the job down in detail.

4. Apply the new method.

Form 14-B

These steps may be applied to improve either ~~a procedure or a method~~.

change to either a method or a procedure

Work analysts use these steps to guide workers thru an analysis of their own tasks in search of ways to improve them. You do not have to wait for your organization to launch a work simplification program in your dept. You can look for ways to work smarter and in turn gain time in which to accept more responsibility. Select only 1 task for improvement at a time.

move Select . . . time to next para after them

Take the initiative to select a task and analyze it, using the ~~five~~ *four* steps for work improvements in the same way a work analyst would use them.

Select a Job to Improve

Any job or task can be improved with directed effort, but some can be improved more than others. When you are looking for a job to improve, choose one that has worthwhile improvement possibilities, one that is important enough to warant the time you will spend studying it.

Recognize that each task consists of three parts: (1) make ready, (2) do, and 3 put away. "Make ready" is the effort and time put into setting up equipment and assembling the necessery materials, "Do" is the actual performance of the work. "Put away" is the storage and clean-up following the actual performance. Scrutinize the "do" operation. If you can eliminate it, you automatically eliminate the "make ready" and "put away" operations which go with it.

change make ready to actual performance

that

insert heading and paragraphs from page 3

Use a Questioning approach

The questioning approach is an attitude. It is essential for ~~anyone~~

change anyone to those

Form 14-B

change
his to their

searching for ways to improve his job performance. Every detail must be questioned for its necessity, possible combination with other details, and simplification.

Begin by asking why the job is done at all. Next examine each "do" operation and ask why it is necessary. Finally question the necessity of the remaining details—those involving "make ready" and "put away".

After you have separated the essential steps from the nonessential, apply the question test to the essential steps, one by one, in order. For each detail, ask, Where & Why? Who & Why? When & Why? How & Why? The expanded questions relative to where become, Where is it done? Why is it done there? Where should it be done? For each detail, apply similar questions concerning who, when, and how.

change
numbers
as
indicated

As you question each detail, keep in mind that you are searching for (1) steps to be elimanated, (2) steps to be performd elsewhere, (3) steps to be combined or rearranged, and (4) steps to be simplified.

Obtain All of the Facts; Break the Job Down in Detail

change
one to
step

move
heading
and
paragraphs
to page 2

Get the facts as the job is being performed. Put each one down detail by detail in the order in which it happens. Get facts, not opinions, and get all the facts. Omisions of facts, excuses, and opinions can lead to wrong conclusions.

To break down the steps of a task as they ocur, prepare a flowchart, Form 14-B the most widely used tool for analyzing work details.

Apply the New Method

move entire section to become last section

After you recieve tentative approval from your employer and in turn from management, conduct a trail run of your new method. Ask your employer and others who are knowledgable about the method to evaluate it and suggest further improvements. Evaluate the new method yourself. Ask, will it work? Will it save time and money? Will it improve quality? Will it increase quantity? Will it be excepted by others who are effected by it?

Develop a New Method

Study the answers indicated as you apply the questions What & Why? When & Why? Where and Why? Who & Why? and How & Why? to each detail.

Write up the proposed method in a meaningful and convincing form. Add comments that will help you to sell your idea. Present the proposed method to your employer. Be prepared to discuss it, answer challenging questions about it, and demonstrate it.

Apply the New Method →

Form 14-B

LETTER FOR CORRECTION

January 10, 20XX

Mr. Roy Baines

Office Equipment Supply

2331 Princess St.

Kingston, ON K7m-3G1

SUBJECT: TRAINING

Dear Mr. Bainis,

Thank you for installing our new office equipment so promptly. The decorater putt the finishing touchs on our offices tody.

Based on what you told us last weak, training on the computer can start immediately. Since both unites have been instaled, can you start training sessions

on Monday?

Mr. Bains, you gave us helpfull advise,and we appreciat it. we are looking foreward to working with the training director next weak.

Sincerely Yours,

Form 14-C

CANADIAN EASTERN BANK
MAIN BRANCH
TORONTO, ON   M6Y 2H5

DATE:	

CREDIT CURRENT ACCOUNT	Account Number:

Please print name

CASH	SILVER		
	X 1		
	X 2		
	X 5		
	X 10		
	X 20		
TOTAL CASH			
CHEQUES	EXCHANGE		
SUB TOTAL **LESS EXCHANGE**			
DEPOSITOR'S **INITIALS**	TOTAL		

Form 15-A-1

CHEQUE REGISTER

Cheque No.	Date	Description	Amount of Cheque		Amount of Deposit		Balance	

Form 15-A-2

MILLENNIUM APPLIANCES, INC.

3431 BLOOR STREET

TORONTO, ON M8X 1G4

TEL: 416-795-2893

147

PAY TO THE
ORDER OF

20

$

/100 DOLLARS

CANADIAN EASTERN BANK
MAIN BRANCH
TORONTO ON M6Y 2H5

MEMO

PER

|| 147|| |: 11779 :509|| 50132111 6||

Form 15-B-1

MILLENNIUM APPLIANCES, INC.

3431 BLOOR STREET

TORONTO, ON M8X 1G4

TEL: 416-795-2893

148

PAY TO THE
ORDER OF

20

$

/100 DOLLARS

CANADIAN EASTERN BANK
MAIN BRANCH
TORONTO ON M6Y 2H5

MEMO

PER

|| 148|| |: 11779 :509|| 50132111 6||

Form 15-B-2

MILLENNIUM APPLIANCES, INC.
3431 BLOOR STREET
TORONTO, ON M8X 1G4
TEL: 416-795-2893

149

20 _____

PAY TO THE
ORDER OF _____

$ _____

_____ /100 DOLLARS

CANADIAN EASTERN BANK
MAIN BRANCH
TORONTO ON M6Y 2H5

PER _____

MEMO _____

|| 149|| |: 11779 :509|| 50132|11 6||

Form 15-B-3

MILLENNIUM APPLIANCES, INC.
3431 BLOOR STREET
TORONTO, ON M8X 1G4
TEL: 416-795-2893

150

20 _____

PAY TO THE
ORDER OF _____

$ _____

_____ /100 DOLLARS

CANADIAN EASTERN BANK
MAIN BRANCH
TORONTO ON M6Y 2H5

PER _____

MEMO _____

|| 150|| |: 11779 :509|| 50132|11 6||

Form 15-B-4

MILLENNIUM APPLIANCES, INC.
3431 BLOOR STREET
TORONTO, ON M8X 1G4
TEL: 416-795-2893

151

20 _____

PAY TO THE
ORDER OF _____

$ _____

_____ /100 DOLLARS

CANADIAN EASTERN BANK
MAIN BRANCH
TORONTO ON M6Y 2H5

PER _____

MEMO _____

|| 151|| |: 11779 :509|| 50132|11 6||

MILLENNIUM APPLIANCES, INC.
3431 BLOOR STREET
TORONTO, ON M8X 1G4
TEL: 416-795-2893

152

20 _____

PAY TO THE
ORDER OF _____

$ _____

_____ /100 DOLLARS

CANADIAN EASTERN BANK
MAIN BRANCH
TORONTO ON M6Y 2H5

PER _____

MEMO _____

|| 152|| |: 11779 :509|| 50132|11 6||

Form 15-B-5

Form 15-B-6

MILLENNIUM APPLIANCES, INC.
3431 BLOOR STREET
TORONTO, ON M8X 1G4
TEL: 416-795-2893

153

PAY TO THE
ORDER OF

20

$

/100 DOLLARS

PER

CANADIAN EASTERN BANK
MAIN BRANCH
TORONTO ON M6Y 2H5

MEMO

|| 153|| |: 11779 :509|| 5013211 6||

Form 15-B-7

MILLENNIUM APPLIANCES, INC.
3431 BLOOR STREET
TORONTO, ON M8X 1G4
TEL: 416-795-2893

154

PAY TO THE
ORDER OF

20

$

/100 DOLLARS

PER

CANADIAN EASTERN BANK
MAIN BRANCH
TORONTO ON M6Y 2H5

MEMO

|| 154|| |: 11779 :509|| 5013211 6||

Form 15-B-8

Cheque 155

MILLENNIUM APPLIANCES, INC.
3431 BLOOR STREET
TORONTO, ON M8X 1G4
TEL: 416-795-2893

155

PAY TO THE
ORDER OF

20 _____

$ _____

_____ /100 DOLLARS

CANADIAN EASTERN BANK
MAIN BRANCH
TORONTO ON M6Y 2H5

MEMO _____

PER _____

|| 155|| |: 11779 :509|| 501321|| 6||

Cheque 156

MILLENNIUM APPLIANCES, INC.
3431 BLOOR STREET
TORONTO, ON M8X 1G4
TEL: 416-795-2893

156

PAY TO THE
ORDER OF

20 _____

$ _____

_____ /100 DOLLARS

CANADIAN EASTERN BANK
MAIN BRANCH
TORONTO ON M6Y 2H5

MEMO _____

PER _____

|| 156|| |: 11779 :509|| 501321|| 6||

MILLENNIUM APPLIANCES, INC.
3431 BLOOR STREET
TORONTO, ON M8X 1G4
TEL: 416-795-2893

157

_____ 20 _____

PAY TO THE
ORDER OF _____

$ _____

_____ /100 DOLLARS

CANADIAN EASTERN BANK
MAIN BRANCH
TORONTO ON M6Y 2H5

PER _____

MEMO _____

|| 157|| |: 11779 :509|| 50132|11 6||

Form 15-B-11

MILLENNIUM APPLIANCES, INC.
3431 BLOOR STREET
TORONTO, ON M8X 1G4
TEL: 416-795-2893

158

_____ 20 _____

PAY TO THE
ORDER OF _____

$ _____

_____ /100 DOLLARS

CANADIAN EASTERN BANK
MAIN BRANCH
TORONTO ON M6Y 2H5

PER _____

MEMO _____

|| 158|| |: 11779 :509|| 50132|11 6||

Form 15-B-12

BANK STATEMENT

NAME: November Sales Seminar c/o William Wilson 3431 Bloor Street, Toronto, ON M8X 1G4	BRANCH: Mississauga Main	

ACCOUNT NO. 08–03261	TRANSIT NO. 3512	BALANCE FORWARD 20xx–11–25	360.27

CODE	DESCRIPTION	DEBIT	CREDIT	DAY/MO	BALANCE
DD	Direct Deposit		300.00	04/11	660.27
DD	Direct Deposit		1500.00	05/11	2160.27
DD	Direct Deposit		3000.00	06/11	5160.27
CH	Cheque No.147	1224.00		07/11	3936.27
CH	Cheque No.148	510.00		08/11	3426.27
CH	Cheque No.149	450.00		08/11	2976.27
DD	Direct Deposit		2250.00	09/11	5226.27
CH	Cheque No.152	1700.00		12/11	3526.27
CH	Cheque No.153	25.00		12/11	3501.27
CH	Cheque No.154	60.00		13/11	3441.27
INC	Interest		17.42	15/11	3458.69
CH	Cheque No.155	300.45		15/11	3158.24
CH	Cheque No.156	500.00		18/11	2658.24
DD	Direct Deposit		600.00	20/11	3258.24
CH	Cheque No.157	500.00		21/11	2758.24

No. of Vouchers This Period	Ø	TOTAL DEBITS	$5269.45	TOTAL CREDITS	$7667.42

Form 15-C

PETTY CASH ENVELOPE

Petty Cash Fund				Explanation	Distribution of Payment								
Received	Paid Out	Date	No.										

Form 15-D-1

Amount _____ Voucher No. _____

PETTY CASH VOUCHER

For: _____

Paid to: _____

Charge to: _____

Date: _____

Approved by: _____

Comments: _____

_____

_____

Form 15-D-2

Amount _____ Voucher No. _____

PETTY CASH VOUCHER

For: _____

Paid to: _____

Charge to: _____

Date: _____

Approved by: _____

Comments: _____

_____

_____

Form 15-D-3

Amount _____ Voucher No. _____

PETTY CASH VOUCHER

For: _____

Paid to: _____

Charge to: _____

Date: _____

Approved by: _____

Comments: _____

_____

_____

Form 15-D-4

Amount _____ Voucher No. _____

PETTY CASH VOUCHER

For: _____

Paid to: _____

Charge to: _____

Date: _____

Approved by: _____

Comments: _____

_____

_____

Form 15-D-5

Amount _____ Voucher No. _____

PETTY CASH VOUCHER

For: _____

Paid to: _____

Charge to: _____

Date: _____

Approved by: _____

Comments: _____

_____

_____

Form 15-D-6

Amount _____ Voucher No. _____

PETTY CASH VOUCHER

For: _____

Paid to: _____

Charge to: _____

Date: _____

Approved by: _____

Comments: _____

_____

_____

Form 15-D-7

Amount _____ Voucher No. _____

PETTY CASH VOUCHER

For: _____

Paid to: _____

Charge to: _____

Date: _____

Approved by: _____

Comments: _____

_____

_____

Form 15-D-8

Amount _____ Voucher No. _____

PETTY CASH VOUCHER

For: _____

Paid to: _____

Charge to: _____

Date: _____

Approved by: _____

Comments: _____

_____

_____

Form 15-D-9

Amount _____ Voucher No. _____

PETTY CASH VOUCHER

For: _____

Paid to: _____

Charge to: _____

Date: _____

Approved by: _____

Comments: _____

_____

_____

Form 15-D-10

Amount _____ Voucher No. _____

PETTY CASH VOUCHER

For: _____

Paid to: _____

Charge to: _____

Date: _____

Approved by: _____

Comments: _____

_____

_____

Form 15-D-11

Amount _____ Voucher No. _____

PETTY CASH VOUCHER

For: _____

Paid to: _____

Charge to: _____

Date: _____

Approved by: _____

Comments: _____

_____

_____

Form 15-D-12

Amount _____ Voucher No. _____

PETTY CASH VOUCHER

For: _____

Paid to: _____

Charge to: _____

Date: _____

Approved by: _____

Comments: _____

_____

_____

Form 15-D-13

PERSONAL INVENTORY
Answer the following questions in preparation for developing your résumé.

PART I: PERSONAL INFORMATION

Name	
Address	
Telephone	
Fax	
E-mail	

PART II: EMPLOYMENT BACKGROUND

Use action verbs to write sentences that list your work-related accomplishments. Begin your sentences with some of the following verbs:

Earned	Developed	Supervised	Organized
Designed	Improved	Analyzed	Trained
Established	Managed	Prepared	Researched

1.

2.

3.

4.

5.

6.

Think of all the employment you have had, both career related and other. Use reverse chronological order (most recent first) to record your answers.

Working Title	
Company Name	
City Where Company Is Located	
Dates Commenced and Ended	
Key Responsibilities	
Working Title	
Company Name	
City Where Company Is Located	
Dates Commenced and Ended	
Key Responsibilities	

Form 16-A

Continue to record information about your employment.	
Working Title	
Company Name	
City Where Company Is Located	
Dates Commenced and Ended	
Key Responsibilities	

PART III: EDUCATION AND TRAINING

Use reverse chronological order to record the following information. Use this area to record postsecondary education (full-time, extension, adult education, etc.).	
Degree/Diploma/Certificate Earned	
Name of Institute	
City Where School Is Located	
Dates Commenced and Ended	
Grade Point Average	
Key Courses Completed	

Use this area to record information about your high school education.	
Diploma/Certificate Earned	
Name of Institute	
City Where School Is Located	
Dates Commenced and Ended	
Grade Point Average	

PART IV: INTERESTS AND ACTIVITIES

List professional organizations that you have held or currently hold membership in.	1. 2. 3.
List volunteer positions you have held or currently hold in your community.	1. 2. 3.
List sports or hobbies you participate in.	1. 2. 3.

Form 16-A

CHECKLIST FOR YOUR JOB CAMPAIGN		
Activity	**Date Due**	**Date Submitted**
1. Prepare a self-appraisal inventory.		
2. Use information available in either the college or public library, or on the internet, to prepare a concise report on a local corporation.		
3. From the placement office, obtain literature that may be helpful to you in your job campaign.		
4. Join a committee to study employment opportunities for administrative assistants in your community. Obtain literature and share your findings with committee members.		
5. Prepare a list of qualifications you plan to emphasize during job interviews. Prepare a list of questions you expect to be asked and their answers. Prepare a list of questions you want to ask the interviewer.		
6. Prepare a résumé.		
7. Write either a prospecting job application letter or a solicited job application letter.		
8. Edit your résumé after your instructor has proofread it.		
9. Prepare a portfolio displaying samples of your work.		
10. Study job advertisements on internet sites as well as government publications and the local newspaper. Analyze the advertisements for administrative assistants.		
11. Write an evaluation of your performance during an early job interview.		
12. Complete the application for employment (Form 13-C-2).		
13. Prepare a job acceptance letter or a job refusal letter.		

Form 16-C-1

APPLICATION FOR EMPLOYMENT

PERSONAL INFORMATION

Social Insurance No.

	Last	First	Middle

NAME:

Street	City	Province	Postal Code

PRESENT ADDRESS:

PHONE: FAX: E-MAIL:

REFERRED BY:

If related to anyone in our employ, state name and department

TYPE OF EMPLOYMENT DESIRED

POSITION   When can you start?   Sarlary Desired

Are you employed now?   May we contact your present employer?

EDUCATION	Name and Location of School	Year Attended	Date Graduated	Major Subjects
UNIVERSITY				
COLLEGE				
HIGH SCHOOL				
OTHER				

List specialized courses

What foreign languages do you speak fluently?   Read?   Write?

Form 16-C-2

FORMER EMPLOYMENT (List employers, starting with last one first.)

Date Month and Year	Company Name and City	Salary	Position	Reason for Leaving
From				
To				
From				
To				
From				
To				

VOLUNTEER ACTIVITIES (List any community service or volunteer work you have done.)

	Position	Name of Organization	Date Commenced and Ended
1			
2			

INTERESTS (List sports where you participate or other activities where you have an interest.)

	Name of Sport or Activity	Level of Interest or Achievement
1		
2		

MEMBERSHIP (List any professional organization where you hold membership.)

	Name of Organization	Position Held
1		
2		

REFERENCES (Give the names of three persons not related to you.)

	Name and Title	Address	Telephone	E-Mail	Years Acquainted
1					
2					
3					

I understand that misrepresentation or omission of facts called for in this application is cause for dismissal.

Date   Signature

Form 16-C-2

Common Proofreaders' Marks

Meaning	Symbol	Example
Insert *(This could be used to indicate you want to insert words, punctuation, or a space.)*	∧ OR ∨	Justyne PDA to the CEO,
Insert Space	#	highschool
Close up the space	◯	every day
Delete	ℓ	Benjamin Ross is the
Let it remain as is *(You may have deleted something and then changed your mind.)*	stet	Benjamin Ross is the stet
Start a new paragraph	¶	policies were accepted. ¶ The no-smoking policy stipulated that
Do not start a new paragraph	no ¶	policies were accepted. ¶ The no-smoking policy stipulated that
Move right	]	The judge insisted on the following penalties: • $5000 fine • 30 days in jail
Move left	[	The judge insisted on the following penalties: • $5000 fine • 30 days in jail

(continued)

Meaning	Symbol	Example
Transpose letters or words	⊓⊔	⌈coloured ⌊red⌋ labels OR colour⌈de⌉
Lower	⊔	H⌊2⌋O
Raise	⊓	E = M C⌈2⌉
Use lowercase	/c	Do (NOT) remove supplies. /c
Capitalize	☰	Do not remove supplies.
Use boldface	bf	Do (not) remove supplies. bf
Underline or use italics	⎯	Do not remove supplies.
Align *(This could be used to indicate the need to align right or left, top or bottom.)*	//	‖ You are invited to attend a business seminar.
Centre	] [	] You are invited to attend a business seminar. [
Spell the word/s out	sp	C.N.I.B. sp
Use parentheses	{ }	Canadian National Institute for the Blind {C.N.I.B.}

Glossary

Abridged Shortened by using fewer words while maintaining the fundamental content.

Ad hoc For a specific purpose and not for general application.

Adjournment A temporary or indefinite halt to a meeting.

Administrative assistant A contemporary secretary whose skill set encompasses office organization, automation, and planning.

Agenda A formal list of items to be achieved or discussed at a meeting.

Almanac A yearly book or calendar of days, weeks, and months, containing statistical information on many subjects.

Ambient lighting Illumination that surrounds us and is not directly focused on one area, as is task lighting.

Ambiguous Having more than one interpretation, thereby causing uncertainty or confusion.

Annotating The process of making notes on a document for comment or criticism.

Application program A program or software that performs a collection of related tasks, such as word processing, and that allows the user to specify the data input and output.

Archiving The act of storing letters, documents, files, or electronic files for historical purposes.

Area code A series of digits placed before the local number to indicate the area in which the call is to be delivered. Also known as a routing code.

Articulation agreement An agreement between two educational institutions through which transfer credits may be used toward an academic credential at either institution.

Automated inquiry system A process where the sender of a registered item of mail may telephone a toll-free number to check the delivery status of the item that has been sent.

Automated teller machine (ATM) A public electronic funds transfer machine for making bank deposits, withdrawals, and accessing information.

Backup A copy of data, often in a separate location from the original. The contents of the hard disk are backed up using CDs, external hard drives, or servers (computers dedicated solely for the backups).

Bibliography A list of details about books, their authors and publishers, used or referred to by another author.

Bit A binary digit. The smallest possible piece of computer information. A 1 or 0 in the binary system represents each bit. A sequence of eight bits forms a byte (*see* **byte**).

Blind advertisements Job advertisements that do not disclose the company placing the advertisement.

Blog This term is short for weblog. A blog can best be described as a journal available on the web.

Brainstorming The unrestrained offering of ideas or suggestions by all members of a conference; the purpose is to find a solution to a problem.

Bridge A virtual facility where conference call participants meet for their exclusive conference.

Broadband Signals are transmitted digitally over a range of frequencies, allowing high-speed access to the internet.

Budget An estimate based on income and expenditures over a set period of time.

Bureaucratic An administrative system that has rigid rules of reporting.

Buyout The purchase of one company by another company.

Byte A unit of data equivalent to one computer character (*see* **bit**).

Call management services A set of telephone-user options provided by the telephone company (e.g., display of incoming call information, call forwarding).

Calling card Similar in appearance to a credit card, but having a unique number that allows users to remotely bill telephone calls to their personal accounts.

Canadian Postal Guide A publication that gives full details of conditions, facilities, and categories of service provided by Canada Post.

Cancelling mail A process where bars are printed over the stamps, and the envelope is stamped to indicate the date, time, and municipality where the mail was processed.

Casual day A working day designated by management as a day when casual, but respectable, attire may be worn in the office.

CD-ROM Compact disk–read only memory; a storage medium capable of retaining large quantities of audio, visual, or textual data.

Central processing unit The part of a computer where the processing actually occurs.

Character A pattern of behaviour built upon the basic values of life.

Charge-out A system of keeping track of materials that have been removed from the office paper files.

Chronological Time-ordered arrangement of events.

Cite To reference something or someone as an example to support what has been said or written.

Clean desk policy An office policy dictating that employees leave their desks clear or tidy when they leave the office.

Code of ethics A formal document that states the organization's primary values and ethical rules of conduct.

Coding A system of symbols and numbers that convey meaning to the users of the system.

Coherence The quality of being consistent or intelligible.

Colloquialism A word or expression that is considered informal speech or writing.

Command An instruction that the operator gives to a computer to tell it what function to perform.

Commuter flight Short, direct flight between two neighbouring cities.

Company merger Joining together two or more companies to conduct business.

Company takeover An individual or organization takes control of another organization.

Compatible The ability of different hardware or software products to function together effectively.

Composure The state of being calm in mind and manner.

Concise Brief and to the point.

Conference A meeting or discussion to exchange ideas.

Conference call A meeting or discussion conducted over the telephone between three or more participants.

Connecting flight A flight on which the passenger, at some point between departure and destination, changes to another flight of the same airline.

Consensus When every team member can support the team decision, the team has reached a consensus. The final decision may not be the choice of each team member; however, all members must agree that they can support it both inside and outside the confines of the meeting.

Contemporary Characteristically modern in style.

Convenience copier A small, inexpensive photocopier.

Copyright The legal right of publishers and artists to control their own work.

Courtesy title A respectful title to be used in formal address (e.g., Mr., Ms., Mrs., Miss, Mayor, Vice-President, Major).

Credenza A sideboard or cabinet used as an extension of a desk.

Cross-referencing A method of locating a single record from two or more file references.

Culture Refers to a system of shared values, beliefs, morals, and social standards embraced by a group of people.

Curriculum vitae A form of résumé, often referred to as a CV. The actual Latin words mean "course of life." The term describes a document that summarizes a person's history and professional qualifications.

Debrief To receive information or to recap a meeting or procedure that has concluded.

Deductive A writing technique that leads the reader from a general idea to a specific concept.

Delete To erase. Text may be deleted by the character, line, paragraph, page, or document.

Desktop computer (Personal Computer) A stand-alone computer used to perform personal or office applications.

Desktop publishing (DTP) A computer application that enables the user to design and create professional documents that integrate text and graphics.

Digital subscriber line (DSL) Lines provided digitally by phone companies to allow subscribers to transmit data at a high rate of speed.

Direct flight A flight on which, regardless of the number of stops en route, the passenger remains on the same plane from departure to arrival at destination.

Directory An electronic directory is a section of the computer system that identifies certain electronic files. It works much like a filing cabinet. (Also called a catalogue or folder.)

Discrimination Showing prejudice or being unfairly partial.

Display A screen or monitor.

Diversity The variety of experiences and perspectives that arise from differences in race, culture, religion, mental or physical abilities, heritage, age, gender, sexual orientation, and other characteristics.

Domestic mail Mailable matter that is transmitted within Canada, which includes the ten provinces, the Yukon, the Northwest Territories, and Nunavut.

Downsizing Reducing the size of an organization, often by laying off employees.

Duplex Printing on both sides of the paper.

E-commerce A broad term that describes the environment in which commercial transactions are conducted over the internet.

Effectiveness The practical and productive effect of a procedure on a process.

Efficiency Producing the desired results with the least output of time, but in a capable and competent fashion.

E-file The electronic storage location and reference name for electronic documents.

Electronic bulletin board A BBS (bulletin board system) is a host computer that can be reached by computer modem for the purpose of sharing or exchanging messages or other files.

Electronic calendar A computer-based personal calendar. When computers are networked, calendars may also be used to schedule and plan on behalf of the user.

Electronic data interchange (EDI) EDI provides a standard exchange of business data from one computer to another.

Electronic funds transfer (EFT) A method of transferring funds via computer and other forms of technology.

Electronic mail (email) A computer network–based message routing, storing, and retrieval system.

Electronic passport (e-passport) A passport with an electronic chip inserted in the back for scanning purposes, replacing the standard paper copy of the passport.

Electronic presentation software Application software that enables you to create individual electronic slides that can be displayed as a slide show. Graphs, charts, and other images created using this software add visual appeal to a presentation.

Empowered To be authorized and trusted to complete a job or task.

Encryption software Security that encodes computer information into something beyond recognition with the use of a software "key."

E-portfolio An electronic version of a portfolio where documents are stored on a personal website or electronic folder.

Equal opportunity employers Employers that provide the same rights and status to all employees.

Ergonomics The study of efficiency, safety, and ease of action between people and their working environment.

Esthetically A way of viewing design that is in good taste and pleasant to look at.

Ethical Agreeing with principles of accepted moral conduct.

Etiquette Customs and rules of social or corporate correct behaviour.

Executive A person who manages or directs the business affairs of an institution or organization.

Facsimile A device that will copy and transmit, over telephone lines, graphical or textual documents to a corresponding remote facsimile. Also called a fax.

Feature-rich A term used to describe a device or system with many features or options.

Fibre optic cable A technology using glass (or plastic) threads (fibres) to transmit data.

Field A field is an area or a location in a unit of data such as a record, message header, or computer instruction. A field can be subdivided into smaller fields.

File A file is a related collection of *records*.

File 13 A euphemism for "the garbage."

Filing The act of storing files in a manual filing system.

Firewall A hardware and software computer security system designed to reduce the threat of unauthorized intrusion.

Flash drive A portable, miniaturized permanent memory device used with the USB ports of a computer. Sometimes called pen drives or memory keys.

Flextime A contraction of "flexible time." Readjusting working hours to accommodate both employee and employer.

Font Complete set of characters that belong to a typeface. They share the same design, size, and style.

Format The arrangement of text and graphics on a page.

Functional department A department within an organization that is structured according to its generic function; for example, the engineering department.

Gazetteer An index of geographical names.

Gigabyte Approximately one billion bytes.

GIGO An acronym for Garbage In, Garbage Out. The acronym means that poor-quality input to a computer will only result in poor-quality output.

Global marketplace The worldwide business environment. An international forum in which to conduct business.

Grammar check A word processing feature that compares the grammar of a keyed document with conventional rules.

Grapevine An informal channel of communication within an organization.

Hard disk drive A large capacity mass storage device that is usually located inside the computer and functions as the primary permanent storage location for your computer work.

Hard skills Technical skills, including working with a variety of technologies, using technology to produce and manage information, and maintaining and troubleshooting problems.

Hardware The physical part(s) of a computer system.

Hidden job market The vibrant job market that exists without advertising. The potential employee must research and network to discover what opportunities are available.

Hierarchy An organization whose employees are ranked by seniority and power.

Hotline A telephone line or special number that is reserved for critical calls such as technical support.

Hotspot This is a site that provides a wireless local area network through the use of a router connected to a link to an internet service provider.

Hyperlink A link from a hypertext document to the same or another hypertext document.

Icon A picture used to represent a computer software function.

Immunization An inoculation that gives selective immunity to infections.

Important records Records or documents that would be challenging to replace if disposed of.

Indexing Classifying and providing an ordered list of items for easy retrieval.

Inductive A writing technique that introduces the reader to a concept and then leads the reader to a reasonable conclusion.

Informal organization An organization or group that develops naturally among personnel without direction from the management of the company within which it operates.

Information A term that is synonymous with data. Data is information translated into a form that is more convenient to manipulate by computers. It is often referred to in terms of *bits* and *bytes*.

Information Age An era in which the timely acquisition, processing, and distribution of information is critical for the growth of business.

Information management The skilful handling or use of information.

Input Data submitted to a computer for processing.

Integrating application software Seamlessly connecting data created in one software with different software to allow all the features of each software to remain. For example, if you integrate an Excel spreadsheet into a Word document, the spreadsheet will appear as a Word table. However, clicking on the table will open the Excel spreadsheet within Word and allow you to make changes to it. Clicking anywhere on the Word page outside the Excel spreadsheet will make the Word document active and display the spreadsheet once again as a Word table.

Interconnect equipment Telephone equipment that organizations purchase or lease from suppliers other than the telephone company.

Interface The software and/or hardware that connects one device or system to another, either electronically or physically.

International mail Canadian mail addressed to points of destination outside Canada and the United States of America.

Internet A global network of computer-based information and services.

Interpersonal communication Personal interaction between individuals or members of a group.

Interpersonal skills Qualities that determine a person's ability to get along with others. Examples are ability to work as a team player, negotiator, customer service provider, and teacher.

Intranet A company's private computer network.

Itinerary A detailed plan for a journey.

Jet lag The disruption of the body's natural rhythm that comes from changing time zones as a result of high-speed jet travel.

Keyboard An input device consisting of an arrangement of keys similar to that on a typewriter.

Kilobyte Approximately one thousand bytes.

Landscaped office An attractive and well-designed open-office plan.

Laptop (notebook) computer A small-scale personal computer. It has all the functionality of a desktop personal computer, but it weighs about three kilograms and is the approximate size of this textbook.

Laser printer A nonimpact printer using an internal laser beam to form characters.

Line organization An organization structure based on authority. Line authority is hierarchical; the president has ultimate authority and reduced authority is given to others down the line to supervisor.

Line-and-staff organization An organizational structure where line managers have operational positions and staff managers have advisory or administrative positions. Line-and-staff organization structures are often found in large, diverse companies.

Local area network (LAN) Two or more local personal computers or terminals connected together by communication lines in order to share common programs and data.

Mail merge The process of combining text (letters/memos) from one file with names and addresses from another file.

Markup An additional monetary value added to the cost price.

Megabyte Approximately one million bytes.

Memory Temporary memory is the place in a computer where programs and data are stored while in use. For permanent memory, *see* **hard disk drive**.

Mentor In a corporate setting, a mentor is a person who usually holds a position of a higher level than yours. This person can offer you career advice, guidance, and information about the organization.

Merger The unification of two or more companies.

Microfilm Micro images on film made by a process that photographs and reduces the size of documents.

Microprocessor chip A processing unit miniaturized to fit on a single integrated circuit (chip).

Mobile banking Chartered banks offer customers with smartphones, tablets, and PDAs access to banking services similar to web-based banking.

Modem A device that converts computer signals to telephone signals and vice versa. It enables communication between computers over telephone lines.

Modular furniture Furniture designed to be used as separate modules or placed together to form larger units.

Monitor Screen output for a computer.

Motivation The inner reason that causes an individual to act.

Mouse Hand-operated input device. It is rolled across a surface to control the movement of a cursor.

Mousing The act of using the PC "mouse" to control software applications.

Multiculturalism The acceptance and appreciation of many integrated cultures within a society.

Negotiating The process of exchanging ideas, information, and opinions with others to work toward agreements; consequently, policies and programs are formulated, and decisions, conclusions, or solutions are the result of a joint effort.

Network Various processors or terminals connected within the same computer environment.

Networking Informal communications between people, departments, divisions, or organizations for the purpose of sharing information.

No-frills flight A flight on which regular services that travellers have come to expect are absent. For example, in-flight cabin services by flight attendants are not provided, and travellers are required to provide their own food and drink.

Nonessential records Documents that if lost or misplaced will not harm the organization's ability to operate.

Nonstop flight A flight that is uninterrupted from point of departure to destination.

Office manual A manual of best procedures to follow in an office.

Office politics The tactics and strategies used in an office to gain an occupational advantage.

Offset printing A printing process in which a rubber cylinder transfers an inked impression from an etched plate to a sheet of paper.

Online Describing a device connected directly to a computer.

Open office An office plan or design without conventional walls, corridors, or floor-to-ceiling partitions.

Open ticket A booking arrangement for some forms of transportation where the scheduling details of the return journey are not specified.

Operating system A computer's fundamental internal commands or instructions needed to operate; the first program loaded upon starting the computer, the operating system enables the application programs to work.

Organization chart A guide to the formal internal structure of an organization.

Orientation Becoming familiar with a situation or environment.

Out folder A substitute folder that replaces an active folder, which has been removed from the filing cabinet.

Out guide A substitute document that replaces an original document temporarily taken from a folder. The out guide provides a description of the removed document.

Output Information resulting from computer processing.

Participatory management A management style that is both permissive and democratic. It involves employees in some aspects of decision making and emphasizes autonomy in work activities.

Passport A travel document, given to citizens by their own government, granting permission to leave the country and to travel in certain specified foreign countries.

Pen drive A portable, miniaturized permanent memory device used with the USB ports of a computer.

Per diem rate A daily allowance for expenses. *Per Diem* is Latin for *by the day*.

Peripheral An external device such as a printer, scanner, or disk drive that is connected to and controlled by the computer.

Personal digital assistant (PDA) A personal pocket-sized electronic organizer with administrative features and functions such as calendar, diary, calculator, filing system, and address book.

Personal qualities Qualities that determine a person's values and sense of what is important, such as attitude, dependability, integrity and honesty, and self-image.

Personal space The distance at which one person feels comfortable talking to another.

Plagiarism Using the words or ideas of someone else as your own without permission or reference to the original source.

Poise Ease and dignity of manner.

Postal code A unique alphanumeric code used to identify the local destination of a mail item.

Prepaid calling cards Cards that are accepted by the telephone company when the holder makes long-distance calls. The cost of the call is deducted from the current balance or value of the card.

Printer A device that produces copy on paper.

Priorities The assignment of precedence of tasks to be accomplished. Typically the tasks will be ranked in order of importance.

Processing Computer manipulation of data.

Procrastination An unproductive behaviour pattern that causes you to delay working on your most important assignments and to focus on tasks that aren't priorities.

Professionalism Aspiring to meet the highest possible standards of your profession rather than a set of minimum requirements.

Project management The process of planning, organizing, securing, managing, leading, and controlling resources to achieve goals.

Proliferation The act of increasing greatly in number.

Prospecting letter An application letter that is written without knowing if a job opening exists.

Random-access memory (RAM) A storage location within the computer, containing data or instructions that can be erased. This area of memory is a temporary storage location.

Raw data Source information in its original form.

Read-only memory (ROM) A storage location within the computer, containing data or instructions that cannot be erased by overwriting or loss of power.

Recession An economic decline in business activity.

Record A record consists of fields of individual data items, such as customer name, customer number, and customer address.

Redundant No longer needed; something that has been superseded and is now considered extra.

Reference A source of information such as a book or an author.

Relative index An alphabetic listing of all topics that appear in a filing system.

Remote access Access to a computer from a remote location; remote communication with a computer.

Removable storage Storage media that can be physically removed from the computer and transported elsewhere. This might include CD-ROMs, pen drives, and floppy disks.

Reprographics Hard-copy reproduction process (copying) of text or graphics.

Rightsizing To adjust the size of the organization, up or down, to meet market and environmental demands. A way of optimizing company resources to achieve efficiency.

Routers Devices that route information from one network to another. Routers allow the independent networks to function as a large virtual network so that users of any network can reach users of any other.

Satellite An object that orbits the earth transmitting a two-way digital signal to receptor dishes located on earth.

Scanner An input device that reads printed material and converts it to computer language.

Screening A procedure used to selectively answer telephone calls.

Secretary An office worker who handles administrative tasks for a person or organization.

Self-confidence The firm belief in one's own abilities.

Short list In an employment scenario, this is a list of applicants that has been reduced to the best possible choices.

Sign on A term used to describe the process of starting the computer, entering a password, and ultimately connecting to the application desired.

Sincerity A quality that demonstrates truthfulness and freedom from pretence.

Smartphone A mobile phone that works on a mobile computing platform.

Social media A general term used to describe web-based tools that encourage exchange of information by users.

Soft skills Personal qualities and interpersonal skills that impact on success in the workplace.

Software The programs, data, or intangible part(s) of a computer system.

Solicited letter An application letter that is written in response to an advertisement.

Solicitors Visitors to business who are attempting to sell products or services.

Spam Unwanted commercial email usually sent out in volume; also called junk mail.

Spam filtering software A software application designed to detect and reduce spam email.

Speculation An opinion based on incomplete information or evidence.

Spell-check A word processing feature that compares each word in a document with the spelling of a built-in dictionary. Words that do not match are highlighted on the screen and changes are suggested.

Spreadsheet A computerized representation of a paper spreadsheet in which data are organized in rows and columns.

Stereotype The oversimplified image held of one thing or person by another.

Stress A mental or physical state of tension.

Subject line A line of text, often appearing in memorandums and letters, that identifies the topic of the communication.

Supervisor A person who watches over or controls the work of others.

Synopsis A statement giving a brief, general review or summary.

Tablet computer A portable personal computer equipped with a touch screen with a virtual keyboard for data input in place of a traditional keyboard.

Talking Yellow Pages A voice mail system that incorporates the Yellow Pages directory and participating businesses. Users can dial numbers and receive recorded commercial information.

Task lighting Directed lighting (illumination) designed to increase visibility of a specific work area.

Teleconference A conference held between people in remote or distant places via telecommunication facilities.

Telephone tag This phenomenon occurs when telephone callers continually leave each other messages to return the call.

Terabyte Approximately one trillion bytes.

Time distribution chart A chart designed to show the distribution of work and time for several workers performing related office tasks.

Time management A skill that enables you to manage time efficiently.

Time-sharing The simultaneous access of a computer by two or more users.

To do list A simple checklist of things to do. It is intended to serve as a reminder and need not be prioritized.

Transmittal sheet Typically the first page of a fax transmission, which provides contact details of the originator and intended recipient.

Travel expense voucher An official (corporate) form that serves as both a record and a claim for expenses incurred while travelling on company business.

Travel fund advance A cash advance paid to an employee prior to a business trip.

Traveller's cheque A special cheque or draft issued by a bank to a traveller who signs it at issuance and again in the presence of the person cashing it.

Unabridged Containing original information, not condensed.

Unethical Contradictory to standards of moral conduct, especially within a profession.

USA mail Canadian mail addressed to points of destination within the United States of America.

Useful records Records or documents that can be considered helpful but not necessary for an organization to operate.

Venue A place where events are held.

Verbatim Repeated or copied word for word.

Videoconference A conference between remote participants in which sound and images are transferred over telephone lines or satellite.

Virtual Something practically real in effect even though it may not be in reality.

Virtual Assistant A virtual assistant, or VA, is a self-employed professional offering administrative support to a variety of clients through his or her home office.

Virtual network A communications connection that may involve routing through several locations and devices. However, it has the appearance and functionality of two computers directly connected with wires.

Virtual receptionist A software application that performs the routine tasks of a receptionist.

Virus A rogue computer program that affects computers with unpredictable and damaging results.

Visa A stamped permit to travel within a given country for a specified length of time. It is granted by the foreign country's government and is usually stamped or attached inside the passport.

Visible filing Paper filing: that which you can feel.

Vital records Records or documents necessary for an organization's operation.

Voice mail A telephone network–based message routing, storing, and retrieval system.

Voice-recognition software Software that transcribes the dictator's words directly to the computer screen.

Web authoring tool A category of software enabling the user to develop or edit a website.

Web-banking Banking services provided online.

Webcasting (or netcasting) Broadcasting live or recorded audio and/or video transmissions via computer.

Web conferencing Meeting over the internet using web conferencing software much as you would meet via telephone to take part in a telephone conferencing call.

Website An address on the World Wide Web, where information or links to other websites can be obtained.

White noise Also known as white sound. A continuous sound formed from many frequencies of equal volume; it has the effect of deadening surrounding sounds.

Wide area network (WAN) Two or more computers and/or local area networks connected together by communications media in order to share programs and data.

Wiki A collaborative website that allows its users to add, modify, or delete its content via a web browser.

Wireless fidelity (Wi-Fi) A wireless network set up for public access. In places like a library, airport, or even a coffee shop you may find a connection for your mobile device.

Windows™ A trademarked name for a graphically interfaced operating system that operates on personal computers. Functions are represented through icons and menus.

Workspace A specific area set aside for individuals to work.

Workstation A personal workspace, often defined by freestanding partitions; a terminal or personal computer.

World Wide Web Often used synonymously with the internet, the World Wide Web is the user interface for finding, viewing, and making use of the vast amount of information on the internet; an international computer network.

Zero-plus dialling A telephone number prefixed with "0" so that the caller can obtain assistance or special service from the operator.

Photo Credits

Introduction: p. 4: © auremar/Shutterstock, p. 5: © Andrey_Popov/Shutterstock

Chapter 1: p. 20: (top) © Konstantin Chagin/Shutterstock (bottom) © StockLite/Shutterstock, p. 22: 22. © Sebastian Gauert/Shutterstock

Chapter 2: p. 30: © Junial Enterprises/Fotolia, p. 33: © rangizzz/Shutterstock, p. 35: © Robert Kneschke/Fotolia

Chapter 3: p. 46: © Tom Davison/Shutterstock, p. 47: Reprinted with Permission from Microsoft Corporation

Chapter 4: p. 70: Dorling Kindersley

Chapter 5: p. 79: © Monkey Business/Fotolia, p. 81: © 06photo/Fotolia

Chapter 6: p. 88: (top) © Daboost/Shutterstock (bottom) © rvlsoft/Shutterstock, p. 89: © Sylvie Bouchard/Shutterstock, p. 90: © Yuri Arcurs/Fotolia, p. 95: Reprinted with Permission from Microsoft Corporation, p. 96: (top) © Monkey Business Images/Shutterstock (bottom) © Kzenon/Fotolia, p. 98: (top) © EDHAR/Fotolia (bottom) © Elena Elisseeva/Shutterstock, p. 101: (top) © Tiler84/Fotolia (bottom) © Supertrooper/Shutterstock

Chapter 7: p. 109: (top left) © Matthias Pahl/Shutterstock (top right) © Rafal Olechowski/Shutterstock (bottom left) © niederhaus.galina/Shutterstock (bottom right) © Andrii Kondiuk/Shutterstock, p. 110: © pzAxe/Shutterstock, p. 112: © Dr. Cloud/Shutterstock, p. 113: © Ron Dale/Shutterstock

Chapter 8: p. 119, 120: Reprinted with permission from Microsoft Corporation. p. 121: © Iakov Filimonov/Shutterstock, p. 137: © auremar/Shutterstock, pp. 140, 141, 142, 143, 144: Reprinted with the kind permission of Canada Post, p. 146: Lkphotographers/Dreamstime.com, p. 147: Reprinted with the kind permission of Canada Post

Chapter 9: p. 157: Definitions courtesy of Project Auditors LLC http://www.projectauditors.com/Dictionary/DictionaryHome.html, p. 158: Reprinted with Permission from Microsoft Corporation, p. 159: © mast3r/Shutterstock

Chapter 10: p. 167: Courtesy of Kardex, p. 168: Reprinted with Permission from Microsoft Corporation, p. 169: © Artuha/Fotolia, p. 170: © michaeljung/Shutterstock, p. 171: (top) © Feng Yu/Shutterstock (bottom) © Chimpinski/Shutterstock, p. 172: (top) © Lasse Kristensen/Fotolia (bottom) © Chad McDermott/Shutterstock, p. 173: © Verisakeet/Fotolia, p. 174: © Stephen Rees/Shutterstock, p. 175: Reprinted with Permission from Microsoft Corporation, p. 187: Teresa Pigeon/Getty

Chapter 11: p. 199: © StockLite/Shutterstock, p. 204: © Volina/Shutterstock, p. 206: Courtesy of US Defense Mapping Agency. US Department of Defense, p. 209: Reprinted with Permission from Microsoft Corporation

Chapter 12: p. 225: © Kikalishvili Mamuka/Shutterstock, p. 227: Digitial Vision/Getty, p. 236: © auremar/Fotolia

Chapter 13: p. 245: altrendo images/Stockbyte/Getty, p. 246: Reprinted with Permission from Microsoft Corporation, p. 250: (bottom) © Yuri Arcurs/Shutterstock (top) © Goodluz/Shutterstock

Chapter 14: p. 278: © Stephen Coburn/Shutterstock

Chapter 16: p. 330: Courtesy of the Conference Board of Canada, p. 347: © Adam Gregor/Shutterstock, p. 349: Source: Adapted from Canadian Human Rights Commission

Chapter 17: p. 374: ZanyZeus/Shutterstock

Index

chamber of commerce directories, 67
change in workplace, 21
change of address, 146
character, 375
charge-out methods for filing, 167–168
chequebooks, 312
cheques
    bank reconciliation and, 316–318
    cancelled, 318
    cash withdrawals and, 314
    certified, 311
    depositing, 315–316
    endorsing, 314–315
    keyed entries on, 313
    stop-payment notification on,
      313–314
    traveller's, 312
    voucher, 312
    writing, 312–313
CHRC. *See* Canadian Human Rights
  Commission
chronological reports, 302
chronological résumés, 336, 337–338, 340
Circular Organization, 78
circulation slips, 129, 131
CIS. *See* Center for Internet Security
Citizen and Immigration Canada, 38
city directories, 67
civic addresses, 141
clean desk policy, 53
COD. *See* collect on delivery
code of ethics, 19
coding, 165
collect on delivery (COD), 136
college placement office, 331
colour coding, 177–178
coloured papers, 54
common knowledge, 68
communication
    See also business letters; reports
    administrative assistant function of, 5
    constructive criticism and, 15,
      274–276
    effective, 270
    eye contact and, 273
    facial expressions and, 274
    image and, 273, 306
    international business and
      interpersonal, 33
    interpersonal, 271
    listening and, 274
    nonverbal, 272–274
    personal space and, 273
    posture and, 273–274
    public speaking and, 276–277
    remote access, 90–91
    teamwork and, 20
    telephone use practice with, 196–197
    verbal, 272
    websites for, 305–306
    written, 277

commuter flights, 227
company mergers, 21, 335
compatibility, 89
complaining customers, 215–216
completing tasks, 50
composure, 17
computerhope.com, 105
computerized postage machine, 145–146
computers
    See also application programs
    accuracy of input information for, 93
    backup for, 94
    CD-ROMs for, 90
    desktop, 86
    flash drives for, 90
    functions of, 88–90
    hard disk drive for, 90
    input and output data of, 88–89, 93
    Internet connection for, 90–91
    laptop, 86–87, 250
    memory of, 88, 90
    networking, 91–92
    notebook, 86–87
    operating system of, 89–90
    PCs, 86
    PDAs, 88
    pen drives for, 168
    for processing, 88–89
    productivity with, 97
    remote access communication and,
      90–91
    smartphones, 88
    storage for, 90, 93–94
    tablet, 87–88
    terminology for, 92
    troubleshooting for, 92–93
    types of, 86–88
    versatility of, 92
    viruses and, 112
Conference Board of Canada, 329, 330, 363
conference calling, 202, 263, 264
conferences, 243
    See also meetings
    international, 265
    teleconferences, 202, 263, 264
    videoconferences, 246, 263, 264
    web, 100, 110, 262–263, 264
confidential information, 15
confidentiality request statement, 123
confidential mail, 125
consensus, 258
consideration of others, 15–16
constructive criticism, 15, 274–276
contemporary office professional, 374
contemporary organization structures, 77–79
convenience copiers, 101
cookies, 113
copiers
    classes of, 101
    convenience, 101
    functions of, 100

    needs survey for, 102
    prices for, 103
    selecting, 101–102
    service for, 103
    vendors for, 102–103
copyright violation, 69
country name, for addressing mail, 143,
  145
courier services, 137
courtesy in telephone use, 199–200
courtesy titles, 286
covering letters, 288
cover letters, 343–345
CP. *See* Canada Post
CPS. *See* Certified Professional Secretary
CPU. *See* central processing unit
CRA. *See* Canada Revenue Agency
creative thinking and planning, 43–44
credenza, 55
credit cards, 232
cross-cultural awareness, 31
cross-cultural competence, 30–31
cross-cultural encounters, 31
cross-referencing, 165–166
cross-training, 371–372
CTS. *See* carpal tunnel syndrome
cultural awareness, 31
cultural competence, 30–31
culture
    blunders with, 36
    gender and, 37
    gift giving and, 37
    international travel arrangements
      and, 238
    system of, 30
    time management in, 32
Cumyn, Alan, 34
currency conversion, 242, 326
currency exchange, international, 323
curriculum vitae (CV), 336, 360
    See also résumés
customer service, 14
CV. *See* curriculum vitae
CVAC. *See* Canadian Virtual Assistants
  Connection
cvtips.com, 364

D

daily plan, for time management, 51–52
dangerous goods, 137
databases
    electronic, 174–175
    reference, 63
data encryption, 114
date stamp, 46
Daylight Saving Time (DST), 205
Day-Timer, 60, 222
DDD. *See* direct-distance dialling
debriefing, in team meetings, 259
decor, 80
deductive arrangement, 302

delivery symbols, 142
dependability, 16–17
deposits, 315–316
deposit slips, 315, 316
deskdemon.com, 8
desktop computers, 86
desktop publishing (DTP), 92, 95–96
desktop publishing reviews, 105
detail management, 46–47
dial-up connection, 107
dictionaries, 64
difficult customers
    abusive customers, 216
    complaining customers, 215–216
    difficult callers, 215
    special needs visitors, 217–218
    tips for success with, 216–217
    unwanted visitors, 215
    visitors with language barriers, 217
difficult people, dealing with, 13–14
difficult tasks, beginning with, 47–48
digital subscriber line (DSL), 107
digression, 12
direct application for jobs, 332
direct-distance dialling (DDD), 204
direction, lack of, 12
directories, 92
    chamber of commerce, 67
    city, 67
    for electronic records, 168
    telephone, 67, 203
direct payroll deposit, 310
direct requests, letters, 282–283
disappointment letters, 283–284
discounting, 13
Discover Canada, 242
discrimination, 367
distributing mail, 129–131
diversity
    benefits of, 31–32
    equity and, 28
    in international business, 32–36
diversityintheworkplace.ca, 38
divisions of work, 78
documentation, for formal reports, 297
domestic long-distance calls, 204–206
domestic mail, 132–135
dominating team members, 12
downsizing, 335
DSL. See digital subscriber line
DST. See Daylight Saving Time
DTP. See desktop publishing
Dun & Bradstreet, 64
duplex, 100

E

e-commerce
    CP and, 131
    legislative protection for, 309
    privacy and, 309
    transactions in, 308–309

ecommerce-guide.com, 326
EDI. See electronic data interchange
education, for professional development, 367–368
effectivemeetings.com, 269
effectiveness, 41–42
efficiency
    See also time management
    CP improving, 131
    effectiveness compared to, 41–42
    work area, 47, 52
    work habits and, 42
e-file, 170
EFT. See electronic funds transfer
electronic bulletin boards, 121
electronic calendars, 51, 208–209
electronic databases, storage of, 174–175
electronic data interchange (EDI), 308
electronic date and time, 47
electronic funds transfer (EFT), 307–308
electronic job search, 357–358, 359
Electronic Medical Records (EMRs), 176
electronic money transfer, 123
Electronic Postage Setting System (EPSS), 145
Electronic Post Office, 124
electronic records
    archiving, 176
    directories for, 168
    filing, 168–170
    retention of, 176
    supplies for, 172
electronic services, from CP, 123–124
The Elements of Style, 305
e-mail
    appointments by, 208
    ethics with, 147–148
    etiquette for, 120–121
    hyperlinks with, 346
    privacy, 132, 147–148
    reports, 292–293
    résumés through, 342
    sending and receiving, 118–121
employability skills, 329
Employability Skills 2000+, 329, 330
employment agencies, 332–333
employment eligibility, 335
Employment Equity Act, 30
employment strategies
    See also job applications; job
      interviews; job prospects
    bouncing back and, 335
    electronic job search for, 357–358, 359
    follow-up correspondence for, 353–357
    international, 360
    websites for, 363–364
empowerment, 12
EMRs. See Electronic Medical Records
encryption software, 114

encyclopedias, 64
encyclopedic filing system, 185
endorsing cheques, 314–315
englishplus.com/grammar, 305
environmental management, 55–56
e-portfolios, 346
EPSS. See Electronic Postage Setting System
equal opportunity employers, 367
equity
    diversity and, 28
    human rights and standards of, 29–30
ergonomics
    acoustics and, 81
    furniture and, 80–81
    lighting and, 81
    position and posture and, 82–83
    websites for, 85
esthetics, 80
ethics
    in accounting, 322
    ambiguity and, 19
    in business letters, 302–303
    code of, 19
    confidential information, 15
    e-mail and, 147–148
    ethical practice, 19–20
    job interview questions and, 348, 349
    job search and, 358, 360
    in meetings, 264–265
    office romance and, 26
    professional development
      committing to, 375–376
    in public speaking, 277
    in records management, 188
    travel expenses and, 237–238
    with visitors, 218
    work, time, and resources, 20
etiquette
    books on, 65
    for business lunch, 24–25, 27
    for e-mail, 120–121
    in foreign countries, 34
    for Internet, 120–121
    netiquette, 151
    for telephone use, 222
    travel and, 242
    websites for business, 269
executive assistants, 4
executives, learning names of, 43
exercises, 85
expandable folders, 171
expedia.ca, 242
external memory, computers, 90
extranet, 108
eye contact, communication and, 273

F

facial expressions, communication with, 274
facilitators, for team meetings, 257
facsimile, 121–123, 342
favourable letters, 282–283

vertical filing cabinet, 172
videoconferences, 246, 263, 264
video display terminal (VDT), 89
viral, 111
virtual assistants, 369
virtual meetings, 92, 262–264
virtual network, 99
virtual offices, 82
virtual receptionists (VRs), 194–196
virtualreferencelibrary.ca, 73
viruses, computer, 112
visas, 226, 230
visible filing, 164–167, 170–171
    See also filing
visitors. *See* receiving office visitors
vital records, 175
vitalrecordsprotection.org, 192
voice mail (VM), 99, 124, 197–198
voice-recognition software, 94
voice recorders, 249–250
voucher cheques, 312
VRs. *See* virtual receptionists

W

WAN. *See* wide area network
Web 2.0, 109–111
web authoring tool, 111
web-banking, 309–310
webcasting, 100, 110
web conferencing, 100, 110, 262–263, 264
webdesignconferencing.com, 116
webinar, 111

web tools, 108–110
Weilinger, Caroline S., 107
wellness in workplace, 21–22
Western Union, 123, 151
Whan, Sandra, 271
What in the World Is Going On? (Cumyn), 34
Whitaker's Books in Print, 64
white noise, 81
WHO. *See* World Health Organization
wide area network (WAN), 91
Wi-Fi. *See* wireless fidelity
wikis, 109
Windows, 89
wireless fidelity (Wi-Fi), 108
wireless networks, 91–92
wireless telephones, 99
wire organizer, 173
word processing, 94–95
work, ethics and, 20
work area efficiency, 47, 52
working environment
    change in, 21
    current office trends in, 1–3
    job titles in, 3–4
workopolis.com, 363
workplace ethics. *See* ethics
workplaces, nontraditional, 55
workspaces, 74
workstation
    clean desk policy for, 53
    for front-line reception, 212

    maximum working area, 52
    normal working area, 52
    organization of, 53–55
    organizing necessary items for,
        53–55
    purging unnecessary items for, 53
    uncluttered desks in, 47, 53
WorldCat, 62
World Clock, 222
World Environmental Organization, 60
World Health Organization (WHO), 231, 242
World Time Server, 242
WorldWeb travel guide, 242
World Wide Web (www), 106
worms, 112
written communication, 277
    See also business letters
www. *See* World Wide Web

X

Xpresspost service, 135

Y

Yahoo! Canada-Reference, 73
yearbooks, 64

Z

zero-plus dialling, 204–205
zero zone, 205